# ★ THE IRAQ PAPERS ★

# THE
# IRAQ
# PAPERS

EDITED BY

JOHN EHRENBERG • J. PATRICE McSHERRY
JOSÉ RAMÓN SÁNCHEZ • CAROLEEN MARJI SAYEJ

OXFORD
UNIVERSITY PRESS

2010

# OXFORD
UNIVERSITY PRESS

Oxford University Press, Inc., publishes works that further
Oxford University's objective of excellence
in research, scholarship, and education.

Oxford   New York
Auckland   Cape Town   Dar es Salaam   Hong Kong   Karachi
Kuala Lumpur   Madrid   Melbourne   Mexico City   Nairobi
New Delhi   Shanghai   Taipei   Toronto

With offices in
Argentina   Austria   Brazil   Chile   Czech Republic   France   Greece
Guatemala   Hungary   Italy   Japan   Poland   Portugal   Singapore
South Korea   Switzerland   Thailand   Turkey   Ukraine   Vietnam

Copyright © 2010 by John Ehrenberg, J. Patrice McSherry,
José Ramón Sánchez, and Caroleen Marji Sayej

Published by Oxford University Press, Inc.
198 Madison Avenue, New York, New York 10016

www.oup.com

Oxford is a registered trademark of Oxford University Press

Library of Congress Cataloging-in-Publication Data
The Iraq papers / edited by John Ehrenberg . . . [et al.].
      p.   cm.
Includes bibliographical references and index.
ISBN 978-0-19-539858-8; 978-0-19-539859-5 (pbk.)
1. Iraq War, 2003—Causes—Sources. 2. Preemptive attack (Military
science)—Government policy—United States—Sources.
I. Ehrenberg, John, 1944–
DS79.76I72628 2010
956.7044'31—dc22      2009019403

9 8 7 6 5 4 3 2 1

Printed in the United States of America
on acid-free paper

# CONTENTS ✭

Contents

**Chapter 5** Insurgency, Counterinsurgency, or Civil War? • 213

U.S. POLICIES AND TACTICS IN THE COUNTERINSURGENCY

IRAQI DOCUMENTS

# PART TWO   CONSEQUENCES OF A PREEMPTIVE WAR

Contents

Contents

**Chapter 9** Policing Terror Versus a War on Terror • 456

### U.S. GOVERNMENT TERRORISM DOCUMENTS

### INTERNATIONAL TERRORISM DOCUMENTS

Contents

# ★ PREFACE ★

THE IDEA FOR this book came out of a retirement dinner for one of our colleagues who was leaving Long Island University after a long and distinguished career. After all the reminiscing had ended, we began talking about what it meant to be teaching political science during a time of crisis. It was early 2007, and the Bush administration's invasion of Iraq was going badly. As civil war was added to national insurgency and the full scope of the invasion's problems was dominating the news at home, the conversation turned to an earlier war and to the failure of official political science to help students navigate its difficult and complex issues. We decided on the spot that, since the lessons of Vietnam seemed to have been forgotten, we would not fail our students the same way.

Four of us—with specializations in comparative analysis and the politics of the Middle East, U.S. foreign policy and international affairs, domestic politics, and political theory—resolved to offer a team-taught course on the Iraq War for advanced undergraduates. Convinced that there were few things we could do that were more important, we spent the next year accumulating information, debating the importance of various factors, refining our understanding, and organizing the semester.

As we began to assemble a reading list, we noticed that, while several useful readers had been published,[1] no comprehensive compilation of key

---

1. See, for example, Christopher Cerf and Micah Sifry, *The Iraq War Reader: History, Documents, Opinions* (New York: Touchstone, 2003).

primary documents had yet appeared. Remembering how important Marvin Gettleman's series of readers on the Vietnam War[2] had been to an earlier generation, we decided to supplement our preparations for the course by gathering a collection of primary sources on the Iraq War and its ramifications, both domestic and international. This book, the first systematic effort of its kind, is the outcome of a semester with our students and some eighteen months of research and intense—sometimes heated!—discussions among ourselves.

We have tried to present the historical, economic, political, moral, and other issues raised by the Bush administration's invasion of Iraq. To accomplish this we have prepared substantive introductions to each chapter, and shorter introductions to each document, to contextualize the material and provide historical and political analysis. We organized the book around the key analytical theme of preemptive war in order to structure the narrative and interpret the documents in a way that revealed the central issues raised by the Bush administration's policies. In this sense, *The Iraq Papers* is an "interpretive reader" that goes beyond the traditional design for books of its kind. While the book has a point of view, it also presents the most important primary documents in a way that honors our obligation to be fair to our readers. We believe that it provides a valuable, if necessarily incomplete, compendium and discussion of some of the burning issues surrounding the war in Iraq.

We do not pretend that our chronological or thematic accounts are exhaustive, but we have been careful to supplement the debates and decisions that originated inside the United States with representative statements from other governments and rarely heard Iraqi voices. For reasons of economy and space, we chose to begin part I with the rise of neoconservatism and the reassessment of containment after the Gulf War of 1991. We believed that this treatment was warranted because it was through the neoconservative movement that preemption gained legitimacy in the previous decade, but we recognized that we could have begun with an earlier historical view. After all, the debates that roiled Washington during the 1990s were not new. We could have begun with the early stages of the Cold War and the struggle between those who supported George Kennan's theory of containment and those who were convinced by John Foster Dulles's embrace of "rollback." In fact, we could have gone back to 1898 and the emergence of the United States as a world power. We did no more than briefly reference this history in the book, having to content ourselves with raising suggestions for broader historical investigation and leaving it to our readers to pursue them.

---

2. See, especially, Marvin E. Gettleman, Jane Franklin, Marilyn Young, H. Bruce Franklin, eds., *Vietnam and America: The Most Comprehensive Documented History of the Vietnam War* (New York: Grove, 1995).

It is likewise true that our thematic presentation is not exhaustive. The questions that we raised in part II were the result of extensive discussions regarding the factors we saw as particularly important. We recognized, though, that we could have addressed many other issues evoked by the war. A long bipartisan commitment to defend Israel, Donald Rumsfeld's plan to reshape the Pentagon, twenty-five years of conservative political dominance, and—who knows?—President Bush's relationship to his father and to his Christian faith might have been as important as the matters that we examined in more detail. And, although we chose to end our account with the close of George W. Bush's presidency, we are well aware that new information about the Iraq War and its ramifications will be coming out for years. After this book entered the production process, for example, several new and graphic "torture memos" were released, too late for inclusion here. Even more explosive was the news in April 2009 that an intelligence officer and an army psychiatrist had disclosed that one reason for the torture of detainees was the pressure from Cheney and Rumsfeld to "prove" a link between Saddam Hussein and al Qaeda.[3] Under these circumstances, we hope that readers will pursue our suggestions for further thought, debate, and investigation—and that they will add their own.

*The Iraq Papers* was shaped by the famous observation that "eternal vigilance is the price of liberty." We hope that the book will raise some important questions, promote a deeper understanding of the issues, and contribute to an open and democratic discussion of the causes and consequences of the preemptive war in Iraq.

---

3. Jonathan S. Landay, "Abusive Tactics Used to Seek Iraq-Al Qaida Link," McClatchy Newspapers, April 22, 2009.

# ★ NOTE TO READERS ★

*THE IRAQ PAPERS* is a book-length documentary essay: an interpretive collection of primary sources. We produced it to help readers understand how the United States got involved in Iraq and to help them consider some of the consequences of that involvement for both countries and for the world. We also focused on some key issues raised by how the war was conducted and how it was presented to the public.

We have been careful to preserve the original documents but have made some minor changes for the sake of consistency, such as standardizing the spelling of Arabic names, indicating redactions or areas of censorship, and excerpting long selections to convey their meaning as accurately as possible. We have also preserved all emphases as they appeared in the original documents. Unless otherwise indicated, Professor Caroleen Marji Sayej translated the Arabic material into English. In a few instances, we used newspaper or journal articles when the primary sources to which they referred were classified or otherwise unavailable. We did so because they provided invaluable information or filled important gaps in the documentary record.

Part I is organized chronologically and takes the reader up to June 2004, when the Coalition Provisional Authority was disbanded and sovereignty handed over to a nominally independent Iraqi government. Many developments occurred after that point, of course, and some of them are presented in the thematically organized part II. The chapters in part II are not necessarily presented or organized chronologically. We believe that combining a chronological account and a thematic discussion can help readers debate the "who, what, when, where, and why" of the preemptive war in Iraq.

We wish to acknowledge the graduate assistants Hope Berndt and Mary Anna Mancuso, who provided invaluable formatting and fact-checking assistance. Jo Ann Faraci, our beloved departmental secretary, helped in more ways than she can imagine. We also thank the three anonymous readers for Oxford University Press, who helped clarify and sharpen our thinking; David McBride, senior editor of politics and law; and Niko Pfund, vice president and publisher of the academic and trade division, for their consistent support of this project.

# INTRODUCTION

## THE DOCTRINE OF PREEMPTION
## AND THE IRAQ WAR

ON MARCH 20, 2003, the Bush administration invaded Iraq to over-throw the government of Saddam Hussein. More than five years later, the United States was still mired in what some alternatively called an insurgency or a civil war, as large numbers of Iraqis resisted the occupation of their country. During this period, academics, politicians, and journalists from around the world were trying to make sense of both the causes and the long-term consequences of the Iraq War on the domestic, regional, and international levels.

The Bush administration used three main arguments for going to war. First was a series of allegations about Saddam Hussein's connections to al Qaeda; next were claims that he had acquired weapons of mass destruction. Lastly, the administration argued for "regime change" by suggesting that it was Washington's duty to spread democracy to countries ruled by dictators. Its specific arguments for war aside, the administration was taking U.S. foreign policy in a new direction.

The organizing theme of this book is "preemption." We examine the invasion of Iraq by considering how particular events, issues, conflicts, ideologies, and interests interacted with changes in the international system to create an environment in which preemptive war became a viable strategy for the U.S. government. We reconstruct both the war planning and implementation through a series of primary documents and historical discussions. We consider the changes in the domestic politics of the United States, the Middle East, and the world that made preemption possible. Finally, we extend the concept of preemption beyond the international security context to show how it was brought to bear on the U.S. Constitution, the democratic political process, and expert knowledge, often in secrecy. The violation of norms and laws in one area, such as international law, affected others, such as democracy at home. We extend the notion of preemption because the concept permeated Bush administration policies. Its breaches of norms and laws in the international arena were intimately connected to breaches of constitutional law and democratic processes at home. The interplay of these factors makes the Iraq case suitable for a multilevel analysis.

We treat the Iraq War as a case study of preemption because U.S. policy shifted from containing Baghdad during the 1990s to preemptively attacking it in 2003. We use the term "preemption" the way it was articulated in the "Bush Doctrine," even though the Iraq War more closely resembled a preventive, not a preemptive, war. A *preventive* war is an attack on a country that may not itself be on the verge of attack but that may, hypothetically, become a threat in the future. A *preemptive* war, on the other hand, is an attack on a country because it poses a demonstrable and imminent threat; the UN Charter, international law, and scholarly literature are explicit about the conditions that warrant preemptive action. The decision to attack Iraq was not based on an impending threat from Saddam Hussein insofar as his political and military behavior had not become more aggressive in the years and months immediately preceding the invasion. Nevertheless, we use the term "preemption" in this book because it best captures the internal ideology and strategy of the Bush administration and because the rationale behind preemption pervaded many of Washington's policies.

President Bush's justifications notwithstanding, the U.S. strike in 2003 was undertaken to secure an advantageous regional and international position for the United States both in the Middle East and in the international system. The invasion violated the international legal rules governing the use of force established by Articles 2 and 51 of the UN Charter. Article 2(4) prohibits the use of force against another country except for self-defense or with specific Security Council authorization to protect international security. On the eve of the war, in February 2003, Secretary of State Colin Powell spoke before the United Nations Security Council, focusing on the alleged risk that Saddam Hussein's government posed to the United States and its allies. In order to justify a preemptive attack on Iraq, the threat would have to be "imminent," for which the standard in international law was "instant, overwhelming, and leaving no choice of means, and no moment for deliberation"—hardly a description of the Iraqi case.[1] President Bush argued that war was legally justified in the post–September 11 world, given the immediacy of new threats and the inadequacy of the "reactive postures" taken to that point. Despite all the discussion, the whole question of whether Iraq was an imminent threat was beside the point since we

---

1. Letter from Daniel Webster, Secretary of State, to Lord Ashburton, August 6, 1842, regarding the *Caroline* affair of 1837, reprinted in John Bassett Moore, *A Digest of International Law* 409 (1906): 412.

now know from the Downing Street Memo and other sources that the decision to invade had been made months before the president announced the beginning of "Operation Iraqi Freedom."

Critics argued that since preemptive military action was not mentioned in the UN Charter, it was illegal under international law. Article 51 of the Charter allows for self-defense only when there is no time to bring the issue before the Security Council, a condition not applicable to the Iraq case; after all, the post-1990 sanctions regime had effectively contained Saddam's aggressive impulses. But some members of the Bush administration argued that the U.S. position was in line with Security Council Resolution 678, passed in November 1990, which authorized the use of force to implement Resolution 660—the demand that Iraq withdraw from Kuwait. Resolution 687 authorized any means necessary not only to uphold Resolution 660, but also to support all subsequent resolutions to restore security in the area. The majority view articulated in the United Nations, however, held that the Security Council, not individual member states, should decide when a resolution had been breached and what proper enforcement would entail.

Most members of the international community were committed to Security Council control over the Iraq issue at every stage. Statements by representatives as varied as France, Russia, China, Ireland, Mexico, Bulgaria, Colombia, Cameroon, and Syria revealed that even states with very different economic and political systems feared the potential consequences of unfettered political and military action. Members of the United Nations were acutely aware that preemptively invading Iraq might damage the stability of the international system by disrupting the norms that had been established over the last few hundred years. United States unilateralism was certain to change the rules of the game, including redefining the boundaries for "regime change" and pressuring the international community to conform to trends suitable to U.S. foreign policy.

Leaders from developed and developing countries, democracies and autocracies alike, worried that U.S. behavior would set a bad precedent for interstate relations. States as varied as Syria, China, and Japan reinforced their commitment to the United Nations in 2002 and 2003. Led by France and Germany, most states followed suit to press for more stringent weapons inspections in Iraq and to engage the United States in a dialogue, not from a position of weakness or in an effort to revive an outdated institution, as the Bush administration argued, but because they understood that bypassing the United Nations meant that all countries could become vulnerable to the whims of U.S. hegemonic power. Despite, or because of, Washington's actions outside the UN framework, other states seemed determined to shore up international law and organization in the ensuing years.

## EXPLAINING THE WAR

Assuming that the invasion would be easy, U.S. war planners ignored many of the difficulties raised by "regime change," the expansion of hegemonic power, and the violation of sovereignty and international norms. Once the early failures of the invasion and occupation were revealed, the war's supporters shifted their focus to the "artificiality of Iraq" and the presence of sectarian violence to explain the unforeseen difficulties the U.S. military project now faced. They argued that these difficulties were the product of long-standing deficiencies in the Iraqi state and society and of the conditions of the broader "war on terror," which they conflated with the Iraqi case to deflect attention from what had happened in Washington. We take issue with this analysis by examining trends and patterns in U.S. foreign policy in order to contextualize the Iraqi case. We continue with a reconstruction of the conflict to illustrate the historical influences, economic imperatives, and political decisions that coalesced in 2003 and continued to shape public affairs for years afterward.

The Iraq War raised the important question of the general conditions under which any state has the right to effect "regime change" in another state and whether there were justifiable reasons for this particular invasion. In 1648, the Peace of Westphalia established the foundation for the system of sovereign states and its core principle of non-intervention. That system structured interstate relations for centuries. While there was nothing new about powerful countries pursuing hegemony and empire, the post–Cold War situation was different from the recent past. During the Cold War, the balance of power between the United States and the USSR was a major deterrent to either country's instigating war. The collapse of the Soviet Union left the United States as the world's only superpower; hence, the previous limitations on foreign policy, such as an opposing bloc in the United Nations, military deterrence, and world public opinion, seemed less relevant.

The Iraq case was notable in that, while U.S. policy toward Iraq was certainly novel in some ways, other elements aligned with traditional U.S. foreign policy. Washington's hegemonic goals were not limited to the Middle East, or to the present. They could be seen in the historical record of U.S. relations with Latin America, for example, where Washington first exercised an expansionist role in pursuit of economic, military, and political interests. The Monroe Doctrine of 1823, the 1901 Platt Amendment, and the 1904 Roosevelt Corollary were all examples of early U.S. efforts to establish a sphere of influence and to control political outcomes in the region. These examples, along with several other parallels in history, help us understand some of the patterns in U.S. foreign policy. But the Iraq War was not simply a case of history repeating itself. There were historically specific developments as well. The international environment and methods of attaining power had changed, including the means and justification for warfare. These developments can be explained by changes in the international system, tendencies in the Middle East, and important individual and state-level developments in the United States. Since the war was a U.S. adventure, special emphasis is placed on the historical continuity of U.S. geostrategic goals and the various policies that reflected them. However, our

analysis is broadened to include the perspectives of the international community and those of Iraqis, alternative patterns of economic development and democratic transition, and the norms that had structured the international community over the last few centuries. Taken together, these factors help explain the sequence of events that shaped the Iraq War.

## LINKING U.S. DEVELOPMENTS WITH INTERNATIONAL/SYSTEM-LEVEL CHANGES

On the system level, changes in the post–Cold War international environment, and the emergence of the United States as the world's sole superpower, were key factors in setting the conditions for preemptive war. Any state's ability to accomplish its goals is affected by other states' interests, their capacities to act, and the larger context of institutions, alliances, and dependencies that mediate relations among global actors. We analyze the shift from a multilateral to a unilateral approach in Iraq, one that made it possible to abandon the strategy of building alliances and imposing sanctions in favor of pursuing a unilateral approach. In addition, we consider the role of international actors and institutions and their efficacy in curbing the power of states.

The 1991 multilateral response to Saddam Hussein's invasion of Kuwait was an example of both collective security as originally envisioned in the UN Charter and a legitimate reaction to aggression, but the ascendancy of the neoconservative movement changed the course of U.S. actions over the next several years. In 1992, soon after the Cold War had ended with the collapse of the USSR, some Pentagon neoconservatives called upon the United States to block the emergence of any challenger to U.S. predominance. That orientation was reflected in an important 1992 Pentagon strategy document and influenced the George W. Bush administration's decision to take preemptive action in Iraq more than a decade later, in a situation made possible by the altered domestic landscape after the September 11 terrorist attacks. Neoconservatives also emphasized the link between rebuilding executive power in domestic politics and waging a more aggressive foreign policy, and argued in favor of curtailing Congress's role in both areas. Once in power in the Bush administration, they moved rapidly to refine arguments they had articulated during the Clinton presidency: that Washington should use force to head off potential challengers, act unilaterally in what they perceived to be self-defense, and avoid delay. After September 11 they argued that a new approach was necessary because the terrorist threat was less visible than, say, a state gathering troops at a border—and, importantly, because the United States could now "preempt" with impunity.

On a more general level, neoconservative advocates of preemptive war claimed that changes after the Cold War meant that the straightforward balance-of-power strategy suitable in a bipolar world was no longer necessary in a unipolar environment shaped by the threat of international

terrorism. They argued that the traditional methods of curbing belligerent states were outdated in both the post–Cold War and post–September 11 political landscape. Sanctions and mediation through institutions like the United Nations and North Atlantic Treaty Organization (NATO) were said to be inadequate for the new enemies and new threats, which required new strategies. The rise of non-state actors such as transnational terrorist networks, they claimed, posed "asymmetric threats" to the "free world" because they were beyond the realm of traditional state warfare and refused to play by the rules of the game. They had the advantage of Internet communication, a reservoir of willing martyrs, and enough technology to coordinate their efforts and recruit new members. Lastly, the neoconservatives argued that terrorists had the support of "rogue" state sponsors such as Iraq, North Korea, or Iran, which could acquire and distribute weapons of mass destruction.

Significantly, some neoconservative members of the Bush administration had been making similar arguments in the decade preceding the invasion of Iraq, even though terrorism was not seen as an imminent threat. With regard to the vital Persian Gulf, they were quite specific long before September 11 that the United States should abandon containment in favor of a preemptive attack on Iraq. Organized by the multinational coalition that had expelled Iraq from Kuwait in 1991, and overseen by the UN Security Council, containment involved "caging" Saddam Hussein by controlling Iraqi airspace, creating no-fly zones in the north and south, and limiting Baghdad's economic relations with the outside world. Arguing that containment was a strategic defeat, the neoconservatives embraced preemption as a quick and clean alternative since it would rapidly topple the Baathist regime and establish a new one. They believed that it was time to take advantage of a unipolar world to preserve and extend U.S. hegemony. A successful preemptive attack on Iraq would be a first step.

Washington's embrace of unilateralism led to an abandonment of institutional cooperation as the Bush administration refused to allow a NATO-led response in Afghanistan following the attacks of September 11, and was uninterested in either UN or NATO participation in its 2003 preemptive attack on Iraq. Having embraced the neoconservative analysis of the international system and the possibilities for U.S. action, the administration sought to extend the American advantage to organize "democracy" in weak and failed states in order to shape their domestic and foreign policy trajectories. This type of nation-building, Washington argued, would reinforce U.S. hegemony and contribute to international stability at the same time. The White House wanted to take advantage of a window of opportunity to act, as many observers argued that system-level changes would not leave the United States as the sole superpower indefinitely. It was, in Charles Krauthammer's words, a "unipolar moment" rather than a fixed power structure that would replace the fifty-year Cold War balance-of-power system.

Not only was the United States departing from a series of international institutions, it was also breaking ranks with important European allies on the proper way to secure post–Cold War peace. In the buildup to the Iraq War, France and Germany offered alternatives to invasion and preemptive war that were in line with long-held international norms and respect for sovereignty. Various European countries effectively worked to strengthen police methods of tracking and dismantling terrorist networks. But the Bush administration had a different vision: to militarize the "war on terror," move away from a criminal justice model, and punish states suspected of sponsoring terrorism. Washington dismissed the European commitment to institutions as reflecting a position of weakness and also disregarded public opinion, Congress, and the Constitution. It feared that cooperation and deliberation would inhibit U.S. options, force it to consider other views, and create an artificial parity between the United States and European countries—an unwelcome reminder of a multipolar system. Some neo-conservative critics, citing President Chirac's speech on *reequilibrage*, accused France of trying to organize a traditional balance against a hegemon. Yet the spirit of "rebalancing" was lost on the Bush administration. The French were calling for the creation of more equality within a transatlantic and international community of values. Their position supported the sharing of, rather than disputes over, leadership, so that states would work together as a check on all state behavior.

## CHANGES IN THE POLITICS OF THE MIDDLE EAST

However, not everything was determined in Washington. The changing political landscape in the Middle East was a key factor in the invasion of Iraq. The general pattern of U.S. geostrategic alliance-building that had functioned in the region for decades had been reconfigured by the time of the September 11 attacks. Though military and diplomatic ties with countries such as Saudi Arabia were still intact, important changes in the domestic landscape of the region threatened the stability of these regimes. Citizens across the Middle Eastern region were increasingly vocal in criticizing what they viewed as complicity with the United States at the expense of the region's people. For example, U.S. support for Israel had long been tolerated by regional allies in exchange for military protection and diplomatic support. Yet there was increasing pressure on these regimes to distance themselves from Washington so as to ensure their own survival. The United States and its Arab allies recognized that unconditional alliances could become a liability for all concerned.

These changes presented a potential break from the long-standing pattern of imperialism that had shaped the modern Middle East. From direct European colonialism after World War I to U.S.–Soviet competition during the Cold War to contemporary U.S. hegemony, no other part of the non-Western world had been so central to superpower intervention. Steadily expanding its influence since the beginning of oil exploration in Saudi Arabia in the 1930s, U.S. foreign policy in the region had always merged economic, military–strategic, and political interests. Washington played a decisive role in the Arab–Israeli conflict for decades, and for many years forged alliances with local regimes to deter the Soviet Union and organize a regional balance of power. United States foreign policy always tried to walk the line between supporting Israel and securing access to Middle Eastern oil. Washington pursued both of these often-contradictory objectives after World War II, although their relationship shifted at particular junctures. During the Cold War, the pursuit of both objectives led the United States to balance regimes against each other, vie with Moscow in regional alliance-building, and offer security and military assistance to U.S. allies.

As was the case in Latin America, these objectives were pursued with little regard for the persistent authoritarianism of most Middle Eastern regimes. Indeed, Washington often seemed to prefer pliable dictators. The United States established alliances with many non-democratic regimes in the region whether they were traditional or modern, religious or secular. The domestic politics of these countries was always secondary, since Washington was largely interested in their compliance with U.S. foreign policy interests. Egypt and Jordan, for example, were considered "friendly" states because they were reliable U.S. allies and made peace with Israel. Iran and Syria, on the contrary, were "rogue" states because they organized opposition to U.S. involvement in the region and remained hostile to Israel. But all four countries routinely violated human rights, suspended civil liberties, jailed dissidents, co-opted the opposition, and ruled by decree. This long history helps explain why U.S. arguments for regime change in Iraq under the banner of democracy were greeted with wide suspicion in the region.

In pursuing its foreign policy objectives, the United States initially tended to forge alliances and relations with local regimes that could organize a balance of power, allowing the United States to avoid direct involvement. That policy's eventual failure helped explain the dramatic shift from Washington's multilateral approach in the 1990 Gulf War to the virtual unilateralism of the 2003 invasion of Iraq. United States policy centered on two principles: securing an alliance with Saudi Arabia beginning in the 1940s and building Iran as a regional symbol of pro-Western secularism and modernization during the 1950s. In both cases, Washington sought access to the Persian Gulf and, after 1948, tried to protect Israel from hostile neighbors. Over time, however, it could not rely on its relationship with either of these autocratic regimes. The Iranian revolution of 1979 and the implications of the Saudi connection to fundamentalist Islamic movements, ignored by U.S. policymakers for decades but made public after September 11, precipitated a new set of policies and strategies for their implementation.

Washington's long-standing relationship with Saudi Arabia served for decades as one leg of its Gulf policy. The kingdom's importance was strictly a function of its oil wealth. Though a member of the Organization of the

Petroleum Exporting Countries (OPEC), Saudi Arabia played a role beyond the capacity of any other supplier. Because it directly controlled about a quarter of the world's proven petroleum reserves and maintained a larger unused capacity than any other country, only Riyadh was in a position to be a "swing producer"; it could therefore influence global oil production and pricing by switching production on to make up for a lag or cutting production back when another producer exceeded its quota. Working closely with the United States, the Saudis maintained this market position for decades, in return for which they received crucial military protection and diplomatic support. Political control and stability in Saudi Arabia were central to the economic fortunes of the entire world, and relations with the kingdom became an important pillar of U.S. foreign policy.

For all of its interest in stability, however, the U.S.–Saudi alliance stimulated the rise of an intensely destabilizing force: Islamic fundamentalism. It is important to understand the dual nature of Saudi Arabia's power structure. The kings always handled political affairs, but they were allied with Wahhabism, the puritanical, militaristic, and intolerant sect of Islam that had been adopted by the al-Saud family at the beginning of the twentieth century. Religion and politics in Saudi Arabia worked together through a compromise that has dominated the domestic political landscape in recent years. The Wahhabis oversaw the state's religious, cultural, and proselytizing activities. To control domestic criticism of their alliance with the United States, the kings accorded the Wahhabis considerable autonomy and funding to pursue their religio-cultural activities. The unintended consequence of this arrangement was that the government, by association, wound up financing many of the fundamentalist schools in Afghanistan and Pakistan that were later linked to terrorism. It was no coincidence that fourteen of the nineteen hijackers in the September 11 attacks were of Saudi origin. Immediately following the attacks, the U.S. airbase at Dhahran, Saudi Arabia, was closed, and the relationship with Riyadh came under strain as news of the Saudi connection to fundamentalist Islam received much attention from U.S. political analysts and the media. Although arms deals continued to be signed and both countries professed a strong diplomatic friendship, their relationship was fundamentally changed by the al Qaeda attack. Saudi Arabia, though dependent on the United States for military support, could no longer contain the domestic unrest that plagued the country. Moreover, the regional consensus was that Saudi Arabia's uncritical alliance with the United States had made regional cooperation more difficult, damaged the possibility of a solution to the Arab–Israeli conflict, and fueled unrest across the Middle East.

Iran had not been a reliable ally in the Gulf for many years. Never averse to regime change and covert operations, the United States had worked with Britain to organize the coup that deposed Iran's democratically elected nationalist prime minister, Mohammed Mossadegh, in 1953—just a year before the CIA's similar subversion of the nationalist government of Jacobo

Arbenz in Guatemala. From 1953 to 1979 Washington acted to strengthen Iran as a pro-Western bulwark against Soviet influence, a guarantor of access to Gulf oil, and a protector of Israel. Under the circumstances, it was not surprising that the symbolism and ideology of the 1979 revolution were so anti-imperialist and anti-American. The revolution's leaders attacked what they called the "westoxication" of Iran, a term coined by Jalal Al-e-Ahmad in response to foreign influence in that country. Millions of Iranians chanted "death to America" as they overthrew Shah Mohammed Reza Pahlavi, the region's most overt ally of the United States. This began a watershed decade for U.S. policymakers. Iran broke relations with Israel and gave its embassy to the Palestine Liberation Organization, withdrew from the Central Treaty Organization (CENTO, the Cold War alliance committing member nations to mutual cooperation in containing the Soviet Union), cancelled $9 billion worth of Western arms contracts, and, in Ayatollah Khomeini's words, challenged regimes that were clients of the "Great Satan," an unambiguous reference to the United States. Saudi Arabia was high on his list.

With the start of the Iran–Iraq War in 1980, Washington discovered that Saddam Hussein could be a useful ally in the Gulf against Iran's anti-Western regime. Vehemently opposed to the newly formed Islamic state in Tehran, Washington supported Iraq during the eight-year war, going so far as to provide Baghdad with military intelligence and chemical weapons for use against Tehran.[2] The Iran–Iraq War caused an estimated four hundred thousand deaths and one million wounded on the Iranian side; three hundred thousand Iraqis died, and eight hundred thousand were wounded. In line with the Cold War balance-of-power strategy, the United States sold weapons to Iran in the late 1980s to fund the Contra rebels in Nicaragua. For Washington, weakening both Iran and Iraq ensured a balance of power in the Gulf, with neither country becoming more powerful than the other.

U.S. support for Saddam Hussein against Iran was not particularly surprising, although U.S.–Iraq relations had gone through ups and downs over the years. Maintaining congenial ties with the nationalist and secular Iraqi Baath Party since the 1950s, Washington had actively supported its coup in 1963, then distanced itself from Iraq during that country's alliance with the Soviet Union in 1972. The United States supported Iraq again for a decade after the Iranian revolution, but finally embarked on a strategy of containment and confrontation after Baghdad attempted to reshape the region with its 1990 invasion of Kuwait.

Saddam Hussein's decision to invade Kuwait was based on three claims: that Kuwait was "slant-drilling" across the border into Iraqi oilfields, that the Kuwaitis should pardon the more than $40 billion debt they were owed for financing Iraq's long war with Iran, and that Kuwait was a natural part

---

2. Julian Borger, "Rumsfeld Offered Help to Saddam," *Guardian*, December 31, 2002.

of Iraq, carved off by the British in the beginning of the twentieth century, and should therefore be returned to Iraq.

Saddam's claims did not receive much international support, however. After all, Iran faced equally devastating economic troubles after the war and also had border disputes with the United Arab Emirates and trouble with Afghanistan, but Tehran did not choose to go to war. The administration of George H. W. Bush reacted to Iraqi aggression by building a broad multinational coalition that included combat forces from more than twenty-five nations, among them Egypt, Saudi Arabia, and Syria. It led the UN Security Council to establish and enforce an embargo on Iraqi imports and exports, with some exceptions for food and humanitarian aid, and agreed to the formation of the UN Special Commission on Iraq (UNSCOM) to monitor and destroy Baghdad's weapons of mass destruction. After a massive air campaign that lasted several weeks and a brief but violent ground war, Iraqi forces were driven from Kuwait. The Iraqi regime was left in place, for the first Bush administration wanted to avoid chaos and disintegration and needed to have a central authority with which it could come to an agreement. Overall, Washington was undoubtedly successful in organizing an effective international response to Saddam's recklessness.

During the 1990s the government of Iraq increasingly resisted inspection and monitoring efforts and occasionally defied the posted no-fly zones, providing the administration of George W. Bush with a pretext for invasion. As the multinationalism of 1990 yielded to the unilateralism of 2003, nationalist responses, reminiscent of the local reactions to colonial powers after World War I, spread across the region. It had always been true of the Middle East that the broadest and most sustained resistance to foreign intervention and occupation had come from indigenous forces. Contrary to some accounts of Arabs as "apathetic and passive masses," more recent Middle Eastern scholarship has traced long-standing nationalist movements in the region.[3] Many Arabs had a sophisticated and highly politicized memory of the not-so-distant imperialism and all its consequences. The combination of U.S. invasion, direct occupation, support for Israel, and cooperation with repressive local regimes created a persistent web of complexities from which it would be difficult for Washington to extricate itself without a complete change of approach.

While U.S. neoconservatives tended to think that political and economic matters were always amenable to military solutions, other governments seemed to understand the limits of force. Middle Eastern oil was vital to dozens of countries, but not all assumed that securing it required resort to arms—unless, of course, more was at stake than oil. Many countries that depended on an uninterrupted flow of oil from the Gulf negotiated mutually

---

3. See the work of Sami Zubaidi, "The Fragments Imagine the Nation: The Case of Iraq," in *International Journal of Middle East Studies* 34, no. 2 (2002); Rashid Khalidi, *Palestinian Identity: The Construction of Modern National Consciousness* (New York: Columbia University Press, 1997).

beneficial economic agreements with producer countries. Recent U.S. policy in the Middle East, however, culminating with the invasion of a sovereign country with a strong national identity, did not sit well with many millions of people who had to suffer the consequences of war. They had a long memory, and they knew better than to believe that the Bush administration was interested solely in bringing democracy to their societies. Over the years, public opinion polls showed that Iraqis overwhelmingly wanted the United States out of their country.[4] By mid-2008, the Iraqi prime minister Nouri al-Maliki—who was cooperating with the United States—had pushed for a guaranteed troop-withdrawal date. The irony was obvious: for all of Washington's talk of spreading democracy, U.S. military policy directly contradicted Iraqi public opinion.

The neoconservative argument for going to war in Iraq, though brewing since the early 1990s, was easier to make in the post–Cold War and post–September 11 Middle Eastern environment. The United States had become less reliant on its allies in the region, and a strong relationship with Saudi Arabia, though desirable, was no longer supported by either U.S. or Saudi public opinion. It was easier for the neoconservatives to push for regime change in view of the fact that appeasing authoritarian leaders, a practice pursued for decades, could no longer guarantee U.S. geostrategic interests. Iraq, which sat on huge oil reserves, was showing no signs of bending to the will of Washington. A long-held desire to remove Saddam Hussein from power would, the neoconservatives argued, build a "democratic," capitalist, and Western-oriented regime in the region that would help promote U.S. objectives and a secure oil supply.

But the arguments for going to war obscured changes that were already occurring in the region, changes that were reducing the very same threats that the Bush administration was emphasizing. In the aftermath of September 11, regional cooperation was on the rise. Jordan, after supporting Saddam Hussein in his ill-fated 1990 invasion of Kuwait, restored relations with both Saudi Arabia and Kuwait. Scholarly research and public-opinion polls in the region recorded increasingly favorable attitudes toward democracy.[5] Saudi Arabia presented an unprecedented peace plan for settling the Arab–Israeli conflict in 2002 that required Israel to withdraw from the Palestinian territories it had occupied in 1967 in exchange for peace with

---

4. See, e.g., Amit R. Paley, "Most Iraqis Favor Immediate Pullout, Polls Show," *Washington Post*, September 27, 2007. The article stated, "A strong majority of Iraqis want U.S.-led military forces to immediately withdraw from the country, saying their swift departure would make Iraq more secure and decrease sectarian violence, according to new polls by the State Department and independent researchers." Three-quarters said they would feel safer if U.S. forces left. See also Cesar G. Soriano and Steven Komarow, "Poll: Iraqis Out of Patience," *USA Today*, April 30, 2004, and a number of other polls.

5. See survey research by Mark Tessler, "Islam and Democracy in the Middle East: The Impact of Religious Orientations on Attitudes Toward Democracy in Four Countries," in *Comparative Politics* 34 (April 2002): 337–354.

all Arab countries—a striking offer since only two Arab countries, Egypt and Jordan, had made peace with Israel since its formation in 1948. The Saudi initiative received very little attention from either the United States or Israel. Most important, Iraq had not acted aggressively toward any of its neighbors in the years leading up to the invasion, a factor that contributed to the international isolation of the United States as it moved toward preemptive war.

There were other policies the United States could have used to secure its geostrategic interests and neutralize old enemies. The United States could have encouraged unfriendly regimes to cooperate. Iran, for example, had cooperated with Washington in the war against Afghanistan because the Taliban was also a threat to Tehran. After helping in the capture of wanted militants across the border, the Iranians were surprised that they were featured in Bush's famous "axis of evil" speech in 2002. In short, there were some promising developments in the region that presented Washington with alternatives to going to war, missed—or rejected—opportunities that helped shape the course and outcome of the Iraq War.

## PLAN OF THE BOOK

This text is organized in two sections. Part I, "The Policy of Preemption," recounts the events surrounding the war, exploring both its causes and the plans that were pursued by the various actors. Part II, "Consequences of a Preemptive War," is thematically organized around some of the ramifications and implications of the war. Each chapter begins with an introduction by the editors, followed by selections from relevant primary documents.

| xxxiii

Chapter 1, "From Containment to Preemptive War: Iraq and the United States in a Unipolar Moment," charts the decision-making process that influenced the Gulf War of 1990 and the invasion of 2003. It documents the ideas and arguments surrounding the debates about containment and preemption. Chapter 2, "Organizing for Preemptive War: Iraq and the Presidency of George W. Bush," discusses the arguments for preemptive war made by an administration that had embraced neoconservatism, examines changes in the power structure among nations, and summarizes the role of international institutions in interpreting Washington's drive toward invasion. Chapter 3, "International Reaction to the War," examines the positions of other countries and looks at the widespread international resistance to the war. Chapter 4, "Liberators or Occupiers? The Coalition Provisional Authority," explores the implementation of law and order in Iraq from 2003, when combat operations formally ended, to the handover of sovereignty to the Iraqis in June 2004. United States officials issued a series of orders through the Coalition Provisional Authority to lay the foundation for how Iraq should be organized once formal power was transferred. Chapter 5, "Insurgency, Counterinsurgency, or Civil War?" examines the factionalization and fractionalization of the Iraqi state and the ensuing violence. While considering the role of the United States in fueling the insurgency, the chapter also emphasizes identity politics in Iraq and the negotiation of power among the various groups.

The thematically organized part II, "Consequences of a Preemptive War," extends the analysis of the Iraq War as a case study in preemption, examining the consequences of preemption in such areas as human rights and international law and state- and nation-building in a post–September 11 world order. The Bush administration, facing important issues surrounding development, democratization, privatization, and international law in Iraq and in the United States, took a unilateral and preemptive approach, which required a rethinking of democratic norms and legal requirements. Chapter 6, "Democratization from Above or Below?" is a discussion of the course of Iraqi state-building, emphasizing the question of whether the state-building process was determined by Iraqi voices or whether U.S. involvement impeded and overshadowed national reconciliation. Chapter 7, "Securing Oil, Preempting Development," addresses Washington's attempts to realize long-held foreign policy goals by privatizing the Iraqi economy and securing "free access" to oil while ignoring Iraqi and alternative development trajectories. Chapter 8, "Human Rights and International Law: U.S. Methods and Operations in Preemptive War," explores the roots of the extralegal practices used by the Bush administration during the Iraq War

and examines the justifications it employed. The roles of constitutional principles, the Geneva Conventions, and human rights covenants are of special concern. Chapter 9, "Policing Terror Versus a War on Terror," reveals that the administration prepared its plan to invade Iraq as part of a broader "war on terror" that adopted a particularly militarized approach to the problem. An additional concern is how this "war" impacted both the judicial system and civil rights in the United States. Chapter 10, "Preemptive Democracy," explores the notion of the "unitary presidency," its effects on democracy at home, and the administration's attempts to circumvent the checks and balances in the U.S. political system. The concluding chapter, "The Limits of Preemption: The United States in the World," provides a historical assessment that is intended to help readers consider the many important questions raised by the preemptive invasion of Iraq. It explores the far-reaching consequences of preemption and unilateralism in world affairs and the consequences of the U.S. drive for hegemony on both interstate relations and democracy at home.

# PART ONE

# THE POLICY OF PREEMPTION

# CHAPTER 1

## FROM CONTAINMENT
## TO PREEMPTIVE WAR

### IRAQ AND THE UNITED STATES
### IN A UNIPOLAR MOMENT

A BROAD BIPARTISAN agreement to keep Saddam Hussein "in his box" lay behind a relatively consistent U.S. policy of containment from 1992 to 2001. Presidents George H. W. Bush and Bill Clinton worked with the United Nations to organize a regime of economic sanctions, oil embargoes, and weapons inspections; enforced northern and southern "no-fly zones"; ringed Iraq with military bases and forces; strengthened Kuwait; ran intelligence and harassment operations in the Kurdish north; occasionally punished Saddam Hussein's armed forces; and supported an Iraqi opposition. The policy did "contain" the Iraqi leader, although Baghdad always sought to undermine it. But Washington's claims that containment was relatively inexpensive in terms of U.S. blood, money, and political capital, and that it prevented Saddam Hussein from challenging vital U.S. interests in the Gulf, ignored the policy's high humanitarian price.

Containment had become the centerpiece of U.S. policy in the Persian Gulf not because Iraq posed an active threat to regional stability but because Baghdad remained an irritant to Washington. An important Gulf power that refused to accept U.S. hegemony, Iraq maintained its militant hostility to Israel; openly challenged the reigning "Washington consensus" on globalization, open markets, and free trade; and actively sought to organize a counterweight to U.S. plans for the region. This challenge to U.S. hegemony was taken particularly seriously by U.S. policymakers because of Iraq's large oil reserves and Saddam Hussein's status as one of the region's last secular Arab nationalists. Washington's claim that the Iraqi leader was still an active threat to international peace and stability was false, for the Gulf War and the sanctions regime had seriously degraded and weakened Iraq. Containment had been designed to serve broad U.S. strategic interests rather than to meet a particular threat, however—and it did so at an enormous cost to Iraqi civilians and to the country's infrastructure. A 1999 UNICEF report documented a 75 percent reduction in Iraq's gross national product, a doubling of the child-mortality rate, and significant increases in malnutrition and mental illness since the embargo had begun, prompting the resignations of three top UN officials responsible for overseeing and coordinating the limited international assistance allowed by the sanctions regime. As the full impact of the sanctions became more broadly known, it undermined Washington's claims that containment did not violate humanitarian standards.

Two successive administrations had worked throughout the 1990s to organize an international response to Baghdad's earlier attempts to redefine Persian Gulf politics. But Baghdad continued to resist inspection and monitoring, circumvent weapons embargoes, undermine the UN "oil for food" program, and defy no-fly zones. While Baghdad was too weak to materially affect the course of events, its behavior provided ammunition to those who were prepared to abandon containment for a more aggressive strategy. Within two months of George W. Bush's election, a changing domestic and international environment provided the opportunity for the redefinition of U.S. foreign policy that made possible his preemptive invasion of Iraq.

This redefinition had developed fitfully through the 1990s as both political parties struggled to articulate a new foreign-policy paradigm. The long crisis and eventual collapse of the Soviet Union left the United States as the world's only superpower. But there was nothing inevitable about George W. Bush's foreign policy. The multilateral coalition that had expelled Iraq from Kuwait had been led by the United States and organized through the United Nations, yet the consensus that had structured U.S. policy was fraying. Important Washington figures continued to defend the containment policies of Presidents George H. W. Bush and Bill Clinton and pointed to fifty years of successful containment of the Soviet Union by way of example. George Kennan's seminal essay "The Sources of Soviet Conduct" had structured Washington's approach to Moscow for some time, but the debates that had roiled the Eisenhower administration reappeared years later. When neoconservatives referred to John Foster Dulles's embrace of "rollback" and claimed that world affairs had taken an entirely new direction, the stage was set for a debate that occupied Washington for the rest of the decade.

Although the George W. Bush administration made statements to the contrary, it did not embrace preemption because containment had failed. The new policy emerged as one part of a general reevaluation of international conditions that resulted from a generation of conservative ascendancy in domestic affairs, the collapse of the Soviet Union, and the emergence of the United States as the world's only superpower. An earlier generation of attacks on President Nixon's commitment to détente and arms control, President Ford's caution in the aftermath of the Vietnam defeat and the Watergate scandal, and President Carter's embrace of negotiations and human rights had produced a coherent right-wing alternative to decades of foreign policy that had helped propel Ronald Reagan to the presidency in 1980. Reagan had abandoned much of his most bellicose language and had come to an understanding with the leadership of the Soviet Union well before the end of his administration, but an updated version of his early positions was taking shape by the end of the 1990s. Refined by outsiders during Clinton's presidency, neoconservatism's second generation presented itself as the muscular, no-nonsense guide to national renewal in a post–Cold War international environment that now provided an unprecedented opportunity to organize a "New American Century." Echoing and adapting the arguments their predecessors had developed, the architects of the invasion of Iraq went to war with a Democratic administration that they claimed had lost its way, was squandering a historic opportunity, and was substituting weakness and naïveté for strength and resolve. If the early neoconservatives had focused on the alleged imminent threat posed by a relentless Soviet Union, the second generation would similarly argue that Iraq posed a "looming" threat. The environment had changed dramatically between the Carter and Clinton administrations, but the neoconservative battle to shape public opinion and acquire political influence rested on very similar claims.

Founded in 1997, the Project for the New American Century (PNAC) appeared during a historical moment that was different from that which had nurtured original neoconservative organizations such as the Committee on the Present Danger. Instead of issuing dire warnings about an imminent threat, | 3 as the first generation had when the USSR was a world power, the PNAC was adapting neoconservatism to an international environment in which the United States stood unchallenged. Rearmament was no longer portrayed as a defensive measure necessary to save a threatened country; now the collapse of the Soviet Union gave Washington the chance to remake the entire world. Francis Fukuyama's triumphalist essay "The End of History?" (1.1) had echoed British prime minister Margaret Thatcher's claim that "there is no alternative" to Western-style capitalism. The *Washington Post* columnist Charles Krauthammer celebrated the arrival of "the unipolar moment" a year later, in an article so titled, arguing that "the center of world power is the unchallenged superpower, the United States, attended by its Western allies. . . . Our best hope for safety in such times, as in difficult times past, is in American strength and will—the strength and will to lead a unipolar world, unashamedly laying down the rules of world order and being prepared to enforce them."[1] Former secretary of state Kissinger counseled caution (1.2), but the 1992 "Defense Planning Guidance" signaled Washington's search for a post–Cold War rationale for a world dominated by U.S. military and political power (1.3). This reevaluation began the process that would place military dominance, preemptive war, and unilateralism at the center of George W. Bush's foreign policy (1.4, 1.6, 1.8–1.11). Years before anyone had heard of al Qaeda or paid much attention to Osama bin Laden, neoconservative spokespeople had articulated the broad

---

1. Charles Krauthammer, "The Unipolar Moment," *Foreign Affairs* (1990), 23–33.

outlines of a foreign policy that featured dramatic increases in military spending, confrontation with unfriendly regimes, a readiness to act unilaterally, and preemptive war.

Buffeted by insistent demands that the Iraqi problem be settled once and for all, the proponents of containment were increasingly on the defensive for the rest of the decade. But, in an important sense, the debate about Iraq was never simply about containment or preemption. Barely hidden in the conflicting recommendations were different assumptions about the nature of the international system and the role of the United States in it. As the Clinton presidency came to a close, the neoconservatives were poised to assume the leadership of a new administration. Prominent Washington insiders who had led the Project for the New American Century soon occupied central positions of power in the U.S. government. Indeed, Elliott Abrams, John Bolton, Dick Cheney, Frank Gaffney, Donald Kagan, Zalmay Khalilzad, Lewis "Scooter" Libby, Donald Rumsfeld, and Paul Wolfowitz had signed the PNAC cofounder William Kristol's "Statement of Principles" (1.8). Sensing an opportunity to take advantage of Krauthammer's "unipolar moment," they swiftly moved to reorganize U.S. foreign policy around the related themes of unilateralism, military supremacy, and preemption. Not long after his election, President George W. Bush made it clear that he was prepared to embrace a distinctly more aggressive foreign policy than had his predecessors. The terrorist attacks of September 11, 2001, provided him the opportunity to deploy the strategy that neoconservative thinkers had articulated for U.S. foreign policy in a unipolar world. Iraq would be the test case.

4 |

# DOCUMENT 1.1

Francis Fukuyama, a minor official in the State Department, burst onto the national scene toward the end of the Reagan presidency when he announced that the age-old struggle of ideologies had come to an end with the triumph of consumerist liberal democracy. His confident assertion was a harbinger of later arguments that the export of U.S.-style democracy and capitalism was part of the march of history and would serve the larger interests of humanity.

FRANCIS FUKUYAMA, "THE END OF HISTORY?"
*NATIONAL INTEREST,* SUMMER 1989 (EXCERPT)

The twentieth century saw the developed world descend into a paroxysm of ideological violence, as liberalism contended first with the remnants of absolutism, then bolshevism and fascism, and finally an updated Marxism that threatened to lead to the ultimate apocalypse of nuclear war. But the century that began full of self-confidence in the ultimate triumph of Western liberal democracy seems at its close to be returning full circle to where it started: not to an "end of ideology" or a convergence between capitalism and socialism, as earlier predicted, but to an unabashed victory of economic and political liberalism.

The triumph of the West, of the Western idea, is evident first of all in the total exhaustion of viable systematic alternatives to Western liberalism. In the past decade, there have been unmistakable changes in the intellectual climate of the world's two largest communist countries, and the beginnings of significant reform movements in both. But this phenomenon extends beyond high politics and it can be seen also in the ineluctable spread of consumerist Western culture in such diverse contexts as the peasants' markets and color television sets now omnipresent throughout China, the cooperative restaurants and clothing stores opened in the past year in Moscow, the Beethoven piped into Japanese department stores, and the rock music enjoyed alike in Prague, Rangoon, and Tehran.

What we may be witnessing is not just the end of the Cold War, or the passing of a particular period of postwar history, but the end of history as such: that is, the end point of mankind's ideological evolution and the universalization of Western liberal democracy as the final form of human government. This is not to say that there will no longer be events to fill the pages of *Foreign Affairs*'s yearly summaries of international relations, for the victory of liberalism has occurred primarily in the realm of ideas or consciousness and is as yet incomplete in the real or material world. But there are powerful reasons for believing that it is the ideal that will govern the material world in the long run.

# DOCUMENT 1.2

Henry Kissinger, the secretary of state in the Nixon and Ford administrations, used the occasion of the Gulf War to issue a veiled warning about President George H. W. Bush's optimism that a "new world order" was at hand. Turning the tables on his longtime neoconservative critics at the same time, he suggested that a messianic desire to remake the world was no substitute for a careful and sober assessment of every given situation. Despite his record of favoring covert action and intervention as national security advisor and secretary of state, Kissinger's "realism" seemed to defend the caution and acceptance of limits that underlay the strategy of containment.

HENRY KISSINGER, "A FALSE DREAM,"
*LOS ANGELES TIMES*, FEBRUARY 24, 1991 (EXCERPT)

America has never been comfortable with fighting wars for limited objectives. World War I was cast as the war to end all wars; World War II was to usher in a new era of permanent peace to be monitored by the United

Nations. Now, the Gulf War is justified in similar terms deeply embedded in the American tradition. In his speech of January 16 announcing hostilities with Iraq, President Bush described the opportunity for building a new world order 'where the rule of law . . . governs the conduct of nations,' and 'in which a credible United Nations can use its peacekeeping role to fulfill the promise and the vision of the UN's founders.'

I have greatly admired President Bush's skill and fortitude in building the coalition. But the new world order cannot possibly fulfill the idealistic expectations expressed by the president; I doubt indeed whether they accurately describe what happened during the Gulf crisis.

American idealism was most eloquently formulated by Woodrow Wilson in his attempt to replace the ever-shifting alignments of the balance of power with an overriding common purpose. In Wilson's words, peace depends 'not on a balance of power but on a community of power. . . . Nations agree that there shall be but one combination and that is the combination of all against the wrongdoer.' In this view, the conduct of international affairs follows objective criteria, not unlike those of the law. All nations are expected to respond to challenges to international order from a common perspective and by united opposition.

That hope was disappointed in the League of Nations and later by the United Nations. And not by accident. While every country has some interest in elaborating a concept that it can invoke in its own defense, the willingness to run risks varies with history, geography, power, in other words, with national interest.

Despite the near unanimity of UN decisions, historians will in all likelihood treat the Gulf crisis as a special case rather than as a watershed. . . .

The key element was American leadership—symbolized by the extraordinary set of personal relations between President Bush and world leaders. Without that American role, the world community would almost certainly have reached different conclusions.

None of this is to deprecate the extraordinary achievement of the administration in coalition-building. It is to warn against counting on being able to repeat this pattern in the future.

Most poignantly, American preeminence cannot last. Had Kuwait been invaded two years later, the American defense budget would have declined so as to preclude a massive overseas deployment. Nor can the American economy indefinitely sustain a policy of essentially unilateral global interventionism—indeed, we had to seek a foreign subsidy of at least $50 billion to sustain this crisis. Therefore, neither the United States nor foreign nations should treat the concept of the new world order as an institutionalization of recent practices.

Any reflection about a new world order must begin with noting its difference from the Cold War period. During the Cold War the principal fissure was between East and West. The ideological conflict led to a more or less uniform perception of the threat, at least among the industrial democ-

racies which produce 72 percent of the world's GNP. The military and—
for the greater period of time—technological predominance of the United
States also shaped a common military policy. Economically, interdepen-
dence moved from a slogan to reality.

The world into which we will be moving will be infinitely more complex. Ideological challenges will be fewer; the danger of nuclear war with
the Soviet Union will be sharply reduced. On the other hand, no one can
know how well Soviet command and control arrangements for nuclear
weapons will withstand domestic upheaval. Elsewhere, local conflicts will
be both more likely and, given modern technology, more lethal. The collapse of the Soviet empire in Eastern Europe and the loosening bonds of
the Western Alliance have unleashed nationalist rivalries not seen since
World War I. The post-colonial period has spawned fanatical fundamentalist forces very hard for the comfortable, if not smug, industrial democracies
to comprehend, much less to master. Economic rivalry among Japan, which
is growing into superpower status, the European Community, which is becoming increasingly assertive, and the United States will no longer be restrained by overriding security concerns. The confluence of these elements
will characterize the new era as one of turmoil, and will require major adjustments in how we think about international relations.

United States policymakers face a number of imperatives:

They must recognize that it is not possible to deal with every issue simultaneously. America must be selective, husbanding its resources as well
as its credibility. Three levels of threat must be distinguished: those we must
be prepared to deal with alone if necessary, those we will deal with only
in association with other nations and those threats that do not sufficiently
challenge American interests to justify any military intervention.

They need to reexamine alliance policy and reallocate responsibility.
Countries associated with us must be brought to understand that the United
States' armed forces are not a mercenary force-for-hire. The special circumstances of the Persian Gulf left President Bush no choice except a disproportionate assumption of risk by the United States. As a general rule in the
future, however, American military forces should be employed only for
causes for which we are prepared to pay ourselves. That, in fact, is a good
working definition of American national interest.

United States policymakers must recognize that the new world order
cannot be built to American specifications. America cannot force feed a
global sense of community where none exists. But it has an opportunity for
creating more limited communities based on a genuine sense of shared purpose. This is why perhaps the most creative—if least well known—foreign
policy initiative of the Bush administration is its effort to create a Western
Hemispheric Free Trade Area, beginning with Mexico, Canada and the
United States.

The list is illustrative, not exhaustive. In the end, the deepest challenge
to America will be philosophical: how to define order. History so far has

| 7

shown us only two roads to international stability: domination or equilibrium. We do not have the resources for domination, nor is such a course compatible with our values. So we are brought back to a concept maligned in much of America's intellectual history—the balance of power.

Of course it is possible to define the issue away by postulating the absence of clashing interests. I would welcome such an outcome, but find little support for it either in history or in the above analysis.

There is no escaping the irony that our triumph in the Cold War has projected us into a world where we must operate by maxims that historically have made Americans uncomfortable. To many Americans, the most objectionable feature of the balance of power is its apparent moral neutrality. For the balance of power is concerned above all with preventing one power or group of powers from achieving hegemony. Winston Churchill described it: 'The policy of England takes no account of which nation it is that seeks the overlordship of Europe. It is concerned solely with whoever is the strongest or the potentially domineering tyrant. It is a law of public policy which we are following, and not a mere expedient dictated by accidental circumstances or likes or dislikes. . . . '

A policy based on such concepts knows few permanent enemies and few permanent friends. In the current Gulf crisis it would avoid branding Iraq as forever beyond the pale. Rather, it would seek to balance rivalries as old as history by striving for an equilibrium between Iraq, Iran, Syria and other regional powers. . . .

These balances all need a balancer—a role the United States can no longer play entirely by itself and in some circumstances may not choose to exercise at all. But it needs criteria to establish priorities.

It is a paradox that no nation is in a better position to contribute to a new world order than the United States: it is domestically cohesive, its economy is less vulnerable to outside forces, its military capacity for the foreseeable future is still the world's largest and most effective. Our challenge is the price of success: triumph in the Cold War has produced a world requiring adjustment of traditional concepts. But the price of success is one for which most other nations would envy us.

# DOCUMENTS 1.3 AND 1.4

In 1991, Defense Secretary Richard Cheney asked his undersecretary for policy, a hawkish intellectual named Paul Wolfowitz, to draft that year's congressionally mandated "Defense Planning Guidance." Wolfowitz and two of his associates—Lewis "Scooter" Libby and Zalmay Khalilzad—produced an exceptionally important foreign policy document. Leaked to the *New York Times* by an official who thought it should be debated in public, then rewritten and softened by an embarrassed administration, its early emphasis on military action and its tentative embrace of preemption and unilateralism would find more forceful expression in the analyses of the Project for the New American Century, statements by Condoleezza Rice, and the invasion and occupation of Iraq (1.5, 1./–1.9, 1.16–1.17).

---

PAUL WOLFOWITZ, LEWIS LIBBY, AND ZALMAY KHALILZAD, "DEFENSE PLANNING GUIDANCE," FEBRUARY 18, 1992 (EXCERPT)

This Defense Planning Guidance addresses the fundamentally new situation which has been created by the collapse of the Soviet Union, the disintegration of the internal as well as the external empire, and the discrediting of Communism as an ideology with global pretensions and influence. The new international environment has also been shaped by the victory of the United States and its Coalition allies over Iraqi aggression—the first post–Cold War conflict and a defining event in U.S. global leadership. In addition to these two victories, there has been a less visible one, the integration of Germany and Japan into a U.S.-led system of collective security and the creation of a democratic "zone of peace."

Our fundamental strategic position and choices are therefore very different from those we have faced in the past. The policies that we adopt in this new situation will set the nation's direction for the next century.

I. Goals and Objectives
   A. National Security Policy Goals
      In the midst of a new era of fundamental worldwide change, ongoing U.S. leadership in global affairs will remain a constant fixture. In support of our international commitments, we will implement defense policies and programs designed to further essential national security policy goals:
      - As a first order of priority, we will ensure the survival of the United States as a free and independent nation, with its fundamental values intact and people secure.
      - We will seek to promote those positive trends which serve to support and reinforce our national interests, principally, promotion, establishment, and expansion of democracy and free market institutions worldwide.
      - We will maintain our security vigilance against national, regional, or global threats (whether ideologically- or technologically-based) which undermine international stability and order.
      - We will continue to support and protect those bilateral, multilateral, international, or regionally-based institutions, processes, and relationships which afford us opportunities to share responsibility

for global and regional security while also allowing for selective engagement when required.

B. Defense Strategy Objectives

These national security policy goals can be translated into two broad strategy objectives that lend further clarity to our overall defense requirements.

Our first objective is to prevent the reemergence of a new rival, either on the territory of the former Soviet Union or elsewhere, that poses a threat on the order of that posed formerly by the Soviet Union. This is a dominant consideration underlying the new regional defense strategy and requires that we endeavor to prevent any hostile power from dominating a region whose resources would, under consolidated control, be sufficient to generate a global power. These regions include Western Europe, East Asia, the territory of the former Soviet Union, and Southwest Asia.

There are three additional aspects to this objective: First, the U.S. must show the leadership necessary to establish and protect a new order that holds the promise of convincing potential competitors that they need not aspire to a greater role or pursue a more aggressive posture to protect their legitimate interests. Second, in the non-defense areas, we must account sufficiently for the interests of the advanced industrial nations to discourage them from challenging our leadership or seeking to overturn the established political and economic order. Finally, we must maintain the mechanisms for deterring potential competitors from even aspiring to a larger regional or global role. An effective reconstitution capability is important here, since it implies that a potential rival could not hope to quickly or easily gain a predominant military position in the world.

The second objective is to address sources of regional conflict and instability in such a way as to promote increasing respect for international law; limit international violence; and encourage the spread of democratic forms of government and open economic systems. These objectives are especially important in deterring conflicts or threats in regions of security importance to the United States because of their proximity (such as Latin America), or where we have treaty obligations or security commitments to other nations. While the U.S. cannot become the world's "policeman," by assuming responsibility for righting every wrong, we will retain the preeminent responsibility for addressing selectively those wrongs which threaten not only our interests, but those of our allies or friends, or which could seriously unsettle international relations. Various types of U.S. interests may be involved in such instances: access to vital raw materials, primarily Persian Gulf oil; proliferation of weapons of mass destruction and ballistic missiles; threats to U.S. citizens from terrorism or regional or local conflict; and threats to U.S. society from narcotics trafficking. . . .

## PATRICK E. TYLER, "U.S. STRATEGY PLAN CALLS FOR INSURING NO RIVALS DEVELOP," *NEW YORK TIMES*, MARCH 8, 1992

In a broad new policy statement that is in its final drafting stage, the Defense Department asserts that America's political and military mission in the post–Cold-War era will be to insure that no rival superpower is allowed to emerge in Western Europe, Asia or the territory of the former Soviet Union.

A 46-page document that has been circulating at the highest levels of the Pentagon for weeks, and which Defense Secretary Dick Cheney expects to release later this month, states that part of the American mission will be "convincing potential competitors that they need not aspire to a greater role or pursue a more aggressive posture to protect their legitimate interests."

The classified document makes the case for a world dominated by one superpower whose position can be perpetuated by constructive behavior and sufficient military might to deter any nation or group of nations from challenging American primacy.

### Rejecting Collective Approach
To perpetuate this role, the United States "must sufficiently account for the interests of the advanced industrial nations to discourage them from challenging our leadership or seeking to overturn the established political and economic order," the document states.

With its focus on this concept of benevolent domination by one power, the Pentagon document articulates the clearest rejection to date of collective internationalism, the strategy that emerged from World War II when the five victorious powers sought to form a United Nations that could mediate disputes and police outbreaks of violence.

Though the document is internal to the Pentagon and is not provided to Congress, its policy statements are developed in conjunction with the National Security Council and in consultation with the President or his senior National Security Advisors. Its drafting has been supervised by Paul D. Wolfowitz, the Pentagon's Under Secretary for Policy. Mr. Wolfowitz often represents the Pentagon on the Deputies Committee, which formulates policy in an interagency process dominated by the State and Defense departments.

The document was provided to the *New York Times* by an official who believes this post–Cold-War strategy debate should be carried out in the public domain. It seems likely to provoke further debate in Congress and among America's allies about Washington's willingness to tolerate greater aspirations for regional leadership from a united Europe or from a more assertive Japan.

Together with its attachments on force levels required to insure America's predominant role, the policy draft is a detailed justification for the Bush administration's "base force" proposal to support a 1.6-million-member military over the next five years, at a cost of about $1.2 trillion. Many Democrats in Congress have criticized the proposal as unnecessarily expensive.

Implicitly, the document foresees building a world security arrangement that pre-empts Germany and Japan from pursuing a course of substantial rearmament, especially nuclear armament, in the future.

In its opening paragraph, the policy document heralds the "less visible" victory at the end of the Cold War, which it defines as "the integration of Germany and Japan into a U.S.-led system of collective security and the creation of a democratic 'zone of peace.'"

The continuation of this strategic goal explains the strong emphasis elsewhere in the document and in other Pentagon planning on using military force, if necessary, to prevent the proliferation of nuclear weapons and other weapons of mass destruction in such countries as North Korea, Iraq, some of the successor republics to the Soviet Union and in Europe.

Nuclear proliferation, if unchecked by superpower action, could tempt Germany, Japan and other industrial powers to acquire nuclear weapons to deter attack from regional foes. This could start them down the road to global competition with the United States and, in a crisis over national interests, military rivalry.

The policy draft appears to be adjusting the role of the American nuclear arsenal in the new era, saying, "Our nuclear forces also provide an important deterrent hedge against the possibility of a revitalized or unforeseen global threat, while at the same time helping to deter third party use of weapons of mass destruction through the threat of retaliation."

## U.N. Action Ignored

The document is conspicuously devoid of references to collective action through the United Nations, which provided the mandate for the allied assault on Iraqi forces in Kuwait and which may soon be asked to provide a new mandate to force President Saddam Hussein to comply with his cease-fire obligations.

The draft notes that coalitions "hold considerable promise for promoting collective action" as in the Persian Gulf War, but that "we should expect future coalitions to be ad hoc assemblies, often not lasting beyond the crisis being confronted, and in many cases carrying only general agreement over the objectives to be accomplished."

What is most important, it says, is "the sense that the world order is ultimately backed by the U.S." and "the United States should be postured to act independently when collective action cannot be orchestrated" or in a crisis that demands quick response.

Bush Administration officials have been saying publicly for some time that they were willing to work within the framework of the United Nations, but that they reserve the option to act unilaterally or through selective coalitions, if necessary, to protect vital American interests.

But this publicly stated strategy did not rule out an eventual leveling of American power as world security stabilizes and as other nations place greater emphasis on collective international action through the United Nations.

In contrast, the new draft sketches a world in which there is one dominant military power whose leaders "must maintain the mechanisms for deterring potential competitors from even aspiring to a larger regional or global role."

### Sent to Administrators

The document is known in Pentagon parlance as the Defense Planning Guidance, an internal Administration policy statement that is distributed to the military leaders and civilian Defense Department heads to instruct them on how to prepare their forces, budgets and strategy for the remainder of the decade. The policy guidance is typically prepared every two years, and the current draft will yield the first such document produced after the end of the Cold War.

| 13

# DOCUMENT 1.5

The former secretary of defense Cheney defended the first Bush administration's decision to keep Saddam Hussein in power after the conclusion of the Gulf War, a position that did not conflict with his role in drafting the earlier "Defense Planning Guidance" (1.3). As vice president, his perspectives dramatically changed as he became a major architect and fierce proponent of "regime change" in Iraq.

---

"DICK CHENEY, SECRETARY OF DEFENSE FOR PRESIDENT GEORGE H. W. BUSH, DEFENDS THE ADMINISTRATION'S DECISION TO KEEP SADDAM HUSSEIN IN POWER," *FRONTLINE* INTERVIEW AIRED ON JANUARY 28, 1997 (EXCERPT)

I was not an enthusiast about getting U.S. forces and going into Iraq. We were there in the southern part of Iraq to the extent we needed to be there to defeat his forces and to get him out of Kuwait but the idea of going into Baghdad for example or trying to topple the regime wasn't anything I was enthusiastic about. I felt there was a real danger here that you would get bogged down in a long drawn-out conflict, that this was a dangerous, difficult part of the world, if you recall we were all worried about the possibility of Iraq coming apart, the Iranians restarting the conflict that they'd had in the eight-year bloody war with the Iranians and the Iraqis over eastern Iraq. We had concerns about the Kurds in the north; the Turks get very nervous every time we start to talk about an independent Kurdistan.

Plus there was the notion that you were going to set yourself a new war aim that we hadn't talked to anybody about. That you hadn't gotten Congress to approve, hadn't talked to the American people about. You're going to find yourself in a situation where you've redefined your war aims and now set up a new war aim that in effect would detract from the enormous success you just had. What we set out to do was to liberate Kuwait and to destroy his offensive capability, that's what I said repeatedly in my public statements. That was the mission I was given by the president. That's what we did. Now you can say, well you should have gone to Baghdad and gotten Saddam. I don't think so I think if we had done that we would have been bogged down there for a very long period of time with the real possibility we might not have succeeded.

# DOCUMENT 1.6

Robert Kagan, who had been a speechwriter for President Reagan's secretary of state George Schultz and was a cofounder of the Project for the New American Century, made an early neoconservative argument for unilateralism in organizing a "beneficial" U.S.-led world order.

ROBERT KAGAN, "AMERICAN POWER—A GUIDE FOR THE PERPLEXED," *COMMENTARY,* APRIL 1996 (EXCERPT)

"A nation's first duty is within its borders," Theodore Roosevelt once declared, but, he went on to say, "it is not thereby absolved from facing its duties in the world as a whole; and if it refuses to do so, it merely forfeits its right to struggle for a place among the people that shape the destiny of mankind." Embedded in that declaration is the idea that the American people should take a hand in shaping mankind's destiny, that playing such a role accords honor, and that the right to such honor must be earned. It is a conception of the national interest entirely alien to today's constricted usage, which gives us nothing to aspire to beyond our material needs.

What, then, ought we do? Any serious understanding of the national interest in our time must begin with the recognition that the world is not as it was in the 19th century or during the Cold War. Through the exercise of its material power and the power of its ideals, the United States has achieved a combination of national security and international mastery unknown since the days of Rome's dominance of the Mediterranean world. Today the international system is build not on a balance of power, but on American hegemony. . . .

The prolongation of this beneficial state of affairs as far into the future as possible would seem to be the best definition of America's national interest in the present era. . . .

If the national interest consists in the preservation of American preeminence, then the same general approach to foreign policy that brought us to our international pinnacle ought to be applied to keeping us there. That means maintaining American military superiority, not only to deter aggression, but also to discourage other great powers from trying to achieve parity with us. (This was the recommendation, unfortunately rejected, of the Pentagon's best policy planners during the Bush administration.) Failure to maintain that superiority will eventually encourage others, even those who do not yet have such ambitions, to challenge American hegemony, and will swiftly bring us back to the more dangerous world we have just departed.

Military strength alone will not avail, however, if we do not use it to maintain a world order which both supports and rests upon American hegemony. This requires a sharp departure from the narrow definition of national interests bequeathed to us by the realists. Their strategy has always been defensive and reactive. . . . Since today's benevolent circumstances are the unique product of our hegemonic influence, any lessening of that influence will allow others to play a much larger part than they do now in shaping the world to suit their needs. The price of American hegemony is that just as it was actively obtained, it must be actively maintained.

| 15

# DOCUMENT 1.7

This important intervention from a bipartisan group of respected and experienced "realists" addressed the accomplishments and the limits of U.S. containment policy in the Gulf. Focusing on the choices that faced the second Clinton administration, it took issue with the neoconservatives and recommended a flexible policy of "dual containment." All three authors had played significant roles in the development of U.S. foreign policy. Brzezinski had served as Carter's national security advisor, Scowcroft had occupied the same position under Presidents Ford and George H. W. Bush, and Murphy had been assistant secretary of state for Near Eastern and South Asian affairs during the Reagan administration. The piece is noteworthy in its understanding of long-range strategic goals and its recognition of the role of domestic public opinion.

ZBIGNIEW BRZEZINSKI, BRENT SCOWCROFT, AND
RICHARD MURPHY, "DIFFERENTIATED CONTAINMENT,"
*FOREIGN AFFAIRS*, MAY–JUNE 1997 (EXCERPT)

The Persian Gulf is one of the few regions whose importance to the United States is obvious. The flow of Gulf oil will continue to be crucial to the economic well-being of the industrialized world for the foreseeable future; developments in the Gulf will have a critical impact on issues ranging from Arab–Israeli relations to terrorism and nuclear nonproliferation. Every U.S. President since Richard Nixon has recognized that ensuring Persian Gulf security and stability is a vital U.S. interest.

The Clinton administration's strategy for achieving this goal during the President's first term was its attempted "dual containment" of Iraq and Iran. This is more a slogan than a strategy, however, and the policy may not be sustainable for much longer. In trying to isolate both of the Gulf's regional powers, the policy lacks strategic viability and carries a high financial and diplomatic cost. Saddam Hussein is still in power six years after his defeat at the hands of a multinational coalition, and the international consensus on continuing the containment of Iraq is fraying. . . . The advent of the Clinton administration's second term, together with the imminent inauguration of a new administration in Iran following this May's elections, provides an opportunity to review U.S. policies toward the Gulf and consider whether midcourse corrections could improve the situation.

When the British withdrew from the Persian Gulf in 1971, the United States became the principal foreign power in the region. For almost three decades it has pursued the goal of preserving regional stability, using a variety of means to that end, particularly regarding the northern Gulf powers of Iraq and Iran.

At first the United States relied on Iran as its chief regional proxy, supporting the Shah's Regime in the hope that it would be a source of stability. This policy collapsed in 1979 with the Iranian Revolution, when Iran switched from staunch ally to implacable foe. During the 1980s, the United States strove to maintain a de facto balance of power between Iraq and Iran so that neither would be able to achieve a regional hegemony that might threaten American interests. The United States provided some help to Iraq during the Iran–Iraq War of 1980–88, moved in other ways to counter the spread of Iranian-backed Islamic militancy, and provided—with Israeli encouragement—some help to Iran, chiefly in the context of seeking the release of American hostages. This era ended with Iraq invading Kuwait in 1990 and the United States leading an international coalition to war to restore Kuwaiti sovereignty and defeat Iraq's bid for dominance.

The Clinton administration came into office in 1993 facing the challenge of ensuring Gulf stability in a new international and regional environment. The disappearance of the Soviet Union gave the United States unprecedented freedom of action, while the Madrid Conference, sponsored by the

Bush administration, inaugurated a fundamentally new phase of the Middle East peace process, offering hope that the Arab–Israeli conflict might eventually prove solvable. The Clinton team's initial Middle East policy had two aspects: continued support for the peace process and dual containment of Iraq and Iran. These strands were seen as reinforcing each other: keeping both Iraq and Iran on the sidelines of regional politics, the administration argued, would protect Saudi Arabia and the smaller Gulf monarchies and enable Israel and the moderate Arab states to move toward peace, while the burgeoning Arab–Israeli detente would demonstrate that the attitudes of the "rejectionist front" were costly and obsolete.

Dual containment was envisaged not as a long-term solution to the problems of Gulf stability but as a way of temporarily isolating the two chief opponents of the American-sponsored regional order. Regarding Iraq, the policy involved maintaining the full-scale international economic sanctions and military containment the administration had inherited, including a no-fly zone in southern Iraq and a protected Kurdish enclave in the north. The Clinton administration stated that it merely sought Iraqi compliance with the post–Gulf War UN Security Council resolutions, particularly those mandating the termination of Iraq's weapons of mass destruction programs. In practice, the administration made it clear that it had no intention of dealing with Saddam Hussein's regime, and seemed content, for lack of a better alternative, to let Iraq stew indefinitely. The administration responded to Iraqi provocations, but saw little opportunity to oust Saddam except at great cost in blood and treasure.

| 17

The dual containment policy initially involved mobilizing international political opposition against Iran, together with limited unilateral economic sanctions. The Clinton administration asserted that it was not trying to change the Iranian regime per se but rather its behavior, particularly its quest for nuclear weapons, its support for terrorism and subversion in the region, and its opposition to the peace process. By early 1995, however, the U.S. attitude toward Iran began to harden. The Iranian behavior at issue had continued. But the real impetus for a shift seems to have come out of American domestic politics, in particular the administration's desire to head off a challenge on Iran policy mounted by an increasingly bellicose Republican Congress. . . .

At the start of President Clinton's second term, therefore, U.S. Persian Gulf policy is at an impasse. Saddam Hussein remains in power in Iraq and has even regained some control over the Kurdish areas of the north, while the Gulf War coalition that defeated him is eroding. Toughened U.S. sanctions against Iran, although doing some damage to the Iranian economy, have produced no major achievements and increasingly isolate America rather than their target. The continued willingness and ability of some members of the GCC [*Editors' Note: Gulf Cooperation Council*] and others to help implement these policies is open to question. What, then, is to be done?

The continued rule of Saddam Hussein poses a danger to the stability and security of the region. He has threatened his neighbors while doing everything possible to acquire weapons of mass destruction in direct violation of international law, even during the last several years, when subject to the most restrictive supervision in the history of international arms control. Although there are real costs involved in maintaining Iraq's pariah status, it is difficult to see how any policy in the military sphere other than continued containment can be adopted so long as Saddam remains in power. The United States should be prepared to maintain Iraq's military containment unilaterally should the will of others falter. Similarly, while there are costs to keeping Iraq's oil off the world market, retaining the economic embargo in general is necessary, because with unrestricted access to large profits Saddam would likely embark on further military development.

The United States may, however, need to consider a revised approach to the political and economic aspects of Iraq's containment, because not all of them can be implemented unilaterally. Furthermore, they have unfortunate consequences on the humanitarian situation in Iraq, which especially concerns some members of the GCC. While America's basic goal should continue to be keeping Saddam's Iraq in a straitjacket, the United States may need to adjust the fit to ensure the straitjacket holds. . . .

However one judges its achievements to date, dual containment cannot provide a sustainable basis for U.S. policy in the Persian Gulf. A more nuanced and differentiated approach to the region is in order, one in tune with America's longer-term interests. This new policy would keep Saddam boxed in, but would supplement such resolve with policy modifications to keep the Gulf War coalition united. The new policy would start with the recognition that the United States' current attempt at unilateral isolation of Iran is costly and ineffective and that its implementation, in the words of one recent study, "lacks the support of U.S. allies and is a leaky sieve." The United States should instead consider the possibilities of creative tradeoffs, such as the relaxation of opposition to the Iranian nuclear program in exchange for rigid and comprehensive inspection and control procedures.

This new course would not involve a dramatic policy reversal and is not likely to yield vast benefits in the immediate future. What it would do is enable the United States to sustain its policy and keep options open for the long term. America may have to consider modifying certain aspects of Iraq's economic containment to keep its military straitjacket securely fastened. On the other hand, flexibility would facilitate diplomatic contacts, presuming an Iranian interest in better relations. Absent such statesmanship, it is all too likely that U.S. policy in the Gulf will continue to be driven by domestic political imperatives rather than national interests, with the hard line of recent years making long-term goals increasingly difficult to achieve. . . .

The foundation of America's policy in the Persian Gulf should continue to be a commitment to ensuring the security of its allies and protecting the flow of oil. Few doubt that the United States has the power to sustain this commitment, but some question whether it has the will. In such circumstances, a recommitment by President Clinton to the principles of the Carter Doctrine—a renewal of U.S. vows to the Gulf—might be both welcome and appropriate. It is imperative that all parties understand an important strategic reality: the United States is in the Persian Gulf to stay. The security and independence of the region is a vital U.S. interest. Any accommodation with a post-Saddam regime in Iraq or with a less hostile government in Iran must be based on that fact.

# DOCUMENT 1.8

Cofounded as "a nonprofit educational organization" by William Kristol and Robert Kagan in early 1997, the Project for the New American Century quickly emerged as the most influential foreign-policy organization of neoconservatives. Its stated goal was "to promote American global leadership," and, to this end, it vigorously criticized the "realism" of President George H. W. Bush and the "incoherence" of President Bill Clinton. Many of its members—among them Dick Cheney, Donald Rumsfeld, Paul Wolfowitz, Paula Dobriansky, Eliot Cohen, Zalmay Khalilzad, and Lewis "Scooter" Libby—went on to occupy key positions in the administration of George W. Bush and played important roles in planning and executing the invasion of Iraq.

PROJECT FOR THE NEW AMERICAN CENTURY,
"STATEMENT OF PRINCIPLES," JUNE 3, 1997

American foreign and defense policy is adrift. Conservatives have criticized the incoherent policies of the Clinton administration. They have also resisted isolationist impulses from within their own ranks. But conservatives have not confidently advanced a strategic vision of America's role in the world. They have not set forth guiding principles for American foreign policy. They have allowed differences over tactics to obscure potential agreement on strategic objectives. And they have not fought for a defense budget that would maintain American security and advance American interests in the new century.

We aim to change this. We aim to make the case and rally support for American global leadership.

As the 20th century draws to a close, the United States stands as the world's preeminent power. Having led the West to victory in the Cold War, America faces an opportunity and a challenge: Does the United States have the vision to build upon the achievements of past decades? Does the United States have the resolve to shape a new century favorable to American principles and interests?

We are in danger of squandering the opportunity and failing the challenge. We are living off the capital—both the military investments and the foreign policy achievements—built up by past administrations. Cuts in foreign affairs and defense spending, inattention to the tools of statecraft, and inconstant leadership are making it increasingly difficult to sustain American influence around the world. And the promise of short-term commercial benefits threatens to override strategic considerations. As a consequence, we are jeopardizing the nation's ability to meet present threats and to deal with potentially greater challenges that lie ahead.

We seem to have forgotten the essential elements of the Reagan administration's success: a military that is strong and ready to meet both present and future challenges; a foreign policy that boldly and purposefully promotes American principles abroad; and national leadership that accepts the United States' global responsibilities.

Of course, the United States must be prudent in how it exercises its power. But we cannot safely avoid the responsibilities of global leadership or the costs that are associated with its exercise. America has a vital role in maintaining peace and security in Europe, Asia, and the Middle East. If we shirk our responsibilities, we invite challenges to our fundamental interests. The history of the 20th century should have taught us that it is important to shape circumstances before crises emerge, and to meet threats before they become dire. The history of this century should have taught us to embrace the cause of American leadership.

Our aim is to remind Americans of these lessons and to draw their consequences for today. Here are four consequences:

1. We need to increase defense spending significantly if we are to carry out our global responsibilities today and modernize our armed forces for the future;
2. we need to strengthen our ties to democratic allies and to challenge regimes hostile to our interests and values;
3. we need to promote the cause of political and economic freedom abroad;
4. we need to accept responsibility for America's unique role in preserving and extending an international order friendly to our security, our prosperity, and our principles.

Such a Reaganite policy of military strength and moral clarity may not be fashionable today. But it is necessary if the United States is to build on the successes of this past century and to ensure our security and our greatness in the next.

# DOCUMENT 1.9

In direct opposition to the Bush-Clinton policy of containment, one of the most important signatories of the PNAC's "Statement of Principles" publicly called for the overthrow of Saddam Hussein as early as November 1997. Five years earlier, Paul Wolfowitz had helped write the "Defense Policy Guidance" (1.3). He had worried for years that the multilateral sanctions regime would be undermined because individual participants would try to make deals with Saddam Hussein in exchange for Iraqi oil. By the end of 1997, he had outlined a new position.

---

PAUL WOLFOWITZ, "REBUILDING THE ANTI-SADDAM COALITION," *WALL STREET JOURNAL*, NOVEMBER 18, 1997

Why has the anti-Saddam coalition become so weak, with the French, Russians and Chinese doing their best to obstruct meaningful action by the United Nations, and even Kuwait making strange noises about being opposed to the use of force? And what might be done to reconstitute a new coalition?

The major reason for other nations' hesitance to join any military effort to force Saddam Hussein to comply with U.N. Security Council resolutions remains unspoken: They do not wish to be associated with a U.S. military effort that is ineffective and that leaves them alone to face Iraq. If the U.S. is to garner support for the military option, it must convince potential allies that its actions are part of a serious strategy. That is the lesson of the original Gulf War coalition. Offering Iraq "little carrots," as the U.S. is now reportedly considering, is precisely the wrong approach.

International condemnation of Saddam's 1990 occupation of Kuwait was almost universal. But that outrage alone would not have been enough to create a consensus for unified action. The actions countries were asked to take were extremely risky, particularly for the nations of the Arabian Peninsula, which faced the direct threat of further Iraqi advances. Their very survival was at risk.

The decisive step in forming the coalition that eventually liberated Kuwait was not the initial condemnation of Iraqi aggression by the U.N. Security Council, but the decision by Saudi Arabia, a few days later, to accept the deployment of a large U.S. armed force on Saudi soil. That Saudi decision was initiated by a telephone call from President Bush to King Fahd on Aug. 4, 1990, in which the president promised that U.S. forces would finish the job of liberating Kuwait. Mr. Bush then dispatched Secretary of Defense Dick Cheney to Jiddah for a meeting with the king on Aug. 6 that sealed the Saudi agreement to the deployment of one of the largest American armed forces ever sent overseas.

In hindsight that Saudi decision has been almost taken for granted, but at the time it was anything but a sure thing. The Saudis had already declined a U.S. offer of a fighter squadron in the immediate aftermath of Iraq's aggression. Even as Mr. Cheney flew to Jiddah, various experts declared that Saudi Arabia would never support military action against Iraq. Based on past behavior, they predicted, the Saudis would seek security by appeasing Iraq rather than confronting it.

The U.S. was asking a country with only modest armed forces of its own to take on a "tiger" in its immediate neighborhood—a tiger that had the fourth-largest army in the world. The Saudis had no interest in merely pulling the tiger's tail. If the U.S. was serious about eliminating a threat to their survival, they would join us. Otherwise, they would do the best they could to persuade the tiger to leave them alone.

As if to underscore the point, immediately after the king's meeting with Mr. Cheney, key Saudi officials came up to me and other members of the secretary's party with a pointed reminder of the time, shortly after the overthrow of the shah of Iran a dozen years earlier, when President Carter dispatched U.S. F-15 fighters to Saudi Arabia as a show of American resolve. As the planes were in the air, the Saudis were shocked to learn—from news reports—that the planes were coming unarmed, by order of the American president. What had started as a show of American resolve had become, instead, a public display of extreme reluctance to use force.

Our Saudi interlocutors told us pointedly: "If this were the United States of Jimmy Carter, which left American helicopters burning in the desert of Iran after the failed attempt to rescue the hostages from the American Embassy, the king would never have agreed to the deployment of American troops." And then, as if to be sure that we didn't think they merely liked Republicans, they added: "Or, if this were the United States of Ronald Reagan, which abandoned Beirut after 241 Marines were killed by terrorists, with nothing more than four ineffective air strikes against those who were responsible, we would never have agreed to take this fateful and dangerous step."

In fact, the resolve that the U.S. had later shown under Mr. Reagan, in persisting with the mission of escorting Kuwaiti tankers in 1987 even after 37 American sailors were killed in the attack on the USS *Stark*, was mentioned as part of the reason for restored confidence in the U.S. What's more, the very magnitude of the force we were proposing to deploy, although daunting, was an important sign of American commitment. When the Saudis were first briefed and told that it might involve hundreds of thousands of U.S. troops, the reaction was: "Well, at least we know you're serious. Now, perhaps, you understand why we refused your offer to send a squadron of fighter jets." Most of all, though, the Saudis were demonstrating their confidence in President Bush and in his promise that he would "finish the job." All of these stories were a way of reminding the U.S. that the Saudis had placed their fate in our hands.

Assembling an international consensus for serious action involves something more than just consulting others for their opinion. If Mr. Bush had sent Mr. Cheney merely to ask the Saudis what they thought we should do, they would almost certainly have said to themselves: If the Americans don't know what to do, then we must send someone to Baghdad on the next plane to see what terms we can negotiate. Instead, the message they got from the U.S. was: We are ready to act to end Iraqi aggression, and we want your help. To that request, the answer was yes.

Like small-businessmen who are asked by the district attorney to help break up the local Mafia—and who worry whether the Mafia will still be around after the prosecutor has gone on to other pursuits—the weaker countries of the Persian Gulf don't need to be persuaded that Saddam Hussein is a menace. They know that already. But they also fear that supporting a U.S. action will earn them additional enmity from Saddam and cause problems with restless elements among their own people. What they need to know is how U.S. action will make a difference.

The anti-Saddam coalition is weak in part because his neighbors, who may have to deal with him someday, fear being the last to make peace. It is becoming weaker also because those who seek to exploit Iraq's oil wealth hope to profit from currying favor with Saddam. Those who fear danger and those who smell profit alike sense weakness in a U.S. position that envisions nothing more than the indefinite continuation of sanctions.

President Bush can be faulted for being slow to recognize that the war was not over simply because Saddam had been driven out of Kuwait—although he had difficulty getting congressional support even for that limited objective. President Clinton is in a stronger position domestically: It appears he could have congressional support for the asking. But the signals coming from his administration are ambiguous. Secretary of Defense William Cohen could not have been clearer in his graphic presentation of the danger posed by Saddam's biological weapons. But talk of using the French and Russians as intermediaries to find a diplomatic "solution" does not inspire confidence.

The present crisis presents both dangers and opportunities. The issue is whether a maniacal and vengeful tyrant, who has already slaughtered tens of thousands of his own people using both chemical weapons and more conventional means, will be allowed to get away with retaining and expanding the chemical, biological and nuclear weapons capabilities that are forbidden under the terms of the Gulf War cease-fire.

If the U.S. has to use force in the present crisis, it should do so in a way that conveys that we have entered a new and entirely different chapter in the struggle with Saddam Hussein. We should not be afraid of "personalizing" this struggle, because it is indeed with him and not with the Iraqi people, most of whom long to be liberated from his tyranny. We should not be afraid to go after targets that constitute the support of Saddam's regime. And we should use this new display of seriousness to convince the greedy that they will not profit from Saddam and to persuade the fearful that we will finish the job.

In that way, we have an opportunity to reconstitute a coalition that will be stronger than we could be on our own—not one that will weaken and water down U.S. policy, reducing it to the lowest common denominator. It has been correctly observed that sometimes, as the leader, the U.S. must act unilaterally. But a willingness to act unilaterally can be the most effective way of securing effective collective action. In the present crisis we may have to act alone at first, or almost alone, because the international consensus is weak. But we must also use action as a means to build a stronger consensus.

# DOCUMENT 1.10

The attack on containment continued with a private letter to President Clinton from the Project for the New American Century. It repeated the position that Washington would be unable to contain Iraq and urged the White House to move toward a unilateral U.S. policy of regime change. The letter was signed by, among others, Elliott Abrams, Richard Armitage, John Bolton, Paula Dobriansky, Robert Kagan, Zalmay Khalilzad, Richard Perle, Donald Rumsfeld, Paul Wolfowitz, and Robert Zoellick—all of whom would play important roles in organizing the 2003 invasion and occupation of Iraq.

PROJECT FOR THE NEW AMERICAN CENTURY,
LETTER TO PRESIDENT CLINTON, JANUARY 26, 1998

Dear Mr. President:

We are writing you because we are convinced that current American policy toward Iraq is not succeeding, and that we may soon face a threat in the Middle East more serious than any we have known since the end of the Cold War. In your upcoming State of the Union Address, you have an opportunity to chart a clear and determined course for meeting this threat. We urge you to seize that opportunity, and to enunciate a new strategy that would secure the interests of the U.S. and our friends and allies around the world. That strategy should aim, above all, at the removal of Saddam Hussein's regime from power. We stand ready to offer our full support in this difficult but necessary endeavor.

The policy of "containment" of Saddam Hussein has been steadily eroding over the past several months. As recent events have demonstrated, we can no longer depend on our partners in the Gulf War coalition to continue to uphold the sanctions or to punish Saddam when he blocks or evades UN inspections. Our ability to ensure that Saddam Hussein is not producing weapons of mass destruction, therefore, has substantially diminished. Even if full inspections were eventually to resume, which now seems highly unlikely, experience has shown that it is difficult if not impossible to monitor Iraq's chemical and biological weapons production. The lengthy period during which the inspectors will have been unable to enter many Iraqi facilities has made it even less likely that they will be able to uncover all of Saddam's secrets. As a result, in the not-too-distant future we will be unable to determine with any reasonable level of confidence whether Iraq does or does not possess such weapons.

Such uncertainty will, by itself, have a seriously destabilizing effect on the entire Middle East. It hardly needs to be added that if Saddam does acquire the capability to deliver weapons of mass destruction, as he is almost certain to do if we continue along the present course, the safety of American troops in the region, of our friends and allies like Israel and the moderate Arab states, and a significant portion of the world's supply of oil will all be put at hazard. As you have rightly declared, Mr. President, the security of the world in the first part of the 21st century will be determined largely by how we handle this threat.

Given the magnitude of the threat, the current policy, which depends for its success upon the steadfastness of our coalition partners and upon the cooperation of Saddam Hussein, is dangerously inadequate. The only acceptable strategy is one that eliminates the possibility that Iraq will be able to use or threaten to use weapons of mass destruction. In the near term, this means a willingness to undertake military action as diplomacy is clearly failing. In the long term, it means removing Saddam Hussein and his regime from power. That now needs to become the aim of American foreign policy.

We urge you to articulate this aim, and to turn your Administration's attention to implementing a strategy for removing Saddam's regime from power. This will require a full complement of diplomatic, political and military efforts. Although we are fully aware of the dangers and difficulties in implementing this policy, we believe the dangers of failing to do so are far greater. We believe the U.S. has the authority under existing UN resolutions to take the necessary steps, including military steps, to protect our vital interests in the Gulf. In any case, American policy cannot continue to be crippled by a misguided insistence on unanimity in the UN Security Council.

We urge you to act decisively. If you act now to end the threat of weapons of mass destruction against the U.S. or its allies, you will be acting in the most fundamental national security interests of the country. If we accept a course of weakness and drift, we put our interests and our future at risk.

## DOCUMENT 1.11

The PNAC continued its public campaign with an op-ed piece in the *New York Times*. In their article, which appeared just four days after PNAC's letter to President Clinton, William Kristol and Robert Kagan continued the attack on containment, called for the overthrow of the Iraqi government, and charged that the Clinton administration was unable to respond to a threat to U.S. interests and security.

---

WILLIAM KRISTOL AND ROBERT KAGAN, "BOMBING IRAQ ISN'T ENOUGH," *NEW YORK TIMES*, JANUARY 30, 1998

Saddam Hussein must go. This imperative may seem too simple for some experts and too daunting for the Clinton Administration. But if the United States is committed, as the President said in his State of the Union Message, to ensuring that the Iraqi leader never again uses weapons of mass destruction, the only way to achieve that goal is to remove Mr. Hussein and his regime from power. Any policy short of that will fail.

The good news is this: The administration has abandoned efforts to win over the Iraqi leader with various carrots. It is clear that Mr. Hussein wants his weapons of mass destruction more than he wants oil revenue or relief for hungry Iraqi children. Now the administration is reportedly planning military action—a three- or four-day bombing campaign against Iraqi weapons sites and other strategic targets. But the bad news is that this too will fail. In fact, when the dust settles, we may be in worse shape than we are today.

Think about what the world will look like the day after the bombing ends. Mr. Hussein will still be in power—if five weeks of heavy bombing in 1991 failed to knock him out, five days of bombing won't either. Can the air attacks ensure that he will never be able to use weapons of mass destruction again? The answer, unfortunately, is no. Even our smart bombs cannot reliably hit and destroy every weapons and storage site in Iraq, for the simple reason that we do not know where all the sites are. After the bombing stops, Mr. Hussein will still be able to manufacture weapons of mass destruction. Pentagon officials admit this.

What will President Clinton do then? Administration officials talk of further punitive measures, like declaring a no-fly zone over all of Iraq, or even more bombing. But the fact is that the United States will have shot its bolt. Mr. Hussein will have proved the futility of American air power. The United Nations inspection regime will have collapsed; American diplomacy will be in disarray. Those who opposed military action all along—the Russians, French and Chinese—will demand the lifting of sanctions, and Mr. Hussein will be out of his box, free to terrorize our allies and threaten our interests.

Mr. Hussein has obviously thought through this scenario, and he likes his chances. That is why he provoked the present crisis, fully aware that it could lead to American bombing strikes. He has survived them before, and he is confident he can survive them again. They will not succeed in forcing him to abandon his efforts to obtain weapons of mass destruction. The only way to remove the threat of those weapons is to remove him, and that means using air power and ground forces, and finishing the task left un-done in 1991.

We can do this job. Mr. Hussein's army is much weaker than before the Persian Gulf War. He has no political support beyond his own bodyguards and generals. An effective military campaign combined with a political strat-egy to support the broad opposition forces in Iraq could well bring his regime down faster than many imagine. And Iraq's Arab neighbors are more likely to support a military effort to remove him than an ineffectual bombing raid that leaves a dangerous man in power.

Does the United States really have to bear this burden? Yes. Unless we act, Saddam Hussein will prevail, the Middle East will be destabilized, other aggressors around the world will follow his example, and American sol-diers will have to pay a far heavier price when the international peace sus-tained by American leadership begins to collapse.

If Mr. Clinton is serious about protecting us and our allies from Iraqi biological and chemical weapons, he will order ground forces to the gulf. Four heavy divisions and two airborne divisions are available for deploy-ment. The President should act, and Congress should support him in the only policy that can succeed.

## DOCUMENT 1.12

A few weeks after the public and private interventions from the Project for the New American Century, former president George H. W. Bush and Brent Scow-croft explained the decision to leave Saddam Hussein in power and maintain Iraq's territorial integrity. A justification of containment, this interview with *Time* magazine defended Bush's commitment to a multilateral policy in the Persian Gulf—a very different orientation from that of the neoconservatives.

GEORGE [H. W.] BUSH AND BRENT SCOWCROFT, "WHY WE DIDN'T REMOVE SADDAM," *TIME*, MARCH 2, 1998

The end of effective Iraqi resistance came with a rapidity which surprised us all, and we were perhaps psychologically unprepared for the sudden transition from fighting to peacemaking. True to the guidelines we had es-tablished, when we had achieved our strategic objectives (ejecting Iraqi forces from Kuwait and eroding Saddam's threat to the region) we stopped the fighting. But the necessary limitations placed on our objectives, the fog of war, and the lack of "battleship Missouri" surrender unfortunately left unresolved problems, and new ones arose.

We were disappointed that Saddam's defeat did not break his hold on power, as many of our Arab allies had predicted and we had come to expect. President Bush repeatedly declared that the fate of Saddam Hussein was up to the Iraqi people. Occasionally, he indicated that removal of Saddam would be welcome, but for very practical reasons there was never a promise to aid an uprising. While we hoped that popular revolt or coup would topple Saddam, neither the U.S. nor the countries of the region wished to see the breakup of the Iraqi state. We were concerned about the long-term balance of power at the head of the Gulf. Trying to eliminate Saddam, extending the ground war into an occupation of Iraq, would have violated our guideline about not changing objectives in midstream, engaging in "mission creep," and would have incurred incalculable human and political costs. Apprehending him was probably impossible. We had been unable to find Noriega in Panama, which we knew intimately. We would have been forced to occupy Baghdad and, in effect, rule Iraq. The coalition would instantly have collapsed, the Arabs deserting it in anger and other allies pulling out as well. Under those circumstances, furthermore, we had been self-consciously trying to set a pattern for handling aggression in the post–Cold War world. Going in and occupying Iraq, thus unilaterally exceeding the UN's mandate, would have destroyed the precedent of international response to aggression we hoped to establish. Had we gone the invasion route, the U.S. could conceivably still be an occupying power in a bitterly hostile land. It would have been a dramatically different—and perhaps barren—outcome.

We discussed at length forcing Saddam himself to accept the terms of Iraqi defeat at Safwan—just north of the Kuwait-Iraq border—and thus the responsibility and political consequences for the humiliation of such a devastating defeat. In the end, we asked ourselves what we would do if he refused. We concluded that we would be left with two options: continue the conflict until he backed down, or retreat from our demands. The latter would have sent a disastrous signal. The former would have split our Arab colleagues from the coalition and, de facto, forced us to change our objectives. Given those unpalatable choices, we allowed Saddam to avoid personal surrender and permitted him to send one of his generals. Perhaps we could have devised a system of selected punishment, such as air strikes on different military units, which would have proved a viable third option, but we had fulfilled our well-defined mission; Safwan was waiting.

As the conflict wound down, we felt a sense of urgency on the part of the coalition Arabs to get it over with and return to normal. This meant quickly withdrawing U.S. forces to an absolute minimum. Earlier there had been some concern in Arab ranks that once they allowed U.S. forces into the Middle East, we would be there to stay. Saddam's propaganda machine fanned these worries. Our prompt withdrawal helped cement our position with our Arab allies, who now trusted us far more than they ever had. We had come to their assistance in their time of need, asked nothing for ourselves, and left again when the job was done. Despite some criticism of our conduct of the war, the Israelis too had their faith in us solidified. We had shown our ability—and willingness—to intervene in the Middle East in a decisive way when our interests were challenged. We had also crippled the military capability of one of their most bitter enemies in the region. Our new credibility (coupled with Yasser Arafat's need to redeem his image after backing the wrong side in the war) had a quick and substantial payoff in the form of a Middle East peace conference in Madrid.

The Gulf War had far greater significance to the emerging post–Cold War world than simply reversing Iraqi aggression and restoring Kuwait. Its magnitude and significance impelled us from the outset to extend our strategic vision beyond the crisis to the kind of precedent we should lay down for the future. From an American foreign-policymaking perspective, we sought to respond in a manner which would win broad domestic support and which could be applied universally to other crises. In international terms, we tried to establish a model for the use of force. First and foremost was the principle that aggression cannot pay. If we dealt properly with Iraq, that should go a long way toward dissuading future would-be aggressors. We also believed that the U.S. should not go it alone, that a multilateral approach was better. This was, in part, a practical matter. Mounting an effective military counter to Iraq's invasion required the backing and bases of Saudi Arabia and other Arab states.

# DOCUMENT 1.13

After the Republican electoral sweep of the 1994 midterm election, the Clinton administration's Iraq policy was affected by an increasingly belligerent Congress. Indeed, the Project for the New American Century had explicitly appealed to the Republican congressional leadership as part of an effort to undermine Clinton's decision to work through the United Nations to contain Iraq. When Congress passed, and Clinton signed, the "Iraq Liberation Act" the following October, the U.S. government seemed to take a step away from containment when it adopted regime change as its official policy. The act stopped short of authorizing direct U.S. military action but appropriated money for the Iraqi opposition and authorized a variety of other measures to undermine the Iraqi government.

"IRAQ LIBERATION ACT,"
OCTOBER 31, 1998 (EXCERPT)

An Act
To establish a program to support a transition to democracy in Iraq.
Be it enacted by the Senate and House of Representatives of the United States of America in Congress assembled,

## SECTION 1. SHORT TITLE.
This Act may be cited as the "Iraq Liberation Act of 1998."

## SECTION 2. FINDINGS.
The Congress makes the following findings:

(1) On September 22, 1980, Iraq invaded Iran, starting an 8 year war in which Iraq employed chemical weapons against Iranian troops and ballistic missiles against Iranian cities.

(2) In February 1988, Iraq forcibly relocated Kurdish civilians from their home villages in the Anfal campaign, killing an estimated 50,000 to 180,000 Kurds.

(3) On March 16, 1988, Iraq used chemical weapons against Iraqi Kurdish civilian opponents in the town of Halabja, killing an estimated 5,000 Kurds and causing numerous birth defects that affect the town today.

(4) On August 2, 1990, Iraq invaded and began a 7 month occupation of Kuwait, killing and committing numerous abuses against Kuwaiti civilians, and setting Kuwait's oil wells ablaze upon retreat.

(5) Hostilities in Operation Desert Storm ended on February 28, 1991, and Iraq subsequently accepted the ceasefire conditions specified in United Nations Security Council Resolution 687 (April 3, 1991) requiring Iraq, among other things, to disclose fully and permit the dismantlement of its weapons of mass destruction programs and submit to long-term monitoring and verification of such dismantlement.

(6) In April 1993, Iraq orchestrated a failed plot to assassinate former President George Bush during his April 14–16, 1993, visit to Kuwait.

(7) In October 1994, Iraq moved 80,000 troops to areas near the border with Kuwait, posing an imminent threat of a renewed invasion of or attack against Kuwait.

(8) On August 31, 1996, Iraq suppressed many of its opponents by helping one Kurdish faction capture Irbil, the seat of the Kurdish regional government.

(9) Since March 1996, Iraq has systematically sought to deny weapons inspectors from the United Nations Special Commission

on Iraq (UNSCOM) access to key facilities and documents, has on several occasions endangered the safe operation of UNSCOM helicopters transporting UNSCOM personnel in Iraq, and has persisted in a pattern of deception and concealment regarding the history of its weapons of mass destruction programs.

(10) On August 5, 1998, Iraq ceased all cooperation with UNSCOM, and subsequently threatened to end long-term monitoring activities by the International Atomic Energy Agency and UNSCOM.

(11) On August 14, 1998, President Clinton signed Public Law 105–235, which declared that "the Government of Iraq is in material and unacceptable breach of its international obligations" and urged the President "to take appropriate action, in accordance with the Constitution and relevant laws of the United States, to bring Iraq into compliance with its international obligations."

(12) May 1, 1998, President Clinton signed Public Law 105–174, which made $5,000,000 available for assistance to the Iraqi democratic opposition for such activities as organization, training, communication and dissemination of information, developing and implementing agreements among opposition groups, compiling information to support the indictment of Iraqi officials for war crimes, and for related purposes.

## SECTION 3. SENSE OF THE CONGRESS REGARDING UNITED STATES POLICY TOWARD IRAQ.

It should be the policy of the United States to support efforts to remove the regime headed by Saddam Hussein from power in Iraq and to promote the emergence of a democratic government to replace that regime.

## SECTION 4. ASSISTANCE TO SUPPORT A TRANSITION TO DEMOCRACY IN IRAQ.

(a) AUTHORITY TO PROVIDE ASSISTANCE—The President may provide to the Iraqi democratic opposition organizations designated in accordance with section 5 the following assistance:

(1) BROADCASTING ASSISTANCE—(A) Grant assistance to such organizations for radio and television broadcasting by such organizations to Iraq. . . .

(B) There is authorized to be appropriated to the United States Information Agency $2,000,000 for fiscal year 1999 to carry out this paragraph.

(2) MILITARY ASSISTANCE—(A) The President is authorized to direct the drawdown of defense articles from the stocks of the Department of Defense, defense services of the Department of Defense, and military education and training for such organizations. . . .

(B) The aggregate value (as defined in section 644(m) of the Foreign Assistance Act of 1961) of assistance provided under this paragraph may not exceed $97,000,000.

(b) HUMANITARIAN ASSISTANCE—The Congress urges the President to use existing authorities under the Foreign Assistance Act of 1961 to provide humanitarian assistance to individuals living in areas of Iraq controlled by organizations designated in accordance with section 5, with emphasis on addressing the needs of individuals who have fled to such areas from areas under the control of the Saddam Hussein regime.

(c) RESTRICTION ON ASSISTANCE—No assistance under this section shall be provided to any group within an organization designated in accordance with section 5 which group is, at the time the assistance is to be provided, engaged in military cooperation with the Saddam Hussein regime. . . .

## SECTION 5. DESIGNATION OF IRAQI DEMOCRATIC OPPOSITION ORGANIZATION.

(a) INITIAL DESIGNATION—Not later than 90 days after the date of the enactment of this Act, the President shall designate one or more Iraqi democratic opposition organizations that the President determines satisfy the criteria set forth in subsection (c) as eligible to receive assistance under section 4.

(b) DESIGNATION OF ADDITIONAL ORGANIZATIONS—At any time subsequent to the initial designation pursuant to subsection (a), the President may designate one or more additional Iraqi democratic opposition organizations that the President determines satisfy the criteria set forth in subsection (c) as eligible to receive assistance under section 4.

(c) CRITERIA FOR DESIGNATION—In designating an organization pursuant to this section, the President shall consider only organizations that—

  (1) include a broad spectrum of Iraqi individuals, groups, or both, opposed to the Saddam Hussein regime; and

  (2) are committed to democratic values, to respect for human rights, to peaceful relations with Iraq's neighbors, to maintaining Iraq's territorial integrity, and to fostering cooperation among democratic opponents of the Saddam Hussein regime. . . .

## SECTION 6. WAR CRIMES TRIBUNAL FOR IRAQ.

Consistent with section 301 of the Foreign Relations Authorization Act, Fiscal Years 1992 and 1993 (Public Law 102–138), House Concurrent Resolution 137, 105th Congress (approved by the House of Representatives on November 13, 1997), and Senate Concurrent Resolution 78, 105th Congress (approved by the Senate on March 13, 1998), the Congress urges the President to call upon the United Nations to establish an international criminal tribunal for the purpose of indicting, prosecuting, and imprisoning Saddam Hussein and other Iraqi officials who are responsible for crimes against humanity, genocide, and other criminal violations of international law.

## SECTION 7. ASSISTANCE FOR IRAQ UPON REPLACEMENT OF SADDAM HUSSEIN REGIME.

It is the sense of the Congress that once the Saddam Hussein regime is removed from power in Iraq, the United States should support Iraq's transition to democracy by providing immediate and substantial humanitarian assistance to the Iraqi people, by providing democracy transition assistance to Iraqi parties and movements with democratic goals, and by convening Iraq's foreign creditors to develop a multilateral response to Iraq's foreign debt incurred by Saddam Hussein's regime.

## SECTION 8. RULE OF CONSTRUCTION.

Nothing in this Act shall be construed to authorize or otherwise speak to the use of United States Armed Forces (except as provided in section 4(a)(2)) in carrying out this Act.

# DOCUMENT 1.14

Saddam Hussein's government had been trying to undermine the UN-organized system of inspections and sanctions for years, and the Iraqi regime's interference accelerated as 1998 drew to a close. Enduring increased pressure from the Republican-led Congress in a number of matters, and facing an impeachment vote in the House of Representatives, President Clinton ordered a series of attacks on Iraq. He explained his decision in a nationally televised speech from the Oval Office.

BILL CLINTON, EXPLANATION OF IRAQ STRIKE, DECEMBER 16, 1998

Good evening.

Earlier today, I ordered America's armed forces to strike military and security targets in Iraq. They are joined by British forces. Their mission is to attack Iraq's nuclear, chemical, and biological weapons programs and its military capacity to threaten its neighbors.

Their purpose is to protect the national interest of the United States, and indeed the interests of people throughout the Middle East and around the world.

Saddam Hussein must not be allowed to threaten his neighbors or the world with nuclear arms, poison gas, or biological weapons.

I want to explain why I have decided, with the unanimous recommendation of my national security team, to use force in Iraq; why we have acted now; and what we aim to accomplish.

Six weeks ago, Saddam Hussein announced that he would no longer cooperate with the United Nations weapons inspectors called UNSCOM. They are highly professional experts from dozens of countries. Their job is to oversee the elimination of Iraq's capability to retain, create, and use weapons of mass destruction, and to verify that Iraq does not attempt to rebuild that capability.

The inspectors undertook this mission first 7.5 years ago at the end of the Gulf War when Iraq agreed to declare and destroy its arsenal as a condition of the ceasefire.

The international community had good reason to set this requirement. Other countries possess weapons of mass destruction and ballistic missiles. With Saddam, there is one big difference: He has used them. Not once, but repeatedly. Unleashing chemical weapons against Iranian troops during a decade-long war. Not only against soldiers, but against civilians, firing Scud missiles at the citizens of Israel, Saudi Arabia, Bahrain, and Iran. And not only against a foreign enemy, but even against his own people, gassing Kurdish civilians in Northern Iraq.

The international community had little doubt then, and I have no doubt today, that left unchecked, Saddam Hussein will use these terrible weapons again.

The United States has patiently worked to preserve UNSCOM as Iraq has sought to avoid its obligation to cooperate with the inspectors. On occasion, we've had to threaten military force, and Saddam has backed down.

Faced with Saddam's latest act of defiance in late October, we built intensive diplomatic pressure on Iraq backed by overwhelming military force in the region. The UN Security Council voted 15 to zero to condemn Saddam's actions and to demand that he immediately come into compliance.

Eight Arab nations—Egypt, Syria, Saudi Arabia, Kuwait, Bahrain, Qatar, United Arab Emirates, and Oman—warned that Iraq alone would bear responsibility for the consequences of defying the UN.

When Saddam still failed to comply, we prepared to act militarily. It was only then at the last possible moment that Iraq backed down. It pledged to the UN that it had made, and I quote, a clear and unconditional decision to resume cooperation with the weapons inspectors.

I decided then to call off the attack with our airplanes already in the air because Saddam had given in to our demands. I concluded then that the right thing to do was to use restraint and give Saddam one last chance to prove his willingness to cooperate.

I made it very clear at that time what unconditional cooperation meant, based on existing UN resolutions and Iraq's own commitments. And along with Prime Minister Blair of Great Britain, I made it equally clear that if Saddam failed to cooperate fully, we would be prepared to act without delay, diplomacy, or warning.

Now over the past three weeks, the UN weapons inspectors have carried out their plan for testing Iraq's cooperation. The testing period ended this weekend, and last night, UNSCOM's chairman, Richard Butler, reported the results to UN Secretary-General Annan.

The conclusions are stark, sobering, and profoundly disturbing.

In four out of the five categories set forth, Iraq has failed to cooperate. Indeed, it actually has placed new restrictions on the inspectors. Here are some of the particulars.

Iraq repeatedly blocked UNSCOM from inspecting suspect sites. For example, it shut off access to the headquarters of its ruling party and said it will deny access to the party's other offices, even though UN resolutions make no exception for them and UNSCOM has inspected them in the past.

Iraq repeatedly restricted UNSCOM's ability to obtain necessary evidence. For example, Iraq obstructed UNSCOM's effort to photograph bombs related to its chemical weapons program.

It tried to stop an UNSCOM biological weapons team from videotaping a site and photocopying documents and prevented Iraqi personnel from answering UNSCOM's questions.

Prior to the inspection of another site, Iraq actually emptied out the building, removing not just documents but even the furniture and the equipment.

Iraq has failed to turn over virtually all the documents requested by the inspectors. Indeed, we know that Iraq ordered the destruction of weapons-related documents in anticipation of an UNSCOM inspection.

So Iraq has abused its final chance.

As the UNSCOM report concludes, and again I quote, "Iraq's conduct ensured that no progress was able to be made in the fields of disarmament.

"In light of this experience, and in the absence of full cooperation by Iraq, it must regrettably be recorded again that the commission is not able to conduct the work mandated to it by the Security Council with respect to Iraq's prohibited weapons program."

In short, the inspectors are saying that even if they could stay in Iraq, their work would be a sham.

Saddam's deception has defeated their effectiveness. Instead of the inspectors disarming Saddam, Saddam has disarmed the inspectors.

This situation presents a clear and present danger to the stability of the Persian Gulf and the safety of people everywhere. The international community gave Saddam one last chance to resume cooperation with the weapons inspectors. Saddam has failed to seize the chance.

And so we had to act and act now.

Let me explain why.

First, without a strong inspection system, Iraq would be free to retain and begin to rebuild its chemical, biological, and nuclear weapons programs in months, not years.

Second, if Saddam can cripple the weapons inspection system and get away with it, he would conclude that the international community—led by the United States—has simply lost its will. He will surmise that he has free rein to rebuild his arsenal of destruction, and someday—make no mistake —he will use it again as he has in the past.

Third, in halting our air strikes in November, I gave Saddam a chance, not a license. If we turn our backs on his defiance, the credibility of U.S. power as a check against Saddam will be destroyed. We will not only have allowed Saddam to shatter the inspection system that controls his weapons of mass destruction program; we also will have fatally undercut the fear of force that stops Saddam from acting to gain domination in the region.

That is why, on the unanimous recommendation of my national security team—including the vice president, the secretary of defense, the chairman of the Joint Chiefs of Staff, the secretary of state, and the national security advisor—I have ordered a strong, sustained series of air strikes against Iraq.

They are designed to degrade Saddam's capacity to develop and deliver weapons of mass destruction, and to degrade his ability to threaten his neighbors.

At the same time, we are delivering a powerful message to Saddam. If you act recklessly, you will pay a heavy price. We acted today because, in the judgment of my military advisors, a swift response would provide the most surprise and the least opportunity for Saddam to prepare.

If we had delayed for even a matter of days from Chairman Butler's report, we would have given Saddam more time to disperse his forces and protect his weapons.

36 |  Also, the Muslim holy month of Ramadan begins this weekend. For us to initiate military action during Ramadan would be profoundly offensive to the Muslim world and, therefore, would damage our relations with Arab countries and the progress we have made in the Middle East.

That is something we wanted very much to avoid without giving Iraq a month's head start to prepare for potential action against it.

Finally, our allies, including Prime Minister Tony Blair of Great Britain, concurred that now is the time to strike. I hope Saddam will come into cooperation with the inspection system now and comply with the relevant UN Security Council resolutions. But we have to be prepared that he will not, and we must deal with the very real danger he poses.

So we will pursue a long-term strategy to contain Iraq and its weapons of mass destruction and work toward the day when Iraq has a government worthy of its people.

First, we must be prepared to use force again if Saddam takes threatening actions, such as trying to reconstitute his weapons of mass destruction or their delivery systems, threatening his neighbors, challenging allied aircraft over Iraq, or moving against his own Kurdish citizens.

The credible threat to use force, and when necessary, the actual use of force, is the surest way to contain Saddam's weapons of mass destruction program, curtail his aggression, and prevent another Gulf War.

Second, so long as Iraq remains out of compliance, we will work with the international community to maintain and enforce economic sanctions.

Sanctions have cost Saddam more than $120 billion—resources that would have been used to rebuild his military. The sanctions system allows Iraq to sell oil for food, for medicine, for other humanitarian supplies for the Iraqi people.

We have no quarrel with them. But without the sanctions, we would see the oil-for-food program become oil-for-tanks, resulting in a greater threat to Iraq's neighbors and less food for its people.

The hard fact is that so long as Saddam remains in power, he threatens the well-being of his people, the peace of his region, the security of the world.

The best way to end that threat once and for all is with a new Iraqi government—a government ready to live in peace with its neighbors, a government that respects the rights of its people. Bringing change in Baghdad will take time and effort. We will strengthen our engagement with the full range of Iraqi opposition forces and work with them effectively and prudently.

The decision to use force is never cost-free. Whenever American forces are placed in harm's way, we risk the loss of life. And while our strikes are focused on Iraq's military capabilities, there will be unintended Iraqi casualties.

Indeed, in the past, Saddam has intentionally placed Iraqi civilians in harm's way in a cynical bid to sway international opinion.

We must be prepared for these realities. At the same time, Saddam should have absolutely no doubt if he lashes out at his neighbors, we will respond forcefully.

Heavy as they are, the costs of action must be weighed against the price of inaction. If Saddam defies the world and we fail to respond, we will face a far greater threat in the future. Saddam will strike again at his neighbors. He will make war on his own people.

And mark my words, he will develop weapons of mass destruction. He will deploy them, and he will use them.

Because we're acting today, it is less likely that we will face these dangers in the future.

Let me close by addressing one other issue. Saddam Hussein and the other enemies of peace may have thought that the serious debate currently before the House of Representatives would distract Americans or weaken our resolve to face him down.

But once more, the United States has proven that although we are never eager to use force, when we must act in America's vital interests, we will do so.

In the century we're leaving, America has often made the difference between chaos and community, fear and hope. Now, in the new century, we'll have a remarkable opportunity to shape a future more peaceful than the past, but only if we stand strong against the enemies of peace.

Tonight, the United States is doing just that. May God bless and protect the brave men and women who are carrying out this vital mission and their families. And may God bless America.

# DOCUMENT 1.15

As the Clinton presidency entered its final year, the president and his spokespeople were relentlessly criticized by the neoconservatives and the Republican-led Congress. The "Iraq Liberation Act" notwithstanding (1.13), Clinton remained broadly committed to containment and sought to portray military action as part of an international effort to keep Saddam Hussein "in his box."

MADELEINE ALBRIGHT, EXPLANATION OF CONTAINMENT, *MEET THE PRESS*, JANUARY 2, 2000

MR. RUSSERT: Another difficult area, Iraq. One year ago, the inspectors were told, "Get out," by Saddam Hussein. Do you believe that Saddam Hussein has more weapons of mass destruction now than he did a year ago?

SECRETARY ALBRIGHT: Well, we are very obviously concerned about his ability to reconstitute and we are keeping him in his box and the no-fly zones are being monitored and, as you know, we occasionally have to take military action as our planes are illuminated or our pilots are in danger.

We are concerned about the fact that there are not inspectors on the ground and, as you know, we tried at the United Nations to ensure that that would happen. There is a new resolution which requires the inspectors to go in and that is the law, the international law at this stage. Saddam Hussein has turned that down. And we, obviously, have reserved the right that if we see that he has or is reconstituting his weapons of mass destruction, that we can take action on that.

We want to make—we have set up a regime whereby the inspectors could go in and that is the way that Saddam Hussein could make sure that sanctions might be suspended.

MR. RUSSERT: Let me show you what the president said a year ago and get your sense of it as we look at it today: "A rather scary threat to regional stability becomes increasingly alarming. Iraq's dictator, Saddam Hussein is successfully staving off attempts at the United Nations to reinstate weapons inspectors in his country."

One year ago, President Clinton himself summed up the likely consequences of allowing Mr. Hussein to go uninspected for too long. "Mark

my words, he will develop weapons of mass destruction, he will deploy them, he will use them."

It's been more than a year. Aren't we concerned what Saddam has done this past year?

**SECRETARY ALBRIGHT:** We are obviously concerned. As I said, I think that we have been successful in keeping him in his box and in terms of the threat to the region. We worked very hard on this resolution. We think it is unfortunate that Saddam Hussein has not taken advantage of it because it—

**MR. RUSSERT:** And the Russians, French, and Chinese oppose us.

**SECRETARY ALBRIGHT:** Well, they abstained. But what's interesting here, Tim, in their as they call it explanation of vote at the United Nations, they made clear that they believed that Saddam Hussein must abide by what the United Nations—the resolution is.

**MR. RUSSERT:** And if he doesn't, what happens?

**SECRETARY ALBRIGHT:** I think that we still continue to have the possibilities that we've had before of taking unilateral or multilateral action if we need to. But I think we should—I can't say that we have accomplished everything we've wanted with Iraq. But we, I think, are on the right track in terms of keeping them, as I've said, in the box, of working with the opposition and working towards regime change, and making quite clear to the neighboring countries and to the rest of the world and our partners at the United Nations that what Saddam Hussein is doing is unacceptable.

# DOCUMENT 1.16

In early 2000, Condoleezza Rice—a professor of political science at Stanford, a fellow at the Hoover Institution, and one of the principal foreign policy advisors to Republican presidential candidate George W. Bush—outlined a post–Cold War foreign policy. Written as part of the Republican Party's campaign, her article suggested that multilateralism, humanitarianism, and particular international obligations made sense only if they were tied to a coherent notion of "the national interest," and it criticized the Clinton administration for its failure to articulate a comprehensive view, its vulnerability to particularistic interest groups, and its consequent instability and undependability. Trained as a Sovietologist, Rice focused her essay on state-to-state relations and paid no attention to the issues of terrorism and non-state actors that would dominate foreign-policy concerns after September 11, 2001. Bush's future national security advisor and secretary of state concentrated on a few key priorities: building a military ready to ensure U.S. power, coping with rogue regimes, and managing Beijing and Moscow. Above all, Rice said, "The next president must be comfortable with America's special role as the world's leader." Her words anticipated her move away from "realism" and toward adoption of the Bush administration's "freedom agenda," which promoted spreading U.S.-style capitalism and democracy worldwide.

---

CONDOLEEZZA RICE, "PROMOTING THE NATIONAL INTEREST," *FOREIGN AFFAIRS,* JANUARY–FEBRUARY 2000 (EXCERPT)

## Life after the Cold War

The United States has found it exceedingly difficult to define its "national interest" in the absence of Soviet power. That we do not know how to think about what follows the U.S.-Soviet confrontation is clear from the continued references to the "post–Cold War period." Yet such periods of transition are important, because they offer strategic opportunities. During these fluid times, one can affect the shape of the world to come.

The enormity of the moment is obvious. The Soviet Union was more than just a traditional global competitor; it strove to lead a universal socialist alternative to markets and democracy. The Soviet Union quarantined itself and many often-unwitting captives and clients from the rigors of international capitalism. In the end, it sowed the seeds of its own destruction, becoming in isolation an economic and technological dinosaur.

But this is only part of the story. The Soviet Union's collapse coincided with another great revolution. Dramatic changes in information technology and the growth of "knowledge-based" industries altered the very basis of economic dynamism, accelerating already noticeable trends in economic interaction that often circumvented and ignored state boundaries. As competition for capital investment has intensified, states have faced difficult choices about their internal economic, political, and social structures. As the prototype of this "new economy," the United States has seen its economic influence grow—and with it, its diplomatic influence. America has emerged as both the principal benefactor of these simultaneous revolutions and their beneficiary.

The process of outlining a new foreign policy must begin by recognizing that the United States is in a remarkable position. Powerful secular trends are moving the world toward economic openness and—more unevenly—democracy and individual liberty. Some states have one foot on the train and the other off. Some states still hope to find a way to decouple democracy and economic progress. Some hold on to old hatreds as diversions from the modernizing task at hand. But the United States and its allies are on the right side of history.

In such an environment, American policies must help further these favorable trends by maintaining a disciplined and consistent foreign policy that separates the important from the trivial. The Clinton administration has assiduously avoided implementing such an agenda. Instead, every issue has been taken on its own terms—crisis by crisis, day by day. It takes courage to set priorities because doing so is an admission that American foreign policy cannot be all things to all people—or rather, to all interest groups. The Clinton administration's approach has its advantages: If priorities and intent are not clear, they cannot be criticized. But there is a high price to pay for this approach. In a democracy as pluralistic as ours, the absence of an articulated "national interest" either produces a fertile ground for those wishing to withdraw from the world or creates a vacuum to be filled by parochial groups and transitory pressures.

## The Alternative
American foreign policy in a Republican administration should refocus the United States on the national interest and the pursuit of key priorities. These tasks are

1. to ensure that America's military can deter war, project power, and fight in defense of its interests if deterrence fails;
2. to promote economic growth and political openness by extending free trade and a stable international monetary system to all committed to these principles, including in the western hemisphere, which has too often been neglected as a vital area of U.S. national interest;
3. to renew strong and intimate relationships with allies who share American values and can thus share the burden of promoting peace, prosperity, and freedom;
4. to focus U.S. energies on comprehensive relationships with the big powers, particularly Russia and China, that can and will mold the character of the international political system; and
5. to deal decisively with the threat of rogue regimes and hostile powers, which is increasingly taking the forms of the potential for terrorism and the development of weapons of mass destruction (WMD).

## Interests and Ideals
Power matters, both the exercise of power by the United States and the ability of others to exercise it. Yet many in the United States are (and have always been) uncomfortable with the notions of power politics, great powers, and power balances. In an extreme form, this discomfort leads to a reflexive appeal instead to notions of international law and norms, and the belief that the support of many states—or even better, of institutions like the United Nations—is essential to the legitimate exercise of power. The "national interest" is replaced with "humanitarian interests" or the interests of "the international community." The belief that the United States is

exercising power legitimately only when it is doing so on behalf of some-one or something else was deeply rooted in Wilsonian thought, and there are strong echoes of it in the Clinton administration. To be sure, there is nothing wrong with doing something that benefits all humanity, but that is, in a sense, a second-order effect. America's pursuit of the national in-terest will create conditions that promote freedom, markets, and peace. Its pursuit of national interests after World War II led to a more prosperous and democratic world. This can happen again.

So multilateral agreements and institutions should not be ends in themselves. U.S. interests are served by having strong alliances and can be promoted within the UN and other multilateral organizations, as well as through well-crafted international agreements. But the Clinton adminis-tration has often been so anxious to find multilateral solutions to problems that it has signed agreements that are not in America's interest. The Kyoto treaty is a case in point: whatever the facts on global warming, a treaty that does not include China and exempts "developing" countries from tough standards while penalizing American industry cannot possibly be in Amer-ica's national interest.

Similarly, the arguments about U.S. ratification of the Comprehensive Test Ban Treaty are instructive. Since 1992, the United States has refrained unilaterally from testing nuclear weapons. It is an example to the rest of the world yet does not tie its own hands "in perpetuity" if testing becomes necessary again. But in pursuit of a "norm" against the acquisition of nu-clear weapons, the United States signed a treaty that was not verifiable, did not deal with the threat of the development of nuclear weapons by rogue states, and threatened the reliability of the nuclear stockpile. Legitimate congressional concerns about the substance of the treaty were ignored dur-ing negotiations. When faced with the defeat of a bad treaty, the adminis-tration attacked the motives of its opponents—incredibly branding long-standing internationalists like Senators Richard Lugar (R-Ind.) and John Warner (R-Va.) as isolationists.

Certainly, Republican presidents have not been immune to the practice of pursuing symbolic agreements of questionable value. According to the Senate Foreign Relations Committee, some 52 conventions, agreements, and treaties still await ratification; some even date back to 1949. But the Clinton administration's attachment to largely symbolic agreements and its pursuit of, at best, illusory "norms" of international behavior have be-come an epidemic. That is not leadership. Neither is it isolationist to suggest that the United States has a special role in the world and should not adhere to every international convention and agreement that someone thinks to propose.

Even those comfortable with notions of the "national interest" are still queasy with a focus on power relationships and great-power politics. The reality is that a few big powers can radically affect international peace, sta-bility, and prosperity. These states are capable of disruption on a grand scale, and their fits of anger or acts of beneficence affect hundreds of millions of people. By reason of size, geographic position, economic potential, and military strength, they are capable of influencing American welfare for good or ill. Moreover, that kind of power is usually accompanied by a sense of entitlement to play a decisive role in international politics. Great powers do not just mind their own business.

Some worry that this view of the world ignores the role of values, particularly human rights and the promotion of democracy. In fact, there are those who would draw a sharp line between power politics and a principled foreign policy based on values. This polarized view—you are either a realist or devoted to norms and values—may be just fine in academic debate, but it is a disaster for American foreign policy. American values are universal. People want to say what they think, worship as they wish, and elect those who govern them; the triumph of these values is most assuredly easier when the international balance of power favors those who believe in them. But sometimes that favorable balance of power takes time to achieve, both internationally and within a society. And in the meantime, it is simply not possible to ignore and isolate other powerful states that do not share those values.

The Cold War is a good example. Few would deny that the collapse of the Soviet Union profoundly transformed the picture of democracy and human rights in eastern and central Europe and the former Soviet territories. Nothing improved human rights as much as the collapse of Soviet power. Throughout the Cold War, the United States pursued a policy that promoted political liberty, using every instrument from the Voice of America to direct presidential intervention on behalf of dissidents. But it lost sight neither of the importance of the geopolitical relationship with Moscow nor of the absolute necessity of retaining robust American military power to deter an all-out military confrontation.

In the 1970s, the Soviet Union was at the height of its power—which it was more than willing to use. Given its weak economic and technological base, the victories of that period turned out to be Pyrrhic. President Reagan's challenge to Soviet power was both resolute and well timed. It included intense substantive engagements with Moscow across the entire range of issues captured in the "four-part agenda" (arms control, human rights, economic issues, and regional conflicts). The Bush administration then focused greater attention on rolling back Soviet power in central and eastern Europe. As the Soviet Union's might waned, it could no longer defend its interests and gave up peacefully (thankfully) to the West—a tremendous victory for Western power and also for human liberty.

## Setting Priorities
The United States has many sources of power in the pursuit of its goals. The global economy demands economic liberalization, greater openness and transparency, and at the very least, access to information technology.

International economic policies that leverage the advantages of the American economy and expand free trade are the decisive tools in shaping international politics. They permit us to reach out to states as varied as South Africa and India and to engage our neighbors in the western hemisphere in a shared interest in economic prosperity. The growth of entrepreneurial classes throughout the world is an asset in the promotion of human rights and individual liberty, and it should be understood and used as such. Yet peace is the first and most important condition for continued prosperity and freedom. America's military power must be secure because the United States is the only guarantor of global peace and stability. The current neglect of America's armed forces threatens its ability to maintain peace.

The Bush administration had been able to reduce defense spending somewhat at the end of the Cold War in 1991. But the Clinton administration witlessly accelerated and deepened these cuts. The results were devastating: military readiness declined, training suffered, military pay slipped 15 percent below civilian equivalents, morale plummeted, and the services cannibalized existing equipment to keep airplanes flying, ships afloat, and tanks moving. The increased difficulty in recruiting people to the armed forces or retaining them is hardly surprising.

Moreover, the administration began deploying American forces abroad at a furious pace—an average of once every nine weeks. As it cut defense spending to its lowest point as a percentage of GDP since Pearl Harbor, the administration deployed the armed forces more often than at any time in the last 50 years. Some of the deployments themselves were questionable, such as in Haiti. But more than anything it was simply unwise to multiply missions in the face of a continuing budget reduction. Means and mission were not matched, and (predictably) the already thinly stretched armed forces came close to a breaking point. When all these trends became so obvious and embarrassing that they could no longer be ignored, the administration finally requested increased defense spending. But the "death spiral," as the administration's own undersecretary of defense called it—robbing procurement and research and development simply to operate the armed forces—was already well under way. That the administration did nothing, choosing instead to live off the fruits of Reagan's military buildup, constitutes an extraordinary neglect of the fiduciary responsibilities of the commander in chief.

Now the next president will be confronted with a prolonged job of repair. Military readiness will have to take center stage, particularly those aspects that affect the living conditions of the troops—military pay, housing—and also training. New weapons will have to be procured in order to give the military the capacity to carry out today's missions. But even in its current state, the American military still enjoys a commanding technological lead and therefore has a battlefield advantage over any competitor. Thus the next president should refocus the Pentagon's priorities on building the military of the 21st century rather than continuing to build on the structure of the Cold War. U.S. technological advantages should be leveraged to build forces that are lighter and more lethal, more mobile and agile, and capable of firing accurately from long distances. In order to do this, Washington must reallocate resources, perhaps in some cases skipping a generation of technology to make leaps rather than incremental improvements in its forces.

The other major concern is a loss of focus on the mission of the armed forces. What does it mean to deter, fight, and win wars and defend the national interest? First, the American military must be able to meet decisively the emergence of any hostile military power in the Asia-Pacific region, the Middle East, the Persian Gulf, and Europe—areas in which not only our interests but also those of our key allies are at stake. America's military is the only one capable of this deterrence function, and it must not be stretched or diverted into areas that weaken these broader responsibilities. It is the role that the United States played when Saddam Hussein threatened the Persian Gulf, and it is the power needed to deter trouble on the Korean Peninsula or across the Taiwan Strait. In the latter cases, the goal is to make it inconceivable for North Korea or China to use force because American military power is a compelling factor in their equations.

Some small-scale conflicts clearly have an impact on American strategic interests. Such was the case with Kosovo, which was in the backyard of America's most important strategic alliance: NATO. In fact, Yugoslav President Slobodan Milosevic's rejection of peaceful coexistence with the Kosovar Albanians threatened to rock the area's fragile ethnic balance. Eastern Europe is a patchwork of ethnic minorities. For the most part, Hungarians and Romanians, Bulgarians and Turks, and even Ukrainians and Russians have found a way since 1991 of preventing their differences from exploding. Milosevic has been the exception, and the United States had an overriding strategic interest in stopping him. There was, of course, a humanitarian disaster looming as well, but in the absence of concerns based on the interests of the alliance, the case for intervention would have been more tenuous.

The Kosovo War was conducted incompetently, in part because the administration's political goals kept shifting and in part because it was not, at the start, committed to the decisive use of military force. That President Clinton was surprised at Milosevic's tenacity is, well, surprising. If there is any lesson from history, it is that small powers with everything to lose are often more stubborn than big powers, for whom the conflict is merely one among many problems. The lesson, too, is that if it is worth fighting for, you had better be prepared to win. Also, there must be a political game plan that will permit the withdrawal of our forces—something that is still completely absent in Kosovo.

But what if our values are attacked in areas that are not arguably of strategic concern? Should the United States not try to save lives in the absence of an overriding strategic rationale? The next American president should be in a position to intervene when he believes, and can make the case, that the United States is duty-bound to do so. "Humanitarian intervention" cannot be ruled out a priori. But a decision to intervene in the absence of strategic concerns should be understood for what it is. Humanitarian problems are rarely only humanitarian problems; the taking of life or withholding of food is almost always a political act. If the United States is not prepared to address the underlying political conflict and to know whose side it is on, the military may end up separating warring parties for an indefinite period. Sometimes one party (or both) can come to see the United States as the enemy. Because the military cannot, by definition, do anything decisive in these "humanitarian" crises, the chances of misreading the situation and ending up in very different circumstances are very high. This was essentially the problem of "mission creep" in Somalia.

The president must remember that the military is a special instrument. It is lethal, and it is meant to be. It is not a civilian police force. It is not a political referee. And it is most certainly not designed to build a civilian society. Military force is best used to support clear political goals, whether limited, such as expelling Saddam from Kuwait, or comprehensive, such as demanding the unconditional surrender of Japan and Germany during World War II. It is one thing to have a limited political goal and to fight decisively for it; it is quite another to apply military force incrementally, hoping to find a political solution somewhere along the way. A president entering these situations must ask whether decisive force is possible and is likely to be effective and must know how and when to get out. These are difficult criteria to meet, so U.S. intervention in these "humanitarian" crises should be, at best, exceedingly rare.

This does not mean that the United States must ignore humanitarian and civil conflicts around the world. But the military cannot be involved everywhere. Often, these tasks might be better carried out by regional actors, as modeled by the Australian-led intervention in East Timor. The U.S. might be able to lend financial, logistical, and intelligence support. Sometimes tough, competent diplomacy in the beginning can prevent the need for military force later. Using the American armed forces as the world's "911" will degrade capabilities, bog soldiers down in peacekeeping roles, and fuel concern among other great powers that the United States has decided to enforce notions of "limited sovereignty" worldwide in the name of humanitarianism. This overly broad definition of America's national interest is bound to backfire as others arrogate the same authority to themselves. Or we will find ourselves looking to the United Nations to sanction the use of American military power in these cases, implying that we will do so even when our vital interests are involved, which would also be a mistake.

## Dealing with the Powerful

Another crucial task for the United States is to focus on relations with other powerful states. Although the United States is fortunate to count among its friends several great powers, it is important not to take them for granted—

so that there is a firm foundation when it comes time to rely on them. The challenges of China and North Korea require coordination and cooperation with Japan and South Korea. The signals that we send to our real partners are important. Never again should an American president go to Beijing for nine days and refuse to stop in Tokyo or Seoul.

There is work to do with the Europeans, too, on defining what holds the transatlantic alliance together in the absence of the Soviet threat. NATO is badly in need of attention in the wake of Kosovo and with the looming question of its further enlargement in 2002 and beyond. The door to NATO for the remaining states of eastern and central Europe should remain open, as many are actively preparing to meet the criteria for membership. But the parallel track of NATO's own evolution, its attention to the definition of its mission, and its ability to digest and then defend new members has been neglected. Moreover, the United States has an interest in shaping the European defense identity—welcoming a greater European military capability as long as it is within the context of NATO. NATO has a very full agenda. Membership in NATO will mean nothing to anyone if the organization is no longer militarily capable and if it is unclear about its mission.

For America and our allies, the most daunting task is to find the right balance in our policy toward Russia and China. Both are equally important to the future of international peace, but the challenges they pose are very different. China is a rising power; in economic terms, that should be good news, because in order to maintain its economic dynamism, China must be more integrated into the international economy. This will require increased openness and transparency and the growth of private industry. The political struggle in Beijing is over how to maintain the Communist Party's monopoly on power. Some see economic reform, growth, and a better life for the Chinese people as the key. Others see the inherent contradiction in loosening economic control and maintaining the party's political dominance. As China's economic problems multiply due to slowing growth rates, failing banks, inert state enterprises, and rising unemployment, this struggle will intensify.

It is in America's interest to strengthen the hands of those who seek economic integration because this will probably lead to sustained and organized pressures for political liberalization. There are no guarantees, but in scores of cases from Chile to Spain to Taiwan, the link between democracy and economic liberalization has proven powerful over the long run. Trade and economic interaction are, in fact, good—not only for America's economic growth but for its political aims as well. Human rights concerns should not move to the sidelines in the meantime. Rather, the American president should press the Chinese leadership for change. But it is wise to remember that our influence through moral arguments and commitment is still limited in the face of Beijing's pervasive political control. The big trends toward the spread of information, the access of young Chinese to American values through educational exchanges and training, and the growth of an entrepreneurial class that does not owe its livelihood to the state are, in the end, likely to have a more powerful effect on life in China. . . .

Even if there is an argument for economic interaction with Beijing, China is still a potential threat to stability in the Asia-Pacific region. Its military power is currently no match for that of the United States. But that condition is not necessarily permanent. What we do know is that China is a great power with unresolved vital interests, particularly concerning Taiwan and the South China Sea. China resents the role of the United States in the Asia-Pacific region. This means that China is not a "status quo" power but one that would like to alter Asia's balance of power in its own favor. That alone makes it a strategic competitor, not the "strategic partner" the Clinton administration once called it. . . .

Some things take time. U.S. policy toward China requires nuance and balance. It is important to promote China's internal transition through economic interaction while containing Chinese power and security ambitions. Cooperation should be pursued, but we should never be afraid to confront Beijing when our interests collide.

### Russian Weakness

Russia presents a different challenge. It still has many of the attributes of a great power: a large population, vast territory, and military potential. But its economic weakness and problems of national identity threaten to overwhelm it. Moscow is determined to assert itself in the world and often does so in ways that are at once haphazard and threatening to American interests. The picture is complicated by Russia's own internal transition—one that the United States wants to see succeed. The old Soviet system has broken down, and some of the basic elements of democratic development are in place. People are free to say what they think, vote for whom they please, and (for the most part) worship freely. But the democratic fragments are not institutionalized—with the exception of the Communist Party, political parties are weak—and the balance of political power is so strongly in favor of the president that he often rules simply by decree. . . .

Now we have a dual credibility problem—with Russians and with Americans. There are signs of life in the Russian economy. The financial crash of August 1998 forced import substitution, and domestic production has increased as the resilient Russian people have taken matters into their own hands. Rising oil prices have helped as well. But these are short-term fixes. There is no longer a consensus in America or Europe on what to do next with Russia. Frustrated expectations and "Russia fatigue" are direct consequences of the "happy talk" in which the Clinton administration engaged.

Russia's economic future is now in the hands of the Russians. The country is not without assets, including its natural resources and an educated population. It is up to Russia to make structural reforms, particularly concerning the rule of law and the tax codes, so that investors—foreign and domestic—will provide the capital needed for economic growth. . . . But the cultural changes ultimately needed to sustain a functioning civil society and a market-based economy may take a generation. Western openness to Russia's people, particularly its youth, in exchange programs and contact with the private sector and educational opportunities can help that process. It is also important to engage the leadership of Russia's diverse regions, where economic and social policies are increasingly pursued independently of Moscow.

In the meantime, U.S. policy must concentrate on the important security agenda with Russia. First, it must recognize that American security is threatened less by Russia's strength than by its weakness and incoherence. This suggests immediate attention to the safety and security of Moscow's nuclear forces and stockpile. . . . Second, Washington must begin a comprehensive discussion with Moscow on the changing nuclear threat. Much has been made by Russian military officials about their increased reliance on nuclear weapons in the face of their declining conventional readiness. The Russian deterrent is more than adequate against the U.S. nuclear arsenal, and vice versa. But that fact need no longer be enshrined in a treaty that is almost 30 years old and is a relic of a profoundly adversarial relationship between the United States and the Soviet Union. The Anti-Ballistic Missile Treaty was intended to prevent the development of national missile defenses in the Cold War security environment. Today, the principal concerns are nuclear threats from the Iraqs and North Koreas of the world and the possibility of unauthorized releases as nuclear weapons spread.

Moscow, in fact, lives closer to those threats than Washington does. It ought to be possible to engage the Russians in a discussion of the changed threat environment, their possible responses, and the relationship of strategic offensive-force reductions to the deployment of defenses. The United States should make clear that it prefers to move cooperatively toward a new offense-defense mix, but that it is prepared to do so unilaterally. Moscow should understand, too, that any possibilities for sharing technology or information in these areas would depend heavily on its record—problematic to date—on the proliferation of ballistic-missile and other technologies related to WMD. It would be foolish in the extreme to share defenses with Moscow if it either leaks or deliberately transfers weapons technologies to the very states against which America is defending. . . .

## Coping with Rogue Regimes

As history marches toward markets and democracy, some states have been left by the side of the road. Iraq is the prototype. Saddam Hussein's regime is isolated, his conventional military power has been severely weakened, his people live in poverty and terror, and he has no useful place in international politics. He is therefore determined to develop WMD. Nothing will change until Saddam is gone, so the United States must mobilize whatever resources it can, including support from his opposition, to remove him.

The regime of Kim Jong Il is so opaque that it is difficult to know its motivations, other than that they are malign. But North Korea also lives outside of the international system. Like East Germany, North Korea is the evil twin of a successful regime just across its border. It must fear its eventual demise from the sheer power and pull of South Korea. Pyongyang, too, has little to gain and everything to lose from engagement in the international economy. The development of WMD thus provides the destructive way out for Kim Jong Il. . . .

One thing is clear: the United States must approach regimes like North Korea resolutely and decisively. The Clinton administration has failed here, sometimes threatening to use force and then backing down, as it often has with Iraq. These regimes are living on borrowed time, so there need be no sense of panic about them. Rather, the first line of defense should be a clear and classical statement of deterrence—if they do acquire WMD, their weapons will be unusable because any attempt to use them will bring national obliteration. Second, we should accelerate efforts to defend against these weapons. This is the most important reason to deploy national and theater missile defenses as soon as possible, to focus attention on U.S. homeland defenses against chemical and biological agents, and to expand intelligence capabilities against terrorism of all kinds.

Finally, there is the Iranian regime. Iran's motivation is not to disrupt simply the development of an international system based on markets and democracy, but to replace it with an alternative: fundamentalist Islam. Fortunately, the Iranians do not have the kind of reach and power that the Soviet Union enjoyed in trying to promote its socialist alternative. But Iran's tactics have posed real problems for U.S. security. It has tried to destabilize moderate Arab states such as Saudi Arabia, though its relations with the Saudis have improved recently. Iran has also supported terrorism against America and Western interests and attempted to develop and transfer sensitive military technologies.

Iran presents special difficulties in the Middle East, a region of core interest to the United States and to our key ally Israel. Iranian weaponry increasingly threatens Israel directly. As important as Israel's efforts to reach peace with its Arab neighbors are to the future of the Middle East, they are not the whole story of stability in the region. Israel has a real security problem, so defense cooperation with the United States—particularly in the area of ballistic missile defense—is critical. That in turn will help Israel protect itself both through agreements and through enhanced military power. . . .

## Building a Consensus for the National Interest

America is blessed with an extraordinary opportunity. It has had no territorial ambitions for nearly a century. Its national interest has been defined instead by a desire to foster the spread of freedom, prosperity, and peace. Both the will of the people and the demands of modern economies accord with that vision of the future. But even America's advantages offer no guarantees of success. It is up to America's presidential leadership and policy to bridge the gap between tomorrow's possibilities and today's realities.

The president must speak to the American people about national priorities and intentions and work with Congress to focus foreign policy around the national interest. The problem today is not an absence of bipartisan spirit in Congress or the American people's disinterest. It is the existence of a vacuum. In the absence of a compelling vision, parochial interests are filling the void.

Foreign policy in a Republican administration will most certainly be internationalist; the leading contenders in the party's presidential race have strong credentials in that regard. But it will also proceed from the firm ground of the national interest, not from the interests of an illusory international community. America can exercise power without arrogance and pursue its interests without hectoring and bluster. When it does so in concert with those who share its core values, the world becomes more prosperous, democratic, and peaceful. That has been America's special role in the past, and it should be again as we enter the next century.

# ★ CHAPTER 2 ★

## ORGANIZING FOR PREEMPTIVE WAR

### IRAQ AND THE PRESIDENCY
### OF GEORGE W. BUSH

THE NEW ADMINISTRATION'S orientation toward foreign policy became apparent soon after the Supreme Court settled the disputed 2000 presidential election. Barely two months after he had taken the oath of office, George W. Bush announced that the United States would withdraw from the Kyoto Protocol on climate change, which President Clinton had signed toward the end of his second term but not submitted for ratification to a hostile Senate. This decision was the administration's first assertion that it did not feel compelled to accept the constraints of international agreements or to accept equal status in multilateral diplomatic relations with other countries. Washington was prepared to take full advantage of the power to act in an international environment where there was no countervailing superpower to challenge it.

On May 1, Bush went further and abandoned one of the foundations of the nuclear age when he announced his intention to withdraw from the 1972 Anti-Ballistic Missile Treaty, marking the first time in modern history that the United States had renounced a major international accord. Five days later, the president informed the United Nations that Washington would not ratify the Rome Statute of 1998, which had established an International Criminal Court with the power to try and to punish individuals for the most serious of international crimes: genocide, crimes against humanity, crimes of aggression, and war crimes. And on July 25, Bush's representative to UN-sponsored talks in Geneva said that he would refuse to sign an international agreement banning the use or development of biological weapons. Within six months of his inauguration and well before September 11, the new president had made it clear that he was prepared to turn his back on decades of diplomacy and intended to reorient U.S. foreign policy to exploit the possibilities of a unipolar world. But Iraq was not yet a subject of major concern, even though prominent members of the government had wanted to overthrow Saddam Hussein for years. Washington's more aggressive stance did not mean preemptive war—not yet.

The terrorist attacks of September 11 gave the administration its chance to change the agenda. Paul Wolfowitz, now the deputy secretary of defense, Lewis Libby, Vice President Cheney's chief of staff, along with their fellow neoconservatives Richard Perle and William Kristol, relentlessly agitated for immediate military action to make an example of Iraq and demonstrate U.S. power to any country that might think of challenging Washington. Bush had prepared the ground with his day-after speech to the nation announcing that "America was attacked because we're the brightest beacon for freedom and opportunity in the world," but the target of the promised retaliation was not yet clear. When the president momentarily sided with Secretary of State Colin Powell and decided to oust the Taliban from Afghanistan, the press reported that administration "moderates" had prevailed over Pentagon "hard-liners" in the struggle for his allegiance. Optimistic accounts suggested that Bush was preparing to abandon his earlier inclination toward unilateralism and was seeking to rebuild old alliances—particularly with Europe. But the president's decision to focus on Afghanistan first did not mean that he had forgotten about Saddam Hussein. Even as *Le Monde* famously declared that "we are all Americans," the administration was preparing for unilateral preemptive war.

By November the military campaign against the Taliban had ousted the regime that had provided sanctuary and support to al Qaeda. United States forces trapped bin Laden in the Tora Bora Mountains of eastern Afghanistan, and the Pentagon unleashed a massive aerial and ground bombardment of the region. But Washington's decision to "outsource" to local warlords the capture of al Qaeda's leaders allowed bin Laden and his followers to escape and regroup in Pakistan. Washington had a chance to organize a long-term reconstruction and rehabilitation effort in Afghanistan, but administration planners had other priorities. The terrorist attack required a coherent and integrated response, and Bush had been talking about Saddam Hussein before September 11 (9.20). Administration policymakers began to search for a conceptual breakthrough and a broader statement of purpose. As internal disagreements were resolved and attention shifted from terrorist groups to states allegedly planning to support them—or even thinking or capable of supporting them—U.S. foreign policy began to pivot toward Iraq. Defense and deterrence yielded to preemption and war as the administration began issuing dire warnings about hidden threats (2.1–2.2, 2.4). When the president gave his "axis of evil" State of the Union address in January 2002, the goal of retaliating against the perpetrators of the September 11 attacks was joined by stopping terrorist groups or "rogue states" from acquiring "weapons of mass destruction." From then on, the claim that Saddam Hussein had, wanted to have, or was trying to develop such weapons became the president's chief argument as he began moving the United States toward preemptive war.

The administration's position was unsupported by the facts. Despite the relentless campaign to convince traumatized Americans that Iraq was a mortal danger to their safety, neither the strategic situation in the Persian Gulf nor the behavior of Saddam Hussein had worsened. A decade of sanctions, isolation, and containment had all but destroyed Baghdad's ability to challenge regional stability or threaten U.S. interests. Preoccupied with defending his isolated and besieged regime, Saddam Hussein had few options or resources. This might explain why he seemed receptive to tentative efforts to reintegrate him into Gulf politics. When Saudi Arabia and Kuwait announced that they were prepared to forgive Baghdad's debts and began to move toward restoring diplomatic relations, observers noted that the region seemed to be looking inward and seeking alternatives to its traditional reliance on U.S. power. When the Saudis floated a Middle East peace plan that included Iraq and indicated that they were prepared to expand their contacts with Baghdad, the Bush administration continued to insist that Saddam Hussein remained an implacable enemy of the United States and a constant threat to world peace. These repeated claims, which remained central to Washington's stated reasons for attacking Iraq, were intended to convince Americans that preemptive war was a justifiable act of self-defense. Bush's intention to reorganize world politics had come down to Saddam Hussein. Little had changed in Baghdad's behavior, but a great deal had changed in Washington.

54 |    When Bush addressed the graduating class at West Point in June (2.5), he hinted that the United States was prepared to attack any country it felt was a threat. The president's claim that feelings and assertions could substitute for the legal requirement of demonstrable imminent threat in justifying military action meant that preemptive war was no longer about self-defense. Throughout the Cold War, Washington had reserved the right of preemptive action, never ruling out the possibility of a first strike on the Soviet Union and carrying out a series of covert actions aimed at overthrowing governments. The United States had been willing before to substitute claims of danger for the traditional requirement of a clear threat. What was novel about Bush's orientation was the explicit and official nature of the new doctrine of preemption. The consequences were clear to other states: if the United States was putting this sort of preemption at the heart of its foreign policy, what nation could be safe from unprovoked attack? What was to prevent other nations from declaring that "everything was different," the old rules no longer applied, and every state was free to act as it chose?

The answer was that the United States, as the world's preeminent military power, was reserving something for itself that it was not prepared to grant to others. The Bush administration was stepping forward as the chief judge and arbiter of the international system, for the West Point speech painted a picture of a world so dominated by U.S. military might that no other power could possibly match it or would even think of trying to do so. The president's willingness to explicitly locate preemption at the center of his foreign policy signaled that Washington was prepared to replace containment's relatively conservative multilateral orientation with the far more radical and unilateral project of preemptive regime change. Charles Krauthammer's belligerent article "The Axis of Petulance" summarized this position as Paul Wolfowitz's 1992 strategic thinking triumphed over alternative views (2.3, 1.3).

As Pentagon war planning became more serious during the spring and summer of 2002, the administration rallied a frightened population to its view of a changed U.S. role in the world. For the next year, new arguments about the Iraqi threat emerged as quickly as earlier claims were debunked: Saddam Hussein was actively cooperating with al Qaeda, or he was quietly protecting it; he had weapons of mass destruction, or he was trying to get them; he was trying to build nuclear bombs, or he might be capable of doing so in the future; he had been deceiving UN weapons inspectors, or the inspectors were incompetent; he had denied his people the blessings of freedom, or his people were too cowed to know what was good for them. When all else failed, it was pointed out that he was a mass murderer and a war criminal.

Brent Scowcroft, James Baker, Lawrence Eagleburger, and other Washington veterans became alarmed as the administration's rhetoric heated up. They had played central roles in organizing the Gulf War a decade earlier and were not amused by the idea of a campaign to spread democracy and reorganize the Middle East. They were old-fashioned "realists," worried that an invasion of Iraq would damage the war on terrorism, get the United States bogged down in a dangerous part of the world, put the Arab–Israeli "peace process" on hold, and harm Washington's relations with its allies. By August they had decided to publicly take issue with the accelerating trend toward war (2.7–2.8). They were not alone. Members of Congress from both parties grew increasingly assertive as the summer wore on, openly questioning whether Iraq really posed a mortal threat to the United States, whether containment had failed, and whether the president had exhausted all options short of war. Democratic senator and chairman of the Senate Armed Services Committee, Carl Levin, said an attack on Iraq might prompt Saddam Hussein to use weapons of mass destruction because he would have nothing to lose. Representative Dick Armey, the Republican majority leader in the House of Representatives, said he did not believe an attack on Iraq would be justified without a clear and unambiguous provocation. Chuck Hagel, a respected senator from Nebraska, expressed reservations about the push to war, a view that was seconded by fellow Republican Richard Lugar. Lee Hamilton, a former Democratic congressman who would later co-chair the Iraq Study Group, told the New York Times "you have not had the president articulate why Saddam needs to be removed," adding, "He has not made the case that Saddam is an imminent threat." When Scott Ritter, a former UN weapons inspector, said that the U.S. position was overstated, leading members of the administration pressed the argument that Saddam Hussein was an active threat to world peace. Vice President Cheney's rare public intervention late in the summer was meant to specifically rebut all the concerns that had been raised during the past two months, serving notice that the administration was growing weary of discussions and negotiations (2.9).

The administration's public positions notwithstanding, Washington had determined its course of action and was preparing domestic and international opinion for an invasion to which it had been committed for some time. A visiting British delegation discovered that the administration had decided on war by the summer of 2002 and was "cherry-picking" its alleged intelligence findings to support a preemptive attack on Iraq, but the now-famous Downing Street Memo did not become public in time to affect the developing debate (2.6). Every subsequent claim the Bush administration made about its willingness to negotiate, its commitment to international law, its support for weapons inspections, its fidelity to the UN Charter, and its determination to protect the world from a criminal Iraqi regime was belied by the explosive information contained in the Downing Street Memo.

The new orientation did not receive explicit, formal sanction until September, when National Security Advisor Condoleezza Rice issued a thirty-one-page document that stood as the authoritative statement of the administration's neoconservative worldview. The three core principles of "The National Security Strategy of the United States of America"—unilateral preemptive war, unchallengeable military superiority, and the spread of U.S.-style capitalism and democracy—now rested at the core of the administration's foreign policy (2.10–2.11). As the debate became increasingly rancorous and long-time allies began protesting, President Bush announced that the United States would ask the United Nations to sanction military action against Iraq. Once again, it seemed that the administration was slowing its rush to war with the president's endorsement of diplomacy. When the Security Council passed Resolution 1441 declaring Iraq in "material breach" of its obligations and demanded that Baghdad cooperate with weapons inspectors and the International Atomic Energy Agency (2.13), the administration claimed victory. But 1441 stopped well short of Washington's desire for authority to act, and Bush's apparent support for Secretary of State Powell masked more than it revealed. Although troops and weapons were streaming into the Persian Gulf and the president had gotten a congressional resolution authorizing the use of force (2.12), the Pentagon was not yet ready for war. As Powell directed an intense diplomatic effort during autumn to get the United Nations to issue tough new resolutions about Iraq, administration spokespeople repeatedly stated that the only way Baghdad could avoid war was for Saddam Hussein to step down and for his government to resign. By this point it really did not matter what the Iraqis did, for the famous "Aznar transcript" documenting a discussion between the Spanish prime minister and President Bush demonstrated conclusively that even the Iraqi leader's resignation and departure would not have avoided war. Nor was Saddam Hussein's December apology to Kuwait for his 1990 invasion enough.

As the administration pushed ahead and made it clear that it would act regardless of what happened in New York, long-time allies publicly broke with

56 |

Washington. Germany and France led a last-ditch UN effort to head off an invasion by insisting on a second resolution from the Security Council, but nothing could deter the president. The conservative Spanish prime minister José María Aznar traveled to President Bush's Crawford, Texas, ranch in late February 2003 to meet with the president and some of his top advisors in an effort to coordinate strategy in the Security Council. British prime minister Blair and his Italian counterpart, Silvio Berlusconi, participated by telephone. When *El País,* the respected Spanish newspaper, published a transcript of the conversation in 2007, it became clear that the administration's repeated assurances that it was seeking a peaceful resolution of the crisis were false. Saddam Hussein had offered to leave Iraq if he could take US$1 billion and some official documents, but it was too late. By the time Secretary of State Powell delivered his famous, and now discredited, speech at the United Nations on February 6, 2003, the die had been cast. By early March there were some 250,000 U.S. troops near Iraq, joined by 45,000 British soldiers and smaller delegations from other members of Bush's "coalition of the willing." The administration's failure to get the Security Council to approve an invasion had changed nothing. When Powell made it clear to French foreign minister Dominique de Villepin that the United States was determined to attack Iraq on the basis of Resolution 1441 no matter what the Security Council decided about a second resolution, he tacitly admitted that six months of diplomacy had ended in failure.

In the end, the neoconservatives' projections had turned out to be wrong. Bush, Cheney, Krauthammer, Wolfowitz, Rice, the Project for the New American Century, and others had argued that if the United States showed resolve, its friends and allies would drop their fantasies about peaceful conflict resolution and fall in line (1.6, 1.8–1.10). Instead, tougher administration action produced only tougher international opposition. The alliance with Europe was strained and Washington's reputation diminished. But the administration did not really care. The only thing that mattered now was U.S. military power and the willingness to use it. By the time President Bush issued an ultimatum and announced the beginning of "Operation Iraqi Freedom," Saddam Hussein had become the justification for unilateral U.S. preemptive war.

# DOCUMENT 2.1

On the evening of September 11, 2001, President Bush delivered an address to a shocked nation. Serving notice that the terrorist attacks of that day would not go unanswered, he assured his fellow citizens that he would lead the country in a war for freedom and "all that is good and just in our world."

## GEORGE W. BUSH, ADDRESS TO THE NATION, SEPTEMBER 11, 2001 (EXCERPT)

Good evening. Today, our fellow citizens, our way of life, our very freedom came under attack in a series of deliberate and deadly terrorist acts. The victims were in airplanes, or in their offices; secretaries, businessmen and women, military and federal workers; moms and dads, friends and neighbors. Thousands of lives were suddenly ended by evil, despicable acts of terror.

The pictures of airplanes flying into buildings, fires burning, huge structures collapsing, have filled us with disbelief, terrible sadness, and a quiet, unyielding anger. These acts of mass murder were intended to frighten our nation into chaos and retreat. But they have failed; our country is strong.

A great people has been moved to defend a great nation. Terrorist attacks can shake the foundations of our biggest buildings, but they cannot touch the foundation of America. These acts shattered steel, but they cannot dent the steel of American resolve.

America was targeted for attack because we're the brightest beacon for freedom and opportunity in the world. And no one will keep that light from shining.

Today, our nation saw evil, the very worst of human nature. And we responded with the best of America—with the daring of our rescue workers, with the caring for strangers and neighbors who came to give blood and help in any way they could.

Immediately following the first attack, I implemented our government's emergency response plans. Our military is powerful, and it's prepared. Our emergency teams are working in New York City and Washington, DC, to help with local rescue efforts.

Our first priority is to get help to those who have been injured, and to take every precaution to protect our citizens at home and around the world from further attacks. . . .

The search is underway for those who are behind these evil acts. I've directed the full resources of our intelligence and law enforcement communities to find those responsible and to bring them to justice. We will make no distinction between the terrorists who committed these acts and those who harbor them. . . .

America and our friends and allies join with all those who want peace and security in the world, and we stand together to win the war against terrorism. Tonight, I ask for your prayers for all those who grieve, for the children whose worlds have been shattered, for all whose sense of safety and security has been threatened. And I pray they will be comforted by a power greater than any of us, spoken through the ages in Psalm 23: "Even though I walk through the valley of the shadow of death, I fear no evil, for You are with me."

This is a day when all Americans from every walk of life unite in our re-solve for justice and peace. America has stood down enemies before, and we will do so this time. None of us will ever forget this day. Yet, we go for-ward to defend freedom and all that is good and just in our world.

Thank you. Good night, and God bless America.

# DOCUMENT 2.2

President Bush's "axis of evil" speech, in which he identified Iraq, North Korea, and Iran as the most dangerous enemies of international peace, added an-other element to a developing argument that would culminate with the pre-emptive invasion of Iraq. Five months after September 11, 2001, the adminis-tration began to move the discussion beyond retaliating against al Qaeda and the Taliban to stopping terrorists from acquiring weapons of mass destruction and preventing states from supplying them with such weapons. Hunting ter-rorists and attacking terrorist organizations were no longer at the center of ad-ministration rhetoric. Now it was the states who were equipping or funding them, or who might do so sometime in the future. Administration allegations that the "axis of evil" supported terrorists and was developing "weapons of mass destruction" comprised their argument that preemptive war was neces-sary to eliminate the Iraqi threat to the United States and its allies.

GEORGE W. BUSH, STATE OF THE UNION ADDRESS, JANUARY 29, 2002 (EXCERPT)

Thank you very much. Mr. Speaker, Vice President Cheney, members of Congress, distinguished guests, fellow citizens: As we gather tonight, our nation is at war, our economy is in recession, and the civilized world faces unprecedented dangers. Yet the state of our Union has never been stronger.

We last met in an hour of shock and suffering. In four short months, our nation has comforted the victims; begun to rebuild New York and the Pen-tagon; rallied a great coalition; captured, arrested, and rid the world of thou-sands of terrorists; destroyed Afghanistan's terrorist training camps; saved a people from starvation; and freed a country from brutal oppression.

The American flag flies again over our embassy in Kabul. Terrorists who once occupied Afghanistan now occupy cells at Guantanamo Bay. And ter-rorist leaders who urged followers to sacrifice their lives are running for their own. . . .

What we have found in Afghanistan confirms that, far from ending there, our war against terror is only beginning. Most of the nineteen men who hi-jacked planes on September the 11th were trained in Afghanistan's camps, and so were tens of thousands of others. Thousands of dangerous killers, schooled in the methods of murder, often supported by outlaw regimes, are now spread throughout the world like ticking time bombs, set to go off without warning.

Thanks to the work of our law enforcement officials and coalition partners, hundreds of terrorists have been arrested. Yet, tens of thousands of trained terrorists are still at large. These enemies view the entire world as a battlefield, and we must pursue them wherever they are. So long as training camps operate, so long as nations harbor terrorists, freedom is at risk. And America and our allies must not, and will not, allow it.

Our nation will continue to be steadfast and patient and persistent in the pursuit of two great objectives. First, we will shut down terrorist camps, disrupt terrorist plans, and bring terrorists to justice. And, second, we must prevent the terrorists and regimes who seek chemical, biological, or nuclear weapons from threatening the United States and the world.

But some governments will be timid in the face of terror. And make no mistake about it: If they do not act, America will.

Our second goal is to prevent regimes that sponsor terror from threatening America or our friends and allies with weapons of mass destruction. Some of these regimes have been pretty quiet since September the 11th. But we know their true nature. North Korea is a regime arming with missiles and weapons of mass destruction, while starving its citizens.

Iran aggressively pursues these weapons and exports terror, while an unelected few repress the Iranian people's hope for freedom.

Iraq continues to flaunt its hostility toward America and to support terror. The Iraqi regime has plotted to develop anthrax, and nerve gas, and nuclear weapons for over a decade. This is a regime that has already used poison gas to murder thousands of its own citizens—leaving the bodies of mothers huddled over their dead children. This is a regime that agreed to international inspections—then kicked out the inspectors. This is a regime that has something to hide from the civilized world.

States like these, and their terrorist allies, constitute an axis of evil, arming to threaten the peace of the world. By seeking weapons of mass destruction, these regimes pose a grave and growing danger. They could provide these arms to terrorists, giving them the means to match their hatred. They could attack our allies or attempt to blackmail the United States. In any of these cases, the price of indifference would be catastrophic.

We will work closely with our coalition to deny terrorists and their state sponsors the materials, technology, and expertise to make and deliver weapons of mass destruction. We will develop and deploy effective missile defenses to protect America and our allies from sudden attack. And all nations should know: America will do what is necessary to ensure our nation's security.

We'll be deliberate, yet time is not on our side. I will not wait on events, while dangers gather. I will not stand by, as peril draws closer and closer.

The United States of America will not permit the world's most dangerous regimes to threaten us with the world's most destructive weapons.

Our war on terror is well begun, but it is only begun. This campaign may not be finished on our watch—yet it must be and it will be waged on our watch.

We can't stop short. If we stop now—leaving terror camps intact and terror states unchecked—our sense of security would be false and temporary. History has called America and our allies to action, and it is both our responsibility and our privilege to fight freedom's fight.

# DOCUMENT 2.3

Charles Krauthammer responded to U.S. allies' misgivings about Bush's speech with a March 1 column in the *Washington Post*. The influential neoconservative applied the lessons of "The Unipolar Moment" to the post–September 11 environment, explicitly embracing "morality, preemption and unilateralism." In doing so, he expressed the emphasis on military power and the impatience with diplomacy that would characterize the Bush administration's general position.

CHARLES KRAUTHAMMER, "THE AXIS OF PETULANCE,"
*WASHINGTON POST*, MARCH 1, 2002 (EXCERPT)

The "axis of evil" caused a sensation around the world because it established a new American foreign policy based on three distinctive principles: morality, preemption, and unilateralism.

Our sophisticated European cousins are aghast. The French led the way, denouncing American *simplisme*. They deem it a breach of manners to call evil by its name. They prefer accommodating to it. They have lots of practice, famously accommodating Nazi Germany in 1940, less famously striking the Gaullist pose of triangulating between the evil empire and primitive Yanks during the Cold War.

The Europeans are not too happy with preemption either. Preemption is the most extreme form of activity, of energy, in foreign policy—anathema to a superannuated continent entirely self-absorbed in its own internal integration. (Hence the paralysis even in the face of fire in its own Balkan backyard.) The Europeans hate preemption all the more because it means America acting on its own. And it is our unilateralism above all that sticks in their craw.

Tough luck. A policy of waiting to be attacked with nuclear (and other genocidal) weapons is suicidal. Moreover, self-defense is the self-evident justification for unilateralism. When under attack, no country is obligated to collect permission slips from allies to strike back. And there is no clearer case of a war of self-defense than America's war on terrorists and allied states for whom "death to America" is not just a slogan but a policy.

I was a unilateralist before it became unfashionable. Long before the axis of evil, long before the Afghan war, long before Sept. 11, I argued that the multilateralism of the Clinton years inevitably produced lowest-common-denominator foreign policy—diluted, ineffective, as feckless as the pinprick cruise missile strikes Clinton liked to launch as an ostentatious pretense of assertiveness.

When the Bush administration came to power advertising its willing-ness to go it alone when necessary, the Democrats were apoplectic. Early last year, for example, when Bush made it clear he would be junking the ABM Treaty, Sen. Carl Levin, now chairman of the Senate Armed Services Committee and thus a man who should know about these things, declared: "I have great concerns about [such] a unilateral decision . . . because I be-lieve that it could risk a second Cold War."

Wrong. Totally wrong. In fact, when Bush did abrogate the ABM Treaty, the Russian response was almost inaudible. Those who'd been bloviating about the diplomatic dangers of such a unilateral decision noted quizzically the lack of reaction. Up in arms over the axis of evil—"it will take years be-fore we can repair the damage done by that statement," said former presi-dent Jimmy Carter—they are warning once again about how the world will rise against us. Wrong again.

Our enemies have already turned against us. Our allies will not. Europe knows that in the end, its security depends on our strength and our pro-tection. Europeans are the ultimate free-riders on American power. We maintain the stability of international commerce, the freedom of the seas, the flow of oil, regional balances of power (in the Pacific Rim, South Asia, the Middle East) and, ultimately, we provide protection against potentially rising hostile superpowers.

The Europeans sit and pout. What else can they do? The ostensible com-plaint is American primitivism. The real problem is their irrelevance.

Being subordinate they can tolerate. Irrelevant they cannot. They may have been subordinate to the United States in the Cold War, but in that great twilight struggle, they manned the front lines, gamely fielding huge land armies against the Warsaw Pact. We provided the nuclear guarantee. They provided the boots on the ground. We were the dominant partner. But we were still partners.

No longer. And they know it. The Soviet threat is gone. Against the new threat of terrorists and terrorist states, the Europeans are sidelined. They are capable of police work but are irrelevant to war-making.

The Afghan war, conducted without them, highlighted how America's 21st century high-tech military made their militaries as obsolete as were the battleships of the 19th century upon the launching of the Dreadnought in 1906.

This is not our fault. We did not force upon them military obsolescence. They chose social spending over defense spending—an understandable choice, perhaps even wise given that America was willing to pick up the slack. But hardly grounds for whining.

We are in a war of self-defense. It is also a war for Western civilization. If the Europeans refuse to see themselves as part of this struggle, fine. If they wish to abdicate, fine. We will let them hold our coats, but not tie our hands.

# DOCUMENT 2.4

As the administration searched for a new strategic vision after September 11, the notion of a unipolar world was adapted to a transformed environment. Officials such as National Security Advisor Condoleezza Rice had been thinking about U.S. foreign policy since the collapse of the Soviet Union, and the problems that accompanied the fall of Communism and the reunification of Germany had taken up most of their attention. As Rice began to consider asymmetric warfare, terrorism, and "non-state actors," she suggested that the United States was doing more than defending itself from terrorism; now it was constructing a new world order that had only begun with the fall of the USSR. She had asserted the centrality of democracy and free markets during the election campaign (1.16) but now began moving closer to the neoconservatives as she embraced a more ideological and assertive foreign policy.

CONDOLEEZZA RICE, REMARKS ON TERRORISM
AND FOREIGN POLICY, JOHNS HOPKINS UNIVERSITY,
APRIL 29, 2002 (EXCERPT)

The international system has been in flux since the collapse of Soviet power. Now it is possible—indeed, probable—that that transition is coming to an end.

If that is right, if the collapse of the Soviet Union and 9/11 bookend a major shift in international politics, then this is a period not just of grave danger, but of enormous opportunity. Before the clay is dry again, America and our friends and our allies must move decisively to take advantage of these new opportunities. This is, then, a period akin to 1945 to 1947, when American leadership expanded the number of free and democratic states—Japan and Germany among the great powers—to create a new balance of power that favored freedom.

It is, indeed, possible to see age-old problems in a new light. . . .

Power matters. Great powers matter. Great powers matter because they can influence international stability for good or for ill due to their size, influence, and their will. Great powers never have, and never will, just mind their own business within their borders.

Thus, the Soviet Union's collapse was important both because it resolved a high-stakes struggle that profoundly affected world peace and security, but also because values and ideas, democracy, markets and freedom triumphed. The socialist alternative that had existed for seventy-plus years, which kept so much of the world isolated from the international economy and deprived so many millions of the benefits of freedom, died alongside the hammer and the sickle.

Our goal today, then, is not just a favorable balance of power, but what President Bush has called a balance of power that favors freedom. . . .

A balance of power that favors freedom is, at its core, a balance of power based on the ascendancy of shared values on every continent. That is why in places such as Russia and China, values matter. They matter in our relations and they matter to the outcome of the balance of power that favors freedom—values like religious freedom, media freedom, and a recognition of the aspirations of long-suffering minority groups. It is not enough for the great powers to share an interest in order; we need to move to sharing an interest in an order that is based on common values.

America today possesses as much power and influence as any nation or entity in the world, and certainly in history. But in stark contrast to the leading powers of centuries past, our ambitions are not territorial. Our military and economic power are complemented by and multiplied by the values that underpin them: democracy, freedom, human rights, the rule of law, honest government, respect for women and children, private property, free speech, equal justice, and religious tolerance.

That is why America seeks a great world beyond the victory over terror. We seek not merely to leave the world safer, but to leave it better; to leave it a world that makes it possible for all men and women to experience the exhilaration and the challenges of freedom. This mission to leave the world safer and better is more important than ever in the face of September 11th. . . .

America cannot impose its vision on the world—yet we will use our influence to favor freedom. There are right and wrong choices and right and wrong acts. And governments are making them every day for their own people and for the people of the world. We can never let the intricacies of cloistered debate—with its many hues of gray and nuance—obscure the need to speak and act with moral clarity. We must recognize that some states or leaders will choose wrongly. We must recognize that truly evil regimes will never be reformed. And we must recognize that such regimes must be confronted, not coddled.

Nations must decide which side they are on in the fault line that divides civilization from terror. They must decide whether to embrace the paradigm of progress: democracy and freedom and human rights, and clean limited government. Together, with others, we can help people and nations make positive choices as they seek a better future, and we can deter those who want to take away a better future for others.

September 11th reintroduced America to a part of itself that some had forgotten, or that some thought we no longer had. We have been reminded that defending freedom was not just the work of the greatest generation, it is the work of every generation. And we will carry this better part of ourselves out into the wider world.

# DOCUMENT 2.5

The administration's post–September 11 turn toward unilateralism and preemption was summarized in the very important speech President Bush gave at West Point. The abandonment of the Anti-Ballistic Missile Treaty, the move away from Cold War strategies of deterrence, new thinking about the role of nuclear weapons in war, and the transformation of the "war on terror" into a war against "weapons of mass destruction" set the background for the first explicit embrace of preemptive war—and a redefinition of what it meant. Bush took the occasion to announce Washington's readiness to attack if it thought it was going to be attacked—or even if it felt threatened or said it felt threatened. In doing so, the administration was discarding a notion embedded in Article 51 of the UN Charter that earlier U.S. leaders had often relied upon: that a nation should go to war only to defend itself against a clear, demonstrable threat.

GEORGE W. BUSH, GRADUATION SPEECH AT WEST POINT, JUNE 1, 2002 (EXCERPT)

. . . The gravest danger to freedom lies at the perilous crossroads of radicalism and technology. When the spread of chemical and biological and nuclear weapons, along with ballistic missile technology—when that occurs, even weak states and small groups could attain a catastrophic power to strike great nations. Our enemies have declared this very intention, and have been caught seeking these terrible weapons. They want the capability to blackmail us, or to harm us, or to harm our friends—and we will oppose them with all our power.

For much of the last century, America's defense relied on the Cold War doctrines of deterrence and containment. In some cases, those strategies still apply. But new threats also require new thinking. Deterrence—the promise of massive retaliation against nations—means nothing against shadowy terrorist networks with no nation or citizens to defend. Containment is not possible when unbalanced dictators with weapons of mass destruction can deliver those weapons on missiles or secretly provide them to terrorist allies.

We cannot defend America and our friends by hoping for the best. We cannot put our faith in the word of tyrants, who solemnly sign nonproliferation treaties, and then systemically break them. If we wait for threats to fully materialize, we will have waited too long.

Homeland defense and missile defense are part of stronger security, and they're essential priorities for America. Yet the war on terror will not be won on the defensive. We must take the battle to the enemy, disrupt his plans, and confront the worst threats before they emerge. In the world we have entered, the only path to safety is the path of action. And this nation will act.

Our security will require the best intelligence, to reveal threats hidden in caves and growing in laboratories. Our security will require modernizing domestic agencies such as the FBI, so they're prepared to act, and act quickly, against danger. Our security will require transforming the military you will lead—a military that must be ready to strike at a moment's notice in any dark corner of the world. And our security will require all Americans to be forward-looking and resolute, to be ready for preemptive action when necessary to defend our liberty and to defend our lives.

66 |  The work ahead is difficult. The choices we will face are complex. We must uncover terror cells in sixty or more countries, using every tool of finance, intelligence, and law enforcement. Along with our friends and allies, we must oppose proliferation and confront regimes that sponsor terror, as each case requires. Some nations need military training to fight terror, and we'll provide it. Other nations oppose terror but tolerate the hatred that leads to terror—and that must change. We will send diplomats where they are needed, and we will send you, our soldiers, where you're needed.

All nations that decide for aggression and terror will pay a price. We will not leave the safety of America and the peace of the planet at the mercy of a few mad terrorists and tyrants. We will lift this dark threat from our country and from the world.

Because the war on terror will require resolve and patience, it will also require firm moral purpose. In this way our struggle is similar to the Cold War. Now, as then, our enemies are totalitarians, holding a creed of power with no place for human dignity. Now, as then, they seek to impose a joyless conformity, to control every life and all of life.

America confronted imperial communism in many different ways— diplomatic, economic, and military. Yet moral clarity was essential to our victory in the Cold War. When leaders like John F. Kennedy and Ronald Reagan refused to gloss over the brutality of tyrants, they gave hope to prisoners and dissidents and exiles, and rallied free nations to a great cause.

Some worry that it is somehow undiplomatic or impolite to speak the language of right and wrong. I disagree. Different circumstances require different methods, but not different moralities. Moral truth is the same in every culture, in every time, and in every place. Targeting innocent civilians for murder is always and everywhere wrong. Brutality against women is always and everywhere wrong. There can be no neutrality between justice and cruelty, between the innocent and the guilty. We are in a conflict between good and evil, and America will call evil by its name. By confronting evil and lawless regimes, we do not create a problem, we reveal a problem. And we will lead the world in opposing it. . . .

The twentieth century ended with a single surviving model of human progress, based on non-negotiable demands of human dignity, the rule of law, limits on the power of the state, respect for women and private property and free speech and equal justice and religious tolerance. America cannot impose this vision—yet we can support and reward governments that make the right choices for their own people. In our development aid, in our diplomatic efforts, in our international broadcasting, and in our educational assistance, the United States will promote moderation and tolerance and human rights. And we will defend the peace that makes all progress possible.

When it comes to the common rights and needs of men and women, there is no clash of civilizations. The requirements of freedom apply fully to Africa and Latin America and the entire Islamic world. The peoples of the Islamic nations want and deserve the same freedoms and opportunities as people in every nation. And their governments should listen to their hopes.

| 67

# DOCUMENT 2.6

On July 23, 2002, eight months before U.S. and British forces invaded Iraq, senior British officials met with Prime Minister Tony Blair. The gathering brought together Defense Secretary Geoffrey Hoon; Foreign Secretary Jack Straw; Attorney General Lord Goldsmith; John Scarlett, the head of the Joint Intelligence Committee, which advises the prime minister; Sir Richard Dearlove, also known as "C," the head of MI6 (the equivalent of the CIA); David Manning, the equivalent of the national security advisor; Admiral Sir Michael Boyce, the chief of the defense staff (or CDS, equivalent to the chairman of the Joint Chiefs of Staff); Jonathan Powell, Blair's chief of staff; Director of Strategy Alastair Campbell (Blair's communications and political advisor); and Director of Government Relations Sally Morgan.

Kept secret for nearly three years, the "Downing Street Memo" was an account of that meeting. Its high point came when "C" reported on his visit to Washington, where he had conducted talks with George Tenet, his counterpart at the CIA, and other high officials. The memo was a revealing description of the Bush administration's determination to go to war, asserted nearly a year before the invasion and months before it asked the Security Council to authorize renewed weapons inspections as an alternative to conflict. It also revealed the president's intention to justify the invasion by connecting terrorism and Iraqi weapons of mass destruction. The memo contained significant British reservations about the legality of Washington's intentions, famously observed that "the intelligence and facts were being fixed around the policy," and noted the lack of planning for the invasion's aftermath. Written by a British foreign-policy aide and addressed to a key advisor to Prime Minister Tony Blair, the memo created a sensation when it was made public in 2005.

---

THE DOWNING STREET MEMO, JULY 23, 2002 (EXCERPT)

SECRET AND STRICTLY PERSONAL—UK EYES ONLY
DAVID MANNING
From: Matthew Rycroft
Date: 23 July 2002
cc: Defence Secretary, Foreign Secretary, Attorney-General, Sir Richard Wilson, John Scarlett, Francis Richards, CDS, C, Jonathan Powell, Sally Morgan, Alastair Campbell

IRAQ: PRIME MINISTER'S MEETING, 23 JULY

Copy addressees and you met the Prime Minister on 23 July to discuss Iraq.

This record is extremely sensitive. No further copies should be made. It should be shown only to those with a genuine need to know its contents.

John Scarlett summarised the intelligence and latest JIC assessment. Saddam's regime was tough and based on extreme fear. The only way to overthrow it was likely to be by massive military action. Saddam was worried and expected an attack, probably by air and land, but he was not convinced that it would be immediate or overwhelming. His regime expected their neighbours to line up with the U.S. Saddam knew that regular army morale was poor. Real support for Saddam among the public was probably narrowly based.

C reported on his recent talks in Washington. There was a perceptible shift in attitude. Military action was now seen as inevitable. Bush wanted to remove Saddam, through military action, justified by the conjunction of terrorism and WMD. But the intelligence and facts were being fixed around the policy. The NSC [*Editors' Note: National Security Council*] had no patience with the UN route, and no enthusiasm for publishing material on the Iraqi regime's record. There was little discussion in Washington of the aftermath after military action. . . .

The Defense Secretary said that the U.S. had already begun "spikes of activity" to put pressure on the regime. No decisions had been taken, but he thought the most likely timing in U.S. minds for military action to begin was January, with the timeline beginning 30 days before the U.S. Congressional elections.

The Foreign Secretary said he would discuss this with Colin Powell this week. It seemed clear that Bush had made up his mind to take military action, even if the timing was not yet decided. But the case was thin. Saddam was not threatening his neighbours, and his WMD capability was less than that of Libya, North Korea or Iran. We should work up a plan for an ultimatum to Saddam to allow back in the UN weapons inspectors. This would also help with the legal justification for the use of force.

The Attorney-General said that the desire for regime change was not a legal base for military action. There were three possible legal bases: self-defence, humanitarian intervention, or UNSC [*Editors' Note: United Nations Security Council*] authorisation. The first and second could not be the base in this case. Relying on UNSCR 1205 of three years ago would be difficult. The situation might of course change.

The Prime Minister said that it would make a big difference politically and legally if Saddam refused to allow in the UN inspectors. Regime change and WMD were linked in the sense that it was the regime that was producing the WMD. There were different strategies for dealing with Libya and Iran. If the political context were right, people would support regime change. The two key issues were whether the military plan worked and whether we had the political strategy to give the military plan the space to work.

On the first, CDS said that we did not know yet if the U.S. battleplan was workable. The military were continuing to ask lots of questions.

For instance, what were the consequences, if Saddam used WMD on day one, or if Baghdad did not collapse and urban warfighting began? You said that Saddam could also use his WMD on Kuwait. Or on Israel, added the Defence Secretary.

The Foreign Secretary thought the U.S. would not go ahead with a military plan unless convinced that it was a winning strategy. On this, U.S. and U.K. interests converged. But on the political strategy, there could be U.S./U.K. differences. Despite U.S. resistance, we should explore discreetly the ultimatum. Saddam would continue to play hard-ball with the UN.

John Scarlett assessed that Saddam would allow the inspectors back in only when he thought the threat of military action was real.

The Defence Secretary said that if the Prime Minister wanted U.K. military involvement, he would need to decide this early. He cautioned that many in the U.S. did not think it worth going down the ultimatum route. It would be important for the Prime Minister to set out the political context to Bush. . . .

MATTHEW RYCROFT

# DOCUMENT 2.7

Most of the domestic debate about Iraq was conducted inside the Republican Party, even though the Democrats controlled the Senate. The Clinton interregnum had failed to produce a consensus about U.S. foreign policy in the aftermath of the Cold War. Most of the neoconservatives had migrated into the Republican Party years earlier, and the internal debate of August 2002 took the form of a struggle between the "realist" veterans of George H. W. Bush's administration and the neoconservatives of his son's. All month, an orchestrated succession of public protests from veteran Republican insiders took issue with the administration's increasingly clear intention to attack Iraq. Brent Scowcroft, the national security advisor to Presidents Gerald Ford and George H. W. Bush, began the offensive with an op-ed piece in the *Wall Street Journal.*

---

BRENT SCOWCROFT, "DON'T ATTACK SADDAM,"
*WALL STREET JOURNAL,* AUGUST 16, 2002

Our nation is presently engaged in a debate about whether to launch a war against Iraq. Leaks of various strategies for an attack on Iraq appear with regularity. The Bush administration vows regime change, but states that no decision has been made whether, much less when, to launch an invasion.

It is beyond dispute that Saddam Hussein is a menace. He terrorizes and brutalizes his own people. He has launched war on two of his neighbors. He devotes enormous effort to rebuilding his military forces and equipping them with weapons of mass destruction. We will all be better off when he is gone.

That said, we need to think through this issue very carefully. We need to analyze the relationship between Iraq and our other pressing priorities— notably the war on terrorism—as well as the best strategy and tactics available were we to move to change the regime in Baghdad.

Saddam's strategic objective appears to be to dominate the Persian Gulf, to control oil from the region, or both.

That clearly poses a real threat to key U.S. interests. But there is scant evidence to tie Saddam to terrorist organizations, and even less to the Sept. 11 attacks. Indeed Saddam's goals have little in common with the terrorists who threaten us, and there is little incentive for him to make common cause with them.

He is unlikely to risk his investment in weapons of mass destruction, much less his country, by handing such weapons to terrorists who would use them for their own purposes and leave Baghdad as the return address. Threatening to use these weapons for blackmail—much less their actual use—would open him and his entire regime to a devastating response by the U.S. While Saddam is thoroughly evil, he is above all a power-hungry survivor.

Saddam is a familiar dictatorial aggressor, with traditional goals for his aggression. There is little evidence to indicate that the United States itself is an object of his aggression. Rather, Saddam's problem with the U.S. appears to be that we stand in the way of his ambitions. He seeks weapons of mass destruction not to arm terrorists, but to deter us from intervening to block his aggressive designs.

Given Saddam's aggressive regional ambitions, as well as his ruthlessness and unpredictability, it may at some point be wise to remove him from power. Whether and when that point should come ought to depend on overall U.S. national security priorities. Our pre-eminent security priority—underscored repeatedly by the president—is the war on terrorism. An attack on Iraq at this time would seriously jeopardize, if not destroy, the global counterterrorist campaign we have undertaken.

The United States could certainly defeat the Iraqi military and destroy Saddam's regime. But it would not be a cakewalk. On the contrary, it undoubtedly would be very expensive—with serious consequences for the U.S. and global economy—and could as well be bloody. In fact, Saddam would be likely to conclude he had nothing left to lose, leading him to unleash whatever weapons of mass destruction he possesses.

Israel would have to expect to be the first casualty, as in 1991 when Saddam sought to bring Israel into the Gulf conflict. This time, using weapons of mass destruction, he might succeed, provoking Israel to respond, perhaps with nuclear weapons, unleashing an Armageddon in the Middle East. Finally, if we are to achieve our strategic objectives in Iraq, a military campaign very likely would have to be followed by a large-scale, long-term military occupation.

But the central point is that any campaign against Iraq, whatever the strategy, cost and risks, is certain to divert us for some indefinite period from our war on terrorism. Worse, there is a virtual consensus in the world against an attack on Iraq at this time. So long as that sentiment persists, it would require the U.S. to pursue a virtual go-it-alone strategy against Iraq, making any military operations correspondingly more difficult and expensive. The most serious cost, however, would be to the war on terrorism. Ignoring that clear sentiment would result in a serious degradation in international cooperation with us against terrorism. And make no mistake, we simply cannot win that war without enthusiastic international cooperation, especially on intelligence.

Possibly the most dire consequences would be the effect in the region. The shared view in the region is that Iraq is principally an obsession of the U.S. The obsession of the region, however, is the Israeli-Palestinian conflict. If we were seen to be turning our backs on that bitter conflict—which the region, rightly or wrongly, perceives to be clearly within our power to resolve—in order to go after Iraq, there would be an explosion of outrage against us. We would be seen as ignoring a key interest of the Muslim world in order to satisfy what is seen to be a narrow American interest.

Even without Israeli involvement, the results could well destabilize Arab regimes in the region, ironically facilitating one of Saddam's strategic objectives. At a minimum, it would stifle any cooperation on terrorism, and could even swell the ranks of the terrorists. Conversely, the more progress we make in the war on terrorism, and the more we are seen to be committed to resolving the Israel-Palestinian issue, the greater will be the international support for going after Saddam.

If we are truly serious about the war on terrorism, it must remain our top priority. However, should Saddam Hussein be found to be clearly implicated in the events of Sept. 11 that could make him a key counter-terrorist target, rather than a competing priority, and significantly shift world opinion toward support for regime change.

In any event, we should be pressing the United Nations Security Council to insist on an effective no-notice inspection regime for Iraq—any time, anywhere, no permission required. On this point, senior administration officials have opined that Saddam Hussein would never agree to such an inspection regime. But if he did, inspections would serve to keep him off balance and under close observation, even if all his weapons of mass destruction capabilities were not uncovered. And if he refused, his rejection could provide the persuasive casus belli which many claim we do not now have. Compelling evidence that Saddam had acquired nuclear-weapons capability could have a similar effect.

In sum, if we will act in full awareness of the intimate interrelationship of the key issues in the region, keeping counterterrorism as our foremost priority, there is much potential for success across the entire range of our security interests—including Iraq. If we reject a comprehensive perspective, however, we put at risk our campaign against terrorism as well as stability and security in a vital region of the world.

## DOCUMENT 2.8

James A. Baker, who had been the chief of staff in the administrations of Presidents Ronald Reagan and George H. W. Bush, secretary of the treasury for Reagan, and secretary of state for George H. W. Bush, seconded Scowcroft's warning with an op-ed piece in the *New York Times* a few days later.

---

JAMES A. BAKER, "THE RIGHT WAY TO CHANGE A REGIME," *NEW YORK TIMES,* AUGUST 25, 2002

While there may be little evidence that Iraq has ties to al Qaeda or to the attacks of Sept. 11, there is no question that its present government, under

Saddam Hussein, is an outlaw regime, is in violation of United Nations Security Council resolutions, is embarked upon a program of developing weapons of mass destruction and is a threat to peace and stability, both in the Middle East and, because of the risk of proliferation of these weapons, in other parts of the globe. Peace-loving nations have a moral responsibility to fight against the development and proliferation of weapons of mass destruction by rogues like Saddam Hussein. We owe it to our children and grandchildren to do so, and leading that fight is, and must continue to be, an important foreign policy priority for America.

And thus regime change in Iraq is the policy of the current administration, just as it was the policy of its predecessor. That being the case, the issue for policymakers to resolve is not whether to use military force to achieve this, but how to go about it.

Covert action has been tried before and failed every time. Iraqi opposition groups are not strong enough to get the job done. It will not happen through internal revolt, either of the army or the civilian population. We would have to be extremely lucky to take out the top leadership through insertion into Iraq of a small rapid-strike force. And this last approach carries significant political risks for the administration, as President Jimmy Carter found out in April 1980.

The only realistic way to effect regime change in Iraq is through the application of military force, including sufficient ground troops to occupy the country (including Baghdad), depose the current leadership and install a successor government. Anyone who thinks we can effect regime change in Iraq with anything less than this is simply not realistic. It cannot be done on the cheap. It will require substantial forces and substantial time to put those forces in place to move. We had over 500,000 Americans, and more soldiers from our many allies, for the Persian Gulf War. There will be casualties, probably quite a few more than in that war, since the Iraqis will be fighting to defend their homeland. Sadly, there also will be civilian deaths. We will face the problem of how long to occupy and administer a big, fractious country and what type of government or administration should follow. Finding Saddam Hussein and his top associates will be difficult. It took us two weeks to locate Manuel Noriega in Panama, a small country where we had military bases.

Unless we do it in the right way, there will be costs to other American foreign policy interests, including our relationships with practically all other Arab countries (and even many of our customary allies in Europe and elsewhere) and perhaps even to our top foreign policy priority, the war on terrorism.

Finally, there will be the cost to the American taxpayer of a military undertaking of this magnitude. The Persian Gulf War cost somewhere in the range of $60 billion, but we were able to convince our many allies in that effort to bear the brunt of the costs.

So how should we proceed to effect regime change in Iraq?

Although the United States could certainly succeed, we should try our best not to have to go it alone, and the President should reject the advice of those who counsel doing so. The costs in all areas will be much greater, as will the political risks, both domestic and international, if we end up going it alone or with only one or two other countries.

The President should do his best to stop his advisors and their surrogates from playing out their differences publicly and try to get everybody on the same page.

The United States should advocate the adoption by the United Nations Security Council of a simple and straightforward resolution requiring that Iraq submit to intrusive inspections anytime, anywhere, with no exceptions, and authorizing all necessary means to enforce it. Although it is technically true that the United Nations already has sufficient legal authority to deal with Iraq, the failure to act when Saddam Hussein ejected the inspectors has weakened that authority. Seeking new authorization now is necessary, politically and practically, and will help build international support.

Some will argue, as was done in 1990, that going for United Nations authority and not getting it will weaken our case. I disagree. By proposing to proceed in such a way, we will be doing the right thing, both politically and substantively. We will occupy the moral high ground and put the burden of supporting an outlaw regime and proliferation of weapons of mass destruction on any countries that vote no. History will be an unkind judge for those who prefer to do business rather than to do the right thing. And even if the administration fails in the Security Council, it is still free—citing Iraq's flouting of the international community's resolutions and perhaps Article 51 of the United Nations Charter, which guarantees a nation's right to self-defense—to weigh the costs versus the benefit of going forward alone.

Others will argue that this approach would give Saddam Hussein a way out because he might agree and then begin the "cheat-and-retreat" tactics he used during the first inspection regime. And so we must not be deterred. The first time he resorts to these tactics, we should apply whatever means are necessary to change the regime. And the international community must know during the Security Council debate that this will be our policy.

We should frankly recognize that our problem in accomplishing regime change in Iraq is made more difficult by the way our policy on the Arab-Israeli dispute is perceived around the world. Sadly, in international politics, as in domestic politics, perception is sometimes more important than reality. We cannot allow our policy toward Iraq to be linked to the Arab-Israeli dispute, as Saddam Hussein will cynically demand, just as he did in 1990 and 1991. But to avoid that, we need to move affirmatively, aggressively, and in a fair and balanced way to implement the President's vision for a settlement of the Arab-Israeli dispute, as laid out in his June speech. That means, of course, reform by Palestinians and an end to terror tactics. But it also means withdrawal by Israeli forces to positions occupied before September 2000 and an immediate end to settlement activity.

74 |

If we are to change the regime in Iraq, we will have to occupy the country militarily. The costs of doing so, politically, economically and in terms of casualties, could be great. They will be lessened if the president brings together an international coalition behind the effort. Doing so would also help in achieving the continuing support of the American people, a necessary prerequisite for any successful foreign policy.

# DOCUMENT 2.9

When Vice President Cheney rejected Scowcroft's and Baker's arguments, he served notice that Washington was abandoning the multilateral emphasis on diplomacy that had characterized the Gulf War a decade earlier and that the administration had placed preemptive regime change at the center of its foreign policy.

---

DICK CHENEY, SPEECH AT VETERANS OF FOREIGN WARS
103RD NATIONAL CONVENTION, NASHVILLE, TENNESSEE,
AUGUST 26, 2002 (EXCERPT)

Much has happened since the attacks of 9/11. But as Secretary Rumsfeld has put it, we are still closer to the beginning of this war than we are to its end. The United States has entered a struggle of years—a new kind of war against a new kind of enemy. The terrorists who struck America are ruthless, they are resourceful, and they hide in many countries. They came into our country to murder thousands of innocent men, women, and children. There is no doubt they wish to strike again and that they are working to acquire the deadliest of all weapons.

Against such enemies, America and the civilized world have only one option: wherever terrorists operate, we must find them where they dwell, stop them in their planning, and one by one bring them to justice. . . .

The combination of advantages already seen in this conflict—precision power from the air, real-time intelligence, special forces, the long reach of naval task forces, and close coordination with local forces—represents a dramatic advance in our ability to engage and defeat the enemy. These advantages will only become more vital in future campaigns. President Bush has often spoken of how America can keep the peace by redefining war on our terms. That means that our armed services must have every tool to answer any threat that forms against us. It means that any enemy conspiring to harm America or our friends must face a swift, a certain and a devastating response. . . .

In this war we've assembled a broad coalition of civilized nations that recognize the danger and are working with us on all fronts. The president has made very clear that there is no neutral ground in the fight against terror. Those who harbor terrorists share guilt for the acts they commit. Under the Bush Doctrine, a regime that harbors or supports terrorists will be regarded as hostile to the United States.

The Taliban has already learned that lesson, but Afghanistan was only the beginning of a lengthy campaign. Were we to stop now, any sense of security we might have would be false and temporary. There is a terrorist underworld out there, spread among more than sixty countries. The job we have will require every tool at our means of diplomacy, of finance, of intelligence, of law enforcement, and of military power. But we will, over time, find and defeat the enemies of the United States. In the case of Osama bin Laden—as President Bush said recently—"If he's alive, we'll get him. If he's not alive—we already got him."

But the challenges to our country involve more than just tracking down a single person or one small group. Nine-eleven and its aftermath awakened this nation to danger, to the true ambitions of the global terror network, and to the reality that weapons of mass destruction are being sought by determined enemies who would not hesitate to use them against us.

It is a certainty that the al Qaeda network is pursuing such weapons and has succeeded in acquiring at least a crude capability to use them. We found evidence of their efforts in the ruins of al Qaeda hideouts in Afghanistan. And we've seen in recent days additional confirmation in videos recently shown on CNN—pictures of al Qaeda members training to commit acts of terror and testing chemical weapons on dogs. Those terrorists who remain at large are determined to use these capabilities against the United States and our friends and allies around the world.

As we face this prospect, old doctrines of security do not apply. In the days of the Cold War, we were able to manage the threat with strategies of deterrence and containment. But it's a lot tougher to deter enemies who have no country to defend. And containment is not possible when dictators obtain weapons of mass destruction and are prepared to share them with terrorists who intend to inflict catastrophic casualties on the United States.

The case of Saddam Hussein, a sworn enemy of our country, requires a candid appraisal of the facts. After his defeat in the Gulf War in 1991, Saddam agreed under UN Security Council Resolution 687 to cease all development of weapons of mass destruction. He agreed to end his nuclear weapons program. He agreed to destroy his chemical and his biological weapons. He further agreed to admit UN inspection teams into his country to ensure that he was in fact complying with these terms.

In the past decade, Saddam has systematically broken each of these agreements. The Iraqi regime has in fact been very busy enhancing its capabilities in the field of chemical and biological agents. And they continue to pursue the nuclear program they began so many years ago. These are not weapons for the purpose of defending Iraq; these are offensive weapons for the purpose of inflicting death on a massive scale, developed so that Saddam can hold the threat over the head of anyone he chooses, in his own region or beyond.

On the nuclear question, many of you will recall that Saddam's nuclear ambitions suffered a severe setback in 1981 when the Israelis bombed the Osirak reactor. They suffered another major blow in Desert Storm and its aftermath.

But we now know that Saddam has resumed his efforts to acquire nuclear weapons. Among other sources, we've gotten this from the firsthand testimony of defectors—including Saddam's own son-in-law, who was subsequently murdered at Saddam's direction. Many of us are convinced that Saddam will acquire nuclear weapons fairly soon.

Just how soon, we cannot really gauge. Intelligence is an uncertain business, even in the best of circumstances. This is especially the case when you are dealing with a totalitarian regime that has made a science out of deceiving the international community. Let me give you just one example of what I mean. Prior to the Gulf War, America's top intelligence analysts would come to my office in the Defense Department and tell me that Saddam Hussein was at least five or perhaps even ten years away from having a nuclear weapon. After the war we learned that he had been much closer than that, perhaps within a year of acquiring such a weapon.

Saddam also devised an elaborate program to conceal his active efforts to build chemical and biological weapons. And one must keep in mind the history of UN inspection teams in Iraq. Even as they were conducting the most intrusive system of arms control in history, the inspectors missed a great deal. Before being barred from the country, the inspectors found and destroyed thousands of chemical weapons, and hundreds of tons of mustard gas and other nerve agents.

Yet Saddam Hussein had sought to frustrate and deceive them at every turn, and was often successful in doing so. I'll cite one instance. During the spring of 1995, the inspectors were actually on the verge of declaring that Saddam's programs to develop chemical weapons and longer-range ballistic missiles had been fully accounted for and shut down. Then Saddam's son-in-law suddenly defected and began sharing information. Within days the inspectors were led to an Iraqi chicken farm. Hidden there were boxes of documents and lots of evidence regarding Iraq's most secret weapons programs. That should serve as a reminder to all that we often learned more as the result of defections than we learned from the inspection regime itself.

To the dismay of the inspectors, they in time discovered that Saddam had kept them largely in the dark about the extent of his program to mass produce VX, one of the deadliest chemicals known to man. And far from having shut down Iraq's prohibited missile programs, the inspectors found that Saddam had continued to test such missiles, almost literally under the noses of the UN inspectors.

Against that background, a person would be right to question any suggestion that we should just get inspectors back into Iraq, and then our worries will be over. Saddam has perfected the game of cheat and retreat, and is very skilled in the art of denial and deception. A return of inspectors would provide no assurance whatsoever of his compliance with UN resolutions. On the contrary, there is a great danger that it would provide false comfort that Saddam was somehow "back in his box."

Meanwhile, he would continue to plot. Nothing in the last dozen years has stopped him—not his agreements; not the discoveries of the inspectors; not the revelations by defectors; not criticism or ostracism by the international community; and not four days of bombings by the U.S. in 1998. What he wants is time and more time to husband his resources, to invest in his ongoing chemical and biological weapons programs, and to gain possession of nuclear arms.

Should all his ambitions be realized, the implications would be enormous for the Middle East, for the United States, and for the peace of the world. The whole range of weapons of mass destruction then would rest in the hands of a dictator who has already shown his willingness to use such weapons, and has done so, both in his war with Iran and against his own people. Armed with an arsenal of these weapons of terror, and seated atop 10 percent of the world's oil reserves, Saddam Hussein could then be expected to seek domination of the entire Middle East, take control of a great portion of the world's energy supplies, directly threaten America's friends throughout the region, and subject the United States or any other nation to nuclear blackmail.

Simply stated, there is no doubt that Saddam Hussein now has weapons of mass destruction. There is no doubt he is amassing them to use against our friends, against our allies, and against us. And there is no doubt that his aggressive regional ambitions will lead him into future confrontations with his neighbors—confrontations that will involve both the weapons he has today, and the ones he will continue to develop with his oil wealth.

Ladies and gentlemen, there is no basis in Saddam Hussein's conduct or history to discount any of the concerns that I am raising this morning. We are, after all, dealing with the same dictator who shoots at American and British pilots in the no-fly zone, on a regular basis; the same dictator who dispatched a team of assassins to murder former President Bush as he traveled abroad; the same dictator who invaded Iran and Kuwait, and has fired ballistic missiles at Iran, Saudi Arabia, and Israel; the same dictator who has been on the State Department's list of state sponsors of terrorism for the better part of two decades. . . .

America in the year 2002 must ask careful questions, not merely about our past, but also about our future. The elected leaders of this country have a responsibility to consider all of the available options. And we are doing so. What we must not do in the face of a mortal threat is give in to wishful thinking or willful blindness. We will not simply look away, hope for the best, and leave the matter for some future administration to resolve. As President Bush has said, time is not on our side. Deliverable weapons of mass destruction in the hands of a terror network, or a murderous dictator, or the two working together, constitutes as grave a threat as can be imagined. The risks of inaction are far greater than the risk of action.

Now and in the future, the United States will work closely with the global coalition to deny terrorists and their state sponsors the materials, technology, and expertise to make and deliver weapons of mass destruction. We will develop and deploy effective missile defenses to protect America and our allies from sudden attack. And the entire world must know that we will take whatever action is necessary to defend our freedom and our security.

As former secretary of state Kissinger recently stated: "The imminence of proliferation of weapons of mass destruction, the huge dangers it involves, the rejection of a viable inspection system, and the demonstrated hostility of Saddam Hussein combine to produce an imperative for preemptive action." If the United States could have preempted 9/11, we would have, no question. Should we be able to prevent another, much more devastating attack, we will, no question. This nation will not live at the mercy of terrorists or terror regimes.

I am familiar with the arguments against taking action in the case of Saddam Hussein. Some concede that Saddam is evil, power-hungry, and a menace—but that, until he crosses the threshold of actually possessing nuclear weapons, we should rule out any preemptive action. That logic seems to me to be deeply flawed. The argument comes down to this: yes, Saddam is as dangerous as we say he is, we just need to let him get stronger before we do anything about it.

Yet if we did wait until that moment, Saddam would simply be emboldened, and it would become even harder for us to gather friends and allies to oppose him. As one of those who worked to assemble the Gulf War coalition, I can tell you that our job then would have been infinitely more difficult in the face of a nuclear-armed Saddam Hussein. And many of those who now argue that we should act only if he gets a nuclear weapon, would then turn around and say that we cannot act because he has a nuclear weapon. At bottom, that argument counsels a course of inaction that itself could have devastating consequences for many countries, including our own.

Another argument holds that opposing Saddam Hussein would cause even greater troubles in that part of the world, and interfere with the larger war against terror. I believe the opposite is true. Regime change in Iraq would bring about a number of benefits to the region. When the gravest of threats are eliminated, the freedom-loving peoples of the region will have a chance to promote the values that can bring lasting peace. As for the reaction of the Arab "street," the Middle East expert Professor Fouad Ajami predicts that after liberation, the streets in Basra and Baghdad are "sure to erupt in joy in the same way the throngs in Kabul greeted the Americans." Extremists in the region would have to rethink their strategy of Jihad. Moderates throughout the region would take heart. And our ability to advance the Israeli-Palestinian peace process would be enhanced, just as it was following the liberation of Kuwait in 1991.

The reality is that these times bring not only dangers but also opportunities. In the Middle East, where so many have known only poverty and oppression, terror and tyranny, we look to the day when people can live in freedom and dignity and the young can grow up free of the conditions that breed despair, hatred, and violence.

In other times the world saw how the United States defeated fierce enemies, then helped rebuild their countries, forming strong bonds between our peoples and our governments. Today in Afghanistan, the world is seeing that America acts not to conquer but to liberate, and remains in friendship to help the people build a future of stability, self-determination, and peace.

We would act in that same spirit after a regime change in Iraq. With our help, a liberated Iraq can be a great nation once again. Iraq is rich in natural resources and human talent, and has unlimited potential for a peaceful, prosperous future. Our goal would be an Iraq that has territorial integrity, a government that is democratic and pluralistic, a nation where the human rights of every ethnic and religious group are recognized and protected. In that troubled land all who seek justice, and dignity, and the chance to live their own lives, can know they have a friend and ally in the United States of America. . . .

80 |

## DOCUMENT 2.10

Vice President Cheney's intervention did not end the debate. His speech repeated many of the administration's talking points about the connection between Iraq and terrorism; Saddam Hussein's pursuit of chemical, biological, and nuclear weapons; his desire to control the Persian Gulf; and the necessity for unwavering U.S. leadership. National Security Advisor Condoleezza Rice brought many of these arguments together when she said that "we don't want the smoking gun to be a mushroom cloud"—but it was "The National Security Strategy of the United States of America," written by her office and issued under the president's signature, that stood as the authoritative statement of the administration's view of the world and of the U.S. role in it.

CONDOLEEZZA RICE AND GEORGE W. BUSH, "THE NATIONAL SECURITY STRATEGY OF THE UNITED STATES OF AMERICA," SEPTEMBER 2002 (EXCERPT)

The great struggles of the twentieth century between liberty and totalitarianism ended with a decisive victory for the forces of freedom—and a single sustainable model for national success: freedom, democracy, and free enterprise. In the twenty-first century, only nations that share a commitment to protecting basic human rights and guaranteeing political and economic freedom will be able to unleash the potential of their people and assure their future prosperity. People everywhere want to be able to speak freely; choose who will govern them; worship as they please; educate their children—male and female; own property; and enjoy the benefits of their labor. These values of freedom are right and true for every person, in every society—and the duty of protecting these values against their enemies is the common calling of freedom-loving people across the globe and across the ages. . . .

The United States possesses unprecedented—and unequaled—strength and influence in the world. Sustained by faith in the principles of liberty, and the value of a free society, this position comes with unparalleled responsibilities, obligations, and opportunity. The great strength of this nation must be used to promote a balance of power that favors freedom.

For most of the twentieth century, the world was divided by a great struggle over ideas: destructive totalitarian visions versus freedom and equality.

That great struggle is over. The militant visions of class, nation, and race which promised utopia and delivered misery have been defeated and discredited. . . .

America must stand firmly for the nonnegotiable demands of human dignity: the rule of law; limits on the absolute power of the state; free speech; freedom of worship; equal justice; respect for women; religious and ethnic tolerance; and respect for private property. . . .

The United States of America is fighting a war against terrorists of global reach. The enemy is not a single political regime or person or religion or ideology. The enemy is terrorism—premeditated, politically motivated violence perpetrated against innocents.

In many regions, legitimate grievances prevent the emergence of a lasting peace. Such grievances deserve to be, and must be, addressed within a political process. But no cause justifies terror. The United States will make no concessions to terrorist demands and strike no deals with them. We make no distinction between terrorists and those who knowingly harbor or provide aid to them.

The struggle against global terrorism is different from any other war in our history. It will be fought on many fronts against a particularly elusive enemy over an extended period of time. Progress will come through the persistent accumulation of successes—some seen, some unseen. . . .

We will disrupt and destroy terrorist organizations by:

direct and continuous action using all the elements of national and international power. Our immediate focus will be those terrorist organizations of global reach and any terrorist or state sponsor of terrorism which attempts to gain or use weapons of mass destruction (WMD) or their precursors;

defending the United States, the American people, and our interests at home and abroad by identifying and destroying the threat before it reaches our borders. While the United States will constantly strive to enlist the support of the international community, we will not hesitate to act alone, if necessary, to exercise our right of self-defense by acting preemptively against such terrorists, to prevent them from doing harm against our people and our country. . . .

At the time of the Gulf War, we acquired irrefutable proof that Iraq's designs were not limited to the chemical weapons it had used against Iran and its own people, but also extended to the acquisition of nuclear weapons and biological agents. In the past decade North Korea has become the world's principal purveyor of ballistic missiles, and has tested increasingly capable missiles while developing its own WMD arsenal. Other rogue regimes seek nuclear, biological, and chemical weapons as well. These states' pursuit of, and global trade in, such weapons has become a looming threat to all nations.

82 |

We must be prepared to stop rogue states and their terrorist clients before they are able to threaten or use weapons of mass destruction against the United States and our allies and friends. Our response must take full advantage of strengthened alliances, the establishment of new partnerships with former adversaries, innovation in the use of military forces, modern technologies, including the development of an effective missile defense system, and increased emphasis on intelligence collection and analysis. . . .

It has taken almost a decade for us to comprehend the true nature of this new threat. Given the goals of rogue states and terrorists, the United States can no longer solely rely on a reactive posture as we have in the past. The inability to deter a potential attacker, the immediacy of today's threats, and the magnitude of potential harm that could be caused by our adversaries' choice of weapons, do not permit that option. We cannot let our enemies strike first.

In the Cold War, especially following the Cuban missile crisis, we faced a generally status quo, risk-averse adversary. Deterrence was an effective defense. But deterrence based only upon the threat of retaliation is less likely to work against leaders of rogue states more willing to take risks, gambling with the lives of their people, and the wealth of their nations.

In the Cold War, weapons of mass destruction were considered weapons of last resort whose use risked the destruction of those who used them. Today, our enemies see weapons of mass destruction as weapons of choice. For rogue states these weapons are tools of intimidation and military aggression against their neighbors. These weapons may also allow these states to attempt to blackmail the United States and our allies to prevent us from deterring or repelling the aggressive behavior of rogue states. Such states also see these weapons as their best means of overcoming the conventional superiority of the United States.

Traditional concepts of deterrence will not work against a terrorist enemy whose avowed tactics are wanton destruction and the targeting of innocents; whose so-called soldiers seek martyrdom in death and whose most potent protection is statelessness. The overlap between states that sponsor terror and those that pursue WMD compels us to action.

For centuries, international law recognized that nations need not suffer an attack before they can lawfully take action to defend themselves against forces that present an imminent danger of attack. Legal scholars and international jurists often conditioned the legitimacy of preemption on the existence of an imminent threat—most often a visible mobilization of armies, navies, and air forces preparing to attack.

We must adapt the concept of imminent threat to the capabilities and objectives of today's adversaries. Rogue states and terrorists do not seek to attack us using conventional means. They know such attacks would fail. Instead, they rely on acts of terror and, potentially, the use of weapons of mass destruction—weapons that can be easily concealed, delivered covertly, and used without warning.

The targets of these attacks are our military forces and our civilian population, in direct violation of one of the principal norms of the law of warfare. As was demonstrated by the losses on September 11, 2001, mass civilian casualties is the specific objective of terrorists and these losses would be exponentially more severe if terrorists acquired and used weapons of mass destruction.

The United States has long maintained the option of preemptive actions to counter a sufficient threat to our national security. The greater the threat, the greater is the risk of inaction—and the more compelling the case for taking anticipatory action to defend ourselves, even if uncertainty remains as to the time and place of the enemy's attack. To forestall or prevent such hostile acts by our adversaries, the United States will, if necessary, act preemptively.

The United States will not use force in all cases to preempt emerging threats, nor should nations use preemption as a pretext for aggression. Yet in an age where the enemies of civilization openly and actively seek the world's most destructive technologies, the United States cannot remain idle while dangers gather. . . .

The major institutions of American national security were designed in a different era to meet different requirements. All of them must be transformed.

It is time to reaffirm the essential role of American military strength. We must build and maintain our defenses beyond challenge. Our military's highest priority is to defend the United States.

The unparalleled strength of the United States armed forces, and their forward presence, have maintained the peace in some of the world's most strategically vital regions. However, the threats and enemies we must confront have changed, and so must our forces. A military structured to deter massive Cold War–era armies must be transformed to focus more on how an adversary might fight rather than where and when a war might occur. We will channel our energies to overcome a host of operational challenges.

The presence of American forces overseas is one of the most profound symbols of the U.S. commitments to allies and friends. Through our willingness to use force in our own defense and in defense of others, the United States demonstrates its resolve to maintain a balance of power that favors freedom. To contend with uncertainty and to meet the many security challenges we face, the United States will require bases and stations within and beyond Western Europe and Northeast Asia, as well as temporary access arrangements for the long-distance deployment of U.S. forces. . . .

We know from history that deterrence can fail; and we know from experience that some enemies cannot be deterred. The United States must and will maintain the capability to defeat any attempt by an enemy—whether a state or non-state actor—to impose its will on the United States, our allies, or our friends. We will maintain the forces sufficient to support our obligations, and to defend freedom. Our forces will be strong enough to dissuade potential adversaries from pursuing a military build-up in hopes of surpassing, or equaling, the power of the United States.

84 |

## DOCUMENT 2.11

As the Joint Resolution authorizing an attack on Iraq was working its way through both houses of Congress (2.12), President Bush delivered one of his most important speeches. Citing all the arguments the administration had been making for months, it warned of the dangers of inaction and called on the nation to support a preemptive war waged in the name of peace. One of the speech's interesting sidelights is that Bush again cited Saddam Hussein's biological and chemical "weapons of mass destruction." Like most of the president's claims, this one was later discredited: it turned out that the "intelligence" behind the president's claims had been fabricated under torture by Ibn al-Shaykih al-Libi, an accused al Qaeda operative whose torture had been "outsourced" by the CIA to Egypt. Four months later, Secretary of State Colin Powell would use this same false information in his address to the UN Security Council as he argued in vain for its support (2.14).

GEORGE W. BUSH, SPEECH OUTLINING IRAQI THREAT,
CINCINNATI, OHIO, OCTOBER 7, 2002

Thank you all. Thank you for that very gracious and warm Cincinnati welcome. I'm honored to be here tonight; I appreciate you all coming.

Tonight I want to take a few minutes to discuss a grave threat to peace,
and America's determination to lead the world in confronting that threat.

The threat comes from Iraq. It arises directly from the Iraqi regime's own
actions—its history of aggression, and its drive toward an arsenal of terror.
Eleven years ago, as a condition for ending the Persian Gulf War, the Iraqi
regime was required to destroy its weapons of mass destruction, to cease all
development of such weapons, and to stop all support for terrorist groups.
The Iraqi regime has violated all of those obligations. It possesses and produces chemical and biological weapons. It is seeking nuclear weapons. It
has given shelter and support to terrorism, and practices terror against its
own people. The entire world has witnessed Iraq's eleven-year history of
defiance, deception, and bad faith.

We also must never forget the most vivid events of recent history. On
September the 11th, 2001, America felt its vulnerability—even to threats
that gather on the other side of the earth. We resolved then, and we are resolved today, to confront every threat, from any source, that could bring
sudden terror and suffering to America.

Members of the Congress of both political parties, and members of the
United Nations Security Council, agree that Saddam Hussein is a threat to
peace and must disarm. We agree that the Iraqi dictator must not be permitted to threaten America and the world with horrible poisons and diseases and gases and atomic weapons. Since we all agree on this goal, the
issue is: how can we best achieve it?

Many Americans have raised legitimate questions: about the nature of
the threat; about the urgency of action—why be concerned now; about the
link between Iraq developing weapons of terror, and the wider war on terror. These are all issues we've discussed broadly and fully within my administration. And tonight, I want to share those discussions with you.

First, some ask why Iraq is different from other countries or regimes that
also have terrible weapons. While there are many dangers in the world, the
threat from Iraq stands alone—because it gathers the most serious dangers
of our age in one place. Iraq's weapons of mass destruction are controlled
by a murderous tyrant who has already used chemical weapons to kill
thousands of people. This same tyrant has tried to dominate the Middle
East, has invaded and brutally occupied a small neighbor, has struck other
nations without warning, and holds an unrelenting hostility toward the
United States.

By its past and present actions, by its technological capabilities, by the
merciless nature of its regime, Iraq is unique. As a former chief weapons
inspector of the UN has said, "The fundamental problem with Iraq remains

the nature of the regime, itself. Saddam Hussein is a homicidal dictator who is addicted to weapons of mass destruction."

Some ask how urgent this danger is to America and the world. The danger is already significant, and it only grows worse with time. If we know Saddam Hussein has dangerous weapons today—and we do—does it make any sense for the world to wait to confront him as he grows even stronger and develops even more dangerous weapons?

In 1995, after several years of deceit by the Iraqi regime, the head of Iraq's military industries defected. It was then that the regime was forced to admit that it had produced more than thirty thousand liters of anthrax and other deadly biological agents. The inspectors, however, concluded that Iraq had likely produced two to four times that amount. This is a massive stockpile of biological weapons that has never been accounted for, and capable of killing millions.

We know that the regime has produced thousands of tons of chemical agents, including mustard gas, sarin nerve gas, VX nerve gas. Saddam Hussein also has experience in using chemical weapons. He has ordered chemical attacks on Iran, and on more than forty villages in his own country. These actions killed or injured at least twenty thousand people, more than six times the number of people who died in the attacks of September the 11th.

And surveillance photos reveal that the regime is rebuilding facilities that it had used to produce chemical and biological weapons. Every chemical and biological weapon that Iraq has or makes is a direct violation of the truce that ended the Persian Gulf War in 1991. Yet Saddam Hussein has chosen to build and keep these weapons despite international sanctions, UN demands, and isolation from the civilized world.

Iraq possesses ballistic missiles with a likely range of hundreds of miles— far enough to strike Saudi Arabia, Israel, Turkey, and other nations—in a region where more than 135,000 American civilians and service members live and work. We've also discovered through intelligence that Iraq has a growing fleet of manned and unmanned aerial vehicles that could be used to disperse chemical or biological weapons across broad areas. We're concerned that Iraq is exploring ways of using these UAVs for missions targeting the United States. And, of course, sophisticated delivery systems aren't required for a chemical or biological attack; all that might be required are a small container and one terrorist or Iraqi intelligence operative to deliver it.

And that is the source of our urgent concern about Saddam Hussein's links to international terrorist groups. Over the years, Iraq has provided safe haven to terrorists such as Abu Nidal, whose terror organization carried out more than ninety terrorist attacks in twenty countries that killed or injured nearly nine hundred people, including twelve Americans. Iraq has also provided safe haven to Abu Abbas, who was responsible for seizing the *Achille Lauro* and killing an American passenger. And we know that Iraq is continuing to finance terror and gives assistance to groups that use terrorism to undermine Middle East peace.

We know that Iraq and the al Qaeda terrorist network share a common enemy—the United States of America. We know that Iraq and al Qaeda have had high-level contacts that go back a decade. Some al Qaeda leaders who fled Afghanistan went to Iraq. These include one very senior al Qaeda leader who received medical treatment in Baghdad this year, and who has been associated with planning for chemical and biological attacks. We've learned that Iraq has trained al Qaeda members in bomb-making and poisons and deadly gases. And we know that after September the 11th, Saddam Hussein's regime gleefully celebrated the terrorist attacks on America.

Iraq could decide on any given day to provide a biological or chemical weapon to a terrorist group or individual terrorists. Alliance with terrorists could allow the Iraqi regime to attack America without leaving any fingerprints.

Some have argued that confronting the threat from Iraq could detract from the war against terror. To the contrary; confronting the threat posed by Iraq is crucial to winning the war on terror. When I spoke to Congress more than a year ago, I said that those who harbor terrorists are as guilty as the terrorists themselves. Saddam Hussein is harboring terrorists and the instruments of terror, the instruments of mass death and destruction. And he cannot be trusted. The risk is simply too great that he will use them or provide them to a terror network.

Terror cells and outlaw regimes building weapons of mass destruction are different faces of the same evil. Our security requires that we confront both. And the United States military is capable of confronting both.

Many people have asked how close Saddam Hussein is to developing a nuclear weapon. Well, we don't know exactly, and that's the problem. Before the Gulf War, the best intelligence indicated that Iraq was eight to ten years away from developing a nuclear weapon. After the war, international inspectors learned that the regime has been much closer—the regime in Iraq would likely have possessed a nuclear weapon no later than 1993. The inspectors discovered that Iraq had an advanced nuclear weapons development program, had a design for a workable nuclear weapon, and was pursuing several different methods of enriching uranium for a bomb.

Before being barred from Iraq in 1998, the International Atomic Energy Agency dismantled extensive nuclear weapons–related facilities, including three uranium enrichment sites. That same year, information from a high-ranking Iraqi nuclear engineer who had defected revealed that despite his public promises, Saddam Hussein had ordered his nuclear program to continue.

The evidence indicates that Iraq is reconstituting its nuclear weapons program. Saddam Hussein has held numerous meetings with Iraqi nuclear scientists, a group he calls his "nuclear mujahideen"—his nuclear holy warriors. Satellite photographs reveal that Iraq is rebuilding facilities at sites that have been part of its nuclear program in the past. Iraq has attempted to purchase high-strength aluminum tubes and other equipment needed for gas centrifuges, which are used to enrich uranium for nuclear weapons.

If the Iraqi regime is able to produce, buy, or steal an amount of highly enriched uranium a little larger than a single softball, it could have a nuclear weapon in less than a year. And if we allow that to happen, a terrible line would be crossed. Saddam Hussein would be in a position to blackmail anyone who opposes his aggression. He would be in a position to dominate the Middle East. He would be in a position to threaten America. And Saddam Hussein would be in a position to pass nuclear technology to terrorists.

Some citizens wonder, after eleven years of living with this problem, why do we need to confront it now? And there's a reason. We've experienced the horror of September the 11th. We have seen that those who hate America are willing to crash airplanes into buildings full of innocent people. Our enemies would be no less willing, in fact, they would be eager, to use a biological or chemical, or a nuclear weapon.

Knowing these realities, America must not ignore the threat gathering against us. Facing clear evidence of peril, we cannot wait for the final proof —the smoking gun—that could come in the form of a mushroom cloud. As President Kennedy said in October of 1962, "Neither the United States of America, nor the world community of nations can tolerate deliberate deception and offensive threats on the part of any nation, large or small. We no longer live in a world," he said, "where only the actual firing of weapons represents a sufficient challenge to a nation's security to constitute maximum peril."

Understanding the threats of our time, knowing the designs and deceptions of the Iraqi regime, we have every reason to assume the worst, and we have an urgent duty to prevent the worst from occurring.

Some believe we can address this danger by simply resuming the old approach to inspections, and applying diplomatic and economic pressure. Yet this is precisely what the world has tried to do since 1991. The UN inspections program was met with systematic deception. The Iraqi regime bugged hotel rooms and offices of inspectors to find where they were going next; they forged documents, destroyed evidence, and developed mobile weapons facilities to keep a step ahead of inspectors. Eight so-called presidential palaces were declared off-limits to unfettered inspections. These sites actually encompass twelve square miles, with hundreds of structures, both above and below the ground, where sensitive materials could be hidden.

The world has also tried economic sanctions—and watched Iraq use billions of dollars in illegal oil revenues to fund more weapons purchases, rather than providing for the needs of the Iraqi people.

The world has tried limited military strikes to destroy Iraq's weapons of mass destruction capabilities—only to see them openly rebuilt, while the regime again denies they even exist.

The world has tried no-fly zones to keep Saddam from terrorizing his own people—and in the last year alone, the Iraqi military has fired upon American and British pilots more than 750 times.

After eleven years during which we have tried containment, sanctions, inspections, even selected military action, the end result is that Saddam Hussein still has chemical and biological weapons and is increasing his capabilities to make more. And he is moving ever closer to developing a nuclear weapon.

Clearly, to actually work, any new inspections, sanctions, or enforcement mechanisms will have to be very different. America wants the UN to be an effective organization that helps keep the peace. And that is why we are urging the Security Council to adopt a new resolution setting out tough, immediate requirements. Among those requirements: the Iraqi regime must reveal and destroy, under UN supervision, all existing weapons of mass destruction. To ensure that we learn the truth, the regime must allow witnesses to its illegal activities to be interviewed outside the country—and these witnesses must be free to bring their families with them so they are all beyond the reach of Saddam Hussein's terror and murder. And inspectors must have access to any site, at any time, without pre-clearance, without delay, without exceptions.

The time for denying, deceiving, and delaying has come to an end. Saddam Hussein must disarm himself—or, for the sake of peace, we will lead a coalition to disarm him.

Many nations are joining us in insisting that Saddam Hussein's regime be held accountable. They are committed to defending the international security that protects the lives of both our citizens and theirs. And that's why America is challenging all nations to take the resolutions of the UN Security Council seriously.

And these resolutions are clear. In addition to declaring and destroying all of its weapons of mass destruction, Iraq must end its support for terrorism. It must cease the persecution of its civilian population. It must stop all illicit trade outside the Oil for Food program. It must release or account for all Gulf War personnel, including an American pilot, whose fate is still unknown.

By taking these steps, and by only taking these steps, the Iraqi regime has an opportunity to avoid conflict. Taking these steps would also change the nature of the Iraqi regime itself. America hopes the regime will make that choice. Unfortunately, at least so far, we have little reason to expect it. And that's why two administrations—mine and President Clinton's—have stated that regime change in Iraq is the only certain means of removing a great danger to our nation.

I hope this will not require military action, but it may. And military conflict could be difficult. An Iraqi regime faced with its own demise may attempt cruel and desperate measures. If Saddam Hussein orders such measures, his generals would be well advised to refuse those orders. If they do not refuse, they must understand that all war criminals will be pursued and punished. If we have to act, we will take every precaution that is possible. We will plan carefully; we will act with the full power of the United States military; we will act with allies at our side, and we will prevail.

There is no easy or risk-free course of action. Some have argued we should wait—and that's an option. In my view, it's the riskiest of all options, because the longer we wait, the stronger and bolder Saddam Hussein will become. We could wait and hope that Saddam does not give weapons to terrorists or develop a nuclear weapon to blackmail the world. But I'm convinced that is a hope against all evidence. As Americans, we want peace— we work and sacrifice for peace. But there can be no peace if our security depends on the will and whims of a ruthless and aggressive dictator. I'm not willing to stake one American life on trusting Saddam Hussein.

Failure to act would embolden other tyrants, allow terrorists access to new weapons and new resources, and make blackmail a permanent feature of world events. The United Nations would betray the purpose of its founding, and prove irrelevant to the problems of our time. And through its inaction, the United States would resign itself to a future of fear.

That is not the America I know. That is not the America I serve. We refuse to live in fear. This nation, in world war and in Cold War, has never permitted the brutal and lawless to set history's course. Now, as before, we will secure our nation, protect our freedom, and help others to find freedom of their own.

Some worry that a change of leadership in Iraq could create instability and make the situation worse. The situation could hardly get worse, for world security and for the people of Iraq. The lives of Iraqi citizens would improve dramatically if Saddam Hussein were no longer in power, just as the lives of Afghanistan's citizens improved after the Taliban. The dictator of Iraq is a student of Stalin, using murder as a tool of terror and control, within his own cabinet, within his own army, and even within his own family.

On Saddam Hussein's orders, opponents have been decapitated, wives and mothers of political opponents have been systematically raped as a method of intimidation, and political prisoners have been forced to watch their own children being tortured.

America believes that all people are entitled to hope and human rights, to the non-negotiable demands of human dignity. People everywhere prefer freedom to slavery; prosperity to squalor; self-government to the rule of terror and torture. America is a friend to the people of Iraq. Our demands are directed only at the regime that enslaves them and threatens us. When these demands are met, the first and greatest benefit will come to Iraqi men, women, and children. The oppression of Kurds, Assyrians, Turkomans, Shia, Sunnis, and others will be lifted. The long captivity of Iraq will end, and an era of new hope will begin.

Iraq is a land rich in culture, resources, and talent. Freed from the weight of oppression, Iraq's people will be able to share in the progress and prosperity of our time. If military action is necessary, the United States and our allies will help the Iraqi people rebuild their economy and create the institutions of liberty in a unified Iraq at peace with its neighbors.

Later this week, the United States Congress will vote on this matter. I have asked Congress to authorize the use of America's military, if it proves necessary, to enforce UN Security Council demands. Approving this resolution does not mean that military action is imminent or unavoidable. The resolution will tell the United Nations, and all nations, that America speaks with one voice and is determined to make the demands of the civilized world mean something. Congress will also be sending a message to the dictator in Iraq: that his only chance—his only choice—is full compliance, and the time remaining for that choice is limited.

Members of Congress are nearing an historic vote. I'm confident they will fully consider the facts and their duties.

The attacks of September the 11th showed our country that vast oceans no longer protect us from danger. Before that tragic date, we had only hints of al Qaeda's plans and designs. Today in Iraq, we see a threat whose outlines are far more clearly defined, and whose consequences could be far more deadly. Saddam Hussein's actions have put us on notice, and there is no refuge from our responsibilities.

We did not ask for this present challenge, but we accept it. Like other generations of Americans, we will meet the responsibility of defending human liberty against violence and aggression. By our resolve, we will give strength to others. By our courage, we will give hope to others. And by our actions, we will secure the peace and lead the world to a better day.

May God bless America.

| 91

# DOCUMENT 2.12

The president's Cincinnati speech and the National Security Strategy document were more than affirmations of President Bush's embrace of preemption, military supremacy, and moralism. They said that the administration wanted to consult with allies, respect the existing balance of power, and strengthen international institutions. But as the Downing Street Memo would later demonstrate, there was no mistaking the new direction that the document laid out. President Bush had been making a bold new set of claims since his election, and the time had come to take action. Neither a divided and hesitant Democratic Party nor accelerating domestic opposition would stand in his way. On October 16, a joint congressional resolution adopted all the administration's arguments and gave the president a "blank check" to deal with Iraq. But congressional consensus stood in sharp contrast to vigorous domestic and international disagreement. On November 8, Secretary of State Colin Powell made a deal with the French, and the United States stepped away from its demand that the Security Council authorize the use of "all necessary means" to bring Iraq into compliance with previous resolutions, settling instead for a threat that Baghdad could be found to be in "material breach." It was widely assumed that this seemingly insignificant change to Resolution 1441 (2.13) would require a second Security Council resolution—one authorizing the use of force—and was seen as a victory for Powell and those nations reluctant to support Washington. But appearances were deceiving. Even though Resolution 1441 organized a very intrusive inspection and disarmament regime, Bush remained intent on toppling Saddam Hussein's government. After Secretary of State Colin Powell gave his famous speech to the Security Council (2.14), the U.S. and British effort to get the Security Council to pass the second resolution, authorizing force, failed. President Bush's ultimatum to Iraq and his announcement of the start of "Operation Iraqi Freedom" marked a new stage in the administration's effort to organize a preemptive war (2.17–2.18).

---

### JOINT CONGRESSIONAL RESOLUTION TO AUTHORIZE THE USE OF UNITED STATES ARMED FORCES AGAINST IRAQ, OCTOBER 16, 2002 (EXCERPT)

Whereas in 1990 in response to Iraq's war of aggression against and illegal occupation of Kuwait, the United States forged a coalition of nations to liberate Kuwait and its people in order to defend the national security of the United States and enforce United Nations Security Council resolutions relating to Iraq;

Whereas after the liberation of Kuwait in 1991, Iraq entered into a United Nations sponsored cease-fire agreement pursuant to which Iraq unequivocally agreed, among other things, to eliminate its nuclear, biological, and chemical weapons programs and the means to deliver and develop them, and to end its support for international terrorism;

Whereas the efforts of international weapons inspectors, United States intelligence agencies, and Iraqi defectors led to the discovery that Iraq had large stockpiles of chemical weapons and a large scale biological weapons program, and that Iraq had an advanced nuclear weapons development program that was much closer to producing a nuclear weapon than intelligence reporting had previously indicated;

Whereas Iraq, in direct and flagrant violation of the cease-fire, attempted to thwart the efforts of weapons inspectors to identify and destroy Iraq's weapons of mass destruction stockpiles and development capabilities, which finally resulted in the withdrawal of inspectors from Iraq on October 31, 1998;

Whereas in 1998 Congress concluded that Iraq's continuing weapons of mass destruction programs threatened vital United States interests and international peace and security, declared Iraq to be in "material and unacceptable breach of its international obligations" and urged the President "to take appropriate action, in accordance with the Constitution and relevant laws of the United States, to bring Iraq into compliance with its international obligations";

Whereas Iraq both poses a continuing threat to the national security of the United States and international peace and security in the Persian Gulf region and remains in material and unacceptable breach of its international obligations by, among other things, continuing to possess and develop a significant chemical and biological weapons capability, actively seeking a nuclear weapons capability, and supporting and harboring terrorist organizations;

Whereas Iraq persists in violating resolutions of the United Nations Security Council by continuing to engage in brutal repression of its civilian population thereby threatening international peace and security in the region, by refusing to release, repatriate, or account for non-Iraqi citizens wrongfully detained by Iraq, including an American serviceman, and by failing to return property wrongfully seized by Iraq from Kuwait;

Whereas the current Iraqi regime has demonstrated its capability and willingness to use weapons of mass destruction against other nations and its own people;

Whereas the current Iraqi regime has demonstrated its continuing hostility toward, and willingness to attack, the United States, including by attempting in 1993 to assassinate former President Bush and by firing on many thousands of occasions on United States and Coalition Armed Forces engaged in enforcing the resolutions of the United Nations Security Council;

Whereas members of al Qaida, an organization bearing responsibility for attacks on the United States, its citizens, and interests, including the attacks that occurred on September 11, 2001, are known to be in Iraq;

Whereas Iraq continues to aid and harbor other international terrorist organizations, including organizations that threaten the lives and safety of American citizens;

Whereas the attacks on the United States of September 11, 2001 underscored the gravity of the threat posed by the acquisition of weapons of mass destruction by international terrorist organizations;

Whereas Iraq's demonstrated capability and willingness to use weapons of mass destruction, the risk that the current Iraqi regime will either employ those weapons to launch a surprise attack against the United States or its Armed Forces or provide them to international terrorists who would do so, and the extreme magnitude of harm that would result to the United States and its citizens from such an attack, combine to justify action by the United States to defend itself;

Whereas United Nations Security Council Resolution 678 authorizes the use of all necessary means to enforce United Nations Security Council Resolution 660 and subsequent relevant resolutions and to compel Iraq to cease certain activities that threaten international peace and security, including the development of weapons of mass destruction and refusal or obstruction of United Nations weapons inspections in violation of United Nations Security Council Resolution 687, repression of its civilian population in violation of United Nations Security Council Resolution 688, and threatening its neighbors or United Nations operations in Iraq in violation of United Nations Security Council Resolution 949;

Whereas Congress in the Authorization for Use of Military Force Against Iraq Resolution (Public Law 102–1) has authorized the President "to use United States Armed Forces pursuant to United Nations Security Council Resolution 678 (1990) in order to achieve implementation of Security Council Resolutions . . .";

Whereas in December 1991, Congress expressed its sense that it "supports the use of all necessary means to achieve the goals of United Nations Security Council Resolution 687 as being consistent with the Authorization of Use of Military Force Against Iraq Resolution (Public Law 102–1)," that Iraq's repression of its civilian population violates United Nations Security Council Resolution 688 and "constitutes a continuing threat to the peace, security, and stability of the Persian Gulf region," and that Congress "supports the use of all necessary means to achieve the goals of United Nations Security Council Resolution 688;"

Whereas the Iraq Liberation Act (Public Law 105–338) expressed the sense of Congress that it should be the policy of the United States to support efforts to remove from power the current Iraqi regime and promote the emergence of a democratic government to replace that regime;

Whereas on September 12, 2002, President Bush committed the United States to "work with the United Nations Security Council to meet our common challenge" posed by Iraq and to "work for the necessary resolutions," while also making clear that "the Security Council resolutions will be enforced, and the just demands of peace and security will be met, or action will be unavoidable";

Whereas the United States is determined to prosecute the war on terrorism and Iraq's ongoing support for international terrorist groups combined with its development of weapons of mass destruction in direct violation of its obligations under the 1991 cease-fire and other United Nations Security Council resolutions make clear that it is in the national security interests of the United States and in furtherance of the war on terrorism that all relevant United Nations Security Council resolutions be enforced, including through the use of force if necessary;

Whereas Congress has taken steps to pursue vigorously the war on terrorism through the provision of authorities and funding requested by the President to take the necessary actions against international terrorists and terrorist organizations, including those nations, organizations or persons who planned, authorized, committed or aided the terrorist attacks that occurred on September 11, 2001 or harbored such persons or organizations;

Whereas the President and Congress are determined to continue to take all appropriate actions against international terrorists and terrorist organizations, including those nations, organizations or persons who planned, authorized, committed or aided the terrorist attacks that occurred on September 11, 2001, or harbored such persons or organizations;

Whereas the President has authority under the Constitution to take action in order to deter and prevent acts of international terrorism against the United States, as Congress recognized in the joint resolution on Authorization for Use of Military Force (Public Law 107–40); and

Whereas it is in the national security of the United States to restore international peace and security to the Persian Gulf region;

Now, therefore, be it resolved by the Senate and House of Representatives of the United States of America in Congress assembled,

SEC. 1. SHORT TITLE.
This joint resolution may be cited as the "Authorization for the Use of Military Force Against Iraq."
SEC. 2. SUPPORT FOR UNITED STATES DIPLOMATIC EFFORTS
The Congress of the United States supports the efforts by the President to–
> (a) strictly enforce through the United Nations Security Council all relevant Security Council resolutions applicable to Iraq and encourages him in those efforts; and
> (b) obtain prompt and decisive action by the Security Council to ensure that Iraq abandons its strategy of delay, evasion and noncompliance and promptly and strictly complies with all relevant Security Council resolutions.

SEC. 3. AUTHORIZATION FOR USE OF UNITED STATES ARMED FORCES.   | 95
> (a) AUTHORIZATION.
> (b) The President is authorized to use the Armed Forces of the United States as he determines to be necessary and appropriate in order to
> > (1) defend the national security of the United States against the continuing threat posed by Iraq; and
> > (2) enforce all relevant United Nations Security Council Resolutions regarding Iraq. . . .

# DOCUMENT 2.13

Security Council Resolution 1441, passed unanimously on November 8, 2002, had been drafted jointly by the United States and Britain after eight weeks of tumultuous negotiations, particularly with Russia and France. It offered Iraq a "final opportunity to comply with its disarmament obligations," which had been specified in a series of earlier resolutions, and declared Baghdad to be in "material breach" of Resolution 687. It went on to warn that "false statements or omissions in the declarations submitted by Iraq pursuant to this resolution and failure by Iraq at any time to comply with, and cooperate fully in the implementation of, this resolution shall constitute a further material breach of Iraq's obligations." France questioned the way Washington was interpreting the phrase "serious consequences" and stated repeatedly that any "material

breach" found by the UN inspectors would require an additional Council resolution before any state could pursue a new course of action.

---

UNITED NATIONS SECURITY COUNCIL RESOLUTION 1441,
NOVEMBER 8, 2002 (EXCERPT)

The Security Council, . . .
Determined to secure full compliance with its decisions,
Acting under Chapter VII of the Charter of the United Nations,

1. Decides that Iraq has been and remains in material breach of its
   obligations under relevant resolutions, . . . in particular through
   Iraq's failure to cooperate with United Nations inspectors and
   the IAEA [Editors' Note: International Atomic Energy Agency], and
   to complete the actions required under paragraphs 8 to 13 of
   resolution 687 (1991);
2. Decides, while acknowledging paragraph 1 above, to afford Iraq,
   by this resolution, a final opportunity to comply with its disarmament obligations under relevant resolutions of the Council;
   and accordingly decides to set up an enhanced inspection
   regime with the aim of bringing to full and verified completion
   the disarmament process established by resolution 687 (1991)
   and subsequent resolutions of the Council;
3. Decides that, in order to begin to comply with its disarmament
   obligations, in addition to submitting the required biannual declarations, the Government of Iraq shall provide to UNMOVIC
   [Editors' Note: United Nations Monitoring, Verification, and Inspection
   Commission], the IAEA, and the Council, not later than 30 days
   from the date of this resolution, a currently accurate, full, and
   complete declaration of all aspects of its programmes to develop
   chemical, biological, and nuclear weapons, ballistic missiles, and
   other delivery systems such as unmanned aerial vehicles and
   dispersal systems designed for use on aircraft, including any
   holdings and precise locations of such weapons, components,
   sub-components, stocks of agents, and related material and
   equipment, the locations and work of its research, development
   and production facilities, as well as all other chemical, biological,
   and nuclear programmes, including any which it claims are for
   purposes not related to weapon production or material;
4. Decides that false statements or omissions in the declarations
   submitted by Iraq pursuant to this resolution and failure by Iraq
   at any time to comply with, and cooperate fully in the implementation of, this resolution shall constitute a further material

breach of Iraq's obligations and will be reported to the Council
for assessment in accordance with paragraphs 11 and 12 below;

5. Decides that Iraq shall provide UNMOVIC and the IAEA immediate, unimpeded, unconditional, and unrestricted access to any
and all, including underground, areas, facilities, buildings,
equipment, records, and means of transport which they wish
to inspect, as well as immediate, unimpeded, unrestricted, and
private access to all officials and other persons whom UNMOVIC
or the IAEA wish to interview in the mode or location of
UNMOVIC's or the IAEA's choice pursuant to any aspect of
their mandates; further decides that UNMOVIC and the IAEA
may at their discretion conduct interviews inside or outside of
Iraq, may facilitate the travel of those interviewed and family
members outside of Iraq, and that, at the sole discretion of
UNMOVIC and the IAEA, such interviews may occur without
the presence of observers from the Iraqi Government; and instructs UNMOVIC and requests the IAEA to resume inspections
no later than 45 days following adoption of this resolution and
to update the Council 60 days thereafter; . . .

7. Decides further that, in view of the prolonged interruption by
Iraq of the presence of UNMOVIC and the IAEA and in order for
them to accomplish the tasks set forth in this resolution and all
previous relevant resolutions and notwithstanding prior understandings, the Council hereby establishes the following revised
or additional authorities, which shall be binding upon Iraq, to
facilitate their work in Iraq:

- UNMOVIC and the IAEA shall determine the composition of
  their inspection teams and ensure that these teams are composed of the most qualified and experienced experts available;
- All UNMOVIC and IAEA personnel shall enjoy the privileges
  and immunities, corresponding to those of experts on mission,
  provided in the Convention on Privileges and Immunities of
  the United Nations and the Agreement on the Privileges and
  Immunities of the IAEA;
- UNMOVIC and the IAEA shall have unrestricted rights of entry
  into and out of Iraq, the right to free, unrestricted, and immediate movement to and from inspection sites, and the right to
  inspect any sites and buildings, including immediate, unimpeded, unconditional, and unrestricted access to Presidential
  Sites equal to that at other sites, notwithstanding the provisions of resolution 1154 (1998);
- UNMOVIC and the IAEA shall have the right to be provided
  by Iraq the names of all personnel currently and formerly associated with Iraq's chemical, biological, nuclear, and ballistic

missile programmes and the associated research, development, and production facilities;

• Security of UNMOVIC and IAEA facilities shall be ensured by sufficient United Nations security guards;

• UNMOVIC and the IAEA shall have the right to declare, for the purposes of freezing a site to be inspected, exclusion zones, including surrounding areas and transit corridors, in which Iraq will suspend ground and aerial movement so that nothing is changed in or taken out of a site being inspected;

• UNMOVIC and the IAEA shall have the free and unrestricted use and landing of fixed- and rotary-winged aircraft, including manned and unmanned reconnaissance vehicles;

• UNMOVIC and the IAEA shall have the right at their sole discretion verifiably to remove, destroy, or render harmless all prohibited weapons, subsystems, components, records, materials, and other related items, and the right to impound or close any facilities or equipment for the production thereof; and

• UNMOVIC and the IAEA shall have the right to free import and use of equipment or materials for inspections and to seize and export any equipment, materials, or documents taken during inspections, without search of UNMOVIC or IAEA personnel or official or personal baggage;

8. Decides further that Iraq shall not take or threaten hostile acts directed against any representative or personnel of the United Nations or the IAEA or of any Member State taking action to uphold any Council resolution;

9. Requests the Secretary-General immediately to notify Iraq of this resolution, which is binding on Iraq; demands that Iraq confirm within seven days of that notification its intention to comply fully with this resolution; and demands further that Iraq cooperate immediately, unconditionally, and actively with UNMOVIC and the IAEA;

10. Requests all Member States to give full support to UNMOVIC and the IAEA in the discharge of their mandates, including by providing any information related to prohibited programmes or other aspects of their mandates, including on Iraqi attempts since 1998 to acquire prohibited items, and by recommending sites to be inspected, persons to be interviewed, conditions of such interviews, and data to be collected, the results of which shall be reported to the Council by UNMOVIC and the IAEA;

11. Directs the Executive Chairman of UNMOVIC and the Director-General of the IAEA to report immediately to the Council any interference by Iraq with inspection activities, as well as any failure by Iraq to comply with its disarmament obligations, including its obligations regarding inspections under this resolution;

12. Decides to convene immediately upon receipt of a report in accordance with paragraphs 4 or 11 above, in order to consider the situation and the need for full compliance with all of the relevant Council resolutions in order to secure international peace and security;

13. Recalls, in that context, that the Council has repeatedly warned Iraq that it will face serious consequences as a result of its continued violations of its obligations;

14. Decides to remain seized of the matter.

# DOCUMENT 2.14

In early February, Secretary of State Colin Powell addressed the Security Council in a last-ditch effort to obtain a second resolution, one that would give the impending U.S. invasion a measure of international legitimacy. He presented a comprehensive portrait of a government bent on acquiring biological, chemical, and nuclear weapons, hiding them from the UN inspectors, and using them when it had a chance. He also painted a picture of a regime actively collaborating with terrorist organizations. Like Bush's speech in Cincinnati four months earlier (2.11), Powell's speech made use of false information obtained through the use of torture, a fact that was unknown publicly at the time. The secretary's address, which featured audio recordings and surveillance photos, was received enthusiastically by broad sections of the U.S. media. Shortly afterward, however, virtually all of its claims about Iraqi weapons programs and connections to terrorist groups were disproven. Powell repeatedly declined interview requests after leaving office but said that his speech had been "painful" for him personally and would stand as a permanent "blot" on his record.

COLIN POWELL, ADDRESS TO THE UNITED NATIONS
SECURITY COUNCIL, FEBRUARY 6, 2003 (EXCERPT)

. . . I asked for this session today for two purposes: First, to support the core assessments made by Dr. Blix [*Editors' Note: Head of UNMOVIC from January 2000 to June 2003*] and Dr. El Baradei [*Editors' Note: Director General of the IAEA and recipient, along with the IAEA, of the Nobel Peace Prize in 2005*]. As Dr. Blix reported to this council on January 27th, "Iraq appears not to have come to a genuine acceptance, not even today, of the disarmament which was demanded of it."

And as Dr. El Baradei reported, Iraq's declaration of December 7 "did not provide any new information relevant to certain questions that have been outstanding since 1998."

My second purpose today is to provide you with additional information, to share with you what the United States knows about Iraq's weapons of mass destruction as well as Iraq's involvement in terrorism, which is also the subject of Resolution 1441 and other earlier resolutions. . . .

The material I will present to you comes from a variety of sources. Some are U.S. sources. And some are those of other countries. Some of the sources are technical, such as intercepted telephone conversations and photos taken by satellites. Other sources are people who have risked their lives to let the world know what Saddam Hussein is really up to.

I cannot tell you everything that we know. But what I can share with you, when combined with what all of us have learned over the years, is deeply troubling.

What you will see is an accumulation of facts and disturbing patterns of behavior. The facts on Iraq's behavior demonstrate that Saddam Hussein and his regime have made no effort—no effort—to disarm as required by the international community. Indeed, the facts and Iraq's behavior show that Saddam Hussein and his regime are concealing their efforts to produce more weapons of mass destruction. . . .

Everything we have seen and heard indicates that, instead of cooperating actively with the inspectors to ensure the success of their mission, Saddam Hussein and his regime are busy doing all they possibly can to ensure that inspectors succeed in finding absolutely nothing. . . .

Saddam Hussein and his regime are not just trying to conceal weapons, they're also trying to hide people. You know the basic facts. Iraq has not complied with its obligation to allow immediate, unimpeded, unrestricted and private access to all officials and other persons as required by Resolution 1441. . . .

As the examples I have just presented show, the information and intelligence we have gathered point to an active and systematic effort on the part of the Iraqi regime to keep key materials and people from the inspectors in direct violation of Resolution 1441. The pattern is not just one of reluctant cooperation, nor is it merely a lack of cooperation. What we see is a deliberate campaign to prevent any meaningful inspection work. . . .

My colleagues, operative paragraph four of UN Resolution 1441, which we lingered over so long last fall, clearly states that false statements and omissions in the declaration and a failure by Iraq at any time to comply with and cooperate fully in the implementation of this resolution shall constitute—the facts speak for themselves—shall constitute a further material breach of its obligation.

We wrote it this way to give Iraq an early test. Would they give an honest declaration and would they early on indicate a willingness to cooperate with the inspectors? . . .

They failed that test. By this standard, the standard of this operative paragraph, I believe that Iraq is now in further material breach of its obligations. I believe this conclusion is irrefutable and undeniable.

Iraq has now placed itself in danger of the serious consequences called for in UN Resolution 1441. And this body places itself in danger of irrelevance if it allows Iraq to continue to defy its will without responding effectively and immediately.

The issue before us is not how much time we are willing to give the inspectors to be frustrated by Iraqi obstruction. But how much longer are we willing to put up with Iraq's noncompliance before we, as a council, we, as the United Nations, say: "Enough. Enough."

The gravity of this moment is matched by the gravity of the threat that Iraq's weapons of mass destruction pose to the world. Let me now turn to those deadly weapons programs and describe why they are real and present dangers to the region and to the world. . . .

The Iraqis have never accounted for all of the biological weapons they admitted they had and we know they had. They have never accounted for all the organic material used to make them. And they have not accounted for many of the weapons filled with these agents such as there are 400 bombs. This is evidence, not conjecture. This is true. This is all well documented.

It should come as no shock . . . that since Saddam Hussein forced out the last inspectors in 1998, we have amassed much intelligence indicating that Iraq is continuing to make these weapons. . . .

Let me turn now to nuclear weapons. We have no indication that Saddam Hussein has ever abandoned his nuclear weapons program.

On the contrary, we have more than a decade of proof that he remains determined to acquire nuclear weapons. . . .

My friends, the information I have presented to you about these terrible weapons and about Iraq's continued flaunting of its obligations under Security Council Resolution 1441 links to a subject I now want to spend a little bit of time on. And that has to do with terrorism. . . .

Our concern is not just about these illicit weapons. It's the way that these illicit weapons can be connected to terrorists and terrorist organizations that have no compunction about using such devices against innocent people around the world.

Iraq and terrorism go back decades. . . .

But what I want to bring to your attention today is the potentially much more sinister nexus between Iraq and the Al Qaida terrorist network, a nexus that combines classic terrorist organizations and modern methods of murder. Iraq today harbors a deadly terrorist network headed by Abu Musab Al-Zarqawi, an associate and collaborator of Osama bin Laden and his Al Qaida lieutenants. . . .

We know that Saddam Hussein is determined to keep his weapons of mass destruction; he's determined to make more. Given Saddam Hussein's history of aggression, given what we know of his grandiose plans, given what we know of his terrorist associations and given his determination to exact revenge on those who oppose him, should we take the risk that he will not some day use these weapons at a time and the place and in the manner of his choosing at a time when the world is in a much weaker position to respond?

The United States will not and cannot run that risk to the American people. Leaving Saddam Hussein in possession of weapons of mass destruction for a few more months or years is not an option, not in a post–September 11th world.

My colleagues, over three months ago this council recognized that Iraq continued to pose a threat to international peace and security, and that Iraq had been and remained in material breach of its disarmament obligations. Today Iraq still poses a threat and Iraq still remains in material breach.

Indeed, by its failure to seize on its one last opportunity to come clean and disarm, Iraq has put itself in deeper material breach and closer to the day when it will face serious consequences for its continued defiance of this council.

My colleagues, we have an obligation to our citizens, we have an obligation to this body to see that our resolutions are complied with. We wrote 1441 not in order to go to war, we wrote 1441 to try to preserve the peace. We wrote 1441 to give Iraq one last chance. Iraq is not so far taking that one last chance.

We must not shrink from whatever is ahead of us. We must not fail in our duty and our responsibility to the citizens of the countries that are represented by this body. . . .

102 |

# DOCUMENT 2.15

Secretary of State Colin Powell's Security Council speech was lauded as a triumph by the administration, most of the country's political leadership, and the media. Long before its inaccuracies became widely known, West Virginia senator Robert C. Byrd took note of the direction in which the administration was moving the country. A long-time defender of congressional prerogatives and a noted constitutional expert, Byrd delivered a prescient warning to his Senate colleagues and to his country.

ROBERT C. BYRD, "WE STAND PASSIVELY MUTE," REMARKS TO THE SENATE, FEBRUARY 12, 2003

To contemplate war is to think about the most horrible of human experiences. On this February day, as this nation stands at the brink of battle, every American on some level must be contemplating the horrors of war.

Yet, this chamber is, for the most part, silent—ominously, dreadfully silent. There is no debate, no discussion, no attempt to lay out for the nation the pros and cons of this particular war. There is nothing.

We stand passively mute in the United States Senate, paralyzed by our own uncertainty, seemingly stunned by the sheer turmoil of events. Only on the editorial pages of our newspapers is there much substantive discussion of the prudence or imprudence of engaging in this particular war.

And this is no small conflagration we contemplate. This is no simple attempt to defang a villain. No. This coming battle, if it materializes, represents a turning point in U.S. foreign policy and possibly a turning point in the recent history of the world.

This nation is about to embark upon the first test of a revolutionary doctrine applied in an extraordinary way at an unfortunate time. The doctrine of preemption—the idea that the United States or any other nation can legitimately attack a nation that is not imminently threatening but may be threatening in the future—is a radical new twist on the traditional idea of self defense. It appears to be in contravention of international law and the UN Charter. And it is being tested at a time of world-wide terrorism, making many countries around the globe wonder if they will soon be on our—or some other nation's—hit list. High-level administration figures recently refused to take nuclear weapons off of the table when discussing a possible attack against Iraq. What could be more destabilizing and unwise than this type of uncertainty, particularly in a world where globalism has tied the vital economic and security interests of many nations so closely together? There are huge cracks emerging in our time-honored alliances, and U.S. intentions are suddenly subject to damaging worldwide speculation. Anti-Americanism based on mistrust, misinformation, suspicion, and alarming rhetoric from U.S. leaders is fracturing the once solid alliance against global terrorism which existed after September 11.

Here at home, people are warned of imminent terrorist attacks with little guidance as to when or where such attacks might occur. Family members are being called to active military duty, with no idea of the duration of their stay or what horrors they may face. Communities are being left with less than adequate police and fire protection. Other essential services are also short-staffed. The mood of the nation is grim. The economy is stumbling. Fuel prices are rising and may soon spike higher.

This administration, now in power for a little over two years, must be judged on its record. I believe that that record is dismal.

In that scant two years, this administration has squandered a large projected surplus of some $5.6 trillion over the next decade and taken us to projected deficits as far as the eye can see. This administration's domestic policy has put many of our states in dire financial condition, under funding scores of essential programs for our people. This administration has fostered policies which have slowed economic growth. This administration has ignored urgent matters such as the crisis in health care for our elderly. This administration has been slow to provide adequate funding for homeland security. This administration has been reluctant to better protect our long and porous borders.

In foreign policy, this administration has failed to find Osama bin Laden. In fact, just yesterday we heard from him again marshaling his forces and urging them to kill. This administration has split traditional alliances, possibly crippling, for all time, international order-keeping entities like the United Nations and NATO. This administration has called into question the traditional worldwide perception of the United States as well-intentioned peacekeeper. This administration has turned the patient art of diplomacy into threats, labeling, and name calling of the sort that reflects quite poorly on the intelligence and sensitivity of our leaders, and which will have consequences for years to come.

Calling heads of state pygmies, labeling whole countries as evil, denigrating powerful European allies as irrelevant—these types of crude insensitivities can do our great nation no good. We may have massive military might, but we cannot fight a global war on terrorism alone. We need the cooperation and friendship of our time-honored allies as well as the newer found friends whom we can attract with our wealth. Our awesome military machine will do us little good if we suffer another devastating attack on our homeland which severely damages our economy. Our military manpower is already stretched thin and we will need the augmenting support of those nations who can supply troop strength, not just sign letters cheering us on.

The war in Afghanistan has cost us $37 billion so far, yet there is evidence that terrorism may already be starting to regain its hold in that region. We have not found bin Laden, and unless we secure the peace in Afghanistan, the dark dens of terrorism may yet again flourish in that remote and devastated land.

Pakistan as well is at risk of destabilizing forces. This administration has not finished the first war against terrorism and yet it is eager to embark on another conflict with perils much greater than those in Afghanistan. Is our attention span that short? Have we not learned that after winning the war one must always secure the peace?

And yet we hear little about the aftermath of war in Iraq. In the absence of plans, speculation abroad is rife. Will we seize Iraq's oil fields, becoming an occupying power which controls the price and supply of that nation's oil for the foreseeable future? To whom do we propose to hand the reins of power after Saddam Hussein?

Will our war inflame the Muslim world, resulting in devastating attacks on Israel? Will Israel retaliate with its own nuclear arsenal? Will the Jordanian and Saudi Arabian governments be toppled by radicals, bolstered by Iran which has much closer ties to terrorism than Iraq?

Could a disruption of the world's oil supply lead to a worldwide recession? Has our senselessly bellicose language and our callous disregard of the interests and opinions of other nations increased the global race to join the nuclear club and made proliferation an even more lucrative practice for nations which need the income?

In only the space of two short years this reckless and arrogant administration has initiated policies which may reap disastrous consequences for years.

One can understand the anger and shock of any president after the savage attacks of September 11. One can appreciate the frustration of having only a shadow to chase and an amorphous, fleeting enemy on which it is nearly impossible to exact retribution.

But to turn one's frustration and anger into the kind of extremely destabilizing and dangerous foreign policy debacle that the world is currently witnessing is inexcusable from any administration charged with the awesome power and responsibility of guiding the destiny of the greatest superpower on the planet. Frankly many of the pronouncements made by this administration are outrageous. There is no other word.

Yet this chamber is hauntingly silent. On what is possibly the eve of horrific infliction of death and destruction on the population of the nation of Iraq—a population, I might add, of which over 50 percent is under age fifteen—this chamber is silent. On what is possibly only days before we send thousands of our own citizens to face unimagined horrors of chemical and biological warfare—this chamber is silent. On the eve of what could possibly be a vicious terrorist attack in retaliation for our attack on Iraq, it is business as usual in the United States Senate.

We are truly "sleepwalking through history." In my heart of hearts I pray that this great nation and its good and trusting citizens are not in for a rudest of awakenings.

To engage in war is always to pick a wild card. And war must always be a last resort, not a first choice. I truly must question the judgment of any president who can say that a massive unprovoked military attack on a nation which is over 50 percent children is "in the highest moral traditions of our country." This war is not necessary at this time. Pressure appears to be having a good result in Iraq. Our mistake was to put ourselves in a corner so quickly. Our challenge is to now find a graceful way out of a box of our own making. Perhaps there is still a way if we allow more time.

# DOCUMENT 2.16

Secretary of State Colin Powell had referred to a January report by Hans Blix to support his claims that Iraq posed an imminent threat, but he was soon to be disappointed. One month after Powell's speech, the United Nations Monitoring, Verification, and Inspection Commission (UNMOVIC) chair briefed the Security Council on the progress of the weapons inspections and disarmament ordered by the Security Council in Resolution 1441 (2.12). Blix presented a very different picture from that of administration spokespeople. His conclusion that Resolution 1441's goals could be achieved in "[not] years, nor weeks, but months" supported the growing international consensus for a halt to the U.S. push for war and was highly unwelcome in Washington.

---

## HANS BLIX, BRIEFING TO THE UNITED NATIONS SECURITY COUNCIL, MARCH 7, 2003

For nearly three years, I have been coming to the Security Council presenting the quarterly reports of UNMOVIC. They have described our many preparations for the resumption of inspections in Iraq. The 12th quarterly report is the first that describes three months of inspections. They come after four years without inspections. The report was finalized ten days ago and a number of relevant events have taken place since then. Today's statement will supplement the circulated report on these points to bring the Council up-to-date.

### Inspection Process

Inspections in Iraq resumed on 27 November 2002. In matters relating to process, notably prompt access to sites, we have faced relatively few difficulties and certainly much less than those that were faced by UNSCOM in the period 1991 to 1998. This may well be due to the strong outside pressure.

Some practical matters, which were not settled by the talks, Dr. El Baradei and I had with the Iraqi side in Vienna prior to inspections or in resolution 1441 (2002), have been resolved at meetings, which we have had in Baghdad. Initial difficulties raised by the Iraqi side about helicopters and aerial surveillance planes operating in the no-fly zones were overcome. This is not to say that the operation of inspections is free from frictions, but at this juncture we are able to perform professional no-notice inspections all over Iraq and to increase aerial surveillance.

American U-2 and French Mirage surveillance aircraft already give us valuable imagery, supplementing satellite pictures and we would expect soon to be able to add night vision capability through an aircraft offered to us by the Russian Federation. We also expect to add low-level, close area surveillance through drones provided by Germany. We are grateful not only to the countries, which place these valuable tools at our disposal, but also to the States, most recently Cyprus, which has agreed to the stationing of aircraft on their territory.

### Documents and Interviews

Iraq, with a highly developed administrative system, should be able to provide more documentary evidence about its proscribed weapons programmes. Only a few new such documents have come to light so far and been handed over since we began inspections. It was a disappointment that Iraq's Declaration of 7 December did not bring new documentary evidence. I hope that efforts in this respect, including the appointment of a governmental commission, will give significant results. When proscribed items are deemed unaccounted for it is above all credible accounts that is needed— or the proscribed items, if they exist.

Where authentic documents do not become available, interviews with persons, who may have relevant knowledge and experience, may be another way of obtaining evidence. UNMOVIC has names of such persons in its records and they are among the people whom we seek to interview. In the last month, Iraq has provided us with the names of many persons, who may be relevant sources of information, in particular, persons who took part in various phases of the unilateral destruction of biological and chemical weapons, and proscribed missiles in 1991. The provision of names prompts two reflections:

The first is that with such detailed information existing regarding those who took part in the unilateral destruction, surely there must also remain records regarding the quantities and other data concerning the various items destroyed.

The second reflection is that with relevant witnesses available it becomes even more important to be able to conduct interviews in modes and locations, which allow us to be confident that the testimony is given without outside influence. While the Iraqi side seems to have encouraged interviewees not to request the presence of Iraqi officials (so-called minders) or the taping of the interviews, conditions ensuring the absence of undue influences are difficult to attain inside Iraq. Interviews outside the country might provide such assurance. It is our intention to request such interviews shortly. Nevertheless, despite remaining shortcomings, interviews are useful. Since we started requesting interviews, 38 individuals were asked for private interviews, of which 10 accepted under our terms, 7 of these during the last week.

As I noted on 14 February, intelligence authorities have claimed that weapons of mass destruction are moved around Iraq by trucks and, in particular, that there are mobile production units for biological weapons. The Iraqi side states that such activities do not exist. Several inspections have taken place at declared and undeclared sites in relation to mobile production facilities. Food testing mobile laboratories and mobile workshops have been seen, as well as large containers with seed processing equipment. No evidence of proscribed activities have so far been found. Iraq is expected to assist in the development of credible ways to conduct random checks of ground transportation.

Inspectors are also engaged in examining Iraq's programme for Remotely Piloted Vehicles (RPVs). A number of sites have been inspected with data being collected to assess the range and other capabilities of the various models found. Inspections are continuing in this area.

There have been reports, denied from the Iraqi side, that proscribed activities are conducted underground. Iraq should provide information on any underground structure suitable for the production or storage of WMD. During inspections of declared or undeclared facilities, inspection teams have examined building structures for any possible underground facilities. In addition, ground penetrating radar equipment was used in several specific locations. No underground facilities for chemical or biological production or storage were found so far.

I should add that, both for the monitoring of ground transportation and for the inspection of underground facilities, we would need to increase our staff in Iraq. I am not talking about a doubling of the staff. I would rather have twice the amount of high quality information about sites to inspect than twice the number of expert inspectors to send.

## Recent Developments

On 14 February, I reported to the Council that the Iraqi side had become more active in taking and proposing steps, which potentially might shed new light on unresolved disarmament issues. Even a week ago, when the current quarterly report was finalized, there was still relatively little tangible progress to note. Hence, the cautious formulations in the report before you.

As of today, there is more. While during our meetings in Baghdad, the Iraqi side tried to persuade us that the Al Samoud 2 missiles they have declared fall within the permissible range set by the Security Council, the calculations of an international panel of experts led us to the opposite conclusion. Iraq has since accepted that these missiles and associated items be destroyed and has started the process of destruction under our supervision. The destruction undertaken constitutes a substantial measure of disarmament—indeed, the first since the middle of the 1990s. We are not watching the breaking of toothpicks. Lethal weapons are being destroyed. However, I must add that no destruction has happened today. I hope it's a temporary break.

To date, 34 Al Samoud 2 missiles, including 4 training missiles, 2 combat warheads, 1 launcher and 5 engines have been destroyed under UNMOVIC supervision. Work is continuing to identify and inventory the parts and equipment associated with the Al Samoud 2 programme.

Two 'reconstituted' casting chambers used in the production of solid propellant missiles have been destroyed and the remnants melted or encased in concrete.

The legality of the Al Fatah missile is still under review, pending further investigation and measurement of various parameters of that missile.

More papers on anthrax, VX and missiles have recently been provided. Many have been found to restate what Iraq had already declared, some will require further study and discussion.

There is a significant Iraqi effort underway to clarify a major source of uncertainty as to the quantities of biological and chemical weapons, which were unilaterally destroyed in 1991. A part of this effort concerns a disposal site, which was deemed too dangerous for full investigation in the past. It is now being re-excavated. To date, Iraq has unearthed eight complete bombs comprising two liquid-filled intact R-400 bombs and six other complete bombs. Bomb fragments were also found. Samples have been taken. The investigation of the destruction site could, in the best case, allow the determination of the number of bombs destroyed at that site. It should be followed by a serious and credible effort to determine the separate issue of how many R-400 type bombs were produced. In this, as in other matters, inspection work is moving on and may yield results.

Iraq proposed an investigation using advanced technology to quantify the amount of unilaterally destroyed anthrax dumped at a site. However, even if the use of advanced technology could quantify the amount of anthrax, said to be dumped at the site, the results would still be open to interpretation. Defining the quantity of anthrax destroyed must, of course, be followed by efforts to establish what quantity was actually produced.

With respect to VX, Iraq has recently suggested a similar method to quantify a VX precursor stated to have been unilaterally destroyed in the summer of 1991.

Iraq has also recently informed us that, following the adoption of the presidential decree prohibiting private individuals and mixed companies from engaging in work related to WMD, further legislation on the subject is to be enacted. This appears to be in response to a letter from UNMOVIC requesting clarification of the issue.

What are we to make of these activities? One can hardly avoid the impression that, after a period of somewhat reluctant cooperation, there has been an acceleration of initiatives from the Iraqi side since the end of January.

This is welcome, but the value of these measures must be soberly judged by how many question marks they actually succeed in straightening out. This is not yet clear.

Against this background, the question is now asked whether Iraq has cooperated "immediately, unconditionally and actively" with UNMOVIC, as required under paragraph 9 of resolution 1441 (2002). The answers can be seen from the factual descriptions I have provided. However, if more direct answers are desired, I would say the following:

The Iraqi side has tried on occasion to attach conditions, as it did regarding helicopters and U-2 planes. Iraq has not, however, so far persisted in these or other conditions for the exercise of any of our inspection rights. If it did, we would report it.

It is obvious that, while the numerous initiatives, which are now taken by the Iraqi side with a view to resolving some long-standing open disarmament issues, can be seen as "active", or even "proactive", these initiatives 3–4 months into the new resolution cannot be said to constitute "immediate" cooperation. Nor do they necessarily cover all areas of relevance. They are nevertheless welcome and UNMOVIC is responding to them in the hope of solving presently unresolved disarmament issues. . . .

How much time would it take to resolve the key remaining disarmament tasks? While cooperation can and is to be immediate, disarmament and at any rate the verification of it cannot be instant. Even with a proactive Iraqi attitude, induced by continued outside pressure, it would still take some time to verify sites and items, analyse documents, interview relevant persons, and draw conclusions. It would not take years, nor weeks, but months. Neither governments nor inspectors would want disarmament inspection to go on forever. However, it must be remembered that in accordance with the governing resolutions, a sustained inspection and monitoring system is to remain in place after verified disarmament to give confidence and to strike an alarm, if signs were seen of the revival of any proscribed weapons programmes.

## DOCUMENT 2.17

UNMOVIC chair Hans Blix's report was a devastating refutation of key administration claims delivered by a respected international civil servant. As opposition to the Bush administration's plans began to harden and domestic critics began to stir once again, the president acted. Ten days after Blix's speech, he issued a unilateral ultimatum to the Iraqi government that no one expected Baghdad to obey. Two days later he announced the start of Operation Iraqi Freedom.

GEORGE W. BUSH, ULTIMATUM TO IRAQ, MARCH 17, 2003

My fellow citizens, events in Iraq have now reached the final days of decision. For more than a decade, the United States and other nations have pursued patient and honorable efforts to disarm the Iraqi regime without war. That regime pledged to reveal and destroy all its weapons of mass destruction as a condition for ending the Persian Gulf War in 1991.

Since then, the world has engaged in twelve years of diplomacy. We have passed more than a dozen resolutions in the United Nations Security Council. We have sent hundreds of weapons inspectors to oversee the disarmament of Iraq. Our good faith has not been returned.

The Iraqi regime has used diplomacy as a ploy to gain time and advantage. It has uniformly defied Security Council resolutions demanding full disarmament. Over the years, UN weapon inspectors have been threatened by Iraqi officials, electronically bugged, and systematically deceived. Peaceful efforts to disarm the Iraqi regime have failed again and again—because we are not dealing with peaceful men.

Intelligence gathered by this and other governments leaves no doubt that the Iraq regime continues to possess and conceal some of the most lethal weapons ever devised. This regime has already used weapons of mass destruction against Iraq's neighbors and against Iraq's people.

The regime has a history of reckless aggression in the Middle East. It has a deep hatred of America and our friends. And it has aided, trained, and harbored terrorists, including operatives of al Qaeda.

The danger is clear: using chemical, biological, or, one day, nuclear weapons, obtained with the help of Iraq, the terrorists could fulfill their stated ambitions and kill thousands or hundreds of thousands of innocent people in our country, or any other.

The United States and other nations did nothing to deserve or invite this threat. But we will do everything to defeat it. Instead of drifting along toward tragedy, we will set a course toward safety. Before the day of horror can come, before it is too late to act, this danger will be removed.

The United States of America has the sovereign authority to use force in assuring its own national security. That duty falls to me, as commander in chief, by the oath I have sworn, by the oath I will keep.

Recognizing the threat to our country, the United States Congress voted overwhelmingly last year to support the use of force against Iraq. America tried to work with the United Nations to address this threat because we wanted to resolve the issue peacefully. We believe in the mission of the United Nations. One reason the UN was founded after the Second World War was to confront aggressive dictators, actively and early, before they can attack the innocent and destroy the peace.

In the case of Iraq, the Security Council did act, in the early 1990s. Under Resolutions 678 and 687—both still in effect—the United States and our allies are authorized to use force in ridding Iraq of weapons of mass destruction. This is not a question of authority, it is a question of will.

Last September, I went to the UN General Assembly and urged the nations of the world to unite and bring an end to this danger. On November 8th, the Security Council unanimously passed Resolution 1441, finding Iraq in material breach of its obligations, and vowing serious consequences if Iraq did not fully and immediately disarm.

Today, no nation can possibly claim that Iraq has disarmed. And it will not disarm so long as Saddam Hussein holds power. For the last four-and-a-half months, the United States and our allies have worked within the Security Council to enforce that Council's long-standing demands. Yet, some permanent members of the Security Council have publicly announced they will veto any resolution that compels the disarmament of Iraq. These governments share our assessment of the danger, but not our resolve to meet it. Many nations, however, do have the resolve and fortitude to act against this threat to peace, and a broad coalition is now gathering to enforce the just demands of the world. The United Nations Security Council has not lived up to its responsibilities, so we will rise to ours.

In recent days, some governments in the Middle East have been doing their part. They have delivered public and private messages urging the dictator to leave Iraq, so that disarmament can proceed peacefully. He has thus far refused. All the decades of deceit and cruelty have now reached an end. Saddam Hussein and his sons must leave Iraq within forty-eight hours. Their refusal to do so will result in military conflict, commenced at a time of our choosing. For their own safety, all foreign nationals—including journalists and inspectors—should leave Iraq immediately.

Many Iraqis can hear me tonight in a translated radio broadcast, and I have a message for them. If we must begin a military campaign, it will be directed against the lawless men who rule your country and not against you. As our coalition takes away their power, we will deliver the food and medicine you need. We will tear down the apparatus of terror and we will help you to build a new Iraq that is prosperous and free. In a free Iraq, there will be no more wars of aggression against your neighbors, no more poison factories, no more executions of dissidents, no more torture chambers and rape rooms. The tyrant will soon be gone. The day of your liberation is near.

It is too late for Saddam Hussein to remain in power. It is not too late for the Iraqi military to act with honor and protect your country by permitting the peaceful entry of coalition forces to eliminate weapons of mass destruction. Our forces will give Iraqi military units clear instructions on actions they can take to avoid being attacked and destroyed. I urge every member of the Iraqi military and intelligence services, if war comes, do not fight for a dying regime that is not worth your own life.

And all Iraqi military and civilian personnel should listen carefully to this warning. In any conflict, your fate will depend on your action. Do not destroy oil wells, a source of wealth that belongs to the Iraqi people. Do not obey any command to use weapons of mass destruction against anyone, including the Iraqi people. War crimes will be prosecuted. War criminals will be punished. And it will be no defense to say, "I was just following orders."

Should Saddam Hussein choose confrontation, the American people can know that every measure has been taken to avoid war, and every measure will be taken to win it. Americans understand the costs of conflict because we have paid them in the past. War has no certainty, except the certainty of sacrifice.

Yet the only way to reduce the harm and duration of war is to apply the full force and might of our military, and we are prepared to do so. If Saddam Hussein attempts to cling to power, he will remain a deadly foe until the end. In desperation, he and terrorist groups might try to conduct terrorist operations against the American people and our friends. These attacks are not inevitable. They are, however, possible. And this very fact underscores the reason we cannot live under the threat of blackmail. The terrorist threat to America and the world will be diminished the moment that Saddam Hussein is disarmed.

Our government is on heightened watch against these dangers. Just as we are preparing to ensure victory in Iraq, we are taking further actions to protect our homeland. In recent days, American authorities have expelled from the country certain individuals with ties to Iraqi intelligence services. Among other measures, I have directed additional security of our airports, and increased Coast Guard patrols of major seaports. The Department of Homeland Security is working closely with the nation's governors to increase armed security at critical facilities across America.

Should enemies strike our country, they would be attempting to shift our attention with panic and weaken our morale with fear. In this, they would fail. No act of theirs can alter the course or shake the resolve of this country. We are a peaceful people—yet we're not a fragile people, and we will not be intimidated by thugs and killers. If our enemies dare to strike us, they and all who have aided them, will face fearful consequences.

We are now acting because the risks of inaction would be far greater. In one year, or five years, the power of Iraq to inflict harm on all free nations would be multiplied many times over. With these capabilities, Saddam Hussein and his terrorist allies could choose the moment of deadly conflict when they are strongest. We choose to meet that threat now, where it arises, before it can appear suddenly in our skies and cities.

The cause of peace requires all free nations to recognize new and undeniable realities. In the twentieth century, some chose to appease murderous dictators, whose threats were allowed to grow into genocide and global war. In this century, when evil men plot chemical, biological, and nuclear terror, a policy of appeasement could bring destruction of a kind never before seen on this earth.

Terrorists and terror states do not reveal these threats with fair notice, in formal declarations—and responding to such enemies only after they have struck first is not self-defense, it is suicide. The security of the world requires disarming Saddam Hussein now.

As we enforce the just demands of the world, we will also honor the deepest commitments of our country. Unlike Saddam Hussein, we believe the Iraqi people are deserving and capable of human liberty. And when the dictator has departed, they can set an example to all the Middle East of a vital and peaceful and self-governing nation.

The United States, with other countries, will work to advance liberty and peace in that region. Our goal will not be achieved overnight, but it can come over time. The power and appeal of human liberty is felt in every life and every land. And the greatest power of freedom is to overcome hatred and violence, and turn the creative gifts of men and women to the pursuits of peace.

That is the future we choose. Free nations have a duty to defend our people by uniting against the violent. And tonight, as we have done before, America and our allies accept that responsibility.

Good night, and may God continue to bless America.

## DOCUMENT 2.18

Two days after his ultimatum to Iraq, President Bush launched his preemptive war.

---

GEORGE W. BUSH, ANNOUNCEMENT OF THE START OF
OPERATION IRAQI FREEDOM, MARCH 19, 2003

My fellow citizens, at this hour, American and coalition forces are in the early stages of military operations to disarm Iraq, to free its people and to defend the world from grave danger.

On my orders, coalition forces have begun striking selected targets of military importance to undermine Saddam Hussein's ability to wage war. These are opening stages of what will be a broad and concerted campaign. More than thirty-five countries are giving crucial support—from the use of naval and air bases, to help with intelligence and logistics, to the deployment of combat units. Every nation in this coalition has chosen to bear the duty and share the honor of serving in our common defense.

To all the men and women of the United States Armed Forces now in the Middle East, the peace of a troubled world and the hopes of an oppressed people now depend on you. That trust is well placed.

The enemies you confront will come to know your skill and bravery. The people you liberate will witness the honorable and decent spirit of the American military. In this conflict, America faces an enemy who has no regard for conventions of war or rules of morality. Saddam Hussein has placed Iraqi troops and equipment in civilian areas, attempting to use innocent men, women and children as shields for his own military—a final atrocity against his people.

I want Americans and all the world to know that coalition forces will make every effort to spare innocent civilians from harm. A campaign on the harsh terrain of a nation as large as California could be longer and more difficult than some predict. And helping Iraqis achieve a united, stable, and free country will require our sustained commitment.

We come to Iraq with respect for its citizens, for their great civilization and for the religious faiths they practice. We have no ambition in Iraq, except to remove a threat and restore control of that country to its own people.

I know that the families of our military are praying that all those who serve will return safely and soon. Millions of Americans are praying with you for the safety of your loved ones and for the protection of the innocent. For your sacrifice, you have the gratitude and respect of the American people. And you can know that our forces will be coming home as soon as their work is done.

Our nation enters this conflict reluctantly—yet, our purpose is sure. The people of the United States and our friends and allies will not live at the mercy of an outlaw regime that threatens the peace with weapons of mass murder. We will meet that threat now, with our Army, Air Force, Navy, Coast Guard, and Marines, so that we do not have to meet it later with armies of fire fighters and police and doctors on the streets of our cities.

Now that conflict has come, the only way to limit its duration is to apply decisive force. And I assure you, this will not be a campaign of half measures, and we will accept no outcome but victory.

My fellow citizens, the dangers to our country and the world will be overcome. We will pass through this time of peril and carry on the work of peace. We will defend our freedom. We will bring freedom to others and we will prevail.

May God bless our country and all who defend her.

# ★ CHAPTER 3 ★

# INTERNATIONAL REACTION
# TO THE WAR

MUCH OF THE WORLD opposed the impending invasion of Iraq. Experts and foreign-policy figures warned in 2002 that an invasion might provoke new terrorist threats against the United States, sidetrack the fight against al Qaeda, and produce a complex and unpredictable situation in the Middle East. On February 15, 2003, millions of people in major cities around the world demonstrated against the imminent war. Even in countries such as Spain and Britain, where leaders aligned themselves with Bush, the majority of citizens opposed the war. In Spain, two million people protested in Barcelona and Madrid alone on February 15; in Britain, up to two million people demonstrated. Nelson Mandela, the legendary South African leader and Nobel Peace Prize laureate, warned that a U.S. invasion of Iraq would plunge the world into a "holocaust."

The Iraq crisis also deepened divisions within the Atlantic alliance. On January 30, 2003, the European Parliament adopted a resolution stating its "opposition to any unilateral military action" and its belief that "a preemptive strike would not be in accordance with international law and the UN Charter and would lead to a deeper crisis involving other countries in the region. . . . [E]verything must be done to avoid military action" (3.1). On the same day, however, eight other European states issued the "Letter of Eight" (3.2), in which the signatories, Tony Blair of the United Kingdom, José María Aznar of Spain, José Manuel Durão Barroso of Portugal, Silvio Berlusconi of Italy, Václav Havel of the Czech Republic, Peter Medgyessy of Hungary, Leszek Miller of Poland, and Anders Fogh Rasmussen of Denmark, called for Europe to stand with the United States and warned that "the Iraqi regime and its weapons of mass destruction represented a clear threat to world security." The fact that five of the fifteen members of the European Union signed the letter—and that Hungary, Poland, and the Czech Republic were scheduled to become members in 2004 —reflected the profound political dissension within the EU about the looming invasion. The EU's "Common Foreign and Security Policy," adopted in 1993 as part of its institutional architecture, had stipulated that all member governments would adhere to a common foreign and security policy, but disagreements about Iraq made it impossible for the Union to arrive at a unified policy on preemptive war.

Colin Powell gave his well-received but later discredited speech on Iraq before the UN Security Council on February 6, 2003 (2.14). That same day, ten states that were in candidacy discussions with the EU endorsed the U.S. policy of regime change in a letter known as the Vilnius Statement (3.3). Albania, Bulgaria, Croatia, Estonia, Latvia, Lithuania, Macedonia, Romania, Slovakia, and Slovenia—all former members of the Soviet bloc—effectively aligned themselves with the military approach of the United States. Their stance, known as "bandwagoning" in international relations theory, deepened the rift within the EU. The French president, Jacques Chirac, sharply criticized the letter, saying, "These countries have been not very well behaved and [are] rather reckless of the danger of aligning themselves too rapidly with the American position. . . . It is not really responsible behavior. . . . I felt they acted frivolously because entry into the European Union implies a minimum of understanding for the others."[1] Defense Secretary Donald Rumsfeld commented that "Old Europe" might be resisting U.S. objectives but that "New Europe" was the wave of the future.

It was not surprising that smaller European states would "bandwagon" when faced with a demand by a powerful and potentially threatening state. This was especially the case in a "unipolar moment," when only one superpower dominated the international system. International relations theory suggests that small, weak states are much more likely to bandwagon because of cost–benefit calculations: they fear costs and negative consequences should they challenge the dominant state, and, conversely, hope to incur benefits from an alliance. As Stephen M. Walt has noted, however, bandwagoning can be a risky strategy. It is often characterized by unequal exchanges and demands, it is asymmetrical, and it is often short-lived; many times it is coerced.[2] Significantly, several of the former Soviet states moved to mend the division within the EU after joining in 2004.

The geopolitical world was shifting. Since the Cold War, when the United States and Western Europe were allies in the anticommunist struggle (admittedly, with distinct tactics, values, and concerns), the two regions had been drifting apart. The neoconservative analyst and Project for the New American Century member Robert Kagan famously wrote in 2002 that "America is from

---

1. "Chirac Lashes Out at 'New Europe,'" *CNN World,* February 18, 2003.
2. Stephen M. Walt, "Testing Theories of Alliance Formation: The Case of Southwest Asia," *International Organization* 42, no. 2 (1988), 275–316.

Mars and Europe is from Venus: they agree on little and understand one another less and less."[3] He contended that Washington was willing to shape the international system for the common good through the aggressive exercise of military power and unilateral action (2.3). Meanwhile, Europe was organizing a peaceful system that deemphasized the use of force and emphasized human rights, conflict resolution through law, and social development. Kagan implied that the European model exemplified military weakness and naïveté, and recommended that the world "readjust to the new reality of American hegemony."

But leading European states moved to reshape the U.S.-dominated unipolar world system by encouraging the European Union to assert itself as a counterbalance to Washington. Prominent European leaders argued that choosing war—especially preemptive war—over peaceful methods of resolving the Iraq crisis was counterproductive. As the German foreign minister pointedly commented, "Those who know our European history understand that we do not live on Venus but, rather, that we are the survivors of Mars. War is terrible." The EU prided itself on its law-governed system and often drew attention to its "values of respect for human dignity, liberty, democracy, equality, the rule of law and respect for human rights, including the rights of persons belonging to minorities. . . . Moreover, the societies of the Member States are characterised by pluralism, non-discrimination, tolerance, justice, solidarity and equality between women and men."[4]

The European Union had introduced the euro in 2001 to encourage the economic integration of the region, and in 2003 France, Germany, Belgium, and Luxembourg called for the Union to draft its own mutual defense treaty and form its own European military force, without the participation of the United States. Washington argued strenuously against that idea, calling it a threat to NATO.[5] The U.S. position had its roots in the secret Pentagon Defense Planning Guidance of 1992, which had argued that Washington "must seek to prevent the emergence of European-only security arrangements which would undermine NATO. . . . Therefore, it is of fundamental importance to preserve NATO as the primary instrument of Western defense and security, as well as the channel for U.S. influence and participation in European security affairs" (1.3). Part of the U.S. strategy to preserve its global hegemony was to maintain its influence and control of military action in Europe through NATO. But the European Union continued to develop the idea of an autonomous defense force.

---

3. Robert Kagan's original article was published in 2002. His 2003 book, *Of Paradise and Power: America vs. Europe in the New World Order* (New York: Knopf, 2003), expanded the argument. In a critique of the book, Anthony Dworkin argued that "international law, Kagan seems to imply, is for sissies." See his review of Kagan at http://writ.news.findlaw.com/books/reviews/20030425_dworkin.html.
4. European Union, "The Founding Principles of the Union," at http://europa.eu/scadplus/constitution/objectives_en.htm.
5. Shada Islam, "Whither NATO? European Defense Force May Counterbalance U.S. Power," *Yale-Global,* October 29, 2003.

The EU also continued its policy of enlargement and held out the prospect of membership to former Soviet bloc countries. A larger European Union meant a larger economic zone, bolstering Europe as a world power and promoting its prosperity, global political influence, and cohesion. However, the U.S. invasion plans drove a wedge between governments that supported U.S. military action and those that opposed it, led by Germany and France. The dissension worked to Washington's short-term advantage: by undercutting European unity the United States could regain political influence there and garner a measure of Continental support for more aggressive positions. Germany and France reacted with annoyance to Rumsfeld's dismissive comments about "Old Europe." But the position of "Old Europe" reflected the views of most of the world's states, which feared the self-proclaimed right of the United States to bypass the United Nations and preemptively intervene in other countries. And, in fact, in its final months the Bush administration moved to reactivate talks with Iran and North Korea—two-thirds of the original "axis of evil"—and asked the United Nations for assistance in the Middle East, thus belatedly recognizing that multilateral diplomacy was, indeed, crucial to U.S. interests.

As the 2003 invasion loomed, most developing countries protested the U.S. doctrine of preemptive war and "regime change." In a session before the Security Council in February, many state delegations expressed opposition to war as a solution to the Iraq crisis (3.4). International nongovernmental organizations (NGOs), including the World Council of Churches, called for a peaceful solution (3.5). The Non-Aligned Movement (NAM), an organization of smaller states in the developing world that seek independence in global affairs, issued a statement calling for a process of negotiation to resolve the crisis. (3.6). Big Arab countries were especially concerned by the Bush administration's determination to enter the region militarily and engineer a "regime change" in Iraq.[6] Syria backed the Security Council resolution offered by France, Germany, and Russia, and its ambassador to the United Nations questioned the evidence that the United States presented on Iraq's weapons of mass destruction, calling it a pretext for a war to advance the interests of Israel and big oil companies. Nevertheless, Syria tried to avoid outright opposition to Washington. Saudi Arabia—long a key ally of the United States—was caught in a difficult situation. The government's close ties with the United States had already provoked anger and rejection within its society (indeed, the U.S. presence in Saudi Arabia after the Gulf War had contributed to the rise of Osama bin Laden and his radical Islamist followers). However, while the Saudi foreign minister called for diplomacy to avoid war, the country did quietly allow U.S. officers to direct operations from Saudi military bases during the invasion.

With the stakes high for the Bush administration, hard-line tactics were used to compel the support of UN members. In the months before the invasion, a

---

6. For useful summaries of key states' positions, see Rick Fawn and Raymond Hinnebusch, eds., *The Iraq War: Causes and Consequences* (Boulder: Lynne Rienner, 2006). This analysis draws from their chapters on Syria and Saudi Arabia.

number of governments and UN delegations had been pressured, threatened with trade sanctions, and even put under surveillance if they declined to fall into line behind the Bush policy. A British whistleblower revealed that the National Security Agency had launched a spying operation in the United Nations at Washington's behest (3.7). In some cases, the Bush administration pressed for the recall of UN diplomats who resisted its push for war. For example, both the Mexican and Chilean UN representatives, who were seated as non-permanent members of the Security Council, worked to broker a compromise to allow more time for the inspectors to work in Iraq. U.S. officials declared their effort "an unfriendly act" and tried to persuade their governments to recall them.[7] The Mexican delegate, Adolfo Aguilar Zinser, assumed the rotating presidency of the Security Council in April and pledged that Mexico would lead an effort in the Council to restore peace in Iraq. President Vicente Fox removed him from his UN post later that year, however, and then forced him out of the Mexican government completely.

In March 2003 it became clear that the Security Council would not support a draft resolution written by Washington, London, and Madrid implicitly authorizing war (3.9). After the Bush administration announced an ultimatum in March for Saddam Hussein to prove he had no weapons of mass destruction (2.17), the secretary general pulled the inspectors and other UN personnel out of Iraq (3.10). While Tony Blair made the case for war (3.11), the French and German representatives spoke out strongly against military action in Iraq (3.12–3.13). In response to the statement issued by those two countries and Russia, National Security Advisor Condoleezza Rice said that U.S. policy would be to "forgive Russia, ignore Germany and punish France."[8]

In the United Nations, the French foreign minister argued that war should be the exception and that the UN weapons inspectors were producing results. Pointedly, he added, "To those who choose to use force and think they can resolve the world's complexity through swift and preventive action, we offer in contrast determined action over time." Similarly, the German foreign minister insisted, "It is possible to disarm Iraq peacefully by upholding these demands with tight deadlines. Peaceful means have therefore not been exhausted. Also for that reason, Germany emphatically rejects the impending war."

After realizing that the Security Council would not support a preemptive invasion of Iraq, the Bush administration dropped its insistence on the joint resolution and claimed that the United States did not need UN authorization for the war. On the day of the invasion, China spoke out against the war (3.14), and a week later a coalition of international NGOs called on the UN to take ac-

---

7. See, e.g., Colum Lynch, "U.S. Pushed Allies on Iraq, Diplomat Writes," *Washington Post*, March 23, 2008. A Chilean diplomat, Héctor Muñoz, wrote a book about his experience in the United Nations at the time and characterized U.S. pressures as generating "bitterness" and "deep mistrust" in Latin America.

8. This quote was widely published but never publicly acknowledged by Rice. See, e.g., Elaine Sciolino, "French Struggle Now with How to Coexist with Bush," *New York Times*, February 8, 2005.

tion to stop it (3.15). In April, Vladimir Putin gave his views on the war and on relations with the United States and called for the strengthening of the United Nations and the system of international law (3.16). In September 2004 Secretary General Kofi Annan stated, somewhat reluctantly, that the invasion had been illegal and had violated the UN Charter (3.17). Secretary of State Colin Powell publicly challenged that view, arguing that U.S. action had been consistent with international law.[9]

# DOCUMENT 3.1

As war approached, the European Parliament of the EU called for stringent weapons inspections and an enhanced inspection regime in Iraq as an alternative to invasion. Arguing strongly that the United Nations—rather than one or several states—should continue to supervise the situation, the Parliament made clear that Europe considered military action to be unjustified at that time. The resolution also called for the International Criminal Court to take up the case of Saddam Hussein. It was significant that Europe was offering a solution to the crisis that was firmly embedded within the system of international institutions and laws.

EUROPEAN PARLIAMENT, RESOLUTION ON
THE SITUATION IN IRAQ, JANUARY 30, 2003

The European Parliament,

- having regard to its previous resolutions on the situation in Iraq, and in particular its resolution of 16 May 2002 on the situation in Iraq eleven years after the Gulf War,
- having regard to all the United Nations Security Council resolutions on Iraq, and in particular Resolution 1441 of 8 November 2002,
- having regard to the report submitted by the Executive Chairman of the UN Monitoring, Verification and Inspection Commission (UNMOVIC) and the Director-General of the International Atomic Energy Agency (IAEA) to the UN Security Council on 27 January 2003,
- having regard to the solemn Franco-German declaration issued in Paris on 22 January 2003,
- having regard to the conclusions of the EU Foreign Affairs Ministers on Iraq of 27 January 2003,

---

9. "Powell Disputes Annan, Insists Iraq War Is Legal," *China Daily*, September 18, 2004.

A. whereas Security Council Resolution 1441 instructed UNMOVIC to impose a stricter disarmament inspection regime on Iraq and demanded that Baghdad provide UNMOVIC and the IAEA with a full and complete declaration of all aspects of its programmes to develop chemical, biological and nuclear weapons and ballistic missiles and all other information concerning its chemical, biological and nuclear weapons programmes,

B. stressing the importance of the complete disarmament of Iraqi chemical, bacteriological, radiological and nuclear weapons of mass destruction under international control, if existing, and of dismantling the possible capacity of Iraq to produce such weapons, according to relevant UN Security Council resolutions,

C. whereas the European Union and its Member States must pursue the same approach with the aim of securing rapid and effective international monitoring of the situation in Iraq,

D. having regard to the Iraqi Government's self-isolation and lack of cooperation with the international community, the extreme militarization of Iraqi society, the widespread and extremely grave violations of human rights and international humanitarian law and the total lack of political and democratic rights in Iraq,

1. Reaffirms its commitment to peace, democracy and respect for human rights and international law and reiterates the need for full application of and compliance with United Nations Security Council resolutions in order to guarantee international peace and security;

2. Fully supports the work of Mr Hans Blix, Executive Chairman of UNMOVIC, Mr El Baradei, Director-General of the IAEA, and their team of inspectors in charge of the UN enhanced inspection regime as stipulated in UNSCR 1441;

3. Believes that breaches of UNSCR 1441 currently identified by the inspectors with regard to weapons of mass destruction do not justify military action and considers that any further steps must be taken by the Security Council after a full assessment of the situation;

4. Calls on the Iraqi Government to comply with UN Security Council resolution (UNSCR) 1441 and continue to allow UNMOVIC inspections, unconditionally and with unimpeded access, and to cooperate fully and respond to the remarks made by the Executive Chairman of UNMOVIC in its report; calls, furthermore, for all available pertinent information, from all sources, to be forwarded without delay to UNMOVIC;

5. Welcomes, in this regard, the conclusions of the General Affairs and External Relations Council held on 27 January 2003 and expects these conclusions to be implemented by the Member States in all the relevant bodies; urges the Council to attempt to reach a common position on Iraq within the framework of the CFSP so that the EU can speak with a single voice on the international stage on the current situation and future development of this conflict; calls on the applicant

countries, by means of appropriate consultations, to fall into line with a European common position;

6. Expresses its opposition to any unilateral military action and believes that a pre-emptive strike would not be in accordance with international law and the UN Charter and would lead to a deeper crisis involving other countries in the region; stresses that everything must be done to avoid military action;

7. Calls for all political and diplomatic avenues to be explored in order to secure a peaceful settlement to the conflict and stresses the necessity of securing and preserving peace and international security;

8. Urges the UN to verify the effects of the embargo, notably the adverse impact on the humanitarian situation of Iraqi civilians, particularly women and children, so that, if required, it would be possible to define the steps towards the lifting of the embargo;

9. Calls on the Council to make every effort to stop war in the Middle East; urges the Council Presidency and the High Representative for the CFSP, in this connection, to make clear to the U.S. Administration that a solution to the Middle East conflict is the EU's top priority and that a strong and convincing international initiative for the speedy implementation of the road map endorsed by the Quartet (EU, U.S., UN and Russia) can no longer be delayed;

10. Stresses the European Union's commitment to the sovereignty and territorial integrity of Iraq, Kuwait and neighbouring countries;

11. Urges the Council and the Member States to take the initiative in proposing that the International Criminal Court should investigate the responsibility of the Iraqi leader's regime for the genocide against the Marsh Arabs and other crimes of war and crimes against humanity;

12. Instructs its President to forward this resolution to the Council, the Commission, the High Representative for the CFSP, the UN Secretary-General and the Government of Iraq.

## DOCUMENT 3.2

Issued on the day the European Parliament passed its resolution, the eight European signatories of this letter presented themselves as speaking for "Europeans," but they parted ways with the EU by challenging its authority and position on the impending war with Iraq. Calling for the enforcement of previous disarmament resolutions without delay, the letter implicitly rejected attempts in the Security Council to postpone a military attack and allow the inspectors more time to work. The letter also lauded the United States, highlighting its role in freeing Europe of Nazism and Communism. Citing Europe's debt to "American bravery, generosity and far-sightedness," it urged Europeans to preserve "the transatlantic relationship."

## THE LETTER OF EIGHT, "EUROPE AND AMERICA MUST STAND UNITED," JANUARY 30, 2003

The real bond between the United States and Europe is the values we share: democracy, individual freedom, human rights and the Rule of Law. These values crossed the Atlantic with those who sailed from Europe to help create the U.S.A. Today they are under greater threat than ever.

The attacks of 11 September showed just how far terrorists—the enemies of our common values—are prepared to go to destroy them. Those outrages were an attack on all of us. In standing firm in defence of these principles, the governments and people of the United States and Europe have amply demonstrated the strength of their convictions. Today more than ever, the transatlantic bond is a guarantee of our freedom.

We in Europe have a relationship with the United States which has stood the test of time. Thanks in large part to American bravery, generosity and far-sightedness, Europe was set free from the two forms of tyranny that devastated our continent in the 20th century: Nazism and Communism. Thanks, too, to the continued cooperation between Europe and the United States we have managed to guarantee peace and freedom on our continent. The transatlantic relationship must not become a casualty of the current Iraqi regime's persistent attempts to threaten world security.

124 |   In today's world, more than ever before, it is vital that we preserve that unity and cohesion. We know that success in the day-to-day battle against terrorism and the proliferation of weapons of mass destruction demands unwavering determination and firm international cohesion on the part of all countries for whom freedom is precious.

The Iraqi regime and its weapons of mass destruction represent a clear threat to world security. This danger has been explicitly recognised by the United Nations. All of us are bound by Security Council Resolution 1441, which was adopted unanimously. We Europeans have since reiterated our backing for Resolution 1441, our wish to pursue the UN route and our support for the Security Council, at the Prague NATO Summit and the Copenhagen European Council.

In doing so, we sent a clear, firm and unequivocal message that we would rid the world of the danger posed by Saddam Hussein's weapons of mass destruction. We must remain united in insisting that his regime is disarmed. The solidarity, cohesion and determination of the international community are our best hope of achieving this peacefully. Our strength lies in unity.

The combination of weapons of mass destruction and terrorism is a threat of incalculable consequences. It is one at which all of us should feel concerned. Resolution 1441 is Saddam Hussein's last chance to disarm using peaceful means. The opportunity to avoid greater confrontation rests with him. Sadly this week the UN weapons inspectors have confirmed that his long-established pattern of deception, denial and non-compliance with UN Security Council resolutions is continuing.

Europe has no quarrel with the Iraqi people. Indeed, they are the first victims of Iraq's current brutal regime. Our goal is to safeguard world peace and security by ensuring that this regime gives up its weapons of mass destruction. Our governments have a common responsibility to face this threat. Failure to do so would be nothing less than negligent to our own citizens and to the wider world.

The United Nations Charter charges the Security Council with the task of preserving international peace and security. To do so, the Security Council must maintain its credibility by ensuring full compliance with its resolutions. We cannot allow a dictator to systematically violate those Resolutions. If they are not complied with, the Security Council will lose its credibility and world peace will suffer as a result.

We are confident that the Security Council will face up to its responsibilities.

*José María Aznar, Spain*
*José Manuel Durão Barroso, Portugal*
*Silvio Berlusconi, Italy*
*Tony Blair, United Kingdom*
*Václav Havel, Czech Republic*
*Peter Medgyessy, Hungary*
*Leszek Miller, Poland*
*Anders Fogh Rasmussen, Denmark*

# DOCUMENT 3.3

Ten former Soviet states issued a statement on the day Colin Powell made his speech at the United Nations accusing Iraq of possessing weapons of mass destruction and of having links to terrorists (2.14). The Vilnius Statement was noticeably more strident than the Letter of Eight, endorsing the Bush administration's rationales for the war with Iraq and urging the Security Council to take immediate "necessary and appropriate action."

THE VILNIUS STATEMENT, FEBRUARY 6, 2003

Statement by the Foreign Ministers of Albania, Bulgaria, Croatia, Estonia, Latvia, Lithuania, Macedonia, Romania, Slovakia and Slovenia in response to the presentation by the United States Secretary of State to the United Nations Security Council concerning Iraq:

Earlier today, the United States presented compelling evidence to the United Nations Security Council detailing Iraq's weapons of mass destruction programs, its active efforts to deceive UN inspectors, and its links to international terrorism.

Our countries understand the dangers posed by tyranny and the special responsibility of democracies to defend our shared values. The trans-Atlantic community, of which we are a part, must stand together to face the threat posed by the nexus of terrorism and dictators with weapons of mass destruction.

We have actively supported the international efforts to achieve a peaceful disarmament of Iraq. However, it has now become clear that Iraq is in material breach of UN Security Council Resolutions, including UN Resolution 1441, passed unanimously on November 8, 2002. As our governments said on the occasion of the NATO Summit in Prague: "We support the goal of the international community for full disarmament of Iraq as stipulated in the UN Security Council Resolution 1441. In the event of non-compliance with the terms of this resolution, we are prepared to contribute to an international coalition to enforce its provisions and the disarmament of Iraq."

The clear and present danger posed by Saddam Hussein's regime requires a united response from the community of democracies. We call upon the UN Security Council to take the necessary and appropriate action in response to Iraq's continuing threat to international peace and security.

## DOCUMENT 3.4

The Non-Aligned Movement began organizing itself in 1955 and took shape in 1961 as an organization of less powerful states seeking to preserve their sovereignty and avoid siding with either the United States or the Soviet Union during the Cold War. Over the years, nearly all the countries in the developing world joined the NAM, which had 118 members in 2007. The NAM called for further debate and discussion on the impending war against Iraq and a session was held in mid-February 2003 before the Security Council. A number of UN member delegations urged that all peaceful measures be exhausted before resorting to war. Several states observed that the inspections had resumed only eleven weeks before and were already yielding positive results (2.16). Some Arab states noted that no evidence of weapons of mass destruction had been discovered in Iraq and that Israel possessed nuclear weapons but was not subject to sanctions. A number of delegates called on UN member states to respect the role of the United Nations as the proper venue for resolving the crisis.

SECURITY COUNCIL PRESS RELEASE SC/7666, "SECURITY
COUNCIL HEARS OVER 60 SPEAKERS IN TWO-DAY DEBATE
ON IRAQ'S DISARMAMENT: MANY SAY USE OF FORCE
SHOULD BE LAST RESORT, OTHERS URGE SWIFT ACTION,"
FEBRUARY 19, 2003 (EXCERPT)

As the Security Council today concluded its debate among non-members
on Iraq's disarmament, many speakers urged the Council to exhaust all
peaceful means before resorting to war, while others insisted that it be prepared to act swiftly and resolutely in the face of Iraq's non-compliance.

The debate, which heard from more than 60 speakers, in two days, was
called for by the Non-Aligned Movement and held in the wake of last Friday's briefing by the Executive Chairman of the United Nations Monitoring, Verification and Inspection Commission (UNMOVIC), Hans Blix, and
the Director-General of the International Atomic Energy Agency (IAEA),
Mohamed ElBaradei. They reported that Iraq's cooperation on procedural
matters had recently improved and they had not found any weapons of
mass destruction. They pointed out, however, that many banned weapons
remained unaccounted for, requiring Iraq's "immediate, unconditional and
active" cooperation. . . .

## Statements

NASSIR ABDULAZIZ AL-NASSER (Qatar) said he was concerned about
the dire unknown consequences in his region caused by the current Iraq
crisis. His country continued to support all efforts to achieve a peaceful solution to the crisis and to accept a formula that would save the Iraqi people.
Any new war would create a new catastrophe for Iraq and its immediate
neighbours, and might lead to a series of changes in geopolitical conditions.
Under the clouds of war, his country, as chair of the ninth Islamic Summit,
had called for an extraordinary summit meeting of the Organization of the
Islamic Conference. . . .

AHMED ABOUL GHEIT (Egypt) said that resolution 1441 (2002) had
been implemented satisfactorily. In turn, two briefings by the chief inspectors had described success in a very short period of time, and further success
was promised in the upcoming period. Iraq's compliance with resolution
1441 and other Council resolutions would lead the way out of a dark tun-
nel, which was now threatening to be transformed into a deep abyss. The
danger of weapons of mass destruction, however, was not confined to Iraq.
All tasks undertaken to disarm Iraq were steps towards ridding the Middle
East of those weapons. The credibility of international legality was not
served by eliminating the proscribed Iraqi weapons, while failing to apply
the same criteria to all other cases. . . .

BRUNO STAGNO (Costa Rica) said that his country had repeatedly demanded that Iraq comply with relevant Council resolutions. At this point,

the peaceful disarmament of Iraq would improve the situation in that region and improve the fate of the Iraqi people. He demanded full, immediate and proactive cooperation from Iraq with the United Nations inspectors. That country should also provide proof of the complete destruction of all its weapons. He was heartened by the inspectors' report regarding Iraq's growing cooperation this week. Since 27 November, when inspections resumed, tangible results had been achieved. It was necessary to fully trust and support the inspectors and give them time to carry out their tasks. The inspectors themselves should determine if the course of inspections had been exhausted. The United Nations Monitoring, Verification and Inspection Commission (UNMOVIC) should be provided with additional assistance and resources in order to enhance its effectiveness. He added that all States should provide the inspectors with intelligence information in their possession. It was essential to achieve peaceful disarmament. He called on Member States to explore all the alternatives before resorting to the use of force. While the Iraqi regime did not deserve another chance, the Iraqi people certainly did.

PIERRE HELG (Switzerland) said he did not think the moment for the use of force had come. His country was fully aware of the dangers inherent in the proliferation of weapons of mass destruction and did not underestimate the risk that such weapons could fall into the hands of international terrorists. It was, however, deeply concerned about the prevailing situation in the region and dreaded the consequences for the civilian population of a military operation. Switzerland had held a humanitarian meeting in Geneva concerning the fate of the civilian population affected by the impending crisis in Iraq, in which 30 countries and 20 humanitarian organizations had participated. He said participants in the meeting had acknowledged that an armed conflict in the region would very probably have grave consequences for the local civilian populations of Iraq and neighbouring countries. Against that background, the resort to force could only be envisaged after all peaceful means to find a solution to the crisis had been exhausted. The inspection regime could be strengthened. He also advocated giving the inspectors additional means to pursue their task with efficiency and speed. In any case, the use of force must be authorized by a Council resolution. He appealed to the Iraqi Government to act in the true interest of its country.

DARMANSJAH DJUMALA (Indonesia) said that the current situation, where the world seemed perched on the thin edge of war, was not hopeless and the objectives of resolution 1441 (2002) could still be met. There was nothing in the reports of UNMOVIC and the IAEA concluding that Iraq was, or was not, in violation of resolution 1441. Both reports had made clear, however, that the work of inspections was continuing according to plan and enjoying cooperation provided by Iraq. At present, that was as much as could be expected. Resolution 1441 was a finely structured text, which provided the disarmament scenario for Iraq and clearly outlined the consequences for default or violations. He said it was only right that, in formulating the next step, the inspectors and the results of their inspections must be taken into account. To authorize war without fulfilling that condition would amount to "preconceived warfare" and seriously undermine the Council's credibility. The problem might be the pace of inspections. Strengthening the inspections regime must be undertaken as a matter of urgency, including hastening the pace of the inspections. What was required, then, was the allocation of broader resources of time, manpower and equipment, in line with 1441. He acknowledged the cooperation provided so far by the Iraqi Government and hoped that would be extended fully and unwaveringly. Diplomacy had not been exhausted and war was not imminent. It was time to close ranks in the Security Council.

ZAINUDDIN YAHYA (Malaysia) favoured the continuation of inspections, as advocated by most Council members and other speakers in the debate. He supported the proposal by France on the need to increase the human and technical capacities of the inspection teams in accordance with resolution 1441, as well as their intention to request another meeting at the ministerial level on 14 March to appraise the situation and progress made. At the same time, the disarmament efforts must be a part of a clear, sanctions-lifting plan, he continued, so that the debilitating humanitarian crisis in Iraq could be brought to an immediate end. The success of the current exercise required the fullest cooperation by the Government of Iraq in every respect, and he welcomed their recent decision to issue a presidential decree containing prohibitions on importation and production of biological, chemical and nuclear weapons, as well as their acceptance of reconnaissance flights. Iraq must continue to cooperate with the inspectors and refrain from giving any pretext to warmongers. Malaysia, like many peace-loving nations, strongly opposed the use of force against Iraq, he said. The crisis could be solved through peaceful means, and the Council must continue to encourage diplomacy to resolve the problem through effective inspections and weapon destruction, as envisaged in resolution 1441. The use of force was more likely to undermine, than maintain or restore, international peace and security. A war on Iraq would have catastrophic consequences on that country's population. Also, there was no precedent in international law for the use of force as a preventive measure, when there had been no actual or imminent attack by the offending State. Massive anti-war rallies over the last few days represented clear testimony that the international community did not wish to support military action against Iraq. Many believed that there was still an alternative to war, and the use of force could only be a last resort.

FAWZI BIN ABDUL MAJEED SHOBOKSHI (Saudi Arabia) said that all reports on the situation bolstered the need for a peaceful solution and for more time for the inspectors. Whatever the reason for war, its results would be disastrous at all levels. By intensifying inspections and continuing political efforts—while stressing the need for Iraqi cooperation with inspectors, and the need to resolve the issue of missing Kuwaitis and other prisoners of war and returning Kuwaiti property—war could be avoided. The Council could not take lightly international objections to war and must urgently seek a peaceful solution. He called for a solution to the Iraqi issue through the implementation of Council resolutions, while maintaining the territorial integrity of Iraq. Even if all available options were exhausted, the extent of military action must be limited. Its intention must not be to punish the Iraqi people. He supported all efforts to destroy weapons of mass destruction in Iraq or in any other State. Israel, the only country in the Middle East with nuclear and prohibited weapons, had refused to subject itself to international oversight. The application of double standards was one of the reasons for violence and extremism in that region.

FELIPE H. PAOLILLO (Uruguay) said the Security Council had sent clear signals to Saddam Hussein's regime that the time for patience and tolerance had run out. The situation was now in another phase and if Iraq wished to avoid being the subject of a grave use of force, it must prove that it did not have banned weapons, or it must destroy them under the auspices of the United Nations. Before recourse to extreme measures of force and the resulting bloody costs of war, however, the international community must exhaust all remaining peaceful paths. Last week, the chief weapons inspectors had informed the Council that the inspections, which had resumed only 11 weeks ago, had already yielded positive results. He said the inspectors should be given more time to complete their extremely complex task. It was well known that Iraq, for 12 years, had been engaging in deceit and scoffing at the efforts of the international community. That could not be allowed to continue. Neither could the situation be "written off" without awaiting the results of the international action now under way. Doing so would have grave and irreversible consequences. War caused death and destruction, which was exactly what the international community sought to prevent by disarming Iraq. The inspections should be continued, expanded and strengthened decisively, so as to extricate Iraq from the position in which it had placed itself.

NDEKHEDEHE EFFIONG NDEKHEDEHE (Nigeria) said that in its painstaking efforts to find a peaceful solution to the issue of disarming Iraq, the Council had come up with a robust inspection regime encapsulated in resolution 1441 (2002). The collective will of the peace-loving Member States of the United Nations had been expressed through the collective wisdom of the Security Council in that unanimous resolution. For that reason, Nigeria had implicit hope in the ability of the Security Council to resolve, amicably, the Iraqi and any other situation that might pose a threat to international peace and security. From all accounts, the inspection teams had been doing wonderful work within a relatively short period of time, he said. Accordingly, Nigeria believed that the inspectors in Iraq must be given time to maximize their efforts and reach the optimum level of their goal. Resolution 1441 was aimed expressly and unequivocally at disarming Iraq peacefully of all chemical, biological and nuclear weapons. There was, therefore, a need to exercise patience with tenacity, as patience was a key ingredient for peace. He urged all concerned to make sustained efforts to avoid the use of force, while ensuring the effective implementation of resolution 1441.

AHMED A. OWN (Libya) said that a war against Iraq would have dire consequences for the Iraqi people, who had already suffered for a long time. It would also have a negative impact on the whole region. His country opposed the use of force in Iraq, as that country was now complying with the inspections and implementing resolution 1441. No proof of the presence or development of weapons of mass destruction in Iraq had been provided to the Council. The inspection process must run its full course, especially as inspections were running smoothly and effectively. It was the wish of the international community, as demonstrated by the debate in the Council and massive demonstrations all over the world. The haste of some countries to remove weapons of mass destruction by force, without any concrete evidence, raised serious questions in the minds of prudent and fair-minded people regarding the existence of a hidden agenda, he continued. While insisting on the implementation of resolutions against Iraq, the Council was turning a blind eye to the non-compliance of Israel. That country was not subjecting its nuclear facilities to the IAEA inspections. Its practices in the occupied territories included random killing of women, children and the elderly, destruction of homes and implementation of the policy of starvation against the Palestinian people. All that took place in the absence of action by the international community. The sense of injustice and double standards in the Middle East would lead to continued instability and jeopardize security all over the world. The international community must take seriously its responsibility in extinguishing hotbeds of tension, including in the Middle East, he said. He hoped a sense of wisdom would prevail. Given sufficient time, the inspections could achieve the goal of disarming Iraq and bringing an end to the suffering of the Iraqi people. The Middle East should become a nuclear-free zone, and all resolutions should be implemented, including those regarding Israel. The region should be saved from a war that would claim the lives of many innocent people. All peaceful means should be exhausted before resorting to war.

FERNANDO YÉPEZ LASSO (Ecuador) said his country was a peaceful country, basing its foreign policy on strict compliance with international law. It, therefore, defended conflict solution by peaceful means. It had always supported the jurisdiction of the Council over the maintenance of international peace and security. He, therefore, urged the Government of Iraq to extend its full cooperation in the effective implementation of resolution 1441 (2002). In that regard, the inspectors of the United Nations must continue their efforts until the process of a peaceful, transparent and verifiable disarmament of Iraq had been completed. He said the situation in Iraq must be handled in conformity with the norms of international law, particularly those contained in Chapter VII of the United Nations Charter. Only the Council, if circumstances warranted, could determine whether or not there were grounds for the use of force, through an explicit resolution outlining the conditions for such use. He warned that the international legal order established after the Second World War was being tested.

CHUCHAI KASEMSARN (Thailand) said he remained hopeful that the centrality of the United Nations in the search for a peaceful solution would continue as events unfolded. He renewed his plea to Iraq to immediately and unconditionally provide complete and proactive cooperation to UNMOVIC (United Nations Monitoring, Verification and Inspection Commission) and the IAEA. Iraq must demonstrate to the world that it was faithfully and completely fulfilling its international obligations under resolution 1441 (2002). Military conflict would have far-reaching consequences. The inevitable disruptions to the global economy would adversely affect the efforts of many nations to recover from financial crises and the recession. Of equal importance, he said, was the impact of military action on the Iraqi people. The Secretary-General's recent initiative to promote discussion with the Council on contingency planning to provide humanitarian assistance to the Iraqi people in the event of armed conflict correctly brought into focus the devastating humanitarian and economic consequences of war. Under any scenario, innocent people of Iraq would be among the first to suffer following an outbreak of armed conflict. It was incumbent upon Iraq, therefore, to be completely forthcoming with the United Nations inspectors, in order to avoid the even greater suffering of its people. The Council should take into account the concerns expressed by the wider United Nations membership and the calls to take the road of peace, by pressing forward on peaceful disarmament and resolving all outstanding issues.

SRGJAN KERIM (The former Yugoslav Republic of Macedonia) said that the debate in the Council and elsewhere did not signify disagreement on the purpose of full and unconditional compliance with resolution 1441, including the clause under which Iraq would face serious consequences if it continued violating its obligations. Although the chief inspectors had noted some progress, the prevailing attitude of the Iraqi regime of delaying and obstructing the inspections in substance had revealed an intention not to cooperate fully. It was not progress that the Council had asked for, but Iraq's full and unconditional compliance with resolution 1441. In addition to that, on 5 February, the United States had presented compelling evidence to the Council, detailing Iraq's weapons of mass destruction, its active efforts to deceive United Nations inspectors and its links to international terrorism. The international community must stand together to face the threat posed by the nexus of terrorism and dictators with weapons of mass destruction. His country had supported international efforts to achieve peaceful disarmament of Iraq, but now it had become clear that Iraq was in material breach of relevant resolutions, including 1441. Iraq must immediately, actively and fully cooperate with UNMOVIC and the IAEA and comply unconditionally with all the relevant resolutions. Maintaining pres-

sure on Iraq had proven to be the only mechanism capable of bringing about certain changes in its behaviour. . . .

AGIM NESHO (Albania) said that the debate about Iraq's cooperation to get rid of its weapons of mass destruction had taken on broad dimensions, and the international community had the responsibility to act in the interest of global peace and stability. The possession and production of weapons of mass destruction, and their potential use for terrorist acts, constituted a real threat for the world. By not immediately, actively and unconditionally cooperating with United Nations weapons inspectors, Iraq had failed to comply with resolution 1441. The issue was not whether Iraq had weapons of mass destruction, but whether it was cooperating to get rid of them. The inspections in Iraq could not go on endlessly because it would then weaken the importance of resolution 1441 and the credibility of the United Nations, he said. He urged the international community to be willing to act without wasting time, to give the necessary message of responsibility and determination for the preservation of international order. "Vain promises and empty rhetoric about peace do not avoid crime and secure peace", he stated.

ALISHER VOHIDOV (Uzbekistan) said the statement of United States Secretary of State Colin Powell on 5 February had provided sufficient and convincing arguments to confirm the correctness of the United States position to use more resolute and cardinal steps to make sure that Iraq possessed no weapons of mass destruction. . . .

ABDULLAH KHAMIS AL-SHAMSI (United Arab Emirates) said a major turning point in Iraq's fulfilment of its commitment to fully disarm itself of banned weapons had been reached. The important briefing by the chief inspectors on 27 January had clearly showed the extent of cooperation and progress by the Iraqi Government in facilitating the inspections. He welcomed the recent important steps taken by the Iraqi side, which had included unconditional cooperation to the inspectors and the opening of all sensitive sites, homes and official institutions. Iraq had also provided the necessary guarantees for UNMOVIC aircraft, as well as private interviews with Iraqi scientists, culminating with a presidential decree against the production and stockpiling of proscribed weapons. He said that those were unprecedented developments in Iraq's cooperation and should be invested in, rather than aborted through war. He had continuously called for the full elimination of Iraq's weapons of mass destruction, in order to avoid the grave consequences those might have on regional security, stability and development. A firm foundation of mutual confidence was needed between Iraq and the inspectors. In that connection, he called on the international community to strengthen the inspections regime and give them the necessary time to complete their mission in a way that respected the sovereignty and territorial integrity of Iraq. Actions should also be aimed at lifting the inhumane sanctions imposed on the Iraqi people. All unilateral non-peaceful

options should be set aside, as those might lead to a new war with grave consequences for the entire region.

MANUEL ACOSTA BONILLA (Honduras) said the United Nations must use all possible means to ensure that Iraq destroyed all weapons of mass destruction and would not be able to acquire them in the future. Such an objective required the United Nations inspectors to get all the needed material and technical support, so that they might determine either that Iraq's aggressive threat did not exist or that it was impossible to reach such a conclusion because of Iraq's lack of cooperation. In the latter case, the Council must take adequate measures to save humanity from criminal and genocidal actions. Hondurans wanted all governments of the world to support peace, the institution of the United Nations and human rights, he said. The dispute among governments because of different perception of facts must not sweep humankind to destruction. Iraq must accept absolutely its obligations to the rest of the world.

OLE PETER KOLBY (Norway) said that time had not run out. The use of force was not unavoidable, and everything must be done to achieve a peaceful solution. That required the immediate, active and unconditional cooperation of Iraq, as stated in resolution 1441 (2002). He was greatly concerned by the reports of the chief weapons inspectors, in particular that there had been no real breakthrough on substance. The UNMOVIC and the IAEA needed urgent answers to their highly important and legitimate questions, namely, what had happened to the weapons of mass destruction that remained unaccounted for? No one should have to beg for those answers. Iraq was required to provide them, and they should have been given long ago. . . .

PAUL HEINBECKER (Canada) said throughout the world people were making their voices heard: no one wanted a war. People were also aware of Iraqi mass violations of human rights and the fact that, equipped with weapons of mass destruction, Saddam Hussein was a threat to the region and to the world. There was no proof Iraq had rid itself of its weapons of mass destruction. On the contrary, there were still weapons of mass destruction unaccounted for. Resolution 1441 (2002) had given Iraq one last chance to answer remaining questions convincingly and to disarm itself. While there was a beginning of Iraqi cooperation, that cooperation was process oriented and given grudgingly, he said. Recent cooperation had only come after intense international pressure and a deliberate build-up of military forces in the region. More time for inspectors could be useful, but only if Iraq decided to cooperate fully and transparently, beginning now. To make clear to Iraq what was expected, the Council must lay out a list of key remaining disarmament tasks. The Council should also establish an early deadline for compliance. That would allow the international community to judge whether Iraq was cooperating on substance, and not just on process. He said the crisis was not only about weapons of mass destruction, but also about the people of Iraq. The humanitarian situation was already grave.

Canada applauded efforts of United Nations agencies and others to undertake preventive measures. He urged all members of the Council to keep the welfare of the Iraqi people at the heart of its deliberations. Canada was fully prepared to accept the judgement of the inspectors and the Council, and would assume its responsibilities accordingly.

HOUSSAM ASAAD DIAB (Lebanon) said that the inspections had not provided any evidence of the presence of weapons of mass destruction in Iraq, and any party of good faith could not but agree to let the inspectors complete their mandate under resolution 1441 (2002). The completion of that process was the only viable option under the Charter and provisions of international law. The overwhelming majority of Member States advocated a peaceful resolution of the crisis. Iraq had been forthcoming in its cooperation with the United Nations, and the latest report by the inspectors showed progress in that respect. While recognizing the cooperation by Iraq, he called on that country to show proactive cooperation with the inspectors. Continuing, he noted with deep regret the application of different criteria when Israel was concerned and called on the Council to ensure the removal of Israel's weapons of mass destruction, which posed a threat to international peace and security. That would render the whole region a nuclear-weapon-free zone, as mandated by relevant United Nations resolutions. All the resolutions should be implemented, in all their aspects. Launching war would put an end to the existing world order, he added. | 135 The war would have dire consequences for all Arab States, which continued to suffer as a result of war and continued Israeli occupation and the racist policies of Israel against the Palestinian people. It was necessary to be guided by the United Nations Charter and the will of the majority of Member States, in order to maintain international peace and security and avoid war.

MISHECK MUCHETWA (Zimbabwe) associated himself with the official position of the African Union that unilateral military action against Iraq would adversely affect Africa's stability and development. During the last few weeks, the Council had witnessed an assault on the principle of multilateralism by a determined and impatient ad hoc coalition, which believed might was right. The unilateralists conveniently forgot that "going it alone" lacked the legitimacy in addressing the challenge at hand. The role of the United Nations could not be overemphasized in the settlement of disputes and preservation of peace and security. Germany had reminded the Council that the sanctions regime imposed to encourage Iraq's compliance with its disarmament obligations had been more effective in ridding Iraq of its weapons of mass destruction than the Gulf war itself, he continued. The sanctions regime had been possible because of cooperation. It was clear that a Member State could engage in individual and collective measures of self-defence, even without the United Nations. As shown by the Iraq case, however, the Security Council's authority had assisted United States policy by adding the teeth of economic sanctions, extending a broad political umbrella, and authorizing on-site monitoring on a foreign State territory. . . .

CELESTINO MIGLIORE (Observer for the Holy See) said that the international community was rightly worried and was addressing a just and urgent cause of the disarmament of arsenals of mass destruction. The threat of weapons of mass destruction was, unfortunately, not restricted to just a single region, but was surfacing in other parts of the world. The Holy See was convinced that, in efforts to draw strength from the wealth of peaceful tools provided by international law, to resort to force would not be a just one. "To the grave consequences of a civilian population that has already been tested long enough are added the dark prospects of tensions and conflicts between peoples and cultures, and the deprecated reintroduction of war as a way to resolve untenable situations", he said. The Holy See was further convinced that even though the process of inspections appeared somewhat slow, it still remained an effective path that could lead to the building of a consensus, which, if widely shared by nations, would make it almost impossible for any government to act otherwise, without risking international isolation. He was thus of the view that it was also the proper path that would lead to an agreed and honourable resolution to the problem, which, in turn, could provide the basis for a real and lasting peace, he said. The vast majority of the international community was calling for a diplomatic resolution of the Iraqi crisis and for exploring all avenues for its peaceful settlement. That call should not be ignored, adding that the Holy See encouraged the parties concerned to keep the dialogue open.

MOHAMMED A. ALDOURI (Iraq) thanked all delegations that had shown such concern for the Iraqi crisis, especially the vast majority who had advocated peace and opposition to war. He also understood those States who favoured the extreme positions of the United States and the United Kingdom. He only called upon them to carefully consider the issue and not move hastily, as war was a grave moral responsibility. He reiterated there were no weapons of mass destruction in Iraq. Iraq would continue to cooperate constructively with the inspections, in substance and process, to disprove allegations that Iraq had such weapons. There were no real problems in the relationship with the inspectors. However, there were outstanding issues regarding disarmament. What was wanted from Iraq was not to hand over weapons of mass destruction, but hand over evidence that it was free of weapons of mass destruction. He was confident that no one would find weapons of mass destruction, because there were none. Iraq had opened all doors and allowed all it could allow. The inspectors just had to do their work in a measured way, away from pressures put upon them, either by the media or by the United States and the United Kingdom.

# DOCUMENT 3.5

A number of churches and religious organizations called for a peaceful solution to the crisis in Iraq. The World Council of Churches (WCC), an umbrella organization of 349 churches, fellowships, and denominations in 110 countries, represented some 560 million Christians in 2003 and included Methodist, Lutheran, Baptist, and other religious traditions. True to its long commitment to social reform and economic justice, the WCC registered its alarm at the mounting military preparations and argued that war against Iraq would be immoral, unwise, and a breach of the UN Charter. It also condemned the human rights violations of the Iraqi government under Saddam Hussein.

---

## WORLD COUNCIL OF CHURCHES, "STATEMENT AGAINST MILITARY ACTION IN IRAQ," FEBRUARY 21, 2003 (EXCERPT)

We believe God made us and all creation. God requires us to seek peace and justice. We believe that with God's grace no work of faith, hope and love is too hard for those who trust God. Therefore, as followers of Jesus Christ, the Prince of Peace, led by His Spirit, we call upon the leaders of the world and all people of faith:

### STOP the threats of war against Iraq!

The Executive Committee of the World Council of Churches, meeting in Bossey, Switzerland, 18–21 February 2003, remains extremely concerned with the continued calls for military action against Iraq by the U.S. and some western governments and strongly deplores the fact that the most powerful nations of this world again regard war as an acceptable instrument of foreign policy.

At the same time, the Executive Committee is equally concerned with the Iraqi violation of fundamental human rights and urges the government of Iraq to comply with international human rights norms and standards and with binding UN Security Council resolutions.

The Executive Committee welcomes the united and consistent message of heads of churches of every Christian tradition around the world against this war. The committee is extremely encouraged that churches are not only taking a leading position in preventing this war, but also preparing to avert a humanitarian catastrophe at the same time through preparedness to respond to the needs of innocent civilians in Iraq.

The Executive Committee affirms the courageous stance of church leaders for peaceful solutions, especially in countries like the USA and the UK in direct opposition to the positions taken by their political leadership.

The Executive Committee welcomes and appreciates the efforts of all church leaders and ecumenical organisations to mobilise public opinion to prevent war in Iraq and to pursue peace. It endorses wholeheartedly the statement adopted by church leaders at a meeting convened by the WCC, in Berlin, Germany, on 5th February 2003, to discuss a common response to the threat of military action against Iraq and expresses its appreciation to the Protestant Church in Germany for hosting the event and arranging a hearing with Germany's Head of Government. It further recognises the recent meetings of U.S. church leaders with government leaders in the UK and France.

Bearing in mind the reality that the 1991 Gulf War did not bring peace to the Iraqi people, but severe suffering under 12 years of economic sanctions; noting the recent developments relating to possible military action in Iraq and the report presented by the United Nations Weapons Inspectors to the UN Security Council on the 14th February; and the mounting public opinion against a war in Iraq evidenced by the turnout of millions of people all over the world who gathered in peace rallies; and

Taking into account that action of the WCC and churches must:

- be guided by the moral obligation to ensure sanctity of life and the ethical conviction that war is not an acceptable way to resolve conflicts,
- follow the need to promote public and international support for the UN as custodian of lawful action regarding Iraq,
- understand that the carefully designed mechanism of the UN weapons inspections is a long term tool and that 20 years of inspections are more effective, less costly and more relevant than 20 days of war,
- recognise the necessity not only to disarm Iraq, but also make the whole Middle East region free from weapons of mass destruction,
- acknowledge the negative impact on Christian-Muslim relations and increased emigration of Christians from the region where Christianity was born,
- highlight the need for a durable and just solution of the Arab-Israeli conflicts, and an end of the illegal occupation of Palestine,
- promote democratisation and compliance with global human rights norms and standards in all Arab countries as well as in Israel.

Recalling the "statement on the threats of military actions against Iraq" by the Central Committee of the World Council of Churches meeting in Geneva 26 August to 3 September 2002; and

Reaffirming that the war against Iraq would be immoral, unwise and in breach of the principles of the UN Charter, the Executive Committee:

- *warns* that war in Iraq will cause a humanitarian crisis of grave magnitude with untold human suffering, especially for the children of Iraq, loss of life, property, environmental destruction and waste of precious resources; it will reinforce and polarise division and hatred between communities resulting in further destabilisation of the region;

- *strongly appeals* to the UN Security Council to uphold the principles of the UN Charter which strictly limit the legitimate use of military force and to refrain from creating negative precedents and lowering the threshold for using violent means to solve international conflicts;
- *further appeals* to the political leaders of the U.S. and the UK to refrain from a unilateral pre-emptive military action against Iraq;
- *calls insistently on* the member nations of the UN Security Council to adequately reinforce and allow reasonable time to UN weapons inspectors to successfully fulfil their mandate to disarm and destroy Iraq's weapons of mass destruction;
- *strongly urges* the government of Iraq to fully cooperate with UN weapons inspectors to ensure that weapons of mass destruction, related research and production facilities are completely destroyed;
- *condemns* the Iraqi government's violations of fundamental rights and freedoms in Iraq and *urges its leadership* to guarantee full respect of the civil and political, economic, social and cultural human rights, including religious rights, of all its citizens;
- *encourages* the churches to continue to challenge and expose any national security policies that promote pre-emptive military strikes as legitimate self-defence undermining the principles and the spirit of the UN Charter;
- *calls on* all churches to intensify further their engagement in efforts for peace; and in turn commends the February 5th Berlin Statement to churches calling them to join this act of witness for a peaceful resolution of this conflict;
- *invites* faithful men, women and children everywhere to engage in earnest prayers that leaders of the nations may be directed along the path to seek peaceful resolution of the conflict in Iraq.
- *proposes* the first day of Lent 2003, a day for reflection and conversion, to be a day of prayer for peace in Iraq in all member churches and worldwide.

# DOCUMENT 3.6

The Non-aligned Movement historically took strong stands against colonialism and neocolonialism, intervention, and racism, and worked to better the economic prospects of less-developed countries. It organized itself as an internal democracy, with a rotating chair, decisions by consensus, and no permanent infrastructure. Its grave concerns about the looming war in Iraq were the direct result of its long opposition to Great Power militarism.

## STATEMENT OF THE NON-ALIGNED MOVEMENT
## ON THE SITUATION IN IRAQ, FEBRUARY 25, 2003

We, the Heads of State or Government of the Non-Aligned Movement, meeting in Kuala Lumpur from 24–25 February 2003, considered with grave concern the precarious and rapidly deteriorating situation arising from the looming threat of war against Iraq.

We are fully cognisant of the concerns expressed by millions in our countries, as well as in other parts of the world, who reject war and believe, like we do, that war against Iraq will be a destabilising factor for the whole region, and that it would have far reaching political, economic and humanitarian consequences for all countries of the world, particularly the States in the region.

We reiterate our commitment to the fundamental principles of the non-use of force and respect for the sovereignty, territorial integrity, political independence and security of all Member States of the United Nations.

We reaffirm our commitment to exert our efforts to achieve a peaceful solution to the current situation. We welcome and support all other efforts exerted to avert war against Iraq and call for the persistent continuation of such efforts based on multilateral as opposed to unilateral actions, and reaffirm the central role of the United Nations and the Security Council in maintaining international peace and security.

We welcome the decision by Iraq to facilitate the unconditional return of, and cooperation with, United Nations inspectors in accordance with Security Council Resolution 1441, which will assure the world in a peaceful way that weapons of mass destruction are eliminated in Iraq.

We call on Iraq to continue to actively comply with Security Council Resolution 1441 and all other relevant Security Council resolutions and to remain engaged in the process. We believe this would be an important step opening the way to a comprehensive and peaceful resolution of all pending issues between Iraq and the United Nations that takes into account the concerns of all affected parties, including Iraq's neighbours.

We stress that the current disarmament efforts in Iraq should not be an end in itself but should also constitute a step towards the lifting of sanctions in accordance with Security Council Resolution 687.

We believe that the peaceful resolution of the Iraqi crisis would ensure that the Security Council will also be in a position to ensure Iraq's sovereignty and the inviolability of its territorial integrity, political independence and security, and compliance with Paragraph 14 of its Resolution 687 on the establishment in the Middle East of a weapons of mass destruction-free zone, which includes Israel.

# DOCUMENT 3.7

In March 2003, a British translator at the Government Communications Head-quarters, a British intelligence agency, leaked a key document to the British newspaper the *Observer.* Katherine Gun had received a National Security Agency memo with details of a covert plan by the U.S. and British governments to spy on members of the Security Council and wiretap their offices and homes before the key vote on Iraq, a surveillance program illegal under the Vienna Conventions governing international diplomacy. The votes of the targeted delegations in the Security Council would determine whether the Bush administration and its allies would win UN approval of an invasion of Iraq. After leaking the document, Gun was fired from her position and later charged under the British Official Secrets Act for passing classified information to unauthorized persons. The case was dropped in 2004.

LEAKED MEMO FROM NATIONAL SECURITY AGENCY
OFFICIAL ASKING FOR COOPERATION IN SURVEILLANCE
OF UNITED NATIONS DELEGATES, MARCH 2, 2003 (EXCERPT)

Sunday March 2, 2003
To: [Recipients withheld]
From: FRANK KOZA, Def Chief of Staff (Regional Targets)
CIV/NSA
Sent on Jan 31 2003 0:16
Subject: Reflections of Iraq Debate/Votes at UN-RT Actions + Potential for Related Contributions
Importance: HIGH
Top Secret//COMINT//X1
All,
    As you've likely heard by now, the Agency is mounting a surge particularly directed at the UN Security Council (UNSC) members (minus U.S. and GBR [*Editors' Note: The United States and Great Britain*] of course) for insights as to how membership is reacting to the on-going debate RE: Iraq, plans to vote on any related resolutions, what related policies/negotiating positions they may be considering, alliances/dependencies, etc—the whole gamut of information that could give U.S. policymakers an edge in obtaining results favorable to U.S. goals or to head off surprises. . . . that means a QRC surge effort[10] to revive/create efforts against UNSC members Angola,

---

10. The term "QRC surge effort" is NSA-military language for a significant intensification of surveillance operations. It is used in U.S. Army documents to refer to the U.S. Army's Quick Reaction Capability (QRC) in SIGINT (signals intelligence) operations. An Army field manual on intelligence (U.S. Army, Field Manual 2–0, 2004, chapter 8, "Signals Intelligence," at https://rdl.train.army.mil/

Cameroon, Chile, Bulgaria and Guinea, as well as extra focus on Pakistan UN matters. . . . We'd appreciate your support in getting the word to your analysts who might have similar, more in-direct access to valuable information from accesses in your product lines. I suspect that you'll be hearing more along these lines in formal channels—especially as this effort will probably peak (at least for this specific focus) in the middle of next week, following the SecState's presentation to the UNSC.

# DOCUMENT 3.8

France, Germany, and Russia took a leading role in resisting the forceful pro-war effort led by the Bush administration. Their joint statement noted that new inspections were producing significant results and that military action was not yet warranted, and they announced their decision to oppose any Security Council resolution authorizing preemptive war.

DECLARATION OF RUSSIA, GERMANY, AND FRANCE ON WAR WITH IRAQ, MARCH 5, 2003

Our common objective remains the full and effective disarmament of Iraq, in compliance with Resolution 1441. We consider that this objective can be achieved by the peaceful means of the inspections. We moreover observe that these inspections are producing increasingly encouraging results:

- The destruction of the Al-Samoud missiles has started and is making progress,
- Iraqis are providing biological and chemical information,
- The interviews with Iraqi scientists are continuing.

Russia, Germany and France resolutely support Messrs Blix and El-Baradei and consider the meeting of the Council on 7 March to be an important step in the process put in place. We firmly call for the Iraqi authorities to co-operate more actively with the inspectors to fully disarm their country. These inspections cannot continue indefinitely. We consequently

---

soldierPortal/atia/adlsc/view/public/10536–1/FM/2–0/chap8.htm;jsessionid=RlynJzFNhrXxgrvQ941 GV6gdyKj1TNVhhkGHwQq1ygwGgTzypfpf!356750119) states "8–8. The Army Technical Control and Analysis Element supports the Army's Quick Reaction Capability (QRC) SIGINT and signals research and target development operations. The QRC systems are responsive to the ground force commander's requirements and allow the ability to conduct SIGINT operations against modern communications systems." It is likely that the NSA and the Army collaborated in this "surge effort," deploying sophisticated intelligence resources to spy on UN delegations for political reasons.

ask that the inspections now be speeded up, in keeping with the proposals put forward in the memorandum submitted to the Security Council by our three countries. We must:

- Specify and prioritise the remaining issues, programme by programme,
- Establish, for each point, detailed timelines.

Using this method, the inspectors have to present without any delay their work programme accompanied by regular progress reports to the Security Council. This programme could provide for a meeting clause to enable the Council to evaluate the overall results of this process.

In these circumstances, we will not let a proposed resolution pass that would authorise the use of force. Russia and France, as permanent members of the Security Council, will assume all their responsibilities on this point.

We are at a turning point. Since our goal is the peaceful and full disarmament of Iraq, we have today the chance to obtain through peaceful means a comprehensive settlement for the Middle-East, starting with a move forward in the peace process, by:

- Publishing and implementing the roadmap;
- Putting together a general framework for the Middle-East, based on stability and security, renunciation of force, arms control and trust building measures.

# DOCUMENT 3.9

The Security Council's rejection of the U.S.-backed resolution—essentially an ultimatum demanding that Iraq surrender weapons of mass destruction by March 17 or face military consequences—signaled that Washington, London, and Madrid had failed in their effort to win international support for an invasion. As a result, the policy of preemptive war stood in direct contradiction to the will of the international community as expressed in the United Nations.

SPAIN, UNITED KINGDOM OF GREAT BRITAIN AND
NORTHERN IRELAND, AND UNITED STATES OF AMERICA:
DRAFT RESOLUTION TO SECURITY COUNCIL, MARCH 7, 2003

The Security Council,
Recalling all its previous relevant resolutions, in particular its resolutions
661 (1990) of August 1990, 678 (1990) of 29 November 1990, 686 (1991)

of 2 March 1991, 687 (1991) of 3 April 1991, 688 (1991) of 5 April 1991, 707 (1991) of 15 August 1991, 715 (1991) of 11 October 1991, 986 (1995) of 14 April 1995, 1284 (1999) of 17 December 1999 and 1441 (2002) of 8 November 2002, and all the relevant statements of its President,

Recalling that in its resolution 687 (1991) the Council declared that a ceasefire would be based on acceptance by Iraq of the provisions of that resolution, including the obligations on Iraq contained therein,

Recalling that its resolution 1441 (2002), while deciding that Iraq has been and remains in material breach of its obligations, afforded Iraq a final opportunity to comply with its disarmament obligations under relevant resolutions,

Recalling that in its resolution 1441 (2002) the Council decided that false statements or omissions in the declaration submitted by Iraq pursuant to that resolution and failure by Iraq at any time to comply with, and cooperate fully in the implementation of, that resolution, would constitute a further material breach,

Noting, in that context, that in its resolution 1441 (2002), the Council recalled that it has repeatedly warned Iraq that it will face serious consequences as a result of its continued violations of its obligations,

Noting that Iraq has submitted a declaration pursuant to its resolution 1441 (2002) containing false statements and omissions and has failed to comply with, and cooperate fully in the implementation of, that resolution,

Reaffirming the commitment of all Member States to the sovereignty and territorial integrity of Iraq, Kuwait, and the neighbouring States,

Mindful of its primary responsibility under the Charter of the United Nations for the maintenance of international peace and security,

Recognizing the threat Iraq's non-compliance with Council resolutions and proliferation of weapons of mass destruction and long-range missiles poses to international peace and security,

Determined to secure full compliance with its decisions and to restore international peace and security in the area,

Acting under Chapter VII of the Charter of the United Nations,

1. Reaffirms the need for full implementation of resolution 1441 (2002);

2. Calls on Iraq immediately to take the decisions necessary in the interests of its people and the region;

3. Decides that Iraq will have failed to take the final opportunity afforded by resolution 1441 (2002) unless, on or before 17 March 2003, the Council concludes that Iraq has demonstrated full, unconditional, immediate and active cooperation in accordance with its disarmament obligations under resolution 1441 (2002) and previous relevant resolutions, and is yielding possession to UNMOVIC and the IAEA of all weapons, weapon delivery and support systems and structures, prohibited by resolution 687

(1991) and all subsequent relevant resolutions, and all information regarding prior destruction of such items;
4. Decides to remain seized of the matter.

# DOCUMENT 3.10

As it became clear that the international community could not prevent the war
that all knew was coming, Secretary General Kofi Annan expressed his sorrow
and resignation, saying he had withdrawn the weapons inspectors and other
UN personnel from Iraq after Washington had advised him that they would no
longer be safe there. The secretary general noted that the humanitarian consequences of the war would be severe and that the legitimacy of any invasion
not approved by the Security Council would be subject to question.

UNITED NATIONS NEWS CENTRE, NEW YORK—"PRESS
ENCOUNTER WITH THE SECRETARY-GENERAL AT THE
SECURITY COUNCIL STAKEOUT," MARCH 17, 2003 (EXCERPT)

**SG:** Good morning, ladies and gentlemen.                                    | 145
    I've just come out of a [Security] Council meeting where we dis-
cussed the situation in Iraq. Obviously the members of the Council who
had hoped for a long time that it ought to be possible to disarm Iraq
peacefully and had hoped to be able to come up with a common position, are today disappointed and frustrated and are worried that they
were not able to muster the collective will to find a common basis to
move ahead. And obviously, we seem to be at the end of the road here.
    Yesterday UNMOVIC, the [International] Atomic [Energy] Agency
and myself got information from the United States authorities that it
would be prudent not to leave our staff in the region. I have just informed the Council that we will withdraw the UNMOVIC and Atomic
Agency inspectors, we will withdraw the UN humanitarian workers, we
will withdraw the UNIKOM [*Editors' Note: United Nations Iraq/Kuwait Observer Mission*] troops on the Iraqi-Kuwaiti border who are also not able
to operate. The implication of these withdrawals will mean that the
mandates will be suspended because it will be inoperable. We can not,
for example, handle the Oil for Food when we do not have inspectors to
monitor the imports, we do not have oil inspectors who will monitor exports of oil, and we don't have the humanitarian personnel who will
monitor the distribution, receipt and distribution of the food supply. So,
I have informed the Council of these suspensions.
    This does not mean that, should war come to Iraq, the UN will sit
back and not do anything to help the Iraqi population. We will find a

way of resuming our humanitarian activities to help the Iraqi people who have suffered for so long and do whatever we can to give them assistance and support. And as you know we have undertaken major contingency planning to be able to move forward as soon as we can.

**Q:** Did you get an authorization from the Security Council to withdraw these inspectors or did you use the measures you have available to you, temporary relocation of the inspectors?

**SG:** It is relocation of the inspectors, and the Council has taken note of my decision.

**Q:** Should the United States go ahead and its allies and use military action against Iraq without UN Security Council authorization, would that be in violation of international law according to you?

**SG:** I think my position on that is very clear. The Council will have to discuss that also.

**Q:** Do you believe part of 1441, is it legal or not legal?

**SG:** I think I have made my position very clear on that and I have indicated to you that if . . . let's have a bit of order and calm here. . . . I have made it very clear that in my judgment if the Council were to be able to manage this process successfully and most of the collective will to handle this operation, its own reputation and credibility would have been enhanced. And I have also said if the action is to take place without the support of the Council, its legitimacy will be questioned and the support for it will be diminished. . . .

**Q:** Is today a very sad day for the UN and for the world?

**SG:** I think almost every government and peoples around the world had hoped that this issue can be resolved peacefully. In the sense that we are not able to do it peacefully, obviously it is a disappointment and a sad day for everybody. War is always a catastrophe—it leads to major human tragedy, lots of people are going to be uprooted, displaced from their homes and nobody wanted that. And this is why we had hoped that the Iraqi leadership would have cooperated fully and would have been able to do this without resort to use of force. But the little window that we seem to have, seems to be closing very, very fast. I'm not sure at this stage the Council can do anything in the next couple of hours.

**Q:** Dr. Blix and [El] Baradei have also been invited, would you fly to Baghdad?

**SG:** I have no plans to fly to Baghdad today.

**Q:** If there is military action, then what happens?

**SG:** Well if there is military action, the Council of course will have to meet to discuss what happens after that. I think I have made it clear that regardless of how this current issue is resolved, the Security Council is going to have a role to play. And I think that was also implied in the communiqué that came out of the Azores. That the UN has an important role to play in the post-conflict Iraq and the Council will have to discuss that. The Council will have to give me a mandate for some of the activities that we will need to undertake. And so this does not mean an end of involvement of the UN in the Iraqi situation. Thank you very much.

## DOCUMENT 3.11

The British prime minister Tony Blair was one of the Bush administration's staunchest allies and strongest supporters of its policy of regime change. When he addressed the British Parliament to make the case that war with Iraq was both necessary and urgent, Blair paid particular attention to the "special partnership" between the United States and Britain. Arguing that France's position was misguided, he asserted that the threat of force was the only thing that motivated Saddam Hussein to respond. He insisted that Saddam Hussein still possessed weapons of mass destruction, despite UN weapons inspectors' recent reports to the contrary (2.16).

TONY BLAIR, STATEMENT BEFORE PARLIAMENT,
MARCH 18, 2003 (EXCERPT)

This is a tough choice. But it is also a stark one: to stand British troops down and turn back; or to hold firm to the course we have set. I believe we must hold firm.

The question most often posed is not why does it matter? But: why does it matter so much? Here we are: the government with its most serious test, its majority at risk, the first Cabinet resignation over an issue of policy. The main parties divided. People who agree on everything else, disagree on this and likewise, those who never agree on anything, finding common cause.

The country and Parliament reflect each other: a debate that, as time has gone on has become less bitter but not less grave. So: why does it matter so much?

Because the outcome of this issue will now determine more than the fate of the Iraqi regime and more than the future of the Iraqi people, for so long brutalised by Saddam. It will determine the way Britain and the world confront the central security threat of the twenty-first century; the development of the UN; the relationship between Europe and the U.S.; the relations within the EU and the way the U.S. engages with the rest of the world. It will determine the pattern of international politics for the next generation.

But first, Iraq and its WMD. In April 1991, after the Gulf War, Iraq was given fifteen days to provide a full and final declaration of all its WMD. Saddam had used the weapons against Iran, against his own people, causing thousands of deaths. He had had plans to use them against allied forces.

It became clear after the Gulf War that the WMD ambitions of Iraq were far more extensive than hitherto thought. This issue was identified by the UN as one for urgent remedy. UNSCOM, the weapons inspection team, was set up [*Editors' Note: UNSCOM is United Nations Special Commission*]. They were expected to complete their task following the declaration at the end of April 1991. . . .

When the inspectors left in 1998, they left unaccounted for:

- ten thousand litres of anthrax
- a far-reaching VX nerve agent programme
- up to 6,500 chemical munitions
- at least 80 tonnes of mustard gas, possibly more than ten times that amount
- unquantifiable amounts of sarin, botulinum toxin, and a host of other biological poisons
- an entire Scud missile programme

We are now seriously asked to accept that in the last few years, contrary to all history, contrary to all intelligence, he decided unilaterally to destroy the weapons. Such a claim is palpably absurd.

1441 is a very clear resolution. It lays down a final opportunity for Saddam to disarm. It rehearses the fact that he has been, for years in material breach of seventeen separate UN resolutions.

It says that this time compliance must be full, unconditional, and immediate. The first step is a full and final declaration of all WMD to be given on 8 December. . . .

Last Friday, France said they could not accept any ultimatum. On Monday, we made final efforts to secure agreement. But they remain utterly opposed to anything which lays down an ultimatum authorising action in the event of non-compliance by Saddam. Just consider the position we are asked to adopt. Those on the Security Council opposed to us say they want Saddam to disarm but will not countenance any new Resolution that authorises force in the event of non-compliance. That is their position. No to any ultimatum; no to any Resolution that stipulates that failure to comply will lead to military action. So we must demand he disarm but relinquish any concept of a threat if he doesn't. From December 1998 to December 2002, no UN inspector was allowed to inspect anything in Iraq. For four years, not a thing. What changed his mind? The threat of force. From December to January and then from January through to February, concessions were made. What changed his mind? The threat of force. . . .

Our fault has not been impatience. The truth is our patience should have been exhausted weeks and months and years ago. Even now, when if the world united and gave [Saddam] an ultimatum: comply or face forcible disarmament, he might just do it, the world hesitates and in that hesitation he senses the weakness and therefore continues to defy. What would any tyrannical regime possessing WMD think viewing the history of the world's diplomatic dance with Saddam? That our capacity to pass firm resolutions is only matched by our feebleness in implementing them. That is why this indulgence has to stop. Because it is dangerous. It is dangerous if such regimes disbelieve us. Dangerous if they think they can use our weakness, our hesitation, even the natural urges of our democracy towards peace, against us. Dangerous because one day they will mistake our innate revulsion against war for permanent incapacity; when in fact, pushed to the limit, we will act. But then when we act, after years of pretence, the action will have to be harder, bigger, more total in its impact. Iraq is not the only regime with WMD. But back away now from this confrontation and future conflicts will be infinitely worse and more devastating.

But, of course, in a sense, any fair observer does not really dispute that Iraq is in breach and that 1441 implies action in such circumstances. The real problem is that, underneath, people dispute that Iraq is a threat; dispute the link between terrorism and WMD; dispute the whole basis of our assertion that the two together constitute a fundamental assault on our way of life. . . .

11 September has changed the psychology of America. It should have changed the psychology of the world. Of course Iraq is not the only part of this threat. But it is the test of whether we treat the threat seriously. Faced with it, the world should unite. The UN should be the focus, both of diplomacy and of action. That is what 1441 said. That was the deal. And I say to you to break it now, to will the ends but not the means that would do more damage in the long term to the UN than any other course. To fall back into the lassitude of the last twelve years, to talk, to discuss, to debate but never act; to declare our will but not enforce it; to combine strong language with weak intentions, a worse outcome than never speaking at all. And then, when the threat returns from Iraq or elsewhere, who will believe us? What price our credibility with the next tyrant? No wonder Japan and South Korea, next to North Korea, has issued such strong statements of support. I have come to the conclusion after much reluctance that the greater danger to the UN is inaction: that to pass Resolution 1441 and then refuse to enforce it would do the most deadly damage to the UN's future strength, confirming it as an instrument of diplomacy but not of action, forcing nations down the very unilateralist path we wish to avoid.

But there will be, in any event, no sound future for the UN, no guarantee against the repetition of these events, unless we recognise the urgent need for a political agenda we can unite upon.

What we have witnessed is indeed the consequence of Europe and the United States dividing from each other. Not all of Europe—Spain, Italy, Holland, Denmark, Portugal—have all strongly supported us. And not a majority of Europe if we include, as we should, Europe's new members who will accede next year, all ten of whom have been in our support.

But the paralysis of the UN has been born out of the division there is. And at the heart of it has been the concept of a world in which there are rival poles of power. The U.S. and its allies in one corner. France, Germany,

Russia and its allies in the other. I do not believe that all of these nations intend such an outcome. But that is what now faces us.

I believe such a vision to be misguided and profoundly dangerous. I know why it arises. There is resentment of U.S. predominance. There is fear of U.S. unilateralism. People ask: does the U.S. listen to us and our pre-occupations? And there is perhaps a lack of full understanding of U.S. pre-occupations after 11th September. I know all of this.

But the way to deal with it is not rivalry but partnership. Partners are not servants but neither are they rivals. I tell you what Europe should have said last September to the U.S. With one voice it should have said: we understand your strategic anxiety over terrorism and WMD and we will help you meet it. We will mean what we say in any UN Resolution we pass and will back it with action if Saddam fails to disarm voluntarily; but in return we ask two things of you: that the U.S. should choose the UN path and you should recognise the fundamental overriding importance of re-starting the MEPP [*Editors' Note: Middle East peace process*], which we will hold you to.

I do not believe there is any other issue with the same power to re-unite the world community than progress on the issues of Israel and Palestine. Of course there is cynicism about recent announcements. But the U.S. is now committed, and, I believe genuinely, to the Roadmap for peace, designed in consultation with the UN. It will now be presented to the parties as Abu Mazen is confirmed in office, hopefully today. All of us are now signed up to its vision: a state of Israel, recognised and accepted by all the world, and a viable Palestinian state.

And that should be part of a larger global agenda. On poverty and sustainable development. On democracy and human rights. On the good governance of nations. That is why what happens after any conflict in Iraq is of such critical significance.

Here again there is a chance to unify around the UN. Let me make it clear. There should be a new UN Resolution following any conflict providing not just for humanitarian help but also for the administration and governance of Iraq. That must now be done under proper UN authorisation. It should protect totally the territorial integrity of Iraq. And let the oil revenues—which people falsely claim we want to seize—be put in a trust fund for the Iraqi people administered through the UN. And let the future government of Iraq be given the chance to begin the process of uniting the nation's disparate groups, on a democratic basis, respecting human rights, as indeed the fledgling democracy in Northern Iraq—protected from Saddam for twelve years by British and American pilots in the No Fly Zone—has done so remarkably.

And the moment that a new government is in place—willing to disarm Iraq of WMD—for which its people have no need or purpose—then let sanctions be lifted in their entirety. I have never put our justification for action as regime change. We have to act within the terms set out in Resolution 1441. That is our legal base. But it is the reason, I say frankly, why if we do act we should do so with a clear conscience and strong heart.

150 |

# DOCUMENT 3.12

As the date specified in the Bush administration's ultimatum to Iraq passed, the French foreign minister spoke before the Security Council to make a last-ditch plea for a peaceful solution to the conflict, lamenting the fact that the inspections, recently restarted, had been cut short. Villepin portrayed the choice between peace and war as between two diametrically opposed visions of the world.

---

DOMINIQUE DE VILLEPIN, ADDRESS BEFORE THE UNITED NATIONS SECURITY COUNCIL, MARCH 19, 2003 (EXCERPT)

We are meeting here today a few hours before the weapons sound. To exchange our convictions again in observance of our respective commitments. But also to outline together the paths that must allow us to recover the spirit of unity. I wish to reiterate here that for France war can only be the exception, and collective responsibility the rule. Whatever our aversion for Saddam Hussein's cruel regime, that holds true for Iraq and for all the crises that we will have to confront together. . . .

| 151

1– To Mr. Blix, who presented his work program to us, and Mr. El Baradei, who was represented today, I want to say thank you for the sustained efforts and results achieved. Their program is a reminder that there is still a clear and credible prospect for disarming Iraq peacefully. It proposes and prioritizes the tasks for such disarmament and presents a realistic timetable for their implementation.

   In doing so the report confirms what we all know here: Yes, the inspections are producing tangible results. Yes, they offer the prospect of effective disarmament through peaceful means and in shorter timeframes. The path we mapped out together in the context of resolution 1441 still exists. In spite of the fact that it has been interrupted today, we know that it will have to resume as soon as possible.

   The Council took note two days ago of the Secretary-General's decision to withdraw the inspectors and all UN personnel from Iraq. The discharge of their mandates has consequently been suspended. It will be necessary when the time comes to complete our knowledge about Iraq's programs and finish disarming Iraq. The contribution of the inspectors will be decisive at that time.

2– Make no mistake about it: the choice is indeed between two visions of the world.

   To those who choose to use force and think they can resolve the world's complexity through swift and preventive action, we offer in contrast determined action over time. For today, to ensure our security, all the dimensions of the problem must be taken into account: both the manifold crises and their many facets, including cultural and religious. Nothing lasting in international relations can be built therefore without dialogue and respect for the other, without exigency and abiding by principles, especially for the democracies that must set the example. To ignore this is to run the risk of misunderstanding, radicalization, and spiraling violence. This is even more true in the Middle East, an area of fractures and ancient conflicts where stability must be a major objective for us.

To those who hope to eliminate the dangers of proliferation through armed intervention in Iraq, I wish to say that we regret that they are depriving themselves of a key tool for other crises of the same type. The Iraq crisis allowed us to craft an instrument, through the inspections regime, which is unprecedented and can serve as an example. Why, on this basis not envision establishing an innovative, permanent structure, a disarmament body under the United Nations?

To those who think that the scourge of terrorism will be eradicated through the case of Iraq, we say they run the risk of failing in their objectives. The outbreak of force in this area which is so unstable can only exacerbate the tensions and fractures on which the terrorists feed.

3– Over and above our division, we have a collective responsibility in the face of these threats, the responsibility to recover the unity of the international community. The United Nations must remain mobilized in Iraq to aid this objective. Together, we have duties to assume in this perspective.

- First of all, to staunch the wounds of war. As always, war brings with it its share of victims, suffering, and displaced people. So it is a matter of urgency to prepare now to provide the requisite humanitarian assistance. This imperative must prevail over our differences. The Secretary-General has already begun to mobilize the various UN agencies to this end. France will take its full part in the collective effort to assist the Iraqi people. The oil-for-food program must be continued under the authority of the Security Council with the necessary adjustments. We are waiting for the Secretary-General's proposals.

- Next, it is necessary to build peace. No country by itself has the means to build Iraq's future. In particular, no state can claim the necessary legitimacy. It is from the United Nations alone that the legal and moral authority can come for such an undertaking. Two principles must guide our action: respect for the unity and territorial integrity of Iraq; and the preservation of its sovereignty.

- By the same token, it is for the United Nations to set out the framework for the country's economic reconstruction. A framework that will have to affirm the two complementary principles of transparency and development of the country's resources for the benefit of the Iraqis themselves.

4– Our mobilization must also extend to the other threats that we have to address together.

Given the very nature of these threats, it is no longer possible today to address them in any old order. By way of example, terrorism is fueled by organized crime networks; it cleaves to the contours of lawless areas; it thrives on regional crises; it garners support from the divisions in the world; it utilizes all available resources, from the most rudimentary to the most sophisticated, from the knife to the weapons of mass destruction it is trying to acquire.

To deal with this reality, we must act in a united way and on all fronts at the same time.

5– So we must remain constantly mobilized.

In this spirit France renews its call for the heads of state and government to meet here in the Security Council to respond to the major challenges confronting us.

Let us intensify our fight against terrorism. Let us fight mercilessly against its networks with all the economic, juridical, and political weapons available to us.

Let us give new impetus to the fight against the proliferation of weapons of mass destruction. France has already proposed that our heads of state and government meet on the sidelines of the next General Assembly to define together the new priorities for our action.

Let us recover the initiative in the regional conflicts that are destabilizing entire regions. I am thinking in particular of the Israeli-Palestinian conflict. How much suffering must the peoples of the region still endure for us to force the doors to peace? Let us not resign ourselves to the irreparable.

In a world where the threat is asymmetrical, where the weak defy the strong, the power of conviction, the capacity to convince, the ability to sway opinion count as much as the number of divisions. They do not replace them. But they are the indispensable aids of a state's influence.

6– Faced with this new world, it is imperative that the action of the international community should be guided by principles.

First of all, respect for law. The keystone of international order, it must apply in all circumstances, but even more so when the gravest decision is to be made: to use force. Only on this condition can force be legitimate. Only on this condition can it restore order and peace.

Next, the defense of freedom and justice. We must not compromise with what is central to our values. We will be listened to and heeded only if we are inspired by the very ideals of the United Nations.

Lastly, the spirit of dialogue and tolerance. Never have the peoples of the world aspired so forcefully to its respect. We must listen to their appeal. . . .

As we see clearly, the United Nations has never been so necessary. It is up to this body to harness all the resolve to meet these challenges.

| 153

Because the United Nations is the place where international rules and legitimacy are founded. Because it speaks in the name of peoples.

In response to the clash of arms there must be a single upwelling of the spirit of responsibility, voice, and gesture from the international community that is gathered here in New York, in the Security Council.

This is in the interest of all: the countries engaged in the conflict, the states and peoples in the region, the international community as a whole. Confronted with a world in crisis, we have a moral and political obligation to restore the threads of hope and unity.

The judgment of future generations will depend on our capacity to meet this great challenge—in furtherance of our values, our common destiny and peace. Thank you.

## DOCUMENT 3.13

The German foreign minister, Joschka Fischer, also strongly protested the impending war on the same day, noting that there was no basis in the UN Charter for regime change by military means. Like the French delegate, he argued that the United Nations, as the most important world deliberative system, was the proper place to resolve international conflicts. Moreover, he expressed fear that the invasion of Iraq would jeopardize the future of the United Nations and the system of international law.

JOSCHKA FISCHER, ADDRESS BEFORE
THE UNITED NATIONS SECURITY COUNCIL,
MARCH 19, 2003 (EXCERPT)

I would like to thank the Security Council Presidency for its excellent work at this difficult time. The Security Council is meeting here today in a dramatic situation. At this moment, the world is facing an imminent war in Iraq. The Security Council cannot remain silent in this situation. Today more than ever, our task must be to safeguard its function and to preserve its relevance. We have come together once more in New York today to emphasize that.

The developments of the last few hours have radically changed the international situation and brought the work of the United Nations on the ground to a standstill. These developments are cause for the deepest concern.

Nevertheless, I would like to thank Dr. Blix for his briefing on the work program. Germany fully supports his approach, even under the current circumstances.

The work program with its realistic description of the unresolved disarmament issues now lies before us. It provides clear and convincing guidelines on how to disarm Iraq peacefully within a short space of time.

I want to stress this fact, particularly today. It is possible to disarm Iraq peacefully by upholding these demands with tight deadlines. Peaceful means have therefore not been exhausted. Also for that reason, Germany emphatically rejects the impending war.

We deeply regret that our considerable efforts to disarm Iraq using peaceful means in accordance with SC Resolution 1441 seem to have no chance of success. Time and again during the last few weeks, we have collaborated with France and Russia to put forward proposals for a more efficient inspections regime consisting of clear disarmament steps with deadlines—most recently on 15 March.

Other members also submitted constructive proposals until the final hours of the negotiations. We are grateful to them for their efforts.

During the last few days, we have moved significantly closer to our common objective: Namely, that of effectively countering the risk posed by Iraqi weapons of mass destruction with complete and comprehensive arms control. Especially in recent weeks, substantial progress was made in disarmament. The scrapping of the Al Samoud missiles made headway: 70 of them have now been destroyed. And—Dr. Blix pointed this out—the regime in Baghdad is beginning under pressure to clear up the unanswered questions on VX and anthrax.

Iraq's readiness to cooperate was unsatisfactory. It was hesitant and slow. The Council agrees on that. But can this seriously be regarded as grounds for war with all its terrible consequences?

| 155

There is no doubt that, particularly in recent weeks, Baghdad has begun to cooperate more. The information Iraq has provided to UNMOVIC and the IAEA are steps in the right direction. Baghdad is meeting more and more of the demands contained in the SC Resolutions. But why should we now—especially now—abandon our plan to disarm Iraq with peaceful means?

The majority of the Security Council members believe that there are no grounds for breaking off the disarmament process carried out under the supervision of the United Nations now.

In this connection, I would like to make the following three points:

- Firstly, the Security Council has not failed. We must counter that myth. The Security Council has made available the instrument to disarm Iraq peacefully. The Security Council is not responsible for what is happening outside the UN.
- Secondly, we have to state clearly under the current circumstances the policy of military intervention has no credibility. It does not have the support of our people. It would not have taken much to safeguard the unity of the Security Council. There is no basis in the UN Charter for a regime change with military means.
- Thirdly, we have to preserve the inspection regime and to endorse the working program because we need both after the end of

military action. Resolutions 1284 and 1441 are still in force, even if some adjustments are needed.

Mr. President,

Germany is convinced that the United Nations and the Security Council must continue to play the central role in the Iraq conflict. This is crucial to world order and must continue to be the case in future. The UN is the key institution for the preservation of peace and stability and for the peaceful reconciliation of interests in the world of today and of tomorrow. There is no substitute for its function as a guardian of peace.

The Security Council bears the primary responsibility for world peace and international security. The negotiations on the Iraq crisis, which were followed by millions of people worldwide during the last few weeks and months, have shown how relevant and how indispensable the peacemaking role of the Security Council is. There is no alternative to this.

We continue to need an effective international non-proliferation and disarmament regime. This can eliminate the risk of the proliferation of weapons of mass destruction using the instruments developed in this process to make the world a safer place. The United Nations is the only appropriate framework for this. No one can seriously believe that disarmament wars are the way forward!

156 |

We are deeply concerned about the humanitarian consequences of a war in Iraq. Our task now is to do everything we possibly can to avert a humanitarian disaster. The UN Secretary-General is to present proposals on this. Yesterday, the Security Council declared its readiness to take up these proposals. With the Oil-for-Food program, the UN has provided 60 percent of the Iraqi population with essential supplies. This experience must be used in future.

Mr. President,

A very large majority of people in Germany and Europe are greatly troubled by the impending war in Iraq. Our continent has experienced the horrors of war only too often. Those who know our European history understand that we do not live on Venus but, rather, that we are the survivors of Mars. War is terrible. It is a great tragedy for those affected and for us all. It can only be the very last resort when all peaceful alternatives really have been exhausted.

Nevertheless, Germany has accepted the necessity of war on two occasions during the last few years because all peaceful alternatives had proved unsuccessful.

Germany fought side by side with its allies in Kosovo to prevent the mass deportation of the Albanian population and to avert an impending genocide. It did likewise in Afghanistan to combat the brutal and dangerous terrorism of the Taliban and al Qaeda after the terrible attacks on the government and the people of the United States. And we will stick to our commitment in this war against terror.

Today, however, we in Germany do not believe that there is no alternative to military force as the last resort. On the contrary, we feel that Iraq can be disarmed using peaceful means. We will therefore seize any opportunity, no matter how small, to bring about a peaceful solution.

# DOCUMENT 3.14

As the invasion began, China—a rising power in the world and a permanent Security Council member—expressed its concern at the Bush administration's bypassing of the Security Council and its refusal to consider a political solution.

FOREIGN MINISTRY OF CHINA, STATEMENT ON WAR
WITH IRAQ, MARCH 20, 2003

On 20 March, bypassing the UN Security Council, the United States and some other countries launched military operations against Iraq. The Chinese government hereby expresses its serious concern.

The Chinese government has all along stood for a political settlement of the Iraq issue within the UN framework, urging the Iraqi government to fully and earnestly implement the relevant Security Council resolutions and calling for respect for Iraq's sovereignty and territorial integrity by the international community.

Security Council Resolution 1441 adopted unanimously last November is an important basis for a political settlement of the Iraq question. It is the widely-held view in the international community that the strict implementation of Resolution 1441 can deny Iraq weapons of mass destruction through peaceful means. The Chinese government has worked tirelessly with various countries to this end.

War will inevitably lead to humanitarian disasters and undermine the security, stability and development of the region and the world at large. People throughout the world detest war and want to see peace preserved. The Chinese government is always committed to peace and stability in the world. We stand for settlement of international disputes by political means and reject the use or threat of force in international affairs. The Chinese government strongly appeals the relevant countries to stop military actions and return to the right path of seeking a political solution to the Iraq question.

# DOCUMENT 3.15

International nongovernmental organizations, including the International Progress Organization, the World Federalist Movement, and the Institute for Global Policy, invoked a 1950 General Assembly resolution in an innovative attempt to stop the war in Iraq. Pointing to the deep division in the Security Council, the organizations called for the General Assembly to take action on the matter. Although the initiative did not bear fruit, it indicated the urgency felt by many nongovernmental organizations worldwide.

---

CALL BY INTERNATIONAL NGOS FOR INVOKING UNITING
FOR PEACE RESOLUTION/2003–03–15/P/RE/18121C-IS,
VIENNA, MARCH 27, 2003

In response to an initiative launched by the International Progress Organization on 15 March 2003, international non-governmental organizations from all continents have endorsed an appeal to the member states of the United Nations General Assembly for invoking the *Uniting for Peace Resolution*. According to the provisions of General Assembly resolution 377A (V), the General Assembly may convene in an emergency session if the Security Council is prevented from discharging its responsibilities for the preservation or restoration of international peace and security.

Because the war of aggression against Iraq is being waged by two veto-wielding members of the Security Council (the United States and the United Kingdom), the Security Council is effectively incapacitated in regard to its enforcement powers for the restoration of peace and security under Chapter VII of the Charter. The Uniting for Peace Resolution—which was adopted by the General Assembly on 3 November 1950 in a similar situation of Security Council paralysis—provides that "if the Security Council, because of the lack of unanimity of the permanent members, fails to exercise its primary responsibility for the maintenance of international peace and security . . . , the General Assembly shall consider the matter immediately with a view to making appropriate recommendations to Members for collective measures . . . to maintain or restore international peace and security."

According to the provisions of the resolution, an emergency session of the General Assembly may be convened within 24 hours if at least nine members of the Security Council or the simply majority of member states of the General Assembly so demand.

In a message delivered on 15 March 2003 to the Secretary-General of the United Nations, Mr. Kofi Annan, and to the President of the General Assembly, Mr. Jan Kavan, the President of the International Progress Organization, Professor Hans Koechler, urged them to support this initiative vis-à-vis the United Nations member states.

A worldwide signature campaign of NGOs is now under way to convince United Nations member states to undertake urgent action for the restoration of international peace and security at a time and in a situation where the Security Council is prevented from acting by the veto power of the very states that undertake the war of aggression against Iraq. The fate of the people of Iraq must not be left to the law of brute force being exercised in defiance of the Security Council. The future and legitimacy of the United Nations Organization as such are at stake. If the invasion of Iraq by the United States and the United Kingdom is left unchallenged, global anarchy will rapidly replace the system of collective security as it has existed in the framework of the United Nations since the end of World War II, the President of the I.P.O. said in a statement commenting on his organization's appeal.

# DOCUMENT 3.16

Russia had collaborated with France and Germany to find ways to avoid war. Here, Russian president Vladimir Putin expressed his views on the war and on U.S.–Russian relations, highlighting the commonalities between the United States and Russia, including a commitment to control weapons of mass destruction and to fight terrorism. In doing so, Putin drew an analogy between the terrorist threats enunciated by the Bush administration and the threats that Chechen rebels, who were seeking to break away from Russia, posed for Putin. Significantly, he emphasized the importance of international law and institutions in resolving global conflicts.

| 159

VLADIMIR PUTIN, PRESS STATEMENT ON IRAQ,
APRIL 3, 2003 (EXCERPT)

. . . . As for the Russian approach to the crisis in Iraq, I set it forth in the Statement two weeks ago. Since then, nothing has changed in our position on Iraq. Moreover, the recent developments confirm the validity of the position we have taken on the issue. We come out for strengthening the foundations and principles of international law and for solving such kind of situations through the United Nations.

As for emotions, I understand the people who are unable to contain them. I understand and to some extent share the opinion of these people, especially after you watch television reports from the combat area. But I don't think that emotions are a good counsel in preparing and passing any decisions.

In recent times Russia—and there have been many crises recently—has not once permitted itself the luxury of being drawn directly in any of these crises. And this time around, I will do everything within my power to prevent Russia being dragged into the Iraq crisis in any form.

As regards political considerations, in approaching any problems, including those of a global character, we of course have always cooperated and will cooperate with the United States.

Politically, the United States and Russia are the biggest nuclear powers in the world and we bear a special responsibility for the maintenance of international peace. We have signed a strategic offensive reductions treaty. The U.S. Senate recently ratified it and we in Russia intend to do the same, we will work together with the deputies of the Federal Assembly. . . .

Secondly—and I am absolutely convinced of this—we must jointly tackle the problem of non-proliferation of mass destruction weapons and means of their delivery. This is one of the most acute problems of the 21st century and, undoubtedly, that problem cannot be solved without positive cooperation and interaction between the United States and Russia.

Finally, the fight against terrorism. It remains highly relevant. Russia knows about it not by hearsay. To give you an example: in spite of the new stage of settlement in Chechnya terrorist acts in the Caucasus continue. This is an international problem. Here, within the anti-terrorist coalition, a stable partnership has been established with the United States and we intend to develop it in the future.

We constantly speak about the need to strengthen the institutions of the United Nations. We often speak of the need to create a new world security architecture in the 21st century. That problem, obviously, cannot be effectively solved without a positive cooperation between the United States and Russia.

As for the economic sphere, everything is fairly simple and, in my view, is understandable even for ordinary Russian citizens. First, the U.S. is our major trade and economic partner. Our trade reached 9.2 billion dollars in 2002 and this year it is moving steadily toward the 10 billion dollar mark. The American economy and the American national currency are an economy and a currency of a global character and the state of the European and Russian economies depends to a large extent on how they develop. If we imagine that the rate of the U.S. dollar starts falling relative to other key national currencies in the world, this would directly affect Russia because today the gold and currency reserves of the Central Bank of the Russian Federation have reached a record 55.5 billion U.S. dollars (as of the beginning of April). The Central Bank keeps three-quarters of its currency reserves in U.S. dollars. If we imagine that the rate will change in a way that is unfavorable for the dollar then the Central Bank of the Russian Federation will suffer direct losses. The same would apply to the savings of Russian citizens who, as we know, keep part of their savings in U.S. dollars.

Finally, we are interested in cooperation in international organizations. We face the challenge of integrating the Russian economy into the world economy. And on this we actively cooperate with our American colleagues.

. . . in our bilateral relations we will proceed from the general principles of building the foreign policy of the Russian Federation, proceeding from the need to strengthen the foundations of international law, and the system of international security with the UN at its center.

If, in respect of the Iraq crisis, the first and the second considerations appear to contradict each other, I am sure that in the final analysis principled work in this direction—on a bilateral and multilateral basis—has a good prospect. Because not only Russia but an overwhelming majority of countries are interested in such a structure of foreign policy. In the final analysis it would benefit the United States.

# DOCUMENT 3.17

In a 2004 interview conducted by the Australian news service ABC, Secretary-General Kofi Annan acknowledged that the invasion of Iraq had been a breach of the UN Charter. The conservative prime minister, John Howard, disagreed with that statement, but Kevin Rudd, then an opposition figure, agreed with Annan. Rudd was elected prime minister in 2007. Colin Powell also took issue with Annan's statement.

| 161

AUSTRALIAN BROADCASTING COMPANY, "THE WORLD TODAY—KOFI ANNAN DECLARES U.S. INVASION OF IRAQ ILLEGAL," SEPTEMBER 16, 2004 (EXCERPT)

**ELEANOR HALL:** The Prime Minister has found himself again defending his policy on Iraq, after the United Nations Secretary-General, Kofi Annan, said today that the U.S.-led invasion was illegal and that the elections planned for Iraq in January would not be credible in the current security environment.

Campaigning in Western Australia, John Howard said he rejected the UN chief's comments and declared that Australia's involvement in the war on Iraq was valid.

From Canberra the ABC's Chief Political Correspondent Catherine McGrath reports.

**CATHERINE McGRATH:** These are the comments by UN General Secretary Kofi Annan on BBC radio that have brought up the Iraq issue up again.

**KOFI ANNAN:** Oh, I hope we do not see another Iraq-type operation for a long time.

**BBC ANNOUNCER:** Done without UN approval or without clear UN approval?

**KOFI ANNAN:** Without UN approval and much broader support from the international community.

**BBC ANNOUNCER:** I wanted to ask you that. Do you think that the resolution that was passed on Iraq before the war did actually give legal authority to do what was done?

**KOFI ANNAN:** Well, I'm one of those who believe that there should have been a second resolution.

**BBC ANNOUNCER:** You don't think there was legal authority for the war?

**KOFI ANNAN:** I have made it. . . . I have stated clearly that it was not in conformity with the Security Council . . . with the UN charter.

**BBC ANNOUNCER:** It was illegal?

**KOFI ANNAN:** Yes, if you wish.

**BBC ANNOUNCER:** It was illegal?

**KOFI ANNAN:** Yes, I've indicated it is not in conformity with the UN Charter from my point, and from the Charter point of view it was illegal.

**CATHERINE McGRATH:** The Government has always maintained the military action was legal—a point repeated by John Howard on Perth radio 6PR this morning.

**JOHN HOWARD:** The legal advice that we had, and I tabled it at the time, was that the action was entirely valid in international law terms. That was a legal opinion we obtained from the relevant people in Australia. There had been a serious [breach] of Security Council resolutions and the advice we had was it was entirely legal.

**CATHERINE McGRATH:** Shadow Foreign Affairs spokesman Kevin Rudd disagrees.

**KEVIN RUDD:** We've always challenged the legality and lawfulness of the Iraq war. The UN Charter outlines two grounds on which you can lawfully engage in armed conflict—one is article 42 of the charter which says that you act together with other states once that action has been explicitly authorized by the United Nations Security Council. That didn't happen in the case of Iraq. The other provision is article 51 of the UN Charter, which is about self-defence. That didn't apply in the case of Iraq either.

**CATHERINE McGRATH:** So how significant is it that Kofi Annan has come out and said that today?

**KEVIN RUDD:** It is a significant contribution by the UN Secretary-General to this debate. As far as Australia is concerned, unfortunately we still have a Prime Minister who is systematically contemptuous of the United Nations as an organization. . . .

# ★ CHAPTER 4 ★

# LIBERATORS OR OCCUPIERS?

## THE COALITION PROVISIONAL AUTHORITY

ON JANUARY 20, 2003, two months before the Bush administration launched its preemptive invasion of Iraq, the Pentagon established the Office for Reconstruction and Humanitarian Assistance (ORHA) to oversee the country's economic and political reorganization. Staffed by representatives from the Departments of State, Defense, Justice, Treasury, Energy, and Agriculture, the U.S. Agency for International Development, and the Office of Management and Budget, ORHA reported directly to Secretary of Defense Donald Rumsfeld. Ret. Lt. Gen. Jay Garner, who had helped coordinate relief operations in northern Iraq after the first Gulf War, was named as its head (4.3).

Garner had been told by Douglas Feith, the Undersecretary of Defense for Policy and Head of the Office of Special Plans, that the ORHA assignment would be short—perhaps ninety days—and relatively easy. By then, Feith predicted, an interim Iraqi government would have been formed, a permanent U.S. ambassador assigned, and the withdrawal of troops begun. Since grateful Iraqis would greet the Americans as liberators, a long-term occupation would be unnecessary.

Shaped by the neoconservative certainty that the "shock and awe" of overwhelming U.S. military power would make it easy to transform Iraq, Feith's optimism was shared by President Bush, Vice President Cheney, Defense Secretary Donald Rumsfeld, and National Security Advisor Condoleezza Rice. They reasoned that if Saddam Hussein was the only obstacle to a U.S.-organized democracy and a free market (2.10), then removing his regime would make it easy to change Iraq, democratize the Middle East, and demonstrate the new structure of international politics. But there was more to victory than Secretary of Defense Rumsfeld's new military tactics. In the absence of sensible plans and accurate knowledge, optimism and blind faith proved dangerous and the distinction between liberators and occupiers became steadily more difficult to sustain. From the moment U.S. troops entered Baghdad and saw civil order collapse amid an orgy of looting and violence, it became clear that things might not go the way Washington had anticipated. Indeed, it was not lost on observers that the oil fields and the Baghdad headquarters of the Oil Ministry were the only facilities that the invading forces had protected.

The administration's failure to consider other possibilities stemmed from its conviction that overwhelming military power would allow it to unilaterally fight a preemptive war without negative consequences. But things began to go wrong from the very beginning. It had been relatively easy to defeat the depleted Iraqi army, but victory on the battlefield only set the stage for an unwelcome and chaotic postwar environment. Despite the neoconservatives' years of harsh attacks on the European preference for "soft power" and on President Clinton's emphasis on the economic dimensions of foreign policy, direct U.S. occupation would result in years of state- and nation-building—a long project that was doomed by the administration's unpreparedness for the complexity of the task. Contrary to Washington's expectations, and made more difficult by a series of mistaken assumptions, almost everything had to be reconstructed: army and police, governmental ministries, banking and education systems, and basic infrastructure for delivering and generating electricity and water, handling sewage, and producing and delivering oil. And reconstruction was the least of it. The rest of the administration's grand Iraqi project—privatizing the economy, opening the country to international investors, and organizing a pro-U.S. liberal democracy—collapsed because Washington had decided beforehand that it did not need to understand Iraqi society. All that was needed was military supremacy, steadiness of purpose, and the willingness to make "tough decisions."

The administration's ideological blinkers had convinced policymakers that the United States was the only actor whose intentions had to be considered. Unencumbered by anything except its flawed projections, Washington organized an incoherent occupation whose policies developed in fits and starts, routinely offended important elements of a deeply traumatized country, and ultimately had to be abandoned. Its plan to deal a body blow to international terrorism, make Iraq into a pro-Western regional guarantor of access to Persian Gulf oil, spread "universal American values," stabilize the Middle East, protect Israel, demonstrate U.S. military supremacy, transform American armed forces, and contain Iran all failed. Amid the wreckage of the Coalition Provisional Authority (CPA), the administration was left with an unpopular salvage operation.

The quagmire in which the Bush administration quickly found itself was all the more surprising in light of the ease with which its invasion had triumphed on the battlefield. But there was more to rapid victory than met the eye, for the occupiers—and occupiers they were—had to take important actions long before they were ready to do so. Garner's initial desire to rely on local Iraqis, and his refusal to abolish the Baath Party, quickly got him into trouble with the Defense Department and with Vice President Cheney's office, both of which made no secret of their desire to install compliant exiles to run the country as soon as Saddam Hussein's government was overthrown. Under the circumstances, it did not take long for ORHA to wear out its Washington mandate, and on April 21 it was dissolved and replaced by the Coalition Provisional Authority. Garner was swiftly dismissed and replaced by L. Paul Bremer on May 11. A former ambassador to the Netherlands, managing director of Kissinger and Associates, member of several corporate boards, and long-time State Department officer, Bremer served as head of the CPA until U.S. occupying forces restored limited sovereignty to an Iraqi interim government on June 28, 2004.

Initially working with only a vague set of guidelines, ORHA had drafted "A Unified Mission Plan for Post-hostilities Iraq" in April. In the introduction, Garner presciently observed that "history will judge the war against Iraq not by the brilliance of its military execution, but by the effectiveness of the post-hostilities activities." Among its key recommendations were organizing an integrated civil–military approach, quickly establishing an interim government, and "internationalizing" the occupation—elementary matters that should have been decided long before U.S. forces entered Baghdad. The report also noted that Iraq's oil revenues alone would not be sufficient to pay for reconstruction and raised the possibility of an extended period of instability in the immediate postwar period. Necessarily vague because it was starting at the very beginning, Garner's plan had very little influence over subsequent CPA policy. And ORHA's task was made much more difficult by the endless fighting and maneuvering surrounding the most prominent of Washington's favored exiles, Ahmed Chalabi.

The Chalabi affair was a good illustration of the hidden weakness that lay at the heart of the administration's embrace of preemption. It has long been a rule of politics that relying on exiles can be dangerous, and the Iraqi case was no exception. Overwhelming U.S. military power and a conviction that history was on Washington's side could not substitute for accurate information, sensible planning, and a modest approach to a complex task. Like the rest of ORHA and the CPA, Garner and Bremer were playing catch-up from the very beginning. Chalabi had been ingratiating himself with the neoconservatives from the middle of the 1980s, when Reagan's Assistant Secretary of Defense Richard Perle had introduced him to his friend Paul Wolfowitz. Chalabi's Westernized, upper-class Shia parents had fled Iraq in 1956 when he was twelve, and he had lived outside his native country until U.S. and British invading forces brought him back to Baghdad forty-six years later.

Chalabi was no stranger to intrigue or controversy. He had founded the Petra Bank in Jordan in 1978 but fled the country eleven years later, just ahead of arrest on suspicion of embezzling US$300 million. Settling in Washington, he became skilled at maneuvering in exile politics, his path to influence smoothed by the evolution of U.S. Mideast policy. By 1992 he had helped found and lead the Iraqi National Congress, the broadest of the exile groups and one of the favored recipients of U.S. aid during the Clinton administration. As President Bush began to intensify the pressure on Baghdad, Chalabi provided a measure of legitimacy at the 2002 State of the Union address, where he was singled out as a "special guest" when the president enrolled Iraq in his soon-to-be famous "axis of evil" (2.2). Washington's allegations about Saddam Hussein's weapons programs, Secretary of State Colin Powell's claims to the Security Council about the Iraqi leader's "mobile biological weapons labs" (2.14), and other information came directly from Chalabi, whose main source—the brother of one of his top lieutenants, code-named "Curveball"—provided a series of "firsthand" accounts that proved useful to the administration as it made its case for war. The Germans had warned that "Curveball" was unreliable and had not been in Iraq when he said he was, but he was useful to Washington anyway. As it turned out, almost all the information Chalabi provided was false.

Having embraced the Iraqi National Congress, the administration ignored persistent questions about its leadership. Cheney, Rumsfeld, Feith, Wolfowitz, and others described Chalabi as a selfless patriot, repeatedly calling him the "George Washington" of his country—and, not coincidentally, the ideal candidate for taking over after U.S. forces left. When William Kristol and Robert Kagan wrote in January 2002 that "the United States should support Ahmad Chalabi,"[1] they were simply expressing a long-held position that overthrowing Saddam Hussein and dismantling the Baathist state apparatus would be a relatively easy first step in the neoconservative project to transform the Middle East and reorganize the world.

But if Chalabi was the darling of the Defense Department and the office of the vice president, he was less beloved by other branches of the U.S. government—and, more to the point, by the Iraqis themselves. Decidedly reluctant to rely on an isolated grouping of exiles, the State Department and the CIA regarded him as an undependable opportunist. They were particularly suspicious of his long-held desire to dissolve Iraq's two most important national institutions, the Baath Party and the army, suspecting that he wanted to install his own people in positions of leadership. They were not alone. In February 2004, a poll of Iraqis found that 0.2 percent trusted Chalabi, and when asked if there were any Iraqi leaders they did not trust at all, he topped the list at 10.3 percent—more than three times the second-most-unpopular figure, Saddam Hussein himself.[2]

Even though ORHA and the CPA reported to Rumsfeld, Garner and Bremer found support in the State Department and tried to maneuver around Chalabi. But Chalabi had better contacts, and he was able to use them so long as his future fit in with the neoconservatives' plans. Garner and Bremer were constantly being whipsawed by the brutal competition between Rumsfeld and

166 |

1. William Kristol and Robert Kagan, "What to Do about Iraq," *Weekly Standard*, January 21, 2002, pp. 23–26.
2. Oxford Research International, "National Survey of Iraq," February 2004, http://news.bbc.co.uk/.

Cheney on the one hand and Powell on the other, a struggle that helped paralyze the occupation even as the question of what to do with the Baath Party and the army turned out to be Bremer's most important, and most bitterly mistaken, early decision (4.6–4.7). But Chalabi's sponsors did not have unlimited patience. When occupying authorities intercepted a message from an Iranian agent in Baghdad saying Chalabi had told him that the United States could read Iran's secret cables, the Pentagon cut off Chalabi's funds and refused to have anything to do with him in public. The rift became permanent when Iraqi police backed by U.S. troops raided Chalabi's Baghdad home in late May 2004 and found counterfeit money and classified information.

The Chalabi episode illustrated the weaknesses of Washington's approach with striking clarity. Convinced that it did not have to do much postwar planning, and repeatedly claiming that U.S. troops would be greeted as liberators by grateful Iraqis, the administration began its formal occupation of the country from a position of political weakness that its military superiority could not hide. Nothing changed when ORHA became the CPA and Garner was replaced by Bremer because the underlying assumptions that were driving policy remained intact.

The yearlong Coalition Provisional Authority marked the collapse of Bush's Iraq project. The administration certainly expected the period of direct occupation to be brief and smooth. But the organizing principles of its preemptive war—that U.S. power was so overwhelming and the U.S. political project so universally admired that Washington could do anything it wanted—doomed the effort from the very beginning. Bremer's year was marked by a series of failures, all of which stemmed from ideological assumptions that had little to do with the realities of Iraqi society and more to do with the Bush administration's desire to remake Iraq in the U.S. image. When incompetence, corruption, bureaucratic rivalry, and bad planning were added to the logic of preemption, the result was confusion and dysfunction in both Washington and Baghdad's Green Zone—the "Emerald City" where the U.S. occupation authorities were housed. Washington planned to privatize the oil industry, reorganize Iraq's system of higher education, oversee the appearance of a "model Arab liberal democracy," copy the District of Columbia's driving code, set up a U.S.-style stock exchange, establish a new radio and television system, and rebuild the country's shattered electrical system. Most of these projects were pursued in the absence of their most fundamental necessary conditions, and almost all of them were organized by unqualified and inexperienced Republican Party members—many of whom had been hired on the basis of how they felt about *Roe v. Wade* or other "wedge" issues. Under the circumstances, it was not surprising that the CPA awkwardly lurched from one ill-conceived policy initiative to another. As one story of arrogance, incompetence, and corruption yielded to the next, it was easy to assume that the CPA was trying to do too much too soon. But the fault lay in the fundamentals. As social collapse, insurgency, and civil war began to swamp the administration's plans, it became clear that almost all of Washington's basic assumptions had been wrong. That was why many of Bremer's decisions, often made in the heat of partisan battle, with little consultation or understanding of their consequences, would come to epitomize the occupation's failures. When the proconsul abruptly left Baghdad after a secret transfer of sovereignty, Washington's goals of a democratic, capitalist, and pro-Western Iraq seemed further from realization than when he had taken over.

Rajiv Chandrasekaran, the *Washington Post* bureau chief in Baghdad, incisively summarized the central failure of preemption. Just before Bremer's hasty departure, Chandrasekaran had breakfast with an Iraqi friend. "As we nibbled from a plate of dates and pastries," Chandrasekaran reported, "I asked him what the CPA's biggest mistake had been. He didn't hesitate. 'The biggest mistake of the occupation,' he said, 'was the occupation itself.'"[3]

## DOCUMENT 4.1

The Second Section of the Hague Convention of 1899, called the Laws and Customs of War on Land, was the first set of international treaties that attempted to codify the laws of warfare. Its section on "military authority over hostile territory" imposes clear responsibilities on occupying powers (8.1) The Convention was expanded in 1907, mostly because of new developments in naval weaponry and tactics. The United States is a signatory to both Conventions. In an effort to establish the legitimacy of the U.S. occupation, Bremer routinely cited "the laws and usages of war" in the preambles to his Orders, Regulations, and Memoranda.

### ARTICLE 43 OF THE HAGUE CONVENTIONS OF 1899 AND 1907

The authority of the legitimate power having actually passed into the hands of the occupant, the latter shall take all steps in his power to re-establish and insure, as far as possible, public order and safety, while respecting, unless absolutely prevented, the laws in force in the country.

## DOCUMENT 4.2

Article 55 of the Hague Convention, also signed by the United States, allows occupying powers to derive benefit from property held by another so long as

---

3. Rajiv Chandrasekaran, *Imperial Life in the Emerald City: Inside Iraq's Green Zone* (New York: Knopf, 2006), 290.

its value is not diminished. This law of "usufruct" establishes the responsibility to leave intact the basic economic structure of the occupied state.

---

ARTICLE 55 OF THE HAGUE CONVENTIONS OF 1899 AND 1907

The occupying State shall only be regarded as administrator and usufructuary of the public buildings, real property, forests, and agricultural works belonging to the hostile State, and situated in the occupied country. It must protect the capital of these properties, and administer it according to the rules of usufruct.

# DOCUMENT 4.3

Less than one month after September 11, the "Future of Iraq Project" organized more than two hundred exiled Iraqi engineers, lawyers, businesspeople, doctors, and others into seventeen working groups whose "nation-building" work centered on topics such as public health and humanitarian needs, transparency and anti-corruption, oil and energy, defense policy and institutions, transitional justice, democratic principles and procedures, local government, civil society, education, media, water, agriculture and environment, and economy and infrastructure (6.1, 7.1). The Project produced a thirteen-volume report that would serve as the most comprehensive U.S. effort at planning for postwar Iraq. Deeply influenced by Iraqi exiles, its many recommendations included the "de-Baathification" of society and the reintegration of party members into Iraqi life, and a 50 percent cut in the size of the army, which would be given responsibility for maintaining internal order, fighting drug smuggling, and combating terrorism.

   The State Department's efforts notwithstanding, the real planning was going on at the Defense Department, where Under Secretary of Defense for Policy Feith's Office of Special Plans had been working on a plan to purge the Baathists, install Chalabi, and determine the future of the Iraqi army. President Bush's still-classified National Security Presidential Directive 24 handed over authority for postwar Iraq to the Defense Department on January 20, 2003, largely at the behest of Secretary Rumsfeld and Vice President Cheney.

---

DOUGLAS J. FEITH, STATEMENT TO THE SENATE COMMITTEE ON FOREIGN RELATIONS, FEBRUARY 11, 2003 (EXCERPT)

I am pleased to have this opportunity to talk with you today about efforts underway in the Defense Department and the U.S. Government to plan for Iraq in the post-conflict period, should war become necessary.

If U.S. and other coalition forces take military action in Iraq, they will, after victory, have contributions to make to the country's temporary administration and the welfare of the Iraqi people. It will be necessary to provide humanitarian relief, organize basic services, and work to establish security for the liberated Iraqis.

Our work will aim to achieve the objectives outlined by my colleague, Under Secretary of State Grossman:

First, demonstrate to the Iraqi people and the world that the United States aspires to liberate, not occupy or control them or their economic resources.

Second, eliminate Iraq's chemical and biological weapons, its nuclear program, the related delivery systems, and the related research and production facilities. This will be a complex, dangerous, and expensive task.

Third, eliminate likewise Iraq's terrorist infrastructure. A key element of U.S. strategy in the global war on terrorism is exploiting the information about terrorist networks that the coalition acquires through our military and law enforcement actions.

Fourth, safeguard the territorial unity of Iraq. The United States does not support Iraq's disintegration or dismemberment.

Fifth, begin the process of economic and political reconstruction, working to put Iraq on a path to become a prosperous and free country. The U.S. government shares with many Iraqis the hope that their country will enjoy the rule of law and other institutions of democracy under a broad-based government that represents the various parts of Iraqi society.

If there is a war, the United States would approach its post-war work with a two-part resolve: a commitment to stay and a commitment to leave.

That is, a commitment to stay as long as required to achieve the objectives I have just listed. The coalition cannot take military action in Iraq—to eliminate weapons of mass destruction and the Iraqi tyranny's threats to the world as an aggressor and supporter of terrorism—and then leave a mess behind for the Iraqi people to clean up without a helping hand. That would ill serve the Iraqis, ourselves, and the world.

But it is important to stress also that the United States would have a commitment to leave as soon as possible, for Iraq belongs to the Iraqi people. Iraq does not and will not belong to the United States, the coalition, or to anyone else.

As Iraqi officials are able to shoulder their country's responsibilities, and they have in place the necessary political and other structures to provide food, security, and the other necessities, the United States and its coalition partners will want them to run their own affairs. We all have an interest in hastening the day when Iraq can become a proud, independent, and respected member of the community of the world's free countries.

U.S. post-war responsibilities will not be easy to fulfill and the United States by no means wishes to tackle them alone. We shall encourage contributions and participation from coalition partners, non-governmental organizations, the UN and other international organizations, and others. And our goal is to transfer as much authority as possible, as soon as possible, to the Iraqis themselves. But the United States will not try to foist burdens onto those who are not in a position to carry them.

## Security and Reconstruction

Administration officials are thinking through the lessons of Afghanistan and other recent history. We have learned that post-conflict reconstruction requires a balance of efforts in the military sphere and the civil sphere. Security is promoted by progress toward economic reconstruction. But economic reconstruction is hardly possible if local business people, foreign investors, and international aid workers do not feel secure in their persons and property.

To encourage the coordinated, balanced progress of economic and security reconstruction in a post-conflict Iraq, President Bush has directed his administration to begin planning now.

The faster the necessary reconstruction tasks are accomplished, the sooner the coalition will be able to withdraw its forces from Iraq, and the sooner the Iraqis will assume complete control of their country. Accordingly, the coalition officials responsible for post-conflict administration of Iraq—whether military or civilian, from the various agencies of the government—will report to the President through General Tom Franks, the Commander of the U.S. Central Command, and the Secretary of Defense.

## The Office of Reconstruction and Humanitarian Assistance

To prepare for all this, the President directed on January 20 the creation of a post-war planning office. Although located within the Policy organization in the Department of Defense, this office is staffed by officials detailed from departments and agencies throughout the government. Its job is detailed planning and implementation. The intention is not to theorize but to do practical work—to prepare for action on the ground, if and when the time comes for such work. In the event of war, most of the people in the office will deploy to Iraq. We have named it the Office of Reconstruction and Humanitarian Assistance and we describe it as an "expeditionary" office. . . .

The immediate responsibility for administering post-war Iraq will fall upon the Commander of the U.S. Central Command, as the commander of the U.S. and coalition forces in the field. The purpose of the Office of Reconstruction and Humanitarian Assistance is to develop the detailed plans that he and his subordinates will draw on in meeting these responsibilities. . . .

Various parts of the government have done a great deal of work on aspects of post-war planning for months now. Several planning efforts are underway.

An interagency working group led by the NSC staff and the Office of Management and Budget has undertaken detailed contingency planning for humanitarian relief in case of conflict with Iraq. The group also includes members from the State Department, USAID, the Office of the Vice-President,

Treasury, the Office of the Secretary of Defense, the Joint Staff, and the CIA. The group is linked to U.S. Central Command. It has also established links with the UN specialized agencies and NGOs involved in humanitarian relief efforts.

This group has developed a concept of operations that would:

- facilitate UN/NGO provision of aid
- establish Civil-Military Operations Centers by means of which U.S. forces would coordinate provision of relief
- restart the UN ration distribution system using U.S. supplies until UN/NGOs arrive.

Other interagency groups are planning for:

- the reconstruction of post-Saddam Iraq,
- vetting current Iraqi officials to determine with whom we should work, and
- post-war elimination of Iraqi Weapons of Mass Destruction.

The new planning office's function is to integrate all these efforts and make them operational. It is building on the work done, not reinventing it.

### Elimination of Weapons of Mass Destruction

Detailed planning is underway for the task of securing, assessing, and dismantling Iraqi WMD capabilities, facilities, and stockpiles. This will be a huge undertaking. The Defense Department is building the necessary capabilities.

This will be a new mission for the Department and for our nation. It is complex and will take place as part of military operations, continuing into the post-conflict period.

We must first locate Iraq's widespread WMD sites. We must then be prepared to secure the relevant weapons or facilities, or rapidly and safely disable them, so they are no longer a threat to coalition forces. This will have to be done in many places and as quickly as possible.

But the mission does not end there. After hostilities, we will have to dismantle, destroy, or dispose of nuclear, chemical, biological, and missile capabilities and infrastructure.

Equally important will be plans to re-direct some of Iraq's dual-use capability and its scientific and managerial talent to legitimate, civilian activities in a new Iraq.

Clearly, this will not be a mission that falls entirely to the U.S. military forces. Other U.S. government personnel, including those within the DoD, the Department of Energy's laboratory system, and in other government agencies can contribute.

Coalition partners, including many NATO allies, have nuclear, chemical, and biological defense-related capabilities and expertise that can play an important role. The UN, IAEA, and other international organizations should be in a position to contribute valuably to the elimination effort and perhaps to ongoing monitoring afterward.

The task of eliminating all nuclear, chemical, and biological stockpiles, facilities, and infrastructure will take time. We cannot now even venture a sensible guess as to the amount. The new Iraqi government will also have an important role to play.

## Oil Infrastructure

The U.S. and its coalition allies may face the necessity of repairing Iraq's oil infrastructure, if Saddam Hussein decides to damage it, as he put the torch to Kuwait's oil fields in 1991. Indeed, we have reason to believe that Saddam's regime is planning to sabotage Iraq's oil fields. But even if there is no sabotage and there is no injury from combat operations, some repair work will likely be necessary to allow the safe resumption of operations at oil facilities after any war-related stoppage.

Detailed planning is underway for resumption of oil production as quickly as possible to help meet the Iraqi people's basic needs. The oil sector is Iraq's primary source of funding. As noted, the United States is committed to preserving Iraq's territorial integrity. So we are intent on ensuring that Iraq's oil resources remain under national Iraqi control, with the proceeds made available to support Iraqis in all parts of the country. No one ethnic or religious group would be allowed to claim exclusive rights to any part of the oil resources or infrastructure. In other words, all of Iraq's oil belongs to all the people of Iraq.

The administration has decided that, in the event of war, the U.S.-led coalition would:

- protect Iraq's oil fields from acts of sabotage and preserve them as a national asset of the Iraqi people, and
- rapidly start reconstruction and operation of the sector, so that its proceeds, together with humanitarian aid from the United States and other countries, can help support the Iraqi people's needs.

The Administration has not yet decided on the organizational mechanisms by which this sector should be operated. We shall be consulting on this important matter with many parties in various countries, including Iraqi experts and groups.

## "No War for Oil"

This is a good point at which to address head-on the accusation that, in this confrontation with the Iraqi regime, the administration's motive is to steal or control Iraq's oil. The accusation is common, reflected in the slogan "No War for Oil." But it is false and malign.

If there is a war, the world will see that the United States will fulfill its administrative responsibilities, including regarding oil, transparently and honestly, respecting the property and other rights of the Iraqi state and people. The record of the United States in military conflicts is open to the world and well known.

The United States became a major world power in World War II. In that war and since, the United States has demonstrated repeatedly and consistently that we covet no other country's property. The United States does not steal from other nations. We did not pillage Germany or Japan; on the contrary, we helped rebuild them after World War II. After Desert Storm, we did not use our military power to take or establish control over the oil resources of Iraq or any other country in the Gulf region. The United States pays for whatever we want to import. Rather than exploit its power to beggar its neighbors, the United States has been a source of large amounts of financial aid and other types of assistance for many countries for decades.

If U.S. motives were in essence financial or commercial, we would not be confronting Saddam Hussein over his weapons of mass destruction. If our motive were cold cash, we would instead downplay the Iraqi regime's weapons of mass destruction and pander to Saddam in hopes of winning contracts for U.S. companies.

The major costs of any confrontation with the Iraqi regime would of course be the human ones. But the financial costs would not be small, either. This confrontation is not, and cannot possibly be, a money-maker for the United States. Only someone ignorant of the easy-to-ascertain realities could think that the United States could profit from such a war, even if we were willing to steal Iraq's oil, which we emphatically are not going to do. . . .

We look forward to consulting with this Committee and with the Congress generally as we develop our ideas and plans for post-conflict Iraqi reconstruction. War is not inevitable, but failing to make contingency plans for its aftermath would be inexcusable.

## DOCUMENT 4.4

On May 1, 2003, President Bush addressed the crew of the USS *Abraham Lincoln* just off the coast of San Diego. Dressed as a fighter pilot and standing before a huge banner proclaiming "Mission Accomplished," he described "the Battle of Iraq" and "the Battle of Afghanistan" as the first two fronts in the new "global war on terror," repeated his administration's arguments for war, and sought to connect his foreign policy with that of Franklin D. Roosevelt, Harry Truman, and Ronald Reagan. The banner's triumphant claim would become one of the most notorious examples of the administration's arrogance and dishonesty.

GEORGE W. BUSH, ANNOUNCEMENT THAT MAJOR COMBAT
OPERATIONS IN IRAQ HAVE ENDED, MAY 1, 2003 (EXCERPT)

Thank you all very much. Admiral Kelly, Captain Card, officers and sailors
of the USS *Abraham Lincoln*, my fellow Americans: Major combat operations in Iraq have ended. In the battle of Iraq, the United States and our
allies have prevailed. And now our coalition is engaged in securing and reconstructing that country.

In this battle, we have fought for the cause of liberty, and for the peace
of the world. Our nation and our coalition are proud of this accomplishment
—yet, it is you, the members of the United States military, who achieved it.
Your courage, your willingness to face danger for your country and for
each other, made this day possible. Because of you, our nation is more secure. Because of you, the tyrant has fallen, and Iraq is free.

Operation Iraqi Freedom was carried out with a combination of precision and speed and boldness the enemy did not expect, and the world had
not seen before. From distant bases or ships at sea, we sent planes and missiles that could destroy an enemy division, or strike a single bunker. Marines
and soldiers charged to Baghdad across 350 miles of hostile ground, in one
of the swiftest advances of heavy arms in history. You have shown the world
the skill and the might of the American Armed Forces.

This nation thanks all the members of our coalition who joined in a
noble cause. We thank the Armed Forces of the United Kingdom, Australia,
and Poland, who shared in the hardships of war. We thank all the citizens
of Iraq who welcomed our troops and joined in the liberation of their own
country. And tonight, I have a special word for Secretary Rumsfeld, for General Franks, and for all the men and women who wear the uniform of the
United States: America is grateful for a job well done.

The character of our military through history—the daring of Normandy,
the fierce courage of Iwo Jima, the decency and idealism that turned enemies into allies—is fully present in this generation. When Iraqi civilians
looked into the faces of our servicemen and women, they saw strength
and kindness and goodwill. When I look at the members of the United
States military, I see the best of our country, and I'm honored to be your
commander-in-chief.

In the images of falling statues, we have witnessed the arrival of a new
era. For a hundred years of war, culminating in the nuclear age, military
technology was designed and deployed to inflict casualties on an ever-
growing scale. In defeating Nazi Germany and Imperial Japan, Allied forces
destroyed entire cities, while enemy leaders who started the conflict were
safe until the final days. Military power was used to end a regime by breaking a nation.

Today, we have the greater power to free a nation by breaking a dangerous and aggressive regime. With new tactics and precision weapons, we

can achieve military objectives without directing violence against civilians. No device of man can remove the tragedy from war; yet it is a great moral advance when the guilty have far more to fear from war than the innocent.

In the images of celebrating Iraqis, we have also seen the ageless appeal of human freedom. Decades of lies and intimidation could not make the Iraqi people love their oppressors or desire their own enslavement. Men and women in every culture need liberty like they need food and water and air. Everywhere that freedom arrives, humanity rejoices; and everywhere that freedom stirs, let tyrants fear.

We have difficult work to do in Iraq. We're bringing order to parts of that country that remain dangerous. We're pursuing and finding leaders of the old regime, who will be held to account for their crimes. We've begun the search for hidden chemical and biological weapons and already know of hundreds of sites that will be investigated. We're helping to rebuild Iraq, where the dictator built palaces for himself, instead of hospitals and schools. And we will stand with the new leaders of Iraq as they establish a government of, by, and for the Iraqi people.

The transition from dictatorship to democracy will take time, but it is worth every effort. Our coalition will stay until our work is done. Then we will leave, and we will leave behind a free Iraq.

The battle of Iraq is one victory in a war on terror that began on September the 11, 2001—and still goes on. That terrible morning, nineteen evil men—the shock troops of a hateful ideology—gave America and the civilized world a glimpse of their ambitions. They imagined, in the words of one terrorist, that September the 11th would be the "beginning of the end of America." By seeking to turn our cities into killing fields, terrorists and their allies believed that they could destroy this nation's resolve, and force our retreat from the world. They have failed.

In the battle of Afghanistan, we destroyed the Taliban, many terrorists, and the camps where they trained. We continue to help the Afghan people lay roads, restore hospitals, and educate all of their children. Yet we also have dangerous work to complete. As I speak, a Special Operations task force, led by the 82nd Airborne, is on the trail of the terrorists and those who seek to undermine the free government of Afghanistan. America and our coalition will finish what we have begun.

From Pakistan to the Philippines to the Horn of Africa, we are hunting down al Qaeda killers. Nineteen months ago, I pledged that the terrorists would not escape the patient justice of the United States. And as of tonight, nearly one-half of al Qaeda's senior operatives have been captured or killed.

The liberation of Iraq is a crucial advance in the campaign against terror. We've removed an ally of al Qaeda and cut off a source of terrorist funding. And this much is certain: No terrorist network will gain weapons of mass destruction from the Iraqi regime, because the regime is no more.

In these nineteen months that changed the world, our actions have been focused and deliberate and proportionate to the offense. We have not forgotten the victims of September the 11th—the last phone calls, the cold murder of children, the searches in the rubble. With those attacks, the terrorists and their supporters declared war on the United States. And war is what they got.

Our war against terror is proceeding according to principles that I have made clear to all: Any person involved in committing or planning terrorist attacks against the American people becomes an enemy of this country, and a target of American justice.

Any person, organization, or government that supports, protects, or harbors terrorists is complicit in the murder of the innocent, and equally guilty of terrorist crimes.

Any outlaw regime that has ties to terrorist groups and seeks or possesses weapons of mass destruction is a grave danger to the civilized world—and will be confronted.

And anyone in the world, including the Arab world, who works and sacrifices for freedom has a loyal friend in the United States of America.

Our commitment to liberty is America's tradition—declared at our founding; affirmed in Franklin Roosevelt's Four Freedoms; asserted in the Truman Doctrine and in Ronald Reagan's challenge to an evil empire. We are committed to freedom in Afghanistan, in Iraq, and in a peaceful Palestine. The advance of freedom is the surest strategy to undermine the appeal of terror in the world. Where freedom takes hold, hatred gives way to hope. When freedom takes hold, men and women turn to the peaceful pursuit of a better life. American values and American interests lead in the same direction: We stand for human liberty.

The United States upholds these principles of security and freedom in many ways—with all the tools of diplomacy, law enforcement, intelligence, and finance. We're working with a broad coalition of nations that understand the threat and our shared responsibility to meet it. The use of force has been—and remains—our last resort. Yet all can know, friend and foe alike, that our nation has a mission: We will answer threats to our security, and we will defend the peace.

Our mission continues. Al Qaeda is wounded, not destroyed. The scattered cells of the terrorist network still operate in many nations, and we know from daily intelligence that they continue to plot against free people. The proliferation of deadly weapons remains a serious danger. The enemies of freedom are not idle, and neither are we. Our government has taken unprecedented measures to defend the homeland. And we will continue to hunt down the enemy before he can strike.

The war on terror is not over; yet it is not endless. We do not know the day of final victory, but we have seen the turning of the tide. No act of the terrorists will change our purpose, or weaken our resolve, or alter their fate. Their cause is lost. Free nations will press on to victory. . . .

# DOCUMENT 4.5

The UN Security Council had refused to sanction the invasion of Iraq, but President Bush's many critics sought to secure some international influence over his conduct of the occupation. For his part, the British prime minister, Tony Blair, had argued that Washington and London needed UN participation if they were to claim any legitimacy at all (2.6). This confluence of interests in international participation produced Security Council Resolution 1483. Periodically renewed, it was the most important, if implicit, international sanction for the Anglo–American occupation. Washington's willingness to seek Security Council authorization for the occupation was an admission that, neoconservative claims to the contrary, the United Nations was an important institution for U.S. foreign-policy objectives, not least because many countries refused to send peacekeeping troops without explicit Security Council authorization.

---

## SECURITY COUNCIL RESOLUTION 1483, MAY 22, 2003 (EXCERPT)

The Security Council,

Recalling all its previous relevant resolutions,

Reaffirming the sovereignty and territorial integrity of Iraq,

Reaffirming also the importance of the disarmament of Iraqi weapons of mass destruction and of eventual confirmation of the disarmament of Iraq,

Stressing the right of the Iraqi people freely to determine their own political future and control their own natural resources, welcoming the commitment of all parties concerned to support the creation of an environment in which they may do so as soon as possible, and expressing resolve that the day when Iraqis govern themselves must come quickly,

Encouraging efforts by the people of Iraq to form a representative government based on the rule of law that affords equal rights and justice to all Iraqi citizens without regard to ethnicity, religion, or gender, and, in this connection. . . .

Resolved that the United Nations should play a vital role in humanitarian relief, the reconstruction of Iraq, and the restoration and establishment of national and local institutions for representative governance,

Noting the statement of 12 April 2003 by the Ministers of Finance and Central Bank Governors of the Group of Seven Industrialized Nations in which the members recognized the need for a multilateral effort to help rebuild and develop Iraq and for the need for assistance from the International Monetary Fund and the World Bank in these efforts,

Welcoming also the resumption of humanitarian assistance and the continuing efforts of the Secretary-General and the specialized agencies to provide food and medicine to the people of Iraq,

Welcoming the appointment by the Secretary-General of his Special Advisor on Iraq,

Affirming the need for accountability for crimes and atrocities committed by the previous Iraqi regime,

Stressing the need for respect for the archaeological, historical, cultural, and religious heritage of Iraq, and for the continued protection of archaeological, historical, cultural, and religious sites, museums, libraries, and monuments,

Noting the letter of 8 May 2003 from the Permanent Representatives of the United States of America and the United Kingdom of Great Britain and Northern Ireland to the President of the Security Council and recognizing the specific authorities, responsibilities, and obligations under applicable international law of these states as occupying powers under unified command. . . .

Noting further that other States that are not occupying powers are working now or in the future may work under the Authority,

Welcoming further the willingness of Member States to contribute to stability and security in Iraq by contributing personnel, equipment, and other resources under the Authority,

Concerned that many Kuwaitis and Third-State Nationals still are not accounted for since 2 August 1990,

Determining that the situation in Iraq, although improved, continues to constitute a threat to international peace and security,

Acting under Chapter VII of the Charter of the United Nations,

1. Appeals to Member States and concerned organizations to assist the people of Iraq in their efforts to reform their institutions and rebuild their country, and to contribute to conditions of stability and security in Iraq in accordance with this resolution;
2. Calls upon all Member States in a position to do so to respond immediately to the humanitarian appeals of the United Nations and other international organizations for Iraq and to help meet the humanitarian and other needs of the Iraqi people by providing food, medical supplies, and resources necessary for reconstruction and rehabilitation of Iraq's economic infrastructure;
3. Appeals to Member States to deny safe haven to those members of the previous Iraqi regime who are alleged to be responsible for crimes and atrocities and to support actions to bring them to justice;
4. Calls upon the Authority, consistent with the Charter of the United Nations and other relevant international law, to promote the welfare of the Iraqi people through the effective administration of the territory, including in particular working towards the restoration of conditions of security and stability and the creation of conditions in which the Iraqi people can freely determine their own political future;

5. Calls upon all concerned to comply fully with their obligations under international law including in particular the Geneva Conventions of 1949 and the Hague Regulations of 1907;

6. Calls upon the Authority and relevant organizations and individuals to continue efforts to locate, identify, and repatriate all Kuwaiti and Third-State Nationals or the remains of those present in Iraq on or after 2 August 1990, as well as the Kuwaiti archives, that the previous Iraqi regime failed to undertake. . . .

7. Decides that all Member States shall take appropriate steps to facilitate the safe return to Iraqi institutions of Iraqi cultural property and other items of archaeological, historical, cultural, rare scientific, and religious importance illegally removed from the Iraq National Museum, the National Library, and other locations in Iraq. . . .

8. Requests the Secretary-General to appoint a Special Representative for Iraq whose independent responsibilities shall involve reporting regularly to the Council on his activities under this resolution, coordinating activities of the United Nations in post-conflict processes in Iraq, coordinating among United Nations and international agencies engaged in humanitarian assistance and reconstruction activities in Iraq, and, in coordination with the Authority, assisting the people of Iraq through:

(a) coordinating humanitarian and reconstruction assistance by United Nations agencies and between United Nations agencies and non-governmental organizations;

(b) promoting the safe, orderly, and voluntary return of refugees and displaced persons;

(c) working intensively with the Authority, the people of Iraq, and others concerned to advance efforts to restore and establish national and local institutions for representative governance, including by working together to facilitate a process leading to an internationally recognized, representative government of Iraq;

(d) facilitating the reconstruction of key infrastructure, in cooperation with other international organizations;

(e) promoting economic reconstruction and the conditions for sustainable development, including through coordination with national and regional organizations, as appropriate, civil society, donors, and the international financial institutions;

(f) encouraging international efforts to contribute to basic civilian administration functions;

(g) promoting the protection of human rights;

(h) encouraging international efforts to rebuild the capacity of the Iraqi civilian police force; and

(i) encouraging international efforts to promote legal and judicial reform;

9. Supports the formation, by the people of Iraq with the help of the Authority and working with the Special Representative, of an Iraqi interim administration as a transitional administration run by Iraqis, until an internationally recognized, representative government is established by the people of Iraq and assumes the responsibilities of the Authority;

10. Decides that. . . . all prohibitions related to trade with Iraq and the provision of financial or economic resources to Iraq. . . . shall no longer apply;

11. Reaffirms that Iraq must meet its disarmament obligations, encourages the United Kingdom of Great Britain and Northern Ireland and the United States of America to keep the Council informed of their activities in this regard, and underlines the intention of the Council to revisit the mandates of the United Nations Monitoring, Verification, and Inspection Commission and the International Atomic Energy Agency. . . .

12. Notes the establishment of a Development Fund for Iraq to be held by the Central Bank of Iraq and to be audited by independent public accountants approved by the International Advisory and Monitoring Board of the Development Fund for Iraq and looks forward to the early meeting of that International Advisory and Monitoring Board, whose members shall include duly qualified representatives of the Secretary-General, of the Managing Director of the International Monetary Fund, of the Director-General of the Arab Fund for Social and Economic Development, and of the President of the World Bank;

13. Notes further that the funds in the Development Fund for Iraq shall be disbursed at the direction of the Authority, in consultation with the Iraqi interim administration, for the purposes set out in paragraph 14 below;

14. Underlines that the Development Fund for Iraq shall be used in a transparent manner to meet the humanitarian needs of the Iraqi people, for the economic reconstruction and repair of Iraq's infrastructure, for the continued disarmament of Iraq, and for the costs of Iraqi civilian administration, and for other purposes benefitting the people of Iraq;

15. Calls upon the international financial institutions to assist the people of Iraq in the reconstruction and development of their economy and to facilitate assistance by the broader donor community, and welcomes the readiness of creditors, including those of the Paris Club, to seek a solution to Iraq's sovereign debt problems;

16. Requests also that the Secretary-General, in coordination with the Authority. . . . terminate. . . . in the most cost effective manner, the ongoing operations of the "Oil-for-Food" Programme. . . .

24. Requests the Secretary-General to report to the Council at regular intervals on the work of the Special Representative with respect to the implementation of this resolution and on the work of the International Advisory and Monitoring Board and encourages the United Kingdom of Great Britain and Northern Ireland and the United States of America to inform the Council at regular intervals of their efforts under this resolution;

25. Decides to review the implementation of this resolution within twelve months of adoption and to consider further steps that might be necessary;

26. Calls upon Member States and international and regional organizations to contribute to the implementation of this resolution;

27. Decides to remain seized of this matter.

## DOCUMENT 4.6

L. Paul Bremer arrived in Baghdad on May 12, 2003, and immediately made it clear that he was in charge. He began his tenure as head of the Coalition Provisional Authority with Orders 1 and 2, which dissolved the Baath Party, the Iraqi government, the armed forces, and a host of other institutions—a project that was dear to Ahmed Chalabi and his patrons in Washington.

The administration had been discussing how far to go with de-Baathification for weeks prior to Bremer's arrival. The State Department advocated a moderate policy of "de-Saddammification," purging the party and the state of those who had committed crimes and those at the very top of the command structure but leaving intact most of the country's national institutions. The Defense Department wanted a more radical purge, since it was looking to install Chalabi and the exiles. The CIA agreed with State, and the vice president's office agreed with Defense. In the end, the dispute ended up in the White House, where National Security Advisor Condoleezza Rice proposed a compromise: those in the highest ranks of the party—about 1 percent of the membership—would be fired and barred from further employment in the public sector. Others would be subject to a "truth and justice" or "truth and reconciliation" process that had been pioneered in Argentina and South Africa. On March 10, Bush held a meeting with his war cabinet—Rice, Cheney, Rumsfeld, and Powell—and accepted Rice's compromise proposal, a clear decision to go easy on the Baathists and preserve some of the institutions that might help organize the occupation and provide for a speedy withdrawal of foreign troops.

But Bremer reported to Rumsfeld, and the neoconservatives triumphed in the end. Powell and Rice said they never saw the drafts of Bremer's first two orders, which many observers later blamed for depriving the occupation of people who knew how Iraq worked and, worse, for fueling the insurgency. Despite considerable opposition from Garner, Maj. Gen. David Petraeus, who com-

manded the 101st Airborne Division, and others in Baghdad, and from Powell and others in Washington, Bremer repeatedly insisted that he had his orders to do away with the Baath Party, the Iraqi government, and the armed forces. With these two orders, hundreds of thousands of skilled, politicized, and armed men were driven into angry and humiliated opposition. In a land of honor and tradition, the incoming viceroy began his work by dissolving the only national institutions that had a shred of legitimacy. The two orders made it clear that the head of the CPA was envisaging a relatively prolonged period of direct rule and an even longer occupation. To add insult to injury, Bremer put Chalabi in charge of de-Baathification.

It remained unclear why Bremer's two orders were issued despite the decision of the president and his advisors. Several well-informed observers suspected that Rumsfeld and Cheney had maneuvered around Bush, Rice, and Powell. Others, Bremer among them, claimed that he had cleared the matter at the highest levels of government.[4]

Petraeus's concern was important, since he was one of the only senior officers who had taken seriously the task of developing an updated counterinsurgency doctrine. Rumsfeld's plan for reinventing the armed forces did not include the concerns that were so troubling to Petraeus. The secretary's interest in refining a "blitzkrieg" strategy of advanced technology, mobile forces, and devastating offensives made him skeptical of the patient, time-consuming, on-the-ground work that nation-building and Petraeus's theory of counterinsurgency required (5.3). Rumsfeld's increasingly stubborn reluctance even to admit that an Iraqi insurgency was taking shape made it difficult for the public to understand what was happening in the late spring of 2003 (4.8). This problem was made worse by the confidence with which the architects of preemptive war had assured the country that both the invasion and the occupation of Iraq would be relatively quick, popular, and inexpensive.

| 183

When Andrew Rathmell, a British defense expert and the CPA's Director of Policy Planning, analyzed Bremer's failures in January 2006, he found that the basic elements of any successful policy were absent. He cited a reluctance to communicate information that deviated from established positions, conflict and confusion between Washington and Baghdad and between Baghdad and other parts of Iraq, a fragmented CPA organization, inadequate communication and debate, a tendency to adopt goals without the necessary resources, and flawed or nonexistent plans in the run-up to the invasion. "The prewar assumption had been that the coalition would be universally welcomed by Iraqis and that Iraq's administrative and physical infrastructures were robust enough not to require too much international assistance," he said. "In reality, the CPA

---

4. See, e.g., L. Paul Bremer, *My Year in Iraq: The Struggle to Build a Future of Hope* (New York: Simon & Schuster, 2006); James Mann, *Rise of the Vulcans: The History of Bush's War Cabinet* (New York: Penguin, 2004); Thomas Ricks, *Fiasco: The American Military Adventure in Iraq* (New York: Penguin, 2006); and Edmund L. Andrews, "Envoy's Letter Counters Bush on Dismantling of Iraq Army," *New York Times*, September 4, 2007.

ended up creating nation-building institutions on the run, governing Iraq at all levels, supporting a counterinsurgency campaign, reconstructing and reforming Iraqi state institutions, and implementing democratic and economic transformation." Rathmell concluded that, even though the task would have been difficult under the best of circumstances, "a greater willingness to question over-optimistic assumptions and more thorough preparation would have given the coalition a running start rather than putting it on the back foot from the outset."[5]

---

## COALITION PROVISIONAL AUTHORITY ORDER NUMBER 1, MAY 16, 2003

### DE-BA'ATHIFICATION OF IRAQI SOCIETY

Pursuant to my authority as Administrator of the Coalition Provisional Authority (CPA), relevant UN Security Council resolutions, and the laws and usages of war,

Recognizing that the Iraqi people have suffered large scale human rights abuses and deprivations over many years at the hands of the Ba'ath Party,

Noting the grave concern of Iraqi society regarding the threat posed by the continuation of Ba'ath Party networks and personnel in the administration of Iraq, and the intimidation of the people of Iraq by Ba'ath Party officials,

Concerned by the continuing threat to the security of the Coalition Forces posed by the Iraqi Ba'ath Party,

I hereby promulgate the following:

*Section 1*

Disestablishment of the Ba'ath Party

1) On April 16, 2003 the Coalition Provisional Authority disestablished the Ba'ath Party of Iraq. This order implements the declaration by eliminating the party's structures and removing its leadership from positions of authority and responsibility in Iraqi society. By this means, the Coalition Provisional Authority will ensure that representative government in Iraq is not threatened by Ba'athist elements returning to power ant [*sic*] that those in positions of authority in the future are acceptable to the people of Iraq.

2) Full members of the Ba'ath Party holding the ranks of 'Udw Qutriyya (Regional Command Member), 'Udw Far' (Branch

---

5. Andrew Rathmell, "Planning Post-Reconstruction in Iraq: What Can We Learn?" *International Affairs* 81, no. 5 (January 2006).

Member). 'Udw Shu'bah (Section Member), and 'Udw Firqah (Group Member) (together, "Senior Party Members") are herby [*sic*] removed from their positions and banned from future employment in the public sector. These Senior Party Members shall be evaluated for criminal conduct or threat to the security of the Coalition. Those suspected of criminal conduct shall be investigated and, if deemed a threat to security or a flight risk, detained or placed under house arrest.

3) Individuals holding positions in the top three layers of management in every national government ministry, affiliated corporations and other government institutions (e.g., universities and hospitals) shall be interviewed for possible affiliation with the Ba'ath Party, and subject to investigation for criminal conduct and risk to security. Any such persons detained to be full members of the Ba'ath Party shall be removed from their employment. This includes those holding the more junior ranks of 'Udw (Member) and 'Udw 'Amil (Active Member), as well as those determined to be Senior Party Members.

4) Displays in government buildings or public spaces of the image or likeness of Saddam Hussein or other readily identifiable members of the former regime or of symbols of the Baath Party or the former regime are hereby prohibited.

5) Rewards shall be made available for information leading to the capture of senior members of the Baath party and individuals complicit in the crimes of the former regime.

6) The Administrator of the Coalition Provisional Authority or his designees may grant exceptions to the above guidance on a case-by-case basis.

*Section 2*

Entry into Force
This order shall enter into force on the date of signature.

# DOCUMENT 4.7

Bremer's Order Number 2 was issued a week after Number 1 and was intended to complete the "de-Baathification" of Iraq.

COALITION PROVISIONAL AUTHORITY ORDER NUMBER 2,
MAY 23, 2003

## DISSOLUTION OF ENTITIES

Pursuant to my authority as Administrator of the Coalition Provisional Authority (CPA), relevant UN Security Council resolutions, including Resolution 1483 (2003), and the laws and usages of war,

Reconfirming all of the provisions of General Franks' Freedom Message to the Iraqi People of April 16, 2003,

Recognizing that the prior Iraqi regime used certain government entities to oppress the Iraqi people and as instruments of torture, repression and corruption,

Reaffirming the Instructions to the Citizens of Iraq regarding Ministry of Youth and Sport of May 8, 2003,

I hereby promulgate the following:

*Section 1*

Dissolved Entities
The entities (the "Dissolved Entities") listed in the attached Annex are hereby dissolved. Additional entities may be added to this list in the future.

186 |    *Section 2*

Assets and Financial Obligations
1) All assets, including records and data, in whatever from [*sic*] maintained and wherever located, of the Dissolved Entities shall be held by the Administrator of the CPA ("the Administrator") on behalf of and for the benefit of the Iraqi people and shall be used to assist the Iraqi people and to support the recovery of Iraq.
2) All financial obligations of the Dissolved Entities are suspended. The Administrator of the CPA will establish procedures whereby persons claiming to be the beneficiaries of such obligations may apply for payment.
3) Persons in possession of assets of the Dissolved Entities shall preserve those assets, promptly inform local Coalition authorities, and immediately turn them over, as directed by those authorities. Continued possession, transfer, sale, use, conversion, or concealment of such assets following the date of this Order is prohibited and may be punished.

*Section 3*

Employees and Service Members
1) Any military or other rank, title, or status granted to a former employee or functionary of a Dissolved Entity by the former Regime is hereby cancelled.

2) All conscripts are released from their service obligations. Conscriptions is suspended indefinitely, subject to decisions by future Iraq governments concerning whether a free Iraq should have conscription.

3) Any person employed by a Dissolved Entity in any form or capacity, is dismissed effective as of April 16, 2003. Any person employed by a Dissolved Entity, in any from or capacity remains accountable for acts committed during such employment.

4) A termination payment in an amount to be determined by the Administrator will be paid to employees so dismissed, except those who are Senior Party Members as defined in the Administrator's May 16, 2003 Order of the Coalition Provisional Authority De-Ba'athification of Iraqi Society, CPA/ORD/2003/01 ("Senior Party Members") (See Section 3.6).

5) Pensions being paid by, or on account of service to, a Dissolved Entity before April 16, 2003 will continue to be paid, including to war widows and disabled veterans, provided that no pension payments will be made to any person who is a Senior Party Member (see Section 3.6) and that the power is reserved to the Administrator and to future Iraqi governments to revoke or reduce pensions as a penalty for past or future illegal conduct or to modify pension arrangements to eliminate improper privileges granted by the Ba'athist regime or for similar reasons.

6) Notwithstanding any provision of this Order, or any other Order, law, or regulation, and consistent with the Administrator's May 16, 2003 Order of the Coalition Provisional Authority De-Ba'athification of Iraqi Society, CPA/ORD/2003/01, no payment, including a termination or pension payment, will be made to any person who is or was a Senior Party Member. Any person holding the rank under the former regime of Colonel or above, or its equivalent, will be deemed a Senior Party Member, provided that such persons may seek, under procedures to be prescribed, to establish to the satisfaction of the Administrator, that they were not a Senior Party Member.

ANNEX: COALITION PROVISIONAL AUTHORITY ORDER NUMBER 2

*DISSOLUTION OF ENTITIES*
Institutions dissolved by the Order referenced (the "Dissolved Entities") are:

The Ministry of Defence
The Ministry of Information
The Ministry of State for Military Affairs
The Iraqi Intelligence Service
The National Security Bureau
The Directorate of National Security (Amn al-'Am)

The Special Security Organization
All entities affiliated with or comprising Saddam Hussein's bodyguards to include:
—Murafaqin (Companions)
—Himaya al Khasa (Special Guard)
The following military organizations:
—The Army, Air Force, Navy, the Air Defence Force, and other regular military services
—The Republican Guard
—The Special Republican Guard
—The Directorate of Military Intelligence
—The Al Quds Force
—Emergency Forces (Quwat al Tawari)
The following paramilitaries:
—Saddam Fedayeen
—Ba'ath Party Militia
—Friends of Saddam
—Saddam's Lion Cubs (Ashbal Saddam)
Other Organizations:
—The Presidential Diwan
—The Presidential Secretariat
—The National Assembly
—The Youth Organization (al-Futuwah)
—National Olympic Committee
—Revolutionary, Special and National Security Courts

All organizations subordinate to the Dissolved Entities are also dissolved. Additional organizations may be added to this list in the future.

## DOCUMENT 4.8

For weeks, the administration insisted that Iraqi resistance to the occupation was limited to criminals, diehards, and terrorists. Secretary Rumsfeld was particularly aggressive in asserting this, repeatedly suggesting that the vast majority of Iraqis saw U.S. forces as liberators and that Washington's preemptive war and occupation were proceeding smoothly.

---

"RUMSFELD BLAMES IRAQ PROBLEMS ON 'POCKETS OF DEAD-ENDERS,'" ASSOCIATED PRESS, JUNE 18, 2003

Defense Secretary Donald Rumsfeld on Wednesday played down recent deadly attacks on Americans in Iraq, equating those losses with everyday violence in large U.S. cities.

Attacks and accidents have killed about 50 American troops—including about a dozen from hostile fire—since major combat was officially declared over on May 1. Between March 20, when the war started, and May 1, 138 Americans died from accidents or hostile fire.

Asked at a Pentagon press conference about the Iraqi resistance, Rumsfeld described it as "small elements" of 10 to 20 people, not large military formations or networks of attackers. He said there "is a little debate" in the administration over whether there is any central control to the resistance, which officials say is coming from Saddam's former Baath Party, Fedayeen paramilitary, and other loyalists.

"In those regions where pockets of dead-enders are trying to reconstitute, Gen. (Tommy) Franks and his team are rooting them out," Rumsfeld said, referring to the U.S. commander in Iraq. "In short, the coalition is making good progress."

While the deaths of U.S. troops generate "a deep sorrow," Rumsfeld said, he believes the American people feel the sacrifices are worthwhile.

"They recognize the difficulty of the task," Rumsfeld said. "You got to remember that if Washington, D.C., were the size of Baghdad, we would be having something like 215 murders a month. There's going to be violence in a big city." Rumsfeld noted that Baghdad has nearly six million residents.

Still, Rumsfeld added, "It tends not to be, at this stage, random killings. . . . What you're seeing instead is what we believe is purposeful attacks against coalition forces, as opposed to simply crime and that type of thing."

On Capitol Hill, Deputy Defense Secretary Paul Wolfowitz said, "We are still in a phase where we need some significant combat power to take on these remnants of the old regime."

"I think these people are the last remnants of a dying cause," he told the House Armed Services Committee. He said U.S. forces "have the sympathy of the population, not the surviving elements of the Baathist regime."

Some lawmakers are increasingly uneasy about the daily killings of soldiers, the stretching thin of troop forces, excessive demands on reservists and the costs of the war.

Wolfowitz and Marine Corps. Gen. Peter Pace, vice chairman of the Joint Chiefs of Staff, said they believed the burden on U.S. forces would ease as more coalition forces enter Iraq. Pace said two additional divisions should be added in August or September to the 120,000 forces now in Iraq.

In Iraq, Maj. Gen. Ray Odierno said raids begun Sunday had resulted in the capture of a number of senior Iraqi figures and the seizure of millions of dollars they were using to finance continued fighting.

At the Pentagon, Rumsfeld defended as "imperfect but good" the intelligence the Bush administration used to build its case for a war to disarm Saddam of weapons of mass destruction.

"I think the intelligence was correct in general," he said. "And you will always find out precisely what it was once you get on the ground and have a chance to talk to people and explore it."

Failure of troops to find any chemical or biological weapons in three months of trying has led critics to suggest the administration exaggerated intelligence findings in order to win support for the war.

Odierno, commander of the 4th Infantry Division, said that troops are pressing forward with patrols and raids to defeat resistance forces and capture former leaders of Saddam's toppled government.

"Although major combat operations have concluded, our soldiers are involved in almost daily contact with noncompliant forces, former regime members and common criminals," said Odierno, whose troops operate north of Baghdad to Kirkuk and east to the Iranian border. The area includes Tikrit, Saddam's former hometown.

"We are seeing military activity throughout our zone, but I really qualify it as militarily insignificant," Odierno told Pentagon reporters in a video conference from Tikrit. He added that the attacks are "having no impact on the way we conduct business on a day-to-day basis."

The commander spoke on the fourth day of Operation Desert Scorpion. Officials had announced Tuesday the capture of 412 people in 69 raids in Baghdad and northern Iraq.

He said 50 more people detained at raids Wednesday were tied to Saddam security or paramilitary groups and included a former Saddam bodyguard.

190 |

## DOCUMENT 4.9

Bremer set about trying to organize a slow-motion transfer of power as soon as he arrived in Baghdad, and he worried that elections might create more problems than they would solve. His first impulse was to appoint a drafting committee that would write a constitution and organize a government friendly to the United States. But he soon found out that it was not easy to rule an occupied country. On June 28, 2003, Ayatollah Ali al-Sistani, the revered Islamic thinker and Shia cleric, issued a "fatwa," or religious ruling, stating that the framers of a permanent Iraqi constitution must be elected by the Iraqi people and not appointed by U.S. officials. "The occupation authorities are not entitled to name the members of the assembly charged with drafting the constitution," Sistani said. "There is no guarantee that such a convention will draft a constitution which upholds the Iraqi people's interests and expresses their national identity." Sistani would hold to that position throughout the yearlong tenure of the CPA and would reinforce it by demanding direct and continuous UN involvement in bringing the occupation to an end.

Sistani's fatwa forced Bremer to revise his plan, and on July 13 the CPA announced the formation of a twenty-five-member Iraq Governing Council. Bremer had rejected Wolfowitz's and Feith's advice that he simply turn power over to Chalabi and the other exiles. Acting under pressure from Sistani and many other Iraqis, he made it clear that the Governing Council would serve as the provisional government. A multiethnic, multireligious group that included tribal leaders, clerics and secular figures, men and women, Shia and Sunnis, Arabs, Kurds, and representatives from minority communities, the Council seemed to be a relatively representative organ that would run the country until elections could be held, a constitution written, and a permanent government organized. Though subject to Bremer's authority, the Council was authorized to draft a temporary constitution that would organize elections for a national assembly, write a permanent constitution, and establish a sovereign government. But it was never clear that legitimate institutions could emerge under the conditions of foreign occupation, and the Council was soon hobbled by internal weaknesses and by the indisputable fact that the U.S. Army and the CPA were the sources of real power in Iraq.

---

COALITION PROVISIONAL AUTHORITY REGULATION NUMBER 6, JULY 13, 2003

## GOVERNING COUNCIL OF IRAQ

Pursuant to my authority as Administrator of the Coalition Provisional Authority (CPA), relevant UN Security Council resolutions, including Resolution 1483 (2003), and the laws and usages of war,

Recognizing that, as stated in paragraph 9 of Resolution 1483, the Security Council supports the formation of an Iraqi interim administration as a transitional administration run by Iraqis, until the people of Iraq establish an internationally recognized, representative government that assumes the responsibilities of the CPA,

Noting that on July 13, 2003, the Governing Council met and announced its formation as the principal body of the Iraqi interim administration referred to in paragraph 9 of Resolution 1483,

Affirming that the CPA and the Special Representative of the UN Secretary General have worked together and will continue to work together in a cooperative and consultative process to support the formation and operation of the Governing Council and welcomed the formation of the Governing Council on July 13, 2003,

Acknowledging that, consistent with Resolution 1483, the Governing Council has certain authorities and responsibilities as representatives of the Iraqi people, including insuring that the Iraqi people's interests are represented in both the interim administration and in determining the means of establishing an internationally recognized, representative government,

Emphasizing that, consistent with Resolution 1483, the Governing Council and the CPA, each in coordination with the Special Representative of the UN Secretary General, undertake to work together in a cooperative and consultative process for the benefit of the Iraqi people,

I promulgate the following:

*Section 1*

Recognition of Governing Council
The CPA recognizes the formation of the Governing Council as the principal body of the Iraqi interim administration, pending the establishment of an internationally recognized, representative government by the people of Iraq, consistent with Resolution 1483.

*Section 2*

Relations between Governing Council and CPA
1) In accordance with Resolution 1483, the Governing Council and the CPA shall consult and coordinate on all matters involving the temporary government of Iraq, including the authorities of the Governing Council.
2) All officials of the CPA are instructed promptly to respond to all requests for experts, technical assistance or other support requested by the Governing Council.

*Section 3*

Entry into Force
The Regulation shall enter into force on the date of signature.

# DOCUMENT 4.10

Despite the CPA's publicly stated claim that a hundred "indicators" showed that the occupation was progressing well, a nationwide insurgency gained strength during the summer of 2003. The Jordanian embassy was bombed on August 7, part of a strategy aimed at U.S. allies and international institutions. On August 19, a cement truck filled with explosives blew up in front of the UN headquarters in Baghdad, killing twenty-two people (among them Sergio Vieira de Mello, the UN Special Representative), wounding many more, and forcing the United Nations to drastically curtail its activities. And on August 29, Ayatollah Mohammed Baqir al-Hakim, one of the Americans' most important Iraqi allies and the highest-ranking Shia cleric to have openly supported the occupation, was killed at the Imam Ali Mosque in the holy city of Najaf. As chaos spread and it became clear that Washington would be unable to organize Iraq as it wanted, Bremer was forced to begin thinking about ending the formal occupation and handing sovereignty over to an Iraqi government. But it proved very difficult to satisfy Sistani's demand for elections, accommodate the requirements of various Iraqi constituencies, and accede to Washington's need to organize an ostensibly sovereign Iraqi government while preserving U.S. political, economic, and military options.

The CPA's conflicting impulses, constituencies, and tasks had initially implied that its tenure would be a long one, a possibility that became increasingly unacceptable as the first summer of the troubled occupation came to a close. By September, Bremer had arrived at a seven-point plan for ending formal U.S. responsibility for Iraqi affairs. Disengagement would develop in three phases: a constitution would be written by Iraqis and national elections would be held, after which the occupation would be dissolved and sovereignty restored. But Bremer had not cleared his plan with his superiors, and when the *Washington Post* ran his op-ed piece on September 8 (4.10), it took the Defense Department, the State Department, and the White House by surprise. As antiwar sentiment in the United States intensified and the White House began thinking about the 2004 midterm elections, the administration grew more concerned about the possibility of a long occupation. Bremer was summoned to Washington, instructed to drop his earlier plan, and told to focus on a rapid transfer of sovereignty (4.11).

---

## L. PAUL BREMER, "IRAQ'S PATH TO SOVEREIGNTY," *WASHINGTON POST,* SEPTEMBER 8, 2003

Five months ago today the brave men and women of our armed forces were completing the liberation of Iraq's 25 million citizens. It was a tremendous military triumph. Gone are Saddam Hussein's torture chambers. Gone are his mass killings and rape rooms. And gone is his threat to America and the international community. The liberation was a great and noble deed.

It is fair to ask: What is next?

No thoughtful person would suggest that the coalition should govern Iraq for long. Although Iraqis have freedoms they have never had before, freedom is not sovereignty and occupation is unpopular with occupier and occupied alike. We believe Iraqis should be given responsibility for their own security, economic development and political system as soon as possible.

So, then, how can we get Iraqis back in charge of Iraq?

Elections are the obvious solution to restoring sovereignty to the Iraqi people. But at the present elections are simply not possible. There are no election rolls, no election law, no political parties' law and no electoral districts.

The current constitution is a Hussein-dictated formula for tyranny. When Hussein loaded two trucks with money and fled the advancing coalition forces, he left behind a vacuum. Electing a government without a permanent constitution defining and limiting government powers invites confusion and eventual abuse.

So, to hold elections Iraq needs a new constitution and it must be written by Iraqis. It must reflect their culture and beliefs. Writing a constitution, as all Americans know, is a solemn and important undertaking. It cannot be done in days or weeks.

Nonetheless, the path to full Iraqi sovereignty is clear. The journey has begun and three of the seven steps on this path have already been taken.

The first step came two months ago with the creation of a 25-member Governing Council broadly representative of Iraqi society. These brave men and women have come forward willingly to help build the new Iraq.

The second step took place last month when the Governing Council named a preparatory committee to devise a way to write a constitution.

The third and most important was putting day-to-day operation of Iraqi government in the hands of Iraqis. Last week the Governing Council named 25 ministers. Now every Iraqi ministry is run by an Iraqi appointed by Iraqis. These ministers, who serve at the pleasure of the Governing Council, conduct the business of government. They set policy.

Even today, they are preparing the 2004 budget and must operate their ministries according to those budgets. The coalition wants them to exercise real power and will thrust authority at them.

Writing Iraq's new constitution is the fourth step. It begins after the preparatory committee recommends a process for writing a constitution to the Governing Council later this month.

Step five, popular ratification of the constitution, is indispensable.

194 |

Once written, the constitution will be widely circulated, discussed and debated among the Iraqi people. All adult Iraqis will have the opportunity to vote for or against it. For the first time in history, Iraq will have a permanent constitution written by and approved by the Iraqi people.

The sixth step, election of a government, follows naturally. Shortly after the constitution is ratified by popular vote there will be an election to fill the elective offices specified in the constitution.

The officials in charge of that government will be chosen through universal adult suffrage in an open election.

When that government is elected, Iraq will have a government designed and selected by Iraqis. It will be unique in Iraq's history and will send a powerful message about democracy to other countries in the region.

The seventh step, dissolving the coalition authority, will follow naturally on the heels of elections. Once Iraq has a freely elected government, the coalition authority will happily yield the remainder of its authority to that sovereign Iraqi government.

The process is straightforward and realistic. No doubt there will be bumps on the path, especially as terrorists have decided to make Iraq a key battlefield in the global war on terrorism. But the Iraqi people, with the full support of the administration and its coalition partners, are on the way to exercising full political sovereignty.

Iraq faces many problems, including decades of under-investment in everything from the oil industry to the sewer system. Security issues are a matter of grave concern. There are other problems as well, but knowing how to turn Iraq into a sovereign state is not one of them.

Last night the president called upon Americans to continue to support the Iraqis in their progress. I am confident that the American people will rise to this challenge as they always do.

# DOCUMENT 4.11

By November 15, 2003, Bremer's plan had run aground. Steps one and two had been accomplished. Step three was progressing. It was step four that proved the plan's undoing. Bremer had been trying to circumvent Sistani's call for elections for weeks, unsure that voters would provide for equality between men and women, the separation of mosque and state, a market economy, and other elements that Washington considered crucial in its drive to make Iraq an example of U.S.-style Arab democracy. When the preparatory committee yielded to Sistani and voted unanimously to require that the constitution be approved in a national election, Bremer was called to Washington. As it became clear that the occupation was unraveling, he hastily made plans for an elected interim government and the early transfer of sovereignty.

The November 15 "Agreement on Political Process" (4.11) between the CPA and the Iraq Governing Council was the Bush administration's admission of defeat. The neoconservative goal of transforming Iraq would have required a much longer occupation than was politically or militarily possible. The new timetable was shorter and abandoned the goal of establishing a permanent constitution and government before the handover of sovereignty. Indeed, the United States would officially dissolve the occupation less than eight months later. Almost every element of Washington's ambitious plans had to be abandoned, among them the timetable for elections, Bremer's caucus system, and the CPA's privatization program (4.12–4.14). From November on, Washington wanted to move as quickly as possible toward the transfer of power. Neoconservative plans for a permanent U.S. presence in the region were put on hold. Like it or not, events would be decided in Iraq.

AGREEMENT ON POLITICAL PROCESS, NOVEMBER 15, 2003

The "Fundamental Law"
To be drafted by the Governing Council, in close consultation with the CPA. Will be approved by both the GC and CPA, and will formally set forth the scope and structure of the sovereign Iraqi transitional administration.

*Elements of the "Fundamental Law":*

- Bill of rights, to include freedom of speech, legislature, religion; statement of equal rights of all Iraqis, regardless of gender, sect, and ethnicity; and guarantees of due process.
- Federal arrangement for Iraq, to include governorates [*Editors' Note: Provinces*] and the separation and specification of powers to be exercised by central and local entities.
- Statement of the independence of the judiciary, and a mechanism for judicial review.
- Statement of civilian political control over Iraqi armed and security forces.
- Statement that Fundamental Law cannot be amended.
- An expiration date for Fundamental Law.
- Timetable for drafting of Iraq's permanent constitution by a body directly elected by the Iraqi people; for ratifying the permanent constitution; and for holding elections under the new constitution.

Drafting and approval of "Fundamental Law" to be complete by February 28, 2004.

## Agreements with Coalition on Security

To be agreed between the CPA and the GC.

Security agreements to cover status of Coalition forces in Iraq, giving wide latitude to provide for the safety and security of the Iraqi people. Approval of bilateral agreements complete by the end of March 2004.

## Selection of Transitional National Assembly

Fundamental Law will specify the bodies of the national structure, and will ultimately spell out the process by which individuals will be selected for these bodies. However, certain guidelines must be agreed in advance.

The transitional assembly will not be an expansion of the GC. The GC will have no formal role in selecting members of the assembly, and will dissolve upon the establishment and recognition of the transitional administration. Individual members of the GC will, however, be eligible to serve in the transitional assembly, if elected according to the process below.

Election of members of the Transitional National Assembly will be conducted through a transparent, participatory, democratic process of caucuses in each of Iraq's 18 governorates.

- In each governorate, the CPA will supervise a process by which an "Organizing Committee" of Iraqis will be formed. This Organizing Committee will include 5 individuals appointed by the Governing Council, 5 individuals appointed by the Provincial Council, and 1 individual appointed by the local council of the five largest cities within the governorate.

- The purpose of the Organizing Committee will be to convene a "Governorate Selection Caucus" of notables from around the governorate. To do so, it will solicit nominations from political parties, provincial/local councils, professional and civic associations, university faculties, tribal and religious groups. Nominees must meet the criteria set out for candidates in the Fundamental Law. To be selected as a member of the Governorate Selection Caucus, any nominee will need to be approved by an 11/15 majority of the Organizing Committee.
- Each Governorate Selection Caucus will elect representatives to represent the governorate in the new transitional assembly based on the governorate's percentage of Iraq's population.

The Transitional National Assembly will be elected no later than May 31, 2004.

### Restoration of Iraq's Sovereignty
Following the selection of members of the transitional assembly, it will meet to elect an executive branch, and to appoint ministers.

By June 30, 2004 the new transitional administration will be recognized by the Coalition, and will assume full sovereign powers for governing Iraq. The CPA will dissolve.

### Process for Adoption of Permanent Constitution
The constitutional process and timeline will ultimately be included in the Fundamental Law, but need to be agreed in advance, as detailed below.

A permanent constitution for Iraq will be prepared by a constitutional convention directly elected by the Iraqi people.

Elections for the convention will be held no later than March 15, 2005.

A draft of the constitution will be circulated for public comment and debate.

A final draft of the constitution will be presented to the public, and a popular referendum will be held to ratify the constitution.

Elections for a new Iraqi government will be held by December 31, 2005, at which point the Fundamental Law will expire and a new government will take power.

# DOCUMENT 4.12

Washington's plan to privatize important areas of the Iraqi economy—particularly the petroleum sector—was expressed in a number of CPA orders (4.12–4.14). Negotiated over a period of several months and intended to extend beyond the formal expiration of the CPA's mandate, privatization was greeted with hostility across the Iraqi political spectrum and was, at least temporarily, abandoned. But later announcements that foreign oil companies had signed preferential contracts for maintaining and modernizing the country's petroleum infrastructure raised the issue once again. Order Number 12 was designed to set the conditions for privatization by opening Iraq to international economic forces.

---

COALITION PROVISIONAL AUTHORITY ORDER NUMBER 12, JUNE 8, 2003

TRADE LIBERALIZATION POLICY

Pursuant to my authority as Administrator of the Coalition Provisional Authority (CPA) and the laws and usages of war, and consistent with relevant UN Security Council resolutions, including Resolution 1483 (2003), and the laws and usages of war,

Reconfirming the provisions of General Franks' Freedom Message to the Iraqi People of April 16, 2003,

Recognizing the central role of international trade in Iraq's recovery and its development of a free market economy,

Acting on behalf, and for the benefit of, the Iraqi people

I hereby promulgate the following:

*Section 1*

Suspension of Tariffs and Trade Restrictions

All tariffs, customs duties, import taxes, licensing fees and similar surcharges for goods entering or leaving Iraq, and all other trade restrictions that may apply to such goods, are suspended until December 31, 2003. For the remainder of this year, the CPA will not collect any such fees for goods entering or leaving Iraq by land, sea or air.

*Section 2*

Exceptions

The suspension directed under Section 1 of this order shall not apply to the goods described in the attached Annex to this Order.

*Section 3*

Entry into Force

This Order shall enter into force on the date of signature.

# DOCUMENT 4.13

Order Number 39 supplemented Bremer's Order Number 12 and the CPA's other privatization measures.

COALITION PROVISIONAL AUTHORITY ORDER NUMBER 39, DECEMBER 20, 2003 (EXCERPT)

## FOREIGN INVESTMENT

Pursuant to my authority as Administrator of the Coalition Provisional Authority (CPA) and the laws and usages of war, and consistent with relevant UN Security Council resolutions, including Resolution 1483 (2003),

Having worked closely with the Governing Council to ensure that economic change occurs in a manner acceptable to the people of Iraq,

Acknowledging the Governing Council's desire to bring about significant change to the Iraqi economic system,

Determined to improve the conditions of life, technical skills, and opportunities for all Iraqis and to fight unemployment with its associated deleterious effect on public security,

Noting that facilitating foreign investment will help to develop infrastructure, foster the growth of Iraqi business, create jobs, raise capital, result in the introduction of new technology into Iraq and promote the transfer of knowledge and skills to Iraqis,

Recognizing the problems arising from Iraq's legal framework regulating commercial activity and the way in which it was implemented by the former regime,

Recognizing the CPA's obligation to provide for the effective administration of Iraq, to ensure the well being of the Iraqi people and to enable the social functions and normal transactions of every day life,

Acting in a manner consistent with the Report of the Secretary General to the Security Council of July 17, 2003, concerning the need for the development of Iraq and its transition from a non-transparent centrally planned economy to a market economy characterized by sustainable economic growth through the establishment of a dynamic private sector, and the need to enact institutional and legal reforms to give it effect,

Having coordinated with the international financial institutions, as referenced in paragraph 8(e) of the UN Security Council Resolution 1483,

In close consultation with and acting in coordination with the Governing Council, I hereby promulgate the following: . . .

*Section 2*

Purposes
This Order promotes and safeguards the general welfare and interests of the Iraqi people by promoting foreign investment through the protection of the rights and property of foreign investors in Iraq and the regulation through transparent processes of matters relating to foreign investment in Iraq. This Order specifies the terms and procedures for making foreign investments and is intended to attract new foreign investment to Iraq.

*Section 3*

Relation to Existing Iraqi Law
   1) This Order replaces all existing foreign investment law.
   2) This Order is subject to revision by the Administrator, or to adoption or replacement by an internationally recognized, representative government established by the people of Iraq.
   3) Future Orders or other guidance will be issued concerning various sectors of the economy.

*Section 4*

Treatment of Foreign Investors
   1) A foreign investor shall be entitled to make foreign investments in Iraq on terms no less favorable than those applicable to an Iraqi investor, unless otherwise provided herein.
   2) The amount of foreign participation in newly formed or existing business entities in Iraq shall not be limited, unless otherwise expressly provided herein.

*Section 5*

Trade Offices & Branches
A foreign investor may open trade representation offices and branches in Iraq; such offices and branches shall be registered with the Iraqi Registrar of Companies.

*Section 6*

Areas of Foreign Investment
   1) Foreign investment may take place with respect to all economic sectors in Iraq, except that foreign direct and indirect ownership of the natural resources sector involving primary extraction and initial processing remains prohibited. In addition, this Order does not apply to banks and insurance companies.
   2) Foreign investment may take place in all parts of Iraq.
   3) A foreign investor shall be prohibited from engaging in retail sales, unless at least 30 days prior to engaging in such retail sales

such foreign investor deposits $100,000 in a non-interest-bearing account in a properly licensed Iraqi bank located in Iraq pursuant to procedures to be promulgated by the Ministry of Trade. Once a deposit is made pursuant to its procedures, the Ministry of Trade shall issue documentation to the foreign investor reflecting the authorization to engage in such retail sales. Such deposit must be maintained during the entire time that the foreign investor is engaged in retail sales; provided however, it shall be returned upon the request of the foreign investor at the completion of the retail sales activity.

## Section 7

Implementing Foreign Investment
  1) A foreign investor may implement foreign investment using, among other things, freely convertible currencies or Iraqi legal tender, in the following forms:
      a) establishing a wholly foreign-owned business entity in Iraq, including as a subsidiary of a foreign investor;
      b) establishing a business entity jointly with an Iraqi investor;
      c) establishing a branch office, as set forth in Section 5 herein; and
      d) directly acquiring an investment.                                    | 201
  2) A foreign investor shall be authorized to:
      a) possess, use, and dispose of its investments;
      b) manage or participate in managing a business entity;
      c) transfer its rights and obligations to other persons in accordance with the law;
      d) transfer abroad without delay all funds associated with its foreign investment, including:
          i)   shares or profits and dividends;
          ii)  proceeds from the sale or other disposition of its foreign investment or a portion thereof;
          iii) interest, royalty payments, management fees, other fees and payments made under a contract; and
          iv)  other transfers approved by the Ministry of Trade;
      e) exercise any other authority conferred upon it by law.
  3) The Finance Minister and the Minister of Planning may jointly issue regulations to assist in the implementation of this Order. . . .

## Section 13

Treatment of Investors
No legal text that impedes the operation of this Order shall hold and all investors, foreign and Iraqi, shall be treated equally under the law, except as otherwise specifically provided in this Order.

*Section 14*

International Agreements
Where an international agreement to which Iraq is a party provides for more favorable terms with respect to foreign investors undertaking investment activities in Iraq, the more favorable terms under the international agreement shall apply.

*Section 16*

Entry into Force
This Order shall enter into force on the date of signature.

## DOCUMENT 4.14

Order Number 46 brought the privatization requirements of Order Number 39 into immediate effect.

COALITION PROVISIONAL AUTHORITY ORDER NUMBER 46, DECEMBER 20, 2003

Pursuant to my authority as Administrator of the Coalition Provisional Authority (CPA) and the laws and usages of war, and consistent with relevant UN Security Council resolutions, including Resolution 1483 (2003),

Recognizing the functions of the Ministry of Trade in providing registration services needed for the establishment of companies, domestic and foreign, wishing to do business in Iraq,

Noting that the registration of companies in accordance with simplified, uniform and transparent procedures is critical to the proper implementation of the Coalition Provisional Authority Order Number 39 on foreign investment,

I hereby promulgate the following:

*Section 1*

Amendment
Coalition Provisional Authority Order Number 39, Section 7, Article 3, on Foreign Investment is hereby amended in its entirety to read as: "The Minister of Trade, in direct consultation with the CPA, shall promptly issue regulations to assist in the implementation of this Order, in coordination with the Minister of Finance and the Minister of Planning."

*Section 2*

Entry into Force
This Order shall enter into force on the date of signature.

# DOCUMENT 4.15

On March 8, 2004, the CPA issued a sixty-two-article Transitional Administrative Law (TAL) to govern the restoration of formal sovereignty by June 30. As an interim constitution foreseen in the November 15 compromise, the TAL specified a series of rights, organized central state institutions, and established federal relations between the capital and the regions, recognizing a measure of autonomy for the Kurds while reserving control of fiscal, defense, and foreign policy for Baghdad. A national assembly would draft a permanent constitution that would be submitted to the electorate to establish a permanent government. Bremer would say later that the TAL was the CPA's most important achievement. Having shelved most of Washington's ambitious plans and delayed decisions about some of the most contentious issues dividing Iraqis, the viceroy had learned the hard lesson that preemption had its limits.

---

LAW OF ADMINISTRATION FOR THE STATE OF IRAQ FOR
THE TRANSITIONAL PERIOD, MARCH 8, 2004 (EXCERPT)

PREAMBLE
The people of Iraq, striving to reclaim their freedom, which was usurped by the previous tyrannical regime, rejecting violence and coercion in all | 203 their forms, and particularly when used as instruments of governance, have determined that they shall hereafter remain a free people governed under the rule of law.

These people, affirming today their respect for international law, especially having been amongst the founders of the United Nations, working to reclaim their legitimate place among nations, have endeavored at the same time to preserve the unity of their homeland in a spirit of fraternity and solidarity in order to draw the features of the future new Iraq, and to establish the mechanisms aiming, amongst other aims, to erase the effects of racist and sectarian policies and practices.

This Law is now established to govern the affairs of Iraq during the transitional period until a duly elected government, operating under a permanent and legitimate constitution achieving full democracy, shall come into being. . . .

*Article 2*
    (A) The term "transitional period" shall refer to the period beginning on 30 June 2004 and lasting until the formation of an elected Iraqi government pursuant to a permanent constitution as set forth in this Law, which in any case shall be no later than 31 December 2005. . . .
    (B) The transitional period shall consist of two phases.
        (1) The first phase shall begin with the formation of a fully sovereign Iraqi Interim Government that takes power on 30 June 2004. This government shall be constituted in accordance with a process of

extensive deliberations and consultations with cross-sections of the Iraqi people conducted by the Governing Council and the Coalition Provisional Authority and possibly in consultation with the United Nations. This government shall exercise authority in accordance with this Law, including the fundamental principles and rights specified herein. . . .

(2) The second phase shall begin after the formation of the Iraqi Transitional Government, which will take place after elections for the National Assembly have been held as stipulated in this Law, provided that, if possible, these elections are not delayed beyond 31 December 2004, and, in any event, beyond 31 January 2005. This second phase shall end upon the formation of an Iraqi government pursuant to a permanent constitution. . . .

(C) This Law shall cease to have effect upon the formation of an elected government pursuant to a permanent constitution.

### Article 4

The system of government in Iraq shall be republican, federal, democratic, and pluralistic, and powers shall be shared between the federal government and the regional governments, governorates, municipalities, and local administrations. The federal system shall be based upon geographic and historical realities and the separation of powers, and not upon origin, race, ethnicity, nationality, or confession. . . .

### Article 6

The Iraqi Transitional Government shall take effective steps to end the vestiges of the oppressive acts of the previous regime arising from forced displacement, deprivation of citizenship, expropriation of financial assets and property, and dismissal from government employment for political, racial, or sectarian reasons.

### Article 7

(A) Islam is the official religion of the State and is to be considered a source of legislation. No law that contradicts the universally agreed tenets of Islam, the principles of democracy, or the rights cited in Chapter Two of this Law may be enacted during the transitional period. This Law respects the Islamic identity of the majority of the Iraqi people and guarantees the full religious rights of all individuals to freedom of religious belief and practice.

(B) Iraq is a country of many nationalities, and the Arab people in Iraq are an inseparable part of the Arab nation. . . .

### Article 9

The Arabic language and the Kurdish language are the two official languages of Iraq. The right of Iraqis to educate their children in their mother tongue, such as Turcoman, Syriac, or Armenian, in government educational institutions in accordance with educational guidelines, or in any other language in private educational institutions, shall be guaranteed. . . .

## CHAPTER TWO—FUNDAMENTAL RIGHTS

*Article 10*

As an expression of the free will and sovereignty of the Iraqi people, their representatives shall form the governmental structures of the State of Iraq. The Iraqi Transitional Government and the governments of the regions, governorates, municipalities, and local administrations shall respect the rights of the Iraqi people, including those rights cited in this Chapter.

*Article 11*

(A) Anyone who carries Iraqi nationality shall be deemed an Iraqi citizen. His citizenship shall grant him all the rights and duties stipulated in this Law and shall be the basis of his relation to the homeland and the State. . . .

*Article 12*

All Iraqis are equal in their rights without regard to gender, sect, opinion, belief, nationality, religion, or origin, and they are equal before the law. Discrimination against an Iraqi citizen on the basis of his gender, nationality, religion, or origin is prohibited. Everyone has the right to life, liberty, and the security of his person. No one may be deprived of his life or liberty, except in accordance with legal procedures. All are equal before the courts.

*Article 13*

(A) Public and private freedoms shall be protected.

(B) The right of free expression shall be protected.

(C) The right of free peaceable assembly and the right to join associations freely, as well as the right to form and join unions and political parties freely, in accordance with the law, shall be guaranteed.

(D) Each Iraqi has the right of free movement in all parts of Iraq and the right to travel abroad and return freely.

(E) Each Iraqi has the right to demonstrate and strike peaceably in accordance with the law.

(F) Each Iraqi has the right to freedom of thought, conscience, and religious belief and practice. Coercion in such matters shall be prohibited.

(G) Slavery, the slave trade, forced labor, and involuntary servitude with or without pay, shall be forbidden.

(H) Each Iraqi has the right to privacy.

*Article 14*

The individual has the right to security, education, health care, and social security. The Iraqi State and its governmental units, including the federal government, the regions, governorates, municipalities, and local administrations, within the limits of their resources and with due regard to other vital needs, shall strive to provide prosperity and employment opportunities to the people.

*Article 15*

(A) No civil law shall have retroactive effect unless the law so stipulates. There shall be neither a crime, nor punishment, except by law in effect at the time the crime is committed.

(B) Police, investigators, or other governmental authorities may not violate the sanctity of private residences, whether these authorities belong to the federal or regional governments, governorates, municipalities, or local administrations, unless a judge or investigating magistrate has issued a search warrant in accordance with applicable law on the basis of information provided by a sworn individual who knew that bearing false witness would render him liable to punishment. Extreme exigent circumstances, as determined by a court of competent jurisdiction, may justify a warrantless search, but such exigencies shall be narrowly construed. In the event that a warrantless search is carried out in the absence of an extreme exigent circumstance, the evidence so seized, and any other evidence found derivatively from such search, shall be inadmissible in connection with a criminal charge, unless the court determines that the person who carried out the warrantless search believed reasonably and in good faith that the search was in accordance with the law.

(C) No one may be unlawfully arrested or detained, and no one may be detained by reason of political or religious beliefs.

(D) All persons shall be guaranteed the right to a fair and public hearing by an independent and impartial tribunal, regardless of whether the proceeding is civil or criminal. Notice of the proceeding and its legal basis must be provided to the accused without delay.

(E) The accused is innocent until proven guilty pursuant to law, and he likewise has the right to engage independent and competent counsel, to remain silent in response to questions addressed to him with no compulsion to testify for any reason, to participate in preparing his defense, and to summon and examine witnesses or to ask the judge to do so. At the time a person is arrested, he must be notified of these rights.

(F) The right to a fair, speedy, and open trial shall be guaranteed.

(G) Every person deprived of his liberty by arrest or detention shall have the right of recourse to a court to determine the legality of his arrest or detention without delay and to order his release if this occurred in an illegal manner.

(H) After being found innocent of a charge, an accused may not be tried once again on the same charge.

(I) Civilians may not be tried before a military tribunal. Special or exceptional courts may not be established.

(J) Torture in all its forms, physical or mental, shall be prohibited under all circumstances, as shall be cruel, inhuman, or degrading treatment. No confession made under compulsion, torture, or threat thereof shall be relied upon or admitted into evidence for any reason in any proceeding, whether criminal or otherwise.

*Article 16*

(A) Public property is sacrosanct, and its protection is the duty of every citizen.

(B) The right to private property shall be protected, and no one may be prevented from disposing of his property except within the limits of law. No one shall be deprived of his property except by eminent domain, in circumstances and in the manner set forth in law, and on condition that he is paid just and timely compensation.

(C) Each Iraqi citizen shall have the full and unfettered right to own real property in all parts of Iraq without restriction.

*Article 17*

It shall not be permitted to possess, bear, buy, or sell arms except on licensure issued in accordance with the law.

*Article 18*

There shall be no taxation or fee except by law.

*Article 19*

No political refugee who has been granted asylum pursuant to applicable law may be surrendered or returned forcibly to the country from which he fled.

*Article 20*

(A) Every Iraqi who fulfills the conditions stipulated in the electoral law has the right to stand for election and cast his ballot secretly in free, open, fair, competitive, and periodic elections.

(B) No Iraqi may be discriminated against for purposes of voting in elections on the basis of gender, religion, sect, race, belief, ethnic origin, language, wealth, or literacy.

*Article 21*

Neither the Iraqi Transitional Government nor the governments and administrations of the regions, governorates, and municipalities, nor local administrations may interfere with the right of the Iraqi people to develop the institutions of civil society, whether in cooperation with international civil society organizations or otherwise.

*Article 22*

If, in the course of his work, an official of any government office, whether in the federal government, the regional governments, the governorate and municipal administrations, or the local administrations, deprives an individual or a group of the rights guaranteed by this Law or any other Iraqi laws in force, this individual or group shall have the right to maintain a cause of action against that employee to seek compensation for the damages caused by such deprivation, to vindicate his rights, and to seek any other legal measure. If the court decides that the official had acted with a sufficient degree of good faith and in the belief that his actions were consistent with the law, then he is not required to pay compensation.

*Article 23*

The enumeration of the foregoing rights must not be interpreted to mean that they are the only rights enjoyed by the Iraqi people. They enjoy all the rights that befit a free people possessed of their human dignity, including the rights stipulated in international treaties and agreements, other instruments of international law that Iraq has signed and to which it has acceded, and others that are deemed binding upon it, and in the law of nations. Non-Iraqis within Iraq shall enjoy all human rights not inconsistent with their status as non-citizens. . . .

## DOCUMENT 4.16

Issued shortly before Bremer's hasty departure from Iraq and the end of the CPA, Order Number 17 dealt with one of the most difficult matters of the CPA period. Some 180,000 private "contractors," about half of whom were providing security and fulfilling other armed functions, operated under the authority of the CPA during the occupation and beyond. The Bush administration, driven by its general desire to "outsource" as much public work to the private sector as possible and avoid congressional and press scrutiny, relied on contractors to a far greater extent than had previous governments. The occupying U.S. Army was also stretched thin. Although political observers warned that using mercenaries was not a good idea, the Bush administration refused to reconsider its deployment of Blackwater, Dyncorp, and Triple Canopy contractors even after explosive episodes such as the mass shooting by Blackwater guards of seventeen Iraqi civilians at a Baghdad intersection in September 2007. Meanwhile, questions of accountability, control, and sovereignty always simmered just beneath the surface, emerging when contractors killed or injured Iraqi civilians, damaged property, insulted and threatened people, or acted offensively.

Among other things, Order Number 17 established impunity for private contractors and made it impossible for a nominally sovereign Iraqi government to hold them to account. Extended past the end of the CPA, the order illustrated the tension between democratic accountability and unilateralist preemption and remained an irritant in U.S.–Iraqi relations until the 2008 Status of Forces Agreement settled the matter by establishing the rule of Iraqi law over crimes committed by most contractors.

---

COALITION PROVISIONAL AUTHORITY ORDER NUMBER 17, JUNE 27, 2004 (EXCERPT)

STATUS OF THE COALITION PROVISIONAL AUTHORITY, MNF-IRAQ, CERTAIN MISSIONS AND PERSONNEL IN IRAQ

Pursuant to my authority as head of the Coalition Provisional Authority (CPA), and under the laws and usages of war, and consistent with relevant UN Security Council resolutions. . . .

Noting the adoption of a process and a timetable for the drafting of an Iraqi constitution by elected representatives of the Iraqi people in the Law of Administration for the State of Iraq for the Transitional Period (TAL) on March 8, 2004,

Conscious that states are contributing personnel, equipment and other resources, both directly and by contract, to the Multinational Force (MNF) and to the reconstruction effort in order to contribute to the security and stability that will enable the relief, recovery and development of Iraq, as well as the completion of the political process set out in the TAL,

Noting that many Foreign Liaison Missions have been established in Iraq that after June 30, 2004 will become Diplomatic and Consular Missions, as defined in the Vienna Conventions on Diplomatic and Consular Relations of 1961 and 1963,

Recalling that there are fundamental agreements that have customarily been adopted to govern the deployment of Multinational Forces in host nations,

Conscious of the need to clarify the status of the CPA, the MNF, Foreign Liaison, Diplomatic and Consular Missions and their Personnel, certain International Consultants, and certain contractors in respect of the Government and the local courts,

Recognizing the need to provide for the circumstances that will pertain following June 30, 2004, and noting the consultations with the incoming Iraqi Interim Government in this regard and in this order,

I hereby promulgate the following: . . .

*Section 2*

Iraqi Legal Process
    1) Unless provided otherwise herein, the MNF, the CPA, Foreign
        Liaison Missions, their personnel, property, funds and assets, and

all International Consultants shall be immune from Iraqi legal process.

2) All MNF, CPA and Foreign Liaison Missions and International Consultants shall respect the Iraqi laws relevant to those Personnel and Consultants in Iraq including the Regulations, Orders, Memoranda and Public Notices issued by the Administrator of the CPA.

3) All MNF, CPA and Foreign Liaison Personnel, and International Consultants shall be subject to the exclusive jurisdiction of their Sending States. They shall be immune from any sort of arrest or detention other than by persons acting on behalf of their Sending States, except that nothing in this provision shall prohibit MNF Personnel from preventing acts of serious misconduct by the above-mentioned Personnel or Consultants, or otherwise temporarily detaining any such Personnel or Consultants who pose a risk of injury to themselves or others, pending expeditious turnover to the appropriate authorities of the Sending State. . . .

*Section 4*

Contractors

1) Sending States may contract for any services, equipment, provisions, supplies, material, other goods, or construction work to be furnished or undertaken in Iraq without restriction as to choice of supplier or Contractor. Such contracts may be awarded in accordance with the Sending State's laws and regulations.

2) Contractors shall not be subject to Iraqi laws or regulations in matters relating to the terms and conditions of their Contracts, including licensing and registering employees, businesses and corporations; provided, however, that Contractors shall comply with such applicable licensing and registration laws and regulations if engaging in business or transactions in Iraq other than Contracts. Notwithstanding any provisions in this Order, Private Security Companies and their employees operating in Iraq must comply with all CPA Orders, Regulations, Memoranda, and any implementing instructions or regulations governing the existence and activities of Private Security Companies in Iraq, including registration and licensing of weapons and firearms.

3) Contractors shall be immune from Iraqi legal process with respect to acts performed by them pursuant to the terms and conditions of a Contract or any sub-contract thereto. Nothing in this provision shall prohibit MNF Personnel from preventing acts of serious misconduct by Contractors, or otherwise temporarily detaining any Contractors who pose a risk of injury to themselves or others, pending expeditious turnover to the appropriate authorities of the Sending Sate. . . .

4) Except as provided in this Order, all Contractors shall respect relevant Iraqi laws, including the Regulations, Orders, Memoranda and Public Notices issued by the Administrator of the CPA

5) Certification by the Sending State that its Contractor acted pursuant to the terms and conditions of the Contract shall, in any Iraqi legal process, be conclusive evidence of the facts so certified. . . .

*Section 7*

Travel and Transport

1) All MNF, CPA and Foreign Liaison Mission Personnel, International Consultants and Contractors, to the extent necessary to perform their Contracts, shall enjoy, together with vehicles, vessels, aircraft and equipment, freedom of movement without delay throughout Iraq. That freedom shall, to the extent practicable with respect to large movement of personnel, stores, vehicles or aircraft through airports or on railways or roads used for general traffic within Iraq, be coordinated with the Government. . . .

*Section 20*

Effective Period

This Order shall enter into force on the date of signature. It shall remain in force for the duration of the mandate authorizing the MNF under UN Security Council Resolutions 1511 and 1546 and any subsequent resolutions and shall not terminate until the departure of the final element of the MNF from Iraq, unless rescinded or amended by legislation duly enacted and having the force of law.

# DOCUMENT 4.17

On June 1, 2004, having been entrusted by all parties with the task, UN envoy Lakhdar Brahimi announced the composition of the interim government to which the Coalition Provisional Authority would yield sovereignty at the end of the month. The interim government was to remain in power until an elected national assembly formed a transitional government and wrote a permanent constitution. Another set of elections would approve the constitution and establish a permanent government.

Bremer seemed pleased with his work in extricating Washington from what threatened to be a long and difficult occupation, but it was during the spring of 2004 that Iraq's nationwide insurgency intensified, public order disintegrated, and the most basic services disappeared. The Battle of Fallujah, the appearance of Shia militias that contested for supremacy with their Sunni counterparts, the breakdown of the fledgling Iraqi army and police forces, and a spasm of sectarian killings and ethnic cleansing testified to the overall failure of the CPA's work and, on a deeper level, of the strategy of preemption and invasion. As Spain, Honduras, the Dominican Republic, and other countries withdrew their token contributions to Bush's "coalition of the willing" and, for the first time, a majority of Americans polled said the war was not going well,[6] official administration spokespeople maintained their public optimism. When General Richard Myers, the chairman of the Joint Chiefs of Staff, called the spring explosion "a symptom of the success we're having in Iraq" and told the House Armed Services Committee that "we're on the brink of success," his view was challenged by an increasingly skeptical press and more than one internationally respected defense analyst. Anthony Cordesman's report for the Center for Strategic and International Studies indicted the Congress, the CPA, the military, and almost every other institution that was responsible for planning and conducting the Bush administration's preemptive war. "No single mission is more important than security, and no popular Iraqi desire is clearer than that this mission be done by Iraqis," said Cordesman. "The U.S. has been guilty of a gross military, administrative, and moral failure."[7] Under the circumstances, it was not surprising that the formal transfer of sovereignty and the dissolution of the CPA happened two days earlier than planned in a five-minute ceremony that was held in secret so it would not be attacked.

PRESS SECRETARY SCOTT McCLELLAN, READING
OF TEXTS OF LETTERS ON IRAQ SOVEREIGNTY,
JUNE 28, 2004 (EXCERPT)

I have a copy of the note that was exchanged between Dr. Rice and the President at the NATO meeting earlier today. We are doing a photo release of the original. But let me read it into the transcript:

Condi wrote: "Mr. President, Iraq is sovereign. Letter was passed from Bremer at 10:26 a.m. Iraq time. Condi"

And then the President wrote back on the note in a black sharpie, "Let Freedom Reign!"

6. Scott Keeter, "Trends in Public Opinion about the War in Iraq, 2003–2007," Pew Research Center, http://pewresearch.org/pubs/431/trends-in-public-opinion-about-the-war-in-iraq-2003–2007.

7. Anthony Cordesman, "Inexcusable Failure: Progress in Training the Iraqi Army and Security Forces as of Mid-July 2004" (Washington, D.C.: Center for Strategic and International Studies, July 20, 2004), 9.

# ★ CHAPTER 5 ★

# INSURGENCY, COUNTERINSURGENCY, OR CIVIL WAR?

THE BUSH ADMINISTRATION'S decision to invade Iraq was in line with both the logic of preemption promoted by its neoconservatives and with its broader approach to military planning (5.1). Washington argued that the United States was obliged, out of moral necessity and national interest, to overthrow a brutal dictator, and that Iraqis would wholeheartedly welcome U.S. intervention. But preemptive war and regime change provoked a reaction that had deep roots in Iraqi history: widespread opposition to foreign occupation. The invasion sparked the rise of anti-occupation and sectarian violence that Secretary of Defense Donald Rumsfeld initially attributed to criminals, "deadenders," foreign fighters, and lingering Baath Party loyalists (4.8). But the Iraqi insurgency was organized and popular, employing sophisticated tactics that adapted to those used by U.S. forces. In 2004 the administration continued to deny the momentum of the insurgency even as it employed counterinsurgency strategies to quell it. Five years after the beginning of the invasion, an organized resistance movement continued to change the political landscape and forced both the Iraqi and U.S. governments to rethink their strategies.

In early 2007, President Bush announced a "surge" in the number of U.S. troops on the ground, from 140,000 to 160,000. A year later, he announced that the policy had been successful, despite repeated warnings from the commander of the Multi-National Force–Iraq (MNF–I), Gen. David Petraeus, that only "fragile" and "reversible" improvements had been made. Other critics argued that the future remained unclear because Iraqi forces were still unable to sustain themselves or defeat the insurgency. They characterized the decline in violence as an illusion since fighting had merely moved from Baghdad to

Basra, in the south, because the government was trying to eliminate the Mahdi Army of Muqtada al-Sadr. Indeed, the U.S. military reported that by mid-2007 attacks had reached fifteen hundred per week, and in 2008 the insurgency was still showing signs of organization, ingenuity, and perseverance despite an overall decline in U.S. deaths and evidence that al Qaeda in Mesopotamia was losing ground (5.7). Others attributed this decline in violence to the rise of the Sunni Awakening, as key tribal groups shifted from supporting the insurgency to cooperating with U.S. and Iraqi authorities.

The U.S. clearly had miscalculated the depth of the insurgency, and this initial error was compounded by several others. Members of both the Sunni and Shia communities simultaneously and spontaneously rose up against the occupying power in separate locations. The resistance took different forms, however, partly in reaction to Washington's counterinsurgency tactics, but also because of cultural and religious differences that were exacerbated by U.S. policies. The Kurds maintained a distance from the fighting. Not pacifists by any means, they had been fighting against the Baath Party, against neighboring Turkey, and against one another in the name of their nationalist aspirations for several decades. Yet they welcomed the U.S. invasion in 2003 as a way to secure their political objectives with the help of a third party.

By 2004, critics had aptly dubbed the violence in Iraq a civil war since it had devolved from resistance against occupation to persistent and organized infighting among Iraqi nationals in a struggle for power. The United States first described the violent Iraqi resistance as an "insurgency," and its response as a strategy of "counterinsurgency" (5.3). Specialists cautioned, however, that since contemporary insurgencies differed from those of previous years, counterinsurgency strategies should likewise adapt. One analyst, David Kilcullen, defined an insurgency as a "struggle to control a contested political space, between a state (or a group of states or occupying powers) and one or more popularly based, non-state challengers."[1] This understanding departed from the classical conception of insurgency as a challenge to an intact, even if fragile, state. Kilcullen's view implied that contemporary insurgencies were likely to emerge in dissolved states when there was a political vacuum.

Counterinsurgency strategies can be dangerous as well. There is always a risk that the measures taken to suppress an insurgency might escalate into uncontrolled violence or coercion against civilians, without either accountability or transparency—which is precisely what happened in the first years of the U.S. occupation. Indeed, U.S. policy initially involved taking preemptive measures to prevent outbreaks of violence. The Department of Defense referred to the conflict with the Iraqi resistance as "irregular warfare," which made it easy to conflate the resistance movement with terrorism, despite the fact that various resistance groups had presented a set of popular nationalist political objectives.

---

1. See David Kilcullen, "Counter-Insurgency Redux," in *Survival* 48, no. 4 (Winter 2006–2007), 111–130. The author builds on Gordon H. McCormick's definition.

United States officials repeatedly argued that countermeasures were used against "terrorists," not Iraqi citizens. They overlooked the fact that the insurgents had a wide popular base and a deeply rooted ability to recruit members. The occupation authorities failed to recognize the depth of the insurgency for some time, making it almost impossible to acknowledge that their policies helped fuel it (5.5). Moreover, the preemptive drive behind U.S. actions resurfaced with the news that the "Salvador Option" was being employed in Iraq, a strategy informed by twelve years of experience in training paramilitaries that acted as death squads in El Salvador during the 1980s (5.2).[2]

These issues were complicated by the fact that the United States lacked a coherent strategy for rebuilding Iraq after combat operations had ended. Beyond seriously underestimating necessary troop levels, the military chain of command suffered from a lack of preparedness and poor communications. Some soldiers were not sure if their mission was to kill insurgents or serve as peacekeepers. These bureaucratic problems were compounded by a wide culture gap as soldiers routinely violated many Islamic honor and gender codes. Contrary to some reports on the ground, early counterinsurgency tactics used by the U.S. military did not urge soldier restraint and often employed harsh, indiscriminate tactics. Systematic abuse was widespread (the most well known being the Abu Ghraib scandal), and the great majority of Iraqis detained were of little intelligence value. Many analysts, Iraqis, and journalists criticized the U.S. tactics of making late-night raids, taking hostages, firing into civilian neighborhoods, and burning orchards as insulting and counterproductive. Yet the administration continued to shift the blame for the escalation of violence to Iraqi leaders and sectarian fighting (5.6). By 2008, Petraeus had modified the counterinsurgency guidance plan to include "winning the hearts and minds of Iraqis," replacing the harsher methods previously used (5.4).

U.S. reconstruction policies also often had the unintended consequence of encouraging infighting among Iraqis. Some Coalition Provisional Authority orders were badly received, and other steps taken by occupation authorities further alienated the Iraqis (chapter 4). First, there was a significant discrepancy between the living conditions of Iraqis and those of CPA officials in Baghdad's Green Zone; in contrast to the rest of the country, the Green Zone enjoyed security, clean water, uninterrupted electricity, and access to medical services. Second, the privatization plans, especially concerning oil, provoked economic insecurities for Iraqis, who then turned on each other and increased their resistance to the occupation. Once Iraqi companies began negotiating with outside investors, they were targeted by those who feared unemployment after decades of service. Third, the de-Baathification policy was incorporated into official Iraqi policy, with punitive provisions that were aimed specifically at Sunnis. Above all, the reconstruction efforts further isolated the Iraqis as Baghdad

---

2. See Michael Hirsh and John Barry, "'The Salvador Option': The Pentagon May Put Special-Forces-led Assassination or Kidnapping Teams in Iraq," *Newsweek*, January 8, 2005.

never had uninterrupted electricity, very few Iraqis were hired for reconstruction projects, oil pipelines were sabotaged every day, and the United States struggled to provide the most basic level of security.

Several preexisting domestic conditions also contributed to the escalation of the crisis. The main U.S. strategy upon removing Saddam Hussein from power was to empower the Shia and Kurds at the expense of the Sunnis. The Shia, once persecuted and disenfranchised by the Baath Party, were given the chance to form a government. They found themselves in a strong position to avenge the deaths of their loved ones under Saddam Hussein's rule. As more than 275 mass grave sites were found, people immediately turned on former Sunni Baathists in ways that were beyond the reach of the CPA. The Sunni response was swift, and their turn toward "ethnic cleansing" forced the Shias to become open partisans in the fighting. By 2004, the U.S. had reacted by supporting what amounted to a weak Shia-dominated government with links to paramilitary groups that committed sectarian atrocities.[3] That situation encouraged some Sunni nationalists to turn to al Qaeda in Mesopotamia, a radical group formed in Iraq by a Jordanian, Abu Musab al Zarqawi, after the invasion (5.9).

Divisions in Iraqi society were accentuated during the U.S. invasion, and intersectarian fighting often exhibited explicit religious overtones. This surprised many observers, since Iraq had been lauded as one of the few Middle Eastern countries with a strong secular middle class throughout the 1980s. Yet the embargo following Iraq's 1990 invasion of Kuwait had fundamentally altered the socioeconomic and political makeup of the country. In fact, both the Sunnis and Shia underwent identity changes during the 1990s as the middle class crumbled and the economic system collapsed. Salaries were unable to keep up with runaway inflation throughout the decade as the Iraqi dinar declined from approximately one dinar to three U.S. dollars in the late 1980s to two thousand dinars to one dollar. A mass exodus ensued as professionals fled the country. In a study of Iraqi living conditions in 2003, the UN Development Program found that nearly half the adult population was illiterate.

The United States seemed totally unaware that Saddam Hussein had altered his policy toward both Shia and Sunnis in response to realities after 1990, a time when the Kurds enjoyed the protection of the United States. Saddam acted to empower the Sunnis. Meanwhile, the Shia were shaped by an event known as the Sha'ban Uprising of 1991, which began days after President George H. W. Bush announced on *Voice of America* radio that Iraqis should "take matters into their own hands" to force Saddam Hussein from power. As defeated Iraqi army units fled to the southern city of Basra, local Shia resisted their presence and took over many administrative buildings. News of the uprising spread

---

3. See, e.g., Zbigniew Brzezinski and Walter Russell Mead's discussion of death squads, *PBS Online NewsHour,* June 14, 2006.

throughout the south, and a full-scale insurrection followed. Mobs, sometimes led by Islamists, killed hundreds of top-ranking security forces from the Baath Party and attacked government agents [4] Within days, Iraq had accepted the resolutions issued by the United Nations and a ceasefire was announced in Washington. The United States withdrew from the picture and the Shia were left to fight the regime on their own.

A similar uprising occurred in Kurdish areas in the north, although the Kurds were much more organized because of contact with the U.S.-led coalition. Once the war had ended, Saddam Hussein regained control of the south (the northern Kurdish area was protected by a no-fly zone) and slaughtered many thousands of Shia there. Though there were no official reports on the number of deaths, Human Rights Watch presented horrifying accounts of the massacres. The new regime slogan became "there will be no Shia after today" ("la Shi'a ba'ad al' youm"). From then on, the south was under subjugation, grand ayatollahs were under house arrest, and many Shia religious shrines were reduced to rubble. On the eve of the 2003 invasion, Deputy Secretary of Defense Paul Wolfowitz expressed remorse for the U.S. abandonment of the Shia in 1991.

Saddam Hussein's brutal policies of repression, discrimination, and isolation of the Shia, who were a majority in Iraq, precipitated an important change in their consciousness. Shia in Iraq and in exile in Western countries and in neighboring Iran began talking about the political rights of the majority. While the Sha'ban uprising brought some of the more militant Islamic groups from underground, it also led to a debate among high-ranking clerical leaders about the proper course for Shia political activism, a debate as old as Shiism itself (chapter 6). The Shia clerics continued to disagree because they held conflicting views about statehood and the roles of religion and politics, differences that were usually expressed through their hierarchy of power. For example, the followers of Muqtada al-Sadr, the fiery anti-U.S. cleric, hoped to politically dominate the Shia realm. The more traditional "quietist" Shia position, embraced by Grand Ayatollah Ali al-Sistani, was distinctly less interested in political leadership, and a variety of other Shia spokesmen expressed other tendencies as well.

A similar transformation occurred among the Sunnis, though it did not express itself through a hierarchical power structure. After the 1990 invasion of Kuwait and ten years of containment, Saddam Hussein's regime was bankrupt. Like other regional leaders faced with a legitimacy crisis, he opted for a strategy of shifting attention away from the regime's deficits by using Islam as a cultural distraction. First he began bolstering his own religious credentials. He also created Islamic symbols in the state, like adding the Islamic crescent moon to the Iraqi flag. Most notably, the regime launched the "Return to Faith Campaign"

---

4. The term "Islamists" is used broadly here to describe a group that proposed a religious solution to a political crisis. It does not refer to a specific Islamic movement.

in 1994 to reintroduce Islam at a local level. Qur'an classes in schools became mandatory, and new training centers for religious study were established. Media outlets began airing religious programming, women were encouraged to wear the Islamic headscarf (*hijab*), new mosques were built, and a new institution, the Saddam University for Islamic Studies (currently called Al-Nahrain University), was opened. The Iraqi leader also encouraged the proliferation of previously banned Sunni political parties and this encouraged the importation of ideas from the rest of the Sunni world. An unintended consequence of the Faith Campaign was the rise of Salafi Islam, a branch of Sunni Islam that called for a strict interpretation of Islam that harkened back to the days of the prophet. The Salafis were intolerant of moderate Muslims, who tried to reconcile religion with modernity. Sometimes known as the "Wahhabi" movement (as in Saudi Arabia), Salafi Islam was puritanical, militaristic, and messianic, seeking to spread the movement worldwide. Many Sunni Iraqi insurgents were inspired by Salafism, which had been building a base in Iraq for more than a decade prior to the U.S.-led invasion. Thus, this type of radicalism was not newly imported from "foreign fighters" in 2003, as U.S. spokespeople repeatedly stated in the news. The insurgency was homegrown, with many of the fighters born out of the Faith Campaign. "Foreign fighters" numbered in the hundreds, a small percentage of the tens of thousands of those participating in the fighting and detained by the United States, which seemed to have no intelligence concerning these developments.

As the insurgency developed, many of the Sunni groups began working together, issuing joint statements and pledging unity with one another (5.8). They also organized the insurgency around common Iraqi nationalist symbols (5.10). Since the Sunni religio-political system lacked a hierarchy, organizations tended to form along tribal lines. The Sunnis also used these tribal affiliations to their advantage as they began turning away from the insurgency in 2007 and organized tribally based "awakening councils" (*sahwat*), which drew many former militants to fight the insurgency. Called "Sons of Iraq" by the U.S. military, the *sahwat* contributed to the move toward national reconciliation after 2007 as they included many former members of al Qaeda in Mesopotamia who had shifted from fighting with the insurgents to fighting against them.

By late 2008, there were more than a hundred thousand Sunnis and eighteen thousand Shia in these *sahwat*. The Sunnis sought to break the stigma of their former association with the Baath Party as they demanded incorporation into the Shia-dominated state-security apparatus. One drawback was their connection to the U.S. military, from which they received a monthly salary of US$300. Sunni militants offered $500 a month for the fighters' participation. By 2007, the government of Iraq, fully aware of its security situation, was working to engage various groups and factions. As the civil war raged on, the Iraqi government issued a national security directive that sought to heal the shattered nation, a goal likely to take years to achieve (5.11).

# U.S. Policies and Tactics in the Counterinsurgency

## DOCUMENT 5.1

Prior to the war in Iraq, the Pentagon had prepared a document that laid out U.S. military standards for implementing military campaigns. It was meant to offer a blueprint and a set of guidelines for planners in Iraq. But almost immediately after the invasion, many critics expressed their dismay at the lack of planning and coordination on the ground. Retired officers began speaking out against a plan written by Gen. George W. Casey, commander of the Multi-National Force–Iraq (MNF–I) from 2004 to 2007, for its vagueness, lack of long-term strategic thinking, and absence of concrete guidelines for implementing some of its most important objectives, such as transitioning power to Iraqi forces. Casey's document remained classified, though the criticism of the retired officers and Casey's own public comments were enough to lead the Pentagon to rethink its counterinsurgency planning. These guidelines distributed for military campaign planning were very general and did not take into account cultural and historic factors on the ground that could complicate any strategy. Signed by Chairman of the Joint Chiefs of Staff Lt. Gen. John Abizaid, they were the product of a joint effort between the U.S. Army and the Marines.

| 219

JOINT DOCTRINE FOR CAMPAIGN PLANNING,
JANUARY 2002 (EXCERPT)

### 1. Scope
This publication provides overarching guidance and principles governing the planning of campaigns at the combatant command and subordinate joint force levels. It focuses on the methodology for translating national and theater strategy into planning actions required to design and synchronize a campaign plan. It describes joint campaign planning across the full range of military operations at the strategic and operational levels of war. It discusses campaign planning within the context of the Joint Operation Planning and Execution System and guides planners to necessary planning references.

Campaign planning is used for combat operations, but also has application in military operations other than war (MOOTW). Campaign planning generally applies to the conduct of combat operations, but can also be used in situations other than war.

### Campaign Plan Design
Because theater-level campaign planning is mostly art, it is inextricably linked with operational art, most notably in the design of the operational concept for the campaign. This is primarily an intellectual exercise based on experience and judgment. The result of this process should be an operational

design that provides the conceptual linkage of ends, ways, and means. To that end, the elements of an operational design are a tool to aid the combatant commander and planners in visualizing what the campaign should look like and shaping the commander's intent. The key to operational design essentially involves (1) understanding the strategic guidance (determining the desired end state and military objective(s)); (2) identifying the critical factors (both principal adversary strengths, including the strategic centers of gravity (COGs), and weaknesses); and (3) developing an operational concept that will achieve the strategic objective(s). . . .

A campaign plan normally consists of an overall operational scheme for the entire campaign, while subordinate component commanders will draw operational schemes for their respective components. The concept should also contain in general terms a scheme of when, where, and under what conditions the combatant commander intends to give or refuse battle, if required. The concept must explicitly state that the focus is on the destruction or neutralization of the adversary's COG(s).

To attack the adversary's COG(s), there are essentially two approaches: either direct or indirect. Direct approaches are used when the adversary's COG is comparatively weaker than the force friendly forces can apply to destroy, overwhelm, neutralize, or defeat it. Conversely, indirect approaches are used when the adversary's COG is not readily assailable, highly protected, or ill-defined. In MOOTW, the adversary's COG(s) are usually difficult to identify and attack directly. Because the adversary's COG will most likely be heavily defended, the indirect approach may offer the most viable method to exploit adversary vulnerabilities and weaknesses by attacking them along decisive points. While decisive points are not COGs, they are essential in attacking COGs. . . .

*FUNDAMENTALS OF CAMPAIGN PLANS*
- Provide broad strategic concepts of operations and sustainment for achieving multinational, national, and theater-strategic objectives.
- Provide an orderly schedule of decisions.
- Achieve unity of effort with air, land, sea, space, and special operations forces, in conjunction with interagency, multinational, nongovernmental, or United Nations forces, as required.
- Incorporate the combatant commander's strategic intent and operational focus.
- Identify any forces or capabilities that the adversary has in the area.
- Identify the adversary strategic and operational centers of gravity and provide guidance for defeating them.
- Identify the friendly strategic and operational centers of gravity and provide guidance to subordinates for protecting them. If required, sequence a series of related major joint operations conducted simultaneously throughout the area of responsibility or joint operations area.

- Establish the organization of subordinate forces and designate command relationships.
- Serve as the basis for subordinate planning.
- Clearly define what constitutes success, including conflict termination objectives and potential post hostilities activities.
- Provide strategic direction, operational focus, and major tasks, objectives, and concepts to subordinates.
- Provide direction for the employment of nuclear weapons as required and authorized by the National Command Authorities.

# DOCUMENT 5.2

Late in 2008, Julian Assange, an investigative editor, reported on WikiLeaks, the online source for previously classified, confidential, and censored political material, on the release of a sensitive U.S. military counterinsurgency manual. Formed in 2007 by journalists and lawyers, WikiLeaks served as a medium for disseminating sensitive materials worldwide. The Web site was routed through Sweden and Belgium because of their stringent shield laws, and it had become an important location for the exposure of information with guarantees for press freedom. This Pentagon manual made clear the historical continuity between U.S. counterinsurgency techniques used in Latin America and Vietnam beginning in the 1960s and those employed in Iraq years later. Informed by the long U.S. involvement in Latin America, the manual was the official U.S. Special Forces doctrine of Foreign Internal Defense (FID). The techniques below reveal the illegal side of counterinsurgency measures, which included the suspension of habeas corpus and breaches of the Geneva Conventions.

---

U.S. SPECIAL FORCES COUNTERINSURGENCY MANUAL
FM 31–20–3, FOREIGN INTERNAL DEFENSE TACTICS
TECHNIQUES AND PROCEDURES FOR SPECIAL FORCES
(1994, 2004) (EXCERPT)

## Counterintelligence

. . . . Most of the counterintelligence measures used will be overt in nature and aimed at protecting installations, units, and information and detecting espionage, sabotage, and subversion. **Examples of counterintelligence measures to use are** background investigations and records checks of persons in sensitive positions and persons whose loyalty may be questionable. Maintenance of files on organizations, locations, and individuals of counterintelligence interest. Internal security inspections of installations and units. Control of civilian movement within government-controlled areas. Identification systems to minimize the chance of insurgents gaining access to installations or moving freely. Unannounced searches and raids on suspected meeting places.

## Censorship

. . . . PSYOP [Psychological Operations] are essential to the success of PRC [Population & Resources Control]. For maximum effectiveness, a strong psychological operations effort is directed toward the families of the insurgents and their popular support base. **The PSYOP aspect of the PRC program tries to make the imposition of control more palatable** to the people by relating the necessity of controls to their safety and well-being. PSYOP efforts also try to create a favorable national or local government image and counter the effects of the insurgent propaganda effort.

## Control Measures

**SF [US Special Forces] can advise and assist HN [Host Nation] forces in developing and implementing control measures. Among these measures are the following:**

Security Forces. Police and other security forces use PRC [Population & Resources Control] measures to deprive the insurgent of support and to identify and locate members of his infrastructure. Appropriate PSYOP [Psychological Operations] help make these measures more acceptable to the population by explaining their need. The government informs the population that the PRC measures may cause an inconvenience but are necessary due to the actions of the insurgents.

## Restrictions

**Rights on the legality of detention or imprisonment of personnel (for example, habeas corpus) may be temporarily suspended.** This measure must be taken as a last resort, since it may provide the insurgents with an effective propaganda theme. PRC [Population & Resources Control] measures can also include curfews or blackouts, travel restrictions, and restricted residential areas such as protected villages or resettlement areas. Registration and pass systems and control of sensitive items (resources control) and critical supplies such as weapons, food, and fuel are other PRC measures. Checkpoints, searches, roadblocks; **surveillance, censorship, and press control;** and **restriction of activity that applies to selected groups (labor unions, political groups and the like) are further PRC measures.** . . .

## Psychological Operations

PSYOP can support the mission by discrediting the insurgent forces to neutral groups, creating dissension among the insurgents themselves, and supporting defector programs. **Divisive programs create dissension, disorganization, low morale, subversion, and defection within the insur-**

gent forces. Also important are national programs to win insurgents over to the government side with offers of amnesty and rewards. Motives for surrendering can range from personal rivalries and bitterness to disillusionment and discouragement. Pressure from the security forces has persuasive power. . . .

The highly specialized and sensitive nature of clandestine intelligence collection demands specially selected and highly trained agents. Information from clandestine sources is often highly sensitive and requires tight control to protect the source. However, tactical information upon which a combat response can be taken should be passed to the appropriate tactical level.

The spotting, assessment, and recruitment of an agent is not a haphazard process regardless of the type agent being sought. During the assessment phase, the case officer determines the individual's degree of intelligence, access to target, available or necessary cover, and motivation. He initiates the recruitment and coding action only after he determines the individual has the necessary attributes to fulfill the needs.

All agents are closely observed and those that are not reliable are relieved. A few well-targeted, reliable agents are better and more economical than a large number of poor ones.

A system is needed to evaluate the agents and the information they submit. The maintenance of an agent master dossier (possibly at the SFOD B level) can be useful in evaluating the agent on the value and quality of information he has submitted. The dossier must contain a copy of the agent's source data report and every intelligence report he submitted.

Security forces can induce individuals among the general populace to become informants. Security forces use various motives (civic-mindedness, patriotism, fear, punishment avoidance, gratitude, revenge or jealousy, financial rewards) as persuasive arguments. They use the assurance of protection from reprisal as a major inducement. Security forces must maintain the informant's anonymity and must conceal the transfer of information from the source to the security agent. The security agent and the informant may prearrange signals to coincide with everyday behavior.

Surveillance, the covert observation of persons and places, is a principal method of gaining and confirming intelligence information. Surveillance techniques naturally vary with the requirements of different situations. The basic procedures include mechanical observation (wiretaps or concealed microphones), observation from fixed locations, and physical surveillance of subjects.

Whenever a suspect is apprehended during an operation, a hasty interrogation takes place to gain immediate information that could be of tactical value. The most frequently used methods for gathering information (map studies and aerial observation), however, are normally unsuccessful. Most PWs cannot read a map. When they are taken on a visual reconnaissance flight, it is usually their first flight and they cannot associate an aerial view with what they saw on the ground.

The most successful interrogation method consists of a map study based on terrain information received from the detainee. The interrogator first asks the detainee what the sun's direction was when he left the base camp. From this information, he can determine a general direction. The interrogator then asks the detainee how long it took him to walk to the point where he was captured. Judging the terrain and the detainee's health, the interrogator can determine a general radius in which the base camp can be found (he can use an overlay for this purpose). He then asks the detainee to identify significant terrain features he saw on each day of his journey, (rivers, open areas, hills, rice paddies, swamps). As the detainee speaks and his memory is jogged, the interrogator finds these terrain features on a current map and gradually plots the detainee's route to finally locate the base camp.

If the interrogator is unable to speak the detainee's language, he interrogates through an interpreter who received a briefing beforehand. A recorder may also assist him. If the interrogator is not familiar with the area, personnel who are familiar with the area brief him before the interrogation and then join the interrogation team. The recorder allows the interrogator a more free-flowing interrogation. The recorder also lets a knowledgeable interpreter elaborate on points the detainee has mentioned without the interrogator interrupting the continuity established during a given sequence. The interpreter can also question certain inaccuracies, keeping pressure on the subject. The interpreter and the interrogator have to be well trained to work as a team. The interpreter has to be familiar with the interrogation procedures. His preinterrogation briefings must include information on the detainee's health, the circumstances resulting in his detention, and the specific information required. A successful interrogation is contingent upon continuity and a well trained interpreter. A tape recorder (or a recorder taking notes) enhances continuity by freeing the interrogator from time-consuming administrative tasks. . . .

## Special Intelligence-gathering Operations

Alternative intelligence-gathering techniques and sources, such as doppelganger or pseudo operations, can be tried and used when it is hard to obtain information from the civilian populace. These pseudo units are usually made up of ex-guerrilla and/or security force personnel posing as insurgents. They circulate among the civilian populace and, in some cases, infiltrate guerrilla units to gather information on guerrilla movements and its support infrastructure.

Much time and effort must be used to persuade insurgents to switch allegiance and serve with the security forces. Prospective candidates must be properly screened and then given a choice of serving with the HN

[Host Nation] security forces or facing prosecution under HN law for terrorist crimes.

Government security force units and teams of varying size have been used in infiltration operations against underground and guerrilla forces. They have been especially effective in getting information on underground security and communications systems, the nature and extent of civilian support and underground liaison, underground supply methods, and possible collusion between local government officials and the underground. Before such a unit can be properly trained and disguised, however, much information about the appearance, mannerisms, and security procedures of enemy units must be gathered. Most of this information comes from defectors or reindoctrinated prisoners. Defectors also make excellent instructors and guides for an infiltrating unit. **In using a disguised team, the selected men should be trained, oriented, and disguised to look and act like authentic underground or guerrilla units.** In addition to acquiring valuable information, the infiltrating units can demoralize the insurgents to the extent that they become overly suspicious and distrustful of their own units. . . . After establishing the cordon and designating a holding area, the screening point or center is established. All civilians in the cordoned area will then pass through the screening center to be classified.

**National police personnel will complete, if census data does not exist in the police files, a basic registration card and photograph all personnel over the age of 15.** They print two copies of each photo—one is pasted to the registration card and the other to the village book (for possible use in later operations and to identify ralliers and informants).

The screening element leader ensures the screeners question relatives, friends, neighbors, and other knowledgeable individuals of guerrilla leaders or functionaries operating in the area on their whereabouts, activities, movements, and expected return. The screening area must include areas where police and military intelligence personnel can privately interview selected individuals. The interrogators try to convince the interviewees that their cooperation will not be detected by the other inhabitants. They also discuss, during the interview, the availability of monetary rewards for certain types of information and equipment. . . .

**Civilian Self-Defense Forces** [*Editors' Note: Paramilitaries, or, especially in a Salvadoran or Colombian civil war context, right-wing "death squads"*]. When a village accepts the CSDF program, the insurgents cannot choose to ignore it. To let the village go unpunished will encourage other villages to accept the government's CSDF program. The insurgents have no choice; they have to attack the CSDF village to provide a lesson to other villages considering CSDF. In a sense, **the psychological effectiveness of the CSDF concept starts by reversing the insurgent strategy of making the government the repressor. It forces the insurgents to cross a critical threshold— that of attacking and killing the very class of people they are supposed**

| 225

to be liberating. To be successful, the CSDF program must have popular support from those directly involved or affected by it. **The average peasant is not normally willing to fight to his death for his national government. His national government may have been a succession of corrupt dictators and inefficient bureaucrats. These governments are not the types of institutions that inspire fight-to-the-death emotions in the peasant.** The village or town, however, is a different matter. The average peasant will fight much harder for his home and for his village than he ever would for his national government. The CSDF concept directly involves the peasant in the war and makes it a fight for the family and village instead of a fight for some faraway irrelevant government.

## DOCUMENT 5.3

One of the problems the United States faced in Iraq was the insurgency's lack of a formal organizational superstructure. Members of the administration began searching for historical precedents and debated whether Vietnam or Latin America served as a better blueprint for counterinsurgency in Iraq. Vice President Dick Cheney reportedly searched the CIA archives for details of the infamous Phoenix Program in Vietnam, organized by the CIA to identify and eliminate the National Liberation Front's civilian infrastructure. The Pentagon had concluded that the vast majority of Vietnamese detainees were of little intelligence value, but after September 11 the Phoenix Program resurfaced as a model for the CIA in Iraq. Reportedly, Cheney liked it because it could allow U.S. intelligence operatives to evade legal repercussions. It was "unconventional" and "stayed below the radar a really long time," remarked a former CIA operative.[5]

In response to the fact that there had been no systematic rethinking of counterinsurgency doctrine for some twenty years, U.S. Army Lt. Gen. David Petraeus and Marine Lt. James Mattis prepared a manual that sought to apply the "lessons" of Vietnam, Latin America, and other regions to Iraq. The manual developed guidelines for counterinsurgency operations (COIN), emphasizing the need to consider not only historical experience but also contemporary social, political, and economic matters. It identified the local population as the "center of gravity," with special emphasis on protecting and engaging civilians while keeping force to a minimum. It appeared to highlight some of the major flaws in the counterinsurgency campaigns in Iraq under Generals George Casey and Ricardo Sanchez, Petraeus's predecessors.

5. Jane Mayer, *The Dark Side: The Inside Story of How the War on Terror Turned into a War on American Ideals* (New York: Doubleday, 2008), 144.

U.S. DEPARTMENT OF DEFENSE, FM3–24,
COUNTERINSURGENCY FINAL DRAFT,
JUNE 16, 2006 (EXCERPT)

## OVERVIEW

Insurgency and counterinsurgency are subsets of war. Though globalization and technological advancement have influenced contemporary conflict, the nature of war in the 21st century is the same as it has been since ancient times, ". . . a violent clash of interests between or among organized groups characterized by the use of military force." Success in war still depends on a group's ability to mobilize support for its political interests and generate sufficient violence to achieve political consequences. Means to achieve these goals are not limited to regular armies employed by a nation-state. At its core, war is a violent struggle between hostile, independent, and irreconcilable wills attempting to impose their desires on another. It is a complex interaction between human beings and is played out in a continuous process of action, reaction, and adaptation. As an extension of both policy and politics with the addition of military force, war can take different forms across the spectrum of conflict. It may range from large-scale forces engaged in conventional warfare to subtler forms of conflict that barely reach the threshold of violence. It is within this spectrum that insurgency and counterinsurgency exist. Insurgency and its tactics are as old as warfare itself. Joint doctrine defines an **insurgency** as an organized movement aimed at the overthrow of a constituted government through the use of subversion and armed conflict (JP 1–02). **Counterinsurgency** is those political, economic, military, paramilitary, psychological, and civic actions taken by a government to defeat an insurgency (JP 1–02). . . .

1–4. Political power is the central issue in an insurgency, and each side has this as its aim. The insurgent attempts to overthrow or subvert an established government or authority; the counterinsurgent uses all of the instruments of national power to support the government in restoring and enforcing the rule of law. Counterinsurgency thus involves the controlled application of national power in political, information, economic, social, military, and diplomatic fields and disciplines. Its scale and complexity should never be underestimated by leaders and planners; indeed, the possible scale and complexity must be understood before the beginning of any such operation. . . .

1–8. Calling the terrorist or guerrilla tactics common to insurgency "unconventional" or "irregular" can be very misleading, since they have been among the most common approaches to warfare throughout history. Any combatant prefers a quick, cheap, overwhelming victory to a long, bloody, protracted struggle. But to achieve success in the face of superior resources and technology, weaker actors have had to adapt. The recent dominant performance of American military forces in major combat operations may lead many future opponents to pursue asymmetric approaches. Because America retains significant advantages in fires and surveillance, a thinking enemy is unlikely to choose to fight U.S. forces in open battle. Opponents who have attempted to do so, such as in Panama in 1989 or Iraq in 1991 and 2003, have been destroyed in conflicts that have been measured in hours or days. Conversely, opponents who have offset America's fire and surveillance advantages by operating close to civilians and news media, such as Somali clans in 1993 and Iraqi insurgents in 2005, have been more successful in achieving their aims. This does not mean that counterinsurgents do not face open warfare. Insurgents resort to conventional military operations if conditions seem right, in addition to using milder means such as nonviolent political mobilization of people, legal political action, and strikes. . . .

1–17. The end of the Cold War has brought a new wave of insurgencies. Many are fueled by more traditional religious or ethnic motivations. They are often based on clan or tribal affiliations, and they differ considerably from the post–World War II approaches. With the collapse of empires in the 20th century and the resulting wave of decolonization, weak and failed states have proliferated, now no longer propped up by Cold War rivalries. These power vacuums breed insurgencies. Similar conditions exist when regimes are changed by force or circumstance. American forces supporting a counterinsurgency often find themselves allied with a struggling nation in its bid to reestablish a functioning government. And the chaotic environment of failed states includes many groups of "spoilers" that counterinsurgents must sort out to develop appropriate responses. . . .

1–19. The contemporary environment also features a new kind of globalized insurgency, represented by Al Qaeda, which seeks to transform the Islamic world and reorder its relationship with the rest of the globe. Such groups feed on local grievances, integrate them into broader ideologies, and link disparate conflicts through globalized communications, finances, and technology. While the scale of the effort is new, the grievances and methods that sustain it are not. As in other insurgencies, terrorism, subversion, propaganda, and open warfare are its tools. But defeating such an enemy requires a similarly globalized response to deal with the array of linked resources and conflicts that sustain it. . . .

## INSURGENT STRATEGIES

1–23. Counterinsurgents not only have to be able to determine what motivates their opponents, which will influence the development of programs designed to attack the root causes of the insurgency, but also what sort of strategy is being used to advance the insurgent cause. Analysis of the insurgent approach shapes counterinsurgent military options. Insurgent strategies include the following:

- Conspiratorial.
- Military-focus.

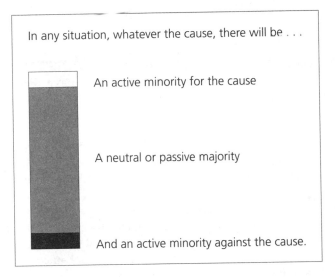

In any situation, whatever the cause, there will be . . .

An active minority for the cause

A neutral or passive majority

And an active minority against the cause.

Support for an insurgency

- Urban warfare.
- Protracted popular war.

## DYNAMICS OF AN INSURGENCY

- Leadership.
- Objectives.
- Ideology.
- Environment and geography.
- External support and sanctuaries.
- Phasing and timing.

These provide a framework for analysis that can reveal the insurgency's strengths and weaknesses. Although analysts can examine the following dynamics separately, they must study their interaction to fully understand an insurgency. . . .

### Understand the Environment

1–101. The local population is a critical center of gravity of an insurgency. Successful conduct of counterinsurgency operations depends on thoroughly understanding the society and culture within which they are being conducted. Soldiers and Marines must understand the following about the population in the area of operations (AO):

- How key groups in the society are organized.
- Relationships and tensions among them.
- Ideologies and narratives that resonate with the groups.
- Group interests and motivations.

- Means by which groups communicate.
- The society's leadership system. . . .

## CONTEMPORARY IMPERATIVES OF COUNTERINSURGENCY
1–112. Recent experiences with counterinsurgency have highlighted an important set of additional imperatives to keep in mind for success. . . .

### Learn and Adapt
1–119. An effective counterinsurgent force is a learning organization. Insurgents constantly shift between military and political phases and approaches. In addition, networked insurgents constantly exchange information about their enemy's vulnerabilities—including with other insurgents in distant theaters. A skillful counterinsurgent is able to adapt at least as fast as the insurgents. Every unit needs to be able to make observations, draw lessons, apply them, and assess results. Headquarters must develop an effective system to circulate best practices throughout the command quickly. Combatant commanders might also need to seek new laws or policies to authorize or resource necessary changes. Insurgents will shift their areas of operations looking for weak links, so widespread competence is required throughout the counterinsurgent force. . . .

230 | PARADOXES OF COUNTERINSURGENCY
1–123. The principles and imperatives discussed above reveal that COIN presents a complex and often unfamiliar set of missions and considerations for a military commander. In many ways, the conduct of counterinsurgency is counterintuitive to the traditional American view of war—although it has actually formed a substantial part of America's actual experience. Some representative paradoxes of COIN are presented here as examples of the different mindset required.

### The More You Protect Your Force, The Less Secure You Are
1–124. Ultimate success in COIN is gained by protecting the populace, not the COIN force. If military forces stay locked up in compounds, they lose touch with the people, appear to be running scared, and cede the initiative to the insurgents. Patrols must be conducted, risk must be shared, and contact maintained. This ensures access to the intelligence needed to drive operations and reinforces the connections with the people that establish real legitimacy.

### More Force Used, the Less Effective It Is
1–125. Any use of force produces many effects, not all of which can be foreseen. The more force applied, the greater the chance of collateral damage and mistakes. It also increases the opportunity for insurgent propaganda to portray lethal military activities as brutal. The precise and discriminate use of force also strengthens the rule of law that needs to be established.

*The More Successful COIN is, the Less Force That Can be Used
and the More Risk That Must Be Accepted*
1–126. This is really a corollary to the previous paradox. As the level of insurgent violence drops, the requirements of international law and the expectations of the populace allow less use of military actions by the counterinsurgent. More reliance is placed on police work. Rules of engagement
get stricter, and troops have to exercise increased restraint. Soldiers and
Marines may also have to accept more risk to maintain involvement with
the people.

*Sometimes Doing Nothing Is the Best Reaction*
1–127. Often an insurgent carries out a terrorist act or guerrilla raid with
the primary purpose of enticing the counterinsurgent to overreact, or at
least to react in a way that can then be exploited. If a careful assessment of
the effects of a course of action concludes that more negative than positive
effects may result, an alternative should be considered—potentially including a decision not to act.

*The Best Weapons for COIN Do Not Shoot*
1–128. Counterinsurgents achieve the most meaningful success by gaining
popular support and legitimacy for the host government, not by killing insurgents. Security plays an important role in setting the stage for other progress, but lasting victory comes from a vibrant economy, political participation, and restored hope. Often dollars and ballots have a more important
impact than bombs and bullets. Soldiers and Marines prepare to engage in
a host of nonmilitary missions to support COIN. Everyone has a role in nation building, not just the State Department or civil affairs soldiers.

*The Host Nation Doing Something Tolerably Is Sometimes
Better Than Us Doing It Well*
1–129. It is just as important to consider who performs an operation as to
assess how well it is done. In cases where the United States is supporting a
host nation, long-term success requires the establishment of viable indigenous leaders and institutions that can carry on without significant American support. The longer that process takes, the more popular support in the
United States will wane, and the more the local populace will question the
legitimacy of their own forces and government. T.E. Lawrence said of his
experience leading the Arab Revolt against the Ottoman Empire, "Do not
try and do too much with your own hands. Better the Arabs do it tolerably
than you do it perfectly. It is their war, and you are to help them, not win
it for them." However, a key word in Lawrence's advice is "tolerably." If the
host nation cannot perform tolerably, the COIN force may have to act. Experience, knowledge of the AO, and cultural sensitivity are essential to deciding when such action is necessary.

*If a Tactic Works This Week, It Might Not Work Next Week;*
*If It Works in This Province, It Might Not Work in the Next*
1–130. Competent insurgents are adaptive and today are often part of a widespread network that constantly and instantly communicates. Insurgents quickly disseminate information about successful COIN practices throughout the insurgency and adapt to them. Indeed, the more effective a COIN tactic is, the faster it becomes out of date because the insurgents have a greater need to counter it. Effective leaders at all levels avoid complacency and are at least as adaptive as their enemies. There is no "silver bullet" set of procedures for COIN. Constantly developing new practices is essential.

*Tactical Success Guarantees Nothing*
1–131. When COL Harry Summers allegedly told a North Vietnamese counterpart in 1975 that "You know you never defeated us on the battlefield," the reply supposedly was, "That may be so, but it is also irrelevant." Military actions by themselves cannot achieve success in COIN. Tactical actions must not only be linked to operational and strategic military objectives, but also to the essential political goals of COIN. Without those connections, lives and resources may be wasted for no real gain.

*Most of the Important Decisions Are Not Made by Generals*
1–132. Successful COIN relies on the competence and judgment of Soldiers and Marines at all levels. Senior leaders set the proper tone for actions by their organizations with thorough training and clear guidance, and then trust their subordinates to do the right thing. Preparation for tactical-level leaders requires more than Service doctrine; they must also be trained and educated to adapt to their local situations, understand the legal and ethical implications of their actions, and exercise subordinates' initiative and sound judgment to meet their senior commanders' intent.

## SUCCESSFUL AND UNSUCCESSFUL PRACTICES

*Successful Practices*
- Emphasize intelligence.
- Focus on the population, their needs, and security.
- Establish and expand secure areas.
- Isolate insurgents from the population (population control).
- Appoint a single authority, usually a dynamic, charismatic leader.
- Conduct effective, pervasive psychological operations.
- Provide amnesty and rehabilitation for insurgents.
- Place police in the lead with military support.
- Expand and diversify the police force.
- Train military forces to conduct counterinsurgency operations.
- Embed special operations forces and advisors with indigenous forces.
- Deny the insurgents sanctuary.

*Unsuccessful Practices*
Place priority on killing and capturing the enemy, not on engaging the population.

- Conduct battalion-sized operations as the norm.
- Concentrate military forces in large bases for protection.
- Focus special operations forces primarily on raiding.
- Place a low priority on assigning quality advisors to host-nation forces.
- Build and train host-nation security forces in the U.S. Army's image.
- Ignore peacetime government processes, including legal procedures.
- Allow open borders, airspace, and coastlines.

# DOCUMENT 5.4

In January 2007 David Petraeus was appointed Commanding General of the Multi-National Force–Iraq (MNF–I), the military command formed to fight the war against the insurgency. As MNF–I commander, he oversaw all coalition forces in Iraq and worked to apply the counterinsurgency doctrine he had been developing for years (5.3). In October 2008, Petraeus was promoted to commander of the U.S. Central Command (CENTCOM) and leadership of MNF–I was transferred to Gen. Raymond Odierno.

MULTI-NATIONAL FORCE–IRAQ COMMANDER'S
COUNTERINSURGENCY GUIDANCE,
JUNE 21, 2008 (EXCERPT)

- **Secure and serve the population.** The Iraqi people are the decisive "terrain." Together with our Iraqi partners, work to provide the people security, to give them respect, to gain their support, and to facilitate establishment of local governance, restoration of basic services, and revival of local economies.
- **Live among the people.** You can't commute to this fight. Position Joint Security Stations, Combat Outposts, and Patrol Bases in the neighborhoods we intend to secure. Living among the people is essential to securing them and defeating the insurgents.
- **Hold areas that have been secured.** Once we clear an area, we must retain it. Develop the plan for holding an area before starting to clear it. The people need to know that we and our Iraqi partners will not abandon their neighborhoods. When reducing forces and presence, gradually thin the line rather than handing

off or withdrawing completely. Ensure situational awareness even after transfer of responsibility to Iraqi forces.

- **Pursue the enemy relentlessly.** Identify and pursue AQI and other extremist elements tenaciously. Do not let them retain support areas or sanctuaries. Force the enemy to respond to us. Deny the enemy the ability to plan and conduct deliberate operations.

- **Generate unity of effort.** Coordinate operations and initiatives with our embassy and interagency partners, our Iraqi counterparts, local governmental leaders, and nongovernmental organizations to ensure all are working to achieve a common purpose.

- **Promote reconciliation.** We cannot kill our way out of this endeavor. We and our Iraqi partners must identify and separate the "reconcilables" from the "irreconcilables" through engagement, population control measures, information operations, kinetic operations, and political activities. We must strive to make the reconcilables a part of the solution, even as we identify, pursue, and kill, capture, or drive out the irreconcilables.

- **Defeat the network, not just the attack.** Defeat the insurgent networks to the "left" of the explosion. Focus intelligence assets to identify the network behind an attack, and go after its leaders, financiers, suppliers, and operators.

234 |

- **Foster Iraqi legitimacy.** Encourage Iraqi leadership and initiative; recognize that their success is our success. Partner in all that we do and support local involvement in security, governance, economic revival, and provision of basic services. Find the right balance between Coalition Forces leading and the Iraqis exercising their leadership and initiative, and encourage the latter. Legitimacy in the eyes of the Iraqi people is essential to overall success.

- **Employ all assets to isolate and defeat the terrorists and insurgents.** Counter-terrorist forces alone cannot defeat Al-Qaeda and the other extremists; success requires all forces and all means at our disposal—non-kinetic as well as kinetic. Employ Coalition and Iraqi conventional and special operations forces, Sons of Iraq, and all other available multipliers. Integrate civilian and military efforts to cement security gains. Resource and fight decentralized. Push assets down to those who most need them and can actually use them.

- **Employ money as a weapon system.** Use a targeting board process to ensure the greatest effect for each "round" expended, and to ensure that each engagement using money contributes to the achievement of the unit's overall objectives. Ensure contracting activities support the security effort, employing locals wherever possible. Employ a "matching fund" concept when feasible in order to ensure Iraqi involvement and commitment.

- **Fight for intelligence.** A nuanced understanding of the situation is everything. Analyze the intelligence that is gathered, share it, and fight for more. Every patrol should have tasks designed to augment understanding of the area of operations and the enemy. Operate on a "need to share" rather than a "need to know" basis; disseminate intelligence as soon as possible to all who can benefit from it.
- **Walk.** Move mounted, work dismounted. Stop by, don't drive by. Patrol on foot and engage the population. Situational awareness can only be gained by interacting with the people face-to-face, not separated by ballistic glass.
- **Understand the neighborhood.** Map the human terrain and study it in detail. Understand local culture and history. Learn about the tribes, formal and informal leaders, governmental structures, and local security forces. Understand how local systems are supposed to work—including governance, basic services, maintenance of infrastructure, and the economy—and how they really work.
- **Build relationships.** Relationships are a critical component of counterinsurgency operations. Together with our Iraqi counterparts, strive to establish productive links with local leaders, tribal sheikhs, governmental officials, religious leaders, and interagency partners.
- **Look for sustainable solutions.** Build mechanisms by which the Iraqi Security Forces, Iraqi community leaders, and local Iraqis under the control of governmental institutions can continue to secure local areas and sustain governance and economic gains in their communities as the Coalition Force presence is reduced. Figure out the Iraqi systems and help Iraqis make them work.
- **Maintain continuity and tempo through transitions.** Start to build the information you'll provide to your successors on the day you take over. Allow those who will follow you to virtually "look over your shoulder" while they're still at home station by giving them access to your daily updates and other items on SIPRNET. Encourage extra time on the ground during transition periods, and strive to maintain operational tempo and local relationships to avoid giving the enemy respite.
- **Manage expectations.** Be cautious and measured in announcing progress. Note what has been accomplished, but also acknowledge what still needs to be done. Avoid premature declarations of success. Ensure our troopers and our partners are aware of our assessments and recognize that any counterinsurgency operation has innumerable challenges that enemies get a vote, and that progress is likely to be slow.
- **Be first with the truth.** Get accurate information of significant activities to your chain of command, to Iraqi leaders, and to the

press as soon as is possible. Beat the insurgents, extremists, and criminals to the headlines, and pre-empt rumors. Integrity is critical to this fight. Don't put lipstick on pigs. Acknowledge setbacks and failures, and then state what we've learned and how we'll respond. Hold the press (and ourselves) accountable for accuracy, characterization, and context. Avoid spin and let facts speak for themselves. Challenge enemy disinformation. Turn our enemies' bankrupt messages, extremist ideologies, oppressive practices, and indiscriminate violence against them.

- **Fight the information war relentlessly.** Realize that we are in a struggle for legitimacy that in the end will be won or lost in the perception of the Iraqi people. Every action taken by the enemy and United States has implications in the public arena. Develop and sustain a narrative that works and continually drive the themes home through all forms of media.
- **Live our values.** Do not hesitate to kill or capture the enemy, but stay true to the values we hold dear. This is what distinguishes us from our enemies. There is no tougher endeavor than the one in which we are engaged. It is often brutal, physically demanding, and frustrating. All of us experience moments of anger, but we can neither give in to dark impulses nor tolerate unacceptable actions by others.
- **Exercise initiative.** In the absence of guidance or orders, determine what they should be and execute aggressively. Higher level leaders will provide broad vision and paint "white lines on the road," but it will be up to those at tactical levels to turn "big ideas" into specific actions.
- **Prepare for and exploit opportunities.** "Luck is what happens when preparation meets opportunity" (Seneca the Younger). Develop concepts (such as that of "reconcilables" and "irreconcilables") in anticipation of possible opportunities, and be prepared to take risk as necessary to take advantage of them.
- **Learn and adapt.** Continually assess the situation and adjust tactics, policies, and programs as required. Share good ideas (none of us is smarter than all of us together). Avoid mental or physical complacency. Never forget that what works in an area today may not work there tomorrow, and may or may not be transferable to another part of Iraq.

# DOCUMENT 5.5

Many commentaries by retired military officials on developments in Iraq contained conflicting reports of success and failure. Ret. Gen. Barry McCaffrey, who had served as commander-in-chief of the U.S. Armed Forces Southern

Command coordinating Pentagon operations in Latin America, delivered his assessment of Iraq to the Foreign Relations Senate Committee in the widely publicized document below. McCaffrey was optimistic about the situation in Iraq and praised the counterinsurgency campaign. He also expressed confidence in U.S. success, arguing that the failures in Iraq were due to Iraqi incompetence.

But McCaffrey's memo, along with others, became the focus of a propaganda controversy that surfaced in 2008. The *New York Times* reported that military analysts hired by ABC, NBC, CBS, CNN, and MSNBC to present unbiased observations of the war in Iraq had undisclosed ties to the Pentagon and to military contractors. Rather than objectively assessing events in Iraq, they were presenting targeted messages that Rumsfeld and his top aides had wanted to disseminate in order to shape public opinion. An intelligence officer anonymously quoted in the *Times* called the program an exercise in PSYOPS (psychological operations).

---

MEMORANDUM FOR SENATE FOREIGN RELATIONS COMMITTEE, JUNE 2005 (EXCERPT)

Subject: Trip Report—Kuwait and Iraq
Saturday, 4 June through Saturday, 11 June 2005

1. PURPOSE:
This memo provides feedback reference visit 4–11 June 2005 by General Barry R. McCaffrey, USA (Ret.) to Kuwait and Iraq.

2. SOURCES:
A. **General George Casey, Commander, MNF-I**—one-on-one discussions and Staff Briefings.
B. **LTG JR Vines, Commander MNC-I**—one-on-one discussions and Staff Briefings.
C. **LTG Dave Petreaus** [*sic*], **Commander, Multinational Security Transition Command**—one-on-one discussions/briefings. . . .

3. THE BOTTOM LINE—OBSERVATIONS FROM OPERATION IRAQI FREEDOM: JUNE 2005:
1st  US Military Forces in Iraq are superb. Our Army-Marine ground combat units with supporting Air and Naval Power are characterized by quality military leadership, solid discipline, high morale, and enormous individual and unit courage. Unit effectiveness is as good as we can get. This is the most competent and battle wise force in our nation's history. They are also beautifully cared for by the chain-of-command—and they

know it. (Food, A/C sleeping areas, medical care, mental health care, home leave, phone/e-mail contact with families, personal equipment, individual and unit training, targeted economic incentives in the battle area, visibility of tactical leadership, home station care for their families, access to news information, etc).

2nd The point of the US war effort is to create legitimate and competent Iraqi national, provincial, and municipal governance. We are at a turning point in the coming six months. The momentum is now clearly with the Iraqi Government and the Coalition Security Forces. The Sunnis are coming into the political process. They will vote in December. Unlike the Balkans—the Iraqis want this to succeed. Foreign fighters are an enormously lethal threat to the Iraqi civilian population, the ISF, and Coalition Forces in that order. However, they will be an increasing political disaster for the insurgency. Over time they are actually adding to the credibility of the emerging Iraqi government. We should expect to see a dwindling number of competent, suicide capable Jihadist. Those who come to Iraq—will be rapidly killed in Iraq. The picture by next summer will be unfavorable to recruiting foreigners to die in Iraq while attacking fellow Arabs.

238 |

The initial US/UK OIF intervention took down a criminal regime and left a nation without an operational State.

The transitional Bremer-appointed Iraqi government created a weak state of warring factions.

The January 2005 Iraqi elections created the beginnings of legitimacy and have fostered a supportive political base to create the new Iraqi Security Forces.

The August Iraqi Constitutional Referendum and the December-January election and formation of a new government will build the prototype for the evolution of an effective, law-based Iraqi State with a reliable Security Force.

January thru September 2006 will be the peak period of the insurgency—and the bottom rung of the new Iraq. The positive trend lines following the January 2006 elections (if they continue) will likely permit the withdrawal of substantial US combat forces by late summer of 2006. With 250,000 Iraqi Security Forces successfully operating in support of a government which includes substantial Sunni participation—the energy will start rapidly draining out of the insurgency.

3rd The Iraqi Security Forces are now a real and hugely significant factor. LTG Dave Petreaus [sic] has done a brilliant job with his supporting trainers.

169,000 Army and Police exist in various stages of readiness. They have uniforms, automatic weapons, body armor, some radios, some armor, light trucks, and battalion-level organization. At least 60,000 are courageous Patriots who are actively fighting. By next summer—250,000 Iraqi troops and 10 division HQS will be the dominant security factor in Iraq.

However, much remains to be done. There is no maintenance or logistics system. There is no national command and control. Corruption is a threat factor of greater long-range danger than the armed insurgency. The Insurgents have widely infiltrated the ISF. The ISF desperately needs more effective, long-term NCO and Officer training.

Finally, the ISF absolutely must have enough helicopter air mobility (120+ Black Hawk UH 60's)—and a substantial number of armored vehicles to lower casualties and give them a competitive edge over the insurgents they will fight. (2000 up-armor Humvee's, 500 ASV's, and 2000 M113A3's with add-on armor package).

## 4. TOP CENTCOM VULNERABILITIES:

1st  Premature drawdown of U.S. ground forces driven by dwindling U.S. domestic political support and the progressive deterioration of Army and Marine manpower. (In particular, the expected melt-down of the Army National Guard and Army Reserve in the coming 36 months.)

2nd  Alienation of the U.S. Congress or the American people caused by Iraqi public ingratitude and corruption.

3rd  Political ineptitude of Shia civil leadership that freezes out the Sunnis and creates a civil war during our drawdown.

4th  "The other shoe"—a war with North Korea, Venezuela, Syria, Iran, or Cuba that draws away U.S. military forces and political energy.

5th  The loss or constraint of our logistics support bases in Kuwait. Clearly we need constant diplomatic attention and care to this vital Ally. If Kuwait became unstable or severely alienated to US Military objectives in the region—then our posture in Iraq would be placed in immediate fatal peril.

6th  Open intervention by Iranian intelligence or military forces to support rogue Shia Iraqi insurgency. (Assassination of Sustani—armed rebellion by Sadr)

7th  Continued under-manning and too rapid turnover in State Department inter-agency representation in Iraq.

8th  Lack of continuity in CENTCOM strategic and operational senior leadership. The CENTCOM military leadership we now have is a collective national treasure.

General Abizaid's value to the War effort based on his credibility to US Military Forces—and ability to communicate and relate to the Iraqi emergent leadership—cannot be overstated.

The combination of a three-star tactical Headquarters (LTG John Vines is the most experienced and effective operational battle leader we have produced in a generation)—and an in-country four-star strategic commander (Gen George Casey) has improved the situation from the overwhelmed, under-resourced Bremer-Sanchez ad hoc arrangement.

LTG Dave Petreaus has done a superb job building the ISF. Relationships are everything in this campaign. We need to lock in our senior team for the coming 24 months.

Suggest that the three key US/Coalition military HQS of Casey-Petreaus-Vines need to stop unit rotation and go to individual replacement rotation.

The very senior U.S. military leadership needs their families based in a Kuwait compound with periodic visits authorized. (We did this with General Abrams and his senior leaders during the final phase of Vietnam.)

240 | 5. THE ENEMY THREAT:

1st The Iraqi Insurgency threat is enormously more complex than Vietnam.

There we faced a single opposing ideology; known enemy leaders; a template enemy organizational structure; an external sanctuary which was vital to the insurgency to bring in fighters, ammunition, resources; and relative security in urban areas under Allied/Vietnamese Government control.

Iraq is much tougher. The enemy forces in this struggle are principally Sunni irredentists—but there is also a substantial criminal class determined to murder, rob, kidnap, and create chaos.

We also face a small but violent foreign Jihadist terrorist element. These terrorists do not depend on foreign sanctuary. They can arm themselves with the incredible mass of munitions and weapons scattered from one end of Iraq to the other.

Finally, Iraq is encircled by six bordering nations—all of whom harbor ill-will for the struggling democratic Iraqi state.

2nd On the positive side of the ledger:

High Sunni voting turnout and political participation in December will likely set the conditions for the down hill slide of the insurgency.

The insurgency can no longer mass against Coalition forces with units greater than squad level— they all get killed in short order by very aggressive US/UK combat Forces. The insurgents have been forced to principally target the weak links—the Iraqi Police and innocent civilians. This will be a counter-productive strategy in the mid-term. It has been forced on them by the effective counter-insurgency operations and information operations of Coalition forces.

Insurgents now have a reduced capability to attack Coalition forces by direct fire: 80% (+) of the attacks are carried out with standoff weapons or suicide bombings (mortars, rockets, IEDs).

Suicide IED attack is enormously effective. However, it will soon likely become a fragile tool. The Jihadists will begin to run short of human bombs. Most are killed or die while carrying out missions which are marginally effective. This must be a prime enemy vulnerability for Coalition information warfare operations.

We must continue to level with the American people. We still have a five year fight facing us in Iraq.

3rd The Fallujah Situation:

The city has huge symbolic importance throughout Mideast.

| 241

Unrealistic expectations were raised on how rapidly the Coalition could rebuild.

The City appears to be an angry disaster. Money doesn't re-build infrastructure—bulldozers and workers and cement do. The Coalition needs an Iraqi/Coalition effort principally executed by military engineers—and thousands of Iraqi workers—to re-build the City. We need a "Pierre L'Enfant" of Fallujah.

Police stations are planned but barely started. The train station is mined and the trains do not function. Roads must be paved. We need to eliminate major signs of US caused war damage, etc.

6. COALITION PUBLIC DIPLOMACY POLICY IS A DISASTER:

1st The US media is putting the second team in Iraq with some exceptions. Unfortunately, the situation is extremely dangerous for journalists. The working conditions for a reporter are terrible. They cannot travel independently of US military forces without risking abduction or death. In some cases, the press has degraded to reporting based on secondary sources, press briefings which they do not believe, and alarmist video of the aftermath of suicide bombings obtained from Iraqi employees of unknown reliability.

**2nd** Our unbelievably competent, articulate, objective, and courageous Battalion, Brigade, and Division Commanders are not on TV. These commanders represent an Army-Marine Corps which is rated as the most trusted institution in America by every poll.

**3rd** We are not aggressively providing support (transportation, security, food, return of film to an upload site, etc) to reporters to allow them to follow the course of the war.

**4th** Military leaders on the ground are talking to people they trust instead of talking to all reporters who command the attention of the American people. (We need to educate and support AP, Reuters, Gannet, Hearst, the Washington Post, the New York Times, etc.)

7. SUMMARY:

   a. This is the darkness before dawn in the efforts to construct a viable Iraqi state. The enterprise was badly launched—but we are now well organized and beginning to develop successful momentum. The future outcomes are largely a function of the degree to which Iraqi men and women will overcome fear and step forward to seize the leadership opportunity to create a new future.

   b. We face some very difficult days in the coming 2–5 years. In my judgment, if we retain the support of the American people—we can achieve our objectives of creating a law-based Iraqi state which will be an influencing example on the entire region.

   c. A successful outcome would potentially usher in a very dramatically changed environment throughout the Middle East and signal in this region the end of an era of incompetent and corrupt government which fosters frustration and violence on the part of much of the population.

   d. It was an honor and a very encouraging experience to visit CENTCOM Forces in Iraq and Kuwait and see the progress achieved by the bravery and dedication of our military forces.

*Barry R. McCaffrey*
*General, USA (Ret)*

# DOCUMENT 5.6

Stephen J. Hadley, the national security advisor for President Bush, prepared this secret memo for administration officials; the document was published by the *New York Times* in November 2006. Hadley assessed the performance of Prime Minister Nouri al-Maliki and his commitment to rise above sectarian agendas. Maliki had reiterated his vision for a Sunni, Shia, and Kurdish partnership, but U.S. commanders on the ground criticized his performance. Hadley's memo addressed Maliki as if he had full control over the government, seeming to assume that the Iraqi head of state had more independence of action than was the case.

---

## STEPHEN J. HADLEY, IRAQ MEMO, NOVEMBER 8, 2006 (EXCERPT)

Makili [*sic*] should:

Compel his ministers to take small steps—such as providing health services and opening bank branches in Sunni neighborhoods—to demonstrate that his government serves all ethnic communities;

Bring his political strategy with Moktada al-Sadr to closure and bring to justice any JAM actors that do not eschew violence;

Shake up his cabinet by appointing nonsectarian, capable technocrats in key service (and security) ministries;

Announce an overhaul of his own personal staff so that "it reflects the face of Iraq";

Demand that all government workers (in ministries, the Council of Representatives and his own offices) publicly renounce all violence for the pursuit of political goals as a condition for keeping their positions;

Declare that Iraq will support the renewal of the U.N. mandate for multinational forces and will seek, as appropriate, to address bilateral issues with the United States through a SOFA [status of forces agreement] to be negotiated over the next year;

Take one or more immediate steps to inject momentum back into the reconciliation process, such as a suspension of de-Baathification measures and the submission to the Parliament or "Council of Representatives" of a draft piece of legislation for a more judicial approach;

Announce plans to expand the Iraqi Army over the next nine months; and

Declare the immediate suspension of suspect Iraqi police units and a robust program of embedding coalition forces into MOI [Ministry of the Interior] units while the MOI is revetted and retrained. . . .

### Moving Ahead

We should waste no time in our efforts to determine Maliki's intentions and, if necessary, to augment his capabilities. We might take the following steps immediately:

Convince Maliki to deliver on key actions that might reassure Sunnis (open banks and direct electricity rebuilding in Sunni areas, depoliticize hospitals);

Tell Maliki that we understand that he is working his own strategy for dealing with the Sadrists and that:

- you have asked General Casey to support Maliki in this effort
- it is important that we see some tangible results in this strategy soon;

Send your personal representative to Baghdad to discuss this strategy with Maliki and to press other leaders to work with him, especially if he determines that he must build an alternative political base;

Ask Casey to develop a plan to empower Maliki, including:

- Formation of National Strike Forces
- Dramatic increase in National Police embedding
- More forces under Maliki command and control

Ask Secretary of Defense and General Casey to make a recommendation about whether more forces are need [*sic*] in Baghdad;

Ask Secretary of Defense and General Casey to devise a more robust embedding plan and a plan to resource it;

Direct your cabinet to begin an intensive press on Saudi Arabia to play a leadership role on Iraq, connecting this role with other areas in which Saudi Arabia wants to see U.S. action;

If Maliki seeks to build an alternative political base:

- Press Sunni and other Iraqi leaders (especially Hakim) [Abdul Aziz al-Hakim, the leader of the Supreme Council for the Islamic Revolution in Iraq, a Maliki rival] to support Maliki
- Engage Sistani to reassure and seek his support for a new non-sectarian political movement.

## DOCUMENT 5.7

Despite all the recommendations and strategic shifts, the success rate of U.S. operations in Iraq, according to the Pentagon, was still mixed as of mid-2008.

DEPARTMENT OF DEFENSE, "MEASURING STABILITY
AND SECURITY IN IRAQ, JUNE 2008," REPORT TO
CONGRESS IN ACCORDANCE WITH THE DEPARTMENT
OF DEFENSE APPROPRIATIONS ACT (SECTION 9010,
PUBLIC LAW 109–289) (EXCERPT)

## Section 1—Stability and Security

While the surge has helped mitigate ethnosectarian tensions and restore stability to many areas, progress remains uneven and fragile. Violence levels vary throughout the country, and Coalition and Iraqi forces continue to confront numerous challenges. With the more recent exception of Basrah, Mosul and Sadr City, overall violence has followed a downward trend, with the greatest recent improvements in the Sunni majority areas of the northern provinces. Elsewhere, Coalition forces and the ISF continue to make incremental security gains, as the ISF grow in numbers, experience and capabilities. Coalition forces, with considerable help from the Sons of Iraq and tribal leaders, continue to combat al Qaeda in Iraq (AQI), maintain a public presence as partners with the ISF and exert pressure on extremists and insurgents. The Iraqi people are responding to this improved security environment and increasingly rejecting indiscriminate violence and extremist ideology. Meanwhile, the ISF are progressively asserting GoI authority over militia extremists and insurgents in cities such as Najaf, Hillah, Nasiriyah, Basrah, Baghdad and elsewhere. The recent security operation in Basrah provided the GoI many constructive lessons. It also served as an important development in the government's efforts to guarantee security for the Iraqi people.

## Overall Assessment of the Security Environment

Improvements in the security environment have been substantial over the past nine months but significant challenges remain. The cumulative effect of Coalition and ISF efforts continues to shrink the areas in which AQI and its insurgent allies enjoy support and sanctuary. In a particularly noteworthy development, Iraqi forces launched clearing operations in Ninewa Province on May 10, 2008, that have disrupted AQI's grip on Mosul. Nevertheless, AQI remains a dangerous and adaptable enemy that seeks to control areas where Coalition and Iraqi force presence is minimal. As AQI comes under increased pressure in Mosul, there have been indications that it is attempting to regroup along the upper Euphrates River. AQI also remains capable of high-profile attacks, though its indiscriminate targeting of civilians continues to alienate AQI from the mainstream Sunni population it claims to represent.

After an increase in attacks related to the late March 2008 activities in Basrah, Baghdad and other southern provinces, most key security indicators have trended downward, though many have yet to reach pre-March 2008 levels. Iraqwide, total monthly security incidents for April 2008 are comparable to the last months of 2007. Coalition and Iraqi efforts to solidify the security gains of the past year continue to gain momentum and manifest themselves not only in security, but also in the political and economic arenas. The ISF continues to grow, train and establish the rule of law in more Iraqi provinces and cities. The ISF also continues to demonstrate improved performance as it gains experience in independent operations.

The cumulative effect of Coalition and ISF efforts continues to shrink the areas in which AQI and its insurgent allies enjoy support and sanctuary.

Most indicators of violence fell continuously from September 2007 through mid-March 2008. However, on March 23, 2008, criminal elements of JAM launched multiple rockets on the International Zone, signaling impatience with the Sadr cease-fire. On March 25, 2008, Prime Minister Maliki launched Operation *Saulat al-Fursan* deploying nearly a division of ISF troops to the Basrah area.[6] The intent of the operation was to wrest control of Basrah from JAM militias and their Special Group (SG) associates. As the operation evolved into a major conflict between ISF and JAM, first in Basrah and subsequently in Baghdad and other southern provinces, attacks and associated casualties rose sharply. By March 30, 2008, the ISF had restored security and freedom of movement in many areas, and a call by Muqtada al-Sadr for JAM forces to cease attacks on ISF and civilians led to further reductions in violence.

In addition to Basrah, the GoI and ISF achieved important gains against Shi'a extremists in Baghdad. As the ISF commenced operations in Basrah, JAM and SGs increased attacks against Coalition and Iraqi forces in Baghdad, to include launching multiple indirect fire attacks into the International Zone on an almost daily basis. Sadr's cease-fire declaration on March 30, 2008, led to a brief lull. Violence levels soon rose again as JAM and SGs resisted Coalition and ISF operations to clear the southern two neighborhoods of Sadr City to diminish the effectiveness of rocket attacks on the International Zone and other parts of Baghdad. Supported by robust intelligence, surveillance and reconnaissance (ISR) assets, Coalition forces effectively employed air weapons teams and armed Predator unmanned aerial vehicles (UAVs) to defeat indirect fire and rocket-propelled grenade launcher teams operating throughout Sadr City. Following negotiations between the United Iraqi Alliance and Sadrist officials, on May 20, 2008, the ISF conducted a largely unopposed entry into Sadr City and began to conduct clearing operations that are still underway. Coalition and Iraqi forces continue to combat illegal militias in additional neighborhoods in Baghdad and throughout southern Iraq.

Subversive foreign influences, primarily from Syria and Iran, continue to exert negative influence on the security environment in Iraq. The Syrian

---

6. "Global Issues: Selections from CQ Researcher" (Washington, D.C.: Congressional Quarterly Press, 2007), 12.

Government continues to take some steps, albeit ineffective ones, to reduce crossborder travel by some extremist fighters. Considerable numbers of foreign terrorists still cross from Syria into Iraq, and Iraqi extremists still use Syria as a safe haven to avoid Iraqi and Coalition forces. The Government of Iran also continues to facilitate large-scale trafficking of arms, ammunition and explosives and fund, train, arm and guide numerous networks that conduct wide-scale insurgency operations. The recent violence in Basra and Baghdad highlighted the lethal role Iran's IRGC-QF plays in Iraq. The number of EFPs and indirect fire incidents from Iranian-supplied rockets increased sharply in late March and April 2008. With increased emplacement of EFPs by SG criminal elements, total EFP incidents in April 2008 were the highest on record.

Though the recent improvements in the security situation across Iraq are significant, the Iraqi Government will have to take deliberate measures to sustain these gains. These measures include the development and employment of a sustained, robust security posture; delivery of humanitarian assistance; progress in reconstruction; and the generation of sustainable employment. Free and fair provincial elections will also be important in facilitating reconciliation and the formation of representative provincial governments. The Coalition is partnering with the GoI to assist the Iraqis in each of these areas. . . .

| 247

## Improvised Explosive Devices and Explosively Formed Penetrators

Weekly improvised explosive device (IED) incidents in Baghdad rose sharply over the months of March and April 2008, as JAM employed many of these devices to restrict Coalition and Iraqi forces' freedom of movement around Sadr City and New Baghdad. Levels for IEDs Iraq-wide remained comparable to early 2006. Despite the spike in Baghdad, the number of IED incidents and casualties has remained below long-term averages for 31 straight weeks. Moreover, the portion of IEDs found and cleared before they detonated has exceeded 50% during all but six weeks in the past seven months. The level of IED incidents and casualties remains low due to the steadily increasing efforts of Coalition and Iraqi forces to disrupt insurgent networks and destroy IED-making facilities and due to the ISF presence among the population, which fosters a great number of tips and often prevents attackers from reaching more heavily populated targets. IEDs constitute the principal threat to Coalition forces, but the number of incidents and Coalition deaths caused by IEDs remains on a consistently low six-month trend. Monthly EFP incidents increased substantially in March and April 2008. Special Groups (SGs) operating in the Baghdad Security Districts of Sadr City and New Baghdad, supported by Iranian training and materiel, were primarily responsible for these increases. The number of EFP incidents declined in May, returning to the level seen in March 2008.

### High-profile Attacks

Monthly high-profile attacks (HPAs) in Iraq decreased in May 2008, falling below the previous two-year low reached in December 2007. HPA explosions for May 2008 are down over 70% from the peak in March 2007. As security improves and Coalition and Iraqi forces focus on enemy networks, there has been a decrease in the effectiveness of HPAs. Nonetheless, AQI retains the intent and capability of carrying out spectacular, high payoff attacks. On April 15, 2008, a series of HPAs throughout Iraq produced 150 civilian casualties, the highest number of casualties attributed to AQI in a single day since February 1, 2008.

The number of deaths due to ethno-sectarian violence remains relatively low, illustrating the enemy's inability to re-ignite the cycle of ethno-sectarian violence. Following a downward trend throughout most of 2007, the number of person-borne IED (PBIED) incidents increased from October 2007 to February 2008, before declining in March and April 2008. AQI's use of PBIEDs and female suicide bombers remains an important tactic, especially as population security measures and local opposition to AQI in some provinces makes effective targeting using suicide vehicle borne IEDs (SVBIEDs) more difficult.

248 |
# Iraqi Documents

Through the use of documents, posters, and other media, Iraqis were able to express their views about insurgency, counterinsurgency, and reconciliation. While most of the following documents were from insurgent groups themselves, the final selection was the Iraqi government's first National Security Strategy Document, which offered an official vision for the state through 2010.

A key point to understand was that the insurgency was homegrown. Some observers said that the differences between Sunnis and Shia were irreconcilable, indicating that these groups were prone to violence in the absence of a strong national leader. Others argued that Iraq was an artificial state, with borders arbitrarily drawn by the colonial powers. Both perspectives were overly simplistic. All states have a level of artificiality, as military conquest and the displacement or shifting of ethnic groups during colonialism were precursors to the modern state system. Further, one could just as soon argue that Sunnis and Shia had a long history of cooperation. The Shia had sided with the Sunnis in their fight for independence against the British during World War 1, for example, and again with their Sunni co-nationals during the 1958 military coup. Iraqi Shia chose their Iraqi identity over their Shia roots when they rejected the 1979 Iranian Revolution's call for Iraqi Shia to secede and join their Persian neighbor. Indeed, there was abundant evidence that Iraqis had a strong sense of nationalism and patriotism that trumped sectarianism before the U.S. invasion. After the occupation began, and prior to the outbreak of sectarian violence, Muqtada al-Sadr's initial communiqués had called for Sunnis and Shia to work together against the occupation. Grand Ayatollah Ali al-Sistani and other leading Shia and Sunni spokesmen issued similar calls. Most importantly, none of the indigenous discussions on Iraqi nationalism called for dismantling or partitioning the state, regardless of sect.

The insurgency contained both Sunni and Shia groups, though the Sunnis tended to take the lead early by having boycotted the political process until 2005 and by being the object of de-Baathification. The Shia tended to fold into the government more easily, while the Sunnis, infuriated by the de-Baathification policy and fearful for their future under a Shia government, were slow to participate. There were several Sunni groups; the four most popular were al Qaeda in Mesopotamia (Tandhim al Qaeda fi Bilad al Rafidayn), Partisans of the Sunni Army (Jaish Ansar al-Sunna), the Islamic Army in Iraq (Al Jaish Islami fil Iraq), and the Islamic Front of the Iraqi Resistance (al-Jabha al-Islamiya lil Muqawama al Iraqiya).

One of the major reasons for the insurgency's strength was its widespread use of Internet, print media, and other technology to unify the anti-occupation coalition. The various insurgent groups published newsletters and training manuals and ran highly sophisticated Web sites, using the Internet to recruit members, disseminate information, and enhance their status. All of their communications highlighted the need to end foreign occupation. Their use of the Internet demonstrated one effect of globalization: jihadism in cyberspace had | 249 steadily mushroomed. *Congressional Quarterly* reported that whereas there were only twelve such jihadi Web sites in the year 2000, there were more than four thousand by 2006.[7]

## DOCUMENT 5.8

In 2004, one of the Sunni insurgent groups, Jaish Muhammad (the Army of Muhammad), offered a window into the logic of the insurgency. Though it claimed responsibility for attacks against occupying troops, it denied any ties to al Qaeda in Mesopotamia. The group's spokesman granted an exclusive interview to a reporter from the Institute for War and Peace Reporting (IWPR) in the town of Bacuba. The reporter was taken to a secret location by a liaison and blindfolded throughout the interview. The bracketed additions in the document here were added by the IWPR for clarification. The interview was translated by Ali Kais al-Rubai, then an IWPR trainee journalist in Iraq.

7. "Global Issues: Selections from CQ Researcher" (Washington, D.C.: Congressional Quarterly Press, 2007), 12.

## ISLAMISTS PLEDGE CONTINUED WAR ON COALITION, MAY 2004

**IWPR:** The United States destroyed Saddam Hussein's regime. Why did you declare war against it?

**Jaish Muhammed:** Yes, the United States rid us of Saddam Hussein's regime. But they did not do it for the sake of the people of Iraq. Rather, they did it for the sake of Iraqi oil and to protect Israel's security. There is another important reason [why we fight them]—ignorance of our traditions that are characterised by their tribal nature; and misbehaviour by elements of these troops towards the Iraqi people—random search operations in houses and the searching of women. They also consider the Sunnis to be a minority, and this is wrong for we are an important part of Iraqi society.

**IWPR:** What is your position regarding the Iraqi Governing Council?

**Jaish Muhammed:** Our position is clear—they are all spies, traitors, and agents for the Americans. First, they do not represent the people of Iraq because they are not elected. They are appointed by their masters, the Americans. Second, the appointed Governing Council members were [in exile during the Saddam regime]. They do not understand Iraqis' suffering and Arab traditions. [They] were distorted by the Western life they lived.

**IWPR:** Your organisation is known as a military one. Do you have a political branch?

**Jaish Muhammed:** Our political orientation is our good Islamic religion, and we have an Islamic party that supports jihadi movements.

**IWPR:** Do you mean the Islamic Party [a Sunni party with a seat on the Governing Council]?

**Jaish Muhammed:** Of course not.

**IWPR:** So what is its name?

**Jaish Muhammed:** I am sorry, I cannot answer that question.

**IWPR:** Do you receive support from foreign countries?

**Jaish Muhammed:** No. But we receive support from honourable and good people in this country.

**IWPR:** What kind of support do you mean?

**Jaish Muhammed:** Financial as well as moral support.

**IWPR:** What do you say about accounts of [non-Iraqi] Arab fighters being among you?

**Jaish Muhammed:** There are some Arab fighters among us, but the US makes this into a bigger issue in the media than it really it is. We are not so few as to need fighters from abroad. Those [Arab fighters] among us are few. They lived with us [before the war], and did not come from abroad after the war.

**IWPR:** Are you responsible for operations targeting the police?

**Jaish Muhammed:** No. A Muslim must not kill a Muslim, no matter what.

IWPR: So, who is responsible?

Jaish Muhammed: I do not know. But [attacks on the police] are an American plan to distort the image of the Iraqi resistance

IWPR: Is there any relationship between you and the Al Qaeda network?

Jaish Muhammed: No. There is no relationship between us and the Al Qaeda network, which has no role in our jihad.

IWPR: But the explosions in Kadhemiyah and Karbala suggest otherwise. [Two attacks on Shia shrines, killing over 180 people, have been blamed on an offshoot of Al Qaeda seeking to trigger a Sunni-Shia civil war.]

Jaish Muhammed: We strongly denounce these organisations. As I said, a Muslim must not kill another Muslim.

IWPR: What does your organisation think of the transfer of sovereignty to an Iraqi government, scheduled for June 30? Will you continue your operations against American forces?

Jaish Muhammed: Handing over of power to Iraqis is in theory a beautiful thing. In practice, it is merely ink on paper. We will continue our operations against the Jews [term often used by Islamic groups to mean the Coalition]. More than one American official has stated that the American forces would stay even after the power handover. I want to tell you something important—we are not after any power. Rather, we want to drive the occupying forces out of the lands of Iraq. We rely on the saying of the Prophet Muhammed, peace be on him—"Drive the polytheists from the Arabian peninsula." That is our goal.

| 251

IWPR: Let's say the Coalition forces left Iraq and transferred power to Iraqis. Would you participate in politics?

Jaish Muhammed: We would go back to our lands and re-plant them. As you can see, most of us are farmers.

IWPR: What is your position regarding the kidnappings carried out by some groups?

Jaish Muhammed: Kidnapping is an obligation. It is not prohibited by religion, if it is done to foreigners who cooperate with the occupation.

IWPR: What is your position regarding the explosion at the United Nations? [August 19, 2003 attack on UN, claimed by a group calling itself the "Armed Vanguards of the Second Army of Mohammed"]

Jaish Muhammed: There is no real United Nations. It is an organisation completely controlled by the United States and its resolutions always serve US interests.

IWPR: Some say that the Sunni Islamist movement did not fight against Saddam, and stood by his side.

Jaish Muhammed: This is wrong, and mere lies. If Saddam killed the first and second Sadrs [two leading Shia clerics killed in 1981 and 1999], he also killed many Sunni preachers. He fought us and sent our faithful to prison.

IWPR: Do you mean the suppression of the [radical Islamic] Wahhabi movement?

**Jaish Muhammed:** We are not Wahhabi [term associated with puritan Islamic trend from Saudi Arabia, in Iraq carries connotation of intolerance towards Shia]. Rather, we are Salafis [more general term used to denote Sunni purist trend]. The answer to your question is yes.

**IWPR:** Any final word?

**Jaish Muhammed:** We want to inform America that its attempt to stir up sectarian discord is a failure. I also want to ask the Governing Council members who talk only about [Saddam-era] mass graves: are the 700 martyrs of Fallujah [*Editors' Note: The civilian death toll given by local sources for the April siege*] not part of the mass graves as well.

# DOCUMENT 5.9

Abu Musab al-Zarqawi was a Jordanian-born Sunni extremist behind a series of attacks, bombings, and beheadings in Iraq during the insurgency. He formed al Qaeda in Iraq, also called al Qaeda in Mesopotamia, after the occupation began to oppose the presence of U.S. and Western military forces in the Islamic world. He perceived his movement as transcending Iraq's borders, pledged allegiance to Osama bin Laden, and joined the broader al Qaeda organization in 2004. Zarqawi wanted to encourage the revival of the Sunnis by indiscriminately attacking Shia, hoping that the reprisals, chaos, and civil war that ensued would speed the withdrawal of U.S. forces. He was killed by coalition forces in 2006.

LETTER FROM ABU MUSAB AL-ZARQAWI
TO OSAMA BIN LADEN, JULY 2005 (EXCERPT)

Here is the current situation as I, with my limited vision, see it. I ask God to forgive my prattle and lapses. I say, having sought help from God, that the Americans, as you know well, entered Iraq on a contractual basis and to create the State of Greater Israel from the Nile to the Euphrates and that this Zionized American Administration believes that accelerating the creation of the State of [Greater] Israel will accelerate the emergence of the Messiah. It came to Iraq with all its people, pride, and haughtiness toward God and his Prophet. It thought that the matter would be somewhat easy. Even if there were to be difficulties, it would be easy. But it collided with a completely different reality. The operations of the brother mujahidin began from the first moment, which mixed things up somewhat. Then, the pace of operations quickened. This was in the Sunni Triangle, if this is the right name for it. This forced the Americans to conclude a deal with the Shi'a, the most evil of mankind. The deal was concluded on [the basis that] the Shi'a would get two-thirds of the booty for having stood in the ranks of the Crusaders against the mujahidin.

## 3. The Shi'a

[They are] the insurmountable obstacle, the lurking snake, the crafty and malicious scorpion, the spying enemy, and the penetrating venom. We here are entering a battle on two levels. One, evident and open, is with an attacking enemy and patent infidelity. [Another is] a difficult, fierce battle with a crafty enemy who wears the garb of a friend, manifests agreement, and calls for comradeship, but harbors ill will and twists up peaks and crests (?). Theirs is the legacy of the Batini bands that traversed the history of Islam and left scars on its face that time cannot erase. The unhurried observer and inquiring onlooker will realize that Shi'ism is the looming danger and the true challenge. "They are the enemy. Beware of them. Fight them. By God, they lie." History's message is validated by the testimony of the current situation, which informs most clearly that Shi'ism is a religion that has nothing in common with Islam except in the way that Jews have something in common with Christians under the banner of the People of the Book. From patent polytheism, worshipping at graves, and circumambulating shrines, to calling the Companions [of the Prophet] infidels and insulting the mothers of the believers and the elite of this [Islamic] nation, [they] arrive at distorting the Qur'an as a product of logic to defame those who know  | 253
it well, in addition to speaking of the infallibility of the [Islamic] nation, the centrality of believing in them, affirming that revelation came down to them, and other forms of infidelity and manifestations of atheism with which their authorized books and original sources—which they continue to print, distribute, and publish—overflow. The dreamers who think that a Shi'i can forget [his] historical legacy and [his] old black hatred of the Nawasib [those who hate the Prophet's lineage], as they fancifully call them, are like someone who calls on the Christians to renounce the idea of the crucifixion of the Messiah. Would a sensible person do this? These are a people who added to their infidelity and augmented their atheism with political cunning and a feverish effort to seize upon the crisis of governance and the balance of power in the state, whose features they are trying to draw and whose new lines they are trying to establish through their political banners and organizations in cooperation with their hidden allies the Americans.

These [have been] a sect of treachery and betrayal throughout history and throughout the ages. It is a creed that aims to combat the Sunnis. When the repulsive Ba'thi regime fell, the slogan of the Shi'a was "Revenge, revenge, from Tikrit to al-Anbar." This shows the extent of their hidden rancor toward the Sunnis. However, their religious and political 'ulama' have been able to control the affairs of their sect, so as not to have the battle between them and the Sunnis become an open sectarian war, because they know that they will not succeed in this way. They know that, if a sectarian war was to take place, many in the [Islamic] nation would rise to defend the Sunnis in Iraq. Since their religion is one of dissimulation, they maliciously and cunningly proceeded another way. They began by taking control of the institutions of the state and their security, military, and economic branches. As you, may God preserve you, know, the basic components of any country are security and the economy. They are deeply embedded inside these institutions and branches. I give an example that brings the matter home: the Badr Brigade, which is the military wing of the Supreme Council of the Islamic Revolution, has shed its Shi'a garb and put on the garb of the police and army in its place. They have placed cadres in these institutions, and, in the name of preserving the homeland and the citizen, have begun to settle their scores with the Sunnis. The American army has begun to disappear from some cities, and its presence is rare. An Iraqi army has begun to take its place, and this is the real problem that we face, since our combat against the Americans is something easy. The enemy is apparent, his back is exposed, and he does not know the land or the current situation of the mujahidin because his intelligence information is weak. We know for certain that these Crusader forces will disappear tomorrow or the day after. He who looks at the current situation [will] see the enemy's haste to constitute the army and the police, which have begun to carry out the missions assigned to them. This enemy, made up of the Shi'a filled out with Sunni agents, is the real danger that we face, for it is [made up of] our fellow countrymen, who know us inside and out. They are more cunning than their Crusader masters, and they have begun, as I have said, to try to take control of the security situation in Iraq. They have liquidated many Sunnis and many of their Ba'th Party enemies and others beholden to the Sunnis in an organized, studied way. They began by killing many mujahid brothers, passing to the liquidation of scientists, thinkers, doctors, engineers, and others. I believe, and God knows best, that the worst will not come to pass until most of the American army is in the rear lines and the secret Shi'i army and its military brigades are fighting as its proxy. They are infiltrating like snakes to reign over the army and police apparatus, which is the strike force and iron fist in our Third World, and to take complete control over the economy like their tutors the Jews. . . . Their greatest [act of] worship is to curse the Muslim friends of God from first to last. These are the people most anxious to divide the Muslims. Among their greatest principles are leveling charges of infidelity and damning and cursing the elite of those who have ruled matters, like the orthodox caliphs and the 'ulama' of the Muslims, because of their belief that anyone who does not believe in the infallible imam, who is not present, does not believe in God and his Prophet, may God bless him and grant him salvation . . .

## 1. The Masses
These masses are the silent majority, absent even though present. "The hooligans following everyone and his brother hungered. They did not seek

enlightenment from the light of science and did not take refuge in a safe corner." These, even if in general they hate the Americans, wish them to vanish and to have their black cloud dissolve. But, despite that, they look forward to a sunny tomorrow, a prosperous future, a carefree life, comfort, and favor. They look ahead to that day and are thus easy prey for cunning information [media] and political enticement whose hiss rings out. . . . In any event, they are people of Iraq. . . .

### 3. The [Muslim] Brothers

As you have observed, they make a profession of trading in the blood of martyrs and build their counterfeit glory on the skulls of the faithful. They have debased the horse, put aside arms, said "no jihad" . . . and lied. Their whole effort is to extend political control and seize the posts of Sunni representation in the government cake whose creation has been decided, while taking care in secret to get control of the mujahidin groups through financial support for two purposes. The first is for propaganda and media work abroad to attract money and sympathy, exactly as they did during the events in Syria, and the second is to control the situation and dissolve these groups when the party ends and the gifts are distributed. They are now intent on creating a Sunni shura body to speak in the name of the Sunnis. It is their habit to grab the stick in the middle and change as the political climate changes. Their religion is mercurial. They have no firm principles, and they do not start from enduring legal bases. God is the one from whom we have sought help.

### D. The Mujahidin

These are the quintessence of the Sunnis and the good sap of this country. In general, they belong to the Sunni doctrine and naturally to the Salafi creed. The Salafis splintered only as the bend curved, and the people of the [distant] regions fell behind the caravan. In general, these mujahidin distinguish themselves by the following:

1. Most of them have little expertise or experience, especially in organized collective work. Doubtlessly, they are the result of a repressive regime that militarized the country, spread dismay, propagated fear and dread, and destroyed confidence among the people. For this reason, most of the groups are working in isolation, with no political horizon, farsightedness, or preparation to inherit the land. Yes, the idea has begun to ripen, and a light whisper has arisen to become noisy talk about the need to band together and unite under one banner. But matters are still in their initial stages. With God's praise, we are trying to ripen them quickly.
2. Jihad here unfortunately [takes the form of] mines planted, rockets launched, and mortars shelling from afar. The Iraqi brothers

still prefer safety and returning to the arms of their wives, where nothing frightens them. Sometimes the groups have boasted among themselves that not one of them has been killed or captured. We have told them in our many sessions with them that safety and victory are incompatible, that the tree of triumph and empowerment cannot grow tall and lofty without blood and defiance of death, that the [Islamic] nation cannot live without the aroma of martyrdom and the perfume of fragrant blood spilled on behalf of God, and that people cannot awaken from their stupor unless talk of martyrdom and martyrs fills their days and nights. The matter needs more patience and conviction. [Our] hope in God is great.

## E. The Immigrant Mujahidin

Their numbers continue to be negligible as compared to the enormity of the expected battle. We know that the convoys of good are many, that the march of jihad continues, and that only confusion over the banner and a muffled reality keep many of them from [answering] the call to battle. What prevents us from [calling] a general alert is that the country has no mountains in which we can take refuge and no forests in whose thickets we can hide. Our backs are exposed and our movements compromised. Eyes are everywhere. The enemy is before us and the sea is behind us. Many an Iraqi will honor you as a guest and give you shelter as a peaceable brother. As for making his house into a base for launching [operations] and a place of movement and battle, this is rarer than red sulphur. For this reason, we have worn ourselves out on many occasions sheltering and protecting the brothers. This makes training the green newcomers like wearing bonds and shackles, even though, praise be to God and with relentless effort and insistent searching, we have taken possession of growing numbers of locations, praise be to God, to be base sites for brothers who are kindling [the fire of] war and drawing the people of the country into the furnace of battle so that a real war will break out, God willing.

## Second: The Current Situation and the Future

There is no doubt that the Americans' losses are very heavy because they are deployed across a wide area and among the people and because it is easy to procure weapons, all of which makes them easy and mouth-watering targets for the believers. But America did not come to leave, and it will not leave no matter how numerous its wounds become and how much of its blood is spilled. It is looking to the near future, when it hopes to disappear into its bases secure and at ease and put the battlefields of Iraq into the hands of the foundling government with an army and police that will bring the behavior of Saddam and his myrmidons back to the people. There is no doubt that the space in which we can move has begun to shrink and that the grip around the throats of the mujahidin has begun to tighten. With the deployment of soldiers and police, the future has become frightening.

### Third: So Where are We?

Despite the paucity of supporters, the desertion of friends, and the toughness of the times, God the Exalted has honored us with good harm to the enemy. Praise be to God, in terms of surveillance, preparation, and planning, we have been the keys to all of the martyrdom operations that have taken place except those in the north. Praise be to God, I have completed 25 [operations] up to now, including among the Shi'a and their symbolic figures, the Americans and their soldiers, the police and soldiers, and the coalition forces. God willing, more are to come. What has prevented us from going public is that we have been waiting until we have weight on the ground and finish preparing integrated structures capable of bearing the consequences of going public so that we appear in strength and do not suffer a reversal. We seek refuge in God. Praise be to God, we have made good strides and completed important stages. As the decisive moment approaches, we feel that [our] body has begun to spread in the security vacuum, gaining locations on the ground that will be the nucleus from which to launch and move out in a serious way, God willing. . . .

### 4. The Shi'a

These in our opinion are the key to change. I mean that targeting and hitting them in [their] religious, political, and military depth will provoke them to show the Sunnis their rabies . . . and bare the teeth of the hidden rancor working in their breasts. . . . Despite their weakness and fragmentation, the Sunnis are the sharpest blades, the most determined, and the most loyal when they meet those Batinis (Shi'a), who are a people of treachery and cowardice. They are arrogant only with the weak and can attack only the broken-winged. Most of the Sunnis are aware of the danger of these people, watch their sides, and fear the consequences of empowering them. Were it not for the enfeebled Sufi shaykhs and [Muslim] Brothers, people would have told a different tale.

This matter, with the anticipated awaking of the slumberer and rousing of the sleeper, also includes neutralizing these [Shi'a] people and pulling out their teeth before the inevitable battle, along with the anticipated incitement of the wrath of the people against the Americans, who brought destruction and were the reason for this miasma. The people must beware of licking the honeycomb and enjoying some of the pleasures from which they were previously deprived, lest they surrender to meekness, stay on the[ir] land, prefer safety, and turn away from the rattle of swords and the neighing of horses.

### 5. The Work Mechanism

. . . . We say that we must drag them into battle for several reasons, which are:

1. They, i.e., the Shi'a, have declared a secret war against the people of Islam. They are the proximate, dangerous enemy of the Sunnis,

even if the Americans are also an archenemy. The danger from the Shi'a, however, is greater and their damage is worse and more destructive to the [Islamic] nation than the Americans, on whom you find a quasi-consensus about killing them as an assailing enemy.

2. They have befriended and supported the Americans and stood in their ranks against the mujahidin. They have spared and are still sparing no effort to put an end to the jihad and the mujahidin.

3. Our fighting against the Shi'a is the way to drag the [Islamic] nation into the battle. We speak here in some detail. We have said before that the Shi'a have put on the uniforms of the Iraqi army, police, and security [forces] and have raised the banner of preserving the homeland and the citizen. Under this banner, they have begun to liquidate the Sunnis under the pretext that they are saboteurs, remnants of the Ba'th, and terrorists spreading evil in the land. With strong media guidance from the Governing Council and the Americans, they have been able to come between the Sunni masses and the mujahidin. I give an example that brings the matter close to home in the area called the Sunni Triangle—if this is the right name for it. The army and police have begun to deploy in those areas and are growing stronger day by day. They have put chiefs [drawn] from among Sunni agents and the people of the land in charge. In other words, this army and police may be linked to the inhabitants of this area by kinship, blood, and honor. In truth, this area is the base from which we set out and to which we return. When the Americans disappear from these areas—and they have begun to do so—and these agents, who are linked by destiny to the people of the land, take their place, what will our situation be?. . .

## DOCUMENT 5.10

The Association of Muslim Scholars (AMS) was founded immediately after the fall of Baghdad. It tried to set itself up as the guardian of Sunni interests, while at the same time reaching out to the Shia who resisted the occupation. The AMS refused to participate in any political process while Iraq was under occupation. In a series of writings, its leaders developed a jurisprudence of resistance (*fiqh al-muqawamma*). Its ideologue Muhammad 'Ayyash al-Kubaisi called the resistance a jihad and declared active resistance to be a religious obligation for all believers. The group denied any major political aspirations beyond its role as an association to bring all Sunnis together. AMS scholars claimed to hold the same power and prestige as the Shia religious authorities, the *marja*. The group was highly organized, disseminating its ideas and rulings through its Web site and its weekly newspaper, *al Sabil*. In response to rising sectarian violence, the AMS issued a binding fatwa in April 2007, calling for a halt to attacks on innocent people and places of worship. The AMS leader Dr. Muhammad Ayyash al-Kubaysi, interviewed by Atif al-Julani and Amjad al-Absi of *al Sabil* newspaper, was killed in March 2007.

## INTERVIEW WITH SHAYKH AHMAD AL-KUBAYSI, LEADER OF THE ASSOCIATION OF MUSLIM SCHOLARS, 2004 (EXCERPT)

[Al-Sabil] Do you think the US Iraq plan has failed and the Americans are about to withdraw from Iraq, especially since the continuation of occupation has become difficult and costly?. . .

I believe that the Americans are in a real dilemma, which started when they discovered that they were deceived by several quarters. These include what was called Iraqi opposition, which provided them with false information about many Iraqi issues. We also believe that the Mossad and the Israeli intelligence services contributed to this deception in order to trick the United States into destroying Iraq and its power, which scared them. . . .

It is obvious that the plans the US leaders had in mind before the war were not in harmony with the Iraqi reality. Therefore, the situation was completely different from what they had expected. They dismantled the security, military, and civil establishments and opened the weapon and ammunition depots for the people, imagining that this will help create internal chaos. This indicates that the US Administration was planning a civil war in Iraq and that it is not a safety valve against the eruption of such a war as it claims and as some rumour. This proves that the occupation sought to entrench sectarian and ethnic tendencies before the start of the war. The western media also began to deal with us as sectarian and ethnic communities like Sunnis, Shi'is, and Kurds rather than Iraqis.

| 259

What surprised the Americans is that the people who seized weapons from the army depots were more rational and enlightened than those who conveyed misleading information to the White House. These weapons were used against the Americans. . . . Back to the question about the failure of the US plan in Iraq, I would like to remind you that when occupation started it had many aims as expressed by the US officials. They expressed their desire to change the map of the region, the school curricula, and many other things related to the identity, culture, religion, and traditions of the Iraqi people. But now all attention is focused on security. Retreat in these aims is another indication of the failure of their plan. . . .

[Al-Sabil] US officials, including the commander of the US forces in Iraq, began to talk about the possible withdrawal of a large number of US forces from Iraq in spring next year. Do you think talk about withdrawal comes within the framework of preparations to change the US strategy in Iraq in order to overcome the impasse and get out of the dilemma?

[Al-Kubaysi] I believe that three things prevented an early and complete US withdrawal from Iraq. . . .

[Al-Kubaysi] First, the Americans declared war on terrorism and did not recognize the Iraqi resistance. They denied the Iraqi people's right to resist. They insisted on talking about a group of infiltrators or "terrorists" coming from across the border. Announcing withdrawal now in accordance with this concept means announcing their defeat at the hands of terrorism rather than people aspiring for freedom. This is a problem and they are trying to avoid it as much as possible. . . .

[Al-Kubaysi] The second issue is that Iraq was besieged and an annihilation war was launched against it. Many children were killed and Iraqi universities and educational institutions were destroyed after 1990. The US Administration was convinced that Iraq became an easy morsel and occupying it would be a picnic for the US Army, which possesses huge military capabilities. Announcing withdrawal in front of the Iraqi people, who are weak financially and who have been besieged for many years, will harm the prestige of the US Army and the entire military institution. This will also harm the reputation and prestige of the United States. They have a thousand apprehensions about this. . . .

260 | [Al-Kubaysi] The third issue is that even if the Americans become sure that their withdrawal is necessary to protect what is left of their reputation and prestige, they must first rearrange some cards in Iraq and the region to secure their economic and political interests in the region. A quick and complete withdrawal from Iraq might make them lose their influence. . . .

[Al-Sabil] Some Americans raise the issue of keeping US military bases in Iraq after withdrawal. Will the Iraqis accept this?

[Al-Kubaysi] The issue is not the size of the US forces in Iraq, but the principle of having these forces there. Any US military presence in Iraq in any form whatsoever is considered occupation. The Iraqi people fought and offered thousands of martyrs for the sake of protecting their sovereignty and dignity. The presence of even a single US soldier in any part of Iraq will be considered occupation and, consequently, this will be a red line that accepts no negotiations or bargaining.

[Al-Sabil] This means resistance will continue even if the United States withdraws its forces from Iraq but keeps some military bases.

[Al-Kubaysi] Resistance will certainly continue and the Americans will then realize that the gains they will make from the presence of their bases in Iraq will be much fewer than the gains they will make in the presence of an agreement based on mutual respect.

[Al-Sabil] Some cast doubts on the seriousness of the Americans in announcing their desire to withdraw from Iraq. They say the Americans withdrew from Vietnam only after leaving tens of thousands of dead soldiers behind them. How do you view this?

[Al-Kubaysi] Observers believe that the Americans were really implicated by their occupation of Iraq. When we compare the Iraqi situation with that of Vietnam, the comparison will be made in view of the changes made. Circumstances have changed and time has changed. The world no longer accepts the idea of occupation and aggression. The American people themselves began to put pressure on their government to withdraw after discovering the size of deception the current administration practised against them. The United States continues to sustain human, military, and economic losses. Its prestige, reputation, and credibility in dealing with many issues, including political, ethical, and legal ones, have been adversely affected and this is not an easy thing. The world is now in a situation that does not tolerate such an abnormal situation. I think the Americans will pay a heavy price if they stay in Iraq. Therefore, it is in their interest to leave Iraq today before tomorrow.

[Al-Sabil] How do you view the US officials' talk about negotiations with the resistance?

[Al-Kubaysi] In principle, there is no resistance whose aim is mere killing. Resistance seeks to pressure the occupying enemy into leaving the country and recognizing the occupied people's right to full sovereignty over their land and to live a free and dignified life on their land just like the other nations. Negotiations over the terms of the occupiers' departure are the natural and final station of every resistance. If we read facts, statements, and information leaked about the size of the US losses, the US impasse, and the US popular pressure, we will discover that the Americans most likely think of leaving Iraq. Negotiations might be the way out of this impasse but we must not be very optimistic in this regard. The Americans might be looking for another type of negotiations to help them get out of this impasse in another way like encouraging illegitimate competition among the resistance factions. This is what the Americans are dreaming of but this is unattainable. The purpose of the negotiations might be obtaining intelligence information, sounding intentions, and collecting information from this and that side. The negotiations might be meant to give some sort of reassurance to the miserable US soldiers who are facing death everyday.

[Al-Sabil] How do you conceive the future of Iraq after withdrawal?

[Al-Kubaysi] The Iraqis tried the one-party totalitarian regimes and paid a heavy price. The Iraqi people have their own character. They are of diverse sectarian and ethnic nationalities. Therefore, we do not think there can be a solution to the situation in Iraq except through our acceptance of one another and through the culture of harmony, freedom of expression, and citizenship right that is guaranteed for all. Also we want an Iraq that reassures its neighbours. We do not want an Iraq that creates problems for any neighbouring country. We believe that the safety and security of neighbouring countries are an Iraqi priority because this will help us build a free and stable Iraq. This stability will eventually contribute to regional stability.

## Federalism

[Al-Sabil] What about federalism, which is a controversial issue at the constitution drafting committee?

[Al-Kubaysi] Actually, the issue of federalism was not proposed at the right time as it gave the Iraqi people a message that there are some who want to benefit from foreign presence and use it to make some private gains. We believe that such plans must be discussed when there is a free, democratic, and pluralistic Iraq. It should not be discussed in the presence of the US tank as if priority goes to making political or economic gains rather than liberating Iraq. This is unacceptable. I think this complicates things and increases tension among the Iraqi people. Let us first try to live in a free and united Iraq away from foreign hegemony. We will then decide if we need a federal system or not. We say let us try. During trial we might or might not need such a federal system. We believe that the culture of separation emerged as a result of the past decade. If we bypass the past, our convictions might change.

[Al-Sabil] What is your position on the Iraqi constitution, which is being drafted these days?

[Al-Kubaysi] Let me first say that in principle we have reservations about any political process that takes place under occupation. This is our right. A few months ago, President Bush called for the withdrawal of all Syrian forces from Lebanon because he said their presence will be detrimental to the credibility and integrity of the elections. Why does he not apply this criterion to Iraq? Therefore, we in principle believe that any political process under occupation will raise many questions about the credibility of such a process.

If we say occupation has its programmes, interests, and influence on some parties participating in the political process, then we have the right to express fears and reservations about the results of this political process whether it pertains to the constitution or the elections. There is another apprehension. The constitution drafting committee depended on the infamous State Administration Law, which entrenched sectarian and ethnic divisions and cancelled Iraq's Arab identity. It only said the Iraqi people in Iraq are part of the Arab nation. The Arab people even in Britain are part of the Arab nation. Where is Iraq's special characteristic as a founding member of the Arab League? If the constitution is drafted in accordance with the State Administration Law, we will then have the right to be pessimistic about it. But if the constitution achieves the key principles of the Iraqi identity and the Iraqi people's aspirations, we will not obstruct its endorsement. As I said, we cannot bestow legitimacy on any political process that takes place under occupation. But there is a difference between voting against the constitution and allowing it to pass if it does not clash with our constants. . . .

## Palestinian "Resistance" Methods

[Al-Kubaysi] First of all, allow me to frankly say that we in Iraq are largely influenced by the Palestinian resistance. The Iraqi resistance literature indicates how much it is affected by the Palestinian resistance. We have not invented something new. The large and great culture of the Palestinian resistance is an important asset. The Palestinian resistance was built on a real methodological basis. It stemmed from a base enjoying some stability and reassurance. The march of the Palestinian resistance is clear. Its vision and aim are clear to all parties.

As for Iraq, the resistance erupted all of a sudden. There was no time between occupation and the start of resistance. The Iraqi people joined the resistance quickly and largely without advance planning as we see in the Palestinian resistance. The Iraqi experience has its advantages and disadvantages. It robbed the occupation of its ability to settle down, develop a realistic vision, and entrench its roots in the Iraqi map. The occupation was shocked by the large scale of resistance. The Iraqi resistance managed to seize the weapon depots as a result of its quick initiative. All this was accompanied—and this is normal—by the weak structure of the Iraqi resistance and poor media means through which it could express itself and by its stance on some challenges. This is due to the fact that the Iraqi popular resistance, unlike the Palestinian resistance, erupted abruptly.

This made us feel the need to serve this resistance by rationalizing it on clear scientific, religious, and political bases. My method was based on reading the Iraqi reality by listening to all parties. I delivered speeches and lectures on issues related to the Iraqi resistance. I then had a clear picture, but regrettably I found scholars and intellectuals with erroneous ideas about what is really taking place in Iraq. The Americans' monopoly of what is presented on the screen contributed to these wrong ideas. The picture the Americans want and the picture that serves them is transmitted through the media while the picture the resistance seeks to project to serve its interests is not carried. There is some sort of confusion in the form of fatwas [Islamic rulings] or advice given to the Iraqi resistance implying some sort of accusation against the resistance forces. These are not based on a true understanding of the situation.

These issues involved us in continuous discussions with intellectuals and politicians. Some of them proceed from a personal agenda towards the resistance and others support the resistance but have reservations about some issues. The discussions gave us a picture of the religious duty

Muslim scholars should carry out by explaining the real situation so that rulings are based on a true vision. We have a religious ruling which says judging things should stem from the way they are perceived.

Therefore, I hope that these articles will not only praise the resistance in Iraq, but also spread some sort of awareness and culture abroad reflecting the legitimacy of the resistance and giving a picture different from that given by the American screen. It is hoped that we can promote this culture on the level of the nation to match the nature of the challenges facing the nation. We believe that the nation is exposed to an overall aggression in Palestine and Iraq and in more than one way. What the aggressor fears most is the spread of the culture of resistance. Therefore, the aggressor is keen on distorting the image of the resistance, casting doubt on its legitimacy and aims, and conveying a bad picture about it. This, in fact, is part of the effort to rob the nation of its ability to react naturally to developments through the resistance. Here lies the importance of the doctrine of resistance, which must prevail not only among the carriers of arms. The whole nation must adopt the culture of resistance, which I consider a duty at this stage. No Muslim should fail to carry out this duty in any way whatsoever. . . .

264 |

# DOCUMENT 5.11

The Iraqi government released a national security program in 2007 that provided an interesting comparison with U.S. counterinsurgency manuals and demonstrated the degree to which Iraqi lawmakers followed U.S. recommendations. After five years of war, the Iraqi government offered an assessment of its security status, its position in the region and the world, and its stance on security arrangements with the United States. The document began with the slogan "Iraq First," a significant expression because it reflected a shift in focus from an external to an internal and introspective perspective that had also characterized a handful of other movements among Middle Eastern states. Like the "Jordan First" campaign, these movements were about domestic parties building their state institutions rather than relying on external parties to do so, and focusing on national rather than regional concerns. Promoting unity and healing Iraq's wounds were strong themes in the document.

---

REPUBLIC OF IRAQ, NATIONAL SECURITY COUNCIL,
"IRAQ FIRST: THE IRAQI NATIONAL SECURITY STRATEGY
2007–2010," JULY 2007 (EXCERPT)

Why a New Strategy?
  1. This strategy will provide for the first time for an Iraqi Government, in a single document, coherent top level direction to all the

Government in its efforts to establish security, promote prosperity, and assure self-reliance.

2. The strategy is named "Iraq First" because it focuses on Iraq, its people, its situation, its challenges, and its enormous potential.
3. This strategy is linked to the International Compact for Iraq that brings into harmony all the international community efforts to assist Iraq.
4. Perhaps most important, the strategy is based on national reconciliation and has a broad understanding of national security.

Key Elements
1. Defines Iraq's national interests (including security, political, economic, and informational).
2. Affirms principles of Federalism, rule of law, human and civil rights.
3. Guides development of Iraq's human resources and natural resources.
4. Protects freedom of the media and expression.
5. Identifies threats to Iraq (terrorism, insurgency, corruption, crime, armed groups and militias, foreign interference, ethnic and sectarian violence, the dictatorial mentality of the past, and serious societal ills).
6. Defines four strategic components for using Iraq's resources to overcome threats and realize its interests:
   a. Security component that includes sovereignty, territorial integrity, and the use of security forces.
   b. Political component that includes national reconciliation, good governance, regional cooperation, and international agreements, that includes promoting human rights, compensating victims, attacking unemployment and poverty, and providing for amnesty.
   c. Economic component that includes reformed societal institutions, combating corruption, and promoting economic growth.
   d. Informational component that provides legal sanctions for free and responsible journalism and confronts incitements to violence and terrorism.

References: This strategy has been formulated based on the Iraqi Constitution, key new agreements such as the International Compact for Iraq, and the Iraqi National Reconciliation and Dialog Project. The strategy is promulgated now following the success of the Constitutional Government and Iraqi Security Forces in operations in Baghdad (Fahrd al Qanoon), the Anbar Awakening (sahwat al Anbar), and success in Diyala Province—in the expectation of "sahwat" throughout the Republic. This strategy will be broadly disseminated in order to stimulate public discussion and debate in which all citizens can participate. . . .

The Iraqi Constitution of 2005—Item 110—second paragraph states that (establishing and implementing national security policy) is one of the specific duties of the federal government. Therefore, Prime Minister Maliki directed the National Security Council to develop a National Security Strategy 2007–2010. The strategy that represents the policy of the Government, in achieving national interests and identifying and deterring threats as part of the political and practical program of the Government, was prepared in a joint national Iraqi effort and high level coordination in meetings that continued for four months in the Ministries and other concerned entities.

The National Security Strategy is a document that the Ministries and other Institutions of the Government use in establishing their policies and plans related to national security. The announcement of this strategy helps in enhancing understanding of the direction and intent of the Government of Iraq in the region and with other countries; assists in establishing positive relationships with the international community and especially in the region; and creates national tie between the people and the Government so as to make the people part of the political, economic, social and security program. . . .

References used in the preparation of this strategy:

a) Iraqi Constitution of 2005
b) International Compact for Iraq Document
c) National Dialogue and Reconciliation Project Document
d) A number of different national security strategies from other countries.

## 1. Introduction

### A. *The Iraqi National Vision*
The Iraqi national vision fulfills the Iraqi people's aspirations for establishing a unified, democratic, federal state, in which both security and stability prevail; all citizens have equal rights and responsibilities under a constitutional government; all look forward to building a prosperous economy opened wide to the world; and the country is an active member in regional and international organizations.

### B. *The Iraqi Strategic Environment*
First. Iraq is experiencing a historically dangerous period which is a transition between the quick collapse of a dictatorial, abusive, totalitarian regime; and the transformation of the Iraqi people into a civilized community. This period is characterized by a number of challenges and opportunities that form the strategic environment for the next few years.

Second. The greatest challenge in this period is that the transformation itself provides a fertile environment for religious, sectarian, and ethnic groupings in a diverse community. This environment permits interference and short-range policies, by regional countries, that are built on special interests and exaggerated fears toward the new Iraq.

Third. The followers of the previous regime represent another big challenge. The previous dictatorial regime relied on a small group of the citizenry that possessed weapons, money, and experience but lacked the simplest of values, ethics, and knowledge. This group will not easily let go of the authority and national resources that they possessed for decades. They are ready to die to retake their past power and authority by any means.

Fourth. The current Government has to protect the newly born democracy from the dangers of conspiracy and intervention, while differentiating between the remainder of those who were misled and those who entered into the disbanded Baath Party in order to live under the previous abusive conditions.

Fifth. Another challenge is represented by the growth of terrorist groups that have adopted Takfirist ideology which has deviated from the ideologies of the region and the world. These groups have found an opportunity for expansion due to the lack of security after the collapse of the previous regime. They also exploited the presence of foreign forces and the general attitude against America in Arab and other regional countries, to get more support from the region.

Sixth. Another challenge stems from the nature of the wars that the previous regime started. Its misguided policies resulted in international sanctions and the complete isolation of Iraq, and left a heavy heritage for the builders of the new Iraq. It left a debt of more than 120 billion dollars; an internally devastated economy that relied solely on oil exports; an infrastructure neglected for more than 20 years; a low level of individual income; an increase in inflation to destructive levels, seriously damaging the middle class and crushing the poor class; an increase in underemployment; a serious increase in the level of administrative and financial corruption; and the emergence of organized crime run by members of the previous regime.

Seventh. The previous regime's policy of minimizing the legitimate roles of government institutions led to their collapse after the collapse of the Head of the Government. All this resulted in significant difficulties and conditions that permitted the growth of corruption and organized crime, especially as the result of the lack of security that followed the collapse of the previous regime. These difficulties came simultaneously with rise of people's expectations for immediate improvement in all aspects of life.

Eighth. With the collapse of the previous regime, and the beginning of building the new Iraq, it is now time to disband the militias that fought the previous regime and reintegrate them into the society. Dealing the issue of militias formed after the collapse of the previous regime due to the lack of security, and the growth of terrorism and mutual fear poses perhaps a more difficult challenge, if the Iraqi Government wishes to confront it.

Ninth. Counterterrorism represents another challenge for the Government in that it cannot set aside human rights and freedoms, or interfere with freedom of expression and an independent media which are among its primary commitments. Nevertheless, these security circumstances should not affect the transparency of the Government.

Tenth. These challenges and dangers are offset by opportunities and national resources: Iraq is a rich country that has a huge reserve of oil and mineral treasures, water, and fertile land; and is also rich with human resources qualified in a way that offers the opportunity for building and a rapid rise of an advanced, multi-resource economy.

Eleventh. The cultural heritage of Iraq, its history of peaceful coexistence by all its societal components, and the rejection of extremism by the people, offer the opportunity to have a unified multi-group society under a federal democratic system.

Twelfth. Although these factors and others do not decide the future of Iraq, yet they represent the strategic environment of the current period in which the new Iraq will develop. Iraq must accommodate these factors as it becomes a secure, stable, and prosperous country.

*B. National Security*

First. National unity
One pillar of the modern Iraq is to safeguard national unity and the Iraqi social structure, including different religions, sects and nationalities. The most important characteristic of Iraqi unity is that all citizens share one national Iraqi identity regardless of other affiliations.

268 |

Second. Security of the nation and its territory
The fundamental responsibility of a state is ensuring the security of the nation and its territory. This responsibility is embedded in Iraq's Constitution and is the responsibility of the Federal Government.

Third. Security of individuals and property
One of the primary commitments of the Government of Iraq is to protect the lives and property of Iraqis and other individuals who are legal residents in Iraq. . . .

### 3. Threats

*A. Terrorism and Insurgency*
These are among the most dangerous threats as they destroy the pillars of the Government and the political process, and weaken the spirit through targeting the community, infrastructure and governmental institutions. They also incite subversion and instability (terrorists and insurgents include Tackfirists and Saddamists).

*B. Sabotage and Corruption*
Sabotage and corruption result in slowing and impeding political, economic and security progress, the application of democratic mechanisms, free trade, the implementation of law, rebuilding, and production of goods. They deplete the national treasures and spread a feeling of inequality among citizens.

## C. Organized Crime

Organized crime in all its types represents a threat to our national security. It develops and grows in the same environment in which terrorism and Insurgency grow.

## D. Regional and International Threats, and Interference in Internal Affairs

Iraq faces dangerous regional and international threats, including terrorists and foreigners who enter Iraq and get support from neighboring countries. Due to the fact that Iraq has a political and military partnership with the Multinational Force in Iraq, these threats do not rise to the level of preparation for or intent to invade Iraq. Iraq will not accept the presence of any terrorist or illegal organizations such as Al Qaeda and other terrorist groups that represent a threat to the security of Iraq and its neighbors. Iraq will not harbor, will not permit, or support the work of such terrorist organizations on its territory. . . .

## F. Mentality of Dictatorship and Isolation of Groups

The mentality of dictatorship and the isolation of groups concentrates power and authorities prevent practicing democracy and, therefore, represent a dangerous threat to our national interests. Due to the fact that the abusive and dictatorial procedures are still present in our memories and cultural heritage, this threat presages the return of this mentality. Although there are some exceptional cases requiring imposing emergency procedures for the purpose of stability according to the Constitution, yet such cases are vulnerable to misuse and consequently threaten the return of the dictatorship.

## G. Sectarian and Ethnic Violence

The feelings of sectarian and ethnic affiliation that grew during decades of dictatorship represent a threat. In addition, terrorists and Takfirist groups attempt to attack religious and political symbols and provoke subversion in order to provoke sectarian violence among the elements of the Iraqi people for the purpose of dividing them and retaking power and authority. . . .

## 4. Strategic Means

*First. General political domain*

### (1) National reconciliation and constitutional review
### (a) National reconciliation

i. The constitutionally-elected Government of Iraqi established a comprehensive project for national reconciliation in which all its aspects are positive and transparent. The project credibly demonstrates openness and active participation by all parties in the political process, especially those that have reservations or reform preferences about the political process. Although the project includes those who bore arms to validate their existence and diverse perspectives, it excludes those criminals and killers who have been involved in killing Iraqis.

ii. The National Committee for Reconciliation and Dialogue was formed and took the responsibility for this project (some meetings and conferences have already been held). The Committee has been taking charge of issues that help in unifying Iraqi people and bringing different viewpoints together.

iii. Although important steps have been taken in this respect, the size of the challenges Iraq faces and the need for an immediate mending of the crack that occurred in the Iraqi community due to many factors including Al Qaeda activities in provoking sectarian conflict, requires exerting more effort to arrive at practical and appropriate strategy, policies, and mechanisms for achieving the mission.

### (b) Constitutional review

Some articles of the Constitution were the subject of dispute and disagreement among political fronts on the one hand, and between the Government and some civil society institutions and parties that did not participate in the political process on the other hand. Some of the objections are substantive and worth reviewing and some are just expressions of disagreement with the government and the political process. In any case, the Council of Representatives, after reaching consensus, formed an inclusive committee to carry out the constitutional review of the articles that are controversial and to make necessary modifications, additions or deletions. This was considered as a gesture of good will towards some of the political fronts to participate in the political process, to support the government, and to complete the national reconciliation process. . . .

### (3) Completing the transition of security responsibility from the Multinational Force in Iraq to the Iraqi constitutional authorities

The Multinational Force in Iraq has been assigned responsibility for security in Iraq by United Nations Security Council Resolution 1546 on 8 June 2004. The Iraqi Government and the Multinational Force in Iraq have been working together to transfer security responsibility to Iraqi constitutional authorities in the provinces that have met the appropriate conditions. The Iraqi Government endeavors with the help of its friends and the Multinational Force to accelerate transfer of security responsibility through achieving the required level of readiness for security forces, reinforcing governance capabilities in the provinces, and reducing the level of the various threats.

### (4) Reducing the requirements for the presence of the Multinational Force in Iraq

The Government of Iraq, after completion of the transfer of security responsibility to the provinces and regions of Iraq, will coordinate with its friends the withdrawal of the Multinational Force from Iraq based on the reduction of requirements for their presence for the purpose of training and support according to the threats and security requirements. . . .

### (6) Adhering to international agreements related to counterterrorism, collective security, and nonproliferation of weapons of mass destruction

Since the establishment of the modern Iraqi Government, Iraq has entered into many international agreements and conventions that ban terrorism and weapons of mass destruction. The former regime violated these agreements and that was one of the reasons for the international intervention. Therefore, the new constitutional Iraqi Government is committed to fighting terrorism in all its forms, and respecting and implementing international commitments of Iraq related to banning the proliferation, production, and use of nuclear, biological, and chemical weapons. In addition to preventing all that relates to their development, manufacture, production, and use of equipment, technology, communications systems and to work with the international community on nonproliferation.

### (7) Concluding bilateral and multilateral security agreements

The Government of Iraq realizes that terrorism and insurgency are being fed from outside Iraq. The long borders Iraq shares with its neighbors cannot be controlled solely by Iraqi Security Forces, and therefore concluding bilateral and multilateral security agreements with regional countries will benefit all these countries.

### (8) Reinforcing the participation of Iraq in the United Nations and international fora

Iraq is an active and founding member of the United Nations. Iraq has substantial international commitments and active participation is one of the bases of the United Nations. . . .

*Second. Political-social Domain*

### . . . . (4) Involving civil society institutions in helping to design, implement, and oversee reform, rebuilding and amassing Iraqi social capital in the process of growth

The Iraqi Constitution states that the Government of Iraq will reinforce the role of civil society institutions, support their development and independence, and support their achieving of their legal objectives. This is accomplished through:

(a) Establishing laws to protect civil society institutions, to legalize their participation in designing Government administrative policy, to protect legal interests of the people, to diminish the effect of social conflicts, and to oversee the work of local governments and the Federal Government;

(b) Enlightening those who establish administrative policies and cadres that are to implement the law, and all the people, of the important role of civil society institutions; through clarifying the authorities and responsibilities, and ensuring participation of everyone in economic and social transformation, including economic freedom and distribution of authorities;. . . .

## Security Domain

*First. Completing the development, missions, and functions of Iraqi Security Forces*

The size and composition of Iraq's Security Forces are based on defeating the identified threats within Iraq's strategic environment. As the first priority in the current period, Iraq's Joint Forces will focus on defeat of terrorism and insurgency as their primary mission, with other threats accorded a lesser priority to the extent that available resources permit. In this current period, Iraq's Joint Forces will achieve self reliance such that only minimal external assistance and support are needed for accomplishing the primary mission. As Iraq's security is reestablished and the terrorist and insurgency threats abate, Iraq's Joint Forces will transition to a conventional defensive posture for ensuring the security of the nation and its territory in conjunction with regional and international security arrangements. Likewise, Iraq's Police and Border Enforcement Forces will transition to conventional maintenance of domestic law and order and maintaining the integrity of Iraq's borders. Iraq's police forces will focus on local police self-reliance except in emergency situations that require reinforcement by National Police or the Iraqi Joint Forces. The capabilities of Iraq's Joint Forces will be such that they do not by their size or capabilities appear as threatening to Iraq's neighbors.

*Second. Enhancing the constitutional civilian command of the security institutions*

Articles (9) and (48) of the first part of the Constitution state that the Security Services and the National Intelligence Service are to be under the command of the civil authority—and should not be a tool for abusing the people and interfering in political affairs or the Government's transfer of authority. The Government is striving to achieve this principle through presenting its draft National Intelligence Law, in addition to continually monitoring the security ministries and directorates through the Security Ministries Reform Committee. The efforts exerted by the security training institutions and academies should be continued to rehabilitate the military and civilian cadres and they should focus on human rights topics, democracy, and constitutional civilian control of the security institutions. . . .

*Sixth. Developing counterterrorism capabilities and programs*
   (1) The Government of Iraq is undertaking increasing and reinforcing its counterterrorism security forces;
   (2) Establishing and implementing a policy to mobilize all national capabilities towards counterterrorism; and

(3) Actively participating in international efforts to counter terrorism through reinforcing Border Enforcement Forces, border
entry and exit points, and security coordination with neigh
boring countries. . . .

*Seventh. Developing a policy to solve the problem of militias*
*and to reintegrate them into the society*
Militias originated in Iraq under different circumstances; some of them
fought the dictatorial Baathist regime, and some originated after the collapse of Saddam's regime for various reasons. The Government is endeav-
oring to establish a program to disband these militias and reintegrate them
into the society in an effort to solve the security problem. This is accomplished through:

(1) Reaching a political agreement and a suitable balanced legislative framework to disband the militias in order to control
weapons possession. In addition, a series of other procedures is
being pursued that lead to building the trust of militia members
with Government authority, such as a legislative decision for
general amnesty based on transitional justice criteria and national loyalty.
(2) Creating political and economic conditions that contribute to
implementation and balance the giving up of weapons with
new social status as an encouraging factor for reintegration.
(3) Adopting—with the assistance of the international community
and commitment to the International Compact with Iraq—a
general program with suitable balanced funding that leads to
disbanding of the militias and reintegrates them into the society
taking into account International experience in post-conflict
situations.
(4) Enhancing economic reforms to establish appropriate conditions
leading to forming programs related to reintegration of the militias and other illegal armed groups. . . .

## C. Economic Domain

. . . . *Fourth. Investing national resources in an optimal,*
*transparent, and fair manner*
According to Article (111) of the Iraqi constitution, oil and gas are the property of all the Iraqi people in all the provinces and regions, since oil wealth
is the main financial source for the budget and other energy and petroleum
products that are necessary for daily continuous consumption for the
people. The management of this sector in an objective, fair and transparent
way is one of the priorities of our national security strategy. The development and organization of the oil sector, in harmony with the objectives of
improving the society and the national economy according to long-range

| 273

plans, decreases reliance on oil and gas revenues. In this context, the Government undertook the drafting of a hydrocarbon law, in addition to encouraging foreign investment in this sector. The provisions of this draft law call for establishment of a national oil company, regional committees which are the competent technical authorities in the regions, a Federal Oil and Gas Council to establish federal oil policies, exploration plans; develop oil fields and major oil pipelines; negotiate licenses and development contracts; and recommend policies and drafts of oil legislation. The Government will also maintain an oil and gas independent advisory office for the same purpose. The Government would also open a single account for oil and gas revenues which would be strictly overseen and audited annually by certified auditing companies with results published regularly. An independent council for auditing and monitoring would be established. A mechanism for managing oil revenues will be established to ensure equitable and transparent distribution based on the federal financial system, taking into consideration the effects of price volatility.

*Fifth. Attracting foreign investment*
This is among the top priorities for the reconstruction of a new Iraq, especially with regard to basic services and projects that fall outside the financial, administrative and technical implementation capabilities of today's Government. Additional funding support from foreign investments, providing all facilities and guarantees, is an important qualitative leap for the new Iraqi economy. Because Iraq is going through a state of instability, with the spread of chaos and financial corruption in governmental institutions, many foreign investors are prevented from investing their money and introducing their companies in the current circumstances. Therefore, the Iraqi government attempts to encourage investment by giving current investors priority in future investment, and facilitating their work in the insecure areas. . . .

*Seventh. Eliminating the national debt, terminating interest payments,*
*and obtaining international aid*
Iraq is attempting to inform the international community of the legacy of debts that resulted from the former regime's procedures and behavior that utilized all funds and resources in wars and suppression of the people. It is difficult for succeeding Iraqi generations to take responsibility for something for which they were not at fault or had a role. The Government of Iraq has succeeded in cooperation with and support from creditor countries, the United Nations, and other friends in attaining nullification of 80% of its external debt, and canceling a portion of the interest on the debt. Successful negotiations are continuing in order to schedule the rest of the debt payment and convince creditor countries to cancel additional interest or undertake mutually valuable exchanges that do not affect the general funding for the implementation of economic reform and growth programs which are

considered among the most important achievements of the Iraqi Government. Iraq has been able to obtain international support in the form of financial grants to rebuild Iraq (Madrid Conference). Therefore, the most important commitment on the Iraqi Government side to terminate these debts and obtain support is to adhere to the agreements and conventions concluded with the international community; and then making good on the promises made to the Iraqi people.

# PART TWO

# CONSEQUENCES OF A PREEMPTIVE WAR

# ★ CHAPTER 6 ★

# DEMOCRATIZATION FROM ABOVE OR BELOW?

ON MARCH 20, 2003, the United States dismantled the regime of Saddam Hussein. The Bush administration claimed it was doing so for a number of reasons, including democracy-building. More than five years after the invasion, observers were trying to make sense of the process in Iraq and to measure it against traditional transitions to democracy. Optimists were quick to point to the positive gains of the Iraqi experience in the areas of participation and contestation, two crucial components of democracy. There was now a multiplicity of voices in the Iraqi political arena, and Iraqi citizens were participating in both state- and nation-building. Average Iraqis risked their lives on a daily basis to go to work, act as responsible members of society, and participate in forming government institutions. All this was occurring while Iraq moved from insurgency to civil war as sectarian violence ripped through the country. It seemed clear that Iraqis were making progress despite the structural constraints of invasion and occupation: an oil crisis, civil war, U.S. pressure to reach benchmarks, foreign control over the country's domestic and foreign policies, and Iraq's position as a weak state in a politically charged region of the world.

United States control of the structure and functioning of the Iraqi government raised some practical concerns regarding the country's ability to democratize and highlighted some of the problematic repercussions of regime change. Because it was formed under the tutelage of the United States, the Iraqi state system had serious legitimacy and credibility problems. First, there was the issue of ethnocentrism: the U.S. assumption seemed to be that in building a specific type of government for a people whose cultural traditions differed, "our way is better than yours." That perspective magnified problems raised by the violation of sovereignty under international law. Consequences followed from the behavior of a hegemonic power that gave itself free rein to remold other states in its own image. In essence, regime change in Iraq seemed to be a stark example of modern imperialism, where invasion, occupation, permanent military bases, and control of natural resources were reminiscent of British and French policy in the region in the previous century.

The Bush administration made the case for war based on ideological and geostrategic calculations that were encouraged by carefully chosen Iraqi exiles and dissidents. Administration officials tried to link the region's persistent authoritarianism to the threat of international terrorism and global insecurity, in an oversimplified version of the theory that "democracies don't fight other democracies."[1] At first, al Qaeda in Afghanistan was targeted as the focal point of the "war on terror," while a broader argument was made that rogue states such as Iraq sponsored terrorism. But soon neoconservatives in the Bush administration subsumed the Iraq case under the "global war on terror."

President Bush repeatedly declared that he was building his entire foreign policy around a "freedom agenda" that would use preemptive war and regime change in Iraq to spread democracy everywhere. He claimed that the United States was responsible to act on behalf of the "free world" and insisted that promoting democracy for oppressed people was a much nobler foundation for foreign policy than appeasing dictators and doing business with autocracies—even if it meant launching a preemptive war.[2] This stance was a surprise to many who recounted the pattern in U.S. foreign policy of building strategic alliances with some of the most brutal leaders in the region, with little regard for regime type. Some had argued that the United States preferred one-man autocratic rule to discordant voices since co-opting one dictator was easier than lobbying for the support of divergent groups.[3] In fact, the U.S. occupation authorities tended to follow a similar pattern when they began to exercise censorship and control of the media, vet preferred political candidates and organizations, and enact other measures that were seemingly undemocratic (6.4). Despite the administration's confident assertion that there was no conflict between the foreign-policy imperatives of the occupying power and democracy in Iraq, it was questionable whether preemptive war and occupation could be compatible with local democracy and self-determination.

Nevertheless, arguments equating continuing autocracy in the Middle East and rogue-state sponsorship of terrorism were important in the administration's case for war in 2003, which rested on Washington-offered "evidence"

---

1. See Spencer Weart, *Never at War: Why Democracies Will Not Fight Each Other* (New Haven, Conn.: Yale University Press, 1998).

2. President Bush seemed to have been impressed by the work of Natan Sharansky and Ron Derfmer, specifically *The Case for Democracy: The Power of Freedom to Overcome Tyranny and Terror* (Green Forest, AR: Balfour, 2006).

3. See Timothy Mitchell, "McJihad: Islam in the U.S. Global Order," *Social Text*, vol. 20, no. 4 (Winter 2002), 1–18.

that Saddam Hussein had participated in global terrorism—arguments that were later refuted. All this came at a time when Middle East scholars were trying to explain the region's "democratic deficit." Indeed, Middle Eastern cases were largely absent from the literature on "transitions to democracy" and what Samuel Huntington called the "third wave of democratization" (the move from nondemocratic to democratic political systems in some thirty-five countries, mostly Asian and Latin American, in the 1970s and 1980s).[4] Experts on the Middle East argued that the region's democratic lag could be explained by several factors: dependence on oil, which resulted in a distributive rather than a productive economy; long-standing tensions between liberal and Islamic political thought; a gender gap in political and social affairs; and, most importantly, the fact that no region of the world had been so thoroughly ensnared in great power struggles as the Middle East.[5] Ignoring the assessment that outside interference was a major factor in the regional lag, key figures in the Bush administration nevertheless argued that the region needed a push from the outside. They predicted that regime change in Iraq would have a "snowball effect," prompting democratization throughout the region and, indeed, all over the world (6.3).

Some scholars and citizens in the Middle East also hoped for regime change to take place. Most agreed, however, that transitions should be homegrown and largely a product of nationalist discourse and local developments rather than of guided changes originating from outside powers. In fact, the region had already been witnessing a steady rise in civil institutions, especially nongovernmental organizations, and the growth of political participation in the form of political party formation and parliamentary participation—a few of the conditions correlated with democratization. Yet the notion that the region was a "penetrated system," independent yet never fully free, reverberated among Middle Eastern scholars as U.S. administrators guided Iraqis toward statehood. Washington's attitude toward regime change in Iraq was aligned with that of some scholars who wrote that allowing free elections or democracy to flourish in the region might result in a system antithetical to U.S. notions of rights. One such writer, Fareed Zakaria, famously warned that people in the region were inclined to elect "illiberal democracies." He contended that upon taking office, those in power would curtail rights, suppress women, and turn states into theocracies. Though this thesis was largely speculative, Bush administration officials argued that U.S. supervision was necessary to prevent such a transition in Iraq.

---

4. See Samuel P. Huntington, *The Third Wave: Democratization in the Late Twentieth Century* (Norman: University of Oklahoma, 1993).

5. For a list of the classical arguments on political development in the Middle East, see Bahgat Korany, Rex Brynen, and Paul Noble, *Political Liberalization and Democratization in the Arab World: Theoretical Perspectives* (Boulder, CO: Lynne Rienner, 1995); Raymond Hinnebusch, *International Politics of the Middle East* (Manchester, UK: University of Manchester Press, 2003); and Rashid Khalidi, *Resurrecting Empire: Western Footprints and America's Perilous Path in the Middle East* (Boston: Beacon, 2005).

As the occupation continued, the construction of permanent state institutions occurred under the tutelage of the United States. This made it difficult to properly gauge the level of Iraqi independence of action. Through close contacts with Iraqi dissidents, the administration initially hoped to transform Iraq along liberal, capitalist free-market lines (6.1–6.2). Indeed, high on Paul Bremer's list was privatizing the economy—an undertaking that he claimed was necessary for political democratization (4.12–4.14). But privatization did not have a large following in Iraqi society, clearly conflicting with local sovereignty and the economic interests of a large number of citizens. Under Saddam Hussein, Iraqis had enjoyed the considerable benefits of a distributive economy: job security, free medical care, salaries for life, and low prices for such basic goods as gasoline and electricity. It soon became clear that a privatized economy would dismantle these state-ensured social goods. Moreover, skilled Iraqis were passed over in favor of foreigners for the reconstruction projects. Hence, a discussion of democracy was always joined to the question of whether Iraq was becoming a neocolonial puppet state, or whether Iraqis themselves could present and implement some initiatives to overcome the country's severe structural constraints. Many state-building possibilities surfaced, including a potential Sunni-Shia compromise alongside a Kurdish desire for federalism and Shia interest in supra-regions. Iraqis also debated whether Iran should serve as a model for Iraq, whether the state should be secular, or whether some new hybrid classification should emerge from the Iraqi experience (6.5).

282 |

The United States assumed that the transition from Saddam Hussein's regime would be smooth because of the presence of a large, secular Iraqi middle class. Secular, however, did not mean democratic. Moreover, the Iraq of 2003 was a very different place than it had been before 1991. Before the sanctions began to hollow out the country's institutions and economy, Iraq's health care and university systems were regarded as the best in the Arab world. There was a vibrant middle class, the United Nations Human Development Index put Iraq third in the region (behind only the United Arab Emirates and Kuwait), and tens of thousands of foreign workers flocked to the country to work on massive infrastructure projects. Profound changes occurred after the Gulf War, however, and they were bound to bring many controversial and unexpected issues to the state-building project. Twelve years of sanctions had had a devastating impact. By 2003, the Iraqi state had insulated itself from a badly atomized society, as once-robust state institutions had deteriorated. The hospitals and schools were dilapidated, raw sewage ran in the streets, and the country's infrastructure was decrepit. After the Bush administration's repeated warnings that Saddam Hussein was an active and menacing threat to international peace and stability, American soldiers were surprised to see how badly the state had been degraded; they had not anticipated coming to Iraq to serve as mechanics and electricians. Clearly, the sanctions—and, by extension, the policy of containment—had crippled the regime. More important, civilian society was suffering badly. Human rights organizations reported that Iraqis were not receiving basic food staples and that five thousand children were dying every month. Not only was the state affected, there were fundamental changes in Iraqi society that were apparent only after Saddam Hussein's ouster created a power vacuum, leaving space for a new and unrestrained political discourse.

The Iraqi discussions that proliferated after 2003 were the product of a multicultural, multireligious environment where building an inclusive and functional government was a top priority. Several competing visions of an Iraqi state became the subject of debate. A strong tradition of secularism was illustrated by the Constitution of 1925, its amendments, and the rise and consolidation of the secular, socialist, left-leaning Baath Party in the 1960s. Yet there was also a profound legacy of religiously organized Shia thought and tradition, since Iraq had served as the academic and cultural focal point of Shiism in the Arab world for centuries (6.6–6.7). On a local level, Shia ayatollahs had been the source of guidance and law for Iraqis and had written extensively on Shia statehood (6.9). While some ayatollahs opted for a quietist approach that separated religion from politics, others called for an activist role in bringing Shiism to the forefront of political life and forming a government with a religious leader as its head (6.8). The Sunnis, by contrast, had maintained a prominent role in government through their loyalty to the Baath Party. Their monopoly of power had shielded them from a theoretical crisis and contentious debates on Sunni state-building trajectories. The Kurds, whose population in Iraq had reached five million, also had plans for statehood. Forced to accept an Iraqi central government in 1920, they had worked their way through periods of cooperation with and resistance to the central government, finally coming to a 2005 post-invasion agreement that gave them considerable veto power in the new state (6.11). These groups, along with the returned Iraqi exiles who composed more than two-thirds of the transitional institutions under the Coalition Provisional Authority (CPA), were certain to have interesting discussions about statehood.

| 283

Before its dissolution, the CPA granted powers to an interim Governing Council, but both were disbanded in June 2004. Sovereignty was then transferred to the interim government that revised the policy of de-Baathification and inherited many of the tasks once held by the CPA. Among those tasks were building a stable financial base for state institutions, controlling government ministries, and handling the oil issue.[6] Though U.S. power continued in other ways, U.S. officials hoped that the interim government would be permanent. The Shia formed an umbrella organization or political party called the United Iraqi Alliance (UIA), headed by a six-person committee, with Ayatollah Ali al-Sistani, the highest-ranking Shia cleric in Iraq, as leader of the party. They put forth 228 candidates for the upcoming elections. Muqtada al-Sadr, the fiery anti-American populist leader, was asked to join but declined in favor of postponing participation during foreign occupation. The United States reportedly covertly supported Ayad Allawi, who had been Iraq's first head of state

---

6. See chapter 7 of this volume about the various debates on how to orient the oil economy. The question of federalism was linked to where oil exploration was taking place in the country as well as whether or not oil would be nationalized or privatized. The United States wanted to privatize oil.

after Saddam Hussein, out of fear that the Sistani bloc would sweep the elections. Allawi had also been a long-time CIA asset.[7] An electoral victory by Sistani would have represented the worst-case scenario for the United States—to watch an ayatollah take power after removing a secular dictator and thereby fulfill Zakaria's prediction. The Sunnis boycotted the elections.

The winners were the UIA and the leading Kurdish party, the Kurdistan Alliance. Together, they put forward a seven-point plan for permanent statehood, which included absorbing the militias into the regime, implementing institutional reform, reconstructing the country, supporting the many Iraqis who had suffered at the hands of Saddam Hussein, and ensuring the Islamic identity of the country in coordination with the office of the highest jurisprudent in Shia Islam (*marja iyya*).

Setting the tone for the new government, the Kurds contributed to the formation of a federalist state and agreed to fold their security forces, the "*pesh merga,*" into the Iraqi army. Other parties soon agreed: The UIA issued a statement in support of federalism and the Supreme Council for the Islamic Revolution in Iraq (SCIRI), led by Ayatollah Hakim, expressed interest in forming "super regions," blocs of Shia-dominated territories, to ensure Shia cohesion. The Sunnis initially rejected both the Kurdish and Shia positions since they would preclude the Sunnis from reconsolidating their power in the future.

In October 2005, Iraq's permanent constitution was ratified. There were articles that protected individual and human rights and that supported a unified Iraqi state, though it would be largely decentralized under a federal system. Power would devolve to the various regions, especially on issues of internal security. The Sunni Arabs felt isolated because de-Baathification had collectively punished hundreds of thousands of Iraqis. As de-Baathification was toned down, Sunnis began participating in the government. The groups started to work together to refine the features of the state (6.12). The United Iraqi Alliance presented a road map for a future viable state that called for the emancipation and empowerment of the Shia, a grand compromise among the three major groups, a radical devolution to local government, and an insistence on democracy, legality, and civil rights. The parties continued to struggle with the definition of citizenship. The Shia demanded a definition that was inclusive, fair, and nonsectarian, given the multiplicity of ethnic and sectarian groups in the country. Yet the constitution claimed Iraqi identity to be personal matter, leading some to fear that it was opening the door to sectarianism.

In the December 2006 elections, the United Iraqi Alliance was composed of SCIRI, the Islamic Dawa Party, the Islamic Supreme Council of Iraq (ISCI), and followers of Muqtada al-Sadr—a mix of former adversaries. Sunnis began to participate, abandoning their previous policy of targeting polling stations in

---

7. See Matt Kelly, "New Iraqi PM a Longtime CIA Source," Associated Press, September 7, 2004; Joel Brinkley, "The Reach of War: New Premier; Ex-C.I.A. Aides Say Iraq Leader Helped Agency in 90's Attacks," *New York Times*, June 9, 2004.

protest. Though politicians were coming to terms with negotiating statehood, the insurgency had devolved into a civil war, with heightened sectarianism and violence—a milieu that was sure to overshadow the important gains Iraqis were making in securing a strong and independent state (6.13). By 2007, Grand Ayatollah Sistani, who had previously issued the famous "democratic fatwa" that criticized Paul Bremer's appointment of constitution drafters and had called for a nationwide boycott until elections were held, had receded from the forefront of politics and distanced himself from direct involvement in the government (6.10).

At the close of 2008, the United States and the government of Iraq signed two bilateral agreements that would determine future relations between the two countries and affect Iraq's ability to gain full sovereignty: the Status of Forces Agreement (SOFA) set the legal terms under which the U.S. military would be allowed to operate in Iraq (6.14), while the Strategic Framework Agreement was broadly aimed at addressing issues not covered by the SOFA (6.15), such as the terms of joint cooperation on energy, information technology, and law enforcement. Both agreements were widely resisted by Iraqis on the grounds that their terms would prolong the occupation and severely limit Iraqi sovereignty.

---

# U.S. Plans for Regime Change

## DOCUMENT 6.1

The Future of Iraq Project (FOIP) was the most comprehensive pre-invasion plan produced in Washington for rebuilding Iraq along "democratic principles" in a post–Saddam Hussein state. The thirteen-volume study was a product of the State Department's organization of more than two hundred Iraqi engineers, lawyers, doctors, businesspeople, and others into seventeen working groups to strategize about such state-building topics as transparency and anticorruption, transitional justice, democratic principles and procedures, local government, civil society building, education, freedom of the press, the economy, and infrastructure. The FOIP remains the most important documented record of U.S.-endorsed reconstruction planning prior to the invasion. Its "democratic principle groups" were featured more prominently than others that were working on education, free speech, local government, refugees, and regional affairs.

The working groups convened between July 2002 and April 2003 to produce reports on the major strategies, issues, and potential roadblocks to rebuilding Iraq. Once marked "For Official Use Only" as a sensitive but unclassified document, fragments of the FOIP were leaked to the press. The complete study became widely available in 2006, with the names and backgrounds of participants excised. There was no data on the background of the participants, except that they were exiles. Many exiles involved in the early state-building discussions on Iraq had been out of that country for decades and most likely had been isolated from important debates as a result. Their discussions served as comparison with the ideas and policies of the indigenous Iraqi politicians who joined the government after the CPA was dissolved. While many FOIP ideas seemed positive in theory, they were the ideas of a "dissident minority" and did not necessarily mesh well with the existing political and social realities Iraqis were experiencing.

---

FUTURE OF IRAQ PROJECT: DEMOCRATIC PRINCIPLES AND PROCEDURES WORKING GROUP, "FINAL REPORT ON THE TRANSITION TO DEMOCRACY IN IRAQ," NOVEMBER 2002 (EXCERPT)

This report takes as its point of departure the resolutions of the 27–31 October 1992 conference of the Iraqi National Congress (the "INC") held in Salahuddin, northern Iraq (Arbil province). In brief, these called for a democratic and federally structured Iraq based on the principle of separation of powers, and the principle of the protection of the individual human rights and group rights. These 1992 Salahuddin principles were reaffirmed by the group of six Iraqi opposition parties that met with senior representatives of the government of the United States on August 9, 2002. . . . That conference will need to adopt a detailed program for the transition from dictatorship to democracy in Iraq.

This report is an attempt to fulfill that need. . . . The ideas presented in this report are feasible on the basis of certain assumptions made by us:

- That the government of the United States actually proceeds with its stated policy of democratic change in Iraq;
- That the unseating of Saddam's regime does not take place at the cost of large scale civilian casualties which could introduce considerable volatility and unpredictability into the political situation;
- That this report, or some variation on it, is actually adopted at a genuinely representative conference of the Iraqi opposition;
- That the government of the United States, as the partner of the Iraqi people in liberating Iraq, itself agrees to support the guiding framework of this report following its adoption by the Iraqi opposition;
- That the international community, including the Government of the United States, by a treaty with a duly constituted Iraqi government, undertakes to guarantee the territorial integrity of Iraq.

Nothing in this report, however, requires of the United Nations or United States to police or manage into existence the new and budding democratic institutions. That is a challenge that the people of Iraq must and will face up to on their own. . . .

## Democratization and Civil Society

In 1991, more than 400 Iraqis put their name to a document that opened with these words; "Civil society in Iraq has been continuously violated by the state in the name of ideology. As a consequence the networks through which civility is normally produced and reproduced have been destroyed. A collapse of values in Iraq has therefore coincided with the destruction of the public realm for uncoerced human association. In these conditions, the first task of a new politics is to reject barbarism and reconstitute civility.". . .

To promote civil society, the Transitional Government (which is the executive entity immediately after regime change) should immediately see that the restrictions on travel in and out of the country for Iraqis and non-Iraqis alike are lifted. The use of the internet, satellite dishes, and the import of foreign publications should be unfettered. A Democracy Fund as suggested in 2.6.2 should also be considered.

At the heart of responsible citizenship, however, lies societal respect for law, which begins with the promulgation of a permanent constitution (which would include a Bill of Rights), and continues through the de-militarization of a society abused by the culture of war and violence, and its de-ideologization in the shape of a comprehensive program of de-Ba'athification.

## Constitutionalism

A constitution that is rooted in the hopes and aspirations of the people of Iraq must arise out of a process of debate and discussion. Such a process may be initiated by individuals or groups in opposition or in exile, but it cannot be completed outside of an Iraq in which the conditions for having such a disucssion have already been established. . . .

With the exception of the first Iraqi constitution of 1925, which followed a three-year process of discussion, no Iraqi constitution has ever been discussed and debated by Iraqis. The prospect of a change in regime in Iraq in the short term raises the issue of how to draft a new constitution and bring it to the forefront of Iraqi political debate and discussion. Or, how to make constitutionalism the central focus of the post-Ba'athist politics. . . .

The governing idea behind any future Iraqi constitution should be that power is not to be trusted; it always needs to be checked. Left to its own re-sources, power corrupts. The sources and symbols of authority, which are often spelled out in constitutional documents, are less important than these checks and balances on the exercise of power.

In the 1977 Legal reform Law promulgated by the regime of the Ba'ath (cited in Section 1.1), the argument was made that because "authority in the State is one, . . . this means the negation of the idea of 'multiplicity of powers,' legislative, executive and judicial." As a matter of historical experience, the negation of multiple sources of power and authority in a state is always the thin end of a wedge in the creation of despotism.

The source of authority in politics, unlike its source in religion, is never "one." Politics has multiple foci (local, regional, central) and various arenas of application (legislative, executive, and judicial). The fundamental point of a constitution is to keep these levels of authority, or powers, separate, while ensuring that they coordinate smoothly in arriving at decisions.

A new Iraqi constitution, if it is to avoid the pitfalls of the post 1958 era, must rest on the concept of the separation of powers among the legislative, the judiciary, and the executive, and it must set forth the relations of these three powers in practical ways.

### An Iraqi Bill of Individual Rights

A permanent Iraqi Constitution must contain a bill of rights, the goal of which would be to define those inviolable individual human rights of all Iraqi citizens, irrespective of their sex, ethnic background, nationality, religion, sect, and political beliefs. This bill must become the fundamental basis for the protection of individuals within Iraq. The point of a bill is to guarantee the equal protection of all individuals, regardless of sex, ethnicity, nationality, or religion. To a very large extent, once the rights of all individuals are protected, the fears of individuals arising from their belonging to a particular sex, nationality, ethnicity, or religion will be abated, albeit gradually. . . .

The protection of such rights entails:

- The inclusion of a bill of rights within the permanent constitution.
- Until a permanent constitution is passed, a bill of rights must be included as part of the governing law of the interim or transitional period.
- There must be laws passed that develop the bill of rights within Iraqi society. Laws must be passed during the transitional period, for instance, that would make it a crime to discriminate on the basis of sex, nationality, ethnicity, or religion. It is not enough to wait for the inclusion of such rights in a permanent constitution.
- The separation of powers must be a fundamental constituent part of the new Iraqi state. It also cannot wait for a permanent constitution but should emerge in nuclear forms at the earliest possible opportunity, namely at the forthcoming conference on the Iraqi opposition.

[*Editors' Note: The working group then moved on to the Bill of Rights of the 1925 Constitution as a basis for the transitional and then permanent constitution of Iraq, even though that constitution had been abrogated following the coup of 1958. Various other interim constitutions had been put in place subsequently, containing articles that abrogated many of these original rights.*]

## Rights Under the 1925 Constitution

- No discrimination among Iraqis: Article 6 provides that there shall be no discrimination in the rights of Iraqis. . . .
- No interference among Iraqis without due process of law: Article 7 provides that the state shall not violate or interfere with the personal liberty of any Iraqis, and provides that no Iraqi shall be arrested, detained, or punished, except in accordance with Iraqi law.
- No torture: Indeed, Article 7 specifically states that "torture and the deportation of Iraqis . . . are specifically forbidden."
- Right to property and no unreasonable search and seizure: Article 8 guarantees that all places of residence are inviolable, and that they may not be entered or searched except in accordance with the manner prescribed by law. This article is in many ways similar to the Fourth Amendment to the U.S. Constitution. . . .

### Civil and Political Rights

- The right to equality before the law (the courts and tribunals);
- The right to be presumed innocent until proven guilty according to law;
- The right to freedom from: Political and extra judicial killing; Disappearance; Torture and other cruel or inhuman treatment and punishment; Arbitrary arrest, detention, or exile; Denial of a fair public trial; Arbitrary interference with privacy, family, and correspondence.
- The rights of citizens to change their government by democratic means;
- The right to vote and to be elected at genuine periodic elections;. . . .

### Economic, Social, and Cultural Rights

- The right of association and form trade unions;
- The right to work (which includes the right and opportunity of everyone to gain his living by work);
- The right to strike;
- The right to organize and bargain collectively;
- The right against slavery;
- Elimination of death penalty;
- Acceptable conditions of work: Minimum wages; Safe and healthy working conditions; Minimum age for employment.
- The right to free education;
- The right to free medical cares.
- The right to social welfare.
- The right to serve in the military and the police.
- Communal and/or National Rights

| 289

As discussed in the introductory paragraph to this section, the transition to democracy and the rule of law must above all be one in which the protection of individual rights stands above all else. However, the composition of Iraqi society is one in which significant members of the Iraqi population (between 20 and 30%) belong to different ethnic or religious groups. More importantly, because of the painful legacy of national and religious discrimination inside Iraq and in the region, many Iraqis have reacted by asserting their national, ethnic, and religious identities. Accordingly, among the rights that need special consideration in Iraq are those collective group rights of certain ethnic, national, and religious groups. These include:

- The right to self-determination, autonomy, and self-government, which does not necessarily extend to sovereignty or statehood.
- The right to freely determine their political status.
- The right to study and be educated in his/her native language.
- The right to establish private media (publications, television, and radio) in local languages specific to some regions of the country and not others.
- The right to display cultural symbols as long as these are not offensive to other religions or national and ethnic groupings.
- The rights of women.

In general, the above group, communal or religious rights mentioned in Section 4.2.3.4, do not override individual human rights wherever these are abused. In particular when or if they come into conflict with the rights of women, they are always deemed subordinate to the rights of women as individuals and as a gender. No group, whether tribal, national, or religious, can make a claim that its customs or traditions allow it to treat women in a way that is contrary to the spirit and letter of the Bill of Rights set out in Section 4.2. The motive of clearing one's family honor, for instance, as a pretext for committing murder against women, will not be permissible as a plea in any Iraqi court of law. Nor can any gender-related restrictions or qualifications be placed on the right to travel, inherit, marry, or engage in any other pursuit allowed under the law. . . .

## The Judicial System

Upon coming to power in 1968, the Ba'ath Party in Iraq (the "Ba'ath Party") introduced a new constitution, and introduced changes to the existing judicial, legal, and policing structures. The effect of these changes, which will be discussed in detail below, was to eliminate the concept of the separation of powers among the executive, legislative, and judicial authorities, and to make the civil court system subservient to the military court systems and extrajudicial authorities, thereby marginalizing it.

The overriding theme of this paper with respect to the judiciary is that the judiciary needs to be reformed in order to become more independent; the

establishment of such an independent judiciary is one of the key prerequi-
sites of the creation of the separation of powers. Indeed, it is the judiciary
which will become the key arbiter with respect to human rights abuses. . . .

Prior to 1968, the Iraqi judiciary had a certain level of independence and
was governed by the High Judicial Council, whose head was the President of the Court of Cassation; the High Judicial Council ensured, at least
de jure, the independence of the judiciary from the executive. After the
Ba'ath Party came to power, pursuant to Law Number 160/1979 (The Law
for the Organization of the Judicial System) and Decree Number 101/1977
of the Minsitry of Justice, the High Judicial Council was dismissed and replaced with the Justice Council, which was chaired by the Minister of Justice and not be the President of the Court of Cassation. Thus, the de jure
independence of the judiciary was eliminated. In addition, at a de facto level,
the Ba'ath Party passed laws and implemented policies which ensured that
the judiciary was made subservient to the executive and simply took orders
from the executive. . . .

Overall, the effect of the Ba'ath Party's laws and policies was not only to
marginalize the role of the judicial system and judges in Iraqi society, but
also to transform the legal system into another part of the Ba'ath Party
machinery, assisting in its plans of controlling Iraqi society. . . .

## Vision of an Iraqi Constitutional State

### Federalism

In 1992, the Kurdish Parliament voted in favor of a federal Iraqi structure.
The National Assembly of the INC adopted this policy in its conference in
Salahuddin in 1992 and reaffirmed it at its 1999 conference in New York.
These votes were the first of their kind in the modern history of Iraq. Taken
together they broke the mold of Iraqi politics. Today, most Iraqi organizations that oppose the regime in Baghdad, whether they are in the PJC or
not, advocate one interpretation or another of federalism. No Iraqi political organization can afford not to support federalism today, especially not
one that calls itself democratic. That should be considered an immense gain
for the people of Iraq, one that should not be frittered away by the differences, which have also broken out over what federalism means.

Two features unite all definitions in play in the Iraqi political arena at the
moment:

- the idea that federalism, whatever else it might mean, is the
  permanent and constitutionally prescribed allocation of certain
  powers to the provinces (regions or governorates). These powers
  cannot then be taken away or diminished once they have been
  constitutionally established (following a national referendum that
  ratifies the new permanent constitution of Iraq, i.e., following the
  transitional period).

• No future state in Iraq will be democratic if it is not at the same time federal in structure.

Federalism is a new word and practice in Arab politics. Its novelty is a reflection of that of the whole phenomenon of the post 1991 Iraqi opposition, an opposition grounded not in issues of "national-liberation," but hostility to home-grown dictatorship. This opposition, which encompasses diverse traditional and modern elements of Iraqi society, has not always been easy to deal with, it is fractious, and prone to in-fighting. Nonetheless it is remarkable that virtually all groups in opposition to the Ba'athist regime agree on the need for representative democracy, the rule of law, a pluralist system of government and federalism. Federalism should therefore become in some form or another a corner stone of the new Iraqi body politic.

However, neither the Kurdish Parliament nor the INC have clarified what they mean by this new idea, nor have they worked out the practical implications of it with regards to the mechanics of power-sharing and resource distribution (most importantly oil revenues). It is in the interests of contributing to such a clarification that section 8.1 has been written.

The driving force behind the injection of this new idea, federalism, has been the Kurdish experience in northern Iraq. For the Kurdish political parties, federalism has become the sine qua non for staying inside a new Iraq, and not trying to secede from it. Without a federal system of government, in which real power is divided, in a constitutionally prescribed and non-negotiable way, the currently autonomous northern region which is populated largely by Kurds will still yearn, and perhaps even one day opt, for separation. After all that has been done to the Kurds in the name of Arabism, no Iraqi should expect otherwise. And certainly no one who calls him or herself a democrat.

As a result there has arisen a purely utilitarian argument for federalism, one derived from a pragmatic calculus of what the balance of power in the immediate aftermath of Saddam's overthrow is going to look like. One must concede federalism, the argument goes among some Arabs, in the interest of getting rid of Saddam and because the Kurds are today in a position to force it upon the rest of Iraq.

The Kurdish corollary of this utilitarian argument goes: we must accept federalism, not because we really want it, but because the regional situation does not allow for us to secede and have our own separate state in northern Iraq.

We do not think that a project as big as restructuring the state of Iraq on a federal basis should be undertaken on the grounds of this kind of utilitarian calculus. No ordinary Iraqi citizen can be expected to opt for federalism on grounds of expediency. Federalism, if it is to become the founding principle of a new beginning in Iraq, must derive from a position of principle. What might that be?

The Coordinating Committee of the Democratic Principles Workshop proposes that federalism in Iraq be understood in the first place as an extension of the principle of the separation of powers, only this time power is being divided instead of separated out into its different branches. Without the separation of powers, there can be no federalism worthy of the name. Because the regime of Saddam Hussein was never willing to relinquish real power except under duress (for example in 1970 when it negotiated the March 11, 1970 Kurdish autonomy accords), none of its "concessions" to the Kurds could ever be taken seriously. They were here one day and gone the next. By contrast a truly federal system of government is a structurally new system in which power itself is from the outset divided.

Federalism is from this point of view the thin end of the wedge of democracy in Iraq. It is the first step towards a state system resting on the principle that the rights of the part, or the minority, should never be sacrificed to the will of the majority. The fundamental principle of human rights is that the rights of the part—be that part defined as a single individual or a whole collectivity of individuals who speak another language and have their own culture—are inviolable by the state. Federalism is about the rights of those collective parts of the mosaic that is Iraqi society. Majority rule is not the essence of a federal democracy; minority rights, or the rights of the part (including ultimately individual human rights) are.

| 293

How should the different parts of the new Iraqi federation be defined? One important definition rests on a national definition of the constituent parts of the federation. The idea is to have Iraq composed of two regions, the first Arab, the second Kurdish. The two largest national groups in Iraq, ought to be, according to this point of view, the basis for federalism in Iraq.

## Problems with National Federalisms

Many Iraqis have raised objections to the formulation in Section 8.1.3. If a federation is defined as being about two national groups, the other smaller national groups argue, then clearly they, who do not have a share in the federation, are being to one degree or another discriminated against. Why should an Armenian or an Assyrian or a Turkmen citizen of Iraq have any less rights as an individual than an Arab or a Kurd in post-Saddam Iraq? Such discrimination in favor of the largest national groups in Iraq is inherently undemocratic.

It is difficult, if not impossible, to refute this argument.

This brings us to another variant of the national or ethnic definition of federalism, namely the idea that a federal system in Iraq should be devised which maps out geographic regions for all the different national and religious communities. . . . Many such maps are in fact circulating among Iraqis.

The problem with this approach is that the demographics in Iraq are such that a mapping exercise of this nature cannot ever be fair to everyone. The communities of Iraq are not all territorially concentrated. There are Kurds in Baghdad and Arabs in Sulaymaniya, and there are Turkmens and Armenians and Assyrians everywhere. Moreover, people have been forcibly deported, and ethnically cleansed, in many parts of Iraq. They may or may not want to move back to their original towns and villages. What map-making skills can ever deal with such a situation?

To even attempt to map such a division of Iraq will turn nationality and/or ethnicity into the basis for making territorial claims and counterclaims, especially with regards to high profit resources located in one region and not another. The fight over Kirkuk is already going in this direction, with Arab, Kurdish and Turkmen claims competing with one another over this oil-rich city. Moreover, the Anfal operations of 1987 and 1988 destroyed Assyrian villages as well as Kurdish villages.

Conclusion: it is extremely unlikely that a federation of many national and ethnic groups would be any kind of an improvement on a federation made up of only two large groups.

### Nationality and the Future State of Iraq

The logical corollary of territoriality as a basis for federalism is to consider what effect this has on the nature of the new Iraqi state which hitherto has been thought of by all and sundry as an Arab state, led by the Arab Ba'ath Socialist Party and part of the Arab League. Can the new federal state of Iraq be an Arab state in the same sense in which Iraq has been thought of as being an Arab state in the past? This is an important question, which goes to the roots of the problem that the idea of federalism was intended to solve. Israel is today a Jewish state in which a substantial number of Arab Palestinians—more than a million—have Israeli citizenship but are not and cannot in principle ever be full-fledged citizens of the state of Israel. The fact that they live in better conditions than their brethren in the West Bank and Gaza, or those in refugee camps all over the Arab world, is not an argument for second-class citizenship. In principle, because they are in a religiously or ethnically defined state, they are second class citizens and one day in the future the two principles upon which the state of Israel was created—ethnicity and democracy—are bound to come into conflict with one another. . . .

### Religion and Statehood

. . . . What, if any, is the relationship which ought to exist between the new Iraqi state and religion, specifically the religion of the overwhelming majority of Iraqis, Islam? This is an important question which ultimately only the people of Iraq can decide upon in the course of their deliberations during the transitional period.

Such a discussion is already underway among Iraqis in exile. One way of thinking about the issues involved is to pose them to each individual Iraqi as a set of questions:

- Do you want your future state of Iraq to be involved in any way in your religious beliefs, either by way of compelling or persuading you towards a particular belief?
- Do you want your future state of Iraq to define individual Iraqi citizens as members of different religious groups (as is the case with the confessional system in Lebanon)? Do you think, in other words, that an individual's religious beliefs are relevant to his or her rights and obligations as a citizen?
- Do you want your future state of Iraq to promote, regulate, direct, or otherwise interfere in matters of religion (through the Ministry of Awqaf', for instance, or through its control over educational programs)?
- Do you trust Iraqi politicians enough to give them any kind of influence or control over your religious affairs?
- Finally, do you think religious scholars, or ulama' (in their religious capacity not as private citizens), have the knowledge and experience required to decide upon your political affairs?

If the answer that Iraqis give to all of these questions is "no," then that means that the people of Iraq have in effect chosen to keep matters of politics and matters of religion separate from one another in order to live truly satisfying and complementary spiritual and political lives. It means that the people of Iraq, precisely out of a sense of their devotion to the life of the spirit, have chosen to keep matters of religion separate from matters of politics. This will have assisted in realizing the creative and spiritual potential present in religious faith when it is not shackled to the ebb and flow of politics.

# DOCUMENT 6.2

As Washington's plans for "regime change" became known, analysts grew increasingly critical of the U.S. objective to remake Iraq under its tutelage, sometimes with questionable tactics. A 101-page classified document detailed the privatization plans for Iraq, dubbed by many as the Bush administration's blueprint for a neoliberal post–Saddam Hussein state. Parts of the plan were leaked to the *Wall Street Journal* in May 2003 and then reproduced by other newspapers. The plan was created by the Treasury Department and the U.S. Agency for International Development (USAID) and given to Peter McPherson, the former president of Michigan State University and the director of economic policy for ORHA, for implementation. McPherson's job was to build capitalist structures in Iraq, under the long-held conservative assumption that "a free society needs free markets." This position reflected the Bush administration's repeated insistence that free enterprise was a prerequisite for democracy and that economic reform would lead to political reform (2.10). The privatization plans for Iraq violated Articles 43 and 55 of the Hague Convention, which required occupying powers to respect the existing property arrangements and laws of the occupied country (4.1, 4.2). Many analysts warned that the outcome in Iraq would likely mimic the force-fed economic transformations that had devastated many of the former Communist states in the 1990s.

TREASURY DEPARTMENT AND THE U.S. AGENCY
FOR INTERNATIONAL DEVELOPMENT (USAID),
MOVING THE IRAQI ECONOMY FROM RECOVERY
TO SUSTAINABLE GROWTH, MAY 2003 (EXCERPT)

**Privatize Iraq's Industries.** Here the United States will attempt to build a consensus for industry privatization during the first year, after which the assets of the Iraqi public sector would be transferred to private ownership over a period of three years. The country did have some limited attempts at privatization in the 1980s, so the concept is not completely foreign to the population at large. The main controversy here is obviously the proposed privatization of the oil industry.

**Modernize the Baghdad Stock Exchange.** Here the goal is to convert Iraq's rudimentary prewar stock market within a year into a world class exchange for trading the shares of newly privatized companies. Tasks would entail developing a centralized share registry as well as a new clearing and settlement system. . . . Presumably, U.S. officials working with AID contractors would write rules for membership in the exchange.

**Reform the Central Bank.** A new charter will be drafted to give the bank independence in pursing monetary policy—as opposed to the policy of underwriting government deficits under the Saddam regime. According to Faleh Daud Salman, Governor of the Iraqi Central Bank (Agence France Presse July 9, 2003), "Independence will help us formulate economic policies that will contribute to encouraging activity in the country and making better use of its resources and revenue, as well as promoting growth." Contractors would help revamp the country's battered banking system by working out problem loans. The traditional Islamic money transfer system, Hawala . . . , would be incorporated into the banking system.

**Establish a New Currency.** Beginning October 15 Iraqis will begin exchanging notes bearing the image of Saddam Hussein for new bills denominated between 50 and 25,000 dinars. This will end the dual currency system that has separated the Kurdish north from the rest of the country.

. . . It is not clear at this point, however, what type of exchange regime the country will adopt. Since exchange rate stability is a key element in the neoliberal model, some type of fixed exchange rate is likely. . . .

**Provide Iraqi Businesses with Fresh Credit.** Initial plans are for extending as much as $8 million in loans to small and medium sized Iraqi businesses within the first year.

**Create a Legal Framework Compatible with Private Ownership, Production, and Distribution.** This essentially involves creating a system of laws protecting private property contracts and all of the supporting infrastructure that is required by a modern market economy.

**Rewrite the Tax and Tariff System.** Here contractors would be designing a comprehensive income tax system and preparing regulations to impose a consumption tax. Presumably the tariff structure would be set quite low or there may even be a tariff holiday for six months or so . . . , preparing the country for a free trade agreement with the United States and eventual membership in the World Trade Organization.

# DOCUMENT 6.3

More than two years after the invasion of Iraq, the Bush administration's plans for rebuilding the country had encountered widespread criticism. The United States wanted to remake Iraq along neoliberal economic lines, but the reconstruction project was not well received by Iraqis, contributing to social discontent and helping fuel the developing insurgency. Nevertheless, U.S. administrators and politicians continued to deliver optimistic assessments of Iraqi state-building. Secretary of State Condoleezza Rice gave the administration's view of the progress in Iraq in both domestic and international politics. Optimistic about the domestic gains made, she plotted the course ahead, strongly emphasizing Iraq's role in the regional and international political systems.

CONDOLEEZZA RICE, OPENING REMARKS BEFORE
THE SENATE FOREIGN RELATIONS COMMITTEE,
OCTOBER 19, 2005 (EXCERPT)

Thank you. I would like to deliver this in full. It's my first opportunity to talk to you specifically about Iraq. I've spoken many times about why we are there, but I would like to talk about how we assure victory. In short, with the Iraqi Government, our political-military strategy has to be to clear, hold, and build: to clear areas from insurgent control, to hold them securely, and to build durable, national Iraqi institutions. In 2003, enforcing UN resolutions, we overthrew a brutal dictator and liberated a nation. Our strategy then emphasized the military defeat of the regime's forces and the creation of a temporary government with the Coalition Provisional Authority and an Iraqi Governing Council.

In 2004, President Bush outlined a five-step plan to end the occupation: transferring sovereignty to an Iraqi interim government, rebuilding Iraq's infrastructure, getting more international support, preparing for Iraq's first national election this past January, and helping to establish security. Our soldiers and marines fought major battles, major battles, against the insurgency in places like Najaf and Sadr City and Fallujah.

In 2005, we emphasized transition: a security transition to greater reliance on Iraqi forces and a political transition to a permanent, constitutional democracy. The just-concluded referendum was a landmark in that process. And now we are preparing for 2006. First we must help Iraqis as they hold another vital election in December. Well over nine million Iraqis voted on Sunday. Whether Iraqis voted yes or no, they were voting for an Iraqi nation, and for Iraqi democracy.

And all their voices, pro and con, will be heard again in December. If the referendum passes, those who voted no this time will realize that their chosen representatives can then participate in the review of the constitution that was agreed upon last week. This process will ultimately lead to Iraqis selecting a lasting government, for a four-year term. We must then have a decisive strategy to help that government set a path toward democracy, stability, and prosperity. . . .

We know our objectives. We and the Iraqi Government will succeed if together we can:

- Break the back of the insurgency so that Iraqis can finish it off without large-scale military help from the United States.
- Keep Iraq from becoming a safe haven from which Islamic extremists can terrorize the region or the world.
- Demonstrate positive potential for democratic change and free expression in the Arab and Muslim worlds, even under the most difficult conditions.
- And turn the corner financially and economically, so there is a sense of hope and a visible path toward self-reliance.

Now, of course, to achieve this, we must know who we are fighting. Some of these people are creatures of a deposed tyrant, others a small number of home-grown and imported Islamist extremists. They feed on a portion of the population that is overwhelmed by feelings of fear, resentment, and despair. . . . They attack infrastructure, like electricity and water, so that average Iraqis will lose hope. . . .

But the enemy strategy has a fatal flaw. The enemy has no positive vision for the future of Iraq. They offer no alternative that could unite Iraq as a nation. And that is why most Iraqis despise the insurgents. . . .

Let me now turn to our political-military strategy. We are moving from a stage of transition toward the strategy to prepare a permanent Iraqi government for a decisive victory. . . .

With our Iraqi allies, we are working to:

- Clear the toughest places—no sanctuaries to the enemy—and to disrupt foreign support for the insurgents.
- We are working to hold and steadily enlarge the secure areas, integrating political and economic outreach with our military operations.
- We are working to build truly national institutions by working with more capable provincial and local authorities. We are challenging them to embody a national compact—not tools of a particular sect or ethnic group. These Iraqi institutions must sustain security forces, bring rule of law, visibly deliver essential services, and offer the Iraqi people hope for a better economic future. . . .

We must build truly national institutions. The institutions of Saddam Hussein's government were violent and corrupt, tearing apart the ties that ordinarily bind communities together. The last two years have seen three temporary governments govern Iraq, making it extremely difficult to build national institutions even under the best of circumstances. The new government that will come can finally set down real roots. To be effective, that government must bridge sects and ethnic groups. And its institutions must not become the tools of a particular sect or group. Let me assure you, the United States will not try to pick winners. We will support parties and politicians in every community who are dedicated to peaceful participation in the future of a democratic Iraq. . . . In sum, we and the Iraqis must seize the vital opportunity provided by the establishment of a permanent government.

Well, what is required?

First, Iraqis must continue to come together in order to build their nation. The state of Iraq was constructed across the fault lines of ancient civilizations, among Arabs and Kurds, Sunni and Shi'a, Muslims and Christians. No one can solve this problem for them. For years these differences were dealt with through violence and repression. Now Iraqis are using compromise and politics.

Second, the Iraqi Government must forge more effective partnerships with foreign governments, particularly in building their ministries and governmental capacity.

- On our side of this partnership, the United States should sustain a maximum effort to help the Iraqi government succeed, tying it more clearly to our immediate political-military objectives.

- On Iraq's side, the government must show us and other assisting countries that critical funds are being well spent—whatever their source. They must show commitment to the professionalization of their government and bureaucracy. And they must demonstrate the willingness to take tough decisions.

Third, Iraq must forge stronger partnerships with the international community beyond the United States.

The Iraqis have made it clear that they want the multinational military coalition to remain. Among many contributors, the soldiers and civilians of the United Kingdom deserve special gratitude for their resolve, their skill, and their sacrifices.

Now the military support from the coalition must be matched by diplomatic, economic, and political support from the entire international community. Earlier this year, in Brussels and Amman, scores of nations gathered to offer more support. NATO has opened a training mission near Baghdad. And now, as Iraq chooses a permanent, constitutional government, it is time for Iraq's neighbors to do more to help.

- The major oil producing states of the Gulf have gained tens of billions of dollars of additional revenue from rising oil prices. They are considering how to invest these gains for the future.
- These governments must be partners in shaping the region's future.
- We understand that across the region, there are needs and multilateral programs in the Palestinian territories, Lebanon, Afghanistan, and Pakistan as well as Iraq. Rather than consider them in a disjointed way, they together form part of a broad regional effort in transforming the Arab and Muslim world. We hope the governments of the region, as well as others in Europe and Asia, will examine these needs and then invest decisively, on an unprecedented scale, to become continuing stakeholders in the future of Iraq and of the region.

Finally, the U.S. Government must deepen and strengthen the integration of our civilian and military activities.

- At the top in Iraq, we have established an effective partnership between the Embassy and Ambassador Khalilzad on the one hand, and the Multinational Forces command and General Casey on the other.
- To be sure, civilian agencies have already made an enormous effort. Hundreds of civilian employees and contractors have lost their lives in Iraq. But more can be done to mobilize the civilian agencies of our government, especially to get more people in the

field, outside of Baghdad's International Zone, to follow up when the fighting stops.

- We will embed our diplomats, police trainers, and aid workers more fully on military bases, traveling with our soldiers and marines.
- To execute our strategy we will restructure a portion of the U.S. mission in Iraq. Learning from successful precedents used in Afghanistan, we will deploy Provincial Reconstruction Teams (PRTs) in key parts of the country. These will be civil-military teams, working in concert with each of the major subordinate commands, training police, setting up courts, and helping local governments with essential services like sewage treatment or irrigation. The first of these new PRTs will take the field next month.

Mr. Chairman, members of the Committee, to succeed, we need most your help and your support, and that of the American people. We seek support across the aisle, from both Democrats and Republicans. . . . But of course, there is a great deal at stake. A free Iraq will be at the heart of a different kind of Middle East. We must defeat the ideology of hatred, the ideology that forms the roots of the extremist threat that we face. Iraq's struggle—the region's struggle—is to show that there is a better way, a freer way, to lasting peace.

Thank you very much, Mr. Chairman.

# DOCUMENT 6.4

In 2005, the *New York Times* revealed the existence of the secret Pentagon Military Analysis Program, which paid Iraqi media outlets to publish articles favorable to the U.S. invasion and occupation. Three years later, the same paper obtained thousands of pages of emails, briefings, tape recordings, and letters that revealed the grand scope of the operation. It reported that the Pentagon had selected retired military officers—who were working as "news analysts" for various television networks and magazines in the United States—to act as a propaganda machine for U.S. policy in Iraq, Guantánamo Bay, and elsewhere. In addition to these covert policies, the Bush administration had attempted to shape U.S. and Iraqi public opinion in other ways, such as with the 2004 launching of a domestically based satellite television channel called al Hurra, "the Free One," which broadcast pro-U.S. information exclusively in the Middle East. (Under the 1948 Smith–Mundt Act, it was forbidden for such stations to broadcast in the United States.)

The following selection offered a tantalizing peek into Defense Secretary Donald Rumsfeld's motives for creating the Pentagon Military Analysis Program.

Rumsfeld clearly sought to influence public opinion and the media, and here discussed with Marine Gen. Peter Pace, chairman of the Joint Chiefs of Staff, the problems he perceived in presenting the situation in Iraq favorably. While the name of the interviewer was undisclosed, his questions suggested that he was not an objective observer or a professional journalist.

---

DONALD H. RUMSFELD AND PETER PACE,
JOINT STATEMENT, APRIL 18, 2008 (EXCERPT)

[Secretary Rumsfeld arrives]

**SECRETARY RUMSFELD:** Stay here, keep talking. Answer the questions.

**GENERAL PACE:** Alright, sir.

**QUESTION:** One of the problems is that the United States Army, United States Marine Corps, DOD, it's at war right now. The rest of it has got to stop. And as a consequence, does that perhaps [inaudible] translate out and it doesn't get out because for the average American—we haven't said to Americans as often as we should have or sought after different ways or caused them to think that they were really at war, so they're going to pay more attention to the Duke Lacrosse team or Michael Jackson or some other damn thing.

**GENERAL PACE:** I think the good news and the bad news is exactly-the-same.

**QUESTION:** So, we're not task organized as a government for war, is what I worry about.

**GENERAL PACE:** The good news and bad news is the same thing which is a lot of Americans don't wake up every day thinking that their country's at war because we have not been attacked since 9/11 here at home and therefore it's been four-plus years since that has happened. So you can see where fellow citizens would not be thinking each day that the country is at war and what are we going to do about it. Whereas the fact of the matter is we are at war; in a very real, tangible, threatening to our society way. That's why any opportunity I get to talk to any group of influencers I like to do that because it gives me a chance at least to put my thoughts on the table so they can blend that in with the rest of the thoughts they've been hearing during the course of that week and determine themselves what's right and what's not.

The Secretary of Defense is here. Mr. Secretary?

**SECRETARY RUMSFELD:** First of all, thank you for coming. It's good to see you. I appreciate those of you who have been out talking and putting in context what's going on in the world. [Inaudible] some things and talk about Iraq and the global war on terror. I don't think you need any long remarks from me. I'd be happy to just answer questions and respond to things that might be on your minds.

QUESTION: Sir, has what's gone on with regard to you and these generals had an impact on your credibility, on this administration and on the military?

SECRETARY RUMSFELD: I guess time will tell. It's awful hard for me to be instantaneously inclusive about something like that. It is clearly a distraction and unhelpful, but our democracy has lots of distractions and things that are unhelpful. If you believe, as I do, that the center of gravity of this war is not in Afghanistan or Iraq or elsewhere, it's in the capitals of Western countries. It's not an accident that Zarqawi and Zawahiri and bin Laden have media committees and they sit down and think how can they impact the body politic in the United States. They're good at it and we're not terribly good at it. So it becomes part of that debate, what's going on. Have we lived through things like this before? Sure. My goodness. The Revolutionary War, the Civil War, World War I, World War II. I can remember when I was Secretary the last time they were digging graves in my front lawn, the Berrigan brothers, and spilling blood on the Pentagon front steps and stuff like that. President Johnson had buses around the White House because they didn't have those concrete revetments in those days and he couldn't go out and give a speech. . . .

QUESTION: Right. One of the things that impressed me about how the initiatives [inaudible] after the hurricane in New Orleans was when Honore chastised the press about getting stuck on stupid. [Laughter]

SECRETARY RUMSFELD: It was wonderful. Can you imagine? I'd like to think I was a genius and I had him located there to—[Laughter]—just in case there was a Katrina. But it was just an accident. The guy is fabulous.

QUESTION: The point is, what is is, the past is the past, it's for historians to review.

SECRETARY RUMSFELD: Sure.

QUESTION: But in the meantime, not only are we trying to do this thing in Iraq but if you look at the polls, the American people to huge numbers, like over 70 percent, believe that Iran is a major threat to this country, and an equally high double digit percentage, 65 to 70 percent, think that a military strike against Iran to keep them from getting nuclear is something that we should be considering. Now it seems to me that doing good in Iraq is one of the best things we could do to off-set a lot of these potential problems with Iran and the focus of the American people ought to be in that future, not—I mean if I were you I wouldn't even be answering a question about this. It's over.

SECRETARY RUMSFELD: Why don't you go down to the press room and tell those folks—[Laughter].

QUESTION: Sir, by most recollections of the press and around, and I asked General Pace about it too. It would appear that we've lost whatever initiative we might have had initially indicating the courses of action that lead to a positive conclusion. After all, as you just said, I hope that the government turns out right. And by the way I hope, and in fact what I'm hearing is they must form a government or it isn't going to work the way we think it should. The same thing at home, more importantly. The initiative at home that would keep the American people focused on the idea that we're moving forward to a positive end. So what are we doing to fix that?

SECRETARY RUMSFELD: Well, the Department of State and the President are on the phone with the people out there frequently. They're trying to do it with a touch that isn't too heavy handed. The goal is to have whatever government is formed look like an Iraqi government and not an American template that we imposed on them. So they're doing it privately. They're doing it I hope successfully, and time will tell. I have no crystal ball. . . . And there is a tension between, on the political side, a tension between being so insistent and so visible and so threatening and so public to the political figures that whatever comes out looks tainted, it looks American. . . .

QUESTION: In terms of the political ties, NSA dropping, all the rest of these things, it seems like the political tide has been kind of ebbing away from you guys for a while. Now we've got a new year, we got a lot more war to fight. But is there some way that you're thinking about to maybe kind of regain the political tide in your favor by going on the offense? Things like, I was encouraged when you said in your press briefing a while ago, you know, maybe we ought to think about the Solomon Amendment. Are you going to go out there and, forgive me for the analogy, but start kind of poking people in the nose politically a little bit—. . . .

SECRETARY RUMSFELD: You're right. I can play it round or square. I can go on offense. I'm not very good on defense. I don't think that makes a heck of a lot of sense. Maybe I should be doing more offense, it's a fair question. The question of what we're doing over there is, think of the dire consequences if that place tanks. Think of it. Having the Zarqawis of the world have that country with that oil and that water and that population and that location, our lives would be miserable if they were training terrorists in that place and financing what's going on in the world. I'd a heck of a lot rather be fighting them over there than fighting them back here.

QUESTION: The point is, back here the media is just all on the negatives, the car bombs. Every time a car bomb goes off people ought to think they're killing innocents. The worst kind of people in the world.

SECRETARY RUMSFELD: They are.

QUESTION: How do we play this and articulate it so again, it comes out. Killing innocents. That's all they know how to do is kill innocents.

SECRETARY RUMSFELD: This is the first war that's ever been run in the twenty-first century in a time of twenty-four-hour news and bloggers and internets and e-mails and digital cameras and Sony cams and God knows all this stuff, and wire transfers, all the electronic things that are going on, and it's a different world. We're not very skillful at it in terms of the media part of the new realities that we're living with. Every time we try to do something someone says it's illegal or immoral, there's nothing the press would rather write about than the press, we all know that. They fall in love with it. So every time someone tries to do some information operations for some public diplomacy or something, they say oh my goodness, it's multiple audiences and if you're talking to them, they're hearing you here as well and therefore that's propagandizing or something or it's not fair or it's not right. We don't have the right rules or the right understandings yet for this century.

QUESTION: I'm an old intel guy and I can sum all of this up, unfortunately, with one word. That is PsyOps. Now most people may hear that and they think oh my God, they're trying to brainwash—

SECRETARY RUMSFELD: What are you, some kind of a nut? You don't believe in the constitution? [Laughter]

QUESTION: You know what they call PsyOps today, they call those public relations firms. [Laughter] So they kind of phase that out.

SECRETARY RUMSFELD: You people should be taking notes. I'm taking all the notes! [Laughter]. . . .

QUESTION: Sir, the danger with the strategy, if I could be so bold, is the next big event that you and General Pace have talked about is the standup of the government. If you allow the Chris Matthews and the Wolf Blitzers of the world to immediately start dissecting the standup of that government and say this guy is bad, Chalabi's a crook, assuming he's part of the government, and on and on and on, and you do not respond immediately, we are going to lose that capability to say what we did was honorable and good and right.

# Iraqi Reactions to Regime Change: Visions of Democracy

This next section of documents is a collection of Iraqi voices on the issues of statehood and national and territorial integrity, both before and after the invasion. It begins with excerpts from the Permanent Constitution of Iraq, ratified in October 2005, followed by documents from the Shia, Kurds, and Sunnis.

# DOCUMENT 6.5

The Iraqi constitution was approved by voters in a referendum on October 15, 2005. It was drafted by members of the Iraqi Constitutional Committee to replace the Transitional Administrative Law (TAL), the law of administration for Iraq prepared by the Coalition Provisional Authority during the transition period (4.15). Prior to the referendum, it was agreed that the first parliament would institute a Constitutional Review Committee to determine amendments to the document. Future amendments would then be ratified by a similar referendum. The document was translated from the Arabic by the UN Office for Constitutional Support. Amendments in parentheses, made too late to be included in the UN-translated text, were translated by the Associated Press.

---

CONSTITUTION OF IRAQ, OCTOBER 2005 (EXCERPT)

THE PREAMBLE
We have honored the sons of Adam.

. . . Acknowledging God's right over us, and in fulfillment of the call of our homeland and citizens, and in response to the call of our religious and national leaderships and the determination of our great (religious) authorities and of our leaders and reformers, and in the midst of an international support from our friends and those who love us, marched for the first time in our history toward the ballot boxes by the millions, men and women, young and old, on the thirtieth of January two thousand and five, invoking the pains of sectarian oppression sufferings inflicted by the autocratic clique and inspired by the tragedies of Iraq's martyrs, Shiite and Sunni, Arabs and Kurds and Turkmen and from all the other components of the people and recollecting the darkness of the ravage of the holy cities and the South in the Sha'abaniyya uprising and burnt by the flames of grief of the mass graves, the marshes, Al-Dujail and others and articulating the sufferings of racial oppression in the massacres of Halabcha, Barzan, Anfal and the Fayli Kurds and inspired by the ordeals of the Turkmen in Basheer and as is the case in the remaining areas of Iraq where the people of the west suffered from the assassinations of their leaders, symbols and elderly and from the displacement of their skilled individuals and from the drying out of their cultural and intellectual wells, so we sought hand in hand and shoulder to shoulder to create our new Iraq, the Iraq of the future free from sectarianism, racism, locality complex, discrimination and exclusion.

Accusations of being infidels, and terrorism did not stop us from marching forward to build a nation of law. Sectarianism and racism have not stopped us from marching together to strengthen our national unity, and to follow the path of peaceful transfer of power and adopt the course of the just distribution of resources and providing equal opportunity for all.

We the people of Iraq who have just risen from our stumble, and who are looking with confidence to the future through a republican, federal, democratic, pluralistic system, have resolved with the determination of our men, women, the elderly and youth, to respect the rules of law, to establish justice and equality to cast aside the politics of aggression, and to tend to the concerns of women and their rights, and to the elderly and their concerns, and to children and their affairs and to spread a culture of diversity and defusing terrorism.

We the people of Iraq of all components and shades have taken upon ourselves to decide freely and with our choice to unite our future and to take lessons from yesterday for tomorrow, to draft, through the values and ideals of the heavenly messages and the findings of science and man's civilization, this lasting constitution. The adherence to this constitution preserves for Iraq its free union, its people, its land and its sovereignty.

## SECTION ONE: FUNDAMENTAL PRINCIPLES
### Article 1:
The Republic of Iraq is a single, independent federal state with full sovereignty. Its system of government is republican, representative Parliamentary and democratic. This Constitution is the guarantor of its unity.
### Article 2:
First: Islam is the official religion of the State and it is a fundamental source of legislation:
  B. No law that contradicts the principles of democracy may be established.
  C. No law that contradicts the rights and basic freedoms stipulated in this constitution may be established.
Second: This Constitution guarantees the Islamic identity of the majority of the Iraqi people and guarantees the full religious rights of all individuals to freedom of religious belief and practice such as Christians, Yazedis, and Mandi Sabeans.
### Article 3:
Iraq is a country of many nationalities, religions and sects and is a founding and active member of the Arab League and is committed to its covenant. Iraq is a part of the Islamic World.
### Article 4:
First: The Arabic language and Kurdish language are the two official languages of Iraq. The right of Iraqis to educate their children in their mother tongue, such as Turkmen, Syriac and Armenian, in government educational institutions in accordance with educational guidelines, or in any other language in private educational institutions, is guaranteed. . . .
Fifth: Each region or governorate may adopt any other local language as an additional official language if the majority of its population so decide in a general referendum.

### Article 5:

The law is sovereign. The people are the source of authorities and its legitimacy, which the people shall exercise in a direct general secret ballot and through their constitutional institutions.

First: No entity or program, under any name, may adopt racism, terrorism, the calling of others infidels, ethnic cleansing, or incite, facilitate, glorify, promote, or justify thereto, especially the Saddamist Baath in Iraq and its symbols, regardless of the name that it adopts. This may not be part of the political pluralism in Iraq. This will be organized by law.

Second: The State shall undertake combating terrorism in all its forms, and shall work to protect its territories from being a base or pathway or field for terrorist activities. . . .

## SECTION TWO: RIGHTS AND LIBERTIES
### CHAPTER ONE: RIGHTS
#### FIRST: Civil and Political Rights
##### Article 14:

Iraqis are equal before the law without discrimination based on gender, race, ethnicity, origin, color, religion, creed, belief or opinion, or economic and social status. . . .

Second: The sanctity of the homes is inviolable and homes may not be entered, searched, or put in danger, except by a judicial decision, and in accordance with the law. . . .

##### Article 18:

First: Iraqi nationality is the right of every Iraqi and shall be the basis of his Citizenship.

Second: An Iraqi is any person born to an Iraqi father or mother. This will regulated by Law. . . .

##### Article 25:

The State guarantees the reform of the Iraqi economy in accordance with modern economic principles to ensure the full investment of its resources, diversification of its sources and the encouragement and the development of the private sector.

##### Article 26:

The state guarantees the encouragement of investments in the various sectors. This will be organized by law. . . .

   A. The family is the foundation of society; the State preserves its entity and its religious, moral and patriotic values.
   B. The State guarantees the protection of motherhood, childhood and old age and shall care for children and youth and provides them with the appropriate conditions to further their talents and abilities.

Second: Children have right over their parents in regard to upbringing, care and education. Parents shall have right over their children in regard to respect and care especially in times of need, disability and old age. . . .

## Article 31:

First: Every citizen has the right to health care. The state takes care of public health and provides the means of prevention and treatment by building different types of hospitals and medical institutions. . . .

## CHAPTER TWO: LIBERTIES
### Article 35

A. The liberty and dignity of man are safeguarded.
B. No person may be kept in custody or interrogated except in the context of a judicial decision.
C. All forms of psychological and physical torture and inhumane treatment shall be prohibited. Any confession coerced by force, threat, or torture shall not be relied on. The victim shall have the right to compensation in accordance with the law for material and moral damages incurred.

Second: The State guarantees the protection of the individual from intellectual, political and religious coercion.

### Article 36:

The state guarantees in a way that does not violate public order and morality:
A. Freedom of expression, through all means. . . .
C. Freedom of assembly and peaceful demonstration. This shall be regulated by law.

### Article 37:

First: The freedom of forming and of joining associations and political parties is guaranteed. This will be organized by law.

Second: It is prohibited to force any person to join any party, society or political entity or force him to continue his membership in it. . . .

### Article 41:

First: The followers of all religions and sects are free in the:
A. Practice of religious rites, including the Husseini ceremonies (Shiite religious ceremonies)
B. Management of the endowments, its affairs and its religious institutions. The law shall regulate this. . . .

### Article 43:

The State shall seek the advancement of the Iraqi clans and tribes and shall attend to their affairs in a manner that is consistent with religion and the law and upholds its noble human values in a way that contributes to the development of society. The State shall prohibit the tribal traditions that are in contradiction with human rights. . . .

## SECTION THREE: FEDERAL POWERS
### Article 45:

The federal powers shall consist of the legislative, the executive and the judicial powers. They exercise their specialization and tasks on the basis of the principle of separation of powers.

CHAPTER ONE: THE LEGISLATIVE POWER:
Article 46:

The federal legislative power shall consist of the Council of Representatives and the Federation Council.

Article 47:

First: The Council of Representatives shall consist of a number of members, at a ratio of one representative per 100,000 Iraqi persons representing the entire Iraqi people. They shall be elected through a direct secret general ballot. The representation of all components of the people in it shall be upheld. Fourth: The elections law aims to achieve a percentage of women representation not less than one-quarter of the Council of Representatives members. . . .

Article 58:

The Council of Representatives specializes in the following:

First: Enacting federal laws.

Second: Monitoring the performance of the executive authority.

Third: Elect the President of the Republic.

Fourth: A law shall regulate the ratification of international treaties and agreements by a two-thirds majority of the members of the Council of Representatives.

Fifth: To approve the appointment of the following:

    A. The President and members of the Federal Court of Cassation, Chief Public Prosecutor and the President of Judicial Oversight Commission based on a proposal from the Higher Juridical Council, by an absolute majority.

    B. Ambassadors and those with special grades based on a proposal from the Cabinet.

    C. The Iraqi Army Chief of Staff, his assistants and those of the rank of division commanders and above and the director of the intelligence service based on a proposal from the Cabinet.

Sixth:

    A. Question the President of the Republic based on a justifiable petition by an absolute majority of the Council of Representatives members.

    B. Relieve the President of the Republic by an absolute majority of the Council of Representatives members after being convicted by the Supreme Federal Court in one of the following cases:

    1. Perjury of the constitutional oath.

    2. Violating the Constitution.

    3. High treason. . . .

SECOND: The Federation Council
Article 62:

A legislative council shall be established named the "Federation Council" to include representatives from the regions and the governorates that are not organized in a region. A law, enacted by a two-third majority of the members of the Council of Representatives, shall regulate the Federation

Council formation, its membership conditions and its specializations and all that is connected with it.

### CHAPTER TWO: THE EXECUTIVE POWER
#### Article 63:

The Federal Executive Power shall consist of the President of the Republic and the Council of Ministers and shall exercise its powers in accordance with the constitution and the law.

#### FIRST: The President of the Republic
#### Article 64:

The President of the Republic is the Head of the State and a symbol of the unity of the country and represents the sovereignty of the country. He safeguards the commitment to the Constitution and the preservation of Iraq's independence, sovereignty, unity, the security of its territories in accordance with the provisions of the Constitution.

#### Article 65:

A nominee to the Presidency must meet the following conditions: . . .

  B. Must be fully eligible and has completed forty years of age.
  C. Must be of good reputation and political experience, and known for his integrity, righteousness, fairness and loyalty to the homeland.
  D. Must not have been convicted of a crime involving moral turpitude. . . .

#### Article 69:

First: The President of the Republic's term in office shall be limited to four years and may be elected for a second time and no more. . . .

#### SECOND: Council of Ministers

First: The conditions for assuming the post of the Prime Minister shall be the same as those for the President of the Republic, provided that he has completed thirty-five years of age and has a college degree or its equivalent. . . .

#### Article 75:

The Prime Minister is the direct executive authority responsible for the general policy of the State and the commander in chief of the armed forces. He directs the Council of Ministers, and presides over its meetings and has the right to dismiss the Ministers on the consent of the Council of Representatives. . . .

### SECTION FOUR: POWERS OF THE FEDERAL GOVERNMENT
#### Article 106:

The federal authorities shall preserve the unity, integrity, independence, sovereignty of Iraq, and its federal democratic system.

#### Article 107:

The federal government shall have exclusive authorities in the following matters:

First: Formulating foreign policy and diplomatic representation; negotiating, signing, and ratifying international treaties and agreements; negotiating,

| 311

signing and ratifying debt policies and formulating foreign sovereign economic and trade policy;

Second: Formulating and executing national security policy, including creating and managing armed forces to secure the protection, and to guarantee the security of Iraq's borders and to defend Iraq;

Third: Formulating fiscal and customs policy, issuing currency, regulating commercial policy across regional and governorate boundaries in Iraq; drawing up the national budget of the State; formulating monetary policy, and establishing and administering a central bank. . . .

### Article 108:

Oil and gas are the ownership of all the people of Iraq in all the regions and governorates.

### Article 109:

First: The federal government with the producing governorates and regional governments shall undertake the management of oil and gas extracted from current fields provided that it distributes oil and gas revenues in a fair manner in proportion to the population distribution in all parts of the country with a set allotment for a set time for the damaged regions that were unjustly deprived by the former regime and the regions that were damaged later on, and in a way that assures balanced development in different areas of the country, and this will be regulated by law.

Second: The federal government with the producing regional and governorate governments shall together formulate the necessary strategic policies to develop the oil and gas wealth in a way that achieves the highest benefit to the Iraqi people using the most advanced techniques of the market principles and encourages investment.

### Article 110:

The following competencies shall be shared between the federal authorities and regional authorities:

First: To administer customs in coordination with the governments of the regions and governorates that are not organized in a region. This will be organized by law. . . .

## SECTION FIVE: POWERS OF THE REGIONS
### CHAPTER ONE: REGIONS
### Article 112:

The federal system in the Republic of Iraq is made up of a decentralized capital, regions and governorates, and local administrations.

### Article 113:

First: This Constitution shall approbate the region of Kurdistan and its existing regional and federal authorities, at the time this constitution comes into force.

Second: This Constitution shall approbate new regions established in accordance with its provisions.

Article 115:

One or more governorates shall have the right to organize into a region based on a request to be voted on in a referendum submitted in one of the following two methods:

A. A request by one-third of the council members of each governorate intending to form a region.

B. A request by one-tenth of the voters in each of the governorates intending to form a region.

# DOCUMENT 6.6

In the 1990s, Iraqi Shia in exile began calling attention to the widespread suffering endured by their co-religionists at the hands of Saddam Hussein's regime. The impetus was the widespread massacre of the Shia of the south after the 1991 Sha'ban uprising. As the government's systematic and disproportionate violence became apparent, a unique Shia consciousness was born.

This manifesto, written by Mowaffaq al-Rubai'e, Ali Allawi, and Sahib al-Hakim before they returned to Iraq after 2003, called for a new Iraq based on the principles of democracy, federalism, and community rights. These three former exiles became prominent Iraqi politicians in 2003. Unlike those who participated in the U.S.-sponsored "democratic principles" working groups in the Future of Iraq Project, they spoke to the realities of Iraqi Shia. Their position was favorable to the idea of forming a distinct Shia region under a federal system, since they viewed the Iraqi state as inherently sectarian. This declaration was a strong statement on the need to end the institutionalized discrimination against the Shia in Iraq. It would later influence Shia cooperation under the Iraqi government, as illustrated by their formation of the UIA in the lead-up to the January 2005 elections.

DECLARATION OF THE SHIA OF IRAQ, JULY 2002 (EXCERPT)

. . . . The Iraqi Shia problem is now a globally recognised fault line and is no longer restricted to the confines of Iraq's territory. It has ceased to be a local issue, for the international community and its organisations (such as Amnesty International, Human Rights Watch, the UN's Special Rapporteur on Iraq) have now acknowledged openly the existence of a serious sectarian problem in Iraq, and have expressed their sympathy and solidarity with the plight of the Shia of Iraq and the sectarian biases that they daily encounter from the authorities. . . .

Iraq's political crisis has nothing to do with either social discrimination or a latent Shia sense of inferiority towards the Sunnis, or vice versa. It is entirely due to the conduct of an overtly sectarian authority determined to pursue a policy of discrimination solely for its own interests of control, a policy that has ultimately led to the total absence of political and cultural liberties and the worse forms of dictatorship. It is not possible for Iraq to emerge out of this cul-de-sac without the complete banishment of official sectarianism from any future political construct, and its replacement by a contract premised on a broad and patriotic definition of citizenship that is far removed from sectarian calculations and divisions. . . .

Any policy that calls for the official adoption of the division of powers on the basis of overt sectarian percentages—such as the situation in Lebanon—cannot be workable in the context of Iraq, given its social and historical experience, and will not resolve the current impasse. It is quite probable that such a solution may well result in further problems, dilemmas and crises being laid in store for the country. The only way out of this conundrum is the total rejection of the anti-Shia practices of the state, and the adoption of an inclusive and equitable system of rule that would define the political direction of the future Iraq. This is what the Shia want and not some bogus solution based on the division of the spoils according to demographic formulae, a condition that would very probably result in communal sectarianism becoming a social and political reality rather than a manifestation of an unscrupulous state authority. . . .

314 | The sectarian issue in Iraq will not be solved by the imposition of a vengeful Shia sectarianism on the state and society. It can only be tackled by defining its nature and boundaries and formulating a complete national programme for its resolution. At the same time, the imperative of national unity should not be used as a pretext to avoid the necessity of dismantling the sectarian state and its harmful policies. . . .

The lessons drawn from Iraq's history are clear—the Shia have at no point sought to establish their own state or unique political entity. Rather, whenever the opportunity was afforded to them, they participated enthusiastically in nation-wide political movements and organisations, ever conscious of the need to maintain national unity and probably more so than other groups inside Iraq. This can be abundantly established by examining the Shia's involvement in the struggle to establish the independent Iraqi state within its current recognised borders. The Shia, both in their islamist and non-islamist manifestations, have avoided being dragged into separatist schemes, and have been steadfast in their commitment to the unitary Iraqi state. The vital support that they gave to the claims of the Sharifian candidate to the Iraqi throne, in addition to the general sympathy that was exhibited to the cause of the Sharifs of Mecca after the Great War, was symptomatic of their patriotism. . . .

This historic position of the Shia in favour of the unitary constitutional Iraqi state was not given its due measure, unfortunately, by successive Iraqi governments. In fact, the Shia role in safeguarding the unity of Iraq was constantly belittled and frequently ignored. The earliest political parties and movements in which the Shia were involved, were clear in their platforms and programmes of an absolute commitment to an independent and constitutional state stretching from the Province of Mosul in the north to the Province of Basra in the south. The slogan, "An Arab Islamic Government", that was demanded by the Shia leadership in the referendum of 1919 is the incontrovertible evidence of the commitment of the Shia to an Arab/Muslim form of rule for Iraq, and the rejection of any status not commensurate with full political independence for the country. . . .

## What Do the Shia Want?

The demands of the Shia can be succinctly summarised as follows:

1. The abolition of dictatorship and its replacement with democracy.
2. The abolition of ethnic discrimination and its replacement with a federal structure for Kurdistan
3. The abolition of the policy of discrimination against the Shia

The Declaration of the Shia of Iraq aims to elaborate on a Shia perspective on the political future of Iraq. Its principal points are as follows:

1. Abolition of ethnic and sectarian discrimination, and the elimination of the effects of these erroneous policies
2. The establishment of a democratic parliamentary constitutional order, that carefully avoids the hegemony of one sect or ethnic group over the others
3. The consolidation of the principles of a single citizenship for all Iraqis, a common citizenship being the basic guarantor of national unity.
4. Full respect for the national, ethnic, religious, and sectarian identities of all Iraqis, and the inculcation of the ideals of true citizenship amongst all of Iraq's communities.
5. Confirmation of the unitary nature of the Iraqi state and people, within the parameters of diversity and pluralism in Iraq's ethnic, religious and sectarian identities.
6. Reconstruction of, and support for, the main elements of a civil society and its community bases.
7. Adoption of the structures of a federal state that would include a high degree of decentralisation and devolution of powers to elected provincial authorities and assemblies.
8. Full respect for the principles of universal human rights.
9. Protection of the Islamic identity of Iraqi society.

# DOCUMENT 6.7

The "Declaration of the Shia of Iraq" received widespread support from leading scholars and jurists in Iraq. Grand Ayatollah Khadim al-Haeri, a firm believer in the principle of "rule of the jurisprudent," called for an active role for Shiism in politics. A prominent ayatollah in Iraq, al-Haeri was exiled from Iraq to Qom, Iran, in the 1970s, where he continued to issue fatwas. He was most well known for his initial support for, and then renunciation of, Muqtada al-Sadr in July 2004. Sadr was stripped of his representation (*wukala*), a privilege granted to him by the religious community because he came from a family of ayatollahs. His father, Muhammad Sadiq al-Sadr, who was killed by Saddam Hussein's regime in 1999, had been a prominent Shia cleric and an important force in Shia politics. Because of his incitement of sectarian violence, Muqtada al-Sadr was deemed no longer qualified to accept or use any religious dues (a form of stipend). Ayatollah al-Haeri's statements here emphasized Shia unity and the healing of the nation.

STATEMENT BY GRAND AYATOLLAH SAYYID
KADHIM AL-HAERI, JULY 2002 (EXCERPT)

I have received your letters regarding the extent of the effort needed to retrieve the rights of Iraq's Shia, and my reply follows. . . .

Firstly: The rights of the Shia have been violated for a long time and up to our period today. This has been caused not by our Sunni brothers but as a result of tyrannical governments. We do not ask the minority sect in Iraq, the Sunnis, to grant rights to the Shia, the majority, for the scholars of Islam have all agreed that Islam does not differentiate between the rights of Muslims, irrespective of their sects.

Each member of a sect recognises and respects the particularities of its own sect, and we as followers of the Household of the Prophet recognise the limits of our sect and respect them.

Secondly: We demand that all tyrannical governments in Iraq cease from trampling the rights of the majority Shia; as we demand from them also that they cease to trample the rights of the minority Sunnis. We say to these governments; We are all Muslims and we enjoy equality of rights under the mantle of Islam.

Thirdly: It is essential that the rights of national minorities such as our brothers the Kurds and Turcomen and others be respected in parallel to the respect of the rights of the Arabs. This is an issue that has no bearing on the issue of sectarian discrimination. And from this perspective, the division of the Iraqi nation into Kurds, Shia and Sunnis is not accurate and mixes between the ethnic issue and the sectarian issue. It would appear to us that this is a deliberate ploy on the part of the international hegemonistic powers.

Fourthly: We demand from any non-Islamic government in Iraq to relinquish power and to allow the Iraqi nation to choose for itself the type of government it wants, which we are sure is an Islamic government.

# DOCUMENT 6.8

A look at ayatollah positions prior to the invasion helps clarify the cleavages that developed during the civil war. Ayatollahs are the highest-ranking religious scholars in Shiism; their positions are based on the required compendium of rulings or fatwas that they issue to the community over time. There are only a handful of ayatollahs in a state at any given time; the title is not granted by an institution but rather, clerics are advanced through a system of peer review, by the number of fatwas decreed, and by the circle of followers in that cleric's law school. Very few clerics reach the position of ayatollah, hence the ayatollahs' importance in guiding the community in everyday affairs. Unlike Sunni Islam, Shiism has a hierarchical religious system that encourages an ongoing debate about the proper relationship between religion and politics. There are few top-ranking ayatollahs with schools and followers, and they tend to disagree on political activism. That means that there is no such thing as an all-encompassing Shia position on statehood. In the spirit of democracy, the ayatollahs offer their differing opinions on the relationship between religion and politics, and the community decides which ayatollah to follow.

Ayatollah Sadiq al-Sadr, the father of Muqtada al-Sadr, wrote for decades on Shia activism and the "usurpation of power" from the secular Baathist adversaries. He wanted to revitalize the role of the ayatollah and called on Shia to participate in political life. After he was killed by Saddam Hussein in 1999, his followers went underground, only to resurface in the aftermath of the U.S. invasion. From that point forward, there were further splits among the Shia. Some followed Muqtada al-Sadr (nephew of Mohammad Baqir al-Sadr) in militant populism and resistance to the U.S. occupation. Others followed Grand Ayatollah Ali al-Sistani, the most prominent living ayatollah in Iraq during the U.S. invasion, who preferred a more conservative approach to political activity. Sistani participated in politics at specific junctures to reorient political activism but thought of himself as only an advisor. He did not, however, call for the creation of an Islamic state with the ayatollah as its head, as neighboring Iran had done in 1979. Others were more neutral. Ayatollah Abdul Qasim al-Khoei issued fatwas about proper conduct, though it was unclear whether he supported or rejected the uprising against the occupation. The invasion caused a split between lay and clerical interpretations of Islam, and contributed to lively debates among the Shia.

Ayatollah Mohammad Baqir al-Hakim was an important Shia leader. He had been exiled to Iran, where he formed the Supreme Council for the Islamic Revolution in Iraq (SCIRI), a political party dedicated to the overthrow of Saddam

Hussein and the Baath Party. Hakim had talks with Washington prior to returning to Iraq in 2003, where—although he expressed his personal belief in an Islamic republic for Iraq—he insisted that he would never impose it by force. His writing on democracy qualified the SCIRI movement as part of the legitimate "democratic opposition," according to the United States. Hakim's premise was that Muslims should choose an Islamic form of government through free and fair elections, but the details of that government were left open. This view led to a proliferation of writings by Islamic intellectuals on the relationship between Islamism and democracy. When Hakim returned to Iraq, he was well received by thousands of Shia as he called for an immediate end to the occupation, the transfer of power to Iraqis, and the formation of a constitutional government with Islamic, not secular, values. He went on to discuss the need to refine the role of the ayatollah, making a distinction between a spiritual and political leader. He sought to carve out a role for himself as an ayatollah in political matters, which was a break from the Iranian interpretation of the ayatollah as both a spiritual and political leader (*velayet e-faqih*). Hakim was killed in a car bombing in Najaf in August 2003. After that, his party was renamed Supreme Islamic Iraqi Council (SIIC) in May 2007, the "revolutionary" part of its mission having been completed.

The statement below was taken from the official Web site of Ayatollah Mohammed Baqir al-Hakim, who, throughout the 1990s and during the invasion, had talked about the role of the Shia and their opposition to Saddam Hussein.

---

STATEMENT BY AYATOLLAH MOHAMMED BAQIR AL-HAKIM, MAY 14, 2001 (EXCERPT)

"The Limits of Implementing Islamism on a State Level"
. . . . "The Third point: clarification of the 'definition' of the Islamism and the model that we adopt; what is the best form of government for Iraq?"

First: We should know that we start (in our work) from the principles and rules of Islam that represent the religious orientation that we follow, and these principles are:

A. The legal position in the performance of the Heavenly Representation [*ayatollah*] in the resistance of tyranny and injustice; that we inspire from the position of our Imam Hussein (peace be upon him) and the positions of our jurisprudents and great references [*The reference here is to the Shia position as a minority struggling to survive. The Shia faced widespread persecution at the hands of Sunnis. For centuries, they practiced "hiding," sometimes pretending to be Sunnis to evade punishment. Many Shia leaders were martyred*

---

Free translation here was provided by Professor Caroleen Marji Sayej; bracketed comments contain her explanation of the translated segment.

*for their commitment to Shia principles and their defense of the Shia state. Imam Hussein, referenced above, was the first leader of the Shia state in the seventh century. The context of tyranny above was a reference to the rule of Saddam Hussein.]* And in the present time from the positions of Imam Khameini (God's peace upon him) and also from the position of Imam Khoei (God's peace upon him) in the uprising of the fifteenth of Shaban and from the position of the martyr Imam Muhammad Baqir al-Sadr who started the Islamic revolution in Iraq, and all of this because we are Muslims who are committed to Islam and its principles, and we must have a legal representation to follow. [*First there is praise for Imam Khomeini, who undertook the task of leading a revolution in Iran in 1979 to replace a secular dictatorship with a Shia Islamic state. Then, Hakim praises the sacrifice of the ayatollahs who were martyred for their belief in politicizing Islam.*]

B. Holding onto Islam and its general principles, because the Iraqi people—in general—are Muslim people, whether its Arabs and its Kurds and its Turkmen, and its Sunnis and Shiites, and even the religious minorities that are present in Iraq are minorities that have lived in the realm of Islam and in the Islamic community, and they should follow this Islamic frame. [*Recognizing that Iraq was multireligious and multicultural, Hakim argued that Islamic principles would be able to incorporate everyone, since the community was mainly composed of Muslims and the culture had pervaded the region for centuries.*]

| 319

C. Loyalty to the prophet's family (peace be upon them) for loyalty to them and to the jurisprudents and religious references and it is an Islamic principle that all Muslims believe in, and that has been parallel to Iraqi history since the inception of Islam, when the Iraqis supported the prophet's family (peace be upon them) and loved them and upheld their traditions and these truths we cannot relinquish.

D. Demanding the humanitarian and legal rights for all Iraqi people, specifically among them, and defending these civil, cultural, and political rights—those rights that the regime [*Saddam Hussein's*] has confiscated without distinguishing between the Sunnis and Shiites, and between Arabs and Kurds and Turkmen, for the regime has usurped all the rights of the Iraqi people. [*Hakim believed that the regime of Saddam Hussein had destroyed unity among Iraqis, regardless of sect. The regime's violations of humanitarian and legal principles had led to a decrease in morale among Iraqis. According to Hakim, Islamic principles could be used to build a tolerant, unified Islamic state.*]

# DOCUMENT 6.9

Grand Ayatollah Ali al-Sistani was the most prominent Shia religious scholar in Iraq at the time of the invasion, based on the number of rulings he had issued over time. Most of his pre-2003 fatwas concerned personal and social, rather than political, issues. After 2003, he issued a series of fatwas calling for an end to the looting of the country and the revenge killings of former Baathists, and urging the immediate return of all stolen property. Sistani played a delicate balancing role, distancing himself from the occupation while at the same time issuing fatwas that would shift the political process according to his religious opinions. He was most known for his fatwa stating that the constitution should be written by elected experts only, taking direct issue with Bremer's reliance on appointed writers (chapter 4).

Underestimating the fatwa's resonance, Bremer thought it would be ignored or revised. But Sistani's commitment to the democratic process and insistence on elections to choose the drafters of the constitution earned the acquiescence of both the populace and the officials in the Governing Council. His official position on the relationship between Islam and the state was never published, though he expressed his ideas through various discussions. While he saw a relationship between Islam and politics, he did not propose that ayatollahs directly involve themselves in government. In October 2007, Sistani issued a fatwa stating, "The foreign security companies working in Iraq belittle innocent Iraqi citizens. . . . The occupying forces do the same in some of their operations, adding to the criminal acts of the *takfiris*" (a reference to Sunni militants). Below is a sampling of Sistani's fatwas after the U.S. occupation began, relayed either through his son, Mohammed Reda Ali al-Sistani, or in written replies to newspapers. Translations from the Arabic were posted on various Web sites.

---

COLLECTION OF FATWAS BY GRAND AYATOLLAH
ALI AL-SISTANI, SEPTEMBER 2002–OCTOBER 2007

*From Fatwa Issued by Sistani, Reported by Iraqi TV, September 2002*
The duty of Muslims in these difficult circumstances is to unite their stands and do all they can to defend beloved Iraq and safeguard it against the schemes of the covetous enemies. . . . Every Muslim should do all he can to defend Muslim Iraq and prevent the aggression against it. . . . Offering any kind of assistance or help to the aggressors is a mortal sin.
*As Quoted by His Son Mohammad Reda Ali Sistani, April 2003*
Our country must be governed by its people, by its best children. It is for Iraqis to choose who governs, we want them to control the country.
*As Quoted by His Son Mohammad Reda Ali Sistani, April 2003*
The coalition forces must assume full responsibility for the lack of security in various parts of Iraq and for allowing looting and theft.
*As Quoted by His Son Mohammad Reda Ali Sistani, June 2003*
We feel great unease over the goals of the occupation forces, and we see that they must make it possible for Iraqis to rule themselves without foreign intervention.

*From Fatwa Signed by Sistani, June 2003*
The occupation authorities are not entitled to name the members of the assembly charged with drafting the constitution. . . . There is no guarantee that such a convention will draft a constitution which upholds the Iraqi people's interests and expresses their national identity.

*From Sistani's Written Answers to Questions Put by the London-based* Al-Zaman *Newspaper, August 2003*
The religious constants and the Iraqi people's moral principles and noble social values should be the main pillars of the coming Iraqi constitution. . . . The principle of shura, pluralism, and respect for the majority view must be enshrined in the new constitution. . . . The religious authority's principal role is to provide believers with the shari'ah fatwas on all aspects of life and to steer the true religion along the course of the imams. . . . Dialogue is the best way to resolve any disagreements.

*Statement from Sistani's Office on the Murder of Ayatollah Mohammed Baqir al-Hakim, August 2003*
Undoubtedly, behind such a horrific and barbaric crime, and also other crimes perpetrated earlier in Najaf and other areas of Iraq, there are those who do not want security and calm to return to this ravaged land. . . . While condemning such barbaric acts, we hold the occupying forces responsible for these operations, the insecurities and inflammatory acts which the people of Iraq are witnessing.

*Sistani's Remarks to Visiting Arab League Delegation as Reported by the Iraqi* al-Zaman *Newspaper, December 2003*
We want what the people want, and we reject what they reject. We want national assembly elections and presidential elections for a specific term. Individual opinions have no value. The value is in what the people choose. The constitution must not be written by the occupier but by Iraqis, based on the Iraqi people's patriotic spirit. . . . Rumours and reports you hear about sectarian or religious conflict in Iraq are not true, we have no differences. We embrace the same position, each one of us respects the other, we live as one people and one family.

*From Statement on Sistani's Web Site after the UN Fact-finding Team's Report on the Feasibility of Elections in Iraq, February 2004*
The religious authority demands clear guarantees—like a UN Security Council resolution—that elections will be held on the set date so that the Iraqi people will be reassured that this issue will not be subject to further delay. The religious authority also demands that the unelected authority, to which power will be handed over on 30 June, should be an interim administration with clear and specific authorities to prepare the country for free and fair elections.

*From Statement by Sistani Reported by London-based Imam Ali Foundation Web Site, June 2004*
For many known reasons, the option of elections has been ruled out. Owing to procrastination, rejection and intimidation, the date of 30 June, on which

Iraqis are supposed to regain sovereignty over their country, is drawing nearer. Members of the new government have been appointed, but do not enjoy the legitimacy of elections. Moreover, not all sectors of the Iraqi community and its political forces are represented appropriately. In spite of this, we hope the new government will prove its efficacy, integrity and unwavering resolve to accomplish its critical duties.

# DOCUMENT 6.10

Grand Ayatollah Sayyid Ali al-Sistani was at the forefront of politics after Washington organized the Coalition Provisional Authority in 2003. In addition to issuing powerful fatwas and forming a political bloc, he continued to issue statements from his office regarding the future of the Iraqi state.

---

SAYYID ALI AL-SISTANI, STATEMENT ON ISLAMIC UNITY
AND THE RENUNCIATION OF SEDITION AND SECTARIANISM,
FEBRUARY 3, 2007

322 |    In the Name of God the Merciful
All united Around God and not divided among yourselves
    The Islamic nation is facing major crises and difficult circumstances and challenges affecting the present and threatening its future, and everyone is aware of this situation and the need to close ranks, renounce division and stay away from sectarianism and avoid stirring up ideological differences, those differences that have continued for centuries—and there seems no way of resolving in a manner satisfactory and acceptable to everyone, so it should not be an issue for debate outside the framework of scientific research. [*Sistani urged all Muslims to conduct their debates with reference to Islamic law. He was concerned that some Sunni groups had issued fatwas that urged the killing of Shias for their religious beliefs. Sistani feared that interpretations outside of the legal Islamic framework would proliferate.*]
    Sober, and particularly that it does not affect the fundamentals of Islam and pillars of belief, for everyone believes in the one and only God, Allah, his the message of the chosen prophet (peace be upon him), and his household in the day of Judgment and in the Noble Quran—that God protected from misinterpretation—With the prophet's tradition, noble source of legitimacy and the example of the Prophet's family (peace be upon them), and

---

Free translation provided by Caroleen Marji Sayej; bracketed comments are her interpretations of the meaning of the document.

so on which generally involve all Muslims, including the pillars of Islam: prayer, fasting, pilgrimage and others.

This is the foundation of the True Islamic unity, they must emphasize for closer bonds of love and friendship between the people of this nation, and not least to work on peaceful coexistence among them based on mutual respect and away from sectarian rivalries and bickering and sectarian whatever their subjects may be. [*Highlighting the commonalities among all Muslims, Sistani reminded Iraqis that all Muslims shared the same fundamental beliefs and traditions.*]

Anyone who cares about preserving the high status of Islam and the refinement of Muslims should do the utmost to bring them together and reduce the severity of tensions arising from some political tugging so as not to lead to more diffusion and scattering and give way to serve the enemy's aspirations to dominate the Islamic country and seize its resources.

But, what is noteworthy—unfortunately—that some people are doing the exact opposite and strive to working far from it and seek to deepen sectarian differences among Muslims, and have increased their efforts in the recent times, after the escalation of political conflicts in the region and the intensification of the conflict over power and influence, So they have worked hard in their attempts to demonstrate their ideological differences and dissemination of the addendum, but from themselves by using slander and sneakiness to achieve what they aim for by abusing a particular sect and diminishing its followers' rights and intimidating others away from the sect.

And under this scheme, some media outlets, including satellite, internet web sites, magazines and others—are broadcasting every now and then strange religious opinions that offend some parties and Islamic teachings, attributing them to Samahat al-Sayid (reference to himself) in a flagrant attempt to tarnish the religious authority and for the purpose of increasing sectarian tensions in order to reach certain goals.

The fatawa (religious opinions) of Samahat al-Sayid (reference to himself) are taken from reliable sources—like his collection of fatawa signed and sealed and it does not contain anything that slanders Muslims from other sects or their doctrines, and anyone who has the least amount of knowledge (of his work) will know the falsehoods of what is being said and published otherwise.

To add to this, that his (Sistani's) positions of discourse and statements issued during his last years on the plight that the injured Iraq lives with, and what he recommends to his followers and imitators in dealing with their fellow Sunni from love and respect, and what he repeatedly emphasized is the sanctity of Muslim blood, but he Sunni or Shiite, introduced the sanctity of his honor and money and distancing from anyone who sheds the sacred blood (of Muslims) no matter whose it is. . . .

This clearly reveals the program of the high religious institution in dealing with the followers of other sects and its views of them, and if everyone

| 323

uses this approach in dealing with those different sects things would not have progressed to what we are witnessing today, from the blind violence everywhere and the horrible killings that does not even spare a small child, an old man, a pregnant woman and all is left to the will of God.

We ask God, high and blessed, to guide everybody to what is for the good of this nation and its reconciliation for he is capable of everything. [*Sistani criticized Islamic radicals and the U.S. occupation. He accused Washington of inciting sectarian hatred through the use of propaganda and media and urged Iraqis not to believe some of the rumors that circulated in the streets. He stated that some of the fatwas that were issued were not legally sound or reliable. Sistani offered a sampling of the proper sources of Islamic positions, with a reference to the religious seal that is stamped on all official legal rulings.*]
The office of Al-Sayyid Sistani (long live)
Noble Najaf
14 / Muharram / 1428
3/2/2007

## DOCUMENT 6.11

324 |

The Kurds are an ethnic group numbering approximately thirty million persons across the Middle East, including five million in Iraq. The 1920 Treaty of Sèvres between the Ottoman Empire and the Allied countries at the end of World War I called for Kurdish automony, but the British and French moved to exclude the Kurds in their respective colonies to suit their strategic interests. The Kurds of Iraq were forced to accept a central government. The 1958 Iraqi coup originally recognized the Kurds and called for a binational state, but the rise of Kurdish nationalist movements led to clashes with the government throughout the 1970s. Kurdish opposition to the Baath Party began to consolidate in the 1980s. After the 1990 invasion of Kuwait, the Kurds were protected by a northern "no-fly zone," in a U.S. plan called Operation Provide Comfort (OPC). The Kurds maintained their autonomy, which included their own language and currency, until the events of 2003 reopened the debate about their future in Iraq. They had been U.S. allies throughout this period, so their position in the constitution, government insitutions, and everyday political life was bound to be favorable, despite their status as a minority group and their distance from Baghdad politics. In fact, the country's first elected president was Jalal Talibani, a Kurd from the Patriotic Union of Kurdistan (PUK). In the constitution, the Kurds were able to secure the elevation of the Kurdish langage to an official language of Iraq and to gain recognition of Kurdistan under a federal system. They were at the forefront of the political process and by 2006 were able to reach a unity agreement in the Kurdish region for the Kurdistan Regional Government, which was composed of several political parties and blocs.

# KURDISTAN REGIONAL GOVERNMENT UNIFICATION AGREEMENT, JANUARY 21, 2006

For these reasons, The Kurdistan Democratic Party (KDP) and the Patriotic Union of Kurdistan (PUK), on the basis of partnership, consensus and equity, agreed to the following:

1. A new post of Vice President of the Region will be established by amendment to the Law of the Presidency of the Region. The Vice President will be from the PUK and will also serve as the Deputy Commander-in-Chief of the Peshmerga forces of the Kurdistan Region.
2. The Prime Minister and his Deputy will be identified by the Kurdistan National Assembly (KNA) and will be charged by the President of the Kurdistan Region with forming a joint cabinet. The Prime Minister will submit the names of his cabinet to the KNA.
3. The Speaker of the KNA will be from the PUK and the Prime Minister will be from the KDP until the next election of the KNA at the end of 2007. For the next election, the KDP and PUK will participate in a joint slate as equals, and at that time the post of the Speaker of the KNA will go to the KDP and the Prime Minister will be from the PUK. This will be for two years. After that, the KDP and PUK will rotate the posts of Speaker and Prime Minister. If by the end of 2007 elections are not conducted due to delay, the posts of Speaker and Prime Minster will rotate.
4. If either of the ministerial blocs withdraws from the joint cabinet, the entire cabinet will be considered as resigned.
5. The ministerial posts will be divided as follows:
    a) The Ministers of Interior, Justice, Education, Health, Social Affairs, Religious Affairs, Water Resources, Transportation, Reconstruction, Planning, and Human Rights will be from the PUK.
    b) The Ministers of Finance, Peshmerga Affairs, Higher Education, Agriculture, Martyrs, Culture, Electricity, Natural Resources, Municipalities, Sports and Youth, and Minister of Region for the affairs of areas outside the Region will be from the KDP.
    c) The remaining ministries will be assigned to other parties of the Kurdistan Region.
    d) The Ministries of Finance, Peshmerga Affairs, Justice, and Interior should unite within one year. These four ministries, until they unite, will have both a cabinet minister and a minister of the region for the affairs of the concerned ministry. Each minister will have responsibility for the part of the ministry which is currently under their control.
6. The budget of 2006 will be managed as it has been decided, but the share of the budget of the Presidency of the Kurdistan Region, the KNA, the Council of Ministers, and the Judicial Council, and any other joint items from each side will be allocated equally. Afterwards, in the coming years, the Kurdistan regional budget will be prepared by the unified

KRG and submitted to the KNA. After approval, the budget will be allocated to various areas according to population percentage and agreement within the unified KRG.

7. Under the auspices of the Presidency of the Kurdistan Region there will be established a Supreme Commission to institutionalize the police and security agencies of the Kurdistan Region. These united agencies will be removed from political considerations. After the unified KRG takes office in the capital of the Kurdistan Region, Erbil, a special program will be instituted for university graduates with the aim of recruiting new candidates to the security services of the governorates for the sake of unification and re-establishment of these important agencies for our people.

8. The KRG representations abroad, according to agreement of both the KDP and PUK, will be assigned by the Prime Minster and his Deputy.

9. In all the Governorates of the Kurdistan Region a joint committee will be established between the KDP and PUK to resolve issues as they may arise.

10. Both sides, KDP and PUK, will present Mr. Jalal Talabani as their candidate for the sovereign post in the Iraqi Federal Government.

*Masoud Barzani, President, KDP*
*Jalal Talabani, Secretary General, PU*


# DOCUMENT 6.12

Levels of Sunni participation in the state-building process in Iraq were lower than those of other groups due to Sunni resistance to the changes in Iraq's power structure after 2003. In fact, they were in a major battle with the government regarding the remnants of the de-Baathification order, which had disenfranchised hundreds of thousands of innocent Iraqis, deprived many Sunnis of their jobs, and depleted Iraq's political and social infrastructure in 2003.

The Sunnis had been in power in Iraq since the military coup of 1958 that overthrew the monarchy. The Baath coup of 1968 further consolidated their power and status, at the expense of both the Kurds and the Shia. The Kurds and some Shia welcomed the U.S. invasion, but the Sunnis were vehemently opposed, since they had wielded the most power under Saddam Hussein's regime. Initially unwilling to share power with the Kurds and Shia, they boycotted the political process until December 2005. The Sunnis remained extremely cautious about sharing power and repeatedly criticized what they described as other factions' attempts to monopolize power. The major Sunni bloc, the National Concord Front, withdrew its ministers from government in a yearlong boycott from July 2007 until July 2008, in hopes of gaining more power in parliament.

A look at the legislative process in Iraq as of February 2008 showed some signs of hope for the Sunnis, although some questions remained unresolved. The most significant piece of legislation, the Accountability and Justice Law, also known as "de-Baathification reform," was passed unanimously in 2008. It set limits to the former, sweeping de-Baathification order (4.6), leading to the reinstatement of lower-ranking Baathists. Other facets of the law were viewed unfavorably by the Sunnis, such as the continuation of a committee that scrutinized rehired Iraqis.[8]

## LAW OF THE SUPREME NATIONAL COMMISSION FOR ACCOUNTABILITY AND JUSTICE, JANUARY 12, 2008 (EXCERPT)

*Article 1*
For the purposes of this law, the following terms shall have the meanings assigned to them hereunder:

First: "The Commission": The Supreme National Commission for Accountability and Justice.

Second: "The Commission Prosecutor": is in charge of supervising crime investigations and collecting evidence, as well as taking all necessary steps to uncover crimes.

| 327

Third: "The Cassation Chamber": is the competent body of the cassation court in charge of applying the law of The Supreme National Commission for Accountability and Justice.

Fourth: "De-Ba'athification": The procedures taken by the Commission in accordance with the provisions of this Law in order to intellectually, administratively, politically, culturally and economically dismantle the Ba'ath Party system in Iraqi society, state institutions, and civil society institutions.

Fifth: "Ba'ath Party": The Arab Ba'ath Socialist Party" which took power on 17/07/1968 and [was] prohibited by article (7) of the Iraqi constitution.

Sixth: "Member": Any individual who joined the Ba'ath Party and gave an oath of allegiance to it.

Seventh: "The defunct regime": The ruling regime in Iraq from 17 July, 1968 to 9 April, 2003.

Eighth: "The security (repressive) agencies": The following agencies during the defunct regime: General Security [al-amn al-'aam], Intelligence [mukhabarat], Special Security [al-amn al-khas], Special Guards [al-hamayat al-khassa], National Security [al-amn al-qawmy], Military Security [al-amn al-'askary], Military Intelligence [al-istikhbarat al-askariyya] and Feda'iyee Saddam.

---

8. This unofficial translation of the law is courtesy of the International Center for Transitional Justice.

Ninth: "Collaborators of the regime": are the members of the Ba'ath Party, the members of the Repressive Agencies, those cooperating with them, or those who benefited from the plunder of the wealth of the country; and were used by the defunct regime to kill, oppress and persecute people.

Tenth: "Security ministries and agencies": (Ministries of Defence, Interior and National Security, the Intelligence Agency and the National Security Advisor and all the other security agencies).

## CHAPTER II: ESTABLISHMENT AND OBJECTIVES

*Article 2*

First: In accordance with this law, the designation Supreme National Commission for Accountability and Justice shall replace the designation Supreme National Council for De-Ba'athification. It shall be a financially and administratively independent body that has all the constitutional prerogatives and enjoys the same legal personality as the previous body. It is linked to the Council of Representatives and shall pursue its works in coordination with the judicial authority and the executive agencies. . . .

Third: The Chairperson of the Commission shall be responsible for the execution of its policies and tasks, and the supervision and follow up of its works. He shall have the right to adopt the necessary decisions, directives and instructions to enforce the work of the Commission and achieve its goals. The Chairperson shall practice all the powers vested in him and shall be at the rank of a minister. He shall be entitled to delegate part of his powers that can be delegated in accordance with the law to his deputy, who shall be at the level of a Deputy Minister.

Fourth: The Commission shall be made up of seven politically and legally experienced members who will have the rank of Director General. The components of the Iraqi society should be represented in the Commission to ensure a balanced composition. This shall be conducted through a proposal from the Council of Ministers, a simple majority approval by the Council of the Representatives and ratification by the Presidency Council. . . .

Eighth: Members of the Commission must:

a. be an Iraqi citizen, legally competent and residing in Iraq;
b. hold a first university degree;
c. not be less than 35-year old;
d. not have been convicted of an offence "prejudicial to honour";
e. not be included in the De-Ba'athification procedures.
f. not be one of the collaborators of the defunct regime or proven to have enriched himself at the expense of public funds.
g. To be honest, of good reputation and integrity.

Ninth: A cassation chamber shall be formed in the court of cassation called "The Cassation Chamber for Accountability and Justice," to be comprised of seven judges nominated by the Higher Judicial Council, ratified by the

Council of Representatives. They shall be headed by the senior judge among them; its decisions shall be by a majority of four votes.

Tenth: The Cassation Chamber shall consider all the claims filed by those who are subject to the stipulated procedures in this law.

Eleventh: The Chamber's headquarters shall be in Baghdad, and the Chamber may open branches inside Iraq.

*Article 3*

The Commission shall aim to realize the following:

First: Prevent the return of the Ba'ath Party to power or to the public life in Iraq whether in its ideas, culture, administration, policies or acts under any name.

Second: Cleanse state institutions, mixed sector institutions, civil society institutions and Iraqi society from any shape or form of the Ba'ath party system.

Third: Refer any member of the dissolved Ba'ath party and repressive agencies, who is incriminated through investigations of committing criminal acts against the Iraqi people, to the competent courts to be fairly dealt with.

Fourth: Enable the victims of the dissolved Ba'ath party and the repressive agencies to claim compensation for the damages that have resulted from such crimes by referring to the competent authorities.

Fifth: Participate in revealing the assets which were illegally seized by elements of the former regime whether inside or outside the country and return it back to the public treasury.

Sixth: Serve the Iraqi memory by documenting all of the crimes and illegal practices committed by members of the Ba'ath party and its repressive agencies and provide a database regarding those elements in order to strengthen the future generations against falling into oppression, tyranny and repression. . . .

## CHAPTER THREE: THE TASKS OF THE COMMISSION

*Article 4*

In order to achieve its goals, the Commission shall adopt the following tasks and means: . . .

Second: Submit evidence and documents available to the Commission concerning the crimes committed by the elements of the Ba'ath Party and its repressive agencies against the citizens to the Iraqi judiciary through the office of the Public Prosecutor. . . .

Fourth: Provide necessary recommendations and studies through coordination with the relevant bodies in order to amend or abolish legislations adopted by the dissolved regime which were specifically adopted for the benefit the elements of that regime excluding other segments of the Iraqi people.

It shall work particularly to achieve the following:

a. Finalize the identification of individuals included in the De-Ba'athification procedures within the period of the Commission's work and to publish a list of the De-Ba'athification procedures stipulated in this Law. The list shall contain names of all individuals subject to these procedures indicating the rank of each and the date of issuing the relevant De-Ba'athification order. This list shall be kept in the dissolved Ba'ath Party archives.
b. All files of the Dissolved Ba'ath Party shall be transferred to the Government in order to be kept until a permanent Iraqi archive is established pursuant to the law.
c. To contribute to the developing of social and cultural programs that reaffirm political pluralism, tolerance and equality, and at the same time condemns the crimes and atrocities committed by the previous regime as well as the culture of one-party system, marginalization and exclusion.

*Article 5*
The Commission shall implement its decisions and directions through establishing a specific mechanism to implement its procedures that includes "investigating the identity", "written innocence" and the commitment to refrain from resuming any party-related activity in any shape or form in accordance with the provisions of this Law.

## CHAPTER FOUR: "PROCEDURES"

*Article 6*
The Commission shall follow the following procedures against those who were members of the Ba'ath Party and the repressive agencies before 09/04/2003 in order to realize the goals of the Commission and accomplish its mission:

First: Dismiss all employees who were at the rank of section member shu'ba and refer them to retirement in accordance with the Employment and Retirement Law.

Second: All civil servants occupying any of the special levels (equivalent to or above Director General) who were at the rank of group member in the Ba'ath Party adw firqa shall be referred to retirement in accordance with the Employment and Retirement Law.

Third: End the service of all the members of the (repressive) security agencies and refer them to retirement in accordance with the Employment and Retirement Law.

Fourth: Feda'iyee Saddam shall not be allowed to benefit from any pension/retirement rights that may arise from their service the mentioned agency.

Fifth: All employees who did not occupy "special levels" posts and who were holding the rank of group member adw firqa or below in the Ba'ath

Party, shall be allowed to return to their previous departments or remain in their jobs.

Sixth: Group members adw firqa shall not be allowed to return to service or remain in their service in the three leadership bodies: the Supreme Judicial Council, security ministries and agencies, and the Ministries of Foreign Affairs, and Finance.

Seventh: Pensions or grants shall not be paid to any person who was a member of the dissolved Ba'ath party after 3/20/2003, and was granted political or humanitarian asylum in any country.

Eighth: Anyone who occupied the rank of member and above in the Ba'ath party and enriched himself at the expense of public funds shall not be allowed to hold special levels posts, equivalent to and above Director General and Director of Administrative Units [Ed: technical term used to denote district leaders, mayors, and governors.]

Ninth: All those not covered by the Employment and Retirement Law shall be assigned to work in government institutions except the three leadership bodies, ministries, security forces, and the foreign and finance ministries. . . .

Tenth: Anyone judicially proven to have committed crimes against the Iraqi People and gained wealth at the expense of public funds will lose all rights stated in the previous paragraphs

| 331

## Article 7
First: All persons eligible for retirement under the provision of Article 6 of this law shall submit official requests to be referred to retirement during 60 days from date this law comes into force, for those who are inside Iraq, and 90 days for those who are abroad, otherwise their pension rights shall become null and void.

Second: All person who are eligible under the provisions of Article 6 of this law for return to their jobs shall submit official requests to return to their jobs within 60 days from the date this law comes into force, for those who are inside Iraq, and 90 days for those who are abroad, otherwise their rights of return to their jobs shall become null and void.

## Article 8
Any former member of the dissolved Ba'ath Party who benefited from this law and was later found by a judicial decision that he submitted false information, joined or returned to organizations of the banned parties, provided assistance or promoted these parties; shall be deprived of all the exceptions and rights and dismissed from service for dishonorable conduct. He shall be requested before the judiciary to reimburse all the entitlements and money that he received. . . .

Any member (of any ranks) of the Ba'ath Party, the repressive agencies or the armed forces, who committed crimes against the Iraqi people or gained wealth at the expense of the public money, shall be referred to the court to be duly prosecuted for their crimes against the Iraqi population.

### Article 11

The dissolved Ba'ath party shall be prosecuted as a party and a system for committing crimes against the Iraqi people.

### Article 12

The Council of Ministers has the right to consider and examine the exceptional cases of reappointment for those who are covered by this law and in accordance with the requirements of the public interest, upon the request of the competent minister and in coordination with the Commission. The Council of Ministers shall take appropriate decisions on these cases which can only come into force after the approval of the Council of Representatives. . . .

### Article 14

The Public Prosecutor shall receive complaints regarding crimes attributed to the members of the Ba'ath Party, the repressive agencies and the "collaborators" of the defunct regime and initiate legal proceeding before the competent courts when probative evidence is available.

## CHAPTER FIVE: (OBJECTIONS)

### Article 15

All persons covered by the provisions of Article 6 of this law, the departments they have joined, the Governorate Council and the government of the province in which the department is located and the office of the public prosecutor of the Commission shall have the right to appeal against the decisions issued by the Commission before the Cassation Chamber within 30 days from the notification of the decision to the concerned person or the date on which he/she is considered notified, in accordance with the notification rules of the Code of Civil Procedure.

### Article 16

Civil servants subject to the procedures of Article 6 of this law by virtue of a decision issued by the Commission shall be considered on a normal leave with full pay during the period in which they are entitled to submit an appeal and until the final decision of the Cassation Chamber in accordance with Article 17 of this Law.

### Article 17

The Cassation Chamber shall issue its final decision on the appeal it receives within a period of sixty 60 days. The decisions shall be final and definitive. . . .

## CHAPTER SEVEN: GENERAL AND FINAL PROVISIONS

*Necessitating Reasons/Justification of the Law*

This law was legislated due to:

The suffering of Iraqis over 35 years during which they were subjected to the worst kinds of persecution, oppression and deprivation on the hands of the most totalitarian, aggressive and criminal of regimes.

The major role that was played by the Ba'athist leadership of that regime and those who worked in its repressive agencies in oppressing the Iraqi people and attempting to weaken their sense of citizenship and national identity.

Taking into consideration the evident sense of serious concern by the Iraqis towards the risk that is represented by the continuation of the participation of the dissolved Ba'ath party and its elements in public life.

Awareness of the pressing necessity to refer elements of the dissolved party who are proved to have committed crimes against Iraq and its people to the relevant courts to receive their fair punishment.

Enable those affected by the Ba'ath party and the repressive agencies to go to relevant courts to seek compensation for damages that were inflected upon them as a result of illegal practices by the Party and the mentioned authorities.

Take into consideration the existence of bogus memberships in the Party of some segments of the populations who do not believe in the Ba'ath dictatorial ideas and its oppressive practices.

Continue the procedures taken by the Supreme National Independent Commission for De-Ba'athification to cleanse the Iraqi society and the State institutions from the dissolved Ba'ath party system.

The desire to document intricate details about groups covered by the De-Ba'athifcation procedures in order to establish a database that would constitute a historic reference to the crimes and atrocities of the dissolved party and Saddam's regime and the extent of the suffering of the people as a result of the practices of the mentioned party.

THIS LAW WAS ENACTED

# DOCUMENT 6.13

By late 2008, Iraqi politicians and clerics had fallen into an alternating pattern of participation in and boycott of the Iraqi government. Although this was partly due to the ongoing civil war and tensions among the groups, lingering U.S. involvement seemed to fuel the disagreements. Ayatollah Sistani's position was that Iraqis should be responsible for their own affairs, especially regarding any long-term pact with the United States, which would likely result in a permanent U.S. presence in Iraq. He was most concerned with safeguarding Iraqis' interests on issues of national sovereignty, national consensus, and parliamentary approval. As the relationship with the United States hovered over their country after 2003, Iraqis remained committed to continue the dialogue among each other.

---

## HELSINKI AGREEMENT, SEPTEMBER 2007

Feuding Shiite and Iraqi groups agreed to meet and discuss the deadlock in determining permanent statehood. These talks took place on Helsinki, Finland surrounding the topic of national reconciliation and resulted in the Helsinki Agreement in September 2007. The participants agreed to the secret talks in order to discuss a more robust framework for statehood. Among the sixteen delegates in attendance were some major players—Nuri al-Maliki (Prime Minister, Shiite), Tariq al-Hashemi (one of two Vice Presidents, Sunni), Muqtada al-Sadr ('fiery' anti-American cleric, Shiite), Abdul-Aziz al-Hakim (head of the largest Shiite coalition), Jalal Talabani (President of Iraq, Kurd, Qadiri Sufi sect of Sunnism), and Massoud Barzani (President of Iraqi Kurdistan, Naqshbandi Sufi sect of Sunnisim). This meeting followed a series of issues in parliament as some blocs returned to parliament only to withdraw, resulting in the forming of new coalitions, and deadlock. This resulted in boycotts of cabinet meetings and full withdrawals of some blocs from government, which became a pattern of politics in Iraqi government. This statement was a commitment to return to the principles of unity.

Representatives of Iraqi parties and blocs held discussions in Finland from August 31 through September 3, 2007 and agreed to consult further on the following recommendations to start negotiations to reach national reconciliation:

1   To resolve all political issues through non-violence and democracy.
2   To prohibit the use of arms for all armed groups during the process of negotiations.
3   To form an independent commission approved by all parties, its task being to supervise the process of disarmament of non-governmental armed groups in a verifiable manner.
4   All parties will commit to accept the results of the negotiations and no party can be subject to a threat of force from any groups that reject all or part of any agreement reached.
5   To work to end international and regional interference in internal Iraqi affairs.
6   To commit to protect human rights.
7   To assure the independence and efficiency of the legal and justice systems, especially the constitutional court.
8   To ensure the full participation of all Iraqi parties and blocs in the political process and agreed governance arrangements.

9 To take all necessary steps to end all violence, killings, forced displacement and any further damage to infrastructure.

10 To establish an independent consultative body to explore ways to deal with the legacy of the past in a way that will unite the nation.

11 All Iraqi parties and blocs have to build Iraq and contribute efficiently to support all the efforts that would make the political process and Iraqi unity successful and to preserve its sovereignty.

12 All participating groups must commit to all of the principles listed here as a complete system of rules.

Political Objectives:

13 To be rational in political speeches, for the national interest, and to move away from sectarian and ethnic dispute.

14 To bring an end to the displacement of Iraqi people and work to take care of those displaced, and secure their safe return, with guarantees of their safety by the national forces in co-operation with political parties and tribal leaders.

15 To deal with the subject of militias under the following procedures:

| 335

A Arming, supplying, training and making sure that the security forces (army/police) are capable of undertaking their duties efficiently. Make sure that the security forces are equipped to adequate levels to achieve an effective national force.

B Activation of economic development across the country, to contain youth unemployment and use the efforts of young people to rebuild in order to improve the quality of life for all citizens.

C Those working outside the law and using military resources inappropriately shall be brought to justice, with no differentiation.

16 The emphasis on the common vision for all Iraqi political entities on the importance of termination of the presence of foreign troops in Iraq through the completion of national sovereignty and rebuilding a national army and security apparatus according to a national vision within a realistic timetable.

17 An emphasis on the continuation of constructive dialogue between different political groups aiming to fulfill national goals.

18 To convince political groups that are currently outside the political process to initiate and activate a constructive dialogue to reach common understandings.

19 To deal with armed groups which are not classified as terrorist, encouraging them to use peaceful political means to address the conflict and to provide their members with jobs and opportunities within state administrations.

20 Working towards correcting the misunderstanding that accompanied the political process and encourage all Iraqi political parties to participate in building Iraq in all aspects.
21 The cessation of the violation of the human rights of Iraqi citizens and their properties by continuous bombardment and military actions by foreign forces. The Iraqi government must take responsibility to protect innocent civilians.

# Joint U.S.–Iraqi Documents

## DOCUMENT 6.14

The Status of Forces Agreement was signed by Iraqi and U.S. officials on November 17, 2008. The agreement was initiated to replace the UN mandate authorizing the presence of foreign forces, which was due to expire at the end of 2008 (4.5). It stated that U.S. combat forces would leave Iraq by June 2009, with the remaining forces out by December 31, 2011. The SOFA included provisions on the holding of prisoners and the use of warrants for searches. It stated that contractors for U.S. forces would be subject to Iraqi criminal law. However, contractors for the State Department and other agencies would retain immunity from Iraqi law, a provision that caused much controversy.

Many Iraqis criticized the agreement as demonstrations ripped through Iraq before and after its signing. Some critics argued that the language of the SOFA had many loopholes, was open to interpretation, and was subject to further amendments and negotiations. Grand Ayatollah Sistani was vocal about its limitations on Iraqi sovereignty, as Iraq would not be able to properly control its borders and shipments. Moreover, Iraq had to compromise on an expansive immunity clause and, most importantly, the agreement did not guarantee full Iraqi sovereignty.

AGREEMENT BETWEEN THE UNITED STATES OF AMERICA AND THE REPUBLIC OF IRAQ ON THE WITHDRAWAL OF THE UNITED STATES FORCES FROM IRAQ AND THE ORGANIZATION OF THEIR ACTIVITIES DURING THEIR TEMPORARY PRESENCE IN IRAQ, NOVEMBER 17, 2008 (EXCERPT)

Preamble
The United States of America and the Republic of Iraq, referred to hereafter as "the Parties": Recognizing the importance of: strengthening their joint security, contributing to world peace and stability, combating terrorism in

Iraq, and cooperating in the security and defense spheres, thereby deterring aggression and threats against the sovereignty, security, and territorial integrity of Iraq and against its democratic, federal, and constitutional system;

Affirming that such cooperation is based on full respect for the sovereignty of each of them in accordance with the purposes and principles of the United Nations Charter;

Out of a desire to reach a common understanding that strengthens cooperation between them;

Without prejudice to Iraqi sovereignty over its territory, waters, and airspace; and Pursuant to joint undertakings as two sovereign, independent, and coequal countries;

Have agreed to the following:

*Article 1: Scope and Purpose*
This Agreement shall determine the principal provisions and requirements that regulate the temporary presence, activities, and withdrawal of the United States Forces from Iraq. . . .

*Article 2: Definition of Terms*
   . . . 2. "United States Forces" means the entity comprising the members of the United States Armed Forces, their associated civilian component, and all property, equipment, and materiel of the United States Armed Forces present in the territory of Iraq.

   3. "Member of the United States Forces" means any individual who is a member of the United States Army, Navy, Air Force, Marine Corps, or Coast Guard.

   4. "Member of the civilian component" means any civilian employed by the United States Department of Defense. This term does not include individuals normally resident in Iraq. . . .

   5. "United States contractors" and "United States contractor employees" mean non-Iraqi persons or legal entities, and their employees, who are citizens of the United States or a third country and who are in Iraq to supply goods, services, and security in Iraq to or on behalf of the United States Forces under a contract or subcontract with or for the United States Forces.

However, the terms do not include persons or legal entities normally resident in the territory of Iraq. . . . .

*Article 3: Laws*
   1. While conducting military operations pursuant to this Agreement, it is the duty of members of the United States Forces and of the civilian component to respect Iraqi laws, customs, traditions, and conventions and to refrain from any activities that are inconsistent with the letter and spirit of this Agreement. It is the

| 337

duty of the United States to take all necessary measures for this purpose.

2. With the exception of members of the United States Forces and of the civilian component, the United States Forces may not transfer any person into or out of Iraq on vehicles, vessels, or aircraft covered by this Agreement, unless in accordance with applicable Iraqi laws and regulations, including implementing arrangements as may be agreed to by the Government of Iraq.

*Article 4: Missions*

1. The Government of Iraq requests the temporary assistance of the United States Forces for the purposes of supporting Iraq in its efforts to maintain security and stability in Iraq, including cooperation in the conduct of operations against al-Qaeda and other terrorist groups, outlaw groups, and remnants of the former regime.

2. All such military operations that are carried out pursuant to this Agreement shall be conducted with the agreement of the Government of Iraq. Such operations shall be fully coordinated with Iraqi authorities. The coordination of all such military operations shall be overseen by a Joint Military Operations Coordination Committee (JMOCC) to be established pursuant to this Agreement. Issues regarding proposed military operations that cannot be resolved by the JMOCC shall be forwarded to the Joint Ministerial Committee.

3. All such operations shall be conducted with full respect for the Iraqi Constitution and the laws of Iraq. Execution of such operations shall not infringe upon the sovereignty of Iraq and its national interests, as defined by the Government of Iraq. It is the duty of the United States Forces to respect the laws, customs, and traditions of Iraq and applicable international law.

4. The Parties shall continue their efforts to cooperate to strengthen Iraq's security capabilities including, as may be mutually agreed, on training, equipping, supporting, supplying, and establishing and upgrading logistical systems, including transportation, housing, and supplies for Iraqi Security Forces.

5. The Parties retain the right to legitimate self defense within Iraq, as defined in applicable international law.

*Article 5: Property Ownership*

. . . 2. Upon their withdrawal, the United States Forces shall return to the Government of Iraq all the facilities and areas provided for the use of the combat forces of the United States, based on two lists. The first list of agreed facilities and areas shall take effect upon the entry into force of the Agreement. The second list shall take effect no later than June 30, 2009, the date for the withdrawal of combat forces from the cities, villages, and localities. The Government of Iraq may agree to allow the United States Forces the use of some necessary facilities for the purposes of this Agreement on withdrawal.

3. The United States shall bear all costs for construction, alterations, or improvements in the agreed facilities and areas provided for its exclusive use. The United States Forces shall consult with the Government of Iraq regarding such construction, alterations, and improvements, and must seek approval of the Government of Iraq for major construction and alteration projects. In the event that the use of agreed facilities and areas is shared, the two Parties shall bear the costs of construction, alterations, or improvements proportionately.

4. The United States shall be responsible for paying the costs for services requested and received in the agreed facilities and areas exclusively used by it, and both Parties shall be proportionally responsible for paying the costs for services requested and received in joint agreed facilities and areas. . . .

## Article 6: Use of Agreed Facilities and Areas

1. With full respect for the sovereignty of Iraq, and as part of exchanging views between the Parties pursuant to this Agreement, Iraq grants access and use of agreed facilities and areas to the United States Forces, United States contractors, United States contractor employees, and other individuals or entities as agreed upon by the Parties.

2. In accordance with this Agreement, Iraq authorizes the United States Forces to exercise within the agreed facilities and areas all rights and powers that may be necessary to establish, use, maintain, and secure such agreed facilities and areas. The Parties shall coordinate and cooperate regarding exercising these rights and powers in the agreed facilities and areas of joint use.

3. The United States Forces shall assume control of entry to agreed facilities and areas that have been provided for its exclusive use. The Parties shall coordinate the control of entry into agreed facilities and areas for joint use and in accordance with mechanisms set forth by the JMOCC. The Parties shall coordinate guard duties in areas adjacent to agreed facilities and areas through the JMOCC. . . .

## Article 8: Protecting the Environment

Both Parties shall implement this Agreement in a manner consistent with protecting the natural environment and human health and safety. The United States reaffirms its commitment to respecting applicable Iraqi environmental laws, regulations, and standards in the course of executing its policies for the purposes of implementing this Agreement.

*Article 9: Movement of Vehicles, Vessels, and Aircraft*

. . . 2. With full respect for relevant rules of safety in aviation and air navigation, United States Government aircraft and civil aircraft that are at the time operating exclusively under a contract with the United States Department of Defense are authorized to over-fly, conduct airborne refueling exclusively for the purposes of implementing this Agreement over, and land and take off within, the territory of Iraq for the purposes of implementing this Agreement. The Iraqi authorities shall grant the aforementioned aircraft permission every year to land in and take off from Iraqi territory exclusively for the purposes of implementing this Agreement. United States Government aircraft and civil aircraft that are at the time operating exclusively under a contract with the United States Department of Defense, vessels, and vehicles shall not have any party boarding them without the consent of the authorities of the United States Forces. The Joint Sub-Committee concerned with this matter shall take appropriate action to facilitate the regulation of such traffic.

3. Surveillance and control over Iraqi airspace shall transfer to Iraqi authority immediately upon entry into force of this Agreement.

4. Iraq may request from the United States Forces temporary support for the Iraqi authorities in the mission of surveillance and control of Iraqi air space.

5. United States Government aircraft and civil aircraft that are at the time operating exclusively under contract to the United States Department of Defense shall not be subject to payment of any taxes, duties, fees, or similar charges, including overflight or navigation fees, landing, and parking fees at government airfields. Vehicles and vessels owned or operated by or at the time exclusively for the United States Forces shall not be subject to payment of any taxes, duties, fees, or similar charges, including for vessels at government ports. Such vehicles, vessels, and aircraft shall be free from registration requirements within Iraq. . . .

*Article 10: Contracting Procedures*

The United States Forces may select contractors and enter into contracts in accordance with United States law for the purchase of materials and services in Iraq, including services of construction and building. The United States Forces shall contract with Iraqi suppliers of materials and services to the extent feasible when their bids are competitive and constitute best value. The United States Forces shall respect Iraqi law when contracting with Iraqi suppliers and contractors and shall provide Iraqi authorities with the names of Iraqi suppliers and contractors, and the amounts of relevant contracts.

### Article 11: Services and Communications

1. The United States Forces may produce and provide water, electricity, and other services to agreed facilities and areas in coordination with the Iraqi authorities through the Joint Sub-Committee concerned with this matter. . . .

3. The United States Forces shall operate their own telecommunications systems in a manner that fully respects the Constitution and laws of Iraq and in accordance with the definition of the term "telecommunications" contained in the Constitution of the International Union of Telecommunications of 1992, including the right to use necessary means and services of their own systems to ensure the full capability to operate systems of telecommunications.

4. For the purposes of this Agreement, the United States Forces are exempt from the payment of fees to use transmission airwaves and existing and future frequencies, including any administrative fees or any other related charges.

5. The United States Forces must obtain the consent of the Government of Iraq regarding any projects of infrastructure for communications that are made outside agreed facilities and areas exclusively for the purposes of this Agreement in accordance with Article 4, except in the case of actual combat operations conducted pursuant to Article 4.

6. The United States Forces shall use telecommunications systems exclusively for the purposes of this Agreement.

### Article 12: Jurisdiction

Recognizing Iraq's sovereign right to determine and enforce the rules of criminal and civil law in its territory, in light of Iraq's request for temporary assistance from the United States Forces set forth in Article 4, and consistent with the duty of the members of the United States Forces and the civilian component to respect Iraqi laws, customs, traditions, and conventions, the Parties have agreed as follows:

Iraq shall have the primary right to exercise jurisdiction over members of the United States Forces and of the civilian component for the grave premeditated felonies enumerated pursuant to paragraph 8, when such crimes are committed outside agreed facilities and areas and outside duty status. Iraq shall have the primary right to exercise jurisdiction over United States contractors and United States contractor employees. The United States shall have the primary right to exercise jurisdiction over members of the United States Forces and of the civilian component for matters arising inside agreed facilities and areas; during duty status outside agreed facilities and areas;

and in circumstances not covered by paragraph 1. At the request of either Party, the Parties shall assist each other in the investigation of incidents and the collection and exchange of evidence to ensure the due course of justice. Members of the United States Forces and of the civilian component arrested or detained by Iraqi authorities shall be notified immediately to United States Forces authorities and handed over to them within 24 hours from the time of detention or arrest. Where Iraq exercises jurisdiction pursuant to paragraph 1 of this Article, custody of an accused member of the United States Forces or of the civilian component shall reside with United States Forces authorities. United States Forces authorities shall make such accused persons available to the Iraqi authorities for purposes of investigation and trial.

The authorities of either Party may request the authorities of the other Party to waive its primary right to jurisdiction in a particular case. The Government of Iraq agrees to exercise jurisdiction under paragraph 1 above, only after it has determined and notifies the United States in writing within 21 days of the discovery of an alleged offense, that it is of particular importance that such jurisdiction be exercised.

  . . . 7. Where the United States exercises jurisdiction pursuant to paragraph 3 of this Article, members of the United States Forces and of the civilian component shall be entitled to due process standards and protections pursuant to the Constitution and laws of the United States. Where the offense arising under paragraph 3 of this Article may involve a victim who is not a member of the United States Forces or of the civilian component, the Parties shall establish procedures through the Joint Committee to keep such persons informed as appropriate of: the status of the investigation of the crime; the bringing of charges against a suspected offender; the scheduling of court proceedings and the results of plea negotiations; opportunity to be heard at public sentencing proceedings, and to confer with the attorney for the prosecution in the case; and, assistance with filing a claim under Article 21 of this Agreement. As mutually agreed by the Parties, United States Forces authorities shall seek to hold the trials of such cases inside Iraq. If the trial of such cases is to be conducted in the United States, efforts will be undertaken to facilitate the personal attendance of the victim at the trial.

   8.  Where Iraq exercises jurisdiction pursuant to paragraph 1 of this Article, members of the United States Forces and of the civilian component shall be entitled to due process Standards and protections consistent with those available under United States and Iraqi law. The Joint Committee shall establish procedures and mechanisms for implementing this Article, including an enu-

meration of the grave premeditated felonies that are subject to
paragraph 1 and procedures that meet such due process standards and protections. Any exercise of jurisdiction pursuant to
paragraph 1 of this Article may proceed only in accordance with
these procedures and mechanisms.

9. Pursuant to paragraphs 1 and 3 of this Article, United States
   Forces authorities shall certify whether an alleged offense arose
   during duty status. In those cases where Iraqi authorities believe
   the circumstances require a review of this determination, the
   Parties shall consult immediately through the Joint Committee,
   and United States Forces authorities shall take full account of
   the facts and circumstances and any information Iraqi authorities may present bearing on the determination by United States
   Forces authorities.

10. The Parties shall review the provisions of this Article every 6
    months including by considering any proposed amendments to
    this Article taking into account the security situation in Iraq, the
    extent to which the United States Forces in Iraq are engaged in
    military operations, the growth and development of the Iraqi
    judicial system, and changes in United States and Iraqi law.

*Article 13: Carrying Weapons and Apparel*  | 343
Members of the United States Forces and of the civilian component may
possess and carry weapons that are owned by the United States while in
Iraq according to the authority granted to them under orders and according to their requirements and duties. Members of the United States Forces
may also wear uniforms during duty in Iraq.

*Article 14: Entry and Exit*

1. For purposes of this Agreement, members of the United States
   Forces and of the civilian component may enter and leave Iraq
   through official places of embarkation and debarkation requiring
   only identification cards and travel orders issued for them by the
   United States. The Joint Committee shall assume the task of setting up a mechanism and a process of verification to be carried
   out by pertinent Iraqi authorities.

2. Iraqi authorities shall have the right to inspect and verify the lists
   of names of members of the United States Forces and of the civilian component entering and leaving Iraq directly through the
   agreed facilities and areas. Said lists shall be submitted to Iraqi
   authorities by the United States Forces. For purposes of this
   Agreement, members of the United States Forces and of the civilian component may enter and leave Iraq through agreed facilities
   and areas requiring only identification cards issued for them by

the United States. The Joint Committee shall assume the task of setting up a mechanism and a process for inspecting and verifying the validity of these documents.

*Article 15: Import and Export*

1. For the exclusive purposes of implementing this Agreement, the United States Forces and United States contractors may import, export (items bought in Iraq), re-export, transport, and use in Iraq any equipment, supplies, materials, and technology, provided that the materials imported or brought in by them are not banned in Iraq as of the date this Agreement enters into force. The importation, re-exportation, transportation, and use of such items shall not be subject to any inspections, licenses, or other restrictions, taxes, customs duties, or any other charges imposed in Iraq, as defined in Article 2, paragraph 10. United States Forces authorities shall provide to relevant Iraqi authorities an appropriate certification that such items are being imported by the United States Forces or United States contractors for use by the United States Forces exclusively for the purposes of this Agreement. Based on security information that becomes available, Iraqi authorities have the right to request the United States Forces to open in their presence any container in which such items are being imported in order to verify its contents. In making such a request, Iraqi authorities shall honor the security requirements of the United States Forces and, if requested to do so by the United States Forces, shall make such verifications in facilities used by the United States Forces. The exportation of Iraqi goods by the United States Forces and United States contractors shall not be subject to inspections or any restrictions other than licensing requirements. The Joint Committee shall work with the Iraqi Ministry of Trade to expedite license requirements consistent with Iraqi law for the export of goods purchased in Iraq by the United States Forces for the purposes of this Agreement. Iraq has the right to demand review of any issues arising out of this paragraph. The Parties shall consult immediately in such cases through the Joint Committee or, if necessary, the Joint Ministerial Committee.

2. Members of the United States Forces and of the civilian component may import into Iraq, re-export, and use personal effect materials and equipment for consumption or personal use. The import into, re-export from, transfer from, and use of such imported items in Iraq shall not be subjected to licenses, other restrictions, taxes, custom duties, or any other charges imposed in Iraq, as defined in Article 2, paragraph 10. The imported quanti-

ties shall be reasonable and proportionate to personal use. United States Forces authorities will take measures to ensure that no items or material of cultural or historic significance to Iraq are being exported. . . .

*Article 16: Taxes*

. . . 2. Members of the United States Forces and of the civilian component shall not be responsible for payment of any tax, duty, or fee that has its value determined and imposed in the territory of Iraq, unless in return for services requested and received. . . .

*Article 19: Support Activities Services*

1. The United States Forces, or others acting on behalf of the United States Forces, may assume the duties of establishing and administering activities and entities inside agreed facilities and areas, through which they can provide services for members of the United States Forces, the civilian component, United States contractors, and United States contractor employees. These entities and activities include military post offices; financial services; shops selling food items, medicine, and other commodities and services; and various areas to provide entertainment and telecommunications services, including radio broadcasts. The establishment of such services does not require permits.

2. Broadcasting, media, and entertainment services that reach beyond the scope of the agreed facilities and areas shall be subject to Iraqi laws.
3. Access to the Support Activities Services shall be limited to members of the United States Forces and of the civilian component, United States contractors, United States contractor employees, and other persons and entities that are agreed upon. The authorities of the United States Forces shall take appropriate actions to prevent misuse of the services provided by the mentioned activities, and prevent the sale or resale of aforementioned goods and services to persons not authorized access to these entities or to benefit from their services. The United States Forces will determine broadcasting and television programs to authorized recipients. . . .

*Article 20: Currency and Foreign Exchange*

1. The United States Forces shall have the right to use any amount of cash in United States currency or financial instruments with a designated value in United States currency exclusively for the purposes of this Agreement. Use of Iraqi currency and special banks by the United States Forces shall be in accordance with Iraqi laws. . . .

*Article 21: Claims*

1. With the exception of claims arising from contracts, each Party shall waive the right to claim compensation against the other Party for any damage, loss, or destruction of property, or compensation for injuries or deaths that could happen to members of the force or civilian component of either Party arising out of the performance of their official duties in Iraq.

2. United States Forces authorities shall pay just and reasonable compensation in settlement of meritorious third party claims arising out of acts, omissions, or negligence of members of the United States Forces and of the civilian component done in the performance of their official duties and incident to the non-combat activities of the United States Forces. United States Forces authorities may also settle meritorious claims not arising from the performance of official duties. All claims in this paragraph shall be settled expeditiously in accordance with the laws and regulations of the United States. In settling claims, United States Forces authorities shall take into account any report of investigation or opinion regarding liability or amount of damages issued by Iraqi authorities. . . .

*Article 22: Detention*

1. No detention or arrest may be carried out by the United States Forces (except with respect to detention or arrest of members of the United States Forces and of the civilian component) except through an Iraqi decision issued in accordance with Iraqi law and pursuant to Article 4.

2. In the event the United States Forces detain or arrest persons as authorized by this Agreement or Iraqi law, such persons must be handed over to competent Iraqi authorities within 24 hours from the time of their detention or arrest.

3. The Iraqi authorities may request assistance from the United States Forces in detaining or arresting wanted individuals.

4. Upon entry into force of this Agreement, the United States Forces shall provide to the Government of Iraq available information on all detainees who are being held by them. Competent Iraqi authorities shall issue arrest warrants for persons who are wanted by them. The United States Forces shall act in full and effective coordination with the Government of Iraq to turn over custody of such wanted detainees to Iraqi authorities pursuant to a valid Iraqi arrest warrant and shall release all the remaining detainees in a safe and orderly manner, unless otherwise requested by the Government of Iraq and in accordance with Article 4 of this Agreement.

5. The United States Forces may not search houses or other real estate properties except by order of an Iraqi judicial warrant and in full coordination with the Government of Iraq, except in the case of actual combat operations conducted pursuant to Article 4. . . .

*Article 24: Withdrawal of the United States Forces from Iraq*
Recognizing the performance and increasing capacity of the Iraqi Security Forces, the assumption of full security responsibility by those Forces, and based upon the strong relationship between the Parties, an agreement on the following has been reached:

1. All the United States Forces shall withdraw from all Iraqi territory no later than December 31, 2011.
2. All United States combat forces shall withdraw from Iraqi cities, villages, and localities no later than the time at which Iraqi Security Forces assume full responsibility for security in an Iraqi province, provided that such withdrawal is completed no later than June 30, 2009.
3. United States combat forces withdrawn pursuant to paragraph 2 above shall be stationed in the agreed facilities and areas outside cities, villages, and localities to be designated by the JMOCC before the date established in paragraph 2 above.
4. The United States recognizes the sovereign right of the Government of Iraq to request the departure of the United States Forces from Iraq at any time. The Government of Iraq recognizes the sovereign right of the United States to withdraw the United States Forces from Iraq at any time.
5. The Parties agree to establish mechanisms and arrangements to reduce the number of the United States Forces during the periods of time that have been determined, and they shall agree on the locations where the United States Forces will be present.

*Article 25: Measures to Terminate the Application of Chapter VII to Iraq*
Acknowledging the right of the Government of Iraq not to request renewal of the Chapter VII authorization for and mandate of the multinational forces contained in United Nations Security Council Resolution 1790 (2007) that ends on December 31, 2008; Taking note of the letters to the UN Security Council from the Prime Minister of Iraq and the Secretary of State of the United States dated December 7 and December 10, 2007, respectively, which are annexed to Resolution 1790; Taking note of section 3 of the Declaration of Principles for a Long-Term Relationship of Cooperation and Friendship, signed by the President of the United States and the Prime Minister of Iraq on November 26, 2007, which memorialized Iraq's call for extension of the above-mentioned mandate for a final period, to end not later than

December 31, 2008: Recognizing also the dramatic and positive developments in Iraq, and noting that the situation in Iraq is fundamentally different than that which existed when the UN Security Council adopted Resolution 661 in 1990, and in particular that the threat to international peace and security posed by the Government of Iraq no longer exists, the Parties affirm in this regard that with the termination on December 31, 2008 of the Chapter VII mandate and authorization for the multinational force contained in Resolution 1790, Iraq should return to the legal and international standing that it enjoyed prior to the adoption of UN Security Council Resolution 661 (1990), and that the United States shall use its best efforts to help Iraq take the steps necessary to achieve this by December 31, 2008.

*Article 26: Iraqi Assets*
1. To enable Iraq to continue to develop its national economy through the rehabilitation of its economic infrastructure, as well as providing necessary essential services to the Iraqi people, and to continue to safeguard Iraq's revenues from oil and gas and other Iraqi resources and its financial and economic assets located abroad, including the Development Fund for Iraq, the United States shall ensure maximum efforts to:
   a. Support Iraq to obtain forgiveness of international debt resulting from the policies of
   b. Support Iraq to achieve a comprehensive and final resolution of outstanding reparation claims inherited from the previous regime, including compensation requirements imposed by the UN Security Council on Iraq.
2. Recognizing and understanding Iraq's concern with claims based on actions perpetrated by the former regime, the President of the United States has exercised his authority to protect from United States judicial process the Development Fund for Iraq and certain other property in which Iraq has an interest. The United States shall remain fully and actively engaged with the Government of Iraq with respect to continuation of such protections and with respect to such claims.
3. Consistent with a letter from the President of the United States to be sent to the Prime Minister of Iraq, the United States remains committed to assist Iraq in connection with its request that the UN Security Council extend the protections and other arrangements established in Resolution 1483 (2003) and Resolution 1546 (2003) for petroleum, petroleum products, and natural gas originating in Iraq, proceeds and obligations from sale thereof, and the Development Fund for Iraq.

*Article 27: Deterrence of Security Threats*
In order to strengthen security and stability in Iraq and to contribute to the maintenance of international peace and stability, the Parties shall work actively to strengthen the political and military capabilities of the Republic of Iraq to deter threats against its sovereignty, political independence, territo-

rial integrity, and its constitutional federal democratic system. To that end, the Parties agree as follows:

In the event of any external or internal threat or aggression against Iraq that would violate its sovereignty, political independence, or territorial integrity, waters, airspace, its democratic system or its elected institutions, and upon request by the Government of Iraq, the Parties shall immediately initiate strategic deliberations and, as may be mutually agreed, the United States shall take appropriate measures, including diplomatic, economic, or military measures, or any other measure, to deter such a threat. The Parties agree to continue close cooperation in strengthening and maintaining military and security institutions and democratic political institutions in Iraq, including, as may be mutually agreed, cooperation in training, equipping, and arming the Iraqi Security Forces, in order to combat domestic and international terrorism and outlaw groups, upon request by the Government of Iraq.

Iraqi land, sea, and air shall not be used as a launching or transit point for attacks against other countries.

*Article 28: The Green Zone*
Upon entry into force of this Agreement the Government of Iraq shall have full responsibility for the Green Zone. The Government of Iraq may request from the United States Forces limited and temporary support for the Iraqi authorities in the mission of security for the Green Zone. Upon such request, | 349
relevant Iraqi authorities shall work jointly with the United States Forces authorities on security for the Green Zone during the period determined by the Government of Iraq.

*Article 29: Implementing Mechanisms*
Whenever the need arises, the Parties shall establish appropriate mechanisms for implementation of Articles of this Agreement, including those that do not contain specific implementation mechanisms.

*Article 30: The Period for Which the Agreement Is Effective*
1. This Agreement shall be effective for a period of three years, unless terminated sooner by either Party pursuant to paragraph 3 of this Article.
2. This Agreement shall be amended only with the official agreement of the Parties in writing and in accordance with the constitutional procedures in effect in both countries.
3. This Agreement shall terminate one year after a Party provides written notification to the other Party to that effect.
4. This Agreement shall enter into force on January 1, 2009, following an exchange of diplomatic notes confirming that the actions by the Parties necessary to bring the Agreement into force in accordance with each Party's respective constitutional procedures have been completed.

Signed in duplicate in Baghdad on this 17th day of November, 2008, in the English and Arabic languages, each text being equally authentic.
FOR THE UNITED STATES OF AMERICA:
FOR THE REPUBLIC OF IRAQ:

## DOCUMENT 6.15

Signed on the same day as the Status of Forces Agreement, the Strategic Framework Agreement covered the issues surrounding a future alliance between Iraq and the United States. These included the U.S. role in defending Iraq from both internal and external threats, U.S. efforts to combat terrorist groups, and U.S. support for political development. The Strategic Framework Agreement also emphasized shaping cultural, economic, and energy cooperation between the two states. This agreement recalled earlier debates on U.S. intentions in Iraq and on whether the shape of the Iraqi state was molded to suit U.S. geostrategic interests.

---

STRATEGIC FRAMEWORK AGREEMENT FOR A RELATIONSHIP OF FRIENDSHIP AND COOPERATION BETWEEN THE UNITED STATES OF AMERICA AND THE REPUBLIC OF IRAQ, NOVEMBER 17, 2008 (EXCERPT)

1. Affirming the genuine desire of the two countries to establish a long-term relationship of cooperation and friendship, based on the principle of equality in sovereignty and the rights and principles that are enshrined in the United Nations Charter and their common interests;
2. Recognizing the major and positive developments in Iraq that have taken place subsequent to April 9, 2003; the courage of the Iraqi people in establishing a democratically elected government under a new constitution; and welcoming no later than December 31, 2008, the termination of the Chapter VII authorization for and mandate of the multinational forces in UNSCR 1790; noting that the situation in Iraq is fundamentally different than that which existed when the UN Security Council adopted Resolution 661 in 1990, and in particular that the threat to international peace and security posed by the Government of Iraq no longer exists; and affirming in that regard that Iraq should return by December 31, 2008 to the legal and international standing that it enjoyed prior to the issuance of UNSCR 661. . . .
4. Recognizing both countries' desire to establish a long-term relationship, the need to support the success of the political process,

reinforce national reconciliation within the framework of a unified and federal Iraq, and to build a diversified and advanced economy that ensures the integration of Iraq into the international community; and

5. Reaffirming that such a long-term relationship in economic, diplomatic, cultural and security fields will contribute to the strengthening and development of democracy in Iraq, as well as ensuring that Iraq will assume full responsibility for its security, the safety of its people, and maintaining peace within Iraq and among the countries of the region have agreed to the following:

## Section I: Principles of Cooperation

This Agreement is based on a number of general principles to establish the course of the future relationship between the two countries as follows:

1. A relationship of friendship and cooperation is based on mutual respect; recognized principles and norms of international law and fulfillment of international obligations: the principle of non-interference in internal affairs; and rejection of the use of violence to settle disputes.
2. A strong Iraq capable of self-defense is essential for achieving stability in the region.
3. The temporary presence of U.S. forces in Iraq is at the request and invitation of the sovereign Government of Iraq and with full respect for the sovereignty of Iraq.
4. The United States shall not use Iraqi land, sea, and air as a launching or transit point for attacks against other countries; nor seek or request permanent bases or a permanent military presence in Iraq.

| 351

## Section II: Political and Diplomatic Cooperation

The Parties share a common understanding that their mutual efforts and cooperation on political and diplomatic issues shall improve and strengthen security and stability in Iraq and the region. In this regard, the United States shall ensure maximum efforts to work with and through the democratically elected Government of Iraq to:

1. Support and strengthen Iraq's democracy and its democratic institutions as defined and established in the Iraqi Constitution, and in so doing, enhance Iraq's capability to protect these institutions against all internal and external threats.
2. Support and enhance Iraq's status in regional and international organizations and institutions so that it may play a positive and constructive role in the international community.
3. Support the Government of Iraq in establishing positive relations with the states of the region, including on issues consequent to

the actions of the former regime that continue to harm Iraq, based on mutual respect and the principles of non-interference and positive dialogue among states, and the resolution of disputes, without the use of force or violence, in a manner that enhances the security and stability of the region and the prosperity of its peoples.

## Section III: Defense and Security Cooperation

In order to strengthen security and stability in Iraq, and thereby contribute to international peace and stability, and to enhance the ability of the Republic of Iraq to deter all threats against its sovereignty, security, and territorial integrity, the Parties shall continue to foster close cooperation concerning defense and security arrangements without prejudice to Iraqi sovereignty over its land, sea, and air territory. Such security and defense cooperation shall be undertaken pursuant to the *Agreement Between the United States of America and the Republic of Iraq on the Withdrawal of United States Forces from Iraq and the Organization of Their Activities during Their Temporary Presence in Iraq.*

## Section IV: Cultural Cooperation

The Parties share the conviction that connections between their citizens, forged through cultural exchanges, educational links and the exploration of their common archeological heritage will forge strong, long lasting bonds of friendship and mutual respect. To that end, the Parties agree to cooperate to:

1. Promote cultural and social exchanges and facilitate cultural activities, such as Citizens Exchanges, the Youth Exchange and Study Program, the Global Connections and Exchange (GCE) program, and the English Language Teaching and Learning program.
2. Promote and facilitate cooperation and coordination in the field of higher education and scientific research, as well as encouraging investment in education, including through the establishment of universities and affiliations between Iraqi and American social and academic institutions such as the U.S. Department of Agriculture's (USDA's) agricultural extension program.
3. Strengthen the development of Iraq's future leaders, through exchanges, training programs, and fellowships, such as the Fulbright program and the International Visitor Leadership Program (IVLP), in fields including science, engineering, medicine, information technology, telecommunications, public administration, and strategic planning.
4. Strengthen and facilitate the application process for U.S visas consistent with U.S. laws and procedures, to enhance the partici-

pation of qualified Iraqi individuals in scientific, educational, and cultural activities.

5. Promote Iraq's efforts in the field of social welfare and human rights.

6. Promote Iraqi efforts and contributions to international efforts to preserve Iraqi cultural heritage and protect archeological antiquities, rehabilitate Iraqi museums, and assist Iraq in recovering and restoring its smuggled artifacts through projects such as the Future of Babylon Project, and measures taken pursuant to the U.S. Emergency Protection for Iraqi Cultural Antiquities Act of 2004.

## Section V: Economic and Energy Cooperation

Building a prosperous, diversified, growing economy in Iraq, integrated in the global economic system, capable of meeting the essential service needs of the Iraqi people, as well as welcoming home Iraqi citizens currently dwelling outside of the country, will require unprecedented capital investment in reconstruction, the development of Iraq's extraordinary natural and human resources, and the integration of Iraq into the international economy and its institutions. To that end the Parties agree to cooperate to:

1. Support Iraq's efforts to invest its resources towards economic development, sustainable development and investment in projects that improve the basic services for the Iraqi people.

   | 353

2. Maintain active bilateral dialogue on measures to increase Iraq's development, including through the Dialogue on Economic Cooperation (DEC) and, upon entry into force, the Trade and Investment Framework Agreement.

3. Promote expansion of bilateral trade through the U.S.-Iraq Business Dialogue, as well as bilateral exchanges, such as trade promotion activities and access to Export-Import Bank programs.

4. Support Iraq's further integration into regional and international financial and economic communities and institutions, including membership in the World Trade Organization and through continued Normal Trade Relations with the United States.

5. Reinforce international efforts to develop the Iraqi economy and Iraqi efforts to reconstruct, rehabilitate, and maintain its economic infrastructure, including continuing cooperation with the Overseas Private Investment Corporation.

6. Urge all parties to abide by commitments made under the International Compact with Iraq with the goal of rehabilitating Iraq's economic institutions and increasing economic growth through the implementation of reforms that lay the foundation for private sector development and job creation.

7. Facilitate the flow of direct investment into Iraq to contribute to the reconstruction and development of its economy.

8. Promote Iraq's development of the Iraqi electricity, oil, and gas sector, including the rehabilitation of vital facilities and institutions and strengthening and rehabilitating Iraqi capabilities.

9. Work with the international community to help locate and reclaim illegally exported funds and properties of Saddam Hussein's family and key members of his regime, as well as its smuggled archeological artifacts and cultural heritage before and after April 9, 2003.

10. Encourage the creation of a positive investment environment to modernize Iraq's private industrial sector to enhance growth and expand industrial production including through encouraging networking with U.S. industrial institutions.

11. Encourage development in the fields of air, land, and sea transportation as well as rehabilitation of Iraqi ports and enhancement of maritime trade between the Parties, including by facilitating cooperation with the U.S. Federal Highway Administration.

12. Maintain an active dialogue on agricultural issues to help Iraq develop its domestic agricultural production and trade policies.

13. Promote access to programs that increase farm, firm, and marketing productivity to generate higher incomes and expanded employment, building on successful programs by the USDA and the USAID programs in agribusiness, agriculture extension, and policy engagement.

14. Encourage increased Iraqi agricultural exports, including through policy engagement and encouraging education of Iraqi exporters on U.S. health and safety regulations.

## Section VI: Health and Environmental Cooperation

In order to improve the health of the citizens of Iraq, as well as protect and improve the extraordinary natural environment of the historic Lands of the Two Rivers, the Parties agree to cooperate to:

1. Support and strengthen Iraq's efforts to build its health infrastructure and to strengthen health systems and networks.

2. Support Iraq's efforts to train health and medical cadres and staff.

3. Maintain dialogue on health policy issues to support Iraq's longterm development. Topics may include controlling the spread of infectious diseases, preventative and mental health, tertiary care, and increasing the efficiency of Iraq's medicine procurement system.

4. Encourage Iraqi and international investment in the health field, and facilitate specialized professional exchanges in order to promote the transfer of expertise and to help foster relationships between medical and health institutions building on existing programs with the U.S. Department of Health and Human Services, including its Centers for Disease Control and Prevention.

5. Encourage Iraqi efforts to strengthen mechanisms for protecting, preserving, improving, and developing the Iraqi environment and encouraging regional and international environmental cooperation.

## Section VII: Information Technology and Communications Cooperation

Communications are the life-blood of economic growth in the twenty-first century, as well as the foundation for the enhancement of democracy and civil society. In order to improve access to information and promote the development of a modern and state of the art communications industry in Iraq, the Parties agree to cooperate to:

1. Support the exchange of information and best practices in the fields of regulating telecommunications services and the development of information technology policies.
2. Exchange views and practices relating to liberalizing information technologies and telecommunications services markets, and the strengthening of an independent regulator.
3. Promote active Iraqi participation in the meetings and initiatives of the Internet Governance Forum, including its next global meetings.

## Section VIII: Law Enforcement and Judicial Cooperation

The Parties agree to cooperate to:

1. Support the further integration and security of the Iraqi criminal justice system, including police, courts, and prisons.
2. Exchange views and best practices related to judicial capacity building and training, including on continuing professional development for judges, judicial investigators, judicial security personnel, and court administrative staff.
3. Enhance law enforcement and judicial relationships to address corruption, and common transnational criminal threats, such as terrorism, trafficking in persons, organized crime, drugs, money laundering, smuggling of archeological artifacts, and cyber crime.

## Section IX: Joint Committees

. . . . b. Propose new cooperation projects and carry out discussions and negotiations as necessary to reach an agreement about details of such cooperation; and

c. Include other governmental departments and ministries for broader coordination from time to time, with meetings in Iraq and the United States, as appropriate.

3. Disputes that may arise under this Agreement, if not resolved within the relevant JCC, and not amenable to resolution within the HCC, are to be settled through diplomatic channels.

## Section X: Implementing Agreements and Arrangements
The Parties may enter into further agreements or arrangements as necessary and appropriate to implement this Agreement.

## Section XI: Final Provisions
1. This Agreement shall enter into force on January 1, 2009, following an exchange of diplomatic notes confirming that the actions by the Parties necessary to bring the Agreement into force in accordance with the respective constitutional procedures in effect in both countries have been completed.
2. This Agreement shall remain in force unless either Party provides written notice to the other of its intent to terminate this Agreement. The termination shall be effective one year after the date of such notification.
3. This Agreement may be amended with the mutual written agreement of the Parties and in accordance with the constitutional procedures in effect in both.
4. All cooperation under this Agreement shall be subject to the laws and regulations of both countries.

Signed in duplicate in Baghdad on this 17th day of November, 2008, in the English and Arabic language, each text being equally authentic.

# ★ CHAPTER 7 ★

# SECURING OIL, PREEMPTING DEVELOPMENT

IN EARLY 2001 the Chevron Corporation took the unusual step of dropping | 357 "Condoleezza Rice" as the name for one of its 129,000-ton tankers. According to some critics, it did so in an attempt to hide the deep connections between the oil industry and the Bush administration. Rice, who had served ten years on the Chevron board and resigned in early 2001 when she was named national security advisor, was not alone in her affiliation with the industry. The president himself, and his vice president, Dick Cheney, had long-standing, direct, and close relations with petroleum companies. Partly due to these particular relations, and more generally because of the role that it played in the U.S. economy, oil seeped into every aspect of U.S. policy in Iraq. The relevance of oil was an underlying question in much speculation about Washington's deeper motives for invading Iraq. But petroleum was important not only to the United States but also to the global economy. It was Iraq's singular, most precious national "patrimony," whose production, ownership, and management would determine whether the country could raise itself from the rubble of Washington's preemptive war.[1]

Soon after toppling Saddam Hussein, the United States began a dogged effort to privatize broad swaths of the Iraqi economy. A long-standing and fervent trust in free markets and a corresponding desire to reduce state involvement in economic matters had driven U.S. foreign policy since the beginning

---

1. Data for 2005–2006 by the U.S. Department of Energy showed the importance of Iraqi oil, which, despite many problems at the time, was the fifteenth-largest world oil producer and twelfth highest in oil exports.

of the Bush administration. Washington hoped that a privatized Iraq could become an example to other Middle Eastern nations, open the country to international trade and investment, encourage democracy, and weaken OPEC (7.1). The looming threat of "peak oil supply"—the exhaustion of world oil resources—was certainly on Cheney's mind when, as head of the Halliburton Corporation, he publicly warned that oil supplies might not be able to satisfy demand as early as 2010 (7.2). A desire to insert U.S. power into the Persian Gulf area so as to counter the oil demands of the emerging economies of India, China, and Southeast Asia was an additional, though unspoken, objective.

With the world's second-largest proven reserves of easily processed oil, Iraq was critically important to the United States and the global economy. There was little doubt that the Bush administration had decided that the war would enable the United States to gain "free access" to Iraq's oil (7.2–7.3). An impressive number of political and media leaders came to the same conclusion, among them figures as different as Alan Greenspan, the former chairman of the Federal Reserve, and Bill Moyers, the PBS (Public Broadcasting Service) journalist.

Preemptive war gave the United States a foothold in Iraq, and the subsequent attempts to privatize Baghdad's oil industry were meant to avoid unwanted congressional scrutiny and public debate both at home and in Iraq. But this strategy also meant missing an opportunity to open consultations with Iraqi and U.S. experts who might have helped Washington avoid some of the complications that soon emerged. The invaders' protection of the Oil Ministry and the oilfields during early explosions of looting made clear the U.S. interest in local petroleum. Along with its initial claims about how easy preemptive war would be, the Bush administration repeatedly promised U.S. citizens, before and during the war, that Iraqi oil revenues would pay for economic reconstruction. Deputy Secretary of Defense Wolfowitz famously assured Congress in March 2003 that Iraq could "finance its own reconstruction and relatively soon" (7.5).

By 2006, U.S. efforts to expand oil production and reconstruct the Iraqi economy were clearly failing, and that lack of success was part of a broader general pattern. Data on unemployment, homelessness, the GDP, and other economic indicators all pointed to real declines in Iraq's national economy after 2003. There was no doubt that a ruined oil sector was a large factor in the slow pace of reconstruction. The lagging effects of the pre-invasion sanctions regime, poor maintenance during the latter stages of Saddam Hussein's rule, widespread corruption, and sabotage by insurgents hostile to foreign occupation also helped explain why oil production remained at or below levels achieved during Saddam Hussein's regime. All of these problems were directly connected to the logic of preemption because they resulted from Washington's desire to sidestep sound policy and expert technical advice and to ignore the will of the Iraqi people. Privatization exacerbated the tensions and differences among Iraqi ethnic and religious groups over the distribution of oil profits. The push to privatize oil, in particular, did much to damage the chances for real Iraqi political unity, national reconciliation, and economic progress.

It soon became clear that, the legal obligations of occupying powers notwithstanding, the Bush administration had wanted to privatize the Iraqi economy long before the invasion (4.2). The State Department's Future of Iraq Project declared that "the economic system most appropriate for Iraq the day after the current regime is a profit-based system" (7.1, 7.8). This privatization plan sat in office drawers far from the Iraqi battlefield during the first months of the war and occupation, but it was not forgotten. President Bush abruptly replaced General Garner with L. Paul Bremer, and the Office for Reconstruction and Humanitarian Assistance with the Coalition Provisional Authority, partly because Garner had tried to move too quickly to transfer sovereignty to an Iraqi government and not quickly enough to transform the Iraqi economy into a model free-market system. Indeed, Garner had argued against privatization because he believed it would slow rebuilding and because the Iraqis and the Kurds would not be convinced that "they had to be privatized."

Bremer's mission was different from Garner's. From the moment he arrived in Baghdad's Green Zone, the Coalition Provisional Authority's "viceroy" made it clear that he intended to implant a free-market economy in Iraq, sell off oil and other economic assets to foreign companies, and prevent the resumption of Baath Party control by firing the incumbent oil technicians and managers. The Bush administration had faith that private ownership would increase oil production, raise much-needed revenue for Iraq's reconstruction, and weaken the OPEC cartel. True to the logic of preemption, administration officials were not particularly interested in the abundant evidence that the vast majority of Iraqis were deeply opposed to privatization—a willful blindness that contributed to the outbreak of national resistance and insurgency in a matter of weeks. Even the U.S. oil industry was not particularly interested in full privatization, preferring Production-Sharing Agreements (PSAs), whereby states retained legal ownership of their oilfields while contracting the exploration, processing, or production of oil to private companies. Indeed, an industry study had recommended that the Bush administration pursue the PSA model in future discussions about Iraqi oil (7.9–7.10).

Bremer's rush to privatize responded to the policy preferences of administration neoconservatives, who were interested in installing an unfettered private market and a U.S.-style democracy in Iraq as a first step toward the transformation of the entire Middle East. But Rice and others in the administration were not especially interested in radical privatization. They agreed with the large U.S. oil companies that saw PSAs as the best possible means to secure access and profits from oil without challenging the nationalist desires of producing countries to have greater control over their own resources. But key figures in the administration were determined to push ahead with privatization as rapidly as possible. Long before an elected Iraqi government had been organized, and before that government agreed in 2007 to continue the privatization goals announced in CPA Order 39, the United States had already decided to sell and divide the Iraqi oil spoils (4.13, 7.9).[2] During the first month of Bremer's administration, for example, British and Australian government officials and oil executives met to discuss which country would be granted control over a large Iraqi oilfield. The Pentagon's decision in the chaotic early days of the occupation to defend the oilfields and the Oil Ministry building while abandoning Iraqi cultural institutions to looters was another indication of U.S. priorities (7.6).

The attempted privatization of the Iraqi oil industry was also fed by a major misconception about the nature of Saddam Hussein's governance. The Baath regime was often violent and brutal, even toward its own citizens. Despite that, it had constructed a system in which most people enjoyed state-subsidized jobs, plentiful consumer goods, housing, and education (chapter 6). The U.S. State Department had recognized before the war that Saddam Hussein's policy of "maintaining low direct and indirect taxes greatly helped the government to impose their policies and peruse [sic] their political agenda" (7.1).[3] The rush to privatize brushed aside complicating factors like these.

Four years after the formal transfer of authority to the Iraqis, Iraqi oil was nominally owned by a weak and unstable national government. New no-bid "technical assistance" oil contracts were signed in 2008 by the Iraqi government, predominantly with "legacy" corporations such as Exxon Mobil, Shell, Total, BP, and Chevron—the same companies that had controlled the oilfields during the colonial period.[4] These contracts were the first results of a new oil law signed in early 2007 and were likely to develop later into PSA contracts that would prove most lucrative for the oil companies.[5] The government of Prime Minister Nouri al-Maliki defended the no-bid process as a temporary measure necessitated by the continuing security concerns that any oil operation would face, and by citing the immediate need for modern skills and infrastructure investments in the fields. Many questioned Iraq's claims that only those few "legacy" corporations had the requisite security and technical skill, especially since there were forty-six foreign oil companies with experience in the Middle East, mostly Chinese, Indian, and Russian, that had already signed pre-invasion memoranda of understanding with the Iraqi Oil Ministry.

2. In 2007, the Iraq Ministry of Planning and Development Cooperation Plan reaffirmed the continuation of the privatization strategy in "Strengthening the Foundations of Economic Growth." http://www.mop-iraq.org/mopdc/index.jsp?sid=1&id=188&pid=152.

3. See "Tax Policy: Guidelines for the Transitional Government of Iraq," chapter in "The Future of Iraq Project: Economy and Infrastructure Working Group" (2002), U.S. Department of State, declassified June 22, 2005, p. 2.

4. Andrew E. Kramer, "Deals with Iraq Are Set to Bring Oil Giants Back," New York Times, June 19, 2008.

5. These contracts were rescinded by the Iraqi government on September 11, 2008, in response to criticism from U.S. senators that the contracts jeopardized Iraqi unity. See Andrew E. Kramer and Campbell Robertson, "Iraq Cancels Six No-Bid Oil Contracts," New York Times, September 11, 2008.

More importantly, as of 2008 there was still no comprehensive agreement or law to organize the distribution of Iraqi oil revenues among the country's regions, factions, and tribes. Iraqi oil technicians and experts had recognized the dangers this posed when they declared in 2007 that the absence of a legitimate and acceptable understanding would "definitely lead to the enforcement of the situation of divisions, anarchy and chaos" (7.12). The failure to arrive at such an understanding not only reinforced social division, but PSAs, such as those signed separately by the Kurds, made it harder for the weak Maliki government to build trust and make progress toward national unity. The U.S. House of Representatives recognized the problem and tried to counter the disruptive effects of separate approaches (7.11).[6] The preferential PSAs also made it hard for the Iraqi government to refute charges that the country's oil was once again being exploited by and for foreign companies and that it would benefit, at best, only some Iraqi factions.

In many ways, preemption was more an ideology than a tactic (9.12). Reconstruction after a war, for instance, usually requires tremendous amounts of time and resources, and occupying powers are obligated to leave existing structures, understandings, and institutions intact (4.2). But the Bush administration had repeatedly promised that its preemptive invasion of Iraq would be easy and cheap. It had come into office opposed to what the neoconservatives contemptuously called "nation-building" and was committed to Defense Secretary Rumsfeld's vision of a transformed U.S. military that would move away from "ponderous, troop-heavy, logistics intensive, open-ended, and costly stabilization and reconstruction campaigns" (7.7). The administration hoped that the military would win a quick preemptive war, get out easily, and not have to worry about reconstruction. Bush officials were not interested in "endless discussions on why 'capitalism triumphs' in some countries and fails in most of the rest of the world," as the Future of Iraq Project put it. "We would rather roll up our sleeves and move heaven and earth to make a workable system of cooperative free enterprise triumph in Iraq in its hour of tremendous need" (7.1). Indeed, CPA chief Bremer and others argued that they had to act quickly and decisively in order to uproot the previous state-controlled economic system in the first months after Saddam Hussein's defeat. Their ideologically driven agenda to unleash a radical new market economy led them to willfully brush aside Iraq's own history, needs, and opposition. They ignored the advice of seasoned U.S. development and military officials and downplayed the documented success of other, sometimes state-driven, models of capitalist economic development, as in South Korea, Singapore, and elsewhere.

Most Iraqis rejected privatization even before it drove a wedge between Iraq's ethnic groups, undermined national sovereignty, sold off the country's other economic assets at bargain-basement prices, and fed the insurgency (7.4). This broad rejection of privatization came from all sectors of a deeply politicized,

---

6. See "Why Iraqis Cannot Agree on an Oil Law," *Council on Foreign Relations*, February 22, 2008.

historically conscious, and broadly nationalist society.[7] Iraqi oil technicians, for example, quickly opposed and criticized the U.S. privatization plan and received support from U.S. steelworkers (7.12–7.13).[8]

There was, of course, no guarantee that reconstruction could have proceeded more quickly and less contentiously had there been no preemptive push to privatize. But it was likely that a more collaborative process and real Iraqi sovereignty over oil and the larger economy would have changed the political situation because it would have given ownership of economic results—positive or negative—to a broader set of Iraqi leaders and groups rather than making it one more issue driving the Iraqis apart (4.13).

Impelled by its initial desire to move quickly and complete the transformation of Iraq in short order, the Bush administration spent a great deal of time on finalizing the privatization of Iraqi oil, increasing production, and securing contracts for U.S. companies. On March 27, 2008, the White House public assessment of Iraqi progress emphasized that oil production had increased in the Kurdish region. It said nothing about the continuing religious and regional fissures in the rest of the country, the lack of an oil-distribution law, and the general failure of its vaunted plans for economic reconstruction (7.14). The report expressed frustration only with the difficulty of effecting the "reforms needed to transition from a command-and-control economy to a modern market-based system" in Iraq (7.14). This assessment clearly contradicted the administration's previously negative view of Iraqi progress, reported to Congress on July 12, 2007. Most analysts suggested that Iraqi conditions reported in the 2007 assessment had not markedly improved by 2008. Thus, though the 2007 report had concluded that sectarian conflict and violence were due to the impact of the oil law, the administration did nothing to reduce the pressure it continued to place on the Iraqis to open their oilfields to foreign companies (7.15, 9.19– 9.20, 10.14). While Washington did everything it could to encourage the Maliki government to pass the Oil Law that legalized privatization, it was clearly less interested in pressing for a companion law to establish equitable distribution of government oil profits.[9] The latter was a difficult, perhaps intractable, issue for a country with so many religious and regional conflicts. But it was pre-

---

7. Privatization led to immediate protest from professionals who condemned it as a destructive and unjust plan. See "Health Workers Protest in Baghdad," *CNN,* May 7, 2003.

8. Iraqis believed the Oil Law transferred control of their oil wealth to foreign companies. David Bacon, "Why Iraqis Oppose US-Backed Oil Law," *San Francisco Chronicle,* August 19, 2007. Bacon reported in *Dollars and Sense* that the largest Iraqi labor union "launched a strike to underline its call for keeping oil in public hands, and to force the government to live up to its economic promises." "Iraq's Workers Strike to Keep Their Oil," September/October 2007.

9. The U.S. State Department placed twenty advisors in the Iraqi Ministry of Oil, eighteen in Finance, and three in Agriculture. See GAO report number GAO-08–117, entitled "Stabilizing and Rebuilding Iraq: U.S. Ministry Capacity Development Efforts Need an Overall Integrated Strategy to Guide Efforts and Manage Risk."

cisely such an agreement that would have been the most effective way to build state legitimacy and Iraqi unity. Instead, any possible Iraqi agreement over oil-profit distribution was vulnerable to U.S. government policy and U.S. oil-company actions (7.11).

As it turned out, the United States could not force the Iraqi government to privatize its economy. But Washington was able to influence Iraq by organizing a friendly regime and by requiring it to use U.S.-defined "benchmarks" and expert advice.[10] The Bush administration constantly assured the U.S. public that "Iraq is making its own investment decisions to address the major challenges it faces." Privately, however, the United States did not leave such matters to the Iraqis. Instead, Washington decided "to use our assistance dollars as leverage in a productive partnership" to shape Iraqi decisions (7.16). Faced with the very real possibility of failure, the administration repeatedly sent emissaries to push Iraq to finalize an Oil Law aimed at privatization. Vice President Cheney and Defense Secretary Gates visited Iraq on separate occasions in April and May of 2007 to pressure the Iraqis on an "American laundry list of must-haves" that made a priority of the "oil law and the rollback of de-Baathification."[11] Washington was joined by international organizations that also pressured Iraq to pass an oil law to speed privatization. In December 2005, the newly sovereign yet internally divided Iraqi government had signed a "first-ever Stand-By Arrangement" with the International Monetary Fund. The IMF contract focused on restructuring Iraq through free-market measures such as the oil law and on advancing "Iraq's transition to a market economy" (7.17). The U.S. Agency for International Development had earlier agreed to provide Baghdad with technical assistance on privatization. The first goal of this USAID contract was to help "the Government of Iraq privatize much of the economy" (7.18).

As of 2008, however, the United States had not achieved its goals of privatizing the Iraqi economy. Faced with overwhelming public opposition and its own nationalist impulses, the Maliki government dragged its feet. Iraqi oil was still nationally owned in 2008, although production was tied to private PSAs. Privatization's biggest failure, however, was a political one: national reconciliation was made almost impossible by the absence of an oil-distribution law. As it turned out, U.S. arms had defeated Saddam Hussein's depleted forces, but securing the country—and its oil—would not be as easy as it first seemed. The true cost of securing access to Iraqi oil with preemptive war and preemptive policies proved to be so expensive, at so many levels, that even conservatives began to question the Bush administration's policy. Writing in the *American Conservative*, Robert Bryce argued that "the U.S. needs to

---

10. Andrew E. Kramer, "U.S. Advised Iraqi Ministry on Oil Deals," *New York Times*, June 30, 2008.

11. David Cloud, Alissa J. Rubin, and Edward Wong, "Gates in Baghdad to Press Iraqis on Reconciliation," *International Herald Tribune*, April 19, 2007; John F. Burns, "Cheney Visits Baghdad and Presses Leaders on Political Progress," *New York Times*, May 10, 2007.

rethink the assumption that secure energy sources depend on militarism."[12] That kind of questioning and opposition, even from within its own ranks, was exactly what the Bush administration had tried to avoid. More than five years after the invasion of Iraq, preemption had produced more failure than success in attempts to privatize the Iraqi economy, reconstruct the country, and secure access to its oil.

# Iraq Economy-planning Documents

## DOCUMENT 7.1

"The Future of Iraq Project" was begun by the State Department in October 2001. It assembled more than two hundred Iraqi exiles and U.S. experts to produce a series of reports suggesting which strategies to follow and which to avoid. One of the reports, from the Economy and Infrastructure Working Group, was declassified in 2005. Though it suggested some caution in moving too fast and without Iraqi input, it also presented a preemptive plan to privatize the Iraqi economy without resorting to fruitless and "endless discussions" with experts and, presumably, with Iraqis.

FUTURE OF IRAQ PROJECT: ECONOMIC AND
INFRASTRUCTURE WORKING GROUP, "AN ECONOMIC
EMPOWERMENT SYSTEM," 2001 (EXCERPT)

Recent findings show that the poor not only save more than had been previously thought, but they also have high rates of debt repayment. According to Hernando de Soto, in Egypt alone the assets of the poor are fifty-five times greater than all foreign investment ever recorded, including the funding of the Suez Canal and the Aswan Dam. Despite this, however, most Third World residents are not able to use their assets to create self-perpetuating increases in productive capital which is the lifeblood of economic progress.

Let others have endless discussions on why "capitalism triumphs" in some countries and fails in most of the rest of the world. **We would rather roll up our sleeves and move heaven and earth to make a working system of cooperative free enterprise triumph in Iraq in its hour of tremendous need.** We can think of no better way to make this happen than by launching first a tailor made economic empowerment system (EES) spon-

---

12. Robert Bryce, "Oil for War: After invading one of the most petroleum-rich countries on earth, the U.S. military is running on empty," *American Conservative*, March 10, 2008.

sored by private parties operating for mutual profit under transparent rules that are fair and beneficial to all concerned.

With strong financial and moral incentives the proposed FFS will pull together four distinct productive elements into covenants of hope and profit which they are free to enter and to leave at any time. **Their sole purpose will be to optimize their economic resources.** The productive elements will consist of potential entrepreneurs, bankers, mentor-technicians, and a credit guarantee fund.

Working together under clearly stated guidelines, this grouping of forces will achieve what was previously deemed impossible. They will enter markets that in times past had been inaccessible to them, adopt technologies most suited to their needs, generate continuing streams of private and social capital, boost their financial returns with reasonable safety, and enjoy a sense of belonging **buy-ins and ownership** of significant private enterprises bestow on them and their families.

Envisioned activities are mentoring and technical assistance to generate the best possible business plans, optimal financing, risk management, and computer-based system administration. The eligible borrowers' ability to compete on a leveled playing field for available financial resources will generate direct benefits to the borrowing entrepreneurs, to the consumers of the goods and services they produce, to the lender-investors who earn handsome profits in financing the proposed projects, and indirect benefits to the community mainly in the form of additional fungible capital and additional resources for social service projects a growing economic pie may be expected to generate. . . .

| 365

## Private Sector and Entrepreneurial Initiatives
Saddam's totalitarian regime has not allowed any large-scale economic endeavors in the private sector. Small and medium sized businesses have continued to operate in niche roles throughout the country, subject to expropriation or exploitation by government officials—if profitable. Many private sector enterprises serve in some adjunct role to support large state owned/controlled industries and are awarded as concessions to Saddam's supporters.

The challenge for the new Iraq will be to foster economic and regulatory conditions that allow new, voluntary, individual business initiatives and entrepreneurial activities, under free, legal, competitive market conditions. Dismantling the current illegal structures and enterprises, removing ruling party cliques from ownership/control, and privatizing some state run enterprises, are the principal economic challenges for planners supporting new free market economics.

## DOCUMENT 7.2

As the chief executive officer of Halliburton in 1999, Dick Cheney warned the oil industry about the looming threat of "peak oil." Though he never used those words, he was very clear that "by 2010 we will need on the order of an additional fifty million barrels a day." He added that, in the future, oil would come mainly from "the Middle East [which had] two thirds of the world's oil and the lowest cost [and which is] still where the prize ultimately lies." Years before he became George W. Bush's vice president, Cheney was thinking about Iraqi oil.

DICK CHENEY, SPEECH AT LONDON INSTITUTE
OF PETROLEUM, NOVEMBER 15, 1999 (EXCERPT)

Thank you very much for that welcome and that introduction. I am delighted to be back in London today and have an opportunity to spend some time with all of you. . . .

From the standpoint of the oil industry obviously and I'll talk a little later on about gas, but obviously for over a hundred years we as an industry have had to deal with the pesky problem that once you find oil and pump it out of the ground you've got to turn around and find more or go out of business. Producing oil is obviously a self-depleting activity. Every year you've got to find and develop reserves equal to your output just to stand still, just to stay even. This is true for companies as well in the broader economic sense as it is for the world. A new merged company like Exxon-Mobil will have to secure over a billion and a half barrels of new oil equivalent reserves every year just to replace existing production. It's like making 100 percent interest discovery in another major field of some five hundred million barrels equivalent every four months or finding two Hibernias a year.

For the world as a whole, oil companies are expected to keep finding and developing enough oil to offset our seventy-one-million plus barrel a day of oil depletion, but also to meet new demand. By some estimates there will be an average of 2 percent annual growth in global oil demand over the years ahead along with conservatively a 3 percent natural decline in production from existing reserves. That means by 2010 we will need on the order of an additional fifty million barrels a day. So where is the oil going to come from?

Governments and the national oil companies are obviously controlling about 90 percent of the assets. Oil remains fundamentally a government business. While many regions of the world offer great oil opportunities, the Middle East with two-thirds of the world's oil and the lowest cost, is still where the prize ultimately lies, even though companies are anxious for greater access there, progress continues to be slow. It is true that technology, privatization, and the opening up of a number of countries have created many new opportunities in areas around the world for various oil companies, but looking back to the early 1990s, expectations were that significant amounts of the world's new resources would come from such areas as the former Soviet Union and from China. Of course that didn't turn out quite as expected. Instead it turned out to be deep water successes that yielded the bonanza of the 1990s.

A fundamental challenge for companies is to do more than replace reserves and production. The trick obviously is also to replace earnings. For most companies the majority of their profits come from core areas, that is areas where they have significant investments, economies of scale, and large license areas locked up, but many of these core areas are now mature and it can be difficult to replace the earnings from the high margin barrels there. Some of the oil being developed in new areas is obviously very high cost and low margin.

Companies that are finding it difficult to create new core areas through exploration are turning to production deals where they can develop reserves that are already known, but where the country doesn't have the capital or the technology to exploit them. In production deals there is less exploration risk but dealing with above ground political risk and commercial and environmental risk are increasing challenges. These include civil strife, transportation routes, labor issues, fiscal terms, sometimes even U.S.-imposed economic sanctions. Many companies are more comfortable dealing with the below ground risk like drilling and reservoir performance than they are with the above ground political risks. The other major element that it is changing is the nature of competition . . .

Increasingly we are seeing international oil and gas companies concentrating on managing investment, financial, commercial and political risk or above ground risk, while service companies are managing technical, completion, and operating risk. Meanwhile, national oil companies are focused on managing their country's national interest and its resources and in the domestic markets. This is part of the new resource rationalism of the 1990s. NOCs may own the resources, but when it is in the national interest to bring in outsiders to help develop them, they do so. Venezuela obviously is a clear example of what I would define as the new resource nationalism. Some NOCs are still looking outside their own borders, but I expect that in the future the emphasis may well be closer to home.

NOCs can focus on becoming regionally dominant players, leveraging off their strong domestic base to move into neighboring countries. This will occur where there are links and synergies with their home business, not just going global for its own sake. I think Petrobras in Brazil may be an example of this in Latin America.

People ask about the future role for OPEC. Certainly the organization represents companies that have a vast amount of oil reserves and it has held together for over a quarter of a century already. OPEC have shown the ability for crisis management every time oil prices have dropped to single-digit levels, but the group may ultimately bring about its own undoing if it shoots for too high a level for oil prices. As observers point out, in the long run, this effectively underwrites higher cost oil exploration and development around the world all at the same time, limiting demand growth below what it might otherwise be. Nonetheless, I believe most of us in the industry have welcomed the restraint in the leadership shown by OPEC in recent months and the improved outlook for the international oil markets. I know I am pleased with the leadership provided by Saudi Arabia, Mexico, and Venezuela and in the long run I think the world will be best served, and the consumer best served as well as producers, by stable prices at reasonable levels. . . .

The Middle East and Africa have over one hundred years' supply of gas reserves at current low usage levels and the former Soviet Union and Latin America have gas reserve to production ratios which should last over seventy years. Even estimates of proved gas reserves understate the volumes involved, since there is plenty of gas still to be found and many existing discoveries have not been booked, usually due to the difficulty of getting gas to market. As companies find more gas, they need to find ways to monetize the remote fields; developing stranded gas often entails new risk involved in building a new market to use the gas. The three main options for moving this gas to market are pipelines, liquefied natural gas, and now gas to liquids. . . .

Oil is unique in that it is so strategic in nature. We are not talking about soapflakes or leisurewear here. Energy is truly fundamental to the world's economy. The Gulf War was a reflection of that reality. The degree of government involvement also makes oil a unique commodity. This is true in both the overwhelming control of oil resources by national oil companies and governments as well as in the consuming nations where oil products are heavily taxed and regulated.

Essentially, the petroleum industry deals with extreme risk and with billions of dollars on the line. Oil is produced in distant lands as a result of huge risk and enormous capital outlays, it is transported over vast distances, refined in expensive refineries with very heavy outlays required to protect the environment and to comply with strict and expensive regulations, distributed through a wide network of pipelines, trucks, and wholesale outlets and sold at stations in prime locations and taxed heavily.

It is the basic, fundamental building block of the world's economy. It is unlike any other commodity. . . .

Frankly the focus in today's economy on globalization and emerging markets is old news to the oil industry. Ours are global companies investing outside the industrialized companies at the turn of the last century. People need to realize that the energy industry often represents the largest foreign investment in many parts of the world and its interest, insights, and experience need to be considered.

Oil is the only large industry whose leverage has not been all that effective in the political arena. Textiles, electronics, agriculture all seem oftentimes to be more influential. Our constituency is not only oilmen from Louisiana and Texas, but software writers in Massachusetts and specialty steel producers in Pennsylvania. I am struck that this industry is so strong technically and financially yet not as politically successful or influential as are often smaller industries. We need to earn credibility to have our views heard.

Another concern is the disruptive volatility of the industry. In the new century the oil business needs to learn how to break out of the boom and bust cycles we have experienced over the last century. Perhaps it is part of being a commodity business, but it wreaks havoc with planning processes and can drive smaller companies out of business and, needless to say, creates problems for consumers as well. . . .

# DOCUMENT 7.3

In February 2005, a report sponsored by the National Energy Technology Laboratory of the U.S. Department of Energy warned that peak oil production would come within twenty years. It suggested that the only way to avoid chaos was to give the peak-oil crisis "immediate, serious attention." The Bush administration, especially Vice President Cheney, did indeed appear to give oil very serious attention, whether or not they accepted the idea of an imminent crisis in oil production.

NATIONAL ENERGY TECHNOLOGY LABORATORY, "PEAKING OF WORLD OIL PRODUCTION: IMPACTS, MITIGATION, AND RISK MANAGEMENT," EXECUTIVE SUMMARY, FEBRUARY 2005

The peaking of world oil production presents the U.S. and the world with an unprecedented risk management problem. As peaking is approached, liquid fuel prices and price volatility will increase dramatically, and, without timely mitigation, the economic, social, and political costs will be unprecedented. Viable mitigation options exist on both the supply and demand sides, but to have substantial impact, they must be initiated more than a decade in advance of peaking.

In 2003, the world consumed just under 80 million barrels per day (MM bpd) of oil. U.S. consumption was almost 20 MM bpd, two-thirds of which was in the transportation sector. The U.S. has a fleet of about 210 million automobiles and light trucks (vans, pick-ups, and SUVs). The average age of U.S. automobiles is nine years. Under normal conditions, replacement of only half the automobile fleet will require 10–15 years. The average age of light trucks is seven years.

Under normal conditions, replacement of one-half of the stock of light trucks will require 9–14 years. While significant improvements in fuel efficiency are possible in automobiles and light trucks, any affordable approach to upgrading will be inherently time-consuming, requiring more than a decade to achieve significant overall fuel efficiency improvement.

Besides further oil exploration, there are commercial options for increasing world oil supply and for the production of substitute liquid fuels: 1) Improved Oil Recovery (IOR) can marginally increase production from existing reservoirs; one of the largest of the IOR opportunities is Enhanced Oil Recovery (EOR), which can help moderate oil production declines from reservoirs that are past their peak production; 2) Heavy oil / oil sands represents a large resource of lower grade oils, now primarily produced in Canada and Venezuela; those resources are capable of significant production increases; 3) Coal liquefaction is a well-established technique for producing clean substitute fuels from the world's abundant coal reserves; and finally, 4) Clean substitute fuels can be produced from remotely located natural gas, but exploitation must compete with the world's growing demand for liquefied natural gas. However, world-scale contributions from these options will require 10–20 years of accelerated effort.

370 |    Dealing with world oil production peaking will be extremely complex, involve literally trillions of dollars and require many years of intense effort. To explore these complexities, three alternative mitigation scenarios were analyzed:

- Scenario I assumed that action is not initiated until peaking occurs.
- Scenario II assumed that action is initiated 10 years before peaking.
- Scenario III assumed action is initiated 20 years before peaking.

For this analysis estimates of the possible contributions of each mitigation option were developed, based on an assumed crash program rate of implementation.

Our approach was simplified in order to provide transparency and promote understanding. Our estimates are approximate, but the mitigation envelope that results is believed to be directionally indicative of the realities of such an enormous undertaking. The inescapable conclusion is that more than a decade will be required for the collective contributions to produce results that significantly impact world supply and demand for liquid fuels.

Important observations and conclusions from this study are as follows:

1. When world oil peaking will occur is not known with certainty.
   A fundamental problem in predicting oil peaking is the poor
   quality of and possible political biases in world oil reserves data.

Some experts believe peaking may occur soon. This study indicates that "soon" is within 20 years.

2. The problems associated with world oil production peaking will not be temporary, and past "energy crisis" experience will provide relatively little guidance. The challenge of oil peaking descrves immediate, serious attention, if risks are to be fully understood and mitigation begun on a timely basis.

3. Oil peaking will create a severe liquid fuels problem for the transportation sector, not an "energy crisis" in the usual sense that term has been used.

4. Peaking will result in dramatically higher oil prices, which will cause protracted economic hardship in the United States and the world. However, the problems are not insoluble. Timely, aggressive mitigation initiatives addressing both the supply and the demand sides of the issue will be required.

5. In the developed nations, the problems will be especially serious. In the developing nations peaking problems have the potential to be much worse.

6. Mitigation will require a minimum of a decade of intense, expensive effort, because the scale of liquid fuels mitigation is inherently extremely large.

7. While greater end-use efficiency is essential, increased efficiency alone will be neither sufficient nor timely enough to solve the problem. Production of large amounts of substitute liquid fuels will be required. A number of commercial or near-commercial substitute fuel production technologies are currently available for deployment, so the production of vast amounts of substitute liquid fuels is feasible with existing technology.

8. Intervention by governments will be required, because the economic and social implications of oil peaking would otherwise be chaotic. The experiences of the 1970s and 1980s offer important guides as to government actions that are desirable and those that are undesirable, but the process will not be easy.

Mitigating the peaking of world conventional oil production presents a classic risk management problem:

- Mitigation initiated earlier than required may turn out to be premature, if peaking is long delayed.
- If peaking is imminent, failure to initiate timely mitigation could be extremely damaging.

Prudent risk management requires the planning and implementation of mitigation well before peaking. Early mitigation will almost certainly be less expensive than delayed mitigation. A unique aspect of the world oil peaking problem is that its timing is uncertain, because of inadequate and potentially biased reserves data from elsewhere around the world. In addition, the onset of peaking may be obscured by the volatile nature of oil prices. Since the potential economic impact of peaking is immense and the uncertainties relating to all facets of the problem are large, detailed quantitative studies to address the uncertainties and to explore mitigation strategies are a critical need.

The purpose of this analysis was to identify the critical issues surrounding the occurrence and mitigation of world oil production peaking. We simplified many of the complexities in an effort to provide a transparent analysis. Nevertheless, our study is neither simple nor brief. We recognize that when oil prices escalate dramatically, there will be demand and economic impacts that will alter our simplified assumptions. Consideration of those feedbacks will be a daunting task but one that should be undertaken.

Our study required that we make a number of assumptions and estimates. We well recognize that in-depth analyses may yield different numbers. Nevertheless, this analysis clearly demonstrates that the key to mitigation of world oil production peaking will be the construction [of] a large number of substitute fuel production facilities, coupled to significant increases in transportation fuel efficiency. The time required to mitigate world oil production peaking is measured on a decade time-scale. Related production facility size is large and capital intensive. How and when governments decide to address these challenges is yet to be determined.

Our focus on existing commercial and near-commercial mitigation technologies illustrates that a number of technologies are currently ready for immediate and extensive implementation. Our analysis was not meant to be limiting. We believe that future research will provide additional mitigation options, some possibly superior to those we considered. Indeed, it would be appropriate to greatly accelerate public and private oil peaking mitigation research. However, the reader must recognize that doing the research required to bring new technologies to commercial readiness takes time under the best of circumstances. Thereafter, more than a decade of intense implementation will be required for world scale impact, because of the inherently large scale of world oil consumption.

In summary, the problem of the peaking of world conventional oil production is unlike any yet faced by modern industrial society. The challenges and uncertainties need to be much better understood. Technologies exist to mitigate the problem. Timely, aggressive risk management will be essential.

# DOCUMENT 7.4

Mandated by Congress and opposed by the Bush administration, the Iraq Study Group, co-chaired by James A. Baker, a former secretary of state, and Lee Hamilton, former chair of the House Foreign Relations Committee, was a bipartisan group of respected political leaders appointed to assess the post-invasion situation in Iraq. It included five Democrats and five Republicans and consulted with 136 people in and out of government before issuing a substantial and well-respected report—which was largely ignored by the administration. Its early warning about the poor economic performance of Iraq post–Saddam Hussein and the failures of reconstruction was prescient.

IRAQ STUDY GROUP REPORT, 2006 (EXCERPT)

## Economic Performance

There are some encouraging signs. Currency reserves are stable and growing at $12 billion. Consumer imports of computers, cell phones, and other appliances have increased dramatically. New businesses are opening, and construction is moving forward in secure areas. Because of Iraq's ample oil reserves, water resources, and fertile lands, significant growth is possible if violence is reduced and the capacity of government improves. For example, wheat yields increased more than 40 percent in Kurdistan during this past year.

The Iraqi government has also made progress in meeting benchmarks set by the International Monetary Fund. Most prominently, subsidies have been reduced—for instance, the price per liter of gas has increased from roughly 1.7 cents to 23 cents (a figure far closer to regional prices). However, energy and food subsidies generally remain a burden, costing Iraq $11 billion per year.

Despite the positive signs, many leading economic indicators are negative. Instead of meeting a target of 10 percent, growth in Iraq is at roughly 4 percent this year. Inflation is above 50 percent. Unemployment estimates range widely from 20 to 60 percent. The investment climate is bleak, with foreign direct investment under 1 percent of GDP. Too many Iraqis do not see tangible improvements in their daily economic situation.

## Oil Sector

Oil production and sales account for nearly 70 percent of Iraq's GDP, and more than 95 percent of government revenues. Iraq produces around 2.2 million barrels per day, and exports about 1.5 million barrels per day. This is below both prewar production levels and the Iraqi government's target of 2.5 million barrels per day, and far short of the vast potential of the Iraqi oil sector. Fortunately for the government, global energy prices have been higher than projected, making it possible for Iraq to meet its budget revenue targets.

Problems with oil production are caused by lack of security, lack of investment, and lack of technical capacity. Insurgents with a detailed knowledge of Iraq's infrastructure target pipelines and oil facilities. There is no metering system for the oil. There is poor maintenance at pumping stations, pipelines, and port facilities, as well as inadequate investment in modern technology. Iraq had a cadre of experts in the oil sector, but intimidation and an extended migration of experts to other countries have eroded technical capacity. Foreign companies have been reluctant to invest, and Iraq's Ministry of Oil has been unable to spend more than 15 percent of its capital budget.

Corruption is also debilitating. Experts estimate that 150,000 to 200,000 —and perhaps as many as 500,000—barrels of oil per day are being stolen. Controlled prices for refined products result in shortages within Iraq, which drive consumers to the thriving black market. One senior U.S. official told us that corruption is more responsible than insurgents for breakdowns in the oil sector.

### The Politics of Oil

The politics of oil has the potential to further damage the country's already fragile efforts to create a unified central government. The Iraqi Constitution leaves the door open for regions to take the lead in developing new oil resources. Article 108 states that "oil and gas are the ownership of all the peoples of Iraq in all the regions and governorates," while Article 109 tasks the federal government with "the management of oil and gas extracted from current fields." This language has led to contention over what constitutes a "new" or an "existing" resource, a question that has profound ramifications for the ultimate control of future oil revenue.

Senior members of Iraq's oil industry argue that a national oil company could reduce political tensions by centralizing revenues and reducing regional or local claims to a percentage of the revenue derived from production. However, regional leaders are suspicious and resist this proposal, affirming the rights of local communities to have direct access to the inflow of oil revenue. Kurdish leaders have been particularly aggressive in asserting independent control of their oil assets, signing and implementing investment deals with foreign oil companies in northern Iraq. Shia politicians are also reported to be negotiating oil investment contracts with foreign companies.

There are proposals to redistribute a portion of oil revenues directly to the population on a per capita basis. These proposals have the potential to give all Iraqi citizens a stake in the nation's chief natural resource, but it would take time to develop a fair distribution system. Oil revenues have been incorporated into state budget projections for the next several years. There is no institution in Iraq at present that could properly implement such a distribution system. It would take substantial time to establish, and would have to be based on a well-developed state census and income tax system, which Iraq currently lacks.

### U.S.-led Reconstruction Efforts

The United States has appropriated a total of about $34 billion to support the reconstruction of Iraq, of which about $21 billion has been appropriated for the "Iraq Relief and Reconstruction Fund." Nearly $16 billion has been spent, and almost all the funds have been committed. The administration requested $1.6 billion for reconstruction in FY 2006, and received $1.485 billion. The administration requested $750 million for FY 2007. The trend line for economic assistance in FY 2008 also appears downward.

Congress has little appetite for appropriating more funds for reconstruction. There is a substantial need for continued reconstruction in Iraq, but serious questions remain about the capacity of the U.S. and Iraqi governments.

The coordination of assistance programs by the Defense Department, State Department, United States Agency for International Development, and other agencies has been ineffective. There are no clear lines establishing who is in charge of reconstruction.

As resources decline, the U.S. reconstruction effort is changing its focus, shifting from infrastructure, education, and health to smaller-scale ventures that are chosen and to some degree managed by local communities. A major attempt is also being made to improve the capacity of government bureaucracies at the national, regional, and provincial levels to provide services to the population as well as to select and manage infrastructure projects.

The United States has people embedded in several Iraqi ministries, but it confronts problems with access and sustainability. Muqtada al-Sadr objects to the U.S. presence in Iraq, and therefore the ministries he controls— Health, Agriculture, and Transportation—will not work with Americans. | 375 It is not clear that Iraqis can or will maintain and operate reconstruction projects launched by the United States.

Several senior military officers commented to us that the Commander's Emergency Response Program, which funds quick-impact projects such as the clearing of sewage and the restoration of basic services, is vital. The U.S. Agency for International Development, in contrast, is focused on long-term economic development and capacity building, but funds have not been committed to support these efforts into the future. The State Department leads seven Provincial Reconstruction Teams operating around the country. These teams can have a positive effect in secure areas, but not in areas where their work is hampered by significant security constraints.

Substantial reconstruction funds have also been provided to contractors, and the Special Inspector General for Iraq Reconstruction has documented numerous instances of waste and abuse. They have not all been put right. Contracting has gradually improved, as more oversight has been exercised and fewer cost-plus contracts have been granted; in addition, the use of Iraqi contractors has enabled the employment of more Iraqis in reconstruction projects.

# DOCUMENT 7.5

Deputy Secretary of Defense Paul D. Wolfowitz testified to the House Appropriations Subcommittee on Defense on March 27, 2003, concerning the

Supplemental Appropriations Act for Iraq and Afghanistan. Congressman Roger F. Wicker, Republican of Mississippi, asked him how much the reconstruction of Iraq would cost U.S. taxpayers. In what turned out to be an infamous miscalculation, Wolfowitz minimized the costs of the war and suggested that Iraq would be able to pay for everything out of its own oil resources. The administration's attempt to convince U.S. taxpayers that preemptive war would not require a great deal of their money was soon shattered. By 2008, the Iraq war was projected to cost $2 trillion to $3 trillion dollars, according to some estimates.[13]

---

PAUL WOLFOWITZ, TESTIMONY TO THE HOUSE
APPROPRIATIONS SUBCOMMITTEE ON DEFENSE
RE FISCAL YEAR 2003 SUPPLEMENTAL APPROPRIATIONS
FOR IRAQ AND AFGHANISTAN, MARCH 27, 2003

**MR. WICKER:** Can you give us that estimate?

**MR. WOLFOWITZ:** I said it covers $12 billion for what we are calling transition in—

**MR. WICKER:** That is for our contribution. But what do you think the entire package is going to be?

**MR. WOLFOWITZ:** Oh, it is—I mean.

**MR. LEWIS:** You don't have that.

**MR. WOLFOWITZ:** We really don't, and the real number would be not what is going to get through the rest of the fiscal year, but what is it going to be over 2 to 3 years. And a rough recollection—well, the oil revenues of that country could bring between $50 and $100 billion dollars over the course of the next two or three years.

Now, there are a lot of claims on that money, but we are not dealing with Afghanistan. It is a personal innocent ward of the international community. We are dealing with a country that can really finance its own reconstruction and relatively soon.

**MR. WICKER:** Thank you.

# DOCUMENT 7.6

On February 7, 2003, a memorandum from the Iraq War planning group to State Department Undersecretary Paula J. Dobriansky warned that "a failure to address short-term public security and humanitarian assistance concerns

---

13. "Cost of the Iraq War," *CQ Researcher* 18, no. 16 (April 25, 2008), 361–384.

could result in serious human rights abuses which would undermine an otherwise successful military campaign and our reputation internationally." One of the planning studies the administration ignored in its preemptive strategy for Iraq, much of the document was redacted for security or political reasons.

---

IRAQ CONTINGENCY PLANNING MEMO—RELEASED
IN PART—UNCLASSIFIED, 2003 (EXCERPT)

United States Department of State, Washington, D.C. February 7, 2003
To: G—Under Secretary Dobriansky
FROM: DRL—Lorne W. Craner, PRM—Arthur E. Dewey, INL—Paul E. Simons, Acting
SUBJECT: Iraq Contingency Planning

As follow-up to your recent visit to CENTCOM, our Bureaus have been actively engaged in the inter-agency and inter-bureau coordination on contingency planning for Iraq. In addition, PDAS Greene has just traveled to Jordan, Kuwait, Qatar and Turkey as Head of the Humanitarian Planning Team, DAS Carpenter has just met with the J-5 at CENTCOM, and INL Acting A/S Simons has just indicated the importance of including short-term civilian public security issues in the military planning process in meetings with the interagency relief and reconstruction working groups and DOD's post-conflict planning group. These visits, and our experience in other post-conflict situations, have alerted us to the fact that there could be the following serious planning gaps for post-conflict public security and humanitarian assistance between the end of the war and the beginning of reconstruction:

[Redacted portion—classified for reasons: E.O. 12958 1.5 (B) and (d)]

Responsibility must remain with coalition military forces until these functions can be turned over to an international public security force or other mechanism to be defined. Although we recognize CENTCOM's focus on its primary military objectives and its reluctance to take on "policing" roles, a failure to address short-term public security and humanitarian assistance concerns could result in serious human rights abuses which would undermine an otherwise successful military campaign, and our reputation internationally. We are willing to provide technical assistance and help CENTCOM develop plans for accomplishing these goals. This will not be possible unless the military is tasked to take on the roles we outlined above.

We have raised these issues with top CENTCOM officials and General Garner, and continue to raise them at the PCC. We understand that D.O.D will brief the Deputies and Principals on rear-area security next week. In addition, we have asked key International Organizations and NGOs to identify activities that the military could be called upon to perform in support of civilian humanitarian and human rights operations. . . .

# Iraq Oil Documents

## DOCUMENT 7.7

The second volume in the United States military's history of the Iraq conflict is based on two hundred interviews conducted by military historians. It documents the problems the military encountered in post–Saddam Hussein Iraq and explains them as the inevitable results of a lack of leadership, time, and coherent civilian policy. Army leaders believed that the administration's failures could be traced to a general reluctance to engage in nation-building, a position explicitly voiced by President Bush in the early days of his term. The lack of prewar planning may have resulted from the Bush administration's focus on privatization as the main strategy for developing Iraq.

---

UNITED STATES COMBINED ARMS CENTER,
"ON POINT II: TRANSITION TO THE NEW CAMPAIGN:
THE UNITED STATES ARMY IN OPERATION IRAQI FREEDOM,"
MAY 2003–JANUARY 2005 (EXCERPT)

378 |

Dr. Donald P. Wright, Colonel Timothy R. Reese with the Contemporary Operations Study Team. Combat Studies Institute Press, US Army Combined Arms Center
Fort Leavenworth, Kansas. June 30, 2008

### The Planning for Phase IV—Operations after Toppling the Saddam Regime

In January 2003 President Bush issued National Security Presidential Directive 24, which formally gave the DOD primacy in the post invasion effort in Iraq. This directive granted the department authority to assert leadership in the planning for operations after the Saddam regime was toppled. What had emerged in 2002, even before the directive, was a series of planning initiatives at various levels in the DOD that reflected a variety of attitudes and approaches toward the overall concept of American involvement in post invasion operations. On the level of strategic policy, the DOD's approach to Iraq was significantly shaped by the Bush administration's overall wary attitude toward what was sometimes called nation building. Bush had taken office in 2001 having campaigned on his dislike for nation-building projects, such as those in the Balkans that had absorbed a great deal of American military resources in the 1990s. For some military theorists at the time, the US Armed Forces existed to fight and win wars and should not have its strength dissipated in missions like SFOR and KFOR.

This stance enforced Secretary Rumsfeld's desire to transform the military into a more agile force that could deploy quickly on a global scale. This vision of a transformed American military implied avoiding commitments to ponderous, troop-heavy, logistics intensive, open-ended, and costly stabilization and reconstruction campaigns. It would be wrong to attach this aversion solely to Rumsfeld or to the Office of the Secretary of Defense. These and other related views about the nature of war in the future and the need for the reinvention of military power were supported by many thinkers in and out of the US Government and the Armed Services in the 1990s. The US Army's much-debated transformation efforts launched by Army Chief of Staff General Shinseki were in some ways an outgrowth of this debate and preceded Rumsfeld's initiatives.

Despite the misgivings about nation building, the DOD did commit resources to the planning of post invasion operations. In retrospect, however, the overall effort appears to have been disjointed and, at times, poorly coordinated, perhaps reflecting the department's ambivalence toward nation building. Within the department, most of the responsibility for the planning would fall on the shoulders of CENTCOM, the combatant command responsible for the overall campaign. And Franks' planners did prepare for operations after the fall of the regime.

Still, given the short time it had to prepare CONPLAN 1003V—and the fact that the command was simultaneously prosecuting the war in Afghanistan—the CENTCOM staff dedicated most of its planning effort to the invasion itself. Also, despite guidance about CENTCOM's role in PH IV of the campaign, Franks did not see postwar Iraq as his long-term responsibility. He later wrote that he expected a huge infusion of civilian experts and other resources to come from the US Government after CENTCOM completed the mission of removing the Saddam regime. Franks' message to the DOD and the Joint Chiefs was, "You pay attention to the day after, and I'll pay attention to the day of."

The Joint Chiefs of Staff, understanding that CENTCOM was focused on winning the conventional portion of the campaign, decided to assist in the planning for PH IV. To do so, in December 2002 the Joint Staff created an organization called Combined Joint Task Force–IV (CJTF-IV) (also designated as CJTF-4) to lead its planning effort for post-Saddam Iraq.

Established by Joint Forces Command and headed by Brigadier General Steve Hawkins, CJTF-IV's relationship to CENTCOM and CFLCC remained unspecified, except that it would help design and prepare the joint task force headquarters that would take over PH IV operations from CENTCOM after the removal of the Baathist regime. Though Hawkins' organization completed some initial planning before the war, its work did not influence CFLCC planning and by early April 2003 it slowly disbanded as its personnel drifted off to join other commands in and out of the theater of operations.

Around the same time CJTF-IV began to organize, the Secretary of Defense established his own organization for the civilian portion of the stabilization and reconstruction effort. By the end of January 2003, Rumsfeld had chosen Lieutenant General (Retired) Jay Garner as the head of what became known as the Office of Reconstruction and Humanitarian Assistance (ORHA). Garner earned his reputation as a smart planner in his work with the Iraqi Kurds during Operation PROVIDE COMFORT in the aftermath of DESERT STORM. While Garner and ORHA officially became the DOD lead for postwar planning, staff officers in CJTF-IV, CFLCC, and CENTCOM continued to develop their own PH IV plans. One reason for this lack of coordination was Garner's struggle to create ORHA from the ground up. He had 61 days between the announcement of ORHA's creation and the start of the war to build an organization, develop interagency plans across the administration, coordinate them with CENTCOM and the still undetermined military headquarters that would assume the military lead in post-Saddam Iraq, and deploy his team to the theater. It proved to be an almost impossible set of tasks.

. . . In retrospect, the ORHA planning effort appears to have suffered from this lack of inter-agency support. Garner has written that in January and February 2003 his staff reviewed various studies of post-Saddam Iraq completed by a number of Government agencies and tried to find the resources to achieve the objectives outlined in these works. Based on the findings in these studies, ORHA created its own plan that focused on preparing for the four most likely crises to occur in Iraq after the toppling of the Baathist regime: oil field fires, large numbers of refugees, food shortages, and the outbreak of epidemics. None of these problems would emerge once Baghdad actually fell in April 2003.

## DOCUMENT 7.8

The Heritage Foundation was one of the most influential conservative policy groups in the United States. The CPA head L. Paul Bremer had formerly chaired its Homeland Security Task Force, which issued a report in 2003 on the future of Iraq's oil industry. It argued not only for privatization but also for Iraq's withdrawal from OPEC. The report exaggerated the prevalence of privatized oil industries globally (only 12 percent of oil-producing states had privatized their petroleum industry) (7.10) and the benefits of leaving OPEC. (Contrary to the Homeland Security Task Force report's assertions, OPEC standards reduce revenues in the short term but expand the productive lifespan of national oilfields.)

---

ARIEL COHEN, "THE ROAD TO ECONOMIC PROSPERITY FOR A POST-SADDAM IRAQ," HERITAGE FOUNDATION REPORT, MARCH 5, 2003 (EXCERPT)

The cost of rebuilding the country will be high. If Operation Desert Storm reconstruction costs are used as the basis for estimation, the cost of rebuilding Iraq after Saddam's regime falls will be in the $50 billion to 100 billion range. Together with repaying the Iraqi foreign debt (estimated at from $60 billion–$140 billion) and compensation costs to Kuwait and other countries (over $20 billion), the more realistic figure is 200 billion. However, as long as structural economic reforms are undertaken, Iraq's vast oil reserves and rebuilt economy, including the revamped oil sector, are likely to provide the funds needed to rebuild and boost economic growth.

Thus, the United States and the people of Iraq have the same interest at heart: maximize Iraq's economic performance. Without private ownership, however, oil will remain politicized and mismanaged. A group of Iraqi-born oil experts stated in December 2002, after a conference on the future of the Iraqi oil sector sponsored by the U.S. State Department, that "the aspiration of the group is a rehabilitated, globally connected oil and gas sector. . . ." Oil will remain the primary source of revenue and will play a pivotal role in the country's economic reconstruction. The group recognized the need to establish a favorable investment climate and attract international and inward capital in the reconstruction and growth of the industry. It saw the importance of introducing modern technology, know-how and management skills. Thus, the exiles fell short of calling for post-Saddam privatization of the Iraqi economy.

Secretary of State Colin Powell has said that "The oil of Iraq belongs to the Iraqi people. . . . [I]t will be held for and used for the people of Iraq. It will not be exploited for the United States' own purpose. . . ." But this does not preclude the United States from offering its guidance to the future government of Iraq on establishing sound economic and trade policies to stimulate growth and recovery. It would be counterproductive to empower either U.N. bureaucrats or Iraqi officials loyal to the Ba'ath party and Saddam to run the Iraqi oil industry.

The Bush Administration, through its executive directors at such IFIs as the IMF and World Bank, as well as other international governmental and non-governmental organizations, should begin to advise the future leaders of Iraq's next government to establish policies that will lead to a thriving modern economy. These policies should be based on "best practices" developed around the world in the 1990s, when the largest government privatizations in history occurred.

During the Iran-Iraq War and the post–Gulf War sanctions period, Iraqi petroleum production declined significantly. Saudi Arabia filled the void, generating a net profit of $100 billion. The funds it generated represent monies that should have benefited the Iraqi people.

Following the demise of Saddam Hussein, it is unlikely that the Saudi kingdom would transfer a fraction of its production quota under the Organization of Petroleum Exporting Countries (OPEC) regime to Iraq to compensate for those lost profits and facilitate its rebuilding. Iraq will need to ensure cash flow for reconstruction regardless of OPEC supply limitations. Combined with the potential privatization of the oil industry, such measures could provide incentives for Iraq to leave the OPEC cartel down the road, which would have long-term, positive implications for global oil supply.

## Potential Benefits of Leaving the OPEC Regime

An Iraq outside of OPEC would find available from its oil trade an ample cash flow for the country's rehabilitation. Its reserves currently stand at 112 billion barrels, but according to the U.S. Energy Information Administration, it may have as much as 200 billion barrels in reserve. Estimates by Iraqi oil officials are even higher: According to Oil Minister Amir Muhammad Rashad and Senior Deputy Oil Minister Taha Hmud, the reserves could be as high as 270 billion to 300 billion barrels, making them equal to Saudi Arabia's.

Iraq's 1990 output prior to the beginning of the Gulf War stood at 3.5 million barrels a day, while oil discovery rates on a few new projects in the 1990s were among the highest in the world: between 50 percent and 75 percent. Given Iraq's own output projections, it may be capable of pumping as much as 6 million barrels (by 2010) to 7 million barrels (by 2020) a day, more than doubling current production levels.

Such a surge in production may be opposed by OPEC countries, which would like to keep its quota around the current 2.8 million barrels per day, while historic market share is taken by the Kingdom of Saudi Arabia, which currently is pumping close to 8 million barrels per day. Depending on the dynamics of global economic growth and world oil output, Iraq's increase in oil production capacity could bring lower oil prices in the long term.

An unencumbered flow of Iraqi oil would be likely to provide a more constant supply of oil to the global market, which would dampen price fluctuations, ensuring stable oil prices in the world market in a price range lower than the current $25 to $30 a barrel. Eventually, this will be a win-win game: Iraq will emerge with a more viable oil industry, while the world will benefit from a more stable and abundant oil supply.

## Privatization: Learning from the Past

Boosting oil exports and oil industry privatization by itself still may not be sufficient for growth over the long haul. To rehabilitate and modernize its economy, a post-Saddam government will need to move simultaneously on a number of economic policy fronts, utilizing the experience of privatization campaigns and structural reforms in other countries to develop a comprehensive policy package.

Several lessons from other countries' privatization experiences are particularly relevant to Iraq's situation. Specifically:

LESSON #1: Privatization works everywhere. Between 1988 and 1993, 2,700 state-owned businesses in 95 countries were sold to private investors. In 1991 alone, $48 billion in state assets were privatized worldwide. Privatizations led to higher productivity, faster growth, increased capacity, and cheaper services for consumers.

In one study, the World Bank reviewed 41 firms privatized by public offerings in 15 countries. This review demonstrates that privatization will increase the return on sales, assets, and equity. As privatized firms grow, they often increase their workforces. In another study, the World Bank reviewed 12 privatization efforts in four countries, and its findings again demonstrate why privatization is good for the economy as a whole, no matter where it is implemented.

LESSON #2: Privatization works best when it is part of a larger structural reform program. Privatization needs to be accompanied by reforms to open markets, removal of price and exchange rate distortions, reductions in barriers to entry, and elimination of monopoly powers. In addition to these policies, governments should enact legislation that protects consumer welfare. Such successful structural reform and privatization programs were implemented in the 1990s in Poland, Hungary, the Czech Republic, and the three Baltic States, particularly Estonia.

LESSON #3: Privatization of large enterprises requires preparation. Successful privatizations of large enterprises may necessitate such advance actions as breaking them into smaller competitive units, recruiting experienced private-sector managers, adopting Generally Accepted Accounting Principles (GAAPs), settling past liabilities, and shedding excess labor.

LESSON #4: Transparency and the rule of law are critical. Opaque privatization and allegations of corruption and cronyism provide political ammunition to the opponents of market-based policies. To eliminate these problems and be successful in its privatization efforts, the government must adopt competitive bidding procedures, objective criteria for selecting bids, and protocols for hiring independent privatization management firms, and establish a privatization authority with minimal bureaucracy to monitor the overall program.

LESSON #5: A minimal safety net is necessary to support laid-off workers and prevent social unrest. Buyouts of the state-owned enterprise's management and labor force, as well as distribution of some of the privatized firm's shares to its management and labor force, can go a long way toward alleviating social tensions that might undermine public support for privatization.

LESSON #6: Privatization is taking place in the Middle East. Privatization is no longer limited to affluent or middle-income countries. From Margaret Thatcher's Great Britain, privatizations of state-owned assets and structural reform policies spread to many countries in Africa, Asia, and Latin America, including the Philippines, Malaysia, Jamaica, and Sri Lanka. An internal study of World Bank managers in the Middle East and North African department found that many were enthusiastic in supporting privatization efforts in their regions. A number of Middle Eastern states, including Iraq's neighbors Turkey and Kuwait, are pursuing privatization of their telecommunications, transportation, utilities, and oil sectors and services, while others, such as Iran and Saudi Arabia, have declared their intentions to privatize assets and are in the policy discussion stage.

## Lessons from Oil and Gas Privatizations

Oil privatization remains a politically painful issue in many countries. Economic nationalists claim oil is a "national patrimony," whereas socialists and radical Islamists call private and foreign ownership of natural resources "imperialist" and other such pejoratives. Such rhetoric has one goal: to keep a precious and profitable resource in the hands of the ruling elite, be it a communist party politburo, a dictator, or a group of mullahs.

In fact, oil is a commodity and should be managed according to the laws of economics and best business practices. Even a country as fiercely nationalist as Russia recognizes this and is undertaking the largest oil-sector privatization in history. The lessons from past experience in oil privatizations are also positive.

# DOCUMENT 7.9

An important 2003 study by BearingPoint, Inc., a company under contract with USAID, recommended Product-Sharing Agreements for Iraqi oil production because they would free up public money for other economic investments. While that might very well have been true, most analysts predicted that Iraq would ultimately receive less revenue with such contracts. PSAs were also far from the norm among the major oil-producing countries (7.10). The Bush administration brushed these concerns aside to push for a more radical privatization, buttressed by this BearingPoint study's advice that the administration should take bold, decisive action.

BEARINGPOINT CORPORATION, "OPTIONS FOR DEVELOPING A LONG TERM SUSTAINABLE IRAQI OIL INDUSTRY," DECEMBER 19, 2003 (EXCERPT)

## Self-financing Reconstruction of Iraq's Oil Sector?

In the past, the state-owned oil entities of Iraq were responsible for the production of virtually all the country's oil and gas. After the Iraq National Oil Company (INOC) was formed in 1964 to develop concession areas taken over from the Iraq Petroleum Company, internal cash flow and sovereign debt financed virtually all oilfield development in the country.

Since 1975, no foreign oil company has operated with equity interests in the country's oil sector. Even after the merger of the oil company into the Oil Ministry in the 1987, the Ministry was able to maintain production of more than 3 mmbd.

Elsewhere in the region, large national oil companies have been built without an equity role by the IOCs. Service contracts and other similarly limited arrangements have provided the sole outlet for IOC involvement in Saudi Arabia, Kuwait and Iran.

It is likely that any substantial role of the World Bank and IMF in Iraq's reconstruction will be accompanied by their "negative pledge" requirement: an agreement that limits the government's ability to pledge oil production or related assets as security for foreign loans. If such a negative pledge requirement is a barrier to MLA involvement, and given the unsettled business climate in Iraq, the probable lack of unsecured external debt financing for oil rehabilitation and expansion would therefore limit the country's investment options to its own cash flow or equity from private investors.

Can Iraq self-finance the rehabilitation and expansion of its petroleum sector from its own cash flow? The answer is yes. At oil prices of $25/bbl, about $12 billion will be available annually as the government's share of oil revenues, after subtracting the real costs of sustaining oil production at 2.5 mmbd, and after accounting for domestic consumption (domestic sales of petroleum products are unlikely in the short to medium term to be a net cash generator for the sector). Industry analysts believe that restoring production to 3–3.5 mmbd over 2 years will require about $5 billion in new investment. Financing such expansion out of current cash flow will take about $2.5 billion annually over 2 years, or about 21% of the government's share of oil revenues.

A more ambitious program, one aimed at reaching production in the 5.5–6 mmbd range is projected to cost about $20–30 billion over 5 years, or $4–6 billion annually. Iraq could afford this as well, though the initial proportion of the government's annual share of revenues could be as high as 50%. However, during periods of unfavorable crude oil prices, say $18/bbl, an ambitious expansion plan could require as much as 85% of the government's take.

There are three obvious economic impacts of self-financing: (i) Iraq's government will emerge from the reconstruction process with much greater equity in its oil industry, (ii) more of the domestic economy will be oriented toward the oil industry than would be the case if external financing were used, and (iii) fiscal policy will be extremely dependent on world oil prices.

To reach ambitious levels of oil production from cash flow, the OGE will need to beef up substantially its accounting, audit, contracting and procurement activities to handle the expected high volume of activity. This will have the effect of focusing business skills needed to rebuild the economy on the oil industry alone. Domestic service industries will likely revolve around the oil contractors, blocking much-needed economic diversification. In addition, OGE will need to maintain a high level of vigilance, given the attractiveness of corruption at such a high level of contracting. The political process for budgeting procedures for the OGE will have to be established firmly within the national planning process. To achieve steady oil field capacity growth in a self-financing strategy, the allocations to the OGE will have to be safeguarded even in times of low oil prices to prevent the highly disruptive effects that stop-start budgeting can have on major long term investment programs.

In the options discussed below, it is possible to have internal cash generation and service contractors replace the investments and activities of the IOCs. This is a matter for the Iraqis to decide. Three of the scenarios developed for this assessment, Lower Production (#1) Business as Usual (#2) and Reserve Producer (#5), implicitly assume lower levels of external investment and activity relative to the two remaining scenarios.

## DOCUMENT 7.10

The International Atomic Energy Agency documented some analysts' warnings that PSAs were rare among oil-producing countries. In the PSA model, the state continues to own the oil reserves, and the state gets revenue from oil sales. Foreign oil companies, however, control exploration, processing, and oil production through long-term (usually generous) contracts that guarantee profits and give the company immunity from local laws. That is, PSAs minimize the risks for and maximize the profits of the oil companies; conversely, they maximize the costs to the host country while minimizing its possible economic gains. The PSA model has never been used by nationally owned oil companies (which are in the majority)—especially for fields, like those in Iraq, where oil can be easily produced. According to economists, oil-producing countries choose PSAs with foreign firms only when oil reserves are small and oil is difficult to extract. This data belied the U.S. assertion that private oil companies were the norm globally and, thus, indispensable to the modernization and improvement of Iraq's oil production.

INTERNATIONAL ATOMIC ENERGY AGENCY, "FOREIGN INVESTMENT IN THE WORLD'S MAJOR OIL RESERVES, 2004"

| | Reserves (billion barrels) end 2004 | Share of world total reserves | Foreign company equity investment? | PSAs? |
|---|---|---|---|---|
| Saudi Arabia | 262.7 | 22.1% | No | No |
| Iran | 132.5 | 11.1% | No | No |
| Iraq | 115.0 | 9.7% | No | No |
| Kuwait | 99.0 | 8.3% | No | No |
| United Arab Emirates | 97.8 | 8.2% | Yes | No |
| Venezuela | 77.2 | 6.5% | Yes[1] | No |
| Russian Federation | 72.3 | 6.1% | Yes[2] | Yes[3] |
| **TOTAL** | **856.6** | **72.1%** | | |

1. In Venezuela, the apertura policy of 1993–1998 to allow foreign oil companies in is now being reversed.
2. Russia also saw massive expansion of the private sector's role in the 1990s; the trend is now in the opposite direction.
3. Only three PSAs have been signed, all during the rapid post-Soviet liberalization of the early mid-1990s. PSAs are now highly controversial and no more are likely to be signed.

# DOCUMENT 7.11

The Select Committee on Energy Independence and Global Warming of the House of Representatives expressed concern about the possibility that Hunt Oil—or any private company—would enter into independent economic contracts with the Kurdish regional government because such contracts might jeopardize the possibility that oil revenues could be used to benefit all Iraqis (especially since a revenue-sharing law had not yet been enacted). Nevertheless, not long after the Energy Committee issued its memo, the Kurds, insisting that Kurdish regional control over oil was not only good for the Kurds but consistent with the Iraq constitution, signed fifteen exploration contracts with foreign companies. In January 2008, the Kurdistan Regional Government went further, hiring the international legal expert James R. Crawford to provide legal opinions to confirm the Kurdish position that oil deals were "in full compliance with [the] Constitution."[14] The House committee's fears were provoked by the sectarian rifts and violence that dominated life in Iraq, divisions that often revolved around the question of how the country's oil wealth was to be distributed. The Kurds refused to cede control of the oilfields in their region. The Sunnis generally resided in areas with few major reserves and desired strong central government control over contracts, development, and distribution. But the Sunnis were suspicious of the Shia majority that controlled the central government. For their part, the Shia were divided between moderate and radical factions (chapter 6). In addition, there was considerable disagreement about whether the central government had constitutional control over existing oilfields, whether the regional government had control over new fields, and what constituted a new field.[15]

---

## U.S. CONGRESSIONAL MEMO ON HUNT OIL PSA WITH KURDISH REGIONAL GOVERNMENT, OCTOBER 18, 2007

Dear Mr. Chairman:

Thank you for your letter regarding the recent signing of an oil production sharing agreement (PSA) between the Hunt Oil Company, its partner Impulse Energy, and the Kurdistan Regional Government (KRG).

Hunt Oil's General Manager for Europe, Africa and the Middle East met with our Regional Reconstruction Team (RRT) in Irbil on September 5 to discuss Hunt's intention to sign a contract with the Kurdistan Regional Government (KRG). Our RRT informed Embassy Baghdad and Washington agencies on September 6. The contract was signed on September 8.

---

14. "International Law Expert Confirms KRG's Authority to Manage Oil & Gas Resources," Ministry for Natural Resources—Erbil, Kurdistan Region, February 5, 2008.

15. See Articles 108 and 109 of the Iraqi Constitution.

The RRT made clear to Hunt Oil's General Manager the same concerns that we have raised with all companies that have spoken with the U.S. Government about investment in Iraq's oil sector. Specifically, the RRT stated that we continue to advise all companies that they incur significant political and legal risk by signing contracts with any party before the Hydrocarbon Framework Law is passed by the Iraqi Parliament and that signature of such contracts would needlessly elevate tensions between the KRG and the Government of Iraq (GOI). We have expressed the same concerns to all companies that have contacted the U.S. Government about investment in Iraq's oil sector, regardless of size or nationality. We have also made the point publicly several times over the last year.

As we have said publicly, the Hunt Oil deal is not helpful because it was signed before the adoption of the Hydrocarbon Framework Law and prior to the delineation of authority over fields and exploration blocs. The Iraqi Federal Government and the KRG have not agreed on the number of exploration blocs, at which locations, nor on the issue of which party has the authority to manage which fields. The KRG's signing contracts before passage of these federal laws complicates the negotiations meant to address these questions. Iraq's political leaders need to resolve the issue of who has the authority under Iraqi law to negotiate, sign, and approve oil contracts. We believe it is in the best interest of Iraq for all interested parties to agree to a single central approver of contracts so that Iraq's oil and gas resources can be developed in accordance with a rational plan. The GOI and KRG will need to discuss what should be done with the numerous contracts already signed by the KRG.

Our understanding is that the draft federal Revenue Sharing Law, a separate piece of legislation from the Hydrocarbon Framework Law, will develop a single national account for the deposit of hydrocarbon revenues. This account would then divide money between national projects, the Federal Government, regions, and provinces. This law has not yet been vetted fully by the Iraqi cabinet, but if passed it would be a trust-building step to ensure that Iraq's oil wealth will be spent to help all areas of Iraq, and not just Baghdad.

Regarding your questions on the President's Foreign Intelligence Advisory Board, the Department of State is not the appropriate agency to respond to these questions. We suggest that you direct these questions to the White House.

We share your interest in the sustainable development of Iraq's oil and gas sector. The U.S. strongly supports the Iraqi Government's policy to reform this sector with the goal of maximizing oil revenues for the benefit of all Iraqis.

Sincerely,

*Jeffrey T. Bergner*
*Assistant Secretary*
*Legislative Affairs*

*Select Committee on Energy Independence, and Global Warming,*
*House of Representatives*
*The Honorable*
*Edward J. Markey, Chairman*

# DOCUMENT 7.12

One hundred and eight Iraqi oil technicians and experts wrote to the Iraqi government in July 2007 to oppose the new oil law because it would "definitely lead to the enforcement of the situation of division, anarchy, and chaos." They begged for caution and deliberation, for consultation with Iraqi technical experts, and, more importantly, for a structure that would maximize the benefits of oil profits for "the whole people of Iraq." There was no official or public reaction from the United States to this plea from Iraqi oil professionals.

LETTER FROM 108 IRAQI TECHNICAL, ACADEMIC,
AND ECONOMIC EXPERTS OPPOSED TO OIL
PRIVATIZATION, ADDRESSED TO THE IRAQI
COUNCIL OF REPRESENTATIVES, JULY 16, 2007                    | 389

*The president and members of the Iraqi Council of Representatives*
During the last six months, the public opinion, including us (oil experts and men of law and economics) were occupied with the procedures and events that accompanied the oil and gas law; many symposiums were held, the most prominent of which may be the symposium that was held by the oil experts in Amman on 17/2/2007 which produced a number of comments and recommendations that was presented at the time to your council.

As everybody knows, the draft of the law took it's [*sic*] path to the State Shoura Council, which gratefully, and in a professional way, redrafted it linguistically as well as suggesting some important notes to improve the efficiency of performance, implementation and to ensure the interest of all the Iraqi people, but it did not tackle some other important aspects.

The Council of Ministers approved on 3/7/2007 the draft of the law and referred it to your Council for the purpose of discussing and enacting. Although the final draft was not published, but it was noted from the available information, as well as from the pronouncements of officials of the central government and the Kurdistan Regional Government, that there are still differences concerning the four annexes, that were included in the law, that contains the classification of the producing fields and the discovered but not yet developed fields that are situated near the production centres, to be under the auspices of the national oil company that is to be created under the law—these differences resulted in the recommendation that these annexes to be deferred later to the federal council of oil and gas to consider; a matter which, in our opinion, does not remedy this important issue.

It is worth noting that the Council of Ministers has lately referred to you the draft of the law of distribution of the financial resources, through which an important part of the claims of the Kurdistan region can be handled; hence, at the present time, concentration may be given to the discussing of this financial law and in isolation of the oil and gas law.

*President and members of the council*

After seeing the draft of the oil and gas law, that was referred to you, we noticed that it does not differ in it's essence from the first draft except the noticeable improvement in the linguists composition. The present draft has ignored the comments presented by the State Shoura Council as well as all other comments such as our comments that we formulated in the Amman symposium, the symposiums held by the oil trade unions and the non-governmental organizations, in addition to many political blocks.

Emanating from our feelings of the extreme importance of the oil and gas law to the present and future of our dear country, we again turn towards you to expend your utmost efforts towards enriching the law with studying and checking and to remove and remedy the sources of faults in it, seeking the help of expert Iraqis of opinions and expertise.

390 |

According to the above, we would like to emphasize to your Council the following observations:

with our conviction for the need of a law to organize the upstream sector and it's development, and due to it's extreme importance, we emphasize the importance of acting steadily and not rushing it's issuance before enriching it with more discussions and carry out amendments that ensure the interest of all the Iraqi people, and not to ignore the sector of the processing industries (refining, distribution and gas processing), with the priority given for the enacting of the Iraq National Oil Company law.

1. there are ongoing discussions aiming to amend the Iraqi Constitution, including the items related to oil and gas; hence we do not see, from the legal and technical point of view, the necessity to enact the law presented to you now before the constitutional amendments are finalized.

2. licensing contracts of exploration, development and production, form the backbone of this law, hence it is vital to emphasize the role of the council of representatives in the approval of such contracts; similar to what is adopted in the rest of the world. It is regrettable to notice that the authority of the council is restricted to the enacting of the law and the approval of international agreements only.

3. as for the four annexes attached to the law, they are of vital importance as well, so we emphasize on the council of representa-

lives, the necessity to discuss them as part and parcel of the proposed law. We emphasize also upon the role of the Iraqi national oil company for the necessity for it to undertake the responsibility of managing all the producing and discovered fields in a form that will safeguard the rights of the Iraqi people completely and not to forsake any of the oil reserves in any contractual format to foreign entities.

4. we assert the importance and necessity to adopt a comprehensive central plan for the whole of Iraq to determine the priorities of explorations and development efforts according to economic and technical basis prevalent in the oil industry; recognizing the importance of the participation of the regions and the governorates in the operations of planning, implementation and management within a comprehensive vision that ensures the maximum benefits for the whole people of Iraq.

5. the passing of this law without paying attention to the expected impacts of competitions between the regions and the governorates, and what that will entail of conflicts, will definitely lead to the enforcement of the situation of divisions, anarchy and chaos; the best example of this, the latest unilateral declaration by the Kurdistan Regional Government offering (40) exploration blocks for foreign investment, without even waiting for the enacting of the federal law and without the existence of a comprehensive and approved central plan for the whole of Iraq, including the Kurdistan region.

Lastly, we call upon the president and the members of the council to take a memorable historical stand that will be remembered and registered for them in protecting the interests of the whole Iraqi people and in defending the rights of its sons in their present and future times.

# Iraq Privatization Documents

## DOCUMENT 7.13

U.S. steelworkers supported the Iraqi oil workers in their actions to prevent privatization of their national oil industry. On July 31, 2007, International President Leo W. Gerard wrote to the chairs of important congressional committees, including Ike Skelton, Duncan Hunter, Tom Lantos, Ileana Ros-Lehtinen, Nita M. Lowey, George Miller, Howard McKeon, John P. Murtha, and C. W. Bill Young in the House, and Carl Levin, Edward M. Kennedy, John McCain, Michael B. Enzi, Joe Biden Jr., Daniel K. Inouye, Richard Lugar, Ted Stevens, Patrick J. Leahy, and Judd Gregg in the Senate. Gerard's letter made it clear that the union's opposition to privatization of Iraqi oil sprang from its belief that Iraqi labor organizations were in a good position to reduce sectarian division and violence in Iraq.

---

## LEO W. GERARD, UNITED STEELWORKERS LETTER TO CONGRESS OPPOSING PRIVATIZATION OF IRAQI OIL INDUSTRY, JULY 31, 2007 (EXCERPT)

I am writing to alert you to two important issues connected with the ongoing occupation and war in Iraq. Though not widely discussed in the U.S., these issues are central to the challenges faced by the Iraqi people. They concern the viability of the Iraqi labor movement and the fate of Iraq's oil.

One of the few benign effects of deposing Saddam Hussein has been the emergence, despite opposition from both the U.S. authority and many parts of the Iraqi government, of a vibrant and growing labor movement. This is crucially important, because to all appearances the labor movement is one of the few organizations structured on a secular basis, has genuine popular support, and has membership across the growing ethnic and sectarian divisions.

This suggests that the labor movement in Iraq is one of the few organizations capable of playing a significant role in lessening and hopefully ending the sectarian strife plaguing their country. We strongly believe the views of this labor movement should be heard much more clearly in Washington than they have been to date. . . .

A number of issues need to be emphasized. First, these leaders believe strongly that sectarian strife will ease, and that unions will be able to act with substantially more freedom when the U.S. military presence has ended.

Second, the unions believe equally strongly that Iraq's oil is a national resource that should not be privatized, and specifically that oil privatization should not be used as any kind of "benchmark" of the Iraqi government's success or failure. They state, and we agree, that the oil privatization law now under consideration by Iraq's government is designed to benefit the multinational oil companies; not the Iraqi people.

Additionally, we believe several policies imposed by the U.S. occupation administration under its former head Paul Bremer and by subsequent Iraqi governments should be rescinded.

These include the continuation in force of a Saddam Hussein–era law banning collective bargaining in Iraq's public sector, an onerously low general wage schedule, and the complete sequestration of union funds by the government.

Therefore we ask that you do all you can to oppose the privatization of Iraq's oil resources, correct the inequities present in Iraqi labor policy, and continue to support an end to the U.S. military presence in Iraq.

Thank you very much for your consideration of these vitally important matters.

# DOCUMENT 7.14

In a press release that accompanied his speech of March 27, 2008, President Bush assessed the political, security, and economic progress being made by Iraq. As usual, he emphasized the positive, especially with regard to oil and the Iraqi economy. He expressed satisfaction with the rise in oil production but warned that more privatization was needed to "transition from a command-and-control economy to a modern market-based system."

---

"FACT SHEET: ACHIEVING POLITICAL AND ECONOMIC PROGRESS IN IRAQ: PRESIDENT BUSH DISCUSSES WAYS THE SURGE IS HELPING IRAQIS RECLAIM SECURITY AND RESTART POLITICAL AND ECONOMIC LIFE," MARCH 27, 2008 (EXCERPT)

## President Bush Visits Dayton, Ohio, Discusses Global War on Terror | 393

Today, President Bush visited the National Museum of the United States Air Force and discussed the political and economic changes currently taking place in Iraq. Last year, the President ordered 30,000 additional soldiers and Marines into Iraq, and gave them a new mission, to focus on protecting the Iraqi people, and to hold the gains that had been made. The other goal of the surge was to open up space for political and economic progress after security returned. So the U.S. deployed additional civilian experts and more than doubled the number of Provincial Reconstruction Teams, with a mission to ensure the security gains were followed by improvements in daily life.

*Civil Society Is Beginning to Grow In Iraq*
The surge is yielding major changes in Iraqi political life. With security improving, local citizens have restarted the political process in neighborhoods, cities, and provinces. Grassroots movements have sprung up all around the country. These groups of citizens are determined to protect their communities, they are determined to fight extremism, and they increasingly participate in civic life.

Today, some 90,000 Iraqis belong to [a] local citizens group bearing the name "Sons of Iraq." The Iraqi Government has pledged to incorporate about 20 to 30 percent of these "Sons of Iraq" into the Iraqi army and police forces.

Leaders in Baghdad are responding and the legislative achievements in Baghdad over the past four months have been remarkable.

In December, the government enacted a pension law that will allow tens of thousands of Sunnis to collect the retirement benefits they were promised.

In January, leaders enacted a de-Ba'athification law that allows mid-level Baath party members to re-enter political and civic life.

In February, leaders enacted a budget that increases spending on security capital reconstruction projects and provincial governments.

The same day in February, leaders enacted an amnesty law to resolves the status of many Iraqis held in Iraqi custody.

Last week, leaders reached agreement on a provincial powers law that helps define Iraqi federalism, and sets the stage for provincial elections later this year. That is an important piece of legislation because it will give Iraqis who boycotted the last provincial elections—such as Sunnis in Anbar or Ninewa provinces—a chance to go to the polls and have a voice in their future.

The U.S. more than doubled the number of Provincial Reconstruction Teams. Karbala PRT helped local residents establish a women's center to provide education and promote equality.

With support of PRTs, Ramadi now has a fully staffed mayor's office and neighborhood councils have formed. Judges are presiding over courts and restoring the rule of law.

394 | *Iraq Has Great Economic Potential*
The improvements in security resulting from the surge are enabling Iraqis to make progress on their economy. Since the surge began:

- Business registrations have increased by more than nine percent;
- Total inflation has fallen by more than 60 percentage points;
- Investment in energy and telecom industries has increased;
- Oil production is up, particularly north of Baghdad;
- The national government has announced a plan to reform the food rationing system; and
- Economic growth is projected to be a robust seven percent this year.

Iraqis still have work to do in their economy. The reforms needed to transition from a command-and-control economy to a modern market-based system are complex and will take more time. Centralized electricity generation is now above pre-war levels, but it is not sufficient to meet the needs of Iraq's growing demand. Other key infrastructure needs to be upgraded, especially energy pipelines and storage facilities. Unemployment is too high, and corruption remains a challenge.

*Iraq's Government Has Stepped Forward to Meet More of Its Own Expenses*
Early in the war, the U.S. funded most of the large-scale reconstruction projects in Iraq. Now the U.S. is focusing on encouraging entrepreneurship. The Iraqi government is stepping up on reconstruction projects. They have

outspent the U.S. in recent budget 11 to one, and soon we expect the Iraqis will cover 100 percent of these expenses.

Initially, the U.S. paid for most of the costs of training and equipping the Iraqi Security Forces. Now Iraq's budget covers three-quarters of the cost of its security forces, which is a total of more than $9 billion in 2008. Soon, we expect Iraq to shoulder the full burden of their security forces.

The national government has now committed $196 million to fund jobs programs so that brave Iraqis who stand up to the extremists and the murders and the criminals can learn the skills they need to help build a free and prosperous nation.

*Iraq Is Strengthening Its Relationship with Other Nations*
Iraq wants to solidify its relationship with the United States. Last year, Iraqi leaders requested to form a long-term strategic partnership with the U.S. This partnership would help assure Iraqis that political and economic and security cooperation between the nations will endure. This partnership would also ensure protections for American troops when the U.N. mandate for Multi-National Forces in Iraq expires this December. This partnership would not bind future Presidents to specific troop levels. This partnership would not establish permanent bases in Iraq.

The surge is helping give Iraq's leaders the confidence to expand their international engagement.

Iraqi leaders are working hard to meet the criterion required to join the World Trade Organization, which would help its entrepreneurs benefit from the opportunities of a global economy.

Iraq has taken steps to attract foreign investment, including hosting its first "Business to Business" expo since the Gulf War.

The government is meeting its pledge to reform its economy in exchange for development assistance and debt relief through the International Compact for Iraq.

Much of the world is increasing its commitment to Iraq. The United Kingdom, Italy, and South Korea are leading PRTs in Iraq. The United Nations is playing an expanded role in Iraq, and will help prepare for this year's provincial elections.

Next month, the third Expanded Neighbors Conference will meet in Kuwait City to discuss ways the region and the world can further support Iraq's political, economic, and security progress. This is a key diplomatic initiative. It will include all of Iraq's neighbors, as well as the permanent members of the United Nations Security Council, the G-8, the Arab League, and the Organization of the Islamic Conference.

*The Progress in Iraq Is Real, It's Substantive, but It's Reversible*
Helping Iraqis defeat their enemies and build a free society would be a strategic victory that would resound far beyond Iraq's borders. If al Qaeda is defeated in Iraq after all the resources it has poured into the battle there,

it will be a powerful blow against the global terrorist movement. If Iran is turned back in its attempt to gain undue influence over Iraq, it will be a setback to its ambitions to dominate the region. If people across the Middle East see freedom prevail in multi-ethnic, multi-sectarian Iraq, it will mark a decisive break from the long reign of tyranny in that region. And if the Middle East grows in freedom and prosperity, the appeal of extremism will decline, the prospects of peace will advance, and the American people will be safer here at home.

Retreating from Iraq would carry enormous strategic costs for the United States. It would increase the likelihood that al Qaeda would gain safe havens that they could use to attack us here at home. It would be a propaganda victory of colossal proportions for the global terrorist movement, which would gain new funds, and find new recruits, and conclude that the way to defeat America is to bleed us into submission. It would signal to Iran that we were not serious about confronting its efforts to impose its will on the region. It would signal to people across the Middle East that the United States cannot be trusted to keep its word. A defeat in Iraq would have consequences far beyond that country—and they would be felt by Americans here at home.

# DOCUMENT 7.15

An important 2007 White House report assessing Iraqi progress on particular benchmarks admitted that sectarian conflict and violence continued to dominate Iraqi life. It also suggested that progress toward an oil law was thwarted by the sectarian conflict, and acknowledged that failure to achieve an equitable distribution of oil profits created a lack of public "confidence" in the Iraqi government. More important was what it failed to say: that the plans to open Iraqi oilfields to foreign firms were an important reason for the sectarian conflict (7.13). Instead, the report indicated that the United States would "move forward" with its economic policies for Iraq.

OFFICE OF THE PRESIDENT, INITIAL BENCHMARK-ASSESSMENT REPORT, JULY 12, 2007 (EXCERPT)

**Political Reconciliation:** Moving key legislation depends on deal making among major players in a society deeply divided along sectarian, ethnic, and other lines. Meaningful and lasting progress on national reconciliation may also require a sustained period of reduced violence in order to build trust. For this reason, most of the major political benchmarks identified in the legislation (i.e., final passage of monumental pieces of legislation through Iraq's Council of Representatives by consensus) are lagging indicators of whether or not the strategy is succeeding or is going to be successful. . . .

(iii) Enacting and implementing legislation to ensure the equitable distribution of hydrocarbon resources to the people of Iraq without regard to the sect or ethnicity of recipients, and enacting and implementing legislation to ensure that the energy resources of Iraq benefit Sunni Arabs, Shi'a Arabs, Kurds, and other Iraqi citizens in an equitable manner.

The final draft of the Revenue Management Law must be approved by the Council of Ministers (COM) and vetted by the Iraqi Government's legal office before submission to the COR. The United States has provided technical advice to the Iraqi Government and is actively engaged in encouraging both sides to expeditiously approve the draft law in the COM and move it to the COR. Prime Minister Maliki intends to submit the Revenue Management Law to the COM soon, for subsequent consideration by the COR along with the framework Hydrocarbon law.

The Government of Iraq has not met its self-imposed goal of May 31 for submitting the framework hydrocarbon and revenue sharing laws to the COR. Although the KRG and the Shi'a parties have agreed to the text of the Revenue Management Law, Council of Ministers' approval has been delayed by a Sunni party boycott. The effect of limited progress toward this benchmark has been to reduce the perceived confidence in, and effectiveness of, the Iraqi Government. This does not, however, necessitate a revision to our current plan and strategy, under which we have assigned a high priority to this subject, and the process overall has continued to move forward.

# DOCUMENT 7.16

In a speech at the U.S. Institute of Peace, Ambassador Charles Ries, the United States Minister for Economic Affairs and Coordinator for Economic Transition in Iraq, explained how the United States influenced economic policy in Iraq by "leveraging" aid dollars. In other words, Washington used "soft power" as well as "hard" (coercive) power to shape policy in its own interest in Iraq. This less well-understood aspect of hegemonic power involved neither guns nor soldiers but relied on technical and financial pressure to create environments in which U.S. objectives and needs would be met.

---

CHARLES P. RIES, "BEYOND BRICKS AND MORTAR: THE 'CIVILIAN SURGE' IN IRAQ," MARCH 11, 2008 (EXCERPT)

. . . But now it's time to change direction. When I took this job last July, the International Zone, where I live and work, was experiencing near-daily alarms warning of mortar volleys. Other parts of Iraq were experiencing the same. But as the 2007 military surge took hold, the threats lessened. Economic activity picked up—slowly but measurably. They were brave, these early entrepreneurs seeking to take back their neighborhoods and government institutions. The security situation was and is extremely fragile.

Effective ministers, deputy ministers and senior officials still risk kidnapping or targeted assassination. But gradually, we saw that the military surge had given us an opening to make important progress on economic and governance issues—if we could direct our resources, fast, where they would have maximum effect. We needed to change our focus from bricks and mortar to giving our Iraqi partners the technical assistance they needed.

Notice that I said "partners." Iraq's national budget doubled from $20 billion in 2004 to $41 billion in 2007, largely as a result of dramatically higher oil prices. Iraq is making its own investment decisions to address the major challenges it faces. We decided it was time to use our assistance dollars as leverage in a productive partnership.

How? By addressing some of the critical economic priorities that would bolster stability and improve the Iraqis' ability to govern. If we could do that—bring even a modest economic revival to neighborhoods now experiencing greater security—the gains of the military surge would be less likely to be undermined by still active insurgents looking for ways to create chaos.

# DOCUMENT 7.17

The first agreement of its kind in Iraq, the 2005 accord with the International Monetary Fund was signed before the new, divided Iraqi government took office. It was established to provide the Iraqi government with the technical assistance needed to transform its economy into a market-based one and to create the legal basis for a privatized oil industry. The IMF used its external institutional resources to try to privatize the economy against the expressed interests of the majority of Iraqis.[16]

---

"IMF EXECUTIVE BOARD APPROVES FIRST EVER STAND-BY ARRANGEMENT FOR IRAQ," PRESS RELEASE NO. 05/307, DECEMBER 23, 2005 (EXCERPT)

The Executive Board of the International Monetary Fund (IMF) today approved the institution's first-ever Stand-By Arrangement for Iraq, which is designed to support the nation's economic program over the next 15 months. The IMF arrangement, for an amount equivalent to SDR 475.4

---

16. See the July 30, 2007, poll conducted by Custom Strategic Research that showed 63 percent of Iraqis opposed to privatization of the oil industry.

million (about US $685 million), is being treated as precautionary by the Iraqi authorities.

Iraq, a founding member country of the IMF, received its first-ever loan from the Fund in September 2004 through Emergency Post Conflict Assistance (see Press Release No. 04/206). The initial credit was designed to facilitate Iraq's negotiations with its Paris Club creditors over a debt-restructuring agreement that is now in place, and to support the nation's economic programs through 2005. Approval of the Stand-By Arrangement is a condition for the second stage of debt reduction agreed with Iraq's Paris Club creditors.

Following the Executive Board's discussion of Iraq, Mr. Takatoshi Kato, Deputy Managing Director and Acting Chair, said:

The Iraqi authorities were successful in promoting macroeconomic stability in 2005, despite the extremely difficult security environment. Economic growth was modest, following the strong rebound recorded in 2004, and inflationary pressures moderated, although prices remained volatile. The Central Bank of Iraq built up reserves and the exchange rate remained stable. The projected fiscal deficit is much lower than expected under the EPCA-supported program, mainly due to higher than projected export prices for crude oil. On the other hand, because of security concerns and capacity constraints, the implementation of structural benchmarks specified in the EPCA-supported program was slower than envisaged.

The authorities' program for 2006 aims to allocate resources towards the planned expansion of the oil sector, redirect expenditures away from general subsidies towards providing improved public services, and strengthen administrative capacity. The program, which envisages an increase in economic growth, a reduction in inflation, and an increase in net international reserves, maintains a focus on macroeconomic stability, while improving governance and advancing Iraq's transition to a market economy.

A critical component of the overall strategy is to contain expenditures within revenues and available financing, by prioritizing expenditures, controlling the wage and pensions bill, reducing subsidies on petroleum products, and expanding the participation of the private sector in the domestic market for petroleum products, while strengthening the social safety net.

The authorities have recently increased prices of refined petroleum products and will need to press ahead with other structural reforms, including measures to enhance the efficiency and transparency of public financial management and the development of a comprehensive restructuring strategy for the state-owned banks. At the same time, the Central Bank of Iraq aims to establish a modern payments system, implement modern supervisory frameworks, facilitate the proper functioning of foreign exchange and money markets, and conduct a monetary policy geared to ensuring financial stability.

"The medium term outlook for Iraq is favorable, but subject to many risks. A strengthening of the security situation will help the authorities to implement the program. Moreover, Iraq remains vulnerable to shocks, particularly those relating to oil production development and oil export price movements," Mr. Kato said.

# DOCUMENT 7.18

This summary of the USAID $5.5 billion contract to rebuild the Iraqi economy made clear that privatization was the preferred tool for reconstruction. It dismissed the state-owned economy that had existed under Saddam Hussein, criticized its mismanagement, and declared the need to remove its barriers to "private sector-led growth." It did not include any mention of the Iraqi public's preferences for their economy. That may have been because most public opinion polls had very clearly demonstrated the Iraqis' preference for publicly owned enterprise.

---

USAID PRIVATE SECTOR DEVELOPMENT PROGRAM
IN IRAQ, 2005

400 |  Historically a society with a strong merchant class, Iraq's private sector was devastated by decades of Ba'athist mismanagement, sanctions, and conflict. Since September 2004, the Private Sector Development Program has helped promote a market-based economy across six areas:

*Privatization.* The majority of economic activity in Iraq is funneled through over 500 state-owned enterprises, creating an unsupportable system. Through technical assistance and support, USAID is helping the Government of Iraq (GOI) privatize much of the economy, removing a major burden from the national budget and revitalizing the private sector. In 2005, USAID helped draft the privatization law and provided assistance to create a Privatization Committee to reduce redundancy, increase efficiency, and ensure a transparent privatization process.

*Trade and Market Access.* Through sector studies and regulatory guidance, USAID is helping reconnect Iraq with the international market, allowing the country to benefit from management acumen, capital, and technology as well as goods and services. In mid-2005, USAID assisted the GOI in submitting the Memorandum on Foreign Trade Regime, the first step in joining the World Trade Organization (WTO). The accession process will oblige Iraq to reform its trade regulations and establish an open, market based economy.

*Investment Promotion.* By promoting foreign investment and removing the barriers to private sector-led growth, USAID helps create a dynamic, market-driven economy that will generate employment. Drawing on USAID support, the Government of Iraq has established Iraqi Investment Promotion Agency (IIPA) and the Iraq Trade Information Center (ITIC) to encourage international investors. The Investor Roadmap and a Competitiveness Study prepared by USAID analyzed investment constraints and outlining corrective policies.

*Capital Markets.* USAID is helping the GOI reform the legal, regulatory, and structural elements of Iraq's non-bank financial markets (e.g., insurance, pension, equity, and commercial debt). To date, USAID has worked with other U.S. Government agencies to establish the Iraq Stock Exchange and Iraqi Securities Commission, essential to attracting foreign direct investment and privatizing state-owned enterprises.

*Business Skills.* USAID support for accounting reform helps integrate Iraqi businesses into the global financial system. As of December 2005, USAID has delivered nearly 40,000 hours of training in international accounting standards, enabling businesses to secure loans and manage accounts.

*Micro, Small and Medium Enterprises.* USAID is working with private banks and microfinance institutions to develop their lending capacity. The availability of loans is essential for private sector growth. Previously, USAID provided technical assistance for Coalition Provisional Authority's $21 million micro-credit program. More recently, USAID awarded long-term grants to three international NGOs to support development of sustainable micro-finance operations, encouraging job creation countrywide. Two indigenous micro-finance institutes in key cities have received essential funding while a third, in Fallujah, will be receiving support in coordination with the U.S. military. Technical advisors are also building capacity at the Iraq Company for Bank Guarantees, an organization that will provide loan guarantees to private banks and microfinance institutions to support lending to micro, small and medium enterprises (MSMEs).

| 401

## Proposed Next Steps (through September 2006)

*Privatization.* USAID advisors will train Iraqi officials in techniques and issues raised by privatization.

*Trade and Market Access.* USAID will support the Government of Iraq in drafting answers to questions on the Memorandum on the Foreign Trade Regime. Work is continuing with the Government of Iraq on developing WTO accession documentation (ACC4, ACC5, ACC8, and ACC9). USAID is also helping ensure that necessary laws—including copyright, customs valuation, intellectual property, and technical barriers to trade—comply with WTO guidelines.

*Investment Promotion.* The Private Sector Development program will continue to support the Investment Promotion Agency (IPA) and follow up on the Competitiveness Survey.

*Capital Markets.* To advance the Iraq securities market, USAID is supporting development of Operational Procedures and Rules based on the existing Interim Law of Securities. An EDGAR-like securities information database is being developed to provide the means to store issuer filings (85 current companies) and make them accessible to the public.

*Business Skills.* USAID will help train 250 credit managers and loan officers in progressive credit management practices, and cash flow based lending. Technical advisors will provide business association training to help associations establish themselves as industry advocates.

*Micro, Small and Medium Enterprises.* USAID will complete the disbursal of three large grants totaling more than $17 million for microfinance. Technical experts will assist in establishing up to seven indigenous MFI's providing $1.8 million in violence-prone areas to help rebuild small enterprises and jump-start provincial economies. USAID will also provide continued support to building capacity at the Iraq Company for Bank Guarantees to facilitate increased lending in the microfinance sector.

# ★ CHAPTER 8 ★

# HUMAN RIGHTS AND INTERNATIONAL LAW

## U.S. METHODS AND OPERATIONS
## IN PREEMPTIVE WAR

AS THE WARS in Afghanistan and Iraq continued, evidence began emerging that Washington was using methods and operations that violated constitutional principles and U.S. law, the Geneva Conventions, and human rights covenants (8.1–8.4). Sources suggested that special counterterrorism units had been authorized to use "enhanced interrogation techniques" and other extralegal methods against prisoners (8.5). Major newspapers such as the *Washington Post* and the *New York Times* published stories in late 2002 and 2003 with accounts of the torture and extrajudicial execution of suspected terrorists or insurgents. Well-known journalists such as Seymour Hersh wrote investigative pieces that drew parallels between U.S. methods in the Middle East and the infamous Phoenix Program of assassination in Vietnam carried out in the 1960s. Latin America experts pointed to similarities between the tactics of disappearance, "rendition," torture, and incommunicado detention used by the United States and the methods used by Latin American military regimes, trained and assisted by the United States during the Cold War (8.6), in such covert intelligence programs as Operation Condor.[1]

The authors wish to thank Michael Ratner, the president of the Center for Constitutional Rights, for his comments on this chapter. Of course, any errors of fact or interpretation remain those of the authors.

1. Condor was a Cold War–era covert network of U.S.-backed Latin American military regimes in Argentina, Brazil, Bolivia, Chile, Paraguay, and Uruguay, later joined by Ecuador and Peru in less central roles. The secret Condor apparatus enabled the militaries to share intelligence—and to seize, torture, and execute political opponents across borders. See J. Patrice McSherry, *Predatory States: Operation Condor and Covert War in Latin America* (Lanham, Md.: Rowman & Littlefield, 2005).

Why did the George W. Bush administration turn to torture and other inhuman and degrading methods in Iraq and elsewhere? The United States had famously outlawed "cruel and unusual punishment" in the Eighth Amendment to the Constitution, ratified in 1791. Abraham Lincoln had prohibited cruelty and torture during the Civil War. The United States had considered "waterboarding"—a torture in which the prisoner is subjected to near-drowning—a war crime for most of its history. In fact, a U.S. officer was convicted in 1901 for "waterboarding" a Filipino detainee during the U.S. occupation of the Philippines. An army officer was court-martialed in 1968 for using the water torture against a Vietnamese prisoner. How was it possible that the United States would turn so quickly to harsh, illegal methods that had been denounced by the civilized world for two hundred years?

Vice President Richard Cheney provided a clue when he said on September 16, 2001, "We also have to work though, sort of the dark side. . . . A lot of what needs to be done here will have to be done quietly, without any discussion, using sources and methods that are available to our intelligence agencies. . . . [I]t's going to be vital for us to use any means at our disposal, basically, to achieve our objective."[2] He added that the United States needed "to make certain that we have not tied the hands, if you will, of our intelligence communities in terms of accomplishing their mission." In short order, legal restraints on U.S. intelligence operations—in place since the scandals of the 1970s, when evidence of CIA assassination plots and foreign interventions had shocked the public—would be superseded. United States operatives would be authorized to employ lawless and brutal methods as part of preemptive war. The United States, unlike other countries, would be above the law. In fact, the CIA and military were no strangers to torture methods, as the historical record indicates.

In April 2004, U.S. practices in the "war on terror" became a major public issue for the first time. An army soldier who was troubled by what he had seen in Abu Ghraib prison decided to turn over graphic photos of detainee abuse to his superiors. As the photographs of Iraqis being sexually humiliated and tortured became public, the world reacted with outrage. In a 2004 internal report, a U.S. Army investigator pointed to the "systemic" nature of the abuses carried out against detainees. Gen. Antonio M. Taguba, appointed by the army to investigate U.S. military detention practices, documented "egregious acts and grave breaches of international law at Abu Ghraib/BCCF [Baghdad Central Confinement Facility] and Camp Bucca, Iraq" in his report (8.7). In June 2008, Taguba wrote, "There is no longer any doubt as to whether the current administration has committed war crimes. The only question that remains to be answered is whether those who ordered the use of torture will be held to account."[3]

---

2. White House transcript of Tim Russert interview with Richard Cheney, September 16, 2001.
3. Taguba wrote the preface for a stunning report by the Physicians for Human Rights, "Broken Laws, Broken Lives: Medical Evidence of Torture by U.S. Personnel and Its Impact," June 2008.

Largely beyond the view of the U.S. public, U.S. forces had begun detaining thousands of Afghans and then Iraqis in 2001, 2002, and 2003. Although figures were difficult to verify, during Senate hearings in 2008 one expert estimated that there were some twenty-five thousand detainees held by the United States worldwide, a number he had calculated from his communications with senior military officers.[4] Most detainees were being held indefinitely, without charges. Two human rights organizations also reported that some 24,661 persons were being detained by the United States in Iraq in 2008, and another 26,472 were being held by the Iraqi government—bringing the total to 51,133, including almost 900 juveniles.[5] During the early years of the war, about eight hundred persons from many countries had been transported to a prison block in Guantánamo Bay, Cuba. Others were held in CIA "black sites," a global network of secret detention centers; in the notorious Abu Ghraib prison in Iraq; in Bagram Air Base in Afghanistan; and elsewhere. As of late 2008, only a handful of detainees in Guantánamo had been charged, and only two had been convicted, under a military commission system widely criticized for not guaranteeing minimal due process.[6]

Over time it became clear that the methods used against detainees, and authorized by the Bush administration, included "waterboarding" (near-drowning and suffocation) (8.8, 8.17); "extraordinary rendition" (disappearance, or extralegal abduction, and transfer, often to countries that used torture) (8.9); use of CIA "black sites" (secret prisons beyond the reach of law); indefinite, incommunicado detention; forcible administering of drugs; and military tribunals that did not guarantee normal legal protections. The policy of preemption was being carried out through the systematic use of methods that the U.S. government had previously denounced when practiced by other states. Human rights organizations issued numerous troubling reports on the violations taking place (8.10–8.11). The relentless, fifty-four-day torture of Saudi detainee Mohammad al-Qahtani—allegedly an accomplice of the September 11 terrorists—was made public in 2006 when *Time* magazine published his harrowing "interrogation log."[7] In Guantánamo, military interrogators had used multiple,

---

4. Statement of Amos N. Guiora, Professor of Law, S. J. Quinney College of Law, University of Utah, Salt Lake City, Utah, Hearing before the Committee on the Judiciary, U.S. Senate, 110th Congress, 2nd Session, June 4, 2008.

5. International Federation for Human Rights and Global Policy Forum, "Open Letter to Members of the Security Council Concerning Detentions in Iraq," April 22, 2008, provided to UN Security Council.

6. One, an Australian, received a nine-month sentence and was released to his country; the other, a Yemeni who had been bin Laden's driver, also received a light sentence. Both had been detained without charge and without due process for many years.

7. Adam Zagorin, "Exclusive: '20th Hijacker' Claims That Torture Made Him Lie," *Time*, March 3, 2006. See also Center for Constitutional Rights, "The Torture of Mohammed al-Qahtani," http://ccrjustice.org/learn-more/reports/publication:-torture-mohammed-al-qahtani. For a well-researched account of the high-level decisions that led to the use of torture, see Philippe Sands, *Torture Team: Rumsfeld's Memo and the Betrayal of American Values* (London: Palgrave MacMillan, 2008).

ruthless, carefully planned techniques on al-Qahtani—including long-term isolation in a cell flooded with light, sleep deprivation, excruciating "stress positions" (which may include hanging), aggressive dogs, nudity, forced injections and intravenous lines, body searches, and enemas—to destroy him through physical and psychological suffering. Approval for the methods came from Defense Secretary Donald Rumsfeld. In February 2008, more than six years later, the Defense Department announced that a death penalty case was being filed against al-Qahtani on charges of murder, terrorism, and other crimes. As the British human rights lawyer Philippe Sands noted in his book exploring this case, the relatively thin information presented as evidence had already been available before his torture.[8] In May 2008, the Convening Authority for Military Commissions "dismissed without prejudice" the charges against al-Qahtani, later stating that her decision was due to the torture he had suffered. But military prosecutors reserved the right to detain him indefinitely and to charge him again.

Several U.S. citizens were also denied their rights and subjected to torture, notably José Padilla. Accused of preparing to detonate a "dirty bomb"—a charge that was later dropped—Padilla spent years in incommunicado detention in military cellblocks in the United States, where he was injected with drugs against his will and subjected to sensory and sleep deprivation, stress positions, freezing temperatures, and other methods of torture.[9] Such practices violated U.S. law, such as Sections 2340 and 2340A of the U.S. Criminal Code, and international prohibitions such as the Convention against Torture, which the United States had ratified in 1994.

Torture has a long history. The torture of prisoners and slaves has been traced to 1300 B.C.; the Greeks and Romans practiced it; indeed, for thousands of years torture was part of many existing legal systems.[10] In the Middle Ages, the Catholic Church used torture during the Inquisition, part of a religious system in which heretics and recent converts or "nonbelievers" (Jews, Muslims, and, later, Protestants) were tortured to force conversion or confession. The torture we know today as "waterboarding" was used in medieval times as well.

Torture has always been used not only to gain information but also to punish, to subjugate, to paralyze, to terrorize, and to demonstrate the power and dominance of rulers over subject populations. Many experts on interrogation state that torture does not produce reliable information, since the tortured per-

---

8. Sands, *Torture Team*, 229.

9. Padilla was arrested on U.S. soil and held without charge as an "enemy combatant." Attorney General John Ashcroft publicly accused him of plotting to explode a dirty bomb in the United States. Yet when the government finally put him on trial, after years of incommunicado detention, there was no mention of a dirty bomb. He was charged with giving "material support to terrorists," and no evidence was offered linking Padilla to actual terrorist acts. He was sentenced on conspiracy charges to seventeen years in prison in January 2008 and given credit for time spent in military cells. The government had asked for life imprisonment.

10. See, e.g., Brian Innes, *The History of Torture* (New York: St. Martin's Press, 1998).

son will often say anything to stop the pain. At times, the objective of torture is simply to produce the information or answers that interrogators want for their own purposes. In most, if not all, cases, torture is justified in terms of the common good, as part of a legitimate, even noble, effort to defeat dangerous outsiders. Dr. Robert Jay Lifton has noted that ordinary individuals "can all too readily be socialized to atrocity." He adds, "These killing projects are never described as such. They are put in terms of the necessity of improving the world, of political and spiritual renewal. You cannot kill large numbers of people without a claim to virtue."[11]

During the Enlightenment, key figures began to raise their voices in opposition to the practice of torture and in favor of ending the Inquisition. Voltaire of France played a leading role in denouncing the excesses of religious intolerance and injustice. In his 1763 "Treatise on Tolerance," Voltaire decried the torture and violent execution of a merchant, Jean Calas, who had been accused on flimsy evidence of killing his own son. Judges sentenced Calas to be "broken on the wheel." The Italian philosopher Cesare Beccaria wrote an essay in 1764 entitled "Of Crimes and Punishments" in which he denounced torture and the death penalty. He methodically dismantled the arguments for torture and pointed to its irrationality:

> that pain should be the test of truth, as if truth resided in the muscles and fibres of a wretch in torture. By this method the robust will escape, and the feeble be condemned. . . . What is the political intention of punishments? To terrify and be an example to others. . . . The impression of pain, then, may increase to such a degree, that, occupying the mind entirely, it will compel the sufferer to use the shortest method of freeing himself from torment. His answer, therefore, will be an effect as necessary as that of fire or boiling water, and he will accuse himself of crimes of which he is innocent: so that the very means employed to distinguish the innocent from the guilty will most effectually destroy all difference between them. . . . It would be superfluous to confirm these reflections by examples of innocent persons who, from the agony of torture, have confessed themselves guilty.[12]

| 407

Torture was formally prohibited throughout Europe by the middle of the eighteenth century, but it was still used extensively by the colonial powers to dominate the peoples of their colonies in Asia, Africa, and even Europe, where the British tortured Irish prisoners until fairly recently. It was a feature of colonization that the narrower the political base of the colonizer's power, and the

---

11. Chris Hedges, "A Skeptic about Wars Intended to Stamp Out Evil," *New York Times*, January 14, 2003.

12. Cesare Beccaria, "Of Torture," in *Dei delitti e delle pene* [An Essay on Crimes and Punishments] (Italy, 1764), ch. 16. Thomas Jefferson and Benjamin Franklin were greatly influenced by Beccaria.

less consent from the colonized, the more violent were the methods used to maintain control. In France, for example, torture was outlawed after the French Revolution but, as the colonial power in Algeria, the French army systematically tortured thousands of Algerians.

Torture became a burning issue after World War II, with the evidence of the inhuman tortures and medical experiments practiced by the Nazis and the Japanese. The Nuremberg Trials exposed the horrors of state-sponsored, organized systems of torture and extermination as tools of absolute power. After the war, the Allies convicted, and executed, eight Japanese soldiers for using water torture against Allied combatants.[13] Worldwide rejection and abhorrence of torture were reflected in the Universal Declaration of Human Rights of 1948, a seminal document whose Article 5 outlawed torture.[14] Other human rights covenants followed. The UN Convention against Torture (8.3), adopted by the General Assembly in 1984, stated unequivocally, "No exceptional circumstances whatsoever, whether a state of war or a threat of war, internal political instability or any other public emergency, may be invoked as a justification of torture. An order from a superior officer or a public authority may not be invoked as a justification of torture."

Official U.S. attitudes had hardened as the Cold War deepened in the 1950s, however. New U.S. security doctrines sanctioned ruthless methods and covert operations in the struggle against revolution and communism. As Cold War fears dominated Washington, influential voices argued that the United States had to leave behind its sense of fair play and adopt harsh methods. The 1954 Doolittle Report commissioned by President Eisenhower argued that the United States "must learn to subvert, sabotage and destroy our enemies by cleverer, more sophisticated and more effective methods than those used against us." It went on to state, "It may become necessary that the American people be made acquainted with, understand and support this fundamentally repugnant philosophy."[15] The CIA began experimenting with torture methods and psychotropic drugs such as LSD in the 1950s.[16] In developing countries where Washington saw subversive threats, U.S. forces worked closely with allied militaries that used brutal methods against political enemies, including "disappearance," torture, and summary execution: the ends were said to justify the means. After September 11, Bush officials again authorized extralegal and ruthless methods in the new "war on terror."

13. Ted Genoways, "If It Amounts to Torture," *Virginia Quarterly Review* 84, no. 1 (Winter 2008), 1–3; see also Evan Wallach (a law professor and judge at the U.S. Court of International Trade), "Waterboarding Used to Be a Crime," *Washington Post*, November 4, 2007.
14. Eleanor Roosevelt chaired the UN Commission on Human Rights, which drafted the Declaration. The United States signed the Declaration in 1948.
15. Lt. Gen. James Doolittle (USAF), "The Report on the Covert Activities of the Central Intelligence Agency," September 30, 1954.
16. Alfred McCoy, *A Question of Torture: CIA Interrogation, From the Cold War to the War on Terror* (New York: Metropolitan Books, 2006).

As the Iraq War continued, some prominent figures offered pro-torture arguments.[17] Alan Dershowitz, a professor at Harvard Law School, contended that judges should grant warrants under which terrorist suspects could be legally tortured, thus adding a veneer of academic respectability to the practice of torture. But major U.S. law associations, such as the American Bar Association, and many legal scholars rejected those arguments and condemned torture as a barbarity and a violation of the Constitution and international law.[18]

The Bush administration argued repeatedly that it did not torture. But the evidence belied such claims, demonstrating that the administration had simply redefined the meaning of torture and then claimed that it was not violating the law because its practices did not contradict its new definition. Various investigations by third parties, and internal administration memoranda leaked to the press or released as a result of lawsuits, showed that the administration had attempted to legalize its practices through legal opinions, executive orders, signing statements, and bills pushed through Congress (8.12–8.15). The CIA resisted an American Civil Liberties Union (ACLU) lawsuit demanding that it release key documents purportedly authorizing torture (8.16). In May 2008, a U.S. judge ordered the CIA to submit one 2002 memo, said to authorize "waterboarding" and other harsh methods, to the court.[19] In July, the CIA turned over this document and others (8.17). The documents made clear that the administration had redefined torture so that it could claim that its interrogation methods were legal.

The Supreme Court, Congress, many major public figures and opinion makers, and much of the public rejected several of the Bush administration's expansive claims (for example, in *Hamdan v. Rumsfeld* the Court ruled, among other things, that Common Article 3 of the Geneva Conventions (8.2) did apply to Taliban and al Qaeda captives). But in 2008, Bush's last year in office, the CIA was still apparently "exempt" (as defined by the president) to new laws passed by Congress and to international statutes outlawing torture (8.18). In March

---

17. A popular television show, *24*, featured a counterterrorism officer who used torture to save the day in almost every episode. The show essentially made the case that torture was legitimate and effective, especially in unlikely "ticking bomb" scenarios. The show was popular and influential within the U.S. public and among military cadets, raising concerns from both human rights groups and military commanders, who worried that it promoted unethical and illegal behavior. The show's right-wing producer, who had ties to the Bush administration, and network officials argued that torture was justified in some circumstances. Most experts, however, said that "ticking bomb" situations as portrayed in the show were no more than fiction. See Jane Mayer, "Whatever It Takes: The Politics of the Man Behind '24,'" *New Yorker*, February 19, 2007.

18. See American Bar Association, Resolution 10-B, 2004, and Recommendation to Congress, August 13–14, 2007; Barry Scheck, President of National Association of Criminal Defense Lawyers, "Abuse of Detainees at Guantánamo Bay," *Champion Magazine*, November 2004; American Civil Liberties Union Web site at http://www.aclu.org/safefree/torture/index.html; National Lawyers Guild, "National Lawyers Guild Calls for Prosecution of President Bush for Role in Torture," June 18, 2004.

19. Reuters, "Judge Orders CIA to Turn Over 'Torture' Memo: ACLU," accessed via *New York Times* Web site, May 8, 2008.

2008, Bush vetoed a bill to ban CIA use of water torture and other methods already prohibited by the army in its most recent field manual. In April 2008, ABC News reported that the top Bush officials—Dick Cheney, Condoleezza Rice, Donald Rumsfeld, Colin Powell, George Tenet, and John Ashcroft—had met secretly and repeatedly in the White House to discuss and approve the details of using particular "coercive interrogation methods," such as "waterboarding," against specific prisoners. In response to the report, President Bush replied, "Yes, I'm aware our national security team met on this issue. And I approved."[20]

In May 2008, the inspector general of the Justice Department released a detailed report on the forms of violence and torture that U.S. forces had used against detainees in Afghanistan, Iraq, and Guantánamo Bay, Cuba, and revealed that, in 2002, FBI officers at Guantánamo had actually begun to prepare a dossier documenting war crimes and other criminal acts of abuse that they had observed.[21] They were ordered to stop by high-level officials in the White House and in the FBI. Also in May 2008, the National Lawyers Guild called on Congress to appoint a special prosecutor, independent of the Department of Justice, to investigate and prosecute top Bush officials, and those who had justified torture in legal opinions, for their roles in the maltreatment of detainees (8.19). What had emerged over time were the outlines of a global U.S. torture regime authorized by the Bush administration.

410 |

# Domestic and International Law

## DOCUMENT 8.1

Article 6, Clause 2, of the Constitution states that treaties and international law become part of U.S. law and are therefore legally binding.

U.S. CONSTITUTION, ARTICLE 6 (EXCERPT)

This Constitution, and the Laws of the United States which shall be made in Pursuance thereof; and all Treaties made, or which shall be made, under

---

20. Jan Crawford Greenburg, Howard L. Rosenberg, and Ariane de Vogue, "Bush Aware of Advisers' Interrogation Talks," *ABC News* Web site, April 11, 2008.

21. U.S. Department of Justice, Office of the Inspector General, "A Review of the FBI's Involvement in and Observations of Detainee Interrogations in Guantanamo Bay, Afghanistan, and Iraq," May 2008.

the Authority of the United States, shall be the supreme Law of the Land; and the Judges in every State shall be bound thereby, anything in the Constitution or Laws of any State to the Contrary notwithstanding.

# DOCUMENT 8.2

This excerpt from one of the 1949 Geneva Conventions—known as Common Article 3 because it appears in all the Geneva Conventions—established the requirement that warring parties in internal conflicts protect civilians and non-combatants and refrain from torture and ill treatment of such populations. The standard interpretation over time became that the article applies in all conflicts, whether internal or not. The United States signed the Convention in 1949 and ratified it in 1955. This Convention and the Geneva Convention Relative to the Treatment of Prisoners of War were of great concern to Bush officials, who sought to circumvent their strictures, as evidenced by memos reproduced in this chapter.

GENEVA CONVENTION RELATIVE TO THE PROTECTION OF PERSONS IN TIME OF WAR, 1949 (EXCERPT)

Article 3: In the case of armed conflict not of an international character occurring in the territory of one of the High Contracting Parties, each party to the conflict shall be bound to apply, as a minimum, the following provisions:

Persons taking no active part in the hostilities, including members of armed forces who have laid down their arms and those placed hors de combat by sickness, wounds, detention, or any other cause, shall in all circumstances be treated humanely, without any adverse distinction founded on race, colour, religion or faith, sex, birth or wealth, or any other similar criteria.

To this end the following acts are and shall remain prohibited at any time and in any place whatsoever with respect to the above-mentioned persons:

(a) Violence to life and person, in particular murder of all kinds, mutilation, cruel treatment and torture;

(b) Taking of hostages;

(c) Outrages upon personal dignity, in particular, humiliating and degrading treatment;

(d) The passing of sentences and the carrying out of executions without previous judgment pronounced by a regularly constituted court affording all the judicial guarantees which are recognized as indispensable by civilized peoples. . . .

2. The wounded and sick shall be collected and cared for.

An impartial humanitarian body, such as the International Committee of the Red Cross, may offer its services to the Parties to the conflict.

The Parties to the conflict should further endeavour to bring into force, by means of special agreements, all or part of the other provisions of the present Convention.

The application of the preceding provisions shall not affect the legal status of the Parties to the conflict.

# DOCUMENT 8.3

The United States played an active role in negotiating the Convention against Torture, and the U.S. government signed it in 1988, under President Ronald Reagan, and then ratified it in 1994. To comply with the provisions of the Convention, the United States enacted two new sections to the U.S. Criminal Code, Sections 2340 and 2340A, which prohibited torture outside of the United States (federal law already outlawed torture within U.S. territory) (8.4). Especially crucial is the clause stating that no exceptional situations whatsoever may ever justify torture.

## THE UNITED NATIONS CONVENTION AGAINST TORTURE AND OTHER CRUEL, INHUMAN, OR DEGRADING TREATMENT OR PUNISHMENT (EXCERPT)

### Article 1

1. For the purposes of this Convention, the term "torture" means any act by which severe pain or suffering, whether physical or mental, is intentionally inflicted on a person for such purposes as obtaining from him or a third person information or a confession, punishing him for an act he or a third person has committed or is suspected of having committed, or intimidating or coercing him or a third person, or for any reason based on discrimination of any kind, when such pain or suffering is inflicted by or at the instigation of or with the consent or acquiescence of a public official or other person acting in an official capacity. It does not include pain or suffering arising only from, inherent in or incidental to lawful sanctions. . . .

### Article 2

1. Each State Party shall take effective legislative, administrative, judicial or other measures to prevent acts of torture in any territory under its jurisdiction.

2. No exceptional circumstances whatsoever, whether a state of war or a threat of war, internal political instability or any other public emergency, may be invoked as a justification of torture.

3. An order from a superior officer or a public authority may not be invoked as a justification of torture. . . .

# DOCUMENT 8.4

These two sections of the U.S. Criminal Code were enacted in order to bring U.S. law into compliance with the Convention against Torture, signed in 1988 and ratified in 1994 by the United States. The legal opinions issued by the Bush administration's lawyers reflected great concern that CIA interrogators might face torture charges based on these legal statutes.

U.S. CRIMINAL CODE, §§2340 AND 2340A (EXCERPTS)

## Section 2340. Definitions

As used in this chapter—

(1) "torture" means an act committed by a person acting under the color of law specifically intended to inflict severe physical or mental pain or suffering (other than pain or suffering incidental to lawful sanctions) upon another person within his custody or physical control;

(2) "severe mental pain or suffering" means the prolonged mental harm caused by or resulting from—

  (A) the intentional infliction or threatened infliction of severe physical pain or suffering;

  (B) the administration or application, or threatened administration or application, of mind-altering substances or other procedures calculated to disrupt profoundly the senses or the personality;

  (C) the threat of imminent death; or

  (D) the threat that another person will imminently be subjected to death, severe physical pain or suffering, or the administration or application of mind-altering substances or other procedures calculated to disrupt profoundly the senses or personality; and . . .

(3) "United States" includes all areas under the jurisdiction of the United States including any of the places described in sections 5 and 7 of this title and section 46501(2) of title 49.

## Section 2340A. Torture

(a) Offense.—Whoever outside the United States commits or attempts to commit torture shall be fined under this title or imprisoned not more than 20 years, or both, and if death results to any person from conduct prohibited by this subsection, shall be punished by death or imprisoned for any term of years or for life.

(b) Jurisdiction.—There is jurisdiction over the activity prohibited in subsection (a) if

(1) the alleged offender is a national of the United States; or

(2) the alleged offender is present in the United States, irrespective of the nationality of the victim or alleged offender.

(c) Conspiracy.—A person who conspires to commit an offense under this section shall be subject to the same penalties (other than the penalty of death) as the penalties prescribed for the offense, the commission of which was the object of the conspiracy.

# Secret Use of "Enhanced Interrogation Techniques"

## DOCUMENT 8.5

After the U.S. attack on Afghanistan in October 2001, the Bush administration began transferring and holding prisoners in a detention center in Guantánamo, Cuba, arguing that the site was beyond the reach of U.S. law. In October 2002, the commander at Guantánamo requested authorization for the use of aggressive coercive techniques taken from the military's SERE (Survival, Evasion, Resistance, and Escape) training program. In fact, the CIA had already been using much harsher torture techniques on detainees,[22] and administration lawyers had already produced secret memos in August 2002 authorizing torture methods. These lawyers, hard-line conservative political appointees, had bypassed normal interagency review processes.

At Guantánamo, the military's SERE program was "reverse-engineered" to create a torture-training and -application program. Ironically, the SERE program was drawn from Soviet and Chinese torture techniques from the 1950s that had been used to force false confessions (called "brainwashing" at the time). Significantly, Secretary of Defense Donald Rumsfeld approved the use of techniques in Categories I and II of the SERE program, and the fourth technique under Category III; he did not question or reject Category III. In fact, Rumsfeld concurred with the opinion of William J. Haynes II, the Defense Department general counsel, that Category III might be legally permissible but was not yet warranted. Moreover, in a handwritten note on Haynes's "action memo," Rumsfeld questioned why forced standing was limited to only four

---

22. See Jane Mayer, *The Dark Side: The Inside Story of How the War on Terror Turned into a War on American Ideals* (New York: Doubleday, 2008).

hours a day—suggesting that no limits applied. Not long after, Gen. Geoffrey Miller, under orders from Rumsfeld, brought the same techniques to Iraq in an effort to "Gitmo-ize" detention and interrogation operations there.

---

LT. COL. JERALD PHIFER, "REQUEST FOR APPROVAL OF COUNTER-RESISTANCE STRATEGIES," OCTOBER 11, 2002

DEPARTMENT OF DEFENSE
JOINT TASK FORCE 170
GUANTANAMO BAY, CUBA
APO AE 09860 JTF -J2

11 October 2002
MEMORANDUM FOR Commander, Joint Task Force 170
SUBJECT: Request for Approval of Counter-Resistance Strategies

1. (U) PROBLEM: The current guidelines for interrogation procedures at GTMO limit the ability of interrogators to counter advanced resistance.
2. (U) Request approval for use of the following interrogation plan.
   a. Category I techniques. During the initial category of interrogation the detainee should be provided a chair and the environment should be generally comfortable. The format of the interrogation is the direct approach. The use of rewards like cookies or cigarettes may be helpful. If the detainee is determined by the interrogator to be uncooperative, the interrogator may use the following techniques.
      (1) Yelling at the detainee (not directly in his ear or to the level that it would cause physical pain or hearing problems).
      (2) Techniques of deception:
          (a) Multiple interrogator techniques.
          (b) Interrogator identity. The interviewer may identify himself as a citizen of a foreign nation or as an interrogator from a country with a reputation for harsh treatment of detainees.
   b. Category II techniques. With the permission of the OIC, Interrogation Section, the interrogator may use the following techniques.
      (1) The use of stress positions (like standing), for a maximum of four hours.
      (2) The use of falsified documents or reports.
      (3) Use of the isolation facility for up to 30 days. Request must be made to through the OIC, Interrogation Section, to the Director, Joint Interrogation Group (JIG). Extensions beyond the initial 30 days must be approved by the Commanding General. For selected detainees, the OIC, Interrogation Section, will approve all contacts with the detainee, to include medical visits of a non-emergent nature.

(4) Interrogating the detainee in an environment other than the standard interrogation booth.

(5) Deprivation of light and auditory stimuli.

(6) The detainee may also have a hood placed over his head during transportation and questioning. The hood should not restrict breathing in any way and the detainee should be under direct observation when hooded.

(7) The use of 20-hour interrogations.

(8) Removal of all comfort items (including religious items).

(9) Switching the detainee from hot rations to MREs.

(10) Removal of clothing.

(11) Forced grooming (shaving of facial hair etc . . . )

(12) Using detainees individual phobias (such as fear of dogs) to induce stress.

  c. Category III techniques. Techniques in this category may be used only by submitting a request through the Director, JIG, for approval by the Commanding General with appropriate legal review and information to Commander, USSOUTHCOM. These techniques are required for a very small percentage of the most uncooperative detainees (less than 3%). The following techniques and other aversive techniques, such as those used in U.S. military interrogation resistance training or by other U.S. government agencies, may be utilized in a carefully coordinated manner to help interrogate exceptionally resistant detainees. Any of these techniques that require more than light grabbing, poking, or pushing, will be administered only by individuals specifically trained in their safe application.

(1) The use of scenarios designed to convince the detainee that death or severely painful consequences are imminent for him and/or his family.

(2) Exposure to cold weather or water (with appropriate medical monitoring).

(3) Use of a wet towel and dripping water to induce the misperception of suffocation.

(4) Use of mild, non-injurious contact, such as grabbing, poking in the chest with the finger, and light pushing.

3. The POC for this memorandum is the undersigned at x3476.

*JERALD PHIFER, LTC, USA, Director, J2*

# Historical Context

## DOCUMENT 8.6

The 1963 KUBARK Manual was used for training Latin American military and intelligence officers during the Cold War counterinsurgency era, when U.S. foreign policy was dominated by fear of communism and revolution in the developing world. KUBARK was the code name for the CIA. The manual shows the historical continuities between the methods of coercive interrogation taught in the early 1960s and those that became notorious in the "war on terror," including the use of sensory deprivation, isolation, freezing and suffocating temperatures, nakedness, forced standing, and so on. One section, still censored, alluded to the use of electric shocks, chemicals, and other forms of "bodily harm." Many scholars have noted the use, or misuse, of psychological insights that were incorporated into coercive interrogation techniques. The manual, highlighting psychological methods to induce regression and destroy the will, discussed how to force the detainee to blame himself or herself rather than the interrogator, an external force, for the suffering being experienced. This training manual was the basis of a second CIA training manual, used in Central America in the 1980s, the 1983 Human Resource Exploitation Training Manual, also declassified in 1997.

CENTRAL INTELLIGENCE AGENCY, KUBARK MANUAL
ON COUNTERINTELLIGENCE INTERROGATION,
JULY 1963 (EXCERPT)

*A. Explanation of Purpose*
This manual cannot teach anyone how to be, or become, a good interrogator. At best it can help readers to avoid the characteristic mistakes of poor interrogators.

Its purpose is to provide guidelines for KUBARK interrogation, and particularly the counterintelligence interrogation of resistant sources. Designed as an aid for interrogators and others immediately concerned, it is based largely upon the published results of extensive research, including scientific inquiries conducted by specialists in closely related subjects.

This study is by no means confined to a resume and interpretation of psychological findings. The approach of the psychologists is customarily manipulative; that is, they suggest methods of imposing controls or alterations upon the interrogatee from the outside. Except within the Communist frame of reference, they have paid less attention to the creation of internal controls—i.e., conversion of the source, so that voluntary cooperation results. Moral considerations aside, the imposition of external techniques of manipulating people carries with it the grave risk of later lawsuits, adverse publicity, or other attempts to strike back. . . .

### III. Legal and Policy Considerations

The legislation which founded KUBARK specifically denied it any law-enforcement or police powers. Yet detention in a controlled environment and perhaps for a lengthy period is frequently essential to a successful counterintelligence interrogation of a recalcitrant source.

[approx. three lines deleted]

This necessity, obviously, should be determined as early as possible. The legality of detaining and questioning a person, and of the methods employed,

[approx. ten lines deleted]

Detention poses the most common of the legal problems. KUBARK has no independent legal authority to detain anyone against his will,

[approx. four lines deleted]

The haste in which some KUBARK interrogations have been conducted has not always been the product of impatience. Some security services, especially those of the Sino-Soviet Bloc, may work at leisure, depending upon time as well as their own methods to melt recalcitrance. KUBARK usually cannot. Accordingly, unless it is considered that the prospective interrogatee is cooperative and will remain so indefinitely, the first step in planning an interrogation is to determine how long the source can be held. The choice of methods depends in part upon the answer to this question. . . .

Interrogations conducted under compulsion or duress are especially likely to involve illegality and to entail damaging consequences for KUBARK. Therefore prior Headquarters approval at the KUDOVE level must be obtained for the interrogation of any source against his will and under any of the following circumstances:

1. If bodily harm is to be inflicted.
2. If medical, chemical, or electrical methods or materials are to be used to induce acquiescence.
3. [approx. three lines deleted]. . . .

Obviously, many resistant subjects of counterintelligence interrogation cannot be brought to cooperation, or even to compliance, merely through pressures which they generate within themselves or through the unreinforced effect of the interrogation situation. Manipulative techniques—still keyed to the individual but brought to bear upon him from outside himself—then become necessary. It is a fundamental hypothesis of this handbook that these techniques, which can succeed even with highly resistant sources, are in essence methods of inducing regression of the personality to whatever earlier and weaker level is required for the dissolution of resistance and the inculcation of dependence. All of the techniques employed to break through an interrogation roadblock, the entire spectrum from simple isolation to hypnosis and narcosis, are essentially ways of speeding up the process of regression. As the interrogatee slips back from maturity toward a more infantile state, his learned or structured personality traits fall away in a reversed chronological order, so that the characteristics most recently acquired—which are also the characteristics drawn upon by the interrogatee in his own defense—are the first to go. As Gill and Brenman have pointed out, regression is basically a loss of autonomy. . . .

Another key to the successful interrogation of the resisting source is the provision of an acceptable rationalization for yielding. As regression proceeds, almost all resisters feel the growing internal stress that results from wanting simultaneously to conceal and to divulge. To escape the mounting tension, the source may grasp at any face-saving reason for compliance— any explanation which will placate both his own conscience and the possible wrath of former superiors and associates if he is returned to Communist control. It is the business of the interrogator to provide the right rationalization at the right time. Here too the importance of understanding the interrogatee is evident; the right rationalization must be an excuse or reason that is tailored to the source's personality. . . .

There are a number of non-coercive techniques for inducing regression. All depend upon the interrogator's control of the environment and, as always, a proper matching of method to source. Some interrogatees can be repressed by persistent manipulation of time, by retarding and advancing clocks and serving meals at odd times—ten minutes or ten hours after the last food was given. Day and night are jumbled. Interrogation sessions are similarly unpatterned, the subject may be brought back for more questioning just a few minutes after being dismissed for the night. Half-hearted efforts to cooperate can be ignored, and conversely he can be rewarded for non-cooperation. (For example, a successfully resisting source may become distraught if given some reward for the "valuable contribution" that he has made.) The Alice in Wonderland technique can reinforce the effect. Two or more interrogators, questioning as a team and in relays (and thoroughly jumbling the timing of both methods) can ask questions which make it impossible for the interrogatee to give sensible, significant answers. A subject who is cut off from the world he knows seeks to recreate it, in some measure, in the new and strange environment. He may try to keep track of time, to live in the familiar past, to cling to old concepts of loyalty, to establish—with one or more interrogators—interpersonal relations resembling those that he has had earlier with other people, and to build other bridges back to the known. Thwarting his attempts to do so is likely to drive him deeper and deeper into himself, until he is no longer able to control his responses in adult fashion. . . .

*D. Detention*

If, through the cooperation of a liaison service or by unilateral means, arrangements have been made for the confinement of a resistant source, the circumstances of detention are arranged to enhance within the subject his feelings of being cut off from the known and the reassuring, and of being plunged into the strange. Usually his own clothes are immediately taken away, because familiar clothing reinforces identity and thus the capacity for resistance. (Prisons give close hair cuts and issue prison garb for the same reason.) If the interrogatee is especially proud or neat, it may be useful to give him an outfit that is one or two sizes too large and to fail to provide a belt, so that he must hold his pants up. . . .

The chief effect of arrest and detention, and particularly of solitary confinement, is to deprive the subject of many or most of the sights, sounds, tastes, smells, and tactile sensations to which he has grown accustomed. John C. Lilly examined eighteen autobiographical accounts written by polar explorers and solitary seafarers. He found " . . . that isolation per se acts on most persons as a powerful stress. . . . In all cases of survivors of isolation at sea or in the polar night, it was the first exposure which caused the greatest fears and hence the greatest danger of giving way to symptoms; previous experience is a powerful aid in going ahead, despite the symptoms. "The symptoms most commonly produced by isolation are superstition, intense love of any other living thing, perceiving inanimate objects as alive, hallucinations, and delusions." . . .

A number of experiments conducted at McGill University, the National Institute of Mental Health, and other sites have attempted to come as close as possible to the elimination of sensory stimuli, or to masking remaining stimuli, chiefly sounds, by a stronger but wholly monotonous overlay. . . .

At the National Institute of Mental Health two subjects were " . . . suspended with the body and all but the top of the head immersed in a tank containing slowly flowing water at 34.5 [degrees] C (94.5 [degrees] F). . . ." Both subjects wore black-out masks, which enclosed the whole head but allowed breathing and nothing else. The sound level was extremely low; the subject heard only his own breathing and some faint sounds of water from the piping. Neither subject stayed in the tank longer than three hours. Both passed quickly from normally directed thinking through a tension resulting from unsatisfied hunger for sensory stimuli and concentration upon the few available sensations to private reveries and fantasies and eventually to visual imagery somewhat resembling hallucinations. . . .

These findings suggest—but by no means prove—the following theories about solitary confinement and isolation:

1. The more completely the place of confinement eliminates sensory stimuli, the more rapidly and deeply will the interrogatee be affected. Results produced only after weeks or months of imprisonment in an ordinary cell can be duplicated in hours or days in a cell which has no light (or weak artificial light which never varies), which is sound-proofed, in which odors are eliminated, etc. An environment still more subject to control, such as water-tank or iron lung, is even more effective.

2. An early effect of such an environment is anxiety. How soon it appears and how strong it is depends upon the psychological characteristics of the individual.

3. The interrogator can benefit from the subject's anxiety. As the interrogator becomes linked in the subject's mind with the reward of lessened anxiety, human contact, and meaningful activity, and thus with providing relief for growing discomfort, the questioner assumes a benevolent role. . . .

4. The deprivation of stimuli induces regression by depriving the subject's mind of contact with an outer world and thus forcing it in upon itself. At the same time, the calculated provision of stimuli during interrogation tends to make the regressed subject view the interrogator as a father-figure. The result, normally, is a strengthening of the subject's tendencies toward compliance. . . .

It has been plausibly suggested that, whereas pain inflicted on a person from outside himself may actually focus or intensify his will to resist, his resistance is likelier to be sapped by pain which he seems to inflict upon himself. "In the simple torture situation the contest is one between the individual and his tormentor (. . . . and he can frequently endure). When the individual is told to stand at attention for long periods, an intervening factor is introduced. The immediate source of pain is not the interrogator but the victim himself. The motivational strength of the individual is likely to exhaust itself in this internal encounter. . . . As long as the subject remains standing, he is attributing to his captor the power to do something worse to him, but there is actually no showdown of the ability of the interrogator to do so." . . .

| 421

### L. Conclusion

A brief summary of the foregoing may help to pull the major concepts of coercive interrogation together:

1. The principal coercive techniques are arrest, detention, the deprivation of sensory stimuli, threats and fear, debility, pain, heightened suggestibility and hypnosis, and drugs.

2. If a coercive technique is to be used, or if two or more are to be employed jointly, they should be chosen for their effect upon the individual and carefully selected to match his personality.

3. The usual effect of coercion is regression. The interrogatee's mature defenses crumbles as he becomes more childlike. During the process of regression the subject may experience feelings of guilt, and it is usually useful to intensify these.

4. When regression has proceeded far enough so that the subject's desire to yield begins to overbalance his resistance, the interrogator should supply a face-saving rationalization. Like the coercive

technique, the rationalization must be carefully chosen to fit the subject's personality. . . .

# Reports on Violations of Law

## DOCUMENT 8.7

Gen. Antonio M. Taguba was appointed by the U.S. Army to investigate detention practices at Abu Ghraib and elsewhere. His report uncovered systematic abuses and torture. Taguba learned that Gen. Geoffrey Miller, commander of the detention center at Guantánamo, had led a team to review "strategic interrogation" practices at Abu Ghraib and had recommended that military prison guards be used to "set the conditions" for interrogation. Military intelligence had been put in charge of the prison and tightly controlled it. Taguba concluded that military intelligence and private contract agents bore responsibility for the abuse and had encouraged military guards to commit acts of violence against detainees. In 2006, he was ordered to retire from the army.

U.S. ARMY, ARTICLE 15–6: INVESTIGATION
OF THE 800TH MILITARY POLICE BRIGADE
(THE TAGUBA REPORT), 2004 (EXCERPT)

1. 5.(S) That between October and December 2003, at the Abu Ghraib Confinement Facility (BCCF), numerous incidents of sadistic, blatant, and wanton criminal abuses were inflicted on several detainees. This systemic and illegal abuse of detainees was intentionally perpetrated by several members of the military police guard force (372nd Military Police Company, 320th Military Police Battalion, 800th MP Brigade), in Tier (section) 1-A of the Abu Ghraib Prison (BCCF). The allegations of abuse were substantiated by detailed witness statements (ANNEX 26) and the discovery of extremely graphic photographic evidence. Due to the extremely sensitive nature of these photographs and videos, the ongoing CID investigation, and the potential for the criminal prosecution of several suspects, the photographic evidence is not included in the body of my investigation. The pictures and videos are available from the Criminal Investigative Command and the CTJF-7 prosecution team. In addition to the aforementioned crimes, there were also abuses committed by members of the 325th MI Battalion, 205th MI Brigade, and Joint Interrogation and Debriefing Center (JIDC). Specifically, on 24 November 2003, SPC Luciana Spencer, 205th MI Brigade, sought to degrade a detainee by having him strip and returned to cell naked. (ANNEXES 26 and 53)

2. 6 included the following acts:
   a. (S) Punching, slapping, and kicking detainees; jumping on their naked feet;
   b. (S) Videotaping and photographing naked male and female detainees;
   c. (S) Forcibly arranging detainees in various sexually explicit positions for photographing;
   d. (S) Forcing detainees to remove their clothing and keeping them naked for several days at a time;
   e. (S) Forcing naked male detainees to wear women's underwear;
   f. (S) Forcing groups of male detainees to masturbate themselves while being photographed and videotaped;
   g. (S) Arranging naked male detainees in a pile and then jumping on them;
   h. (S) Positioning a naked detainee on a MRE Box, with a sandbag on his head, and attaching wires to his fingers, toes, and penis to simulate electric torture;
   i. (S) Writing "I am a Rapest" [sic] on the leg of a detainee alleged to have forcibly raped a 15-year old fellow detainee, and then photographing him naked;
   j. (S) Placing a dog chain or strap around a naked detainee's neck and having a female Soldier pose for a picture;
   k. (S) A male MP guard having sex with a female detainee;
   l. (S) Using military working dogs (without muzzles) to intimidate and frighten detainees, and in at least one case biting and severely injuring a detainee;
   m. (S) Taking photographs of dead Iraqi detainees.

(ANNEXES 25 and 26). . . .
1. 8. (U) In addition, several detainees also described the following acts of abuse, which under the circumstances, I find credible based on the clarity of their statements and supporting evidence provided by other witnesses (ANNEX 26):
   a. (U) Breaking chemical lights and pouring the phosphoric liquid on detainees;
   b. (U) Threatening detainees with a charged 9mm pistol;
   c. (U) Pouring cold water on naked detainees;
   d. (U) Beating detainees with a broom handle and a chair;
   e. (U) Threatening male detainees with rape;
   f. (U) Allowing a military police guard to stitch the wound of a detainee who was injured after being slammed against the wall in his cell;
   g. (U) Sodomizing a detainee with a chemical light and perhaps a broom stick.
   h. (U) Using military working dogs to frighten and intimidate detainees with threats of attack, and in one instance actually biting a detainee. . . .

10. (U) I find that contrary to the provision of AR 190–8, and the findings found in MG Ryder's Report, Military Intelligence (MI) interrogators and Other US Government Agency's (OGA) interrogators [*Editors' Note: OGA is code that means Central Intelligence Agency, CIA, or private contractors*] actively requested that MP guards set physical and mental conditions for favorable interrogation of witnesses. Contrary to the findings of MG Ryder's Report, I find that personnel assigned to the 372nd MP Company, 800th MP Brigade were directed to change facility procedures to "set the conditions" for MI interrogations. I find no direct evidence that MP personnel actually participated in those MI interrogations. (ANNEXES 19, 21, 25, and 26).

11. (U) I reach this finding based on the actual proven abuse that I find was inflicted on detainees and by the following witness statements. (ANNEXES 25 and 26):

   a. (U) SPC Sabrina Harman, 372nd MP Company, stated in her sworn statement regarding the incident where a detainee was placed on a box with wires attached to his fingers, toes, and penis, "that her job was to keep detainees awake." She stated that MI was talking to CPL Grainer. She stated: "MI wanted to get them to talk. It is Grainer and Frederick's job to do things for MI and OGA to get these people to talk."

   b. (U) SGT Javal S. Davis, 372nd MP Company, stated in his sworn statement as follows: "I witnessed prisoners in the MI hold section, wing 1A being made to do various things that I would question morally. In Wing 1A we were told that they had different rules and different SOP [*Editors' Note: Standard Operating Procedure*] for treatment. I never saw a set of rules or SOP for that section just word of mouth. The Soldier in charge of 1A was Corporal Granier. He stated that the Agents and MI Soldiers would ask him to do things, but nothing was ever in writing he would complain [*sic*]." When asked why the rules in 1A/1B were different than the rest of the wings, SGT Davis stated: "The rest of the wings are regular prisoners and 1A/B are Military Intelligence (MI) holds." When asked why he did not inform his chain of command about this abuse, SGT Davis stated: "Because I assumed that if they were doing things out of the ordinary or outside the guidelines, someone would have said something. Also the wing belongs to MI and it appeared MI personnel approved of the abuse." SGT Davis also stated that he had heard MI insinuate to the guards to abuse the inmates. When asked what MI said he stated: "Loosen this guy up for us." "Make sure he has a bad night." "Make sure he gets the treatment." He claimed these comments were made to CPL Granier and SSG Frederick. Finally, SGT Davis stated that: "the MI staffs to my understanding have been giving Granier compliments on the way he has been handling the MI holds. Example being statements like, 'Good job, they're breaking down real fast. They answer every question. . . .'"

424 |

13. (U) I find that there is sufficient credible information to warrant an Inquiry UP Procedure 15, AR 381–10, US Army Intelligence Activities, be conducted to determine the extent of culpability of MI personnel, assigned to the 205th MI Brigade and the Joint Interrogation and Debriefing Center (JIDC) at Abu Ghraib (BCCF).

Specifically, I suspect that COL Thomas M. Pappas, LTC Steve L. Jordan, Mr. Steven Stephanowicz, and Mr. John Israel [*Editors' Note: These last two men were contract agents from CACI, the private security and intelligence enterprise*] were either directly or indirectly responsible for the abuses at Abu Ghraib (BCCF) and strongly recommend immediate disciplinary action as described in the preceding paragraphs as well as the initiation of a Procedure 15 Inquiry to determine the full extent of their culpability. (ANNEX 36)


# DOCUMENT 8.8

Malcolm Nance, a U.S. Navy counterterrorism specialist, testified before a House judiciary subcommittee hearing and before international commissions on torture. He was graphic in his explanation as to why "waterboarding" clearly constituted torture. In this piece, he argued that many of the debates aired on television talk shows were uninformed and misguided. Nance called the redefinition, use, and defense of torture "a crisis of honor" for the United States.

MALCOLM NANCE, "WATERBOARDING IS TORTURE . . . PERIOD," *SMALL WARS JOURNAL* BLOG, OCTOBER 2007

I'd like to digress from my usual analysis of insurgent strategy and tactics to speak out on an issue of grave importance to *Small Wars Journal* readers. We, as a nation, are having a crisis of honor.

Last week the Attorney General nominee Judge Michael Mukasey refused to define waterboarding terror suspects as torture. On the same day MSNBC television pundit and former Republican Congressman Joe Scarborough quickly *spoke out in its favor*. On his morning television broadcast,

The founders of the professional publication *Small Wars Journal* were U.S. Marines, but the blog's home page stated that the journal was private and tried to transcend the perspective of any one branch of the service, presenting an approach that blended the views on small wars of "the full joint, allied, and coalition military with their governments' federal or national agencies, nongovernmental agencies, and private organizations."

he asserted, without any basis in fact, that the efficacy of the waterboard a viable tool to be used on Al Qaeda suspects.

Scarborough said, "For those who don't know, waterboarding is what we did to Khalid Sheikh Mohammed, who is the Al Qaeda number two guy that planned 9/11. And he talked . . ." He then speculated that "If you ask Americans whether they think it's okay for us to waterboard in a controlled environment . . . 90% of Americans will say 'yes.'" Sensing that what he was saying sounded extreme, he then claimed he did not support torture but that waterboarding was debatable as a technique: "You know, that's the debate. Is waterboarding torture? . . . I don't want the United States to engage in the type of torture that [Senator] John McCain had to endure."

In fact, waterboarding is just the type of torture then Lt. Commander John McCain had to endure at the hands of the North Vietnamese. As a former Master Instructor and Chief of Training at the US Navy Survival, Evasion, Resistance and Escape School (SERE) in San Diego, California I know the waterboard personally and intimately. SERE staff were required [to] undergo the waterboard at its fullest. I was no exception. I have personally led, witnessed and supervised waterboarding of hundreds of people. *It has been reported* that both the Army and Navy SERE school's interrogation manuals were used to form the interrogation techniques used by the US army and the CIA for its terror suspects. What was not mentioned in most articles was that SERE was designed to show how an evil, totalitarian enemy would use torture at the slightest whim. If this is the case, then waterboarding is unquestionably being used as torture technique.

The carnival-like he-said, she-said of the legality of Enhanced Interrogation Techniques has become a form of doublespeak worthy of Catch-22. Having been subjected to them all, I know these techniques, if in fact they are actually being used, are not dangerous when applied in training for short periods. However, when performed with even moderate intensity over an extended time on an unsuspecting prisoner—it is torture, without doubt. Couple that with waterboarding and the entire medley not only *"shock the conscience"* as the statute forbids—it would terrify you. Most people cannot stand to watch a high intensity kinetic interrogation. One has to overcome basic human decency to endure watching or causing the effects. The brutality would force you into a personal moral dilemma between humanity and hatred. It would leave you to question the meaning of what it is to be an American.

We live at a time where Americans, completely uninformed by an incurious media and enthralled by vengeance-based fantasy television shows like "24", are actually cheering and encouraging such torture as justifiable revenge for the September 11 attacks. Having been a rescuer in one of those incidents and personally affected by both attacks, I am bewildered at how casually we have thrown off the mantle of world leader in justice and honor. Who we have [sic] become? Because at this juncture, after Abu

426 |

Ghraieb [*sic*] and other undignified exposed incidents of murder and torture, we appear to have become no better than our opponents.

With regards to the waterboard, I want to set the record straight so the apologists can finally embrace the fact that they condone and encourage torture. . . .

1. Waterboarding is a torture technique. Period. There is no way to gloss over it or sugarcoat it. It has no justification outside of its limited role as a training demonstrator. Our service members have to learn that the will to survive requires them [to] accept and understand that they may be subjected to torture, but that America is better than its enemies and it is one's duty to trust in your nation and God, endure the hardships and return home with honor.
2. Waterboarding is not a simulation. Unless you have been strapped down to the board, have endured the agonizing feeling of the water overpowering your gag reflex, and then feel your throat open and allow pint after pint of water to involuntarily fill your lungs, you will not know the meaning of the word.

Waterboarding is a controlled drowning that, in the American model, occurs under the watch of a doctor, a psychologist, an interrogator and a trained strap-in/strap-out team. It does not simulate drowning, as the lungs are actually filling with water. There is no way to simulate that. The victim is drowning. How much the victim is to drown depends on the desired result (in the form of answers to questions shouted into the victim's face) and the obstinacy of the subject. A team doctor watches the quantity of water that is ingested and for the physiological signs which show when the drowning effect goes from painful psychological experience, to horrific suffocating punishment to the final death spiral.

Waterboarding is slow motion suffocation with enough time to contemplate the inevitability of black out and expiration—usually the person goes into hysterics on the board. For the uninitiated, it is horrifying to watch and if it goes wrong, it can lead straight to terminal hypoxia. When done right it is controlled death. Its lack of physical scarring allows the victim to recover and be threatened with its use again and again.

Call it "Chinese Water Torture," "the Barrel," or "the Waterfall," it is all the same. Whether the victim is allowed to comply or not is usually left up to the interrogator. Many waterboard team members, even in training, enjoy the sadistic power of making the victim suffer and often ask questions as an afterthought. These people are dangerous and predictable and when left unshackled, unsupervised or undetected they bring us the murderous abuses seen at Abu Ghraieb, Baghram and Guantanamo. No doubt, to avoid human factors like fear and guilt someone has created a one-button version that probably looks like an MRI machine with high intensity waterjets. . . .

It is outrageous that American officials, including the Attorney General and a legion of minions of lower rank have not only embraced this torture but have actually justified it, redefined it to a misdemeanor, brought it down to the level of a college prank and then bragged about it. The echo chamber that is the American media now views torture as . . . heroic and macho. . . .

Congressional leaders from both sides of the aisle need to stand up for American values and clearly specify that coercive interrogation using the waterboard is torture and, except for limited examples of training our service members and intelligence officers, it should be stopped completely and finally—oh, and this time without a Presidential signing statement reinterpreting the law.

## DOCUMENT 8.9

The American Civil Liberties Union published on its Web site the testimony of a German victim of "extraordinary rendition," describing his illegal abduction by a U.S. rendition team and subsequent incommunicado detention and torture in a secret CIA detention center, or "black site." The German chancellor Angela Merkel noted that U.S. officials later acknowledged that a mistake had been made. Even some CIA officers involved in the German citizen's ongoing detention believed he was innocent. The ACLU brought a suit against the CIA on his behalf, but a U.S. court decided not to hear the case on grounds of state secrecy, and the Supreme Court declined to review the case.

AMERICAN CIVIL LIBERTIES UNION, KHALID EL-MASRI
TESTIMONY ON "RENDITION" (EXCERPT)

Khaled El-Masri is a German citizen who resides near Neu Ulm, Germany. El-Masri was born in Kuwait in 1963 to Lebanese parents. He moved to Germany in 1985 to escape the Lebanese War. He became a German citizen in 1995, married in 1996 and has six young children. He is a carpenter by trade and prior to his abduction was employed as a car salesman. El-Masri was detained from December 31, 2003 through May 28, 2004 in Macedonia and Afghanistan where he was held in the CIA prison known as the "Salt Pit." Currently El-Masri is unable to find employment.

STATEMENT. WASHINGTON—I have come to America seeking three things: an acknowledgement that the United States government is responsible for kidnapping, abusing and rendering me to a CIA "black site" prison; an explanation as to why I was singled out for this treatment; and an apology, because I am an innocent man who has never been charged with any crime.

Almost one year ago the American Civil Liberties Union, on my behalf, filed a lawsuit against George Tenet, the former director of the CIA, other CIA officials and U.S.-based aviation corporations that owned and operated the airplanes used in my abduction. For reasons I do not fully understand, the court decided not to hear my case because the government claimed that allowing the case to proceed would reveal state secrets, even though the facts of my mistreatment have been widely reported in American and international media.

This is not democracy. In my opinion, this is how you establish a dictatorial regime. Countries are occupied, people are killed, and we cannot say anything because it's all considered a state secret. Freedom and justice are disrespected, as are basic morals and values. And if you don't keep quiet after you are abused, you are considered a threat to international or national security. But I will not be scared into being silent. I will continue to fight for this case until I prevail or until I die. And I will fight for morality, for principles, for the values I believe in, and for my family.

Here is my story. On December 31, 2003, I boarded a bus in Ulm, Germany for a holiday in Skopje, Macedonia. When the bus crossed the border into Macedonia, Macedonian officials confiscated my passport and detained me for several hours. Eventually, I was transferred to a hotel where I was held for 23 days. I was guarded at all times, the curtains were always drawn, I was never permitted to leave the room, I was threatened with guns, and I was not allowed to contact anyone. At the hotel, I was repeatedly questioned about my activities in Ulm, my associates, my mosque, meetings with people that had never occurred, or associations with people I had never met. I answered all of their questions truthfully, emphatically denying their accusations. After 13 days I went on a hunger strike to protest my confinement.

On January 23, 2004, seven or eight men entered the hotel room and forced me to record a video saying I had been treated well and would soon be flown back to Germany. I was handcuffed, blindfolded, and placed in a car. The car eventually stopped and I heard airplanes. I was taken from the car, and led to a building where I was severely beaten by people's fists and what felt like a thick stick. Someone sliced the clothes off my body, and when I would not remove my underwear, I was beaten again until someone forcibly removed them from me. I was thrown on the floor, my hands were pulled behind me, and someone's boot was placed on my back. Then I felt something firm being forced inside my anus.

I was dragged across the floor and my blindfold was removed. I saw seven or eight men dressed in black and wearing black ski masks. One of the men placed me in a diaper and a track suit. I was put in a belt with chains that attached to my wrists and ankles, earmuffs were placed over my ears, eye pads over my eyes, and then I was blindfolded and hooded. After being marched to a plane, I was thrown to the floor face down and my legs and arms were spread-eagled and secured to the sides of the plane. I felt two injections, and I was rendered nearly unconscious. At some point, I felt the plane land and take off again. When it landed again, I was unchained and taken off the plane. It felt very warm outside, and so I knew I had not been returned to Germany. I learned later that I was in Afghanistan. . . .

That first night I was interrogated by six or eight men dressed in the same black clothing and ski masks, as well as a masked American doctor and a translator. They stripped me of my clothes, photographed me, and took blood and urine samples. I was returned to my cell, where I would remain in solitary confinement, with no reading or writing materials, and without once being permitted outside to breathe fresh air, for more than four months. Ultimately, I was interrogated three or four times, always by the same man, with others who were dressed in black clothing and ski masks, and always at night. The man who interrogated me threatened me, insulted me, and shoved me. He interrogated me about whether I had taken a trip to Jalalabad using a false passport; whether I had attended Palestinian training camps; and whether I knew September 11 conspirators or other alleged extremists. As in Macedonia, I truthfully denied their accusations. Two men who participated in my interrogations identified themselves as Americans. My requests to meet with a representative of the German government, a lawyer, or to be brought before a court, were repeatedly ignored.

In March, I, along with several other inmates, commenced a hunger strike to protest our confinement without charges. After 27 days without food, I was allowed to meet with two unmasked Americans, one of whom was the prison director and the second an even higher official whom other inmates referred to as "the Boss." I pleaded with them to either release me or bring me to court, but the American prison director replied that he could not release me without permission from Washington. He also said that I should not be detained in the prison. On day 37 of my hunger strike I was dragged into an interrogation room, tied to a chair, and a feeding tube was forced through my nose to my stomach. After the force-feeding, I became extremely ill and suffered the worst pain of my life.

Near the beginning of May, I was brought into the interrogation room to meet an American who identified himself as a psychologist. He told me he had traveled from Washington D.C. to check on me, and promised I would soon be released. Soon thereafter, I was interrogated again by a native German speaker named "Sam," the American prison director, and an American translator. I was warned that as a condition of my release, I was never to mention what had happened to me, because the Americans were determined to keep the affair a secret.

On May 28, I was led out of my cell, blindfolded and handcuffed. I was put on a plane and chained to the seat. I was accompanied by Sam and also heard the voices of two or three Americans. Sam informed me that the plane would land in a European country other than Germany, because the

Americans did not want to leave clear traces of their involvement in my ordeal, but that I would eventually continue on to Germany. I believed I would be executed rather than returned home.

When the plane landed, I was placed in a car, still blindfolded, and driven up and down mountains for hours. Eventually, I was removed from the car and my blindfold removed. My captors gave me my passport and belongings, sliced off my handcuffs, and told me to walk down a dark, deserted road and not to look back. I believed I would be shot in the back and left to die, but when I turned the bend, there were armed men who asked me why I was in Albania and took my passport. The Albanians took me to the airport, and only when the plane took off did I believe I was actually returning to Germany. When I returned I had long hair and beard, and had lost 40 pounds. My wife and children had left our house in Ulm, believing I had left them and was not coming back. Now we are together again in Germany.

## DOCUMENT 8.10

The International Committee of the Red Cross (ICRC) compiled this confidential report documenting serious and deliberate violations of international humanitarian law by U.S. forces in Iraq in 2003. The report called upon Coalition Forces to treat detainees humanely, as obligated by law. It documented severe abuses of Iraqi prisoners "tantamount to torture," such as brutality, hooding, humiliation, and threats of "imminent execution," and noted that some 70–90 percent of Iraqi detainees had been arrested by mistake. The ICRC submitted its report to state authorities under a strict condition of confidentiality, meaning it was not to be transmitted or used in proceedings of a judicial nature. However, it was leaked to the press without the knowledge or consent of the ICRC after the Abu Ghraib photos were released.

INTERNATIONAL COMMITTEE OF THE RED CROSS,
REPORT ON THE TREATMENT BY THE COALITION
FORCES OF PRISONERS OF WAR AND OTHER PROTECTED
PERSONS BY THE GENEVA CONVENTIONS IN IRAQ
DURING ARREST, INTERNMENT, AND INTERROGATION,
FEBRUARY 2004 (EXCERPT)

2. TREATMENT DURING TRANSFER AND INITIAL CUSTODY
... 15. The ICRC collected several allegations indicating that following arrest, persons deprived of their liberty were ill-treated, sometimes during transfer from their place of arrest to their initial internment facility. This ill-treatment would normally stop by

the time the persons reached a regular internment facility, such as Camp Cropper, Camp Bucca or Abu Ghraib. The ICRC also collected one allegation of death resulting from harsh conditions of interment and ill-treatment during initial custody.

16. One allegation collected by the ICRC concerned the arrest of nine men by the CF in a hotel in Basrah on 13 September 2003. Following their arrest, the nine men were made to kneel, face and hands against the ground, as if in a prayer position. The soldiers stamped on the back of the neck of those raising their head. They confiscated their money without issuing a receipt. The suspects were taken to Al-Hakimiya, a former office previously used by the mukhabarat in Basrah and then beaten severely by CF personnel. One of the arrestees died following the ill-treatment (################ aged 28, married, father of two children). Prior to his death, his co-arrestees heard him screaming and asking for assistance.

The issued "International Death Certificate" mentioned "Cardio-respiratory arrest—asphyxia" as the condition directly leading to the death. As to the cause of that condition, it mentioned "Unknown" and "Refer to the coroner". The certificate did not bear any other mention. An eyewitness' description of the body given to the ICRC mentioned a broken nose, several broken ribs and skin lesions on the face consistent with beatings. The father of the victim was informed of his death on 18 September, and was invited to identify the body of his son. On 3 October, the commander of the CF in Basrah presented to him his condolences and informed him that an investigation had been launched and that those responsible would be punished. Two other persons deprived of their liberty were hospitalised with severe injuries. Similarly, a week later, an ICRC medical doctor examined them in the hospital and observed large haematomas with dried scabs on the abdomen, buttocks, sides, thigh, wrists, nose and forehead consistent with their accounts of beatings received.

17. During a visit of the ICRC in Camp Bucca on 22 September 2003, a 61-year old person deprived of his liberty alleged that he had been tied, hooded and forced to sit on the hot surface of what he surmised to be the engine of a vehicle, which had caused severe burns to his buttocks. The victim had lost consciousness. The ICRC observed large crusted lesions consistent with his allegation.

18. The ICRC examined another person deprived of his liberty in the "High Value Detainees" Section in October 2003 who had been subjected to a similar treatment. He had been hooded, handcuffed in the back, and made to lie face down, on a hot

surface during transportation. This had caused severe skin burns that required three months hospitalization. At the time of the interview he had been recently discharged from hospital. He had to undergo several skin grafts, the amputation of his right index finger, and suffered the permanent loss of the use of his left fifth finger secondary to burn-induced skin retraction. He also suffered extensive burns over the abdomen, anterior aspects of the lower extremities, the palm of his right hand and the sole of his left foot. The ICRC recommended to the CF that the case be investigated to determine the cause and circumstances of the injuries and the authority responsible for the ill-treatment. At the time of writing the results of the report were still pending.

19. During transportation following arrest, persons deprived of their liberty were almost always hooded and tightly restrained with flexi-cuffs. They were occasionally [MISSING SECTION] haematoma and linear marks compatible with repeated whipping or beating. He had wrist marks compatible with tight flexi-cuffs.

The ICRC also collected allegations of deaths as a result of harsh internment conditions, ill-treatment, lack of medical attention, or the combination thereof, notably in Tikrit holding area formerly known as the Saddam Hussein Islamic School. . . .       | 433

## 3. TREATMENT DURING INTERROGATION

. . . 24. Arrests were usually followed by temporary internment at battle group level or at initial interrogation facilities managed by military intelligence personnel, but accessible to other intelligence personnel (especially in the case of security detainees). The ill treatment by the CF personnel during interrogation was not systematic, except with regard to persons arrested in connection with suspected security offences or deemed to have an "intelligence" value. In those cases, persons deprived of their liberty supervised by the military intelligence were subjected to a variety of ill-treatments ranging from insults and humiliation to both physical and psychological coercion that in some cases might amount to torture in order to force them to cooperate with their interrogators. In certain cases, such as in Abu Ghraib military intelligence section, methods of physical and psychological coercion used by the interrogators appeared to be part of the standard operating procedures by military intelligence personnel to obtain confessions and extract information. Several military intelligence officers confirmed to the ICRC that it was part of the military intelligence process to hold a person deprived of his liberty naked in a completely dark and empty cell for a prolonged period to use inhumane and degrading treatment, including physical and psychological coercion, against persons deprived of their liberty to secure their cooperation.

### 3.1 Methods of Ill-treatment

25. The methods of ill-treatment most frequently alleged during interrogation included

—Hooding, used to prevent people from seeing and to disorient them, and also to prevent them from breathing freely. One or sometimes two bags, sometimes with an elastic blindfold over the eyes which, when slipped down, further impeded proper breathing. Hooding was sometimes used in conjunction with beatings thus increasing anxiety as to when blows would came. The practice of hooding also allowed the interrogators to remain anonymous and thus to act with impunity. Hooding could last for periods from a few hours to up to 2 to 4 consecutive days, during which hoods were lifted only for drinking, eating or going to the toilets;

—Handcuffing with flexi-cuffs, which were sometimes made so tight and used for extended periods that they caused skin lesions and long term after effects on the hands (nerve damage), as observed by the ICRC;

—Beatings with hard objects (including pistols and rifles), slapping, punching, kicking with knees or feet on various parts of the body (legs, sides, lower back, groin);

—Pressing the face into the ground with boots;

—Threats (of ill-treatment, reprisals against family members, imminent execution or transfer to Guantanamo);

—Being stripped naked for several days while held in solitary confinement in an empty and completely dark cell that included a latrine;

—Being held in solitary confinement combined with threats (to intern the individual indefinitely, to arrest other family members, to transfer the individual to Guantanamo), insufficient sleep, food or water deprivation, minimal access to showers (twice a week), denial of access to open air and prohibition of contacts with other persons deprived of their liberty;

—Being paraded naked outside cells in front of other persons deprived of their liberty, and guards, sometimes hooded or with women's underwear over the head;

—Acts of humiliation such as being made to stand naked against the wall of the cell with arms raised or with women's underwear over the head for prolonged periods while being laughed at by guards, including female guards, and sometimes photographed in this position;

—Being attached repeatedly over several days, for several hours each time, with handcuffs to the bars of their cell door in humiliating (i.e. naked or in underwear) and/or uncomfortable position causing physical pain;

—Exposure while hooded to loud noise or music, prolonged exposure while hooded to the sun over several hours, including during the hottest time of the day when temperatures could reach 50 degrees Celsius (122 degrees Fahrenheit) or higher;

—Being forced to remain for prolonged periods in stress positions such as squatting or standing with or without the arms lifted. . . .

# DOCUMENT 8.11

Arguing that the Bush administration was pursuing a policy to evade international law, Human Rights Watch presented early evidence of a pattern of abuse at Abu Ghraib and elsewhere that belied the administration's claims that the brutality could be blamed on "a few bad apples." The organization traced the appearance of such human rights violations to three policy decisions by the Bush administration: the decision to suspend the Geneva Conventions and international law, thus creating a lawless environment with no limits to interrogation; the decision to authorize the use of physically coercive methods against detainees to cause pain and disorientation; and the decision to suppress reports of ill treatment. Footnotes originally in the report are omitted for readability.

| 435

---

HUMAN RIGHTS WATCH, "THE ROAD TO ABU GHRAIB,"
JUNE 2004 (EXCERPT)

## II. Guantánamo: America's "Black Hole"
The secrecy surrounding detention practices at the U.S. Naval Base at Guantánamo Bay, Cuba, the U.S. government's refusal to grant POW status to the Taliban detainees there or to even recognize that Al Qaeda detainees are covered by the Geneva Conventions, the approval of harsh interrogation techniques, and the allegations of abuse by some released detainees combine to raise concerns about mistreatment of detainees at the base. While Human Rights Watch has no information of Abu-Ghraib-level abuses at Guantánamo, there is a lot that remains to be learned. [*Editors' Note: Much information has become public since 2004.*]

The United States has carefully controlled information about the detainees at Guantánamo, barring them from most contact with the outside world. As a result, little is publicly known about the more than 700 detainees from forty-four countries, including children as young as 13, who have been held at Guantánamo. Human Rights Watch, and others, have had access only to detainees released from U.S. custody—and those released thus far are people whom U.S. authorities did not consider to be a security risk or indictable for criminal offenses. That is, none of them are the sort of high value or important detainees who might have been treated more harshly. What the world has been allowed to see of the Guantánamo detention facility are highly controlled tours for journalists (who have not been able to talk to detainees), and occasional video material released by the U.S. Department of Defense. Guantánamo has been described as a "legal black hole" by Lord Johan Steyn, a judicial member of Britain's House of Lords.

Incommunicado detention has been consistently condemned by international human rights bodies as facilitating conditions under which torture and other mistreatment may take place.

Statements by U.S. officials that the Geneva Conventions do not apply to Al Qaeda detainees—indeed, the Bush administration's refusal to acknowledge that any law applies to them—and that harsher methods of interrogation are therefore permissible, only heighten this concern. In his January 2002 memo to the president, for instance, White House Counsel Gonzales endorsed not applying the Conventions to Guantánamo to avoid "Geneva's strict limitations on questioning of enemy prisoners."

It was the failure to obtain sufficient information using non-coercive methods on Guantánamo detainees which reportedly led to the creation of the working group which informed Secretary Rumsfeld in April 2003 that the president, as commander in chief, could authorize torture notwithstanding domestic and international legal prohibitions. According to the *Wall Street Journal*, a U.S. official who helped prepared [sic] the report said "We'd been at this for a year-plus and got nothing out of them [certain Guantánamo detainees] . . . we need to have a less-cramped view of what torture is and is not." According to the official, interrogation techniques including drawing on prisoners' bodies, putting women's underwear on their heads, and threatening imminent harm to their families had not borne fruit and there was a need to "ratchet up the pressure."

The *Washington Post* reported that in April 2003, officials at the highest levels of the Defense and Justice Departments approved a list of about twenty interrogation techniques for use at Guantánamo Bay that permit, among other things, reversing the normal sleep patterns of detainees and exposing them to heat, cold and "sensory assault," including loud music and bright lights, according to defense officials. The use of the techniques, according to the *Post*, must be justified as "militarily necessary," and must be accompanied by "appropriate medical monitoring," and requires the approval of senior Pentagon officials, and in some cases, of the Defense Secretary. CBS News reported that Secretary Rumsfeld had approved such treatment for Mohammed Khatani [*Editors' Note: This is the individual known also as al-Qahtani*], who in August 2001 allegedly tried unsuccessfully to enter the United States as part of the 9-11 plot. The treatment included reversing Khatani's sleep patterns, cutting off his beard, playing loud music, and subjecting him to interrogation sessions lasting up to twenty hours. The head of U.S. Southern Command, General James Hill, whose responsibilities include Guantánamo Bay, said in June 2004 that Rumsfeld approved unspecified intensive interrogation techniques on two prisoners at Guantánamo. The *Wall Street Journal* has reported that interrogation methods now used at Guantánamo include "limiting prisoners' food, denying them clothing, subjecting them to body-cavity searches, depriving them of sleep for as much as ninety-six hours and shackling them in so-called stress positions.". . . .

# The Documentary Record: Key Memos by Members of the George W. Bush Administration

## DOCUMENT 8.12

Responding to pressures from above, particularly from the vice president's office, John Yoo, the deputy assistant attorney general of the Office of Legal Counsel from 2001 to 2003, and Special Counsel Robert J. Delahunty wrote the original legal memo justifying the withholding from alleged al Qaeda or Taliban prisoners the protections provided under the Geneva Convention for the treatment of prisoners of war. The administration did not want to be subject to any limits or legal constraints in its war on terror. The lawyers' memo was the basis for the legal opinion provided by White House Counsel Alberto Gonzales to the president, which advised that Geneva be declared inapplicable for al Qaeda or Taliban prisoners. Warning that the administration's authorization of aggressive coercive methods might expose top officials to war crimes charges, Gonzales wrote that declaring that detainees were members of the Taliban or al Qaeda and were not protected by the Geneva Convention "substantially reduces the threat of domestic criminal prosecution under the War Crimes Act" of 1996. Gonzales continued, "Your determination would create a reasonable basis in law that [the War Crimes Act] does not apply, which would provide a solid defense to any future prosecution."

Secretary of State Colin Powell strongly opposed the policy and called its legal justification seriously flawed, arguing that the United States had previously recognized the Taliban as the legitimate government of Afghanistan. But on February 7, 2002, George W. Bush announced the new policy of suspending the Geneva Conventions for "unlawful combatants."

ALBERTO GONZALES, MEMORANDUM TO THE PRESIDENT, "DECISION RE APPLICATION OF THE GENEVA CONVENTION ON PRISONERS OF WAR TO THE CONFLICT WITH AL QAEDA AND THE TALIBAN," JANUARY 25, 2002 (EXCERPT)

## Purpose

On January 18, I advised you that the Department of Justice had issued a formal legal opinion concluding that the Geneva Convention III on the Treatment of Prisoners of War (GPW) does not apply to the conflict with al Qaeda. I also advised you that DOJ's opinion concludes that there are reasonable grounds for you to conclude that GPW does not apply with respect to the conflict with the Taliban. I understand that you decided that GPW does not apply and, accordingly, that al Qaeda and Taliban detainees are not prisoners of war under the GPW.

The Secretary of State has requested that you reconsider that decision. Specifically, he has asked that you conclude the GPW does apply to both al Qaeda and the Taliban. I understand, however, that he would agree that al Qaeda and Taliban fighters could be determined not to be prisoners of war (POWs) but only on a case-by-case basis following individual hearing before a military board.

This memorandum outlines the ramifications of your decision and the Secretary's request for reconsideration.

## Legal Background

As an initial matter, I note that you have the constitutional authority to make the determination you made on January 18 that the GPW does not apply to al Qaeda and the Taliban. (Of course, you could nevertheless, as a matter of policy, decide to apply the principles of GPW to the conflict with al Qaeda and the Taliban.) The Office of Legal Counsel of the Department of Justice has opined that, as a matter of international and domestic law, GPW does not apply to the conflict with al Qaeda. OLC has further opined that you have the authority to determine that GPW does not apply to the Taliban. As I discussed with you, the grounds for such a determination may include:

A determination that Afghanistan was a failed state because the Taliban did not exercise full control over the territory and people, was not recognized by the international community, and was not capable of fulfilling its international obligations (e.g., was in widespread material breach of its international obligations).

A determination that the Taliban and its forces were, in fact, not a government, but a militant, terrorist-like group.

OLC's interpretation of this legal issue is definitive. The Attorney General is charged by statute with interpreting the law for the Executive Branch. This interpretive authority extends to both domestic and international law. He has, in turn, delegated this role to the OLC.

Nevertheless, you should be aware that the Legal Advisor to the Secretary of State has expressed a different view.

## Ramifications of Determination That GPW Does Not Apply

The consequences of a decision to adhere to what I understood to be your earlier determination that the GPW does not apply to the Taliban include the following:

Positive:

Preserves flexibility:

As you have said, the war against terrorism is a new kind of war. It is not the traditional clash between nations adhering to the laws of war that formed the backdrop for GPW. The nature of the new war places a high premium on other factors, such as the ability to quickly obtain information from captured terrorists and their sponsors in order to avoid further atrocities against American civilians, and the need to try terrorists for war crimes such as wantonly killing civilians. In my judgment, this new paradigm renders obsolete Geneva's strict limitations on questioning of enemy prisoners and renders quaint some of its provisions requiring that captured enemy be afforded such things as commissary privileges, scrip (i.e., advances of monthly pay), athletic uniforms, and scientific instruments.

Although some of these provisions do not apply to detainees who are not POWs, a determination that GPW does not apply to al Qaeda and the Taliban eliminates any argument regarding the need for case-by-case determinations of POW status. It also holds open options for the future conflicts in which it may be more difficult to determine whether an enemy force as a whole meets the standard for POW status.

By concluding that GPW does not apply to al Qaeda and the Taliban eliminates any argument regarding the need for case-by-case determinations of POW status. It also holds open options for the future conflicts in which it may be more difficult to determine whether an enemy force as a whole meets the standard for POW status.

Substantially reduces the threat of domestic criminal
prosecution under the War Crimes Act (18 U.S.C. 2441).

That statute, enacted in 1996, prohibits the commission of a "war crime" by or against a U.S. person, including U.S. officials. "War crime" for these purposes is defined to include any grave breach of GPW or any violation of common Article 3 thereof (such as "outrages against personal dignity"). Some of these provisions apply (if the GPW applies) regardless of whether the individual being detained qualifies as a POW. Punishments for violations of Section 2441 include the death penalty. A determination that the GPW is not applicable to the Taliban would mean that Section 2441 would not apply to actions taken with respect to the Taliban.

Adhering to your determination that GPW does not apply would guard effectively against misconstruction or misapplication of Section 2441 for several reasons.

First, some of the language of GPW is undefined (it prohibits, for example, "outrages upon personal dignity" and "inhuman treatment"), and it is difficult to predict with confidence what actions might be deemed to constitute violations of the relevant provisions of GPW.

Second, it is difficult to predict the needs and circumstances that could arise in the course of the war on terrorism.

Third, it is difficult to predict the motives of prosecutors and independent counsels who may in the future decide to pursue unwarranted charges based on Section 2441. Your determination would create a reasonable basis in law that Section 2441 does not apply, which would provide a solid defense to any future prosecution.

Negative:

On the other hand, the following arguments would support reconsideration and reversal of your decision that the GPW does not apply to either al Qaeda or the Taliban:

Since the Geneva Conventions were concluded in 1949, the United States has never denied their applicability to either U.S. or opposing forces engaged in armed conflict, despite several opportunities to do so. During the last Bush Administration, the United States stated that it "has a policy of applying the Geneva Conventions of 1949 whenever armed hostilities occur with regular foreign armed forces, even if arguments could be made that the threshold standards for the applicability of the Conventions . . . are not met."

The United States could not invoke the GPW if enemy forces threatened to mistreat or mistreated U.S. or coalition forces captured during operations in Afghanistan, or if they denied Red Cross access or other POW privileges.

The War Crimes Act could not be used against the enemy, although other criminal statutes and the customary law of war would still be available.

Our position would likely provoke widespread condemnation among our allies and in some domestic quarters, even if we make clear that we will comply with the core humanitarian principles of the treaty as a matter of policy.

Concluding that the Geneva Convention does not apply may encourage other countries to look for technical "loopholes" in future conflicts to conclude that they are not bound by GPW either.

Other countries may be less inclined to turn over terrorists or provide legal assistance to us if we do not recognize a legal obligation to comply with the GPW.

A determination that GPW does not apply to al Qaeda and the Taliban could undermine U.S. military culture which emphasizes maintaining the highest standards of conduct in combat, and could introduce an element of uncertainty in status of adversaries. . . .

On balance, I believe that the arguments for reconsideration and reversal are unpersuasive. . . .

# DOCUMENT 8.13

John Yoo of the Office of Legal Counsel was a political appointee who shared the ideology of top Bush officials. He contended that extreme interrogation methods would not violate domestic and international laws prohibiting torture. This memo, like others reproduced here, suggested that the administration was concerned about the illegality of the harsh interrogation methods it intended to use, or was already using (e.g., against detainee Abu Zubaydah),[23] and whether they would violate domestic and international laws prohibiting torture, thus opening individuals to possible prosecution under federal law (§§2340–2340A), the Convention against Torture, or the International Criminal Court. They sought to establish a legal framework that would protect individuals from accountability. To this end, Yoo reviewed Section 2340, which defined torture under federal law, and Section 2340A, which made it a criminal offense for a person outside the United States to commit or attempt to commit torture, and examined various treaties to which the United States is a party.

JOHN YOO, LETTER TO ALBERTO GONZALES,
"INTERROGATION METHODS TO BE USED,"
AUGUST 1, 2002 (EXCERPT)

Dear Judge Gonzales:

You have requested the views of our Office concerning the legality, under international law, of interrogation methods to be used during the current war on terrorism. More specifically, you have asked whether interrogation methods used on captured al Qaeda operatives, which do not violate the prohibition on torture found in 18 U.S.C. 2340–2340A, would either: a) violate our obligations under the Torture Convention, or b) create the basis for a prosecution under the Rome Statute establishing the International Criminal Court (ICC). We believe that interrogation methods that comply with 2340 would not violate our international obligations under the Torture Convention, because of a specific understanding attached by the United States to its instrument of ratification. We also conclude that actions taken as part of the interrogation of al Qaeda operatives cannot fall within the jurisdiction of the ICC, although it would be impossible to control the actions of a rogue prosecutor or judge. . . .

Despite the apparent differences in language between the Convention and 2340, international law clearly could not hold the United States to an obligation different than that expressed in 2340. When it acceded to the

---

23. Yoo acknowledged that the August 2002 memo was the basis for the coercive interrogation of Zubaydah. Jeffrey Rosen, "Conscience of a Conservative," *New York Times Magazine,* September 9, 2007.

Convention, the United States attached to its instrument of ratification a clear understanding that defined torture in the exact terms used by 2340. The first Bush administration submitted the following understanding of the treaty:

> The United States understands that, in order to constitute torture, an act must be *specifically intended* to inflict severe physical or mental pain or suffering and that mental pain or suffering refers to prolonged mental pain caused by or resulting from (1) the intentional infliction or threatened infliction of severe physical pain or suffering; (2) administration or application, or threatened administration or application, of mind altering substances or other procedures calculated to disrupt profoundly the senses or the personality; (3) the threat of imminent death; or (4) the threat that another person will imminently be subjected to death, severe physical pain or suffering, or the administration or application of mind-altering substances or other procedures calculated to disrupt profoundly the senses or personality.

. . . . as noted earlier, one of the most established principles of international law is that a state cannot be bound by treaties to which it has not consented. Although President Clinton signed the Rome Statute, the United States has withdrawn its signature from the agreement before submitting it to the Senate for advice and consent—effectively terminating it. The United States, therefore, cannot be bound by the provisions of the ICC Treaty nor can U.S. nationals be subject to ICC prosecution. We acknowledge, however, that the binding nature of the ICC Treaty on non-parties is a complicated issue and do not attempt to definitively answer it here. . . .

442 |

## DOCUMENT 8.14

The administration's lawyers, responding to pressures from the top, issued another legal opinion, which became known as the "torture memo." The opinion, signed by Assistant Attorney General Jay Bybee, drew directly from the one authored by Yoo (8.13). The "Bybee memo" redefined torture in order to legally permit "cruel, inhuman, or degrading" interrogation methods, which were construed to fall under the threshold of torture—thus overturning two centuries of constitutional law. The legal opinion then provided "justification defenses" to "potentially eliminate criminal liability" for those who used the extreme methods. Harold Koh, the dean of Yale Law School and the assistant secretary of state for human rights under President Bill Clinton, noted that according to these definitions, many of the atrocities that Saddam Hussein had committed against his people would not be called torture.[24]

---

24. Harold Koh, "Can the President Be Torturer in Chief?" *Indiana Law Journal* 81 (2006), 1145, 1165.

The memo also argued that as a wartime commander-in-chief, the president was authorized to sanction torture, superseding federal and international laws. Defending the idea of the "unitary executive," the memo posited that the president's power was unlimited by checks and balances and that any attempts by Congress or the courts to restrict that power represented unconstitutional infringements of the president's authority (chapter 10).

---

JAY BYBEE TO ALBERTO GONZALES, "STANDARDS OF CONDUCT FOR INTERROGATION UNDER 18 U.S.C. §§2340–2340A," AUGUST 1, 2002 (EXCERPT)

You have asked for our Office's views regarding the standards of conduct under the Convention Against Torture and Other Cruel, Inhuman and Degrading Treatment of Punishment as implemented by Sections 2340–2340A of title 18 of the United States Code. As we understand it, this question has arisen in the context of the conduct of interrogations outside of the United States. We conclude below that Section 2340A proscribes acts inflicting, and that are specifically intended to inflict, severe pain or suffering, whether mental of physical. Those acts must be of an extreme nature to rise to the level of torture within the meaning of Section 2340A and the Convention. We further conclude that certain acts may be cruel, inhuman, or degrading, but still not produce pain and suffering of the requisite intensity to fall within Section 2340A's proscription against torture. We conclude by examining possible defenses that would negate any claim that certain interrogation methods violate the statute.

In Part I, we examine the criminal statute's text and history. We conclude that for an act to constitute torture as defined in Section 2340, it must inflict pain that is difficult to endure. Physical pain amounting to torture must be equivalent in intensity to the pain accompanying serious physical injury, such as organ failure, impairment of bodily function, or even death. For purely mental pain or suffering to amount to torture under Section 2340, it must result in significant psychological harm of significant duration, e.g., lasting for months or even years. We conclude that the mental harm must also result from one of the predicate acts listed in the statute, namely: threats of imminent death; threats of infliction of the kind of pain that would amount to physical torture; infliction of such physical pain as a means of psychological torture; use of drugs or other procedures designed to deeply disrupt the senses, or fundamentally alter an individual's personality; or threatening to do any of these things to a third party. . . .

In Part IV, we examine international decisions regarding the use of sensory deprivation techniques. These cases make clear that while many of these techniques may amount to cruel, inhuman or degrading treatment, they do not produce pain or suffering of the necessary intensity to meet the definition of torture. From these decisions, we conclude that there is a wide range of such techniques that will not rise to the level of torture. . . .

In order to respect the president's inherent constitutional authority to manage a military campaign against al Qaeda and its allies, Section 2340A must be construed as not applying to interrogations undertaken pursuant to his Commander-in-Chief authority. As our Office has consistently held during this Administration and previous Administrations, Congress lacks authority under Article I to set the terms and conditions under which the President may exercise his authority as Commander in Chief to control the conduct of operations during a war. . . .

A review of the Executive branch's interpretation of CAT reveals that Congress codified the view that torture included only the most extreme forms of physical or mental harm. When it submitted the Convention to the Senate, the Reagan administration took the position that CAT reached only the most heinous acts. The Reagan administration included the following understanding:

The United States understands that, in order to constitute torture, an act must be a deliberate and calculated act of an extremely cruel and inhuman nature, specifically intended to inflict excruciating and agonizing physical or mental pain or suffering.

Even if an interrogation method arguably were to violate Section 2340A, the statute would be unconstitutional if it impermissibly encroached on the President's constitutional power to conduct a military campaign. As Commander-in-Chief, the President has the constitutional authority to order interrogations of enemy combatants to gain intelligence information concerning the military plans of the enemy. The demands of the Commander-in-Chief power are especially pronounced in the middle of a war in which the nation has already suffered a direct attack . . . Any effort to apply Section 2340A in a manner that interferes with the President's direction of such core war matters as the detention and interrogation of enemy combatants thus would be unconstitutional. . . .

If the right to defend the national government can be raised as a defense in an individual prosecution, as *Neagle* suggests, then a government defendant, acting in his official capacity, should be able to argue that any conduct that arguably violated Section 2340A was undertaken pursuant to more than just individual self-defense or defense of another. In addition, the defendant could claim that he was fulfilling the Executive Branch's authority to protect the federal government, and the nation, from attack . . . we conclude that a government defendant may also argue that his conduct of an interrogation, if properly authorized, is justified on the basis of protecting the nation from attack. . . .

# DOCUMENT 8.15

In October 2003, Jack Goldsmith replaced John Yoo as head of the Office of Legal Counsel. He soon judged that the August "torture memos" had no basis in law—he called them "an advance pardon" for those responsible for torture —and he decided that they should be rescinded. He thus refused to supply administration officials with the justifications they were seeking to supersede, or rewrite, the law. Goldsmith first withdrew a March 2003 memo written by Yoo that had served as the basis for the Pentagon's harsh interrogation program. After the Abu Ghraib torture photos became public in April 2004, Yoo's August 2002 "torture memo" was leaked to the press. It had served as the legal "golden shield" for the CIA's coercive interrogation program. A week later, Goldsmith revoked that legal opinion.[25] He resigned the same day in order to ensure that the memo's withdrawal would be accepted, especially by the powerful vice president's office. That office, particularly Cheney's influential legal advisor, David Addington, had already reacted with outrage to several previous interpretations of the law provided by Goldsmith that had challenged the sweeping view of presidential power (the "unitary executive theory") advocated within the administration. In December 2004, Goldsmith's acting successor, Daniel Levin, issued a formal replacement memorandum, addressed to Deputy Attorney General James B. Comey, for the rescinded August "torture memo"—although he was pressured to include a footnote that apparently exonerated those who had acted under Yoo's legal opinions.

DANIEL LEVIN, MEMORANDUM FOR JAMES B. COMEY, "LEGAL STANDARDS APPLICABLE UNDER 18 U.S.C. §§2340–2340A," DECEMBER 30, 2004 (EXCERPT)

Torture is abhorrent both to American law and values and to international norms. This universal repudiation of torture is reflected in our criminal law, for example, 18 U.S.C. §§2340–2340A; international agreements, exemplified by the United Nations Convention Against Torture (the "CAT")'; customary international law; centuries of Anglo-American law; and the longstanding policy of the United States, repeatedly and recently reaffirmed by the President. This Office interpreted the federal criminal prohibition against torture—codified at 18 U.S.C. §§2340–2340A—in *Standards of Conduct for Interrogation under 18 U.S.C. §§2340–2340A* (Aug. 1, 2002) ("August 2002 Memorandum"). The August 2002 Memorandum also addressed a number of issues beyond interpretation of those statutory provisions, including the President's Commander-in-Chief power, and various defenses

---

25. This account draws from Rosen, "Conscience of a Conservative," September 9, 2007.

that might be asserted to avoid potential liability under sections 2340–2340A. *See id.* at 31–46.

Questions have since been raised, both by this Office and by others, about the appropriateness and relevance of the non-statutory discussion in the August 2002 Memorandum, and also about various aspects of the statutory analysis, in particular the statement that "severe" pain under the statute was limited to pain "equivalent in intensity to the pain accompanying serious physical injury, such as organ failure, impairment of bodily function, or even death." *Id.* at I. We decided to withdraw the August 2002 Memorandum, a decision you announced in June 2004. At that time, you directed this Office to prepare a replacement memorandum. Because of the importance of—and public interest in—these issues, you asked that this memorandum be prepared in a form that could be released to the public so that interested parties could understand our analysis of the statute.

This memorandum supersedes the August 2002 Memorandum in its entirety. Because the discussion in that memorandum concerning the President's Commander-in-Chief power and the potential defenses to liability was—and remains—unnecessary, it has been eliminated from the analysis that follows. Consideration of the bounds of any such authority would be inconsistent with the President's unequivocal directive that United States personnel not engage in torture. We have also modified in some important respects our analysis of the legal standards applicable under 18 U.S.C. §§2340–2340A. For example, we disagree with statements in the August 2002 Memorandum limiting "severe" pain under the statute to "excruciating and agonizing" pain, *id.* at 19, or to pain "equivalent in intensity to the pain accompanying serious physical injury, such as organ failure, impairment of bodily function, or even death," *id.* at 1. There are additional areas where we disagree with or modify the analysis in the August 2002 Memorandum, as identified in the discussion below. The Criminal Division of the Department of Justice has reviewed this memorandum and concurs in the analysis set forth below. . . .

446 |

# DOCUMENT 8.16

This American Civil Liberties Union press release outlined the significance of the still-classified memos on coercive interrogation techniques, authored by administration officials, and decried the secrecy surrounding top policy decisions made by President Bush and other officials after September 11, 2001. Using the Freedom of Information Act, the ACLU obtained substantial information about the documents, one of which authorized the CIA to use specific torture techniques. That secret memo, dated August 1, 2002, the same day as the Bybee memo (8.13), was the one a U.S. judge had directed should be turned over to the court in May 2008. It should be noted that the Associated Press in

2005 had reported that, according to government data, at least 108 prisoners had died in U.S. custody in Iraq and Afghanistan, most of them violently.

---

AMERICAN CIVIL LIBERTIES UNION, PRESS RELEASE, "CIA PROVIDES FURTHER DETAILS ON SECRET INTERROGATION MEMOS," JANUARY 10, 2007

## August 2002 Memo Discussed "Alternative Interrogation Methods"

NEW YORK In an ongoing lawsuit with the American Civil Liberties Union, the CIA has filed a declaration arguing that the agency should not be compelled to release two Justice Department memos discussing interrogation methods and a presidential order concerning the CIA's authorization to set up detention facilities outside the United States.

"The CIA's declaration uses national security as a pretext for withholding evidence that high-level government officials in all likelihood authorized abusive techniques that amount to torture," said ACLU attorney Amrit Singh. "This declaration is especially disturbing because it suggests that unlawful interrogation techniques cleared by the Justice Department for use by the CIA still remain in effect. The American public has a right to know how the government is treating its prisoners."

One of the documents is described as a "14-page memorandum dated 17 September 2001 from President Bush to the Director of the CIA pertaining to the CIA's authorization to detain terrorists." According to the brief, of the 14 pages, 12 pages are "a notification memorandum" from the president to the National Security Council regarding a "clandestine intelligence activity." The ACLU said this revelation raises questions regarding the extent to which Condoleezza Rice was involved in establishing the CIA detention program as National Security Advisor.

In its declaration, the CIA also says that the Bush memo is so "Top Secret" that National Security Council officials created a "special access program" governing access to the document. It states that "the name of the special access program is itself classified SECRET," meaning that the CIA believes that the disclosure of the program's name "could be expected to result in serious danger to the nation's security."

The other two documents are legal memoranda prepared for the CIA by the Justice Department's Office of Legal Counsel. One is an 18-page legal memorandum dated August 1, 2002 "advising the CIA regarding interrogation methods it may use against al Qaeda members." It includes information "regarding potential interrogation methods and the context in which their use was contemplated." It also discusses "alternative interrogation methods," a phrase that was echoed by President Bush in a September 2006 speech promoting the Military Commissions Act. According to news reports, interrogation methods specifically authorized by the undisclosed Justice Department memo and used by the CIA include "waterboarding," a technique meant to induce the perception of drowning, and the use of "stress positions."

The ACLU said that the CIA's declaration suggests that the August 1, 2002 memo remains in effect. In particular, the CIA argues that public disclosure of the methods cleared by the Justice Department would allow terrorists "to resist cooperation."

The second Office of Legal Counsel document being withheld is a "31-page undated, unsigned, draft legal memorandum . . . that interprets the Convention Against Torture." According to the CIA, the document is a "preliminary" version of an August 1, 2002 memo prepared for Alberto Gonzales by Assistant Attorney General Jay S. Bybee. The CIA said it is withholding the document on attorney work-product and "deliberative process" grounds, noting that disclosure of the draft would permit the public to compare versions and "identify the similarities and differences between the draft and final legal documents."

The final Bybee memorandum contended that abuse does not rise to the level of torture under U.S. law unless it inflicts pain "equivalent in intensity to the pain accompanying serious physical injury, such as organ failure, impairment of bodily function, or even death." After public outcry, that memorandum was rescinded by the administration in December 2004.

The CIA previously claimed that it could neither deny nor confirm the mere existence of the documents without jeopardizing national security. But the agency backed away from that claim after President Bush acknowledged in his September speech that the CIA does in fact detain and interrogate terrorism suspects overseas.

"Through these memos, the president and Office of Legal Counsel created a legal framework that was specifically intended to allow the CIA to violate both U.S. and international law," said Jameel Jaffer, Deputy Director of the ACLU's National Security Program. "While national security sometimes requires secrecy, it is increasingly clear that these documents are being kept secret not for national security reasons but for political ones."

The documents discussed in the CIA's declaration have been the subject of Congressional interest as well. In a November 16, 2006 letter to Attorney General Alberto Gonzales, Senator Patrick Leahy requested these among other documents, and also sought clarification from the Justice Department on whether the August 1, 2002 interrogation techniques memo has been modified or withdrawn since 2002. In a letter dated December 22, 2006, the Justice Department refused to release the documents to Senator Leahy and did not deny that the August 1, 2002 interrogation techniques memo remains in effect.

# DOCUMENT 8.17

The ACLU reprinted three key, and heavily redacted, documents on its Web site after the CIA and the Department of Justice complied with the judicial order to release them. The first, signed by CIA Director George Tenet and dated January 28, 2003, was almost completely blacked out, though it did show that the Office of Legal Counsel had authorized the CIA to use "enhanced interrogation techniques," with detailed reporting requirements, by that date. The second document, dated August 4, 2004, stated that the Justice Department had ruled that "waterboarding" and other methods did not violate the Torture Statute. The third—a fifteen-page memo dated August 1, 2002, and also signed by Bybee—was almost completely blacked out but indicated that near-drowning and other harsh methods would not be considered torture unless the perpetrators "intended" to inflict severe harm. "The absence of specific intent negates the charge of torture," it stated. Thus, the administration and its lawyers sought to provide a loophole for CIA interrogators to escape future legal charges. A key paragraph of that top-secret memo is reprinted here. The censored parts of the memo directly discussed, at length, a particular case of torture, apparently that of Abu Zubaydah, who was repeatedly subjected to "waterboarding." (Legal references have been removed for readability.)

CIA AND JUSTICE DEPARTMENT, DOCUMENTS
RELEASED IN RESPONSE TO ACLU LAWSUIT, JULY 2008

U.S. Department of Justice
Office of Legal Counsel
August 1, 2002
Memorandum for [2 LINES REDACTED]
Interrogation of [WORDS REDACTED]
You have asked for this Office's views on whether certain proposed conduct would violate the prohibition against torture found at Section 2340A of title 18 of the United States Criminal Code. You have asked for this advice [REST OF PARAGRAPH BLACKED OUT]
[FROM PAGE 16—MOST PREVIOUS PAGES COMPLETELY REDACTED]
Specific Intent. To violate the statute, an individual must have the specific intent to inflict severe pain or suffering. Because specific intent is an element of the offense, the absence of specific intent negates the charge of torture. As we previously opined, to have the required specific intent, an individual must expressly intend to cause such severe pain and suffering. . . . We have further found that if a defendant acts with the good faith belief that his actions will not cause such suffering, he has not acted with specific intent. . . . A defendant acts in good faith when he has an honest

belief that his actions will not result in severe pain and suffering. . . . Although an honest belief need not be reasonable, such a belief is easier to establish where there is a reasonable basis for it. . . . Good faith may be established by, among other things, the reliance on the advice of experts.

Based on the information you have provided us, we believe that those carrying out these procedures would not have the specific intent to inflict severe pain or suffering. The objective of these techniques is not to cause severe pain. [REST OF PAGE BLACKED OUT]

# DOCUMENT 8.18

This ABC News report discussed six in the list of still-classified aggressive interrogation methods used by CIA units against suspected terrorists. In 2005, as Congress debated Senator John McCain's defense bill amendment to outlaw torture and abuse of prisoners, George W. Bush and other administration officials argued that the CIA should be exempt. After the bill passed, Bush officials said that they did not consider the CIA to be bound by the new law. In December 2007, the CIA revealed that in 2005 it had destroyed videos of interrogations conducted in 2002 that used "enhanced interrogation techniques." Bush vetoed a bill to prohibit CIA use of near-drowning and other aggressive methods in March 2008.

BRIAN ROSS AND RICHARD ESPOSITO, "CIA'S
HARSH INTERROGATION TECHNIQUES DESCRIBED,"
ABC NEWS REPORT ON SIX "ENHANCED INTERROGATION
TECHNIQUES," NOVEMBER 18, 2005

Harsh interrogation techniques authorized by top officials of the CIA have led to questionable confessions and the death of a detainee since the techniques were first authorized in mid-March 2002, ABC News has been told by former and current intelligence officers and supervisors.

They say they are revealing specific details of the techniques, and their impact on confessions, because the public needs to know the direction their agency has chosen. All gave their accounts on the condition that their names and identities not be revealed. Portions of their accounts are corroborated by public statements of former CIA officers and by reports recently published that cite a classified CIA Inspector General's report. Other portions of their accounts echo the accounts of escaped prisoners from one CIA prison in Afghanistan.

"They would not let you rest, day or night. Stand up, sit down, stand up, sit down. Don't sleep. Don't lie on the floor," one prisoner said through a translator. The detainees were also forced to listen to rap artist Eminem's

"Slim Shady" album. The music was so foreign to them it made them frantic, sources said.

Contacted after the completion of the ABC News investigation, CIA officials would neither confirm nor deny the accounts. They simply declined to comment.

The CIA sources described a list of six "Enhanced Interrogation Techniques" instituted in mid-March 2002 and used, they said, on a dozen top al Qaeda targets incarcerated in isolation at secret locations on military bases in regions from Asia to Eastern Europe. According to the sources, only a handful of CIA interrogators are trained and authorized to use the techniques:

1. **The Attention Grab:** The interrogator forcefully grabs the shirt front of the prisoner and shakes him.
2. **Attention Slap:** An open-handed slap aimed at causing pain and triggering fear.
3. **The Belly Slap:** A hard open-handed slap to the stomach. The aim is to cause pain, but not internal injury. Doctors consulted advised against using a punch, which could cause lasting internal damage.
4. **Long Time Standing:** This technique is described as among the most effective. Prisoners are forced to stand, handcuffed and with their feet shackled to an eye bolt in the floor for more than 40 hours. Exhaustion and sleep deprivation are effective in yielding confessions. [*Editors' Note: This torture technique, known as the plantón, was used extensively by Latin American military regimes in the 1970s.*]
5. **The Cold Cell:** The prisoner is left to stand naked in a cell kept near 50 degrees. Throughout the time in the cell the prisoner is doused with cold water.
6. **Water Boarding:** The prisoner is bound to an inclined board, feet raised and head slightly below the feet. Cellophane is wrapped over the prisoner's face and water is poured over him. Unavoidably, the gag reflex kicks in and a terrifying fear of drowning leads to almost instant pleas to bring the treatment to a halt. . . .

"The person believes they are being killed, and as such, it really amounts to a mock execution, which is illegal under international law," said John Sifton of Human Rights Watch.

The techniques are controversial among experienced intelligence agency and military interrogators. Many feel that a confession obtained this way is an unreliable tool. Two experienced officers have told ABC that there is little to be gained by these techniques that could not be more effectively gained by a methodical, careful, psychologically based interrogation.

According to a classified report prepared by the CIA Inspector General John Helgerwon and issued in 2004, the techniques "appeared to constitute cruel and degrading treatment under the (Geneva) convention," the *New York Times* reported on Nov. 9, 2005.

It is "bad interrogation. I mean you can get anyone to confess to anything if the torture's bad enough," said former CIA officer Bob Baer.

Larry Johnson, a former CIA officer and a deputy director of the State Department's office of counterterrorism, recently wrote in the *Los Angeles Times*, "What real CIA field officers know firsthand is that it is better to build a relationship of trust . . . than to extract quick confessions through tactics such as those used by the Nazis and the Soviets.". . .

However, ABC News was told that at least three CIA officers declined to be trained in the techniques before a cadre of 14 were selected to use them on a dozen top al Qaeda suspects in order to obtain critical information. In at least one instance, ABC News was told that the techniques led to questionable information aimed at pleasing the interrogators and that this information had a significant impact on U.S. actions in Iraq.

According to CIA sources, Ibn al Shaykh al Libbi, after two weeks of enhanced interrogation, made statements that were designed to tell the interrogators what they wanted to hear. Sources say Al Libbi had been subjected to each of the progressively harsher techniques in turn and finally broke after being water boarded and then left to stand naked in his cold cell overnight where he was doused with cold water at regular intervals.

His statements became part of the basis for the Bush administration claims that Iraq trained al Qaeda members to use biochemical weapons. Sources tell ABC that it was later established that Al Libbi had no knowledge of such training or weapons and fabricated the statements because he was terrified of further harsh treatment. "This is the problem with using the waterboard. They get so desperate that they begin telling you what they think you want to hear," one source said.

Two sources also told ABC that the techniques—authorized for use by only a handful of trained CIA officers—have been misapplied in at least one instance. The sources said that in that case a young, untrained junior officer caused the death of one detainee at a mud fort dubbed the "salt pit" that is used as a prison. They say the death occurred when the prisoner was left to stand naked throughout the harsh Afghanistan night after being doused with cold water. He died, they say, of hypothermia. According to the sources, a second CIA detainee died in Iraq and a third detainee died following harsh interrogation by Department of Defense personnel and contractors in Iraq. CIA sources said that in the DOD case, the interrogation was harsh, but did not involve the CIA.

The Kabul fort has also been the subject of confusion. Several intelligence sources involved in both the enhanced interrogation program and the program to ship detainees back to their own country for interrogation—a process described as rendition, say that the number of detainees in each program has been added together to suggest as many as 100 detainees are moved around the world from one secret CIA facility to another. In the rendition program, foreign nationals captured in the conflict zones are shipped back to their own countries on occasion for interrogation and prosecution.

There have been several dozen instances of rendition. There have been a little over a dozen authorized enhanced interrogations. As a result, the enhanced interrogation program has been described as one encompassing 100 or more prisoners. . . .

## DOCUMENT 8.19

The National Lawyers Guild and International Association of Democratic Lawyers called for the investigation and prosecution of White House lawyers such as John Yoo, David Addington, and Jay Bybee, who had "counseled the White House on how to get away with war crimes," and challenged a number of the legal claims made by these officials. (Extensive footnotes have been removed for readability.)

---

NATIONAL LAWYERS GUILD AND INTERNATIONAL | 453
ASSOCIATION OF DEMOCRATIC LAWYERS, "WHITE PAPER
ON THE LAW OF TORTURE AND HOLDING ACCOUNTABLE
THOSE WHO ARE COMPLICIT IN APPROVING TORTURE
OF PERSONS IN U.S. CUSTODY," MAY 2008 (EXCERPT)

This paper provides the background to the legal issues underpinning the call by the National Lawyers Guild (NLG) to prosecute and dismiss from their jobs people like then Deputy Assistant Attorney General John Choon Yoo, then Assistant Attorney General Jay Bybee and others who participated in the drafting of memoranda claimed to be based on sound legal precedent that purported to authorize the commitment of acts of torture or other cruel, inhuman or degrading treatment on behalf of the U.S. government. The memoranda were written at the request of high ranking U.S. officials in order to insulate them from the risk of future prosecution for subjecting detainees in U.S. custody to torture. By logical extension, this paper explains why all those who approved the use of torture and committed it—whether ordering it, approving it or giving purported legal advice to justify it—are subject to prosecution under international and U.S. domestic law.

The prohibition of torture is a *jus cogens* norm (these are principles of international law so fundamental that no nation may ignore them or attempt to contract out of them through treaties). The United States has consistently prohibited the use of torture through its Constitution, laws, executive statements and judicial decisions and by ratifying international treaties that prohibit it. The prohibition against torture applies to all persons in U.S. custody in times of peace, armed conflict, or state of emergency. In other words, the prohibition is absolute. However, the legal memoranda drafted by government lawyers purposely or recklessly misconstrued and/or ignored *jus cogens,* customary international law, and various U.S. treaty obligations in order to justify the unjustifiable, claiming that clearly unlawful interrogation "techniques" were lawful.

## I. THE PROHIBITION AGAINST TORTURE IS A *JUS COGENS* NORM

The prohibition against torture is a *jus cogens* norm. *Jus cogens* are defined as norms "accepted and recognized by the international community of states as a whole . . . from which no derogation is permitted . . ." In international criminal law, the legal duties that arise in connection with crimes designated as violations of *jus cogens* norms include the duty to prosecute or extradite, the non-applicability of statutes of limitations, the non-applicability of any immunities up to and including those enjoyed by Heads of State, the non-applicability of the defense of "obedience to superior orders" and universal jurisdiction over perpetrators of such crimes. Other *jus cogens* norms include the prohibitions against slavery, genocide, and wars of aggression. *Jus cogens* norms, like customary international law norms, are legally binding. No affirmative executive act may undercut the force of these prohibitions nor may a legislature legalize crimes designated as violating *jus cogens* norms or immunizing from prosecution those responsible. *Jus cogens* norms differ from norms which have attained the status of customary international law by dint of their universal and non-derogable character and the fact that *jus cogens* norms are peremptory, that is, they trump any other inconsistent international law. . . .

454 |

## THE CONVENTION AGAINST TORTURE, THE TORTURE STATUTE, AND THE WAR CRIMES ACT

As noted above, one of the processes which helped confer *jus cogens* status on torture was the ratification by the U.S. of the International Covenant on Civil and Political Rights (ICCPR) and the Torture Convention. The U.N. General Assembly adopted the CAT in 1984 to strengthen existing prohibitions against torture and other cruel, inhuman, or degrading treatment. On October 21, 1994, the United States ratified Convention, which expressly prohibits torture under all circumstances. The 1999 decision by the House of Lords to extradite Augusto Pinochet for prosecution for promoting and condoning acts of torture committed during his regime was based in part on the existence of the Convention and its contribution to the recognition of torture as a *jus cogens* norm. . . .

As a ratified convention, the CAT is a treaty which, through Article VI, Section 2 of the United States Constitution (Supremacy clause), is "the

Supreme Law of the Land" in domestic U.S. law. Pursuant to the dictates of the CAT, Congress criminalized torture for actions outside the United States. The language of the Torture Statute tracks to a large degree the language of the Torture Convention and punishes conspiracy to commit torture as well as torture itself. While the U.S. included various "understandings" along with its ratification of the Convention, international law does not permit such "understandings" to undercut the force and language of the Convention.

## II. THE UNITED STATES PROHIBITS TORTURE AND OTHER CRUEL, INHUMAN, OR DEGRADING TREATMENT

The U.S. Court of Appeals for the Second Circuit declared more than 25 years ago that the prohibition against torture is universal, obligatory, specific, and definable. Since then, every U.S. circuit court has held that torture violates universal and well-established customary international law, with the Eleventh Circuit finding that official torture is now prohibited by the law of nations, including U.S. law. . . .

Nor does the attorney-client privilege extend to keeping silent about planned criminal action. Even conceding Yoo and his co-conspirators actually believed their position was correct, no competent lawyer could have believed it unassailable. Giving real advice necessarily meant advising of the risks as well as the arguments favoring torture. And, it should be noted, their incredibly narrow definition of torture completely ignored the prohibition against other cruel, inhuman or degrading treatment or punishment, which would be obvious to anyone who chose to read even the full name of the CAT. It is impossible to believe this was the result of incompetence, leaving only the conclusion that they were willing participants in a conspiracy to violate *a jus cogens* norm. Professor Yoo and Judge Bybee, as well as the other lawyers who provided cover for illegal torture, are not protected by their right to free speech or academic freedom. They were not expressing their unsupportable legal opinions in scholarly journals or in classrooms. They were asked to justify what the administration wanted to do and they willingly did it, knowing the inevitable results. . . .

# ★ CHAPTER 9 ★

## POLICING TERROR VERSUS
## A WAR ON TERROR

SEPTEMBER 11 CHANGED EVERYTHING, not least by stoking fear of terrorism throughout U.S. society and prompting debates about how to fight it. Nevertheless, the government properly bore most of the responsibility for its failure to identify and prepare for the danger, despite years of large counterterrorism budgets. The George W. Bush administration had at first downplayed the terrorist threat, then was surprised by it, and finally began to exploit it, conceptualizing matters in such a way as to advance its larger goals of centralizing power in the presidency and reshaping the Middle East. Bush officials used the "war on terror" to carry out the administration's long-standing plans to topple Saddam Hussein, fusing Iraq with al Qaeda and international terrorism as they sought to marshal domestic and international support for preemption. In a similar vein, the administration later stated that the emergent Iraqi insurgency was directed by al Qaeda, an inaccurate assertion that served its short-run purposes but made it harder to fight an increasingly diverse terrorist threat (9.18, 9.19).

Other means short of war could have been employed to track down the terrorists who attacked on September 11. But the Bush administration had ideological reasons for viewing existing antiterrorism measures as mere police work or "swatting at flies."[1] As National Security Advisor Condoleezza Rice later testified, President Bush decided to eliminate al Qaeda by entirely restructuring

---

1. "Transcript of Condoleezza Rice's 9/11 Commission statement," CNN, May 19, 2004.

the Middle East. That long-standing orientation was expressed with particular clarity when, on May 1, 2001, the president delivered a major speech on U.S. security priorities at the National Defense University. Declaring that "rogue" states like Iraq—not terrorist groups like al Qaeda—"hate our friends, they hate our values, they hate democracy and freedom," he implied that such states were the primary threats to U.S. security (9.20). But the president's focus changed dramatically after September 11, as a generalized threat from state-less terrorist groups became the primary justification for preemptive war against Iraq. The administration then made terrorism into a black and white moral issue that pitted the "haters of freedom" abroad against the "lovers of freedom" in the United States (2.5, 9.10). Members of the administration repeatedly insisted that the American people faced a sinister enemy and that the fight against terrorism was an epic struggle of "good versus evil" (9.11). Allegations linking Iraq to al Qaeda and to the September 11 attacks were quickly transformed into a crusade of moral clarity and repeatedly used, particularly in Bush's State of the Union addresses, to justify preemptive war in Iraq (9.12).

The administration presented terrorism as an "existential" danger. But the measures it took, according to many observers, often exacerbated the threat rather than reduced it. This was partly due to the administration's unwillingness to admit that "rogue" leaders do not necessarily support terrorist groups. In fact, as a secular and nationalist leader, Saddam Hussein had been hostile to domestic and regional Islamist movements in the past.

| 457

The occupation of Iraq soon ran into problems for many reasons, prominent among which was the Bush administration's conflation of Osama bin Laden's al Qaeda organization with the developing Iraqi insurgency movement—even though al Qaeda did not operate in Iraq and had no bases there. The Iraqi insurgency was a widespread movement resisting foreign occupation and included a variety of orientations ranging from secular nationalism to religiously organized Islamism. Al Qaeda in Mesopotamia, formed by the radical Jordanian Abu Musab al-Zarqawi only after the U.S. invasion, was a separate organization with limited ties to the larger al Qaeda. In fact, Islamic groups were not tolerated in Saddam Hussein's Iraq since he viewed them as an unacceptable alternative to his secular, socialist Baath leadership. The Bush administration's insistence on labeling the U.S. invasion and occupation of Iraq as part of the war on terror disregarded the realities of the situation and helped fuel anti-occupation and anti-U.S. sentiment that did not exist in Iraq before 2003.

Societies can be terrorized by ordinary criminals, tribal groups, insurgents, renegade police, revolutionaries, or even their own governments. Historically, Washington had employed a variety of definitions of terrorism, depending on circumstances and political interests. Thus, it was no real surprise when the Bush administration claimed that September 11 had made preexisting criminal approaches obsolete. As it pursued its broad strategic objectives after the attacks, the administration discounted much counterterrorism expertise inside and outside of government, disregarded many of the lessons learned by U.S.

and European security agencies before September 11, and acted as if a "war on terror" could be "won" through military means. It argued that it was dealing with an act of war rather than a criminal act and that new groups, like al Qaeda, required new approaches. These groups were stateless, often operated outside national borders and beyond the knowledge and control of their host countries, and sometimes enjoyed the protection and support of "rogue states." They were often intent on acquiring and using weapons of mass destruction and, unlike ordinary criminals, did not pursue individual or monetary gain. Islamist terrorists were sometimes inspired by a cult of martyrdom that made it difficult to deter them with criminal penalties as they sought to undermine the effectiveness, legitimacy, and will of state institutions. All this, argued the administration, made contemporary terrorist groups so menacing that new assumptions, new policies, and new weapons were required to combat them.

Most international and U.S. security agencies had treated "terrorism" as a criminal tactic used by particular actors, however, not as a discrete entity that could be fought. The U.S. National Security Council, for instance, defined it not as "one person" or "a single political regime" but as "premeditated, politically motivated violence perpetrated against noncombatant targets by sub-national groups or clandestine agents" (9.1). In similar fashion, the Federal Bureau of Investigation defined terrorism in 1998 as "the unlawful use of force and violence against persons or property to intimidate or coerce a government, the civilian population, or any segment thereof, in furtherance of political or social objectives" (9.3). Like other law enforcement agencies, the FBI traditionally subjected accused terrorists to existing criminal statutes and gave them access to legal counsel and normal judicial procedures, including Fifth Amendment guarantees—an approach that had been quite successful in thwarting terrorist acts in the late 1990s (9.4). Criminalizing terrorism was effective because police work and public criminal trials tended to deprive individuals and groups of the attention and recognition they desired, and would likely receive, if their acts were defined as political.

458 |

Driven by its larger project, the Bush administration insisted that terrorist groups enjoyed "state sponsorship," a claim that supported its strategy of preemption and "regime change." If Saddam Hussein's regime harbored and supported terrorist groups like al Qaeda, the lifeline to terrorists would be cut once the regime was toppled. Yet, since the basic assumption was inaccurate, subsequent policies were flawed as well. Even if the administration had been correct in its assertions, many experts believed that terrorist groups could survive even in the absence of state sponsorship. It followed that "regime change" in Iraq might not be the best way to combat terrorism. But the administration's approach to terrorism after September 11 was driven by its general approach to international affairs.

By removing contemporary political terrorism from the category of criminal behavior, the United States announced its rejection of European strategies that were based on existing law and institutions and gave notice that it intended to act alone. Given the shock of September 11, the Bush administration might be excused for its first reaction. British, Italian, and German authorities had likewise initially overreacted to a series of bombings and killings by domestic groups operating between the 1960s and the 1980s. But Washington's embrace of neoconservatism made it difficult for it to modify its original decision to fold the "war on terror" into its larger goal of reshaping the Middle East.

Several European governments confronting terrorism in the 1970s and 1980s had initially imposed restrictions on civil liberties and sought to broadly expand government power, acting as if their countries were at war. Those measures proved to be counterproductive, and they soon returned to criminal justice approaches. In England and Germany, popular opinion and the courts successfully opposed the suspension of civil liberties. London, Rome, and Berlin discovered that it was a mistake to fight terrorism by relying exclusively—or even mainly—on a militarized approach. They realized that overreaction elevated the standing of terrorist groups and made it easier for them to gain additional support and recruits. It also unleashed unprecedented violence and counterviolence in their societies. In the end, legal prosecution under existing criminal statutes and international cooperation proved more effective than brute force in reducing the threat of terrorist violence. That government commitment to using normal police methods to fight terrorism and to protect civil liberties became so strong in Germany that in 2004 a Frankfurt deputy police chief was prosecuted for merely threatening to use force against a suspect in a child kidnapping case.[2] Criminal approaches also dominated FBI and police security practices and analysis in the United States during the 1990s.

One landmark 1994 report by the U.S. Department of Defense's Special Operations Unit accurately predicted the declining relevance of state-sponsored terrorism and the increasing importance of stateless terrorist groups. "Terror 2000: The Future Face of Terrorism" correctly forecast most of the major elements of the September 11 attacks and made important policy recommendations, centered on a criminal justice approach, that were largely ignored by the president and his advisors (9.5). Before the administration launched its preemptive war against Iraq, political leaders like Al Gore and the president's own National Security Council (NSC) had suggested a complex strategy for fighting terrorism that was significantly broader than an exclusively military approach (9.6). The 2003 NSC report stated that the United States would "not triumph solely or even primarily through military might" (9.1). Its next report, in 2006, expanded on strategies to "deny terrorists access to the materials, expertise, and other enabling capabilities required to develop WMD [weapons of mass destruction]."[3]

---

2. Kidnapping is considered a terrorist act in Germany. See Shawn Boyne, "Preserving the Rule of Law in a Time of Terror: Germany's Response to Terrorism," 2005.
3. See National Security Council, "National Strategy for Combating Terrorism," September 2006.

Though many in the Bush administration claimed that September 11 was sufficient justification for abandoning past practices and taking unilateral action, the reality was that earlier intelligence and police work had produced several warnings about al Qaeda. As early as January 25, 2001—just a few days after Bush took office—Richard A. Clarke, the chief counterterrorism advisor on the National Security Council from 1992 to 2003, had warned President Bush and his National Security Advisor Condoleezza Rice not to "underestimate" the threat posed by al Qaeda, but he was disregarded (9.6). The President's Daily Brief of August 6, 2001—an intelligence report prepared by the CIA that drew on various intelligence sources—was titled "Bin Laden Determined to Strike in U.S." It warned that there had been "suspicious activity in this country consistent with preparations for hijackings or other types of attacks, including recent surveillance of federal buildings in New York" and that "a group of bin Laden supporters was in the U.S. planning attacks with explosives" (9.8).

Condoleezza Rice was present at that crucial August 6 briefing. Afterward, she dismissed questions about why the administration had not responded to that intelligence, suggesting that the briefings had not provided enough detail. The administration did not act, she said, because the intelligence reports did not "tell us when; they [did not] tell us where; they [did not] tell us who; and they [did not] tell us how" al Qaeda would strike.[4]

Rice was partially correct in pointing to shortcomings in the functioning of the country's many intelligence agencies. Information was often not shared among them and there were far too few language and area specialists working on the Middle East. Richard Clarke and Michael F. Scheuer, the chief of the bin Laden Unit at the CIA from 2001 to 2004, provided personal testimony on the lack of focus and poor management in the intelligence agencies. So did the 9/11 Commission (9.9).

But the problem was deeper than bureaucratic confusion and mismanagement. The administration's move toward a preemptive and militaristic approach in its "war on terror" was driven by its general approach to foreign policy. Pushed by their desire to take advantage of the "unipolar moment," Bush administration neoconservatives had long-standing plans, dating from the early 1990s, to overthrow Saddam Hussein. As early as January 2001, in the first weeks of the new administration, two meetings of the National Security Council were dedicated to finding a way to oust Saddam Hussein, according to Treasury Secretary Paul O'Neill.[5] In May 2001, Bush himself gave clear signs that the administration was preparing for war with Iraq (chapter 2, 9.11, 9.20). The political climate after September 11, 2001, erased prior constraints on uni-

---

4. "Transcript of Rice's 9/11 Commission statement," CNN, May 19, 2004.
5. CBS News, "Bush Sought 'Way' to Invade Iraq? O'Neill Tells *60 Minutes* Iraq Was 'Topic A' 8 Months Before 9–11."

lateral action against Iraq and opened the door to pushing the definitional limits to incorporate war with Iraq into the "war on terror."

Primed by the administration's portrayal of Iraq as a compelling threat, by 2003 much of the public was ready to accept a more militarized approach to fighting terrorism, one that was particularly attuned to the opportunities and advantages made possible by sole superpower status. The choice of military tactics reflected the new approach. A key goal of the "shock and awe" campaign was to terrorize both the civilian population of Iraq and Saddam Hussein's military (9.13). The "shock and awe" approach originated in the 1996 work of the military strategists Harlan K. Ullman and James P. Wade Jr. Presented at the National Defense University, the preeminent institution for military education for all the armed services, their 1996 book portrayed "shock and awe" as massive psychological and physical violence against an entire society. Evoking the devastating psychological impact of the World War II nuclear bombing of Hiroshima and Nagasaki on Japan's political leaders and civilians, the authors wrote that the goal was to "impose a regime of Shock and Awe through delivery of instant, nearly incomprehensible levels of massive destruction directed at influencing society writ large, meaning its leadership and public, rather than targeting directly against military or strategic objectives" (9.13).

The invasion of Iraq was the first real application of "shock and awe." Secretary Donald Rumsfeld and others in the Defense Department argued that the "Powell Doctrine" of using overwhelming force to accomplish a conventional mission with a clear exit strategy was no longer effective for dealing with the asymmetric conditions of warfare involving stateless terrorists and other new enemies. These Pentagon officials further argued that conventional military force could not wring easy submission from a terrorist enemy that blended into the population. The "shock and awe" strategy also was designed to have a "demonstration effect," aiming to convince other "rogue" states and potential sub-state enemies that the United States would strike in a devastating manner if and when it chose. The objective was to stun the enemy by paralyzing its military capability through a combination of simultaneous attacks. Psychological shock was as important as the destruction of human beings and physical military capability. While the strategy seemed initially effective in Afghanistan and Iraq, U.S. soldiers were surprised later by the resilience of the civilian populations. Afghans and Iraqis often continued with their daily affairs while bombs dropped around them.

An additional objective of Ullman and Wade's approach was to influence the American people. Ullman and Wade recognized that the U.S. public, like most people in the world, did not want war. Without a compelling threat— equivalent to the perceived threat personified by the USSR during the early Cold War—Americans were not willing to "tolerate pain," they argued. Where the Powell doctrine highlighted the importance of gaining public support before going to war, "shock and awe" now recommended that the government deploy overwhelming preemptive military and political strikes to defeat the enemy *before* domestic public opposition could develop. In the future, Ullman and Wade suggested, "preemption may become a more realistic option along the lines of Israel's strikes against Syria's nuclear reactors in 1982" (9.13).

"Shock and awe" might have dramatic short-term effects, but wars often become considerably more complex than envisaged by military planners and political leaders. The Iraqi insurgency, which developed after President Bush's famous 2003 declaration that combat operations had ended, made a quick U.S. exit impossible (4.4). From that time on, the administration was faced with the difficult task of explaining what had gone wrong. In response to emerging doubts and questions, it continued to suggest that the Iraqi insurgency was linked to al Qaeda (9.14; see also chapters 2 and 5). The administration also stressed that there had been no new attacks in the United States since its invasion of Iraq, arguing that this proved that "we must defeat the terrorists overseas so we do not face them in the United States" (9.14).

But this argument ignored several important issues. First, there was no real way of knowing whether the Bush policies had succeeded or whether, instead, no new terrorist attacks against the United States had been planned. That is, the administration's claim of success through war was not provable. Second, there was a real possibility that the preemptive rush into Iraq may have been welcomed by an al Qaeda force with few options for taking on the United States, despite al Qaeda's public denunciations of the invasion. Indeed, the U.S. invasion and occupation of Iraq might have served as an effective recruiting tool for al Qaeda (9.15). There was some evidence that by inflating al Qaeda's importance with the argument that it was the biggest foe the United States faced in Iraq, the administration might have actually helped it attract new members and validate its assertion that the United States was the main enemy of Islam. Some evidence later indicated that al Qaeda had wanted to battle the United States in Iraq (9.15). Its leaders believed that keeping the United States in a long, drawn-out war would be the best way of weakening the United States by extracting treasure and blood (9.17). At the same time, as the administration correctly pointed out, al Qaeda had also promised to "expel the Americans from Iraq." Indeed, this became a central part of the government's circular argument to "stay the course."

Moreover, despite the administration's claims about the proper way to deal with non-state actors, the world was still organized by states. Laws, interstate relations, and international norms continued to structure the international system. Even if non-state actors violated the international legal framework, their illegal behavior did not give governments free rein to defy international law and did not mean that unilateral measures would be successful. The administration's preemptive acts and the extralegal methods it employed (such as "extraordinary rendition" and torture) damaged U.S. moral stature in the world and degraded the international legal framework. The behavior of the United States was widely regarded with dismay by sectors of the public at home and by the international community abroad. There were urgent calls for Washington to return to the values of multilateralism, respect for law, and participation in an international political community—particularly because there was ample evidence that such an orientation would be a more effective way of combating terrorism than Washington's unilateralism and preemption.

Many people also questioned the truth and morality of the administration's logic of "fighting them over there." It seemed to make the tens of thousands of deaths, the millions of injured and displaced, and the enormous destruction inflicted on Iraq nothing more than the necessary collateral damage designed to satisfy an attempt to preserve U.S. safety at home at the expense of countless others overseas. Such considerations again raised the question of whether other means of fighting terrorism could have been used more productively in order to avoid the catastrophic effects of war. Finally, the invasion—"fighting over there"—had stimulated the appearance of insurgency in Iraq, thus undermining the entire argument and contributing to the growing perception at home that, even in the absence of an attack since September 11, 2001, the war in Iraq had made the United States more vulnerable, not less, to terrorism.

By late 2007, the violence in Iraq had diminished to some extent. Though many attributed the reduction of violence to the "troop surge" that had begun early that year, other analysts argued that the larger U.S. military presence was not the key factor (9.21). They pointed instead to a pre-surge initiative in which the United States had begun delivering dollars to Sunni tribal leaders who formed "Awakening Councils" to fight insurgents (5.4). Many former insurgents, in fact, switched sides and joined the Councils. Though Paul Bremer had dismissed the Councils as an irrelevant pre-democratic "vestige" when he headed the CPA, the fact was that, without them, many individuals would have continued their violent opposition to the United States and the Iraqi government. The U.S. decision to stop fighting the tribes and to provide them instead with both respect and financial and security assistance had positive effects (9.21; see also chapter 5).[6] Indeed, winning the "hearts and minds" of the Iraqi people was the strategy recommended in the National Strategy for Combating Terrorism in 2003, by key military leaders, and even by some figures in the Bush administration. The United States, these voices suggested, should aim for "progress" rather than the traditional military goal of complete "victory" (9.1, 9.21). It was worth noting that General Petraeus and others adopted this strategy after the occupation of Iraq began to face sustained and violent resistance (5.4).

As the administration's second term drew to a close, it seemed trapped by its own policies and rhetoric. Even British counterterrorism experts—historically the administration's strongest allies—criticized its militarized approach to fighting terrorism. The former director general of Britain's domestic intelligence agency MI5 said she hoped the next president "would stop using the phrase

6. Center for Strategic and International Studies, "Success or Failure? Iraq's Insurgency and Civil Violence and U.S. Strategy: Developments through June 2007" July 9, 2007, p. 88.

| 463

'war on terror,'" arguing that "it got us off on the wrong foot because it made people think terrorism was something you could deal with by force of arms primarily." Another British official publicly rejected what he called "the Guantánamo model" as a way to defeat terrorism, arguing that "our rights are priceless . . . the best way to face down those threats is to strengthen our institutions rather than to degrade them."[7] Yet, against voices like these, the Bush administration continued to insist that its militarized approach in Iraq and elsewhere was central to "the global war on terror."

# U.S. Government Terrorism Documents

## DOCUMENT 9.1

A statement crafted by the National Security Council in 2003 presented a nuanced and sophisticated analysis of the nature of the terrorist threat and how to deal with it. Its connections to the Bush doctrine of preemption were revealed in its declaration that the United States would not hesitate "to act alone." The Bush administration agreed with that claim as it launched the war in Iraq. It largely ignored, however, the report's broader analysis and the multipronged approach, "using all the tools of statecraft," that it recommended.

464 |

U.S. NATIONAL SECURITY COUNCIL, "NATIONAL STRATEGY FOR COMBATING TERRORISM," FEBRUARY 2003 (EXCERPT)

Introduction

The terrorist attacks of September 11, 2001, in Washington, D.C., New York City, and Pennsylvania were acts of war against the United States of America and its allies, and against the very idea of civilized society. No cause justifies terrorism. The world must respond and fight this evil that is intent on threatening and destroying our basic freedoms and our way of life. Freedom and fear are at war.

The enemy is not one person. It is not a single political regime. Certainly it is not a religion. The enemy is terrorism—premeditated, politically motivated violence perpetrated against noncombatant targets by sub national groups or clandestine agents. Those who employ terrorism, regardless of their specific secular or religious objectives, strive to subvert the rule of law and effect change through violence and fear. These terrorists also share the

---

7. Raymond Bonner, "2 British Antiterror Experts Say U.S. Takes Wrong Path," *New York Times,* October 22, 2008.

misguided belief that killing, kidnapping, extorting, robbing, and wreaking havoc to terrorize people are legitimate forms of political action.

The struggle against international terrorism is different from any other war in our history. We will not triumph solely or even primarily through military might. We must fight terrorist networks, and all those who support their efforts to spread fear around the world, using every instrument of national power—diplomatic, economic, law enforcement, financial, information, intelligence, and military. Progress will come through the persistent accumulation of successes—some seen, some unseen. And we will always remain vigilant against new terrorist threats. Our goal will be reached when Americans and other civilized people around the world can lead their lives free of fear from terrorist attacks.

There will be no quick or easy end to this conflict. At the same time, the United States, will not allow itself to be held hostage by terrorists. Combating terrorism and securing the U.S. homeland from future attacks are our top priorities. But they will not be our only priorities. This strategy supports the National Security Strategy of the United States. As the National Security Strategy highlights, we live in an age with tremendous opportunities to foster a world consistent with interests and values embraced by the United States and freedom-loving people around the world. And we will seize these opportunities.

This combating terrorism strategy further elaborates on Section III of the National Security Strategy by expounding on our need to destroy terrorist organizations, win the "war of ideas," and strengthen America's security at home and abroad. While the National Strategy for Homeland Security focuses on preventing terrorist attacks within the United States, the National Strategy for Combating Terrorism focuses on identifying and defusing threats before they reach our borders.

| 465

While we appreciate the nature of the difficult challenge before us, our strategy is based on the belief that sometimes the most difficult tasks are accomplished by the most direct means.

Ours is a strategy of direct and continuous action against terrorist groups, the cumulative effect of which will initially disrupt, over time degrade, and ultimately destroy the terrorist organizations. The more frequently and relentlessly we strike the terrorists across all fronts, using all the tools of statecraft, the more effective we will be.

The United States, with its unique ability to build partnerships and project power, will lead the fight against terrorist organizations of global reach. By striking constantly and ensuring that terrorists have no place to hide, we will compress their scope and reduce the capability of these organizations. By adapting old alliances and creating new partnerships, we will facilitate regional solutions that further isolate the spread of terrorism. Concurrently, as the scope of terrorism becomes more localized, unorganized and relegated to the criminal domain, we will rely upon and assist other states to eradicate terrorism at its root.

The United States will constantly strive to enlist the support of the international community in this fight against a common foe. If necessary, however, we will not hesitate to act alone, to exercise our right to self-defense, including acting preemptively against terrorists to prevent them from doing harm to our people and our country.

The war on terrorism is asymmetric in nature but the advantage belongs to us, not the terrorists. We will fight this campaign using our strengths against the enemy's weaknesses. We will use the power of our values to shape a free and more prosperous world. We will employ the legitimacy of our government and our cause to craft strong and agile partnerships. Our economic strength will help failing states and assist weak countries in ridding themselves of terrorism. Our technology will help identify and locate terrorist organizations, and our global reach will eliminate them where they hide. And as always, we will rely on the strength of the American people to remain resolute in the face of adversity.

We will never forget what we are ultimately fighting for—our fundamental democratic values and way of life. In leading the campaign against terrorism, we are forging new international relationships and redefining existing ones in terms suited to the transnational challenges of the 21st century. We seek to integrate nations and peoples into the mutually beneficial democratic relationships that protect against the forces of disorder and violence. By harnessing the power of humanity to defeat terrorism in all its forms, we promote a freer, more prosperous, and more secure world and give hope to our children and generations to come. Ultimately, our fight against terrorism will help foster an international environment where our democratic interests are secure and the values of liberty are respected around the world. . . .

## The Changing Nature of Terrorism

While retaining this basic structure, the terrorist challenge has changed considerably over the past decade and likely will continue to evolve. Ironically, the particular nature of the terrorist threat we face today springs in large part from some of our past successes.

In the 1970s and 1980s, the United States and its allies combated generally secular and nationalist terrorist groups, many of which depended upon active state sponsors.

While problems of state sponsorship of terrorism continue, years of sustained counterterrorism efforts, including diplomatic and economic isolation, have convinced some governments to curtail or even abandon support for terrorism as a tool of statecraft. The collapse of the Soviet Union—which provided critical backing to terrorist groups and certain state sponsors—accelerated the decline in state sponsorship. Many terrorist organizations were effectively destroyed or neutralized, including the Red Army Faction, Direct Action, and Communist Combatant Cells in Europe, and the Japanese Red Army in Asia. Such past successes provide valuable lessons for the future.

With the end of the Cold War, we also saw dramatic improvements in the ease of transnational communication, commerce, and travel. Unfortunately, the terrorists adapted to this new international environment and turned the advances of the 20th century into the destructive enablers of the 21st century.

## A New Global Environment

Al-Qaida exemplifies how terrorist networks have twisted the benefits and conveniences of our increasingly open, integrated, and modernized world to serve their destructive agenda. The *Al Qaida* network is a multinational enterprise with operations in more than 60 countries. Its camps in Afghanistan provided sanctuary and its bank accounts served as a trust fund for terrorism. Its global activities are coordinated through the use of personal couriers and communication technologies emblematic of our era—cellular and satellite phones, encrypted e-mail, Internet chat rooms, videotape, and CD-ROMs. Like a skilled publicist, Usama bin Laden and Al Qaida have exploited the international media to project his image and message worldwide.

Members of Al Qaida have traveled from continent to continent with the ease of a vacationer or business traveler. Despite our coalition's successes in Afghanistan and around the world, some Al Qaida operatives have escaped to plan additional terrorist attacks. In an age marked by unprecedented mobility and migration, they readily blend into communities wherever they move.

They pay their way with funds raised through front businesses, drug trafficking, credit card fraud, extortion, and money from covert supporters. They use ostensibly charitable organizations and non-governmental organizations (NGOs) for funding and recruitment. Money for their operations is transferred surreptitiously through numerous banks, money exchanges, and alternate remittance systems (often known as "hawalas")—some legitimate and unwitting, others not.

## DOCUMENT 9.2

UN Security Council Resolution 1566 of 2004 followed its Resolution 1373 of 2001, passed in response to the September 11, 2001, attacks. Cosponsored by the United States, China, and Russia, Resolution 1566 defined terrorism as a set of specific criminal acts, recommended how states should respond, and condemned all acts of terrorism, no matter what the motivation. It also declared that states' efforts to counter terrorism must "comply with all their obligations under international law." Despite its support of 1566, however, the Bush administration employed many methods that violated international norms in its "war on terror" (see chapter 8).

UNITED NATIONS SECURITY COUNCIL RESOLUTION 1566,
OCTOBER 8, 2004

The Security Council,
*Reaffirming* its resolutions 1267 (1999) of 15 October 1999 and 1373 (2001)
of 28 September 2001 as well as its other resolutions concerning threats to
international peace and security caused by terrorism,
*Recalling* in this regard its resolution 1540 (2004) of 28 April 2004,
*Reaffirming* also the imperative to combat terrorism in all its forms and
manifestations by all means, in accordance with the Charter of the United
Nations and international law,
Deeply concerned by the increasing number of victims, including children,
caused by acts of terrorism motivated by intolerance or extremism in various regions of the world,
*Calling upon* States to cooperate fully with the Counter-Terrorism Committee (CTC) established pursuant to resolution 1373 (2001), including the
recently established Counter-Terrorism Committee Executive Directorate
(CTED), the "Al-Qaida/Taliban Sanctions Committee" established pursuant
to resolution 1267 (1999) and its Analytical Support and Sanctions Monitoring Team, and the Committee established pursuant to resolution 1540
(2004), and further calling upon such bodies to enhance cooperation with
each other,
*Reminding* States that they must ensure that any measures taken to combat
terrorism comply with all their obligations under international law, and
should adopt such measures in accordance with international law, in particular international human rights, refugee, and humanitarian law,
*Reaffirming* that terrorism in all its forms and manifestations constitutes one
of the most serious threats to peace and security,
*Considering* that acts of terrorism seriously impair the enjoyment of human
rights and threaten the social and economic development of all States and
undermine global stability and prosperity,
*Emphasizing* that enhancing dialogue and broadening the understanding
among civilizations, in an effort to prevent the indiscriminate targeting of
different religions and cultures, and addressing unresolved regional conflicts
and the full range of global issues, including development issues, will contribute to international cooperation, which by itself is necessary to sustain
the broadest possible fight against terrorism,
*Reaffirming* its profound solidarity with victims of terrorism and their
families,
*Acting* under Chapter VII of the Charter of the United Nations,

1. *Condemns* in the strongest terms all acts of terrorism irrespective
   of their motivation, whenever and by whomsoever committed,
   as one of the most serious threats to peace and security;
2. *Calls upon* States to cooperate fully in the fight against terrorism,
   especially with those States where or against whose citizens ter-

rorist acts are committed, in accordance with their obligations under international law, in order to find, deny safe haven and bring to justice, on the basis of the principle to extradite or prosecute, any person who supports, facilitates, participates or attempts to participate in the financing, planning, preparation or commission of terrorist acts or provides safe havens;

3. *Recalls* that criminal acts, including against civilians, committed with the intent to cause death or serious bodily injury, or taking of hostages, with the purpose to provoke a state of terror in the general public or in a group of persons or particular persons, intimidate a population or compel a government or an international organization to do or to abstain from doing any act, which constitute offences within the scope of and as defined in the international conventions and protocols relating to terrorism, are under no circumstances justifiable by considerations of a political, philosophical, ideological, racial, ethnic, religious or other similar nature, and calls upon all States to prevent such acts and, if not prevented, to ensure that such acts are punished by penalties consistent with their grave nature;

4. *Calls upon* all States to become party, as a matter of urgency, to the relevant international conventions and protocols whether or not they are a party to regional conventions on the matter . . .    | 469

# DOCUMENT 9.3

An important 1998 FBI report presented a U.S. counterterrorism policy based on criminal prosecution and documented its success, even against al Qaeda. In the aftermath of the September 11, 2001, attacks the Bush administration abandoned the criminal justice approach in favor of a militarized policy that was closely linked to its embrace of unilateralism and preemption.

---

COUNTERTERRORISM THREAT ASSESSMENT AND
WARNING UNIT, NATIONAL SECURITY DIVISION, FBI,
"TERRORISM IN THE UNITED STATES 1998" (EXCERPT)

The year 1998 demonstrated the wide range of terrorist threats confronting the United States. Terrorists in Colombia continued to target private American interests, kidnapping seven U.S. citizens throughout the year and carrying out 77 bombings against multinational oil pipelines, many of which are used by U.S. oil companies. On August 7, 1998, the U.S. embassies in Nairobi, Kenya, and Dar es Salaam, Tanzania, were attacked in nearly simultaneous truck bombings that left 224 persons dead, including 12 U.S.

citizens (all victims of the Nairobi attack). The bombings also wounded over 4,500 persons.

In the United States, the FBI recorded five terrorist incidents in 1998. Within the same year, 12 planned acts of terrorism were prevented in the United States. There were no suspected incidents of terrorism in the United States during 1998. . . .

Likewise, the 12 acts of terrorism prevented in the United States during the year were being planned by domestic extremists. Nine of these planned acts were prevented as a result of the arrest of several members of the white supremacist group The New Order, based in Illinois. The six men, who were arrested on weapons violations charges in February 1998, planned to conduct a crime spree that was to include bombings, assassinations, and robberies. Consistent with a steady increase in cases involving the use or threatened use of chemical and biological agents, two additional terrorist preventions involved the planned use of biological toxins. The final prevention involved a plan to detonate a bomb at an unspecified target in Washington, D.C.

The United States continued to pursue an aggressive policy toward terrorism in 1998. In January, international terrorist Ramzi Ahmed Yousef received a lengthy prison sentence for masterminding the February 26, 1993 World Trade Center bombing, as well as a foiled plot to bomb U.S. commercial aircraft transiting the Far East in 1995. A Yousef accomplice in the World Trade Center bombing was also sentenced in 1998. Eyad Mahmoud Ismail Najim, who drove the bomb-laden van into the parking garage of the World Trade Center, was sentenced to 240 years in prison and ordered to pay 10 million dollars in restitution and a 250-thousand dollar fine. An associate of the plotters, Mohammad Abouhalima, who drove his brother (Mahmud) to Kennedy International Airport after the 1993 World Trade Center bombing, was sentenced to eight years in prison. In addition, Ibrahim Ahmad Suleiman received a 10-month sentence for providing false statements to the grand jury investigating the bombing. In May, Abdul Hakim Murad, an accomplice in Ramzi Yousef's plot to bomb U.S. airliners, was sentenced to life plus 60 years in prison, without parole. In June, international terrorist Mohammed Rashid was rendered to the United States from overseas to stand trial on charges related to the detonation of a bomb on Pan Am flight 830 in 1982, which killed one passenger and wounded 15 others.

In addition, a number of domestic terrorists and extremists were convicted and/or sentenced for their illicit activities throughout the year. These included Terry Lynn Nichols, who was sentenced to life in prison for his role in the Oklahoma City bombing, and 21 individuals convicted of charges related to the 1996 Montana Freemen siege.

In the immediate aftermath of the August 7 U.S. embassy bombings in East Africa, the FBI launched the largest extraterritorial investigation in its history. Two subjects, Mohammed Sadeek Odeh and Mohammed Rashed

Daoud al-Owhali, were arrested in Kenya within 20 days of the bombings and, shortly thereafter, were rendered to the United States. Information obtained from these subjects, as well as information collected through other investigative leads, quickly focused investigative attention on terrorist financier Usama Bin Laden and his terrorist network Al-Qaeda (the base), as allegedly being behind the embassy bombings. On November 4, 1998, Bin Laden and several members of his network, including his military commander Muhammad Atef, as well as Odeh and al-Owhali, were named in an indictment unsealed in the Southern District of New York. Another subject, Mamdouh Mahmud Salim, who had been arrested in Germany in September 1998, was extradited to the United States on December 20. In addition, Wadih El-Hage, a naturalized American citizen who was living in Arlington, Texas, at the time of the bombings, was arrested by the FBI for making false statements during questioning. El-Hage is believed to be a key member of the Al-Qeada network.

## DOCUMENT 9.4

This chart in an FBI report (9.3) demonstrated the increasing success of the legal and criminal justice approach to combating terrorism in the United States before the Bush administration came to power.

| 471

COUNTERTERRORISM THREAT ASSESSMENT AND WARNING UNIT, NATIONAL SECURITY DIVISION, FBI, "TERRORISM IN THE UNITED STATES, 1990–1998" (GRAPHIC)

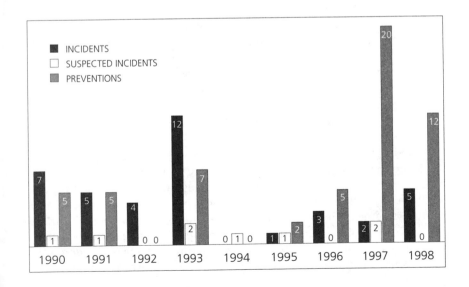

# DOCUMENT 9.5

An important 1994 report commissioned by the U.S. Department of Defense predicted the rise of religiously based non-state terrorism. Arguing that terrorism "would grow more common, not less so," it advised that it "would not be sponsored by states, but increasingly by Muslim extremists motivated by a bitter hatred of the west in general and America in particular." It also argued that these new terrorist groups would not be reluctant to kill masses of innocent people in pursuit of their goals. While "Terror 2000" presented extremist networks as a major terrorist threat, it did not recommend military approaches to deal with them. One of several similar reports produced in the years before September 11, 2001, this one was disregarded by the Bush administration, partly because of administrative problems concerning coordination among the intelligence agencies, but also because the administration at first minimized the threat posed by extremist terrorist networks.

MARVIN J. CETRON AND PETER S. PROBST,
"TERROR 2000: THE FUTURE FACE OF TERRORISM,"
U.S. DEPARTMENT OF DEFENSE, JUNE 24, 1994 (EXCERPT)

. . . recently, we have seen the rise of terrorist affinity groups, small bands of like-minded individuals with little in the way of a formal structure. It may well have been one such group that bombed the New York World Trade Center. The bombers met in the New Jersey and Brooklyn mosques of Sheik Omar Abdel Rahman. They received aid from experience terrorists in the Islamic immigrant community, many of who received on-the-job training in the Afghan war . . .

In a simple, straight-line projection, the number of international terrorist incidents each year will rise and fall in the decades to come, yet will grow over all at an average rate of 15 percent per year. However, because of the growing social and political instability, we expect international terrorist attacks to increase two- or three-fold over the next decade. Moreover, we expect an even greater increase in "local terrorism;" that is, terrorism that is confined to a single country and which involves only the nationals and targets of that country . . .

Religious and ethnically motivated terrorists are more willing than most to pursue their aims by whatever means necessary. Unlike politically motivated terrorists, they do not shrink from mass murder, because they are struggling against the forces of darkness or to preserve such quasi-mystical concepts as "the purity of the race." Mass casualties are not to be shunned, because they could alienate marginal supporters, but sought, because they demonstrate to unbelievers the cataclysmic nature of divine retribution. And if innocents suffer, *God* will sort them out. Hussein Mussawi, the Hezbollah leader who was killed in an Israeli helicopter assault, once commented: "We are not fighting so that the enemy recognizes us and offers us something. We are fighting to wipe out the enemy." Radical Islam not only attacks moderate Arab regimes, but has spread beyond the Middle East. It now has significant followings in Muslim communities in Africa, Asia, Europe and the Americas. . . .

# DOCUMENT 9.6

During the first week of the Bush administration and almost nine months before the attacks of September 11, the counterterrorism coordinator Richard Clarke, a holdover from the Clinton administration, informed National Security Advisor Condoleezza Rice that al Qaeda was a serious threat. He made it very clear that Osama bin Laden's organization was no "narrow, little terrorist [group]" and offered strategies for addressing the threat that it posed. The meeting of administration "principals" that Clarke recommended to decide how to handle al Qaeda did not happen before September 11, however. After leaving government, Clarke became a strong critic of the Bush administration's pre–September 11 attitude toward counterterrorism. He testified before the 9/11 Commission in March 2004 and became the only administration official to apologize: "To the loved ones of the victims of 9/11, to those who are here in this room, to those who are watching on television, your government failed you. Those entrusted with protecting you failed you. And I failed you. We tried hard, but that doesn't matter because we failed."[9]

RICHARD A. CLARKE, "MEMORANDUM FOR CONDOLEEZZA RICE, SUBJECT: PRESIDENTIAL POLICY INITIATIVE/REVIEW—THE AL QUIDA [*SIC*] NETWORK," NATIONAL SECURITY COUNCIL, JANUARY 25, 2001 (EXCERPT)

Steve [*Editors' Note: Stephen Hadley, Rice's deputy at the NSC*] asked today that we propose major Presidential policy reviews or initiatives. We urgently need such a Principals level review on the al Qaeda network.

## Just Some Terrorist Group?
As we noted in our briefings for you, al Qaeda is not some narrow, little terrorist issue that needs to be included in broader regional policy. Rather, several of our regional policies need to address centrally the transnational challenge to the US and our interests posed by the al Qaeda network. . . .

9. Clarke expanded on his apology in *Your Government Failed You: Breaking the Cycle of National Security Disasters* (New York: HarperCollins, 2008).

al Qaeda is the active, organized, major force that is using a distorted version of Islam as its vehicle to achieve two goals:

- to drive the US out of the Muslim world, forcing the withdrawal of our military and economic presence in countries from Morocco to Indonesia;
- to replace moderate, modern, Western regime in Muslim countries with theocracies modeled along the lines of the Taliban.

al Qaeda affects centrally our policies on Pakistan, Afghanistan, Central Asia, North Africa and the GCC. Leaders in Jordan and Saudi Arabia see al Qaeda as a direct threat to them. The strength of the network of organizations limits the scope of support friendly Arab regimes can give to a range of US policies, including Iraq policy and the Peace Process. We would make a major error if we underestimate the challenge al Qaeda poses. Or over estimated the stability of the moderate, friendly regimes al Qaeda threatens.

## Pending Time Sensitive Decisions
At the close of the Clinton Administration, two decisions about al Qaeda were deferred to the Bush Administration.

- First, should we provide the Afghan Northern Alliance enough assistance to maintain it as a viable opposition force to the Taliban/al Qaeda? If we do not, I believe that the Northern Alliance may be effectively taken out of action this Spring when fighting resumes after the winter thaw. The al Qaeda 55th Brigade, which has been a key fighting force for the Taliban, would then be freed to sent its personnel elsewhere, where they would likely threaten US interests. For any assistance to get there in time to effect the spring fighting, a decision is needed now.
- Second, should we increase assistance to Uzbekistan to allow them to deal with the al Qaeda/IMU threat? [Operational detail, removed at the request of the CIA]

Three other issues awaiting addressal now are:

- First, what the new Administration says to the Taliban and Pakistan about the importance we attach to ending the al Qaeda sanctuary in Afghanistan. We are separately proposing early, strong messages to both.
- Second, do we propose significant program growth in the FY02 budget for anti–al Qaeda operations by CIA and counter-terrorism training and assistance by State and CIA?
- Third, when and how does the Administration choose to respond to the attack on the USS Cole. That decision is obviously complex. We can make some decisions, such as those above, now without

yet coming to grips with the harder decision about the Cole. On the Cole, we should take advantage of the policy that we "will respond at a time, place, and manner of our own choosing" and not be forced into knee jerk responses.

I recommend that you have a Principals discussion of al Qaeda soon and address the following issues:

1. Threat magnitude: Do the Principals agree that the al Qaeda network poses a first order threat to US interests in a number or regions, or is this analysis a "chicken little" over reaching and can we proceed without major new initiatives and by handling this issue in a more routine manner?
2. Strategy: If it is a first order issue, how should the existing strategy be modified or strengthened? Two elements of the existing strategy that have not been made to work effectively are a) going after al Qaeda's money and b) public information to counter al Qaeda propaganda.
3. FY02 Budget: Should we continue the funding increases into FY02 for State and CIA programs designed to implement the al Qaeda strategy?
4. Immediate [Redacted] Decisions: Should we initiate [Redacted] funding to the Northern Alliance and to the Uzbek's?

| 475

Please let us know if you would like such a decision/discussion paper or any modifications to the background paper.
Concurrences by: Mary McCarthy, Dan Fried, Bruce Reidel, Don Camp
Attachment—Tab A December 2000 Paper: Strategy for Eliminating the Threat from the Jihadist Networks of Al Qida: Status and Prospects—Tab B September 1998 Paper: Pol-Mil Plan for Al Qida


# DOCUMENT 9.7

The former vice president Al Gore warned, on September 23, 2002, that a war with Iraq would distract the United States from pursuing Osama bin Laden, who had praised the September 11 attacks and whose al Qaeda network was responsible for planning and executing them. Gore predicted that a war would unleash forces that would complicate the situation in the Middle East and make terrorism worse. He did not reject the possibility that Saddam Hussein had "weapons of mass destruction" but reminded his listeners that Iraq was far from being the only such state to possess them. Robert Parry's article, summarizing and quoting from the Gore speech, is the best summary we have of this prescient speech.

ROBERT PARRY, "GORE'S OTHER GLOBAL WARNING:
IRAQ WAR," CONSORTIUMNEWS.COM,
FEBRUARY 25, 2007 (EXCERPT)

. . . in fall 2002 Gore sought to warn the American people about another "inconvenient truth," the folly of invading Iraq.

The former Vice President did so at a time when it was considered madness or almost treason to object to George W. Bush's war plans. But Gore was one of a small number of national political figures who took that risk and paid a price, subjected to widespread ridicule and disdain from the Washington news media.

On Sept. 23, 2002, in a speech at the Commonwealth Club in San Francisco, Gore laid out a series of concerns and differences that he had with Bush's policy of "preemptive war" and specifically Bush's decision to refashion the "war on terror" into an imminent invasion of Iraq.

Gore, who had supported the Persian Gulf War in 1990–91, criticized Bush's failure to enlist the international community as his father had. Gore also warned about the negative impact that alienating other nations was having on the broader war against terrorists.

"I am deeply concerned that the course of action that we are presently embarking upon with respect to Iraq has the potential to seriously damage our ability to win the war against terrorism and to weaken our ability to lead the world in this new century," Gore said. "To put first things first, I believe that we ought to be focusing our efforts first and foremost against those who attacked us on Sept. 11. . . .

"Great nations persevere and then prevail. They do not jump from one unfinished task to another. We should remain focused on the war against terrorism."

Instead of keeping after al Qaeda and stabilizing Afghanistan, Bush had chosen to start a new war against Iraq as the first example of his policy of preemption, Gore said.

"He is telling us that our most urgent task right now is to shift our focus and concentrate on immediately launching a new war against Saddam Hussein," Gore said. "And the President is proclaiming a new uniquely American right to preemptively attack whomsoever he may deem represents a potential future threat."

Gore also objected to the timing of the vote on war with Iraq.

"President Bush is demanding, in this high political season, that Congress speedily affirm that he has the necessary authority to proceed immediately against Iraq and, for that matter, under the language of his resolution, against any other nation in the region regardless of subsequent developments or emerging circumstances," Gore said.

The former Vice President staked out a position with subtle but important differences from Bush's broad assertion that the United States has the right to override international law on the President's command. Gore argued that U.S. unilateral power should be used sparingly, only in extreme situations.

"There's no international law that can prevent the United States from taking action to protect our vital interests when it is manifestly clear that there's a choice to be made between law and our survival," Gore said. "Indeed, international law itself recognizes that such choices stay within the purview of all nations. I believe, however, that such a choice is not presented in the case of Iraq."

## Lost Good Will

Gore bemoaned, too, that Bush's actions had dissipated the international good will that surrounded the United States after the 9/11 attacks.

"That has been squandered in a year's time and replaced with great anxiety all around the world, not primarily about what the terrorist networks are going to do, but about what we're going to do," Gore said. "Now, my point is not that they're right to feel that way, but that they do feel that way."

Gore also took aim at Bush's unilateral assertion of his right to imprison American citizens without trial or legal representation simply by labeling them "enemy combatants."

"The very idea that an American citizen can be imprisoned without recourse to judicial process or remedy, and that this can be done on the sole say-so of the President of the United States or those acting in his name, is beyond the pale and un-American, and ought to be stopped," Gore said.

Gore raised, too, practical concerns about the dangers that might follow the overthrow of Hussein, if chaos in Iraq followed. Gore cited the deteriorating political condition in Afghanistan where the new central government exerted real control only in parts of Kabul while ceding effective power to warlords in the countryside.

"What if, in the aftermath of a war against Iraq, we faced a situation like that, because we've washed our hands of it?" Gore asked. "What if the al Qaeda members infiltrated across the borders of Iraq the way they are in Afghanistan? . . .

"Now, I just think that if we end the war in Iraq the way we ended the war in Afghanistan, we could very well be much worse off than we are today. . . ."

# DOCUMENT 9.8

The classified President's Daily Brief was prepared by the Central Intelligence Agency every day to alert the president to the most pressing intelligence developments. The August 6, 2001, briefing drew on FBI intelligence to provide an explicit warning of an impending al Qaeda attack, even mentioning the

World Trade Center and a possible plane hijacking. Though the memo cautioned that the intelligence agencies had not been able to corroborate the hijacking threat with certitude, its overall message was that Osama bin Laden was "determined to strike" in the United States sometime soon. Condoleezza Rice, Bush's national security advisor at the time, justified the administration's lack of a response in her testimony before Congress by stating that the document contained mere "historical information based on old reporting," adding, "There was no new threat information."

CIA, PRESIDENT'S DAILY BRIEF, "BIN LADIN [*SIC*]
DETERMINED TO STRIKE IN U.S.," AUGUST 6, 2001

Clandestine, foreign government, and media reports indicate Bin Ladin since 1997 has wanted to conduct terrorist attacks in the US. Bin Ladin implied in US television interviews in 1997 and 1998 that his followers would follow the example of World Trade Center bomber Ramzi Yousef and "bring the fighting to America."

After US missile strikes on his base in Afghanistan in 1998, Bin Ladin told followers he wanted to retaliate in Washington, according to a [Redacted] service.

An Egyptian Islamic Jihad (EIJ) operative told an [Redacted] service at the same time that Bin Ladin was planning to exploit the operative's access to the US to mount a terrorist strike.

*The millennium plotting in Canada in 1999 may have been part of Bin Ladin's first serious attempt to implement a terrorist strike in the US.* Convicted plotter Ahmed Ressam has told the FBI that he conceived the idea to attack Los Angeles International Airport himself, but that Bin Ladin lieutenant Abu Zuhaydah encouraged him and helped facilitate the operation. Ressam also said that in 1998 Abu Zubaydah was planning his own US attack.

Ressam says Bin Ladin was aware of the Los Angeles operation.

Although Bin Ladin has not succeeded, his attacks against the US Embassies in Kenya and Tanzania in 1998 demonstrate that he prepares operations years in advance and is not deterred by setbacks. Bin Ladin associates surveilled our Embassies in Nairobi and Dar es Salaam as early as 1993, and some members of the Nairobi cell planning the bombings were arrested and deported in 1997.

Al-Qa'ida members—including some who are US citizens—have resided in or traveled to the US for years, and the group apparently maintains a support structure that could aid attacks. Two Al Qa'ida members found guilty in the conspiracy to bomb our Embassies in East Africa were US citizens, and a senior EIJ member lived in California in the mid-1990s.

A clandestine source said in 1998 that a Bin Ladin cell in New York was recruiting Muslim-American youth for attacks.

We have not been able to corroborate some of the more sensational threat reporting, such as that from a [redacted] service in 1998 saying that Bin Ladin wanted to hijack a US aircraft to gain the release of "Blind Shaykh" 'Umar 'Abd al-Rahman and other US-held extremists.
Declassified and Approved for Release, 10 April 2004.

# DOCUMENT 9.9

The 9/11 Commission Report, mandated by Congress and the president in late 2002 to provide an independent and bipartisan analysis of the events of that day, explained that the failure to anticipate and prevent the attacks was not a failure of traditional law enforcement techniques but the result of their improper administration. It concluded that the intelligence agencies had exposed many of the plotters and their activities but had failed to stop the attacks because of poor coordination among the agencies and inefficient management. There was no mention of Iraqi involvement.

---

THE 9/11 COMMISSION REPORT, 2004 (EXCERPT)

### Government Response to the Threats

National Security Advisor Rice told us that the CSG [*Editors' Note: Counterterrorism Security Group*] was the "nerve center" for running the crisis, although other senior officials were involved over the course of the summer. In addition to his daily meetings with President Bush, and weekly meetings to go over other issues with Rice, Tenet was speaking regularly with Secretary of State Colin Powell and Secretary of Defense Donald Rumsfeld. The foreign policy principals routinely talked on the telephone every day on a variety of topics. Hadley told us that before 9/11, he and Rice did not feel they had the job of coordinating domestic agencies. They felt that Clarke and the CSG (part of the NSC) were the NSC's bridge between foreign and domestic threats.

There was a clear disparity in the levels of response to foreign versus domestic threats. Numerous actions were taken overseas to disrupt possible attacks—enlisting foreign partners to upset terrorist plans, closing embassies, moving military assets out of the way of possible harm. Far less was done domestically—in part, surely, because to the extent that specifics did exist, they pertained to threats overseas. As noted earlier, a threat against the embassy in Yemen quickly resulted in its closing. Possible domestic threats were more vague. When reports did not specify where the attacks were to take place, officials presumed that they would again be overseas, though they did not rule out a target in the United States. Each of the FBI threat advisories made this point.

Clarke mentioned to National Security Advisor Rice at least twice that al Qaeda sleeper cells were likely in the United States. In January 2001, Clarke forwarded a strategy paper to Rice warning that al Qaeda had a presence in the United States. He noted that two key al Qaeda members in the Jordanian cell involved in the millennium plot were naturalized U.S. citizens and that one jihadist suspected in the East Africa bombings had "informed the FBI that an extensive network of al Qida 'sleeper agents' currently exists in the US." He added that Ressam's abortive December 1999 attack revealed al Qaeda supporters in the United States. . . . His analysis, however, was based not on new threat reporting but on past experience.

The September 11 attacks fell into the void between the foreign and domestic threats. The foreign intelligence agencies were watching overseas, alert to foreign threats to U.S. interests there. The domestic agencies were waiting for evidence of a domestic threat from sleeper cells within the United States. No one was looking for a foreign threat to domestic targets. The threat that was coming was not from sleeper cells. It was foreign—but from foreigners who had infiltrated into the United States.

A second cause of this disparity in response is that domestic agencies did not know what to do, and no one gave them direction. Cressey told us that the CSG did not tell the agencies how to respond to the threats. He noted that the agencies that were operating overseas did not need direction on how to respond; they had experience with such threats and had a "playbook." In contrast, the domestic agencies did not have a game plan. Neither the NSC (including the CSG) nor anyone else instructed them to create one.

This lack of direction was evident in the July 5 meeting with representatives from the domestic agencies. The briefing focused on overseas threats. The domestic agencies were not questioned about how they planned to address the threat and were not told what was expected of them. Indeed, as noted earlier, they were specifically told they could not issue advisories based on the briefing. The domestic agencies' limited response indicates that they did not perceive a call to action.

Clarke reflected a different perspective in an email to Rice on September 15, 2001. He summarized the steps taken by the CSG to alert domestic agencies to the possibility of an attack in the United States. Clarke concluded that domestic agencies, including the FAA, knew that the CSG believed a major al Qaeda attack was coming and could be in the United States. Although the FAA had authority to issue security directives mandating new security procedures, none of the few that were released during the summer of 2001 increased security at checkpoints or on board aircraft. The information circulars mostly urged air carriers to "exercise prudence" and be alert. Prior to 9/11, the FAA did present a CD-ROM to air carriers and airport authorities describing the increased threat to civil aviation. The presentation mentioned the possibility of suicide hijackings but said that "fortunately, we have no indication that any group is currently thinking in that direction." The FAA conducted 27 special security briefings for specific air carriers between May 1, 2001, and September 11, 2001. Two of these briefings discussed the hijacking threat overseas. None discussed the possibility of suicide hijackings or the use of aircraft as weapons. No new security measures were instituted.

Rice told us she understood that the FBI had tasked its 56 U.S. field offices to increase surveillance of suspected terrorists and to reach out to informants who might have information about terrorist plots. An NSC staff document at the time describes such a tasking as having occurred in late June but does not indicate whether it was generated by the NSC or the FBI. Other than the previously described April 13 communication sent to all FBI field offices, however, the FBI could not find any record of having received such a directive. The April 13 document asking field offices to gather information on Sunni extremism did not mention any possible threat within the United States and did not order surveillance of suspected operatives. The NSC did not specify what the FBI's directives should contain and did not review what had been issued earlier.

Acting FBI Director Pickard told us that in addition to his July 19 conference call, he mentioned the heightened terrorist threat in individual calls with the special agents in charge of field offices during their annual performance review discussions. In speaking with agents around the country, we found little evidence that any such concerns had reached FBI personnel beyond the New York Field Office.

The head of counterterrorism at the FBI, Dale Watson, said he had many discussions about possible attacks with Cofer Black at the CIA. They had expected an attack on July 4. Watson said he felt deeply that something was going to happen. But he told us the threat information was "nebulous." He wished he had known more. He wished he had had "500 analysts looking at Usama Bin Ladin threat information instead of two."

Attorney General Ashcroft was briefed by the CIA in May and by Pickard in early July about the danger. Pickard said he met with Ashcroft once a week in late June, through July, and twice in August. There is a dispute regarding Ashcroft's interest in Pickard's briefings about the terrorist threat situation. Pickard told us that after two such briefings Ashcroft told him that he did not want to hear about the threats anymore. Ashcroft denies Pickard's charge. Pickard says he continued to present terrorism information during further briefings that summer, but nothing further on the "chatter" the U.S. government was receiving.

The Attorney General told us he asked Pickard whether there was intelligence about attacks in the United States and that Pickard said no. Pickard said he replied that he could not assure Ashcroft that there would be no attacks in the United States, although the reports of threats were related to overseas targets. Ashcroft said he therefore assumed the FBI was doing what it needed to do. He acknowledged that in retrospect, this was a dangerous assumption. He did not ask the FBI what it was doing in response to the threats and did not task it to take any specific action. He also did not direct the INS, then still part of the Department of Justice, to take any specific action.

In sum, the domestic agencies never mobilized in response to the threat. They did not have direction, and did not have a plan to institute. The borders were not hardened. Transportation systems were not fortified. Electronic surveillance was not targeted against a domestic threat. State and local law enforcement were not marshaled to augment the FBI's efforts. The public was not warned.

The terrorists exploited deep institutional failings within our government. The question is whether extra vigilance might have turned up an opportunity to disrupt the plot. . . . Al Qaeda's operatives made mistakes. At least two such mistakes created opportunities during 2001, especially in late August.

## DOCUMENT 9.10

On September 15, 2001, President Bush explained his administration's plan to locate and eliminate terrorists. No matter where they hide, he said, "we're going to get them." His speech was noteworthy because he made the prosecution of terrorism into a "war" and stated that while he and the military would "do what it takes" to capture the terrorists, the American people should carry on as usual.

---

"GEORGE W. BUSH, COLIN POWELL, AND JOHN ASHCROFT, PRESIDENT URGES READINESS AND PATIENCE," SEPTEMBER 15, 2001

Camp David—Thurmont, Maryland
For Immediate Release, Office of the Press Secretary, September 15, 2001
9:19 A.M. EDT

**THE PRESIDENT:** I've asked the highest levels of our government to come to discuss the current tragedy that has so deeply affected our nation. Our country mourns for the loss of life and for those whose lives have been so deeply affected by this despicable act of terror.

I am going to describe to our leadership what I saw: the wreckage of New York City, the signs of the first battle of war.

We're going to meet and deliberate and discuss—but there's no question about it, this act will not stand; we will find those who did it; we will smoke them out of their holes; we will get them running and we'll bring them to justice. We will not only deal with those who dare attack America, we will deal with those who harbor them and feed them and house them.

Make no mistake about it: underneath our tears is the strong determination of America to win this war. And we will win it. . . .

Q Sir, what do you say to Americans who are worried that the longer it takes to retaliate, the more chance the perpetrators have to escape and hide and just escape justice?

THE PRESIDENT: They will try to hide, they will try to avoid the United States and our allies—but we're not going to let them. They run to the hills; they find holes to get in. And we will do whatever it takes to smoke them out and get them running, and we'll get them.

Listen, this is a great nation; we're a kind people. None of us could have envisioned the barbaric acts of these terrorists. But they have stirred up the might of the American people, and we're going to get them, no matter what it takes.

In my radio address today I explained to the American people that this effort may require patience. But we're going to—

Q How long—

THE PRESIDENT: As long as it takes. And it's not just one person. We're talking about those who fed them, those who house them, those who harbor terrorists will be held accountable for this action.

Q Sir, are you satisfied that Osama bin Laden is at least a kingpin of this operation? | 483

THE PRESIDENT: There is no question he is what we would call a prime suspect. And if he thinks he can hide and run from the United States and our allies, he will be sorely mistaken.

Q Mr. President, do you have a message for the reservists that you called up yesterday? Can you tell us whether you think more may have to be called up?

THE PRESIDENT: The message is for everybody who wears the uniform: get ready. The United States will do what it takes to win this war. And I ask patience of the American people. There is no question in my mind we'll have the resolve—I witnessed it yesterday on the construction site. Behind the sadness and the exhaustion, there is a desire by the American people to not seek only revenge, but to win a war against barbaric behavior, people that hate freedom and hate what we stand for.

And this is an administration that is going to dedicate ourselves to winning that war. . . .

Q What is the risk of additional attacks on us at this point?

THE PRESIDENT: I would think the American people need to be—go about their business on Monday, but with a heightened sense of awareness that a group of barbarians have declared war on the American people.

Q Sir, how much of a sacrifice are ordinary Americans going to have to be expected to make in their daily lives, in their daily routines?

**THE PRESIDENT:** Our hope, of course, is that they make no sacrifice whatsoever. We would like to see life return to normal in America. But these people have declared war on us and we will do whatever it takes to make sure that we're safe internally. So, therefore, people may not be able to board flights as quickly. Our borders are tighter than they've ever been before. We're taken a variety of measures to make sure that the American people are safe, just as the Attorney General spoke about.

But we hope, obviously, that the measures we take will allow the American economy to continue on. I urge people to go to their businesses on Monday. I understand major league baseball is going to start playing again. It is important for America to get on about its life. But our government will be on full alert and we'll be tracing every lead, every potential to make sure that the American people are safe.

**Q** How long do you envision—

**THE PRESIDENT:** The definition is whatever it takes.

END 9:28 A.M. EDT

## DOCUMENT 9.11

In these 2001 remarks, President Bush provided the earliest indication that the U.S. objective in the unconventional war on terror was to go after any state that "harbored" terrorists. At a White House reception for Japanese Prime Minister Junichiro Koisumi, Bush explained to the people of Japan, who were worried about the militarized solution to terrorism proposed by the administration, that terrorists were motivated by evil and hated "freedom and legitimate governments." The president also championed his own will and determination to bring the terrorists to justice.

GEORGE W. BUSH, "INTERNATIONAL CAMPAIGN AGAINST TERROR GROWS," SEPTEMBER 25, 2001 (EXCERPT)

**Q** Mr. President, according to opinion poll, about 90 percent of the Japanese are concerned that Japan support of the U.S. military action could trigger terrorist attacks on Japan, itself. Do you have anything to say to them to, to their concern?

**PRESIDENT BUSH:** Well, I think this: I think 100 percent of the Japanese people ought to understand that we're dealing with evil people who hate freedom and legitimate governments, and that now is the time for freedom-loving people to come together to fight terrorist activity. We cannot be—we cannot fear terrorists. We can't let terrorism dictate our course of action. And we will not let a terrorist dictate the course of action in the United States; and I'm sure the prime minister feels the same way about Japan.

No threat, no threat will prevent freedom-loving people from defending freedom. And make no mistake about it: This is good versus evil. These are evildoers. They have no justification for their actions. There's no religious justification, there's no political justification. The only motivation is evil. And the prime minister understands that, and the Japanese people, I think, understand that as well.

Q Mr. President, amid signs of increasing turmoil in Afghanistan and signs that there may be splits within the Taliban regime itself, do you believe that the people of Afghanistan, themselves, are trying to liberate themselves from the Taliban rule, and would you support that as part of your campaign against terrorism?

PRESIDENT BUSH: We have no issue and no anger toward the citizens of Afghanistan. We have obviously serious problems with the Taliban government. They're an incredibly repressive government, a government that has a value system that's hard for many in America, or in Japan, for that matter, to relate to. Incredibly repressive toward women.

They have made the decision to harbor terrorists. The mission is to rout terrorists, to find them and bring them to justice. Or, as I explained to the prime minister in Western terms, to smoke them out of their caves, to get them running so we can get them.

The best way to do that, and one way to do that is to ask for the cooperation of citizens within Afghanistan who may be tired of having the Taliban in place, or tired of having Osama bin Laden, people from foreign soils, in their own land, willing to finance this repressive government. | 485

I understand the reality of what's taking place inside Afghanistan, and we're going to have a—listen, as I've told the prime minister, we're angry, but we've got a clear vision. We're upset, but we know what we've got to do. And the mission is to bring these particular terrorists to justice, and at the same time, send a clear signal, Terry, that says if you harbor a terrorist, if you aid a terrorist, if you hide terrorists, you're just as guilty as the terrorists.

And this is an administration—we're not into nation building, we're focused on justice. And we're going to get justice. It's going to take a while, probably. But I'm a patient man. Nothing will diminish my will and my determination—nothing.

Q Mr. President, do you expect any financial support also from Japan, including—

PRESIDENT BUSH: Financial proposals?

Q Yes.

PRESIDENT BUSH: You mean, related to our—

Q For the entire mission against terrorism.

PRESIDENT BUSH: For our—well, first of all, the prime minister, as he said, talked about $40 million of aid to Pakistan. That's a very important contribution. And I repeat the reason why: a stable Pakistan is very important to a stable world. After all, Pakistan has nuclear weapons, and we want stability in countries that may have nuclear weapons. And so that's a very important financial contribution.

Remember, this war will be fought on a variety of fronts. It is not like wars that we're used to. There's very little that's conventional about it. It's different. And so, for example, the sharing of information is vital to find and rout out terrorism. It's vital that we have a cooperative relationship. It's vital that if we hear anything that may affect the security of Japan, that we're forthcoming with that information. And vice versa.

And so the resources—again, you—the tendency is to think in terms of a conventional war, where people might put money in to support a military operation. That's not the kind of war we're talking about now. And so resources will be deployed in different ways—intelligence-gathering, diplomacy, humanitarian aid, as well as cutting off resources. And one effective tool in getting these people is to cut off their money. And yesterday I made an announcement here about how we intend to do so. . . .

**PRESIDENT BUSH:** Thank you all very much.

END 12:03 P.M. EDT


# DOCUMENT 9.12

The words repeatedly used by President Bush in all of his State of the Union addresses showed a persistent and selective set of references to terrorism, Saddam Hussein, and al Qaeda. An interesting aspect of this charting of Bush's words was that, while he spoke often about terrorism in general, he largely ignored al Qaeda's leader, Osama bin Laden, who remained in hiding, probably in Pakistan rather than in Iraq, throughout President Bush's tenure in office.

# "THE WORDS THAT WERE USED,"
## *NEW YORK TIMES*, JANUARY 29, 2008

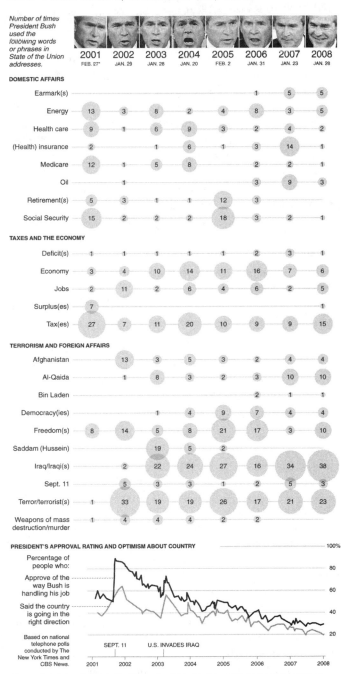

Number of times President Bush used the following words or phrases in State of the Union addresses.

| | 2001 FEB. 27* | 2002 JAN. 29 | 2003 JAN. 28 | 2004 JAN. 20 | 2005 FEB. 2 | 2006 JAN. 31 | 2007 JAN. 23 | 2008 JAN. 28 |
|---|---|---|---|---|---|---|---|---|
| **DOMESTIC AFFAIRS** | | | | | | | | |
| Earmark(s) | | | | | | 1 | 5 | 5 |
| Energy | 13 | 3 | 8 | 2 | 4 | 8 | 3 | 5 |
| Health care | 9 | 1 | 6 | 9 | 3 | 2 | 4 | 2 |
| (Health) insurance | 2 | | 1 | 6 | 1 | 3 | 14 | 1 |
| Medicare | 12 | 1 | 5 | 8 | | 2 | 2 | 1 |
| Oil | | 1 | | | | 3 | 9 | 3 |
| Retirement(s) | 5 | 3 | 1 | 1 | 12 | 3 | | |
| Social Security | 15 | 2 | 2 | 2 | 18 | 3 | 2 | 1 |
| **TAXES AND THE ECONOMY** | | | | | | | | |
| Deficit(s) | 1 | 1 | 1 | 1 | 1 | 2 | 3 | 1 |
| Economy | 3 | 4 | 10 | 14 | 11 | 16 | 7 | 6 |
| Jobs | 2 | 11 | 2 | 6 | 4 | 6 | 2 | 5 |
| Surplus(es) | 7 | | | | | | | 1 |
| Tax(es) | 27 | 7 | 11 | 20 | 10 | 9 | 9 | 15 |
| **TERRORISM AND FOREIGN AFFAIRS** | | | | | | | | |
| Afghanistan | | 13 | 3 | 5 | 3 | 2 | 4 | 4 |
| Al-Qaida | | 1 | 8 | 3 | 2 | 3 | 10 | 10 |
| Bin Laden | | | | | | 2 | 1 | 1 |
| Democracy(ies) | | | 1 | 4 | 9 | 7 | 4 | 4 |
| Freedom(s) | 8 | 14 | 5 | 8 | 21 | 17 | 3 | 10 |
| Saddam (Hussein) | | | 19 | 5 | 2 | | | |
| Iraq/Iraqi(s) | | 2 | 22 | 24 | 27 | 16 | 34 | 38 |
| Sept. 11 | | 5 | 3 | 3 | 1 | 2 | 5 | 3 |
| Terror/terrorist(s) | 1 | 33 | 19 | 19 | 26 | 17 | 21 | 23 |
| Weapons of mass destruction/murder | 1 | 4 | 4 | 4 | 2 | 2 | | |

**PRESIDENT'S APPROVAL RATING AND OPTIMISM ABOUT COUNTRY** ────────────── 100%

Percentage of people who:

Approve of the way Bush is handling his job

Said the country is going in the right direction

Based on national telephone polls conducted by The New York Times and CBS News.

SEPT. 11      U.S. INVADES IRAQ

2001   2002   2003   2004   2005   2006   2007   2008

\* As a newly elected president, Bush did not deliver a formal State of the Union address in 2001. His Feb. 27 speech to a joint session of Congress was analogous to the State of the Union, but without the title.

# DOCUMENT 9.13

According to many people who were inside and outside the Pentagon, the strategy of "Rapid Dominance through Shock and Awe" was based on a 1996 document by Harlan Ullman and James P. Wade that was developed at the National Defense University. Secretary Rumsfeld and others argued that the "Powell Doctrine" of using overwhelming force to accomplish a conventional mission with a clear exit strategy was no longer effective for dealing with the asymmetric conditions of warfare involving stateless terrorists and other new enemies. Ullman himself told CBS News in 2003, "We want them to quit. We want them not to fight. . . . You have this simultaneous effect, rather like the nuclear weapons at Hiroshima, not taking days or weeks but in minutes." The strategy's use in Iraq seemed to be initially effective, as massive bombing and a rapid charge to Baghdad led to the quick toppling of Saddam Hussein's regime. This selection spelled out the general objective of creating terror both in the enemy society and in the enemy military through quick strikes that caused "shock and awe." The document also argued that this new way of conducting war required that the domestic public also perceive a "compelling threat" because only this would persuade U.S. citizens to accept military engagement abroad.

HARLAN K. ULLMAN AND JAMES P. WADE, "SHOCK AND AWE: ACHIEVING RAPID DOMINANCE," NATIONAL DEFENSE UNIVERSITY REPORT, OCTOBER 1996 (EXCERPT)

. . . . Certainly, Rapid Dominance seeks to achieve certain objectives that are similar to those of current doctrine. A major distinction is that Rapid Dominance envisages a wider application of force across a broader spectrum of leverage points to impose Shock and Awe. This breadth should lead to a more comprehensive and integrated interaction among all the specific components and units that produce aggregate military capability and must include training and education, as well as new ways to exploit our technical and industrial capacity. It is possible that in these resource, technical, and commercial industrial areas that Rapid Dominance may provide particular utility that otherwise may constrain the effectiveness of Decisive Force.

The second example is "Hiroshima and Nagasaki" noted earlier. The intent here is to impose a regime of Shock and Awe through delivery of instant, nearly incomprehensible levels of massive destruction directed at influencing society writ large, meaning its leadership and public, rather than targeting directly against military or strategic objectives even with relatively few numbers or systems. The employment of this capability against society and its values, called "counter-value" in the nuclear deterrent jargon, is massively destructive, strikes directly at the public will of the adversary to resist, and ideally or theoretically, would instantly or quickly incapacitate that will over the space of a few hours or days. . . .

In assessing the future utility and applicability of Rapid Dominance, it is crucial to consider the political context in which force is likely to be employed. As we enter the next century, the probability is low that an overriding, massive, direct threat posed by a peer-competitor to the U.S. will emerge in the near term. Without compelling reasons, public tolerance toward American sacrifice abroad will remain low and may even decrease. This reluctance on the part of Americans to tolerate pain is directly correlated to perceptions of threat to U.S. interests. Without a clear and present danger, the definition of national interest may remain narrow.

Americans have always appreciated rapid and decisive military solutions. But, many challenges or crises in the future are likely to be marginal to U.S. interests and therefore may not be resolvable before American political staying power is exhausted. In this period, political micromanagement and fine tuning are likely to be even more prevalent as administrations respond to public sentiments for minimizing casualties and, without a threat or compelling reason, U.S. involvement.

Future actions and measures may likely reflect "politically correct" alternatives. In 1991, the Gulf War came close to presenting the nearly optimal situation for prosecution to a decisive and irreversible conclusion. Such a course, however, was not politically feasible because it would have shattered the allied coalition while exceeding the authority of the UN mandate. Military operations that impact across a whole population or cause "innocent civilians" to suffer (e.g., some economic sanctions, collateral damage from raids) also are likely to be only politically acceptable in aggravated situations. For example, if economic sanctions cause malnutrition or other health problems or collateral damage from bombing or shelling impacts hospitals, schools, orphanages, or refugee camps, the policy may be the ultimate victim. . . .

Americans prefer not to intervene, especially when the direct threat to the U.S. is ambiguous, tenuous, or difficult to define. Therefore, when intervention is necessary there is likely to be both a political and practical imperative to have allied or international involvement or at least the political cover of the UN, NATO, or appropriate NGOs.

As more states (and sub national groups) acquire nuclear, chemical, and biological weapons of mass destruction (WMD) capabilities and longer range delivery means, the ability for rogues to inflict pain will increase, as will the ability to ratchet up the political risks. WMD can easily complicate our ability to influence positive and constructive behavior of possessors. Because of the threat of retaliation, WMD capabilities may become politically acceptable targets provided collateral damage to civilians is minimized. Preemption may become a more realistic option along the lines of Israel's strikes against Syria's nuclear reactors in 1982. It is, however, a responsible state's worst nightmare to have successfully struck a chemical, biological, or nuclear production facility with precision only to learn the next day that hundreds of civilians have been killed due to the inadvertent release of chemical, biological, or nuclear materials.

There must also be an appropriate political context that justifies the use of preemptive force, as opposed to less destructive or nonlethal types of sanctions (e.g., responses to terrorism in the case of Libya, invasion of Kuwait by Iraq, exports of WMD to a threatening country such as Iran, the North Korean threat to South Korea and Japan).

The U.S. will, nevertheless, need to maintain the capability to deter and defeat both strategic and other direct threats to its vital interests, preferably on a decisive basis. In an unsettled, less structured, and volatile world, the ability to use force with precision, effectiveness, impunity, and, when needed, rapidity, will still be a powerful influence on cooperation, stability, and, where relevant, submission. . . .

In considering how Rapid Dominance might apply and might be used, it is first important to know what it is that we want to achieve with military force. We need to consider whether the application of force will allow us to influence and control an adversary's will or merely exacerbate a bad situation. Therefore, it is essential to know what is of value to that adversary. An objective, realistic, and in depth situational grasp will be essential to such an understanding. For example, disarming or destroying may produce unintended consequences. For a conventional foe that values its military and depends on technology, Rapid Dominance should be particularly effective and persuasive. In the case of less developed nations, however, the opportunity for exercising influence in this way and against military formations may be considerably less and must be carefully assessed.

As noted, in cases of marginal direct threats to U.S. security, the cost in casualties needs to be low. To be effective, we must take away an opponent's ability to make it cost us in terms of casualty levels we consider intolerable. In applying Rapid Dominance, we also must be defending something that is of value to us. The lower the value in terms of our national interests, the lower the price we are likely to be willing to pay.

In MRC [*Editors' Note: Major Regional Contingency*] situations, we need to have the capability to defeat, destroy, or incapacitate an opponent. On the other hand, in OOTW [*Editors' Note: Operations Other Than War*], other nonmilitary factors are likely to be involved and goals made more limited. For example, it may be necessary to intimidate or capture the leadership in order to restore order or reverse an action, or it may simply be necessary to anticipate, prevent, and counter opposition to conduct of a more limited mission (e.g., feeding the starving or protecting innocent people from genocide). . . .

Whether in an MRC or in OOTW, we first will need to know what we want to achieve with Rapid Dominance. This is a task for political leadership that is informed with military advice concerning what is feasible, what is not, and what is uncertain. The extent of the mission must be clearly defined. Is it to defeat an enemy so that it will no longer pose a threat? Do we only need to stop an adversary from carrying out a particular act? Must we control a situation entirely or only sufficiently to be able to carry out a specific mission? Can we really affect the adversary's will?

# International Terrorism Documents

## DOCUMENT 9.14

In 2007, President Bush reaffirmed the need for a U.S. presence in Iraq by referring to the statements of al Qaeda leaders who viewed Iraq as their main stage for fighting the United States. The administration's insistence that its preemptive war was still about targeting terrorism failed to account for the fact that there was no insurgency and no al Qaeda in Iraq (also known as al Qaeda in Mesopotamia) before the U.S. invasion. The Iraqi Sunni and Shia insurgents carrying out most of the violence were not affiliated with al Qaeda. The president also made no mention, although he no doubt knew, of other statements by al Qaeda fighters, in which they indicated a desire to combat the United States "over there" in Iraq (see 9.15, 9.17).

| 491

"PRESIDENT BUSH ATTENDS VETERANS OF FOREIGN WARS NATIONAL CONVENTION, DISCUSSES WAR ON TERROR," KANSAS CITY, AUGUST 22, 2007 (EXCERPT)

. . . There was another price to our withdrawal from Vietnam, and we can hear it in the words of the enemy we face in today's struggle—those who came to our soil and killed thousands of citizens on September the 11th, 2001. In an interview with a Pakistani newspaper after the 9/11 attacks, Osama bin Laden declared that "the American people had risen against their government's war in Vietnam. And they must do the same today."

His number two man, Zawahiri, has also invoked Vietnam. In a letter to al Qaeda's chief of operations in Iraq, Zawahiri pointed to "the aftermath of the collapse of the American power in Vietnam and how they ran and left their agents."

Zawahiri later returned to this theme, declaring that the Americans "know better than others that there is no hope in victory. The Vietnam specter is closing every outlet." Here at home, some can argue our withdrawal from Vietnam carried no price to American credibility—but the terrorists see it differently.

We must remember the words of the enemy. We must listen to what they say. Bin Laden has declared that "the war [in Iraq] is for you or us to win. If we win it, it means your disgrace and defeat forever." Iraq is one of several fronts in the war on terror—but it's the central front—it's the central front for the enemy that attacked us and wants to attack us again. And it's the central front for the United States and to withdraw without getting the job done would be devastating.

If we were to abandon the Iraqi people, the terrorists would be emboldened, and use their victory to gain new recruits. As we saw on September the 11th, a terrorist safe haven on the other side of the world can bring death and destruction to the streets of our own cities. Unlike in Vietnam, if we withdraw before the job is done, this enemy will follow us home. And that is why, for the security of the United States of America, we must defeat them overseas so we do not face them in the United States of America. . . .

I recognize that history cannot predict the future with absolute certainty. I understand that. But history does remind us that there are lessons applicable to our time. And we can learn something from history. In Asia, we saw freedom triumph over violent ideologies after the sacrifice of tens of thousands of American lives—and that freedom has yielded peace for generations . . .

## DOCUMENT 9.15

492 |

A U.S. military air strike on an al Qaeda safe house near Bacuba on June 7, 2006, killed Abu Musab al-Zarqawi, the commander of the Iraq-based al Qaeda in Mesopotamia. Apparently, the Iraqi military discovered several documents there. Iraqi national security advisor Muwaffaq al-Rabi'i released one of them, a letter, to the Iraqi media on September 18, 2006. An unknown al Qaeda fighter named Atiyah was said to have composed the letter, but the U.S. military's Combating Terrorism Center at West Point believed it was actually written by Osama bin Laden's deputy, Ayman al-Zawahiri. The letter—whose authenticity was questioned by some Middle East experts—gave details about an al Qaeda strategy in Iraq that advised caution, listening, mercy, and love, instructing fighters to go beyond bombs and killing. It recommended to the independent and recalcitrant al-Zarqawi group that it try to win the hearts and minds of the Iraqi people by not degrading or frightening them. The letter also indicated that al Qaeda believed that it was engaged in a protracted struggle in Iraq and that the war might even have to be prolonged in order to achieve the organization's goals.

ATIYAH LETTER EXPOSING NEW LEADER IN AL QA'IDA
HIGH COMMAND, SEPTEMBER 25, 2006 (EXCERPT)

My dear brother, you are achieving successes and striking the enemies of God and hitting and doing much, which is a good and great thing that we are not lowering at all and we ask God to bless and increase, but this isn't everything. The path is long and difficult, and the enemy isn't easy, for he is great and numerous and he can take quite a bit of punishment as well. However, true victory is the triumph of principles and values, the triumph of the call to Islam. True conquest is the conquest of the hearts of people, and the regard for seeing the Treaty of Hudaybiyah as a victory.

Policy must be dominant over militarism. This is one of the pillars of war that is agreed upon by all nations, whether they are Muslims or unbelievers. That is to say, that military action is a servant to policy. We as people of Islam are people of policy, wisdom, reason, and are good at applying its fundamentals of justice, mercy, good deeds, et cetera . . .

I will speak further about embracing the people and bringing them together and winning them over and placating them and so forth, for this, my brother, is a great way towards victory and triumph that is not lesser than military operations, but rather in truth is the foundation while military operations must be a servant that is complementary to it.

Therefore, when you embrace the people and enjoin them through your morals, kind words, your conduct and upbringing, you will have gained a greater means of victory over your enemy, with God's permission. If the people love you and are grand in their love of you and affection, and God brings their hearts to you, then that is more successful and helpful to you, and more safeguarding of you against all harm that your enemy is planning . . .

Winning over the people, bringing them close, being cautious about alienating them, befriending them, helping them, accepting their foibles (which means [accepting] what they possess, including strength, weakness, propriety, impropriety, goodness, and ill; which doesn't negate the continuation of guiding them towards goodness and betterment), molding them, gaining their sympathy at all their levels and ranks, using the utmost caution to not be harsh with them or degrade them or frighten them or be hasty in judging them or even be hasty in reforming them in a way that they might not comprehend, which might cause them provocation, wherein they would turn on us and you with hostile animosity. However, [you should do this] with gentleness, gradual open-mindedness, while overlooking and being quiet about many of their mistakes and flaws, and while tolerating a great deal of harm from them for the sake of not having them turn away and turn into enemies on any level . . .

Brother Abu-Musa'b, may God protect and guide you. Bless you, my brother. Know that we, like all the mujahidin, are still weak. We are in the stage of weakness and a state of paucity. We have not yet reached a level of stability. We have no alternative but to not squander any element of the foundations of strength, or any helper or supporter. We are unceasing in our efforts to unite our nation's strength and resources . . .

Among these, meaning the elements, is the fact that our strength lies in our weakness and determination, being as we are a part of this great nation, the nation of Muhammad, whom God has blessed, and being as the

Muslim nation is with us, loving us, harboring us, supporting us, sympathizing with us, and concurring with us. Also among these are our mettle and the mettle of our soldiers, which are the waters that our fish inhabits. So on, and so forth of that which is obvious. So, if we waste this great foundation, then we would be remiss, profligate, and liable to fail. . . .

Among its lessons are when we ought to speak and when silence is better; what we should say in every situation, position, and stage, what issues we should lay on people and what we should postpone, and so forth . . .

I say: the most important thing is that you be patient, forbearing, and persevere until the final moment, for indeed your enemy is also patient and he is betting that there will be a moment in which you are weak, that you fail and fall apart internally, may God not make this His judgment. Therefore, seek aid in God and frustrate your enemies and achieve the hope of your loved ones and friends. Be as God the Almighty said, "Humble towards the believers, mighty against the disbelievers." But gently, gently, remember what the prophet, peace be upon him, said on the authority of 'Ali, "Penetrate [the enemy] through your messengers." There is a meaning in there, if you ruminate on it!

Let us not merely be people of killing, slaughter, blood, cursing, insult, and harshness; but rather, people of this, who are unopposed to mercy and gentleness. Let us put everything in perspective. Let our mercy overcome our anger and precede it. We need to give our followers and our coming young meanings that have balance, completeness, and moderation in ethics and concepts. It is wisdom and perfection, my dear brother, to combine several things, especially for those of us who are looked up to, such as your elevated position; may God advance your rank among his virtuous worshipers, Amen.

494 |

You are a political leader, a chief, and an administrator, especially in your own surroundings. You have other jobs and great missions. The most important thing is for you to be a successful leader to the mujahidin, and then, to practice what is available to you, and what is within your ability, in terms of moral and ethical leadership, for the benefit of the Muslim nation. . . .

One of your important jobs is to bring closer together the people of scholarship and the people of jihad in all sectors of Muslims. By that I mean the good people of scholarship, the people of good works who work hard for God, even if they disagree with us or if we disagree with them in some or many issues, opinions, and positions such as a position regarding a certain government or another, and such; exactly as I said regarding the people of jihad, the people of jihad who are virtuous, truthful, and disciplined towards the shari'a of the Lord of the two realms.

One of your important jobs is to educate our jihadi cohort in good conduct, by providing them with a good model in manners, respect, modesty, the giving of advice, accepting advice, admitting mistakes, respecting others, proficiency in dialogue, politeness with those who disagree, mercy, justice, kindness, et cetera. These are the good qualities that are required, and from which our jihadi cohort is suffering a deficiency, as professed by all of our brothers who are shaykhs among the mujahidin and their leaders. As mentioned, we need to make a great effort to educate and guide our cohort, because there are within our mujahidin cohort a lot of bad qualities that need to be treated . . .

Therefore, you, as a leader and a jihadist political organization who wants to destroy a power and a state and erect on its rubble an Islamic state, or at least form the building block on the right path towards that, need all of these people; and it is imperative for someone like this to get along with everyone in various degrees as well, for the brothers are of varying calibers, in my belief . . .

Whenever the people feel that we value them and appreciate their efforts and that we respect them and want the best for them and that we sympathize with them, this is what will draw their hearts to us, just as there are people we bring close through gift giving and money, but that is another matter. . . .

We warn against all acts that alienate, from killing to any sort of other treatment. Even insofar as the corrupt ones and traitors from among the Sunnis, we shouldn't kill them unless the people would understand and think that it was a good thing due to the obviousness of their corruption, their treason, and their evil. However, if we come and kill some people whom we know to be corrupt and treasonous, but who are respected and beloved by the people, then this leads to great trouble and it is an act against all of the fundamentals of politics and leadership. So be warned of that, my dear brother, as God knows best and is wiser . . . | 495

The most important thing is that you continue in your jihad in Iraq, and that you be patient and forbearing, even in weakness, and even with fewer operations; even if each day had half of the number of current daily operations, that is not a problem, or even less than that. So, do not be hasty. The most important thing is that the jihad continues with steadfastness and firm rooting, and that it grows in terms of supporters, strength, clarity of justification, and visible proof each day. Indeed, prolonging the war is in our interest, with God's permission. The best acts are those that last, however few they may be, provided that we guard against mistakes building up and that we have integration in the jihadist enterprise. The only thing that you have to fear is yourselves and your own mistakes, not your enemy. By God, your enemy will never defeat you as long as you are patient and steadfast, not having caused damage that is great or frequent; and you seek help in God. It is the grace of God and the grace of the Supporter, and the Almighty will not neglect us. "Now surely the help of God is nigh" . . .

Goodbye and God bless you.

Your brother, 'Atiyah. 10th of Dhu Qa'dah, 1426.

# DOCUMENT 9.16

In 2000, the Manchester (England) Metropolitan Police searched the home of an alleged al Qaeda member and found what they said was an al Qaeda training manual translated into English and entitled "The Declaration of Jihad against the Country's Tyrants." It was introduced as evidence in the 2001 trial in New York on the 1998 bombings of the U.S. embassies in Kenya and Tanzania (*United States of America v. Usama bin Laden et al.*). The manual forbade its users from removing it from its safe house, indicating that it was meant for internal use. It suggested that al Qaeda acted not because it "hated freedom," as the Bush administration repeatedly asserted, but because it hated the policies, the corruption, and the oppression of its own "apostate rulers," many of whom enjoyed U.S. support. It was difficult to determine if the words of al Qaeda's leaders in the manual were sincere, but it did seem clear that the group's leadership was attempting to exploit real, existing complaints among Muslims in the Middle East.

---

THE AL QAEDA MANUAL, INTRODUCTION, 2000 (EXCERPT)

496 |   Martyrs were killed, women were widowed, children were orphaned, men were handcuffed, chaste women's heads were shaved, harlots' heads were crowned, atrocities were inflicted on the innocent, gifts were given to the wicked, virgins were raped on the prostitution alter . . .

After the fall of our orthodox caliphates on March 3, 1924 and after expelling the colonialists, our Islamic nation was afflicted with apostate rulers who took over in the Moslem nation. These rulers turned out to be more infidel and criminal than the colonialists themselves. Moslems have endured all kinds of harm, oppression, and torture at their hands.

Those apostate rulers threw thousands of the Haraka Al-Islamyia (Islamic Movement) youth in gloomy jails and detention centers that were equipped with the most modern torture devices and [manned with] experts in oppression and torture. Those youth had refused to move in the rulers' orbit, obscure matters to the youth, and oppose the idea of rebelling against the rulers. But they [the rulers] did not stop there; they started to fragment the essence of the Islamic nation by trying to eradicate its Moslem identity. Thus, they started spreading godless and atheistic views among the youth. We found some that claimed that socialism was from Islam, democracy was the [religious] council, and the prophet—God bless and keep him—propagandized communism.

Colonialism and its followers, the apostate rulers, then started to openly erect crusader centers, societies, and organizations like Masonic Lodges, Lions and Rotary clubs, and foreign schools. They aimed at producing a wasted generation that pursued everything that is western and produced rulers, ministers, leaders, physicians, engineers, businessmen, politicians, journalists, and information specialists. [Koranic verse:] "And Allah's enemies plotted and planned, and Allah too planned, and the best of planners is Allah."

They [the rulers] tried, using every means and [kind of] seduction, to produce a generation of young men that did not know [anything] except what they [the rulers] want, did not say except what they [the rulers] think about, did not live except according to their [the rulers'] way, and did not dress except in their [the rulers'] clothes. However, majestic Allah turned their deception back on them, as a large group of those young men who were raised by them [the rulers] woke up from their sleep and returned to Allah, regretting and repenting.

The young men returning to Allah realized that Islam is not just performing rituals but a complete system: Religion and government, worship and Jihad [holy war], ethics and dealing with people, and the Koran and sword. The bitter situation that the nation has reached is a result of its divergence from Allah's course and his righteous law for all places and times. That [bitter situation] came about as a result of its children's love for the world, their loathing of death, and their abandonment of Jihad [holy war].

Unbelief is still the same. It pushed Abou Jahl—may Allah curse him—and Kureish's valiant infidels to battle the prophet—God bless and keep him—and to torture his companions—may Allah's grace be on them. It is the same unbelief that drove Sadat, Hosni Mubarak, Gadhafi, Hafez Assad, Saleh, Fahed-Allah's curse be upon the non-believing leaders—and all the apostate Arab rulers to torture, kill, imprison, and torment Moslems. | 497

These young men realized that an Islamic government would never be established except by the bomb and rifle. Islam does not coincide or make a truce with unbelief, but rather confronts it.

The confrontation that Islam calls for with these godless and apostate regimes, does not know Socratic debates, Platonic ideals nor Aristotelian diplomacy. But it knows the dialogue of bullets, the ideals of assassination, bombing, and destruction, and the diplomacy of the cannon and machine-gun.

The young came to prepare themselves for Jihad [holy war], commanded by the majestic Allah's order in the holy Koran. [Koranic verse:] "Against them make ready your strength to the utmost of your power, including steeds of war, to strike terror into (the hearts of) the enemies of Allah and your enemies, and others besides whom ye may not know, but whom Allah doth know."

# DOCUMENT 9.17

An address by Osama bin Laden to the U.S. people was produced by the Al-Sahab Institute for Media Production and broadcast on October 30, 2004, by al Jazeera, the Arabic-language news network, just days before the U.S. presidential election. Bin Laden's statement explained that al Qaeda was battling the United States because of its policies in the Middle East, and claimed a comparative spending advantage for al Qaeda. It also suggested that al Qaeda had baited the United States into Afghanistan and Iraq in an attempt to "bleed" the United States of lives and treasure.

---

## OSAMA BIN LADEN, SPEECH BROADCAST BY AL JAZEERA ON OCTOBER 30, 2004 (EXCERPT)

O American people, I address these words to you regarding the best way of avoiding another Manhattan, and regarding the war, its causes and its consequences. But before this, I say to you: Security is one of the important pillars of human life, and free men do not take their security lightly, contrary to Bush's claim that we hate freedom. Let him explain why we did not attack Sweden, for example. Clearly, those who hate freedom—unlike the nineteen, may Allah have mercy on them—have no self-esteem. We have been fighting you because we are free men who do not remain silent in the face of injustice. We want to restore our [Islamic] nation's freedom. Just as you violate our security, we violate yours. Whoever toys with the security of others, deluding himself that he will remain secure, is nothing but a foolish thief. One of the most important things rational people do when calamities occur is to look for their causes so as to avoid them.

But I am amazed at you. Although we have entered the fourth year after the events of 9/11, Bush is still practicing distortion and deception against you and he is still concealing the true cause from you. Consequentially, the motives for its reoccurrence still exist. I will tell you about the causes underlying these events and I will tell you the truth about the moments this decision was taken, to allow you to reflect.

I say to you, as Allah is my witness: We had not considered attacking the towers, but things reached the breaking point when we witnessed the iniquity and tyranny of the American-Israeli coalition against our people in Palestine and Lebanon—then I got this idea.

The events that had a direct influence on me occurred in 1982, and the subsequent events, when the U.S. permitted the Israelis to invade Lebanon with the aid of the American sixth fleet. They started shelling, and many were killed and wounded, while others were terrorized into fleeing. I still remember those moving scenes—blood, torn limbs, and dead women and children; ruined homes everywhere, and high-rises being demolished on top of their residents; bombs raining down mercilessly on our homes. It was as though a crocodile swallowed a child, and he could do nothing but cry. But does a crocodile understand any language other than arms? The entire world saw and heard, but did not respond.

In those critical moments, I was overwhelmed by ideas that are hard to describe, but they awakened a powerful impulse to reject injustice and gave birth to a firm resolve to punish the oppressors. As I was looking at those destroyed towers in Lebanon, I was struck by the idea of punishing the oppressor in the same manner and destroying towers in the U.S., to give it a taste of what we have tasted and to deter it from killing our children and women. That day I became convinced that iniquity and the premeditated murder of innocent children and women is an established American principle, and that terror is [the real meaning of] "freedom" and "democracy," while they call the resistance "terrorism" and "reaction." America stands for iniquity and for imposing sanctions on millions of people, resulting in the death of many, as Bush Sr. did, causing the mass slaughter of children in Iraq, [the worst] that humanity has ever known. It stands for dropping millions of pounds of bombs and explosives on millions of children in Iraq again, as Bush Jr. did, in order to depose an old agent and to appoint a new agent to help him steal Iraq's oil, and other sorts of horrible things.

It was against the backdrop of these and similar images that 9/11 came in response to these terrible iniquities. Should a man be blamed for protecting his own? And is defending oneself and punishing the wicked an eye for an eye—is that reprehensible terrorism? Even if it is reprehensible terrorism, we have no other choice. This is the message that we have tried to convey to you, in words and in deeds, more than once in the years preceding 9/11. . . .

As for its results, they are very positive, with Allah's grace. They surpassed all expectations by all criteria for many reasons, one of the most important of which is that we had no difficulty dealing with Bush and his administration, because it resembles the regimes in our [Arab] countries, half of which are ruled by the military, and the other half are ruled by the sons of kings and presidents with whom we have had a lot of experience. Among both types, there are many who are known for their conceit, arrogance, greed, and for taking money unrightfully. . . .

As previously mentioned, it was easy for us to provoke this administration and to drag it [after us]. It was enough for us to send two Jihad fighters to the farthest east to hoist a rag on which "Al-Qa'ida" was written—that was enough to cause generals to rush off to this place, thereby causing America human and financial and political losses, without it accomplishing anything worthy of mention, apart from giving business to [the generals'] private corporations. Besides, we gained experience in guerilla warfare and in conducting a war of attrition in our fight with the iniquitous, great power, that is, when we conducted a war of attrition against Russia with Jihad fighters for ten years until they went bankrupt, with Allah's grace; as a result, they were forced to withdraw in defeat, all praise and thanks to Allah. We are continuing in the same policy—to make America bleed profusely to the point of bankruptcy, Allah willing. And that is not too difficult for Allah.

Whoever says that Al-Qa'ida triumphed over the White House administration, or that the White House administration lost this war—this is not
entirely accurate, for if we look carefully at the results, it is impossible to
say that Al-Qa'ida is the only cause for these amazing gains. The White
House policy, which strove to open war fronts so as to give business to their
various corporations—be they in the field of armament, of oil, or of construction—also helped in accomplishing these astonishing achievements
for Al-Qa'ida. It appeared to some analysts and diplomats as though we and
the White House play as one team to score a goal against the United States
of America, even though our intentions differ. Such ideas, and some others,
were pointed out by a British diplomat in the course of a lecture at the
Royal Institute for International Affairs; for example, that Al-Qa'ida spent
$500,000 on the event [9/11] while America lost in the event and its sub-
sequent effects more than 500 billion dollars; that is to say that each of Al-
Qa'ida's dollars defeated one million American dollars, thanks to Allah's
grace. This is in addition to the fact that America lost a large number of
jobs, and as for the [federal] deficit, it lost a record number estimated at a
trillion dollars.

Even more serious for America is the fact that the Jihad fighters have
recently forced Bush to resort to an emergency budget in order to continue
the fighting in Afghanistan and in Iraq, which proves the success of the
plan of bleeding [America] to the point of bankruptcy, Allah willing.

Indeed, all of this makes it clear that Al-Qa'ida won gains; but on the
other hand, it also makes it clear that the Bush administration won gains
as well, since anyone who looks at the scope of the contracts won by large
dubious corporations like Halliburton and other similar ones that have ties
to Bush and to his administration will become convinced that the losing
side is in fact you, the American people, and your economy.

We agreed with the general commander Muhammad Atta, may Allah
have mercy on him, that all operations should be carried out within twenty
minutes, before Bush and his administration would become aware. We
never imagined that the Commander in Chief of the American armed
forces would abandon fifty thousand of his citizens in the twin towers to
face this great horror alone when they needed him most. It seemed to him
that a girl's story about her goat and its butting was more important than
dealing with planes and their "butting" into skyscrapers. This allowed us
three times the amount of time needed for the operations, Allah be praised.

It should be no secret to you that American thinkers and intellectuals
warned Bush before the war: all that you [Bush] need in order to assure
America's security by ridding [Iraq] of weapons of mass destruction, assuming there were any, is at your disposal, and all the countries of the world
are with you in the matter of carrying out inspections, and the U.S.'s interest does not require you to drive it into an unjustified war, whose end
you cannot know.

However, the blackness of black gold blinded his sight and his perception and he gave preference to private interests over America's public interest. And so there was war and many died. The American economy bled and Bush became embroiled in the quagmire of Iraq, which now threatens his future.

His case is like that [described in the parable]: He is like the ill-tempered goat that dug out of the ground the sharp knife [with which it would be slaughtered].

I say to you: more than fifteen thousand of our people were killed and tens of thousands were wounded, just as more than one thousand of you were killed and more than ten thousand wounded, and Bush's hands are sullied with the blood of all of these casualties on both sides, for the sake of oil and to give business to his private companies. You should know that a nation that punishes a weak person if he is instrumental in killing one of that nation's sons for money, while letting go free a high-class man who was instrumental in killing more than one thousand of its sons, also for money. Similarly your allies in Palestine intimidate women and children and murder and imprison men. . . .

Keep in mind that every action has a reaction, and finally you should consider the last wills and testaments of the thousands who left you on 9/11, waving their hands in despair. These are inspiring wills, which deserve to be published and studied thoroughly. One of the most important things I have read regarding their hand-waving signals before they fell is that they were saying "We were wrong to let the White House carry out unchecked its aggressive foreign policy against oppressed people." As though they were telling you, the American people, "You should call to task those who caused our death." Happy is he who learns a lesson from the experience of others. A verse that I have read is also relevant to their [last] signals:

> Evil kills those who perpetrate it,
> And the pastures of iniquity are harmful.

There is a saying: a small amount spent on prevention is better than a great amount spent on treatment. You should know that it is better to return to that which is right than to persist in that which is wrong. A rational man would not neglect his security, property, or home for the sake of the liar in the White House.

Your security is not in the hands of Kerry or Bush or Al-Qa'ida. Your security is in your own hands, and any [U.S.] state [wilaya] that does not toy with our security automatically guarantees its own security.

Allah is our guardian but you have none.
Peace be upon whoever follows the true guidance.

# DOCUMENT 9.18

The 2006 National Intelligence Estimate—an assessment representing the authoritative intelligence analysis of all sixteen U.S. intelligence agencies—reported that al Qaeda had been weakened as the organizational leader of the jihadist movement but that the overall terrorist threat had increased both in numbers and in geographic dispersion. It concluded that al Qaeda had become decentralized, organized more by self-radicalized cells than by a central leadership. That new development made the terrorist threat more dangerous and implied that a wide variety of legal, political, economic, and diplomatic methods would be necessary to replace strict reliance on military strategies.

---

"TRENDS IN GLOBAL TERRORISM: IMPLICATIONS FOR THE UNITED STATES," DECLASSIFIED KEY JUDGMENTS OF THE NATIONAL INTELLIGENCE ESTIMATE, APRIL 2006 (EXCERPT)

United States–led counterterrorism efforts have seriously damaged the leadership of Al Qa'ida and disrupted its operations; however, we judge that Al Qa'ida will continue to pose the greatest threat to the Homeland and US interests abroad by a single terrorist organization. We also assess that the global jihadist movement—which includes Al Qa'ida, affiliated and independent terrorist groups, and emerging networks and cells—is spreading and adapting to counterterrorism efforts.

- Although we cannot measure the extent of the spread with precision, a large body of all-source reporting indicates that activists identifying themselves as jihadists, although a small percentage of Muslims, are increasing in both number and geographic dispersion.
- If this trend continues, threats to US interests at home and abroad will become more diverse, leading to increasing attacks worldwide.
- Greater pluralism and more responsive political systems in Muslim majority nations would alleviate some of the grievances jihadists exploit. Over time, such progress, together with sustained, multifaceted programs targeting the vulnerabilities of the jihadist movement and continued pressure on Al Qa'ida, could erode support for the jihadists.

We assess that the global jihadist movement is decentralized, lacks a coherent global strategy, and is becoming more diffuse. New jihadist networks and cells, with anti-American agendas, are increasingly likely to emerge. The confluence of shared purpose and dispersed actors will make it harder to find and undermine jihadist groups.

- We assess that the operational threat from self-radicalized cells will grow in importance to US counterterrorism efforts, particularly abroad but also in the Homeland.
- The jihadists regard Europe as an important venue for attacking Western interests. Extremist networks inside the extensive Muslim diasporas in Europe facilitate recruitment and staging for urban attacks, as illustrated by the 2004 Madrid and 2005 London bombings.

We assess that the Iraq jihad is shaping a new generation of terrorist leaders and operatives; perceived jihadist success there would inspire more fighters to continue the struggle elsewhere.

- The Iraq conflict has become the "cause celebre" for jihadists, breeding a deep resentment of US involvement in the Muslim world and cultivating supporters for the global jihadist movement. Should jihadists leaving Iraq perceive themselves, and be perceived, to have failed, we judge fewer fighters will be inspired to carry on the fight.

We assess that the underlying factors fueling the spread of the movement outweigh its vulnerabilities and are likely to do so for the duration of the timeframe of this Estimate.

- Four underlying factors are fueling the spread of the jihadist movement: (1) Entrenched grievances, such as corruption, injustice, and fear of Western domination, leading to anger, humiliation, and a sense of powerlessness; (2) the Iraq "jihad"; (3) the slow pace of real and sustained economic, social, and political reforms in many Muslim majority nations; and (4) pervasive anti-US sentiment among most Muslims—all of which jihadist exploit.

Concomitant vulnerabilities in the jihadist movement have emerged that, if fully exposed and exploited, could begin to slow the spread of the movement. They include dependence on the continuation of Muslim-related conflicts, the limited appeal of jihadists' radical ideology, the emergence of respected voices of moderation, and criticism of the violent tactics employed against mostly Muslim citizens.

- The jihadists' greatest vulnerability is that their ultimate political solution—an ultra-conservative interpretation of *shari'a*-based governance spanning the Muslim world—is unpopular with the vast majority of Muslims. Exposing the religious and political straitjacket that is implied by the jihadists' propaganda would help to divide them from the audiences they seek to persuade.

- Recent condemnations of violence and extremist religious interpretations by a few notable Muslim clerics signal a trend that could facilitate the growth of a constructive alternative to jihadist ideology: peaceful political activism. This also could lead to the consistent and dynamic participation of broader Muslim communities in rejecting violence, reducing the ability of radicals to capitalize on passive community support. In this way, the Muslim mainstream emerges as the most powerful weapon in the war on terror.
- Countering the spread of the jihadist movement will require coordinated multilateral efforts that go well beyond operations to capture or kill terrorist leaders.

If democratic reform efforts in Muslim majority nations progress over the next five years political participation probably would drive a wedge between intransigent extremists and groups willing to use the political process to achieve their local objectives. Nonetheless, attendant reforms and potentially destabilizing transitions will create new opportunities for jihadists to exploit.

Al-Qa'ida, now merged with Abu Mus'ab al-Zarqawi's network, is exploiting the situation in Iraq to attract new recruits and donors and to maintain its leadership role.

- The loss of key leaders, particularly Usama Bin Ladin, Ayman al-Zawahiri, and al-Zarqawi, in rapid succession, probably would cause the group to fracture into smaller groups. Although like-minded individuals would endeavor to carry on the mission, the loss of these key leaders would exacerbate strains and disagreements. We assess that the resulting splinter groups would, at least for a time, pose a less serious threat to US interests than does Al Qa'ida.
- Should al-Zarqawi continue to evade capture and scale back attacks against Muslims, we assess he could broaden his popular appeal and present a global threat.
- The increased role of Iraqis in managing the operations of Al Qa'ida in Iraq might lead veteran foreign jihadists to focus their efforts on external operations.

Other affiliated Sunni extremist organizations, such as Jemaah Islamiya, Ansar al-Sunnah, and several North American groups, unless countered, are likely to expand their reach and become more capable of multiple and/or mass-casualty attacks outside their traditional areas of operation.

- We assess that such groups pose less of a danger to the Homeland than does al Qa'ida but will pose varying degrees of threat to our allies and to US interests abroad. The focus of their attacks is likely to ebb and flow between local regime targets and regional or global ones.

We judge that most jihadist groups—both well-known and newly formed —will use improvised explosive devices and suicide attacks focused primarily on soft targets to implement their asymmetric warfare strategy, and that they will attempt to conduct sustained terrorist attacks in urban environments. Fighters with experience in Iraq are a potential source of leadership for jihadists pursuing these tactics. . . .

While Iran, and to a lesser extent Syria, remain the most active state sponsors of terrorism, many other states will be unable to prevent territory or resources from being exploited by terrorists.

Anti-US and anti-globalization sentiment is on the rise and fueling other radical ideologies. This could prompt some leftist, nationalist, or separatist groups to adopt terrorist methods to attack US interests. The radicalization process is occurring more quickly, more widely, and more anonymously in the Internet age, raising the likelihood of surprise attacks by unknown groups whose members and supporters may be difficult to pinpoint.

- We judge that groups of all stripes will increasingly use the Internet to communicate, propagandize, recruit, train, and obtain logistical and financial support.

# DOCUMENT 9.19

Mandated by Congress and initially opposed by the Bush administration, the Iraq Study Group was a bipartisan body of ten prominent political figures, half of them Republicans and half Democrats. Co-chaired by James A. Baker and Lee H. Hamilton, the group consulted 136 people in and out of government and issued a comprehensive report. Its recommendations were largely disregarded by the Bush administration. This excerpt documented what most reporters and other observers had already noted: that the vast majority of oppositional violence and fighting in Iraq was being conducted by non–al Qaeda, mostly native Iraqi insurgent forces.

IRAQ STUDY GROUP REPORT, 2006 (EXCERPT)

Violence is increasing in scope, complexity, and lethality. There are multiple sources of violence in Iraq: the Sunni Arab insurgency, al Qaeda and affiliated jihadist groups, Shiite militias and death squads, and organized criminality. Sectarian violence—particularly in and around Baghdad—has become the principal challenge to stability.

Most attacks on Americans still come from the Sunni Arab insurgency. The insurgency comprises former elements of the Saddam Hussein regime, disaffected Sunni Arab Iraqis, and common criminals. It has significant support within the Sunni Arab community. The insurgency has no single leadership but is a network of networks. It benefits from participants' detailed knowledge of Iraq's infrastructure, and arms and financing are supplied primarily from within Iraq. The insurgents have different goals, although nearly all oppose the presence of U.S. forces in Iraq. Most wish to restore Sunni Arab rule in the country. Some aim at winning local power and control.

Al Qaeda is responsible for a small portion of the violence in Iraq, but that includes some of the more spectacular acts: suicide attacks, large truck bombs, and attacks on significant religious or political targets. Al Qaeda in Iraq is now largely Iraqi-run and composed of Sunni Arabs. Foreign fighters —numbering an estimated 1,300—play a supporting role or carry out suicide operations. Al Qaeda's goals include instigating a wider sectarian war between Iraq's Sunni and Shia, and driving the United States out of Iraq.

Sectarian violence causes the largest number of Iraqi civilian casualties. Iraq is in the grip of a deadly cycle: Sunni insurgent attacks spark large-scale Shia reprisals, and vice versa. Groups of Iraqis are often found bound and executed, their bodies dumped in rivers or fields. The perception of unchecked violence emboldens militias, shakes confidence in the government, and leads Iraqis to flee to places where their sect is the majority and where they feel they are in less danger. In some parts of Iraq—notably in Baghdad—sectarian cleansing is taking place. The United Nations estimates that 1.6 million are displaced within Iraq, and up to 1.8 million Iraqis have fled the country.

Shiite militias engaging in sectarian violence pose a substantial threat to immediate and long-term stability. These militias are diverse. Some are affiliated with the government, some are highly localized, and some are wholly outside the law. They are fragmenting, with an increasing breakdown in command structure. The militias target Sunni Arab civilians, and some struggle for power in clashes with one another. Some even target government ministries. They undermine the authority of the Iraqi government and security forces, as well as the ability of Sunnis to join a peaceful political process. The prevalence of militias sends a powerful message: political leaders can preserve and expand their power only if backed by armed force.

The Mahdi Army, led by Muqtada al-Sadr, may number as many as 60,000 fighters. It has directly challenged U.S. and Iraqi government forces, and it is widely believed to engage in regular violence against Sunni Arab civilians. Mahdi fighters patrol certain Shia enclaves, notably northeast Baghdad's teeming neighborhood of 2.5 million known as "Sadr City." As the Mahdi Army has grown in size and influence, some elements have moved beyond Sadr's control.

The Badr Brigade is affiliated with the Supreme Council for the Islamic Revolution in Iraq (SCIRI), which is led by Abdul Aziz al-Hakim. The Badr Brigade has longstanding ties with the Iranian Revolutionary Guard Corps. Many Badr members have become integrated into the Iraqi police, and others play policing roles in southern Iraqi cities. While wearing the uniform of the security services, Badr fighters have targeted Sunni Arab civilians. Badr fighters have also clashed with the Mahdi Army, particularly in southern Iraq.

Criminality also makes daily life unbearable for many Iraqis. Robberies, kidnappings, and murder are commonplace in much of the country. Organized criminal rackets thrive, particularly in unstable areas like Anbar province. Some criminal gangs cooperate with, finance, or purport to be part of the Sunni insurgency or a Shiite militia in order to gain legitimacy. As one knowledgeable American official put it, "If there were foreign forces in New Jersey, Tony Soprano would be an insurgent leader."

Four of Iraq's eighteen provinces are highly insecure—Baghdad, Anbar, Diyala, and Salah ad Din. These provinces account for about 40 percent of Iraq's population of 26 million. In Baghdad, the violence is largely between Sunni and Shia. In Anbar, the violence is attributable to the Sunni insurgency and to al Qaeda, and the situation is deteriorating.

In Kirkuk, the struggle is between Kurds, Arabs, and Turkmen. In Basra and the south, the violence is largely an intra-Shia power struggle. The most stable parts of the country are the three provinces of the Kurdish north and parts of the Shia south. However, most of Iraq's cities have a sectarian mix and are plagued by persistent violence.

# Opposition to U.S. Terrorism Policy

## DOCUMENT 9.20

In this May 1, 2001, speech, President Bush pointed to "rogue" states such as Iraq rather than terrorist groups such as al Qaeda as the major security threat facing the United States. Interestingly, he declared that those rogue states threatened the United States because they "hated our values." After September 11, the administration linked Iraq and al Qaeda in its rhetoric, and this argument became one of its standard explanations for al Qaeda's threatening and attacking the United States.

## GEORGE W. BUSH, REMARKS TO STUDENTS AND FACULTY, NATIONAL DEFENSE UNIVERSITY, MAY 1, 2001 (EXCERPT)

. . . This afternoon, I want us to think back some thirty years to a far different time in a far different world. The United States and the Soviet Union were locked in a hostile rivalry. The Soviet Union was our unquestioned enemy: a highly armed threat to freedom and democracy. Far more than that wall in Berlin divided us.

Our highest ideal was—and remains—individual liberty. Theirs was the construction of a vast communist empire. Their totalitarian regime held much of Europe captive behind an iron curtain.

We didn't trust them, and for good reason. Our deep differences were expressed in a dangerous military confrontation that resulted in thousands of nuclear weapons pointed at each other on hair-trigger alert. Security of both the United States and the Soviet Union was based on a grim premise: that neither side would fire nuclear weapons at each other, because doing so would mean the end of both nations.

We even went so far as to codify this relationship in a 1972 ABM Treaty, based on the doctrine that our very survival would best be ensured by leaving both sides completely open and vulnerable to nuclear attack. The threat was real and vivid. The Strategic Air Command had an airborne command post called the Looking Glass, aloft twenty-four hours a day, ready in case the president ordered our strategic forces to move toward their targets and release their nuclear ordnance.

The Soviet Union had almost 1.5 million troops deep in the heart of Europe, in Poland and Czechoslovakia, Hungary and East Germany. We used our nuclear weapons not just to prevent the Soviet Union from using their nuclear weapons, but also to contain their conventional military forces, to prevent them from extending the Iron Curtain into parts of Europe and Asia that were still free.

In that world, few other nations had nuclear weapons and most of those who did were responsible allies, such as Britain and France. We worried about the proliferation of nuclear weapons to other countries, but it was mostly a distant threat, not yet a reality.

Today, the sun comes up on a vastly different world. The Wall is gone, and so is the Soviet Union. Today's Russia is not yesterday's Soviet Union. Its government is no longer Communist. Its president is elected. Today's Russia is not our enemy, but a country in transition with an opportunity to emerge as a great nation, democratic, at peace with itself and its neighbors. The Iron Curtain no longer exists. Poland, Hungary and the Czech Republic are free nations, and they are now our allies in NATO, together with a reunited Germany.

Yet, this is still a dangerous world, a less certain, a less predictable one. More nations have nuclear weapons and still more have nuclear aspirations.

Many have chemical and biological weapons. Some already have developed the ballistic missile technology that would allow them to deliver weapons of mass destruction at long distances and at incredible speeds. And a number of these countries are spreading these technologies around the world.

Most troubling of all, the list of these countries includes some of the world's least-responsible states. Unlike the Cold War, today's most urgent threat stems not from thousands of ballistic missiles in the Soviet hands, but from a small number of missiles in the hands of these states, states for whom terror and blackmail are a way of life. They seek weapons of mass destruction to intimidate their neighbors, and to keep the United States and other responsible nations from helping allies and friends in strategic parts of the world.

When Saddam Hussein invaded Kuwait in 1990, the world joined forces to turn him back. But the international community would have faced a very different situation had Hussein been able to blackmail with nuclear weapons. Like Saddam Hussein, some of today's tyrants are gripped by an implacable hatred of the United States of America. They hate our friends, they hate our values, they hate democracy and freedom and individual liberty. Many care little for the lives of their own people. In such a world, Cold War deterrence is no longer enough.

To maintain peace, to protect our own citizens and our own allies and friends, we must seek security based on more than the grim premise that we can destroy those who seek to destroy us. This is an important opportunity for the world to re-think the unthinkable, and to find new ways to keep the peace.

Today's world requires a new policy, a broad strategy of active nonproliferation, counter proliferation and defenses. We must work together with other like-minded nations to deny weapons of terror from those seeking to acquire them. We must work with allies and friends who wish to join with us to defend against the harm they can inflict. And together we must deter anyone who would contemplate their use.

We need new concepts of deterrence that rely on both offensive and defensive forces. Deterrence can no longer be based solely on the threat of nuclear retaliation. Defenses can strengthen deterrence by reducing the incentive for proliferation. . . .

# DOCUMENT 9.21

A 2008 Rand Corporation study of terrorist groups active since 1968 concluded that criminal justice approaches worked best and suggested that the United States had exacerbated the terrorist threat by employing an overly militarized strategy to the exclusion of other means. The U.S. Army Air Forces had originally established Rand in 1946. The corporation later became an independent and widely respected nonprofit think tank that specialized in national security issues.

---

SETH G. JONES AND M. C. LIBICKI, "HOW TERRORIST GROUPS END: LESSONS FOR COUNTERING AL QA'EDA," RAND CORPORATION, 2008 (EXCERPT)

Our quantitative analysis looked at groups that have ended since 1968 or are still active. It yielded several other interesting findings:

> Religious terrorist groups take longer to eliminate than other groups. Approximately 62 percent of all terrorist groups have ended since 1968, but only 32 percent of religious terrorist groups have ended.
>
> Religious groups rarely achieve their objectives. No religious group that has ended achieved victory since 1968.
>
> Size is a significant determinant of a group's fate. Big groups of more than 10,000 members have been victorious more than 25 percent of the time, while victory is rare when groups are smaller than 1,000 members.
>
> There is no statistical correlation between the duration of a terrorist group and ideological motivation, economic conditions, regime type, or the breadth of terrorist goals. But there appears to be some correlation between the size of a terrorist group and duration: Larger groups tend to last longer than smaller groups.
>
> When a terrorist group becomes involved in an insurgency, it does not end easily. Nearly 50 percent of the time, groups ended by negotiating a settlement with the government; 25 percent of the time, they achieved victory; and 19 percent of the time, military forces defeated them.
>
> Terrorist groups from upper-income countries are much more likely to be left wing or nationalist and much less likely to be motivated by religion.

## Implications for al Qa'ida

What does this mean for counterterrorism efforts against al Qa'ida? After September 11, 2001, the U.S. strategy against al Qa'ida centered on the use of military force. Indeed, U.S. policymakers and key national-security documents referred to operations against al Qa'ida as the war on terrorism. Other instruments were also used, such as cutting off terrorist financing, providing foreign assistance, engaging in diplomacy, and sharing information with foreign governments. But military force was the primary instrument.

The evidence by 2008 suggested that the U.S. strategy was not successful in undermining al Qa'ida's capabilities. Our assessment concludes that al Qa'ida remained a strong and competent organization. Its goals were the same: uniting Muslims to fight the United States and its allies (the far enemy) and overthrowing western-friendly regimes in the Middle East (the near enemy) to establish a pan-Islamic caliphate. Al Qa'ida has been involved in more terrorist attacks since September 11, 2001, than it was during its prior history. These attacks spanned Europe, Asia, the Middle East, and Africa. Al Qa'ida's modus operandi also evolved and included a repertoire of more-sophisticated improvised explosive devices (IEDs) and a growing use of suicide attacks. Its organizational structure evolved, making it a more dangerous enemy. This included a bottom-up approach (encouraging independent action from low-level operatives) and a top-down one (issuing strategy and operations from a central hub in Pakistan).

# ★ CHAPTER 10 ★

# PREEMPTIVE DEMOCRACY

WHATEVER THE RESULTS IN IRAQ, for many U.S. citizens the attempt to export democracy through a "war on terror" carried real risks for democracy in the United States. It was difficult to reconcile a foreign policy based on unilateralism and secrecy with the openness and transparency that keep government accountable at home. As details surfaced about the George W. Bush administration's activities, it became clear that a doctrine of preemption abroad coupled with a theory of a "unitary executive" at home threatened to preempt democratic freedoms in exchange for promises of increased domestic security. The administration repeatedly suggested that only unrestrained presidential power could wage the "war on terror" and protect citizens at the same time. But many observers saw its efforts to expand executive powers over secret surveillance, treatment of detainees, speech, and privacy as threats to constitutional rule that produced no added security (10.1).

The Bush administration's attempts to enhance the powers of the executive were not without historical precedent. International or domestic crises always tend to strengthen centralizing tendencies and encourage authoritarianism. An early example of executive overreach came when the United States was a young republic and vulnerable to foreign powers. In 1798, President John Adams pushed for passage of the Alien and Sedition Act because he believed that the only way to meet the threat of foreign invasion was to suppress dissent at home. The Act gave the federal government preemptive authority to arrest and deport foreign-born residents without due process of law. Mere suspicion of wrongdoing was enough to land a person in jail. Adams and the Federalists argued that the General Welfare clause in the Constitution gave the

Congress carte blanche to restrict freedom in order to further the "common good." But the drive for partisan political advantage was certainly not absent from their calculations. Thomas Jefferson considered the Act unconstitutional and released those arrested after his election in 1800.

Other presidents have claimed that enhancing security in times of crisis can come only at the expense of civil liberties. Abraham Lincoln justified the suspension of habeas corpus during the Civil War, Woodrow Wilson signed the Espionage Act penalizing "disloyalty" during World War I, Franklin D. Roosevelt ordered the internment of Japanese Americans during World War II, and Harry Truman supported loyalty oaths and purges in the early stages of the Cold War. It was a testament to the strength of democracy that these efforts were often publicly debated and defeated through social protest, a free press, new elections, the courts, or Congress. But the struggle to preserve and expand democratic rights continued, giving substance to the abolitionist Wendell Phillips's famous warning that "eternal vigilance is the price of liberty."

James Madison once observed, "If men were angels, no government would be necessary. If angels were to govern men, neither external nor internal controls on government would be necessary."[1] He was explaining why a government based on law required separate and shared power among its three federal branches. People require law, and for that they need a state. But they also need protection from the same state that creates and enforces the law. Madison knew better than to expect any political leader to practice self-restraint. The Constitution's division of sovereignty and its deliberately complex federalism testified to the founders' deep suspicion of centralized power. It expressed a pair of contradictory impulses that remain important in the political culture of the United States: while it organized a strong federal government, it also viewed centralized power as a necessary evil and built in safeguards to prevent abuses of power.

The U.S. democratic experiment elevated laws above individual rulers and created a cumbersome and divided government in order to forestall the rise of arbitrary central power. Checks and balances in government also created the space and friction that permitted citizens to oppose the government. Periods of popular action, such as the civil rights movement, brought the country closer to the ideals of democracy precisely because they channeled democratic pressures from society into the political system from outside the formal institutions of state power. The crosscutting impulses of central authority and popular sovereignty have marked U.S. history since the earliest debates about legislatures and kings, the Articles of Confederation, and the Constitution. Even in periods of great crisis and national emergency, many presidents have understood the importance of combining decisive leadership with respect for the Constitution's checks and balances.

But the Bush administration was notably different from its predecessors in its relentless attempts to circumvent and preempt limitations on executive

---

1. James Madison, *The Federalist* No. 51, 1788.

power. This was a particular priority of Vice President Cheney and his staff. A persistent drive to implement a "unitary" theory of inherent presidential power came to be one of the Bush administration's most important legacies. Cheney had come away from the Vietnam War, the Church and Pike committee hearings, the Watergate scandal, Nixon's resignation, and the Iran–Contra Affair determined to roll back what he saw as an overemphasis on rights and dissent in society and excessive congressional restraints on executive power. Echoing Alexander Hamilton's desire for an "energetic" presidential system, Cheney made a general argument that only the president, and not Congress or the courts, could move aggressively on behalf of the nation's interests, particularly—but not exclusively—in times of war or crisis. President Bush shared Cheney's view. The administration claimed greatly enhanced powers to spy on average Americans and foreigners, to bypass Congress if the president thought it necessary, and to conduct foreign policy with greatly diminished domestic oversight (10.3, 10.13). The administration further argued that new threats to domestic security required an extraordinary concentration of executive power to fight the "long war" against international terrorism, basing its position on an expansive interpretation of the Constitution (8.12, 8.13).

The administration's argument for a "unitary executive" centered on the assertion that Article 2 vested all execution of the laws in the president, named him as commander-in-chief of the armed forces, and gave him authority to conduct foreign relations. Assistant Attorney General Jay Bybee argued in 2002 with regard to the Iraq War that "any effort by the Congress to regulate the interrogation of battlefield combatants would violate the Constitution's sole vesting of the Commander in Chief authority in the President" (8.14). Bybee's claim rested at the heart of the administration's attempt to counter, skirt, or preempt lawful limitations on executive prerogatives. It was put to additional use as well, since it served the administration's drive to extend presidential power beyond the traditional duties and rights of the commander-in-chief. That memo, and others produced by the administration, interpreted the president's constitutional authority so broadly that it seemed both unlimited and intended to relegate Congress and the Courts to minor roles in the execution of the laws (10.13). Despite widespread criticism of its position by legal scholars and others, the administration continued to insist that a unitary executive was not only constitutionally valid but also necessary, particularly because September 11 and terrorism had "changed everything" (9.10, 9.20). But since Americans desired freedom and security equally, the matter of balancing the two often became a question of degree. How should the exact calibration between acceptable degrees of security and freedom be determined, and, more critically, who should make that determination (10.3)? The Bush administration's answer was that it was the executive branch alone (10.5).

President Bush invoked the "unitary executive" doctrine hundreds of times when signing legislation, issuing executive orders, or overriding other branches of government (10.6). Some of his advisors went so far as to argue that even the Supreme Court did not have the last word on legal rulings, an interpretation that would place the president above the law.[2] After White House Counsel (later Attorney General) Alberto Gonzales wrote in an internal memo that the Geneva Conventions were obsolete and "quaint," his words became famous as a stark reminder of the administration's thinking—and of the dangers of presidential overreach (see chapter 8).

In 2002 and 2003, the administration's lawyers provided legal arguments to justify torture, exposing the broad implications of the theory of almost limitless executive power under the unitary presidency (8.12). One memo, drafted by Cheney's chief counsel, David Addington, stated, "Congress may no more regulate the president's ability to detain and interrogate enemy combatants than it may regulate his ability to direct troop movements on the battlefield" (10.3). Addington had shared Cheney's views on presidential power for years, as had Bybee and other key figures in the administration. In another example, the administration claimed the right to indefinitely detain even U.S. citizens if they were deemed to be "enemy combatants." Many legal scholars concluded that such interpretations of presidential power were so sweeping that they virtually nullified the Constitution's carefully constructed system of checks and balances. The controversy went even beyond the treatment of "enemy combatants" to involve such matters as the organization of a broad system of secret surveillance of U.S. citizens.[3]

The legal profession received the administration's claims of expansive executive power with considerable skepticism. The Supreme Court, whose majority consisted of conservative jurists generally sympathetic to the executive, overruled the administration's positions several times. It decided in *Hamdi v. Rumsfeld* that accused "enemy combatants" who were U.S. citizens did have the right to due process, including the right to contest the accusations against them in court. Justice Sandra Day O'Connor famously wrote: "A state of war is not a blank check for the president when it comes to the rights of the nation's citizens." On the same day, the Supreme Court also ruled in *Rasul v. Bush* that non-citizens held at Guantánamo had the basic right of habeas corpus: to know the evidence against them and to challenge their imprisonment because, the Court held, Guantánamo Bay was "territory over which the United States exercises exclusive jurisdiction and control."

Yet, even when Congress passed a law outlawing torture, Bush secretly evaded it by invoking national security to assert that he, as president, had the power to waive the torture ban if he so wished. While publicly signing the Defense Authorization Act, the president simultaneously issued a "signing statement" that unilaterally gave him the right to ignore the very bill he had just

2. Dana Milbank, "In Cheney's Shadow, Counsel Pushes the Conservative Cause," *Washington Post*, October 11, 2004. See also the *Post* series by Barton Gellman and Jo Becker, "Pushing the Envelope on Presidential Power," June 25, 2007.

3. See, e.g., Curtis Bradley, David Cole, Walter Dellinger, Ronald Dworkin, Richard Epstein, Philip B. Heymann et al. "On NSA Spying: A Letter to Congress," *New York Review of Books* 53, no. 2, February 9, 2006.

signed (10.8). Signing statements proved to be an important tool deployed by the Bush administration in support of its drive to create a "unitary executive." Such statements were not unknown previously. Other presidents, from James Monroe to Bill Clinton, had used them, but they had done so rarely. Indeed, the forty-two presidents who preceded Bush had issued a total of 322 signing statements, whereas Bush signed 435 in his first term alone, and by 2006 had claimed the right to disobey or disregard over 750 laws.[4] In expanding the number of situations in which he used such statements, President Bush also broadened their applicability, using them to circumvent restrictions on his actions and to challenge, ignore, and reverse laws without resorting to the constitutional power to veto. Using signing statements allowed Bush to bypass laws while also avoiding the risk of a potential congressional override of his veto (10.6, 10.7).

It soon became clear that the president's signing statements went far beyond the conduct of the Iraq War. One allowed the president to disregard a law requiring reports to Congress on FBI searches under the Patriot Act. Another announced the president's intention to ignore a law mandating the preparation of uncensored reports by government researchers for Congress. Others allowed the president to evade a law prohibiting the military from using illegal methods to compile intelligence files on Americans, a law establishing affirmative action guarantees for women and minorities in government hiring, and a law to protect whistleblowers in the nuclear power industry (10.6). There were many other examples, illustrating the link between the administration's conduct of both domestic and foreign policy. The administration's unitary vision of an executive-dominated government at home was organically linked to its belief in unilateral action abroad and to the preemptive attack on Iraq. Secrecy in one sphere inevitably carried over to the other as well (10.14).

Shortly after September 11, 2001, Congress approved (with little debate) the USA Patriot Act, which granted the president, law enforcement, and intelligence agencies new, wide-ranging powers to fight terrorism (10.4). Secret searches and spying without judicial authorization were approved, immigrants could be detained indefinitely, and even the library records and e-mails of Americans could be secretly monitored by government agencies (10.9). In 2005, the *New York Times* reported that since 2001 the administration had been carrying out a broad program of domestic spying, without obtaining warrants from the so-called FISA court as mandated by the 1978 Foreign Intelligence Surveillance Act (10.1). The investigation revealed that, unbeknownst to the public, the administration had secretly instituted the "Terrorist Surveillance Program" in 2001 (10.2). Additionally, a Terrorist Screening Center was created in 2004, consolidating government watch lists that were used to check individuals coming into the country or even traveling within the country. A 2007

---

4. Charlie Savage, "Bush Challenges Hundreds of Laws," *Boston Globe,* April 30, 2006. Savage received a 2007 Pulitzer Prize for his reporting on this issue.

U.S. Justice Department audit stated that some twenty thousand new names were added to the list every month. People in the government's secret database had no way of knowing they were there and no way of contesting false information in their files. The Justice Department audit found that 38 percent of the records contained "errors and inconsistencies," that too many of the one million people in the database were "individuals that should not be watchlisted," and that many "known or suspected terrorists were not appropriately watchlisted on screening databases" at all (10.10). Meanwhile, some twenty thousand U.S. citizens and foreigners were detained as suspected terrorists in 2006 alone, many of them falsely listed, their records full of errors.[5]

Criticism from within the government itself shed light on the administration's attempts to preempt constitutional safeguards.[6] Those revelations helped fan the flames of dissent as retired military officers, former members of the administration, prominent lawyers, celebrities, and media professionals began to oppose the war. It was ordinary citizens, however, who fought early to uphold constitutional democracy, long before the press and "official" Washington began speaking out. Soldiers, too, dared to question policies that they believed were wrong.

Katherine Jashinski became the first female soldier to refuse orders in 2004 and file as a conscientious objector. Stephen Funk, a Marine Corps reservist, was the first soldier imprisoned for refusing to follow orders in 2004. S. Sgt. Camilo Mejia of the U.S. Army was the first noncommissioned officer jailed for refusing to return to Iraq after applying for conscientious-objector status. The first officer to file for objector status, Lt. Ehren Watada, was imprisoned in 2006 for refusing deployment to Iraq. In August 2007, seven noncommissioned officers serving in Iraq with the 82nd Airborne Division signed a statement of protest against the war after coming to believe that they were fighting as "an army of occupation" (10.11). Sadly, two of them, S. Sgt. Yance T. Gray and Sgt. Omar Mora, were killed in service less than one month after their brave voices were heard.

Army lawyers sent to process detainees at Guantánamo Bay in Cuba tried to follow orders, but some soon realized that the rights enumerated in the Bill of Rights and the Geneva Conventions were being violated. Many military and private lawyers opposed the military tribunals set up after September 11, 2001. In one example, the twenty-six-year veteran military lawyer Lt. Col. Stephen Abraham filed an affidavit in June 2007 charging the government with using vague and incomplete evidence. Retired generals spoke out as well. By April 2006, six retired generals had made public statements against the Iraq War and the secrecy with which it was being conducted. Four-star former general and commander of the Central Command Marine Gen. Anthony Zinni charged

---

5. Ellen Nakashima, "Terror Suspect List Yields Few Arrests," *Washington Post*, August 25, 2007.

6. See, e.g., Jack L. Goldsmith, *The Terror President: Law and Judgment inside the Bush Administration* (New York: W. W. Norton, 2007).

that the Bush administration's behavior ranged from "true dereliction, negligence and irresponsibility" to "lying, incompetence and corruption."[7]

These citizens reminded everyone that faith in democratic processes and the willingness to stand up for them have always been indispensable to preserving the country's democratic legacy. But more was required, and important institutions proved inadequate to their responsibilities. The media, for the most part, reported the run-up to the invasion and the administration's handling of the war with far too little criticism and skepticism. *New York Times* reports by Judith Miller were the most telling. Her articles claiming that Saddam Hussein possessed weapons of mass destruction and had ties to al Qaeda were based on misinformation, but they served to buttress the administration's case for war with Iraq when they were published. By May 2004, the *Times* had recognized the serious mistakes it had made in reporting on the administration's case for preemptive war. After protracted negotiations, Miller left the paper. The *Times* then apologized to its readers and established a public editor to audit its own reporting (10.12).

In 2006, Bush signed the Military Commissions Act, which gave the president the unchecked power to decide who was an enemy combatant and who could be imprisoned without the protection of habeas corpus.[8] The law also denied "enemy combatants" the right to invoke the Geneva Conventions— essentially opening the door for the use of torture. The U.S. courts continued to resist these sweeping claims. The Supreme Court's *Boumediene v. Bush* decision rejected the administration's denial of habeas corpus and established a set of procedures to allow federal courts to hear habeas challenges from Guantánamo detainees. In another case, a judge in Oregon ruled in September 2007 that sections of the Patriot Act on search and surveillance were unconstitutional because they ignored the Supreme Court's requirement of probable cause. She stated, "For over 200 years, this nation has adhered to the rule of law—with unparalleled success. A shift to a nation based on extra-constitutional authority is prohibited, as well as ill advised."[9]

The struggle over how to balance security and democracy went beyond even executive claims, legislative actions, and constitutional interpretation. In order for democracy to function, a level of social trust between government and citizens, and among citizens themselves, may be as important as formal laws and constitutions. Some countries, such as Great Britain, have no written constitutions but are stable, well-developed democracies. Others, like Colombia, have long, detailed constitutions but are dominated by small oligarchies and are full of violent political conflict. The United States, in contrast to both,

---

7. See also David S. Cloud, "Ex-Commander Says Iraq Effort Is 'a Nightmare,'" *New York Times,* October 13, 2007.

8. The "Military Commissions Act of 2006," HR-6166, was signed by President George W. Bush on October 17, 2006, as a response to the Supreme Court's decision on *Hamdan v. Rumsfeld.*

9. Susan Jo Keller, "Patriot Act Sections on Search and Surveillance Are Ruled Unconstitutional," *New York Times,* September 27, 2007.

has a relatively short constitution that is accessible and open to interpretation. All these examples suggest that successful societies require more than explicit documents and formal institutions, as important as they are. Societies also function on the basis of a set of informal understandings, practices, institutions, and habits that comprise a social system.[10] While many U.S. citizens continued to have faith in constitutional democracy even when they questioned the president, Congress, or the press, there were signs that the administration had damaged those deeper bonds of social trust and solidarity.

Even as the Bush administration moved to stretch constitutional principles at home in the name of a "unitary" presidency, it claimed that it was creating a constitutional democracy in Iraq. But its efforts to narrow civil rights and constitutional democracy at home exposed a crucial shortcoming in its approach to foreign and domestic affairs alike. Its attempts to push beyond the outer limits of the Constitution could be repaired, in time, by the courts, by Congress, or, possibly, by the executive itself. But it could take longer to repair public confidence in the ability of government institutions to manage power and provide security without injuring liberty.

# U.S. Government Documents

## DOCUMENT 10.1

The Department of Justice, headed by Attorney General Alberto Gonzales, issued a document to explain the legal basis for the warrantless surveillance program being carried out by the National Security Agency (NSA). The document's argument was conceptualized by David Addington, the vice president's powerful legal counsel and chief of staff, and John Yoo, the head attorney in the Office of Legal Counsel, both of whom relentlessly pushed for expansive executive power under the theory of the "unitary presidency." A wide variety of civil liberties organizations, lawyers, and political figures had strongly criticized the program after the New York Times exposé because it bypassed the Foreign Intelligence Surveillance Act and the FISA court established in 1978 to provide judicial warrants for surveillance (10.13). While the Justice Department document claimed that the program intercepted only international communications into and out of the United States of persons linked to al Qaeda or related terrorist organizations, experts noted that the program was actually a massive data-mining project that scooped up hundreds of millions of e-mails, telephone calls, and other communications of U.S. citizens (10.2). The administration

---

10. There is an enormous literature on the importance of a vibrant civil society in fortifying democracy. See, for example, Robert Putnam, *Bowling Alone: The Collapse and Revival of American Community* (New York: Simon & Schuster, 2000).

claimed that these intercepts would establish an early-warning system to prevent another terrorist attack in the United States. Because the program came after all the revelations about torture and abuses in Abu Ghraib prison and elsewhere, the Justice Department took pains to present the warrantless surveillance as legal, through appeals to the Constitution and the Congressional Authorization for Use of Military Force (2.12). The administration opposed attempts by Congress to apply FISA and other existing laws, claiming that the executive's "inherent authority" to protect national security permitted it to ignore laws that constrained the president.

---

## LEGAL AUTHORITIES SUPPORTING THE ACTIVITIES OF THE NATIONAL SECURITY AGENCY DESCRIBED BY THE PRESIDENT, JANUARY 19, 2006 (EXCERPT)

### SUMMARY

... In response to the September 11th attacks and the continuing threat, the President, with broad congressional approval, has acted to protect the Nation from another terrorist attack. In the immediate aftermath of September 11th, the President promised that "[w]e will direct every resource at our command—every means of diplomacy, every tool of intelligence, every tool of law enforcement, every financial influence, and every weapon of war—to the destruction of and to the defeat of the global terrorist network." The NSA activities are an indispensable aspect of this defense of the Nation. By targeting the international communications into and out of the United States of persons reasonably believed to be linked to al Qaeda, these activities provide the United States with an early warning system to help avert the next attack. For the following reasons, the NSA activities are lawful and consistent with civil liberties.

The NSA activities are supported by the President's well-recognized inherent constitutional authority as Commander in Chief and sole organ for the Nation in foreign affairs to conduct warrantless surveillance of enemy forces for intelligence purposes to detect and disrupt armed attacks on the United States. The President has the chief responsibility under the Constitution to protect America from attack, and the Constitution gives the President the authority necessary to fulfill that solemn responsibility. The President has made clear that he will exercise all authority available to him, consistent with the Constitution, to protect the people of the United States.

In the specific context of the current armed conflict with al Qaeda and related terrorist organizations, Congress by statute has confirmed and supplemented the President's recognized authority under Article II of the Constitution to conduct such warrantless surveillance to prevent further catastrophic attacks on the homeland. In its first legislative response to the terrorist attacks of September 11th, Congress authorized the President to "use all necessary and appropriate force against those nations, organizations, or persons he determines planned, authorized, committed, or aided the terrorist attacks" of September 11th in order to prevent "any future acts of international terrorism against the United States." Authorization for Use of Military Force, Pub. L. No. 107–40, §2(a), 115 Stat. 224, 224 (Sept. 18, 2001) (reported as a note to 50 U.S.C.A. §1541) ("AUMF"). History conclusively demonstrates that warrantless communications intelligence targeted at the enemy in time of armed conflict is a traditional and fundamental incident of the use of military force authorized by the AUMF. The Supreme Court's interpretation of the AUMF in Hamdi v. Rumsfeld, 542 U.S. 507 (2004), confirms that Congress in the AUMF gave its express approval to the military conflict against al Qaeda and its allies and thereby to the President's use of all traditional and accepted incidents of force in this current military conflict—including warrantless electronic surveillance to intercept enemy communications both at home and abroad. This understanding of the AUMF demonstrates Congress's support for the President's authority to protect the Nation and, at the same time, adheres to Justice O'Connor's admonition that "a state of war is not a blank check for the President," Hamdi, 542 U.S. at 536 (plurality opinion), particularly in view of the narrow scope of the NSA activities.

The AUMF places the President at the zenith of his powers in authorizing the NSA activities. Under the tripartite framework set forth by Justice Jackson in Youngstown Sheet & Tube Co. v. Sawyer, 343 U.S. 579, 635–38 (1952) (Jackson, J., concurring), Presidential authority is analyzed to determine whether the President is acting in accordance with congressional authorization (category I), whether he acts in the absence of a grant or denial of authority by Congress (category II), or whether he uses his own authority under the Constitution to take actions incompatible with congressional measures (category III). Because of the broad authorization provided in the AUMF, the President's action here falls within category I of Justice Jackson's framework. Accordingly, the President's power in authorizing the NSA activities is at its height because he acted "pursuant to an express or implied authorization of Congress," and his power "includes all that he possesses in his own right plus all that Congress can delegate."

The NSA activities are consistent with the preexisting statutory framework generally applicable to the interception of communications in the United States—the Foreign Intelligence Surveillance Act ("FISA"), as amended, 50 U.S.C. §§1801–1862 (2000 & Supp. II 2002), and relevant related provisions in chapter 119 of title 18. Although FISA generally requires judicial approval of electronic surveillance, FISA also contemplates that Congress may authorize such surveillance by a statute other than FISA. See 50 U.S.C. §1809(a) (prohibiting any person from intentionally "engag[ing] . . . in electronic surveillance under color of law except as authorized by statute"). The AUMF, as construed by the Supreme Court in Hamdi and as confirmed by the history and tradition of armed conflict, is just such a statute. Accordingly, electronic surveillance conducted by the President pursuant to the AUMF, including the NSA activities, is fully consistent with FISA and falls within category I of Justice Jackson's framework.

Even if there were ambiguity about whether FISA, read together with the AUMF, permits the President to authorize the NSA activities, the canon of constitutional avoidance requires reading these statutes in harmony to overcome any restrictions in FISA and Title III, at least as they might otherwise apply to the congressionally authorized armed conflict with al Qaeda. Indeed, were FISA and Title III interpreted to impede the President's ability to use the traditional tool of electronic surveillance to detect and prevent future attacks by a declared enemy that has already struck at the homeland and is engaged in ongoing operations against the United States, the constitutionality of FISA, as applied to that situation, would be called into very serious doubt.

In fact, if this difficult constitutional question had to be addressed, FISA would be unconstitutional as applied to this narrow context. Importantly, the FISA Court of Review itself recognized just three years ago that the President retains constitutional authority to conduct foreign surveillance apart from the FISA framework, and the President is certainly entitled, at a minimum, to rely on that judicial interpretation of the Constitution and FISA.

Finally, the NSA activities fully comply with the requirements of the Fourth Amendment. The interception of communications described by the President falls within a well-established exception to the warrant requirement and satisfies the Fourth Amendment's fundamental requirement of reasonableness. The NSA activities are thus constitutionally permissible and fully protective of civil liberties.

522 |

## DOCUMENT 10.2

A former National Security Agency analyst provided this assessment of the Bush administration's warrantless surveillance program, which was based on massive data-mining operations affecting the entire U.S. population. He pointed out the dangers of the program to U.S. civil liberties and the ways in which the program inhibited, rather than assisted, the search for terrorists. Giving legal and technical arguments for keeping surveillance programs within the requirements imposed by FISA and other existing laws, the analyst argued that those legal requirements did not constrain intelligence gathering or compromise security, and he rejected administration justifications for warrantless, and thus illegal, surveillance.

IRA WINKLER, "WHY NSA SPYING PUTS THE U.S. IN DANGER:
A FORMER NSA ANALYST SPEAKS OUT AT THE ILLEGAL
PRACTICE OF WARRANTLESS SPYING," *COMPUTERWORLD*,
MAY 18, 2006

As a former NSA analyst, I'm dismayed by the continuing revelations of the
National Security Agency's warrantless—and therefore illegal—spying. The
case involves fundamental issues related to NSA's missions and longstanding rules of engagement. What's even more dismaying is the lack of public
reaction to this.

Fundamentally, this is an issue of law. FISA, the Foreign Intelligence
Surveillance Act, was established in 1978 to address a wide variety of issues
revolving around Watergate, during which a President used foreign intelligence agencies to collect data on US citizens. As part of FISA, NSA has to
get warrants to analyse and maintain collections of data involving US citizens. FISA has withstood all tests until now, and it involves a fundamental
aspect of the US Constitution—its system of checks and balances.

The FISA law allows NSA to request those warrants up to 72 hours after
the fact—that is, after the data has been analyzed. And lest you think that
the courts from which such warrants are requested are staffed by a bunch
of liberal, activist, criminal-coddling judges, they have reportedly turned
down only five warrants in the last 28 years. So when President Bush says
"If Osama bin Laden is calling someone in the United States, we want to
know about it," followed by his nervous laugh, he's laughing at the American public, as "knowing about it" is a totally irrelevant issue. FISA blocks
no legitimate acquisition of knowledge.

It doesn't even slow the process down. The issue is not that NSA cannot
examine calls into the US from terrorist suspects—FISA provides for that—
but that the agency must justify acting on the results and keeping the information within 72 hours. The President claims that the process of getting
those warrants—of complying with the law—is too time-consuming. Normally that would sound like simple laziness, but the reality is that the programme is so large that they would need an army of lawyers to get all the
warrants they'd need to be in compliance with FISA. But the law is the law.
No president has the right to pick and choose which laws they find con-
venient to follow.

If Bush didn't like the FISA laws, he could have asked Congress to amend
them. After all, after 9/11 Congress passed a wide variety of laws (without,
for the most part, reading them) that were supposed to prevent another
attack. They could have easily slipped something modifying FISA into all of
that legislation. They did not, though recent revelations about this administration's use of signing statements may indicate that they simply didn't
want to raise the possibility of questions.

Ignoring FISA's rules concerning warrants is illegal. It also weakens national security, since the process of obtaining the warrants has an effect on

quality control. To date, FBI agents have been sent out to do thousands of investigations based on this warrantless wiretapping. None of those investigations turned up a legitimate lead. I have spoken to about a dozen agents, and they all roll their eyes and indicate disgust with the man-years of wasted effort being put into physically examining NSA "leads."

This scattershot attempt at data mining drags FBI agents away from real investigations, while destroying NSA's credibility in the eyes of law enforcement and the public in general. That loss of credibility makes NSA the agency that cried 'wolf'—and after so many false leads, should they provide something useful, the data will be looked at skeptically and perhaps given lower priority by law enforcement than it would otherwise have been given.

Worse, FBI agents working real and pressing investigations such as organised crime, child pornography, and missing persons are being pulled away from their normal law enforcement duties to follow up on NSA leads. Nobody wants another September 11th, of course, but we experience real crimes on a daily basis that, over the course of even one year, cause far greater loss of life and damage than the September 11th attacks did. There are children abused on a daily basis to facilitate online child pornography, yet I know of at least two agents who were pulled from their duties tracking down child abusers to investigate everyone who called the same pizza parlour as a person who received a call from a person who received an overseas call. There are plenty of similar examples.

We have snakes in our midst, yet we are chasing a mythical beast with completely unreliable evidence. And now we discover that NSA is searching through every possible phone call made in the US. They claim that NSA is not receiving any personally identifying information. Frankly you have to be a complete moron to believe that. It is trivial to narrow down access to a phone number to just a few members of a household, if not in fact to exactly one person.

The government claims that it got the information legally since it was given the data or bought it from the telecommunications companies. Perhaps, but *USA Today* reports that at least one company (Qwest) received threats from the US government for not cooperating. That's extortion—another crime.

Congress is not exercising any backbone at all, and neither is their constituents—aka you. Every time we receive new information about the NSA domestic spying programme, it gets exponentially worse, and it's clear that we still have no clue as to the full extent of the programme. More importantly, the courts and Congress do not appear to have a clue as to the full extent of the programme, and those bodies are constitutionally required to exercise checks and balances over the NSA. The actions taken by the executive branch after September 11th aren't protecting our freedom. They are usurping it.

So, besides knowing that it's illegal, that [it] provides useless information, that it takes law enforcement agents away from investigating and preventing crimes actually being committed, and that it erodes civil liberties, we have no clue how bad it really is. The arguments I hear for it are that 1) I have nothing to worry about so I don't care if they investigate me, or 2) we need to do everything we can to protect ourselves, or 3) the NSA isn't listening to the content of the calls, so there's no harm.

Addressing the first point, people who did nothing wrong have been investigated and jailed in this country and others over the years. Additionally, I believe that Saddam Hussein would cheerfully agree with the tired allegation that if you did nothing wrong, you shouldn't mind the government looking at your calls. I think Lenin, Stalin, Hitler, and the Chinese government would also agree with that line of thought. Is this the company we consent to keep in the name of safety?

To doing everything we can to protect ourselves, we have, again, pulled law enforcement agents away from real ongoing crimes to investigate poor and scattered "intelligence." This definition of "protection," again, leaves us watching for dragons while very real snakes multiply freely in our midst.

And so what if the NSA isn't listening to the calls themselves? An intelligence agency doesn't need to hear your chatter to invade your privacy. By simply tying numbers together—an intelligence discipline of traffic analysis—I assure you I can put together a portrait of your life. I'll know your friends, your hobbies, where your children go to school, if you're having an affair, whether you plan to take a trip, and even when you're awake or asleep. Give me a list of whom you're calling and I can tell most of the critical things I need to know about you.

| 525

Unnerved at the prospect of one person holding that data? You should be. While I can personally attest to the fact that the vast majority of NSA employees are good and honest people, NSA has more than its share of bitter, vindictive mid- and senior-level bureaucrats. I would not trust my personal information with these people as I have personally seen them use internal information against their enemies.

At the same time, we have seen the Bush administration personally go after Joseph Wilson, the ambassador who spoke out against the Bush administration, by leaking potentially classified information about him. They vigorously tried to undermine the credibility of Richard Clarke and others who spoke out against them. Now consider that the NSA telephone call database is not classified; there's no legal reason that they can't use this database as vindictively as they did, even when the data was [sic] potentially classified, as in releasing the information that Valerie Plame, Wilson's wife, worked for the CIA.

Over the years, I have defended NSA and its employees as reasonable and law abiding. I was all for invading Afghanistan, deployment of the Clipper Chip, and many other controversial government programmes. NSA domestic spying is against everything I was ever taught working at NSA. I might be more for it if there was any credible evidence that this somehow provides useful information that couldn't otherwise be had. However, the domestic spying programme has gotten so massive that the well established process of getting a warrant cannot be followed—and quantity most certainly doesn't translate to quality. Quite the opposite.

Again, I'm not arguing against allowing the NSA or other intelligence agencies to collect information on terrorists. My problem is that they are bypassing legally required oversight mechanisms. This implies that the operations are massive, and go well beyond the scope of looking at terrorists. Not only is this diminishing what makes America unique and worth preserving, it removes all quality control and puts the country at increased risks by moving resources away from critical investigations of more substantial threats.

I think Senator Jon Kyl, a strong supporter of the NSA domestic spying programme, said it best, "We have got to collect intelligence on the enemy." I fully agree. But the enemy numbers in the hundreds at best. NSA is collecting data on hundreds of millions of people who are clearly not the enemy. These numbers speak for themselves.

## DOCUMENT 10.3

This report was issued by a Defense Department working group, consisting of legal counsel from different branches of the military. It was the earliest indication of the administration's attempts to provide legal justification for and institutional support to the use of torture. It was also important because it established the legal reasoning behind the theory of the unitary executive. The Constitution declares in Article II, section 2, that "the President shall be Commander in Chief of the Army and Navy of the United States, and of the Militia of the several States, when called into the actual Service of the United States." The Bush administration interpreted this to mean that the president had more than the power to command the Army and Navy. It believed that as long as there was any connection to national security, the president had the power to ignore any law or treaty.

---

WORKING GROUP REPORT ON DETAINEE INTERROGATIONS
IN THE GLOBAL WAR ON TERRORISM: ASSESSMENT
OF LEGAL, HISTORICAL, POLICY, AND OPERATIONAL
CONSIDERATIONS, DECLASSIFIED BY THE U.S. DEPARTMENT
OF DEFENSE, MARCH 6, 2003 (EXCERPT)

. . . a. Commander-in-Chief Authority

(U) As the Supreme Court has recognized, and as we will explain further below, the President enjoys complete discretion in the exercise of his Commander-in-Chief authority including in conducting operations against hostile forces. Because both "[t]he executive power and the command of the military and naval forces is vested in the President," the Supreme Court has unanimously stated that it is "the President alone who is constitutionally invested with the entire charge of hostile operations." *Hamilton v. Dillin*, 88 U.S. (21 Wall.) 73, 87 (1874) (emphasis added).

(U) In light of the President's complete authority over the conduct of war without a clear statement otherwise, criminal statutes are not read as infringing on the President's ultimate authority in these areas. The Supreme Court has established a canon of statutory construction that statutes are to be construed in a manner that avoids constitutional difficulties so long as a reasonable alternative construction is available. *See, e.g., Edward J. DeBartolo Corp. v. Florida Gulf Coast Bldg. & Constr. Trades Council*, 485 U.S. 568, 575 (1988) (citing *NLRB v. Catholic Bishop of Chicago*, 440 U.S. 490, 499–501, 504 (1979)) ("[W]here an otherwise acceptable construction of a statute would raise serious constitutional problems, [courts] will construe [a] statute to avoid such problems unless such construction is plainly contrary to the intent of Congress.") This canon of construction applies especially where an act of Congress could be read to encroach upon powers constitutionally committed to a coordinate branch of government. *See, e.g., Franklin v. Massachusetts*, 505 U.S. 788, 800–1 (1992) (citation omitted) ("Out of respect for the separation of powers and the unique constitutional position of the President, we find that textual silence is not enough to subject the President to the provisions of the [Administrative Procedure Act]. We would require an express statement by Congress before assuming it intended the President's performance of his statutory duties to be reviewed for abuse of discretion."); *Public Citizen v. United States Dep't of Justice*, 491 U.S. 440, 465–67 (1989) (construing Federal Advisory Committee Act not to apply to advice potential constitutional question regarding encroachment on Presidential power to appoint judges).

(U) In the area of foreign affairs, and war powers in particular, the avoidance canon has special force. *See, e.g. Dept of Navy v. Egan*, 485 U.S. 518, 530 (1988) ("unless Congress specifically has provided otherwise, courts traditionally have been reluctant to intrude upon the authority of the Executive in military and national security affairs."); *Japan Whaling Ass'n v. American Cetacean Sacy*, 478 U.S. 221, 232–33 (1986) (construing federal statutes to avoid curtailment of traditional presidential prerogatives in foreign affairs). It should not be lightly assumed that Congress has acted to interfere with the President's constitutionally superior position as Chief Executive and Commander-in-Chief in the area of military operations. *See Egan*, 484 U.S. at 529 . . . (deference to Executive Branch is "especially" appropriate "in the area of national security").

(U) In order to respect the President's inherent constitutional authority to manage a military campaign, 18 U.S.C. §2340A (the prohibition against torture) must be construed as inapplicable to interrogations undertaken pursuant to his Commander-in-Chief authority. Congress lacks authority under Article I to set the terms and conditions under which the President may exercise his authority as Commander-in-Chief to control the conduct of operations during a war. The President's power to detain and interrogate enemy combatants arises out of his constitutional authority as Commander-in-Chief. A construction of Section 2340A that applied the provision to regulate the President's authority as Commander-in-Chief to determine the interrogation and treatment of enemy combatants would raise serious constitutional questions. Congress may no more regulate the President's ability to detain and interrogate enemy combatants than it may regulate his ability to direct troop movements on the battlefield. Accordingly, we would construe Section 2340A to avoid this constitutional difficulty, and conclude that it does not apply to the President's detention and interrogation of enemy combatants pursuant to his Commander-in-Chief authority. . . .

*Prosecution for Contempt of Congress of an Executive Branch Official Who Has Asserted A Claim of Executive Privilege,* 8:Op O.L.C. 101, 134 (May 30, 1984). Likewise, if executive officials were subject to prosecution for conducting interrogations when they were carrying out the President's Commander-in-Chief powers, "it would significantly burden and immeasurably impair the President's ability to fulfill his constitutional duties." These constitutional principles preclude an application of Section 2340A to punish officials for aiding the President in exercising his exclusive constitutional authorities. . . .

## DOCUMENT 10.4

The Wisconsin senator Russell Feingold's statement to the Senate on October 25, 2001, declared the need to fight terrorism without jeopardizing liberty. He argued that a police state would provide almost perfect security but would not be the kind of place in which most Americans would want to live. He also suggested that the preemptive ethos in the White House created a "demand for haste" that was "inappropriate" and likely to produce errors that endangered civil liberties. Feingold made it clear that the danger was not just that the broad scope of unchecked government spying would gather vast amounts of information on innocent citizens but also that government, even a well-meaning one, would inevitably harm citizens with that information. The "Anti-Terrorism Bill," signed by President Bush the day after Senator Feingold's speech, is known as the "USA Patriot Act."

RUSS FEINGOLD, STATEMENT ON THE ANTI-TERRORISM BILL (USA PATRIOT ACT), OCTOBER 25, 2001 (EXCERPT)

Mr. President, I have asked for this time to speak about the anti-terrorism bill before us, H.R. 3162. As we address this bill, we are especially mindful of the terrible events of September 11 and beyond, which led to the bill's proposal and its quick consideration in the Congress. . . .

The first caution was that we must continue to respect our Constitution and protect our civil liberties in the wake of the attacks. As the chairman of the Constitution Subcommittee of the Judiciary Committee, I recognize that this is a different world with different technologies, different issues, and different threats. Yet we must examine every item that is proposed in response to these events to be sure we are not rewarding these terrorists and weakening ourselves by giving up the cherished freedoms that they seek to destroy. . . .

But upon reviewing the case itself, *Kennedy v. Mendoza-Martinez*, I found that Justice Arthur Goldberg had made this statement but then ruled in favor of the civil liberties position in the case, which was about draft evasion. He elaborated:

> It is fundamental that the great powers of Congress to conduct war and to regulate the Nation's foreign relations are subject to the constitutional requirements of due process. The imperative necessity for safeguarding these rights to procedural due process under the gravest of emergencies has existed throughout our constitutional history, for it is then, under the pressing exigencies of crisis, that there is the greatest temptation to dispense with fundamental constitutional guarantees which, it is feared, will inhibit governmental action. "The Constitution of the United States is a law for rulers and people, equally in war and peace, and covers with the shield of its protection all classes of men, at all times, and under all circumstances . . . In no other way can we transmit to posterity unimpaired the blessings of liberty, consecrated by the sacrifices of the Revolution."

| 529

I have approached the events of the past month and my role in proposing and reviewing legislation relating to it in this spirit. I believe we must redouble our vigilance. We must redouble our vigilance to ensure our security and to prevent further acts of terror. But we must also redouble our vigilance to preserve our values and the basic rights that make us who we are.

The Founders who wrote our Constitution and Bill of Rights exercised that vigilance even though they had recently fought and won the Revolutionary War. They did not live in comfortable and easy times of hypothetical enemies. They wrote a Constitution of limited powers and an explicit Bill of Rights to protect liberty in times of war, as well as in times of peace.

There have been periods in our nation's history when civil liberties have taken a back seat to what appeared at the time to be the legitimate exigencies of war. Our national consciousness still bears the stain and the scars of those events: The Alien and Sedition Acts; the suspension of habeas corpus during the Civil War; the internment of Japanese-Americans, German-Americans, and Italian-Americans during World War II; the blacklisting of supposed communist sympathizers during the McCarthy era; and the surveillance and harassment of antiwar protesters, including Dr. Martin Luther King Jr., during the Vietnam War. We must not allow these pieces of our past to become prologue. . . .

Now some may say, indeed we may hope, that we have come a long way since those days of infringements on civil liberties. But there is ample reason for concern. And I have been troubled in the past six weeks by the potential loss of commitment in the Congress and the country to traditional civil liberties.

As it seeks to combat terrorism, the Justice Department is making extraordinary use of its power to arrest and detain individuals, jailing hundreds of people on immigration violations and arresting more than a dozen "material witnesses" not charged with any crime. Although the government has used these authorities before, it has not done so on such a broad scale. Judging from government announcements, the government has not brought any criminal charges related to the attacks with regard to the overwhelming majority of these detainees.

For example, the FBI arrested as a material witness the San Antonio radiologist Albader Al-Hazmi, who has a name like two of the hijackers, and who tried to book a flight to San Diego for a medical conference. According to his lawyer, the government held Al-Hazmi incommunicado after his arrest, and it took six days for lawyers to get access to him. After the FBI released him, his lawyer said, "This is a good lesson about how frail our processes are. It's how we treat people in difficult times like these that is the true test of the democracy and civil liberties that we brag so much about throughout the world." I agree with those statements. . . .

Of course, there is no doubt that if we lived in a police state, it would be easier to catch terrorists. If we lived in a country that allowed the police to search your home at any time for any reason; if we lived in a country that allowed the government to open your mail, eavesdrop on your phone conversations, or intercept your email communications; if we lived in a country that allowed the government to hold people in jail indefinitely based on what they write or think, or based on mere suspicion that they are up to no good, then the government would no doubt discover and arrest more terrorists.

But that probably would not be a country in which we would want to live. And that would not be a country for which we could, in good conscience, ask our young people to fight and die. In short, that would not be America.

Preserving our freedom is one of the main reasons that we are now engaged in this new war on terrorism. We will lose that war without firing a shot if we sacrifice the liberties of the American people. That is why I found the antiterrorism bill originally proposed by Attorney General Ashcroft and President Bush to be troubling.

The administration's proposed bill contained vast new powers for law enforcement, some seemingly drafted in haste and others that came from the FBI's wish list that Congress has rejected in the past. You may remember that the attorney general announced his intention to introduce a bill shortly after the September 11 attacks. He provided the text of the bill the following Wednesday, and urged Congress to enact it by the end of the week. That was plainly impossible, but the pressure to move on this bill quickly, without deliberation and debate, has been relentless ever since.

It is one thing to shortcut the legislative process in order to get federal financial aid to the cities hit by terrorism. We did that, and no one complained that we moved too quickly. It is quite another to press for the enactment of sweeping new powers for law enforcement that directly affect the civil liberties of the American people without due deliberation by the peoples' elected representatives.

Fortunately, cooler heads prevailed at least to some extent, and while this bill has been on a fast track, there has been time to make some changes and reach agreement on a bill that is less objectionable than the bill that the administration originally proposed.

As I will discuss in a moment, I have concluded that this bill still does not strike the right balance between empowering law enforcement and protecting civil liberties. But that does not mean that I oppose everything in the bill. Indeed many of its provisions are entirely reasonable, and I hope they will help law enforcement more effectively counter the threat of terrorism.

For example, it is entirely appropriate that with a warrant the FBI be able to seize voice mail messages as well as tap a phone. It is also reasonable, even necessary, to update the federal criminal offense relating to possession and use of biological weapons. It made sense to make sure that phone conversations carried over cables would not have more protection from surveillance than conversations carried over phone lines. And it made sense to stiffen penalties and lengthen or eliminate statutes of limitation for certain terrorist crimes.

There are other non-controversial provisions in the bill that I support; those to assist the victims of crime, to streamline the application process for public safety officers' benefits and increase those benefits, to provide more funds to strengthen immigration controls at our northern borders, to expedite the hiring of translators at the FBI, and many others.

In the end, however, my focus on this bill, as Chair of the Constitution Subcommittee of the Judiciary Committee in the Senate, was on those provisions that implicate our constitutional freedoms. And it was in reviewing those provisions that I came to feel that the administration's demand for haste was inappropriate; indeed, it was dangerous. Our process in the Senate, as truncated as it was, did lead to the elimination or significant rewriting of a number of audacious proposals that I and many other members found objectionable.

For example, the original administration proposal contained a provision that would have allowed the use in U.S. criminal proceedings against U.S. citizens of information obtained by foreign law enforcement agencies in wiretaps that would be illegal in this country. In other words, evidence obtained in an unconstitutional search overseas was to be allowed in a U.S. court.

Another provision would have broadened the criminal forfeiture laws to permit—prior to conviction—the freezing of assets entirely unrelated to an alleged crime. The Justice Department has wanted this authority for years, and Congress has never been willing to give it. For one thing, it touches on the right to counsel, since assets that are frozen cannot be used to pay a lawyer. The courts have almost uniformly rejected efforts to restrain assets before conviction unless they are assets gained in the alleged criminal enterprise. This proposal, in my view, was simply an effort on the part of the department to take advantage of the emergency situation and get something that they've wanted to get for a long time.

The foreign wiretap and criminal forfeiture provisions were dropped from the bill that we considered in the Senate. Other provisions were rewritten based on objections that I and others raised about them. For example, the

original bill contained sweeping permission for the attorney general to get copies of educational records without a court order. The final bill requires a court order and a certification by the attorney general that he has reason to believe that the records contain information that is relevant to an investigation of terrorism.

So the bill before us is certainly improved from the bill that the administration sent to us on September 19, and wanted us to pass on September 21. But again, in my judgment, it does not strike the right balance between empowering law enforcement and protecting constitutional freedoms. Let me take a moment to discuss some of the shortcomings of the bill.

First, the bill contains some very significant changes in criminal procedure that will apply to every federal criminal investigation in this country, not just those involving terrorism. One provision would greatly expand the circumstances in which law enforcement agencies can search homes and offices without notifying the owner prior to the search. The longstanding practice under the Fourth Amendment of serving a warrant prior to executing a search could be easily avoided in virtually every case, because the government would simply have to show that it has "reasonable cause to believe" that providing notice "may" "seriously jeopardize an investigation." This is a significant infringement on personal liberty.

Notice is a key element of Fourth Amendment protections. It allows a person to point out mistakes in a warrant and to make sure that a search is limited to the terms of a warrant. Just think about the possibility of the police showing up at your door with a warrant to search your house. You look at the warrant and say, "Yes, that's my address, but the name on the warrant isn't me." And the police realize a mistake has been made and go away. If you're not home, and the police have received permission to do a "sneak and peak" search, they can come in your house, look around, and leave, and may never have to tell you.

Another very troubling provision has to do with the effort to combat computer crime. The bill allows law enforcement to monitor a computer with the permission of its owner or operator, without the need to get a warrant or show probable cause. That's fine in the case of a so-called "denial of service attack" or plain old computer hacking. A computer owner should be able to give the police permission to monitor communications coming from what amounts to a trespasser on the computer.

As drafted in the Senate bill, however, the provision might permit an employer to give permission to the police to monitor the e-mails of an employee who has used her computer at work to shop for Christmas gifts. Or someone who uses a computer at a library or at school and happens to go to a gambling or pornography site in violation of the Internet use policies of the library or the university might also be subjected to government surveillance—without probable cause and without any time limit. With this one provision, Fourth Amendment protections are potentially eliminated for a broad spectrum of electronic communications.

I am also very troubled by the broad expansion of government power under the Foreign Intelligence Surveillance Act, known as FISA. When Congress passed FISA in 1978 it granted to the executive branch the power to conduct surveillance in foreign intelligence investigations without meeting the rigorous probable cause standard under the Fourth Amendment that is required for criminal investigations. There is a lower threshold for obtaining a wiretap order from the FISA court because the FBI is not investigating a crime, it is investigating foreign intelligence activities. But the law currently requires that intelligence gathering be the primary purpose of the investigation in order for this lower standard to apply.

This bill changes that requirement. The government now will only have to show that intelligence is a "significant purpose" of the investigation. So even if the *primary* purpose is a criminal investigation, the heightened protections of the Fourth Amendment won't apply.

It seems obvious that with this lower standard, the FBI will try to use FISA as much as it can. And of course, with terrorism investigations that won't be difficult, because the terrorists are apparently sponsored or at least supported by foreign governments. This means that the Fourth Amendment rights will be significantly curtailed in many investigations of terrorist acts.

The significance of the breakdown of the distinction between intelligence and criminal investigations becomes apparent when you see the other expansions of government power under FISA in this bill. One provision that troubles me a great deal is a provision that permits the government under FISA to compel the production of records from any business regarding any person, if that information is sought in connection with an investigation of terrorism or espionage.

Now we're not talking here about travel records pertaining to a terrorist suspect, which we all can see can be highly relevant to an investigation of a terrorist plot. FISA already gives the FBI the power to get airline, train, hotel, car rental and other records of a suspect. But under this bill, the government can compel the disclosure of the personal records of anyone—perhaps someone who worked with, or lived next door to, or went to school with, or sat on an airplane with, or has been seen in the company of, or whose phone number was called by—the target of the investigation.

And under this new provision *all* business records can be compelled, including those containing sensitive personal information like medical records from hospitals or doctors, or educational records, or records of what books someone has taken out of the library. This is an enormous expansion of authority, under a law that provides only minimal judicial supervision.

Under this provision, the government can apparently go on a fishing expedition and collect information on virtually anyone. All it has to allege in order to get an order for these records from the court is that the information is sought for an investigation of international terrorism or clandestine intelligence gathering. That's it. On that minimal showing in an ex parte application to a secret court, with no showing even that the information is *relevant* to the investigation, the government can lawfully compel a doctor or hospital to release medical records, or a library to release circulation records. This is a truly breathtaking expansion of police power. . . .

Another provision in the bill that deeply troubles me allows the detention and deportation of people engaging in innocent associational activity. It would allow for the detention and deportation of individuals who provide lawful assistance to groups that are not even designated by the secretary of state as terrorist organizations, but instead have engaged in vaguely defined "terrorist activity" sometime in the past. To avoid deportation, the immigrant is required to prove a negative: that he or she did not know, and should not have known, that the assistance would further terrorist activity.

This language creates a very real risk that truly innocent individuals could be deported for innocent associations with humanitarian or political groups that the government later chooses to regard as terrorist organizations. Groups that might fit this definition could include Operation Rescue, Greenpeace, and even the Northern Alliance fighting the Taliban in northern Afghanistan. This provision amounts to "guilt by association," which I believe violates the First Amendment.

And speaking of the First Amendment, under this bill, a lawful permanent resident who makes a controversial speech that the government deems to be supportive of terrorism might be barred from returning to his or her family after taking a trip abroad. . . .

When concerns of this kind have been raised with the administration and supporters of this bill they have told us, "Don't worry, the FBI would never do that." I call on the attorney general and the Justice Department to ensure that my fears are not borne out.

The anti-terrorism bill that we consider in the Senate today highlights the march of technology, and how that march cuts both for and against personal liberty. Justice Brandeis foresaw some of the future in a 1928 dissent, when he wrote:

> The progress of science in furnishing the Government with means of espionage is not likely to stop with wire-tapping. Ways may some day be developed by which the Government, without removing papers from secret drawers, can reproduce them in court, and by which it will be enabled to expose to a jury the most intimate occurrences of the home. . . . Can it be that the Constitution affords no protection against such invasions of individual security?

We must grant law enforcement the tools that it needs to stop this terrible threat. But we must give them only those extraordinary tools that they need and that relate specifically to the task at hand.

We must maintain our vigilance to preserve our laws and our basic rights.

We in this body have a duty to analyze, to test, to weigh new laws that the zealous and often sincere advocates of security would suggest to us. This is what I have tried to do with this anti-terrorism bill. And that is why I will vote against this bill when the roll is called.

Protecting the safety of the American people is a solemn duty of the Congress; we must work tirelessly to prevent more tragedies like the devastating attacks of September 11th. We must prevent more children from losing their mothers, more wives from losing their husbands, and more firefighters from losing their heroic colleagues. But the Congress will fulfill its duty only when it protects *both* the American people and the freedoms at the foundation of American society. So let us preserve our heritage of basic rights. Let us practice as well as preach that liberty. And let us fight to maintain that freedom that we call America.

I yield the floor.

## DOCUMENT 10.5

In this important case, the Fourth Circuit Appeals Court argued in *Al-Marri v. Wright* that the federal government could not hold Ali Saleh Kahlah al-Marri, a resident of Qatar who was arrested as a student at Bradley University in the United States and accused of aiding al Qaeda, in indefinite detention as an "enemy combatant." Any prosecution for alleged crimes must be made in the civilian criminal court system, the court ruled. More importantly, this mostly conservative Court, two-thirds of whose members were appointed by the two Bush administrations, stated that although it did not "minimize the grave threat international terrorism poses to our country and our national security . . . [it] specifically cautioned against 'break[ing] faith with this Nation's tradition . . . [as] firmly embodied in the Constitution.'" Most importantly, it warned that "the President cannot eliminate constitutional protections with the stroke of a pen."

---

## U.S. COURT OF APPEALS FOR THE 4TH CIRCUIT, *AL-MARRI V. WRIGHT*, JUNE 11, 2007 (EXCERPT)

In light of al-Marri's due process rights under our Constitution and Congress's express prohibition in the Patriot Act on the indefinite detention of those civilians arrested as "terrorist aliens" within this country, we can only conclude that in the case at hand, the President claims power that far exceeds that granted him by the Constitution.

We do not question the President's war-time authority over enemy combatants; but absent suspension of the writ of habeas corpus or declaration of martial law, the Constitution simply does not provide the President the power to exercise military authority over civilians within the United States. See Toth, 350 U.S. at 14 ("[A]ssertion of military authority over civilians cannot rest on the President's power as commander-in-chief, or on any theory of martial law."). The President cannot eliminate constitutional protections with the stroke of a pen by proclaiming a civilian, even a criminal civilian, an enemy combatant subject to indefinite military detention. Put simply, the Constitution does not allow the President to order the military to seize civilians residing within the United States and detain them indefinitely without criminal process, and this is so even if he calls them "enemy combatants."

A "well-established purpose of the Founders" was "to keep the military strictly within its proper sphere, subordinate to civil authority." Reid, 354 U.S. at 30. In the Declaration of Independence our forefathers lodged the complaint that the King of Great Britain had "affected to render the Military independent of and superior to the Civil power" and objected that the King had "depriv[ed] us in many cases, of the benefits of Trial by Jury." The Declaration of Independence paras. 14, 20 (U.S. 1776). A resolute conviction that civilian authority should govern the military animated the framing of the Constitution. As Alexander Hamilton, no foe of Executive power, observed, the President's Commander-in-Chief powers "amount to nothing more than the supreme command and direction of the military and naval forces." The Federalist No. 69, at 386 (Alexander Hamilton) (Clinton Rossiter ed., 1961). "That military powers of the Commander in Chief were not to supersede representative government of internal affairs seems obvious from the Constitution and from elementary American history." Youngstown, 343 U.S. at 644 (Jackson, J., concurring) (emphasis added). For this reason, the Supreme Court rejected the President's claim to "inherent power" to use the military even to seize property within the United States, despite the Government's argument that the refusal would "endanger the well-being and safety of the Nation." Id. at 584 (majority opinion).

Of course, this does not mean that the President lacks power to protect our national interests and defend our people, only that in doing so he must abide by the Constitution. We understand and do not in any way minimize the grave threat international terrorism poses to our country and our national security. But as Milligan teaches, "the government, within the Constitution, has all the powers granted to it, which are necessary to preserve its existence." Milligan, 71 U.S. at 121. Those words resound as clearly in the twenty-first century as they did in the nineteenth.

Thus, the President plainly has plenary authority to deploy our military against terrorist enemies overseas. See Curtiss-Wright, 299 U.S. at 319–20; see also Eisentrager, 339 U.S. at 789. Similarly, the Government remains free to defend our country against terrorist enemies within, using all the considerable powers "the well-stocked statutory arsenal" of domestic law affords.

Hamdi, 542 U.S. at 547 (Souter, J., concurring in the judgment) (citing numerous federal statutes criminalizing terrorist acts). Civilian law enforcement officers may always use deadly force whenever reasonable. See Scott v. Harris, 127 S. Ct. 1769, 1776–78 (2007). Furthermore, in the wake of September 11th, Congress has specifically authorized the President to deploy the armed forces at home to protect the country in the event of actual "terrorist attack[s] or incident[s]" within the United States meeting certain conditions. See 10 U.S.C.A. §333(a)(A) (2007) (amending the Insurrection Act to provide the President with this authority, notwithstanding the Posse Comitatus Act, 18 U.S.C. §1385).

But in this nation, military control cannot subsume the constitutional rights of civilians. Rather, the Supreme Court has repeatedly catalogued our country's "deeply rooted and ancient opposition . . . to the extension of military control over civilians." Reid, 354 U.S. at 33; see also Laird v. Tatum, 408 U.S. 1, 15 (1972) (Burger, C.J.) (recognizing "a traditional and strong resistance of Americans to any military intrusion into civilian affairs" that "has deep roots in our history and found early expression . . . in the constitutional provisions for civilian control of the military"). The Court has specifically cautioned against "break[ing] faith with this Nation's tradition"—"firmly embodied in the Constitution"—"of keeping military power subservient to civilian authority." Reid, 354 U.S. at 40. When the Court wrote these words in 1957, it explained that "[t]he country ha[d] remained true to that faith for almost one hundred seventy years." Id. Another half century has passed but the necessity of "remain[ing] true to that faith" remains as important today as it was at our founding.

# DOCUMENT 10.6

The American Bar Association (ABA) found that presidential signing statements and executive orders "undermine the rule of law and our constitutional system of separation of powers." It was particularly clear about how the White House was challenging congressional power even when there was "no serious issue" at stake. The ABA further argued that the president's record of challenging Congress with signing statements amounted to a "consistent and audacious" rejection of the constitutional authority of the legislative branch. That legal assessment by the largest professional association of lawyers in the United States embodied a substantial rebuke to President Bush's efforts to amass more power for a "unitary executive."

AMERICAN BAR ASSOCIATION TASK FORCE ON
PRESIDENTIAL SIGNING STATEMENTS AND THE SEPARATION
OF POWERS DOCTRINE REPORT, JULY 2006 (EXCERPT)

### 3. The Bush II Era

From the inception of the Republic until 2000, Presidents produced signing statements containing fewer than 600 challenges to the bills they signed. According to the most recent update, in his one-and-a-half terms so far, President George W. Bush (Bush II) has produced more than 800.

He asserted constitutional objections to over 500 in his first term: 82 of these related to his theory of the "unitary executive," 77 to the President's exclusive power over foreign affairs, 48 to his power to withhold information required by Congress to protect national security, 37 to his Commander in Chief powers.

Whereas President Clinton on occasion asked for memoranda from the Office of Legal Counsel on his authority to challenge or reject controversial provisions in bills presented to him, it is reported that in the Bush II Administration all bills are routed through Vice President Cheney's office to be searched for perceived threats to the "unitary executive"—the theory that the President has the sole power to control the execution of powers delegated to him in the Constitution and encapsulated in his Commander in Chief powers and in his constitutional mandate to see that "the laws are faithfully executed."

Some examples of signing statements in which President Bush has indicated he will not follow the law are: bills banning the use of U.S. troops in combat against rebels in Colombia; bills requiring reports to Congress when money from regular appropriations is diverted to secret operations; two bills forbidding the use in military intelligence of materials "not lawfully collected" in violation of the Fourth Amendment; a post–Abu Ghraib bill mandating new regulations for military prisons in which military lawyers were permitted to advise commanders on the legality of certain kinds of treatment even if the Department of Justice lawyers did not agree; bills requiring the retraining of prison guards in humane treatment under the Geneva Conventions, requiring background checks for civilian contractors in Iraq and banning contractors from performing security, law enforcement, intelligence and criminal justice functions. Perhaps the most prominent signing statements which conveyed refusals to carry out laws involved:

- Congressional requirements to report back to Congress on the use of Patriot Act authority to secretly search homes and seize private papers;
- The McCain amendment forbidding any U.S. officials to use torture or cruel, inhuman, or degrading treatment on prisoners (the President said in his statement that as Commander in Chief he could waive any such requirement if necessary to prevent terrorist attacks);
- A requirement that government scientists transmit their findings to Congress uncensored, along with a guarantee that whistleblower employees at the Department of Energy and the Nuclear Regulatory Commission will not be punished for providing information to Congress about safety issues in the planned nuclear waste repository at Yucca Mountain.

| 539

President Bush has been particularly adamant about preventing any of his subordinates from reporting directly to Congress even though there is Supreme Court precedent to the effect that Congress may authorize a subordinate official to act directly or to report directly to Congress. When Congress set up an educational research institute to generate independent statistics about student performance, and to publish reports "without the approval" of the Secretary of Education, President Bush asserted in his signing statement that "the Institute director would be subject to the supervision and direction of the Secretary."

In another bill, Congress said no U.S. official shall prevent the Inspector General for the Coalition Provisional Authority in Iraq from carrying out his investigations and he should report any attempt directly to Congress. President Bush insisted in his signing statement that the Inspector General "refrain" from any investigation involving national security or intelligence already being investigated by the Pentagon and the Inspector General himself could not tell Congress anything without going through the President.

The Intelligence Authorization Act of 2002 required that the Congress be given regular reports on special matters. The signing statement treated this requirement as "advisory" or "precatory" only stating that the requirement "would be construed in a manner consistent with the President's constitutional authority to withhold information, the disclosure of which could impair foreign relations, the national security, the deliberative processes of the Executive or the performance of the Executive's constitutional duties."

This exact phraseology has been repeated in Bush signing statements innumerable times. Scholars have noted that it is a hallmark of the Bush II signing statements that the objections are ritualistic, mechanical and generally carry no citation of authority or detailed explanation.

"These boilerplate objections [are] placed over and over again in signing statements." A frustrated Congress finally enacted a law requiring the Attorney General to submit to Congress a report of any instance in which that official or any officer of the Department of Justice established or pursued a policy of refraining from enforcing any provision of any federal statute, but this too was subjected to a ritual signing statement insisting on the President's authority to withhold information whenever he deemed it necessary.

Even action deadlines set in the National Homeland Security Act were rejected as contravening the unitary executive function. The Intelligence Authorization Act of 2003 setting up the 9/11 Commission provoked the same signing statement retaining the President's power to withhold information—a claim which later became a major bone of contention between the White House and the Commission. A December 2004 intelligence bill required reports on the use of national security wiretaps on U.S. soil as well as reports on civil liberties, security clearances, border security and counter narcotics efforts. All were subjected to the same treatment by signing statement. Even the Homeland Security Act requirements for reports to Congress about airport screening chemical plant vulnerabilities and visa services suffered a similar fate.

President Bush's signing statements have consistently refused to honor Congressional attempts to impose affirmative action or diversity requirements on federal hiring. Fifteen times the Bush signing statements have objected to such provisions, proclaiming that they would be construed "in a manner consistent with the Constitution's guarantee of equal protection." This included directions by Congress to recruit and train women and minorities in the intelligence agencies and promote diversity in the Export-Import bank operations.

One learned commentator sums up the Bush II use of signing statements as follows: "When in doubt challenge the legislative process whether there is a serious issue or not." He labels the Bush record on signing statements as "an audacious claim to constitutional authority; the scope of the claims and the sweeping formulae used to present them are little short of breathtaking." They are "dramatic declaratory judgments holding acts of Congress unconstitutional and purporting to interpret not only Article II Presidential powers but those of the legislators under Article I."

# DOCUMENT 10.7

A July 2006 report by the American Bar Association found that presidential signing statements were "contrary to the rule of law and our constitutional system of separation of powers" (10.6). The resolutions below were included as an addendum to that report and adopted, by voice vote, by the ABA. The ABA recommendations prompted Republican senator Arlen Specter of Pennsylvania to propose the "Presidential Signing Statements Act of 2006," which would have instructed all state and federal courts to deny any source of authority to presidential signing statements. It never passed the Senate judiciary committee, of which Specter was the chair. Opponents believed the measure was too strong, and they were confident that the president would always enforce the law correctly. Proponents argued that signing statements rejecting parts or all of a law amounted to a line-item veto, a practice the Supreme Court had already declared unconstitutional in its 1998 *Clinton v. New York* decision.

---

AMERICAN BAR ASSOCIATION TASK FORCE,
RECOMMENDATION ON PRESIDENTIAL SIGNING STATEMENTS
AND THE SEPARATION OF POWERS DOCTRINE, 2006                | 541

RESOLVED, That the American Bar Association opposes, as contrary to the rule of law and our constitutional system of separation of powers, the issuance of presidential signing statements that claim the authority or state the intention to disregard or decline to enforce all or part of a law the President has signed, or to interpret such a law in a manner inconsistent with the clear intent of Congress;

FURTHER RESOLVED, That the American Bar Association urges the President, if he believes that any provision of a bill pending before Congress would be unconstitutional if enacted, to communicate such concerns to Congress prior to passage;

FURTHER RESOLVED, That the American Bar Association urges the President to confine any signing statements to his views regarding the meaning, purpose and significance of bills presented by Congress, and if he believes that all or part of a bill is unconstitutional, to veto the bill in accordance with Article I, §7 of the Constitution of the United States, which directs him to approve or disapprove each bill in its entirety;

FURTHER RESOLVED, That the American Bar Association urges Congress to enact legislation requiring the President promptly to submit to Congress an official copy of all signing statements he issues, and in any instance in which he claims the authority, or states the intention, to disregard or decline to enforce all or part of a law he has signed, or to interpret such a law in a manner inconsistent with the clear intent of Congress, to submit to Congress a report setting forth in full the reasons and legal basis for the statement; and further requiring 23 that all such submissions be available in a publicly accessible database; and

FURTHER RESOLVED, That the American Bar Association urges Congress to enact legislation enabling the President, Congress, or other entities or individuals, to seek judicial review, to the extent constitutionally permissible, in any instance in which the President claims the authority, or states the intention, to disregard or decline to enforce all or part of a law he has signed, or interprets such a law in a manner inconsistent with the clear intent of Congress, and urges Congress and the President to support a judicial resolution of the President's claim or interpretation.

# DOCUMENT 10.8

This presidential signing statement pertaining to the 2006 Defense Authorization Act stated that the president would implement its provisions only "in a manner consistent with the president's constitutional authority." That language meant that the president reserved the right, against an express congressional order, to decide whether or not to honor the Act's prohibition of "cruel, inhuman, or degrading treatment or punishment of detainees under custody or control of the United States government." More broadly, such signing statements, based on the "unitary executive" theory, claimed not just the right to implement laws according to the president's interpretation of the Constitution, but also the right to reject the actual intent of any law. In the case of the Defense Authorization Act, President Bush indicated that the Congress could not mandate that the executive consult with Congress on defense matters.

GEORGE W. BUSH, STATEMENT ON H.R. 1815,
"NATIONAL DEFENSE AUTHORIZATION ACT
FOR FISCAL YEAR 2006," JANUARY 6, 2006

Today, I have signed into law H.R. 1815, the "National Defense Authorization Act for Fiscal Year 2006." The Act authorizes funding for the defense of the United States and its interests abroad, for military construction, and for national security–related energy programs.

Several provisions of the Act, including sections 352, 360, 403, 562, 818, and 2822, call for executive branch officials to submit to the Congress proposals for legislation, including budget proposals for enactment of appropriations, or purport to regulate or require disclosure of the manner in which the president formulates recommendations to the Congress for legislation.

The executive branch shall implement these provisions in a manner consistent with the president's constitutional authority to supervise the unitary executive branch and to recommend for the consideration of the Congress such measures as the president judges necessary and expedient. Also, the executive branch shall construe section 1206(d) of the Act, which purports to regulate formulation by executive branch officials of proposed programs for the president to direct, in a manner consistent with the president's constitutional authority to supervise the unitary executive branch and to require the opinions of heads of executive departments. In addition, the executive branch shall construe section 1513(d) of the Act, which purports to make consultation with specified members of Congress a precondition to the execution of the law, as calling for but not mandating such consultation, as is consistent with the Constitution's provisions concerning the separate powers of the Congress to legislate and the president to execute the laws.

A number of provisions of the Act, including sections 905, 932, 1004, 1212, 1224, 1227, and 1304, call for the executive branch to furnish information to the Congress on various subjects. The executive branch shall construe such provisions in a manner consistent with the president's constitutional authority to withhold information the disclosure of which could impair foreign relations, national security, the deliberative processes of the Executive, or the performance of the Executive's constitutional duties.

# DOCUMENT 10.9

Until 2001, National Security Letters were used mainly by the FBI in investigations of credit and financial institutions. Section 505 of the 2001 USA Patriot Act expanded and broadened their use in the "war on terror." The letters required particular entities or organizations to turn over to the government various records and data pertaining to individuals. A contentious aspect of the letters was that they were issued without judicial oversight or approval. Equally troublesome was the fact that recipients and targets were prohibited, under threat of criminal prosecution, from revealing that they had received a letter or disclosing its contents to family, friends, or agents. The wide surveillance net cast, the lack of judicial oversight, and the silencing provisions of the letters put severe stress on civil liberties by preventing recipients from consulting with lawyers, hiding the scope of government surveillance from public scrutiny, and outlawing resistance to government abuses.

---

FEDERAL BUREAU OF INVESTIGATION, SAMPLE NATIONAL SECURITY LETTER, DECLASSIFIED ON AUGUST 3, 2004

Dear [Mr/Mrs] [LAST NAME]

Under the authority of Executive Order 12333, dated December 4, 1981, and pursuant to Title 18, United States Code (US.C), Section 2709 (as amended, October 26, 2001), you are hereby directed to provide the Federal Bureau of Investigation. [REDACTED PORTION]

In accordance with Title 18, U.S.C., Section 2709 (b), I certify that the information sought is relevant to an authorized investigation to protect against international terrorism of clandestine intelligence activities, and that such an investigation of a United States person is not conducted solely on the basis of activities protected by the first amendment of the Constitution of the United States.

You are further advised that Title 18, U.S.C, Section 2709 (c), prohibits any officer, employee or agent of yours from disclosing to any person that the FBI has sought or obtained access to information or records under these provisions. [REDACTED PORTION]

# DOCUMENT 10.10

The Inspector General of the Justice Department prepared an audit in 2007 of the Terrorist Screening Center (the FBI-administered organization, an outgrowth of Homeland Security, which consolidated terrorist watch-list information in the United States). The audit indicated that there were close to a million names in the center's database. The list, which was growing by an average of more than twenty thousand records per month, was rife with mistakes. Many innocent people, including Nelson Mandela—the antiapartheid leader, former president of South Africa, and Nobel Peace Prize recipient—were on the list, while many known terrorists were not. The secret screening program created tremendous opportunities for abuse and the arbitrary exercise of power and represented the kind of grave threat to civil liberties that the Constitution and the Bill of Rights were designed to prevent.

U.S. DEPARTMENT OF JUSTICE, OFFICE OF THE INSPECTOR GENERAL, AUDIT DIVISION, "FOLLOW-UP AUDIT OF THE TERRORIST SCREENING CENTER," AUDIT REPORT 07-41, SEPTEMBER 2007 (EXCERPT)

Results in Brief
Overall, this follow-up audit found that the TSC has enhanced its efforts to ensure the quality of watchlist data, has increased staff assigned to data quality management, and has developed a process and a separate office to address complaints filed by persons seeking relief from adverse effects related to terrorist watchlist screening. However, we also determined that the TSC's management of the watchlist continues to have weaknesses. For example, the TSC is relying on two interconnected versions of the watchlist database. As a result of this and other conditions, we identified several known or suspected terrorists who were not watchlisted appropriately.

Specifically, we identified 20 watchlist records on suspected or known terrorists that were not made available to the frontline screening agents (such as a border patrol officer, visa application reviewer, or local police officer) for use during watchlist screening encounters (such as at a border crossing, through the visa application process, or during a routine traffic stop). We also found that the number of duplicate records in the database has significantly increased since our last review. . . .

We also concluded that the TSC needs to further improve its efforts for ensuring the accuracy of the watchlist records. We found that, in general, the TSC's actions to review records as part of a targeted special project successfully ensured the quality of the data. In contrast, our examination of the routine quality assurance reviews revealed continued problems. We examined 105 records subject to the routine quality assurance review and found that 38 percent of the records we tested continued to contain errors or inconsistencies that were not identified through the TSC's quality assurance efforts. Although the TSC had clearly increased its quality assurance efforts since our last review, it continues to lack important safeguards for ensuring data integrity, including a comprehensive protocol outlining the agency's quality assurance procedures and a method for regularly reviewing the work of its staff. Additionally, the TSC needs to work with partner agencies to develop clearly defined areas of responsibility and timeframes for quality assurance matters.

A single omission of a terrorist identity or an inaccuracy in the identifying information contained in a watchlist record can have enormous consequences. Deficiencies in the accuracy of watchlist data increase the possibility that reliable information will not be available to frontline screening agents, which could prevent them from successfully identifying a known or suspected terrorist during an encounter or place their safety at greater risk by providing inappropriate handling instructions for a suspected terrorist.

Furthermore, inaccurate, incomplete, and obsolete watchlist information increases the chances of innocent persons being stopped or detained during an encounter because of being misidentified as a watchlist identity. . . .

Our audit further determined that the TSC was following its procedures and reaching appropriate resolutions in its review of complaints filed by individuals seeking redress from further adverse experiences that they believed were the result of terrorist watchlist screening. However, we found that the redress reviews were not always completed in a timely manner, and we recommend that the TSC and partner agencies develop timeliness measures for each phase in the redress process.

Additionally, the TSC's redress reviews have identified that the database contains records for individuals that should not be watchlisted and that some watchlist records are inaccurate or incomplete. We believe that these results provide a further indicator that watchlist data needs continuous monitoring and attention. We also believe that the TSC should use information related to terrorist watchlist identities that are frequently the subject of watchlist encounters to proactively initiate redress reviews before complaints are filed.

## Summary of Watchlist Nomination, Screening, and Redress Processes

. . . In 2005, the TSC created a process for resolving complaints from individuals who were adversely affected by terrorist watchlist-related screenings and who were seeking relief or "redress." Since the creation of a unit dedicated to processing such complaints in 2005, the TSC Redress Office has received 438 terrorist watchlist-related redress complaints.

## Known or Suspected Terrorists Missing from Watchlist

Our review revealed continued instances where known or suspected terrorists were not appropriately watchlisted on screening databases that frontline screening agents use to identify terrorists and obtain instruction on how to appropriately handle the subjects. Even a single omission of a suspected or known terrorist from the watchlist is a serious matter. We found at least 20 watchlist records that were not appropriately watchlisted to downstream screening databases. These watchlisting errors are discussed in detail below.

Due to technological differences and capabilities of the various systems used in the watchlist process, the TSC maintains two interconnected versions of the TSDB to allow for the electronic import and export of data. Although the TSC is developing an upgraded TSDB to eliminate the need for the two systems, in the meantime TSC officials informed us that these two databases should be identical in content and therefore should contain the same number of records. However, we discovered during our review that these two systems had differing record counts. Specifically, on one day that we tested the databases the difference was 18 records, and on a subsequent day the difference was 38 records. . . .

During the course of our review, we were also informed by TSC officials that in September 2006 they had identified 2,682 records in the TSDB that were not being exported to any screening database. Working with NCTC, the TSC determined that 2,118 of these records should not have been watchlisted in any system and needed to be removed from the TSDB. TSC officials conducted a manual review of the remaining 564 records and determined that 8 had not been appropriately watchlisted and needed to be renominated to the TSDB.

However, despite being responsible for removing outdated or obsolete data from the TSDB, the TSC did not have a process for regularly reviewing the contents of the TSDB to ensure that only appropriate records were included on the watchlist. TSC officials told us that they intend to begin performing a monthly review of the database to identify any records that are being stored in the TSDB that are not being exported to any downstream systems. We believe it is essential that the TSC regularly review the

TSDB to ensure that all outdated information is removed, as well as to affirm that all records are appropriately watchlisted.

# DOCUMENT 10.11

Seven noncommissioned officers serving in Iraq with the 82nd Airborne Division in August 2007 wrote this *New York Times* opinion piece. In it, they protested the war in Iraq, making an insightful analysis of conditions on Iraqi soil while remaining committed to serving their nation. The significance of the piece went beyond its eloquence as an example of reasoned protest by soldiers at war. Two of them, S. Sgt. Yance T. Gray and Sgt. Omar Mora, were killed in service less than one month after the article was published. In October 2, 2007, a resolution was passed in the U.S. House of Representatives honoring their "service and sacrifice" along with that of other U.S. military officers and soldiers who had raised questions about the war. This resolution included a criticism of the radio commentator Rush Limbaugh for his alleged assertion that military critics of the war were "phony soldiers."

---

BUDDHIKA JAYAMAHA, WESLEY D. SMITH, JEREMY ROEBUCK, OMAR MORA, EDWARD SANDMEIER, YANCE T. GRAY, AND JEREMY A. MURPHY, "THE WAR AS WE SAW IT," *NEW YORK TIMES*, AUGUST 19, 2007

Viewed from Iraq at the tail end of a 15-month deployment, the political debate in Washington is indeed surreal. Counterinsurgency is, by definition, a competition between insurgents and counterinsurgents for the control and support of a population. To believe that Americans, with an occupying force that long ago outlived its reluctant welcome, can win over a recalcitrant local population and win this counterinsurgency is far-fetched. As responsible infantrymen and noncommissioned officers with the 82nd Airborne Division soon heading back home, we are skeptical of recent press coverage portraying the conflict as increasingly manageable and feel it has neglected the mounting civil, political and social unrest we see every day. (Obviously, these are our personal views and should not be seen as official within our chain of command.)

The claim that we are increasingly in control of the battlefields in Iraq is an assessment arrived at through a flawed, American-centered framework. Yes, we are militarily superior, but our successes are offset by failures elsewhere. What soldiers call the "battle space" remains the same, with changes only at the margins. It is crowded with actors who do not fit neatly into boxes: Sunni extremists, Al Qaeda terrorists, Shiite militiamen, criminals and armed tribes. This situation is made more complex by the questionable loyalties and Janus-faced role of the Iraqi police and Iraqi Army, which have been trained and armed at United States taxpayers' expense.

A few nights ago, for example, we witnessed the death of one American soldier and the critical wounding of two others when a lethal armor-piercing explosive was detonated between an Iraqi Army checkpoint and a police one. Local Iraqis readily testified to American investigators that Iraqi police and Army officers escorted the triggermen and helped plant the bomb. These civilians highlighted their own predicament: had they informed the Americans of the bomb before the incident, the Iraqi Army, the police or the local Shiite militia would have killed their families.

As many grunts will tell you, this is a near-routine event. Reports that a majority of Iraqi Army commanders are now reliable partners can be considered only misleading rhetoric. The truth is that battalion commanders, even if well meaning, have little to no influence over the thousands of obstinate men under them, in an incoherent chain of command, who are really loyal only to their militias.

Similarly, Sunnis, who have been underrepresented in the new Iraqi armed forces, now find themselves forming militias, sometimes with our tacit support. Sunnis recognize that the best guarantee they may have against Shiite militias and the Shiite-dominated government is to form their own armed bands. We arm them to aid in our fight against Al Qaeda.

However, while creating proxies is essential in winning a counterinsurgency, it requires that the proxies are loyal to the center that we claim to support. Armed Sunni tribes have indeed become effective surrogates, but the enduring question is where their loyalties would lie in our absence. The Iraqi government finds itself working at cross purposes with us on this issue because it is justifiably fearful that Sunni militias will turn on it should the Americans leave.

In short, we operate in a bewildering context of determined enemies and questionable allies, one where the balance of forces on the ground remains entirely unclear. (In the course of writing this article, this fact became all too clear: one of us, Staff Sergeant Murphy, an Army Ranger and reconnaissance team leader, was shot in the head during a "time-sensitive target acquisition mission" on Aug. 12; he is expected to survive and is being flown to a military hospital in the United States.) While we have the will and the resources to fight in this context, we are effectively hamstrung because realities on the ground require measures we will always refuse—namely, the widespread use of lethal and brutal force.

Given the situation, it is important not to assess security from an American-centered perspective. The ability of, say, American observers to safely walk down the streets of formerly violent towns is not a resounding indicator of security. What matters is the experience of the local citizenry and the future of our counterinsurgency. When we take this view, we see that a vast majority of Iraqis feel increasingly insecure and view us as an occupation force that has failed to produce normalcy after four years and is increasingly unlikely to do so as we continue to arm each warring side.

Coupling our military strategy to an insistence that the Iraqis meet political benchmarks for reconciliation is also unhelpful. The morass in the government has fueled impatience and confusion while providing no semblance of security to average Iraqis. Leaders are far from arriving at a lasting political settlement. This should not be surprising, since a lasting political solution will not be possible while the military situation remains in constant flux.

The Iraqi government is run by the main coalition partners of the Shiite-dominated United Iraqi Alliance, with Kurds as minority members. The Shiite clerical establishment formed the alliance to make sure its people did not succumb to the same mistake as in 1920: rebelling against the occupying Western force (then the British) and losing what they believed was their inherent right to rule Iraq as the majority. The qualified and reluctant welcome we received from the Shiites since the invasion has to be seen in that historical context. They saw in us something useful for the moment.

Now that moment is passing, as the Shiites have achieved what they believe is rightfully theirs. Their next task is to figure out how best to consolidate the gains, because reconciliation without consolidation risks losing it all. Washington's insistence that the Iraqis correct the three gravest mistakes we made—de-Baathification, the dismantling of the Iraqi Army and the creation of a loose federalist system of government—places us at cross purposes with the government we have committed to support.

Political reconciliation in Iraq will occur, but not at our insistence or in ways that meet our benchmarks. It will happen on Iraqi terms when the reality on the battlefield is congruent with that in the political sphere. There will be no magnanimous solutions that please every party the way we expect, and there will be winners and losers. The choice we have left is to decide which side we will take. Trying to please every party in the conflict —as we do now—will only ensure we are hated by all in the long run.

At the same time, the most important front in the counterinsurgency, improving basic social and economic conditions, is the one on which we have failed most miserably. Two million Iraqis are in refugee camps in bordering countries. Close to two million more are internally displaced and now fill many urban slums. Cities lack regular electricity, telephone services and sanitation. "Lucky" Iraqis live in gated communities barricaded with concrete blast walls that provide them with a sense of communal claustrophobia rather than any sense of security we would consider normal.

In a lawless environment where men with guns rule the streets, engaging in the banalities of life has become a death-defying act. Four years into our occupation, we have failed on every promise, while we have substituted

Baath Party tyranny with a tyranny of Islamist, militia and criminal violence. When the primary preoccupation of average Iraqis is when and how
they are likely to be killed, we can hardly feel smug as we hand out care
packages. As an Iraqi man told us a few days ago with deep resignation,
"We need security, not free food."

In the end, we need to recognize that our presence may have released
Iraqis from the grip of a tyrant, but that it has also robbed them of their self-
respect. They will soon realize that the best way to regain dignity is to call
us what we are—an army of occupation—and force our withdrawal.

Until that happens, it would be prudent for us to increasingly let Iraqis
take center stage in all matters, to come up with a nuanced policy in which
we assist them from the margins but let them resolve their differences as
they see fit. This suggestion is not meant to be defeatist, but rather to highlight our pursuit of incompatible policies to absurd ends without recognizing the incongruities.

We need not talk about our morale. As committed soldiers, we will see
this mission through.

[Buddhika Jayamaha is an Army specialist. Wesley D. Smith is a sergeant.
Jeremy Roebuck is a sergeant. Omar Mora is a sergeant. Edward Sandmeier is a sergeant. Yance T. Gray is a staff sergeant. Jeremy A. Murphy is
a staff sergeant.]

# DOCUMENT 10.12

In this long editorial statement, the *New York Times* admitted to serious and
harmful errors in its reporting of the war in Iraq. It did not name reporter Judith
Miller, but she had a hand in four of the six news reports—often front-page
articles—that the *Times* acknowledged had been particularly egregious in their
inaccuracy. The *Times*'s mea culpa was notable in its recognition that the mistakes made went far beyond those committed by a particular reporter. The
newspaper admitted that the problematic articles "depended at least in part
on information from a circle of Iraqi informants, defectors and exiles bent on
'regime change' in Iraq." The *Times* was not the only news organization that
failed to investigate or challenge the claims made by the administration or
by Iraqi exiles. Many others uncritically accepted "misinformation from exile
sources" or unsubstantiated assertions by the Bush administration. The *Times*
was the only news organization to apologize, however, and to create a mechanism, the new post of public editor, to reduce the possibility of a recurrence.

## "FROM THE EDITORS: *THE TIMES* AND IRAQ," MAY 26, 2004

Over the last year this newspaper has shone the bright light of hindsight on decisions that led the United States into Iraq. We have examined the failings of American and allied intelligence, especially on the issue of Iraq's weapons and possible Iraqi connections to international terrorists. We have studied the allegations of official gullibility and hype. It is past time we turned the same light on ourselves.

In doing so—reviewing hundreds of articles written during the prelude to war and into the early stages of the occupation—we found an enormous amount of journalism that we are proud of. In most cases, what we reported was an accurate reflection of the state of our knowledge at the time, much of it painstakingly extracted from intelligence agencies that were themselves dependent on sketchy information. And where those articles included incomplete information or pointed in a wrong direction, they were later overtaken by more and stronger information. That is how news coverage normally unfolds.

But we have found a number of instances of coverage that was not as rigorous as it should have been. In some cases, information that was controversial then, and seems questionable now, was insufficiently qualified or allowed to stand unchallenged. Looking back, we wish we had been more aggressive in re-examining the claims as new evidence emerged—or failed to emerge.

The problematic articles varied in authorship and subject matter, but many shared a common feature. They depended at least in part on information from a circle of Iraqi informants, defectors and exiles bent on "regime change" in Iraq, people whose credibility has come under increasing public debate in recent weeks. (The most prominent of the anti-Saddam campaigners, Ahmed Chalabi, has been named as an occasional source in *Times* articles since at least 1991, and has introduced reporters to other exiles. He became a favorite of hard-liners within the Bush administration and a paid broker of information from Iraqi exiles, until his payments were cut off last week.) Complicating matters for journalists, the accounts of these exiles were often eagerly confirmed by United States officials convinced of the need to intervene in Iraq. Administration officials now acknowledge that they sometimes fell for misinformation from these exile sources. So did many news organizations—in particular, this one.

Some critics of our coverage during that time have focused blame on individual reporters. Our examination, however, indicates that the problem was more complicated. Editors at several levels who should have been challenging reporters and pressing for more skepticism were perhaps too intent on rushing scoops into the paper. Accounts of Iraqi defectors were not always weighed against their strong desire to have Saddam Hussein ousted. Articles based on dire claims about Iraq tended to get prominent display, while follow-up articles that called the original ones into question were sometimes buried. In some cases, there was no follow-up at all.

On Oct. 26 and Nov. 8, 2001, for example, Page 1 articles cited Iraqi defectors who described a secret Iraqi camp where Islamic terrorists were trained and biological weapons produced. These accounts have never been independently verified.

On Dec. 20, 2001, another front-page article began, "An Iraqi defector who described himself as a civil engineer said he personally worked on renovations of secret facilities for biological, chemical and nuclear weapons in underground wells, private villas and under the Saddam Hussein Hospital in Baghdad as recently as a year ago." Knight Ridder Newspapers reported last week that American officials took that defector—his name is Adnan Ihsan Saeed al-Haideri—to Iraq earlier this year to point out the sites where he claimed to have worked, and that the officials failed to find evidence of their use for weapons programs. It is still possible that chemical or biological weapons will be unearthed in Iraq, but in this case it looks as if we, along with the administration, were taken in. And until now we have not reported that to our readers.

On Sept. 8, 2002, the lead article of the paper was headlined "U.S. Says Hussein Intensified Quest for A-Bomb Parts." That report concerned the aluminum tubes that the administration advertised insistently as components for the manufacture of nuclear weapons fuel. The claim came not from defectors but from the best American intelligence sources available at the time. Still, it should have been presented more cautiously. There were hints that the usefulness of the tubes in making nuclear fuel was not a sure thing, but the hints were buried deep, 1,700 words into a 3,600-word article. Administration officials were allowed to hold forth at length on why this evidence of Iraq's nuclear intentions demanded that Saddam Hussein be dislodged from power: "The first sign of a 'smoking gun,' they argue, may be a mushroom cloud."

Five days later, the *Times* reporters learned that the tubes were in fact a subject of debate among intelligence agencies. The misgivings appeared deep in an article on Page A13, under a headline that gave no inkling that we were revising our earlier view ("White House Lists Iraq Steps to Build Banned Weapons"). The *Times* gave voice to skeptics of the tubes on Jan. 9, when the key piece of evidence was challenged by the International Atomic Energy Agency. That challenge was reported on Page A10; it might well have belonged on Page A1.

On April 21, 2003, as American weapons-hunters followed American troops into Iraq, another front-page article declared, "Illicit Arms Kept Till Eve of War, an Iraqi Scientist Is Said to Assert." It began this way: "A scientist who claims to have worked in Iraq's chemical weapons program for more than a decade has told an American military team that Iraq destroyed chemical weapons and biological warfare equipment only days before the war began, members of the team said."

The informant also claimed that Iraq had sent unconventional weapons to Syria and had been cooperating with Al Qaeda—two claims that were then, and remain, highly controversial. But the tone of the article suggested that this Iraqi "scientist"—who in a later article described himself as an official of military intelligence—had provided the justification the Americans had been seeking for the invasion.

The *Times* never followed up on the veracity of this source or the attempts to verify his claims. . . . We consider the story of Iraq's weapons, and of the pattern of misinformation, to be unfinished business. And we fully intend to continue aggressive reporting aimed at setting the record straight.

# DOCUMENT 10.13

The Senate Judiciary Committee, chaired by then-Republican senator Arlen Specter of Pennsylvania, questioned Attorney General Alberto Gonzales in a 2006 hearing, held in response to Bush administration actions and claims that it could defy any law that conflicted with its interpretation of the executive's constitutional power. In some cases, the Bush administration claimed justification for exempting itself from existing laws because of the president's role as head of the executive branch and as commander-in-chief. The Bush administration exercised this right mostly through "signing statements" that created guidelines for how the executive would implement the law. It rarely used the veto power. In other cases, as in the National Security Agency's surveillance program, the administration simply interpreted legislation in a way that would not "infringe upon the president's constitutional authority." The questioning in this hearing centered on critical constitutional issues: why the administration could not make use of the existing FISA process to pursue antiterrorist surveillance needs, whether the administration had begun the NSA program before the passage of the Patriot Act, why the administration did not pursue changes in the FISA law if it found the law inadequate, whether wiretaps were placed on purely domestic calls, and whether there had been any abuses or mistakes in implementing the NSA program. Attorney General Gonzales refused to answer most of these questions, claiming that they entered into "operational" areas that were subject to national security protection. Democratic senator Dianne Feinstein of California opened an important line of questioning about the theory of the "unitary executive," which seemed to elevate presidential authority above Congress and the courts. Democratic senator Richard Durbin of Illinois and Republican senator Lindsey Graham of South Carolina asked whether the claim of inherent executive power gave the executive a blank check to ignore whatever law it pleased, while Democratic senators Patrick Leahy of Vermont and Charles Schumer of New York brought their criticisms to bear on specific instances of executive overreach.

U.S. SENATE JUDICIARY COMMITTEE, HEARING ON
WARTIME EXECUTIVE POWER AND THE NATIONAL
SECURITY AGENCY'S SURVEILLANCE AUTHORITY,
FEBRUARY 6, 2006 (EXCERPT)

FEINSTEIN: Thanks very much, Mr. Chairman.

I'd like to make clear that, for me, at least, this hearing isn't about whether our nation should aggressively combat terrorism; I think we all agree on that. And it's not about whether we should use sophisticated electronic surveillance to learn about terrorist plans and intentions and capabilities; we all agree on that. And it's not about whether we should use those techniques inside the United States to guard against attacks; we all agree on that. But this administration is effectively saying, and the attorney general has said it today, it doesn't have to follow the law. And this, Mr. Attorney General, I believe, is a very slippery slope. It's fraught with consequences.

The Intelligence Committees have not been briefed on the scope and nature of the program. They have not been able to explore what is a link or an affiliate to Al Qaida or what minimization procedures are in place. We know nothing about the program other than what we read in the newspapers. . . .

554 | FEINSTEIN: You have advanced what I think is a radical legal theory here today. The theory compels the conclusion that the president's power to defend the nation is unchecked by law, that he acts alone and according to his own discretion, and that the Congress's role, at best, is advisory.

FEINSTEIN: You say that the authorization for use of military force allows the president to circumvent the Foreign Intelligence Surveillance Act and that if the AUMF [*Editors' Note: Authorization for the Use of Military Force*] doesn't, then the Constitution does. Senator Daschle has testified that when he was majority leader, the administration came to him shortly before the AUMF came to the floor and asked that the words "inside the United States" be added to the authorization, and that he said, "Absolutely not," and it was withdrawn.

The question I have is how do you interpret congressional intent from the passage of the AUMF that it gave the administration the authority to order electronic surveillance of Americans in contravention to the FISA law?

GONZALES: Senator, it is not in contravention of the FISA law. We believe the authorization to use military force is the kind of congressional action that the FISA law anticipated. It has never been our position that somehow the AUMF amended FISA. It's never been our position that somehow FISA has been overridden. Quite the contrary: We believe that the president's authorizations are fully consistent with the provisions of FISA. . . .

FEINSTEIN: Senator Kennedy asked you about first-class mail, has it been opened, and you declined answering. Let me ask this way: Has any other secret order or directive been issued by the president or any other senior administration official which authorizes conduct which would otherwise be prohibited by law? Yes or no will do. . . .

GONZALES: Senator, I am not comfortable going down the road of saying yes or no as to what the president has or has not authorized. I'm here to . . .

GRAHAM: Now, to the inherent authority argument, taken to its logical conclusion, it concerns me that it could basically neuter the Congress and weaken the courts. And I'd like to focus a minute on the inherent authority of the president during a time of war concept.

I'll give you a hypothetical and you can answer it if you choose to. And I understand if you won't. There's a detainee in our charge, an enemy prisoner, a high-value target. We reasonably believe that this person possesses information that could save millions or thousands of American lives.

The president, as commander in chief, tells the military authorities in charge, "You have my permission, my authority, I'm ordering you to do all things necessary and these five things, I'm authorizing. Do it because I'm commander in chief and we've got to protect the country."

There's a preexisting statute on the book, passed by the Congress, called the Uniform Code of Military Justice and it tells our troops that, "If you have a prisoner in your charge, you're not to do these things," and they are the same five things. What do we do?

GONZALES: Well, of course, Senator, the president has already said that we're not going to engage in torture.

That is a categorical statement by the president. As to whether or not the statute that you referred to would be constitutional, these kinds of questions are very, very difficult. One could make the argument, for example, that the provision in the Constitution that talks about Congress under Section 8 of Article I, giving Congress the specific authority to make rules regarding captures, that that would give Congress the authority to legislate in this area.

This is really a big deal for the people fighting the war. And if you take your inherent authority argument too far, then I am really concerned that there is no check and balance.

GRAHAM: And when the nation's at war, I would argue, Mr. Attorney General, you need checks and balances more than ever, because within the law we put a whole group of people in jail who just looked like the enemy.

GONZALES: Senator, if I could just respond. I'm not—maybe I haven't been as precise with my words as I might have been. . . .

GRAHAM: I don't think I've talked about inherent exclusive authority. I talked inherent authority under the Constitution and the commander in chief. Congress, of course, and I've said in response to other questions, they have a constitutional role to play also during a time of war. . . .

The FISA statute said, basically, "This is the exclusive means to conduct foreign surveillance where American citizens are involved." And the Congress, seems to me, gave you a one-lane highway, not a two-lane highway. They took the inherent authority argument, they thought about it, they debated it, and they passed a statute—if you look at the legislative language—saying, "This shall be the exclusive means." And it's different than 1401.

So I guess what I'm saying, Mr. Attorney General, if I buy your argument about FISA, I can't think of a reason you wouldn't have the ability if you chose to set aside the statute on torture if you believed it impeded the war effort.

GONZALES: Well, Senator, whether or not we set aside a statute, of course . . .

GRAHAM: But inherent authority sets aside the statute.

GONZALES: That's what we're talking about here. We don't need to get to that tough question.

GRAHAM: If you don't buy the force resolution argument, if we somehow magically took that off the table, that's all you're left with is the inherent authority. And Congress could tomorrow change that resolution, and that's dangerous for the country if we get in a political fight over that. All I'm saying is that the inherent authority argument, in its application, to me, seems to have no boundaries when it comes to executive decisions in a time of war. It deals the Congress out, it deals the courts out. And, Mr. Attorney General, there is a better way. And on our next round of questioning we will talk about that better way.

GONZALES: Can I simply make one quick response?

SPECTER: You may respond, Attorney General.

GONZALES: Well, the fact that the president, again, may have inherent authority doesn't mean that Congress has no authority in a particular area. And when we look at the words of the Constitution, and there are clear grants of authority to the Congress in a time of war. . . .

DURBIN: And so I have to ask you point-blank, as Senator Feingold asked you earlier. You knew when you answered my question that this administration had decided that it was going to basically find a way around the FISA law, based on the president's, as you called it, inherent constitutional powers. So how can your response be valid today in light of what we now know?

GONZALES: Oh, it's absolutely valid, Senator. And this is going to sound repetitious, but it has never been our position that we are circumventing or ignoring FISA. Quite the contrary, the president has authorized activities that are totally consistent with FISA, with what FISA contemplates. I have indicated that I believe that, putting aside the question of the authorization to use military force, that, while it's a tough legal question as to whether or not Congress has the authority under the Constitution to cabin or to limit the president's constitutional authority to engage in electronic surveillance of the enemy, that is not a question that we even need to get to. It has always been our position that FISA

556 |

can be and must be read in a way that it doesn't infringe upon the president's constitutional authority. . . .

DURBIN: But I'll tell you something else, Mr. Attorney General. If you then read, I think, the fine reasoning of Justice O'Connor, she comes to a point which brings us here today. And I thank the chairman for allowing us to be here today. And this is what she says, in the course of this decision: "It is during our most challenging and uncertain moments that our nation's commitment to due process is most severely tested and it is in those times that we must preserve our commitment at home to the principles for which we fight abroad."

We have said repeatedly, as nominees for the Supreme Court have come here, "Do you accept the basis of Hamdi that a war is not a blank check for a president?" They have said, "Yes; that's consistent with Johnson and Youngstown." And now, what we hear from you is that you are going to take this decision in Hamdi and build it into a way to avoid the most basic statute when it comes to electronic surveillance in America, a statute which describes itself as the exclusive means by which this government can legally do this. . . .

LEAHY: We're asking for a legal analysis. I mean, obviously you had to make a determination that you had the right to do this. When did you make the determination that AUMF gave you the right to do this?

GONZALES: From the very outset, before the program actually commenced, it has always been the position that FISA cannot be interpreted in a way that infringes upon the president's constitutional authority, that FISA must be interpreted, can be interpreted in a way . . .

LEAHY: Did you tell anybody that when you were up here seeking the Patriot Act and seeking the changes in FISA?

Did you tell anybody you had already determined—it was your testimony here today that you made the determination, virtually immediately —that you had this power without using FISA? . . .

GONZALES: Sir, I don't recall. Did I tell anyone in Congress or tell. . . .

FEINSTEIN: I am puzzled—and I want to go back to why you didn't come for a change in FISA. Let me just read off a few of the changes that we have made to FISA.

We extended the emergency exemption from 24 to 72 hours. We lowered the legal standard for surveillance to the significant purpose test. We allowed for John Doe roving wiretaps. We lowered the standard for FISA pen traps. We expanded their scope to include Internet routing information. We extended the scope of business records that could be sought under FISA. We extended the duration of FISA warrants. We broadened FISA to enable the surveillance of lone wolf terrorists. And we made the director of national intelligence the lead authority.

Now, in view of the changes that we have made, I cannot understand why you didn't come to the committee unless the program was much broader and you believed it would not be authorized. That's the only reason I can figure you didn't come to the committee. Because if the program is as the president has said and you have said, to this date you haven't briefed the Intelligence Committee, you haven't let us ask the question, "What is a link? What is an affiliate? How many people are covered? What are the precise—and I don't believe in the briefings those questions were asked—what are the precise numbers? What happens to the data? How long is it retained in a database? When are innocent people taken out of the database?" And I can only believe—and this is my honest view—that this program is much bigger and much broader than you want anyone to know.

GONZALES: Well, Senator, of course, I cannot talk about aspects here that are beyond what the president has already confirmed. What I can say is that those members of Congress who have received briefings know—I think they know; and, of course, I don't know what they actually know—but they have been briefed on all the details about all of the activities. So they know what's going on. . . .

SCHUMER: OK. Good. Now, here's the next question I have: Has the government done this? Has the government searched someone's home, an American citizen, or office, without a warrant since 9/11, let's say?

GONZALES: To my knowledge, that has not happened under the terrorist surveillance program, and I'm not going to go beyond that.

SCHUMER: I don't know what that—what does that mean, under the terrorist surveillance program? The terrorist surveillance program is about wiretaps. This is about searching someone's home. It's different. So it wouldn't be done under the surveillance program. I'm asking you if it has been done, period.

GONZALES: But now you're asking me questions about operations or possible operations, and I'm not going to get into that, Senator.

SCHUMER: I'm not asking you about any operation. I'm not asking you how many times. I'm not asking you where . . .

GONZALES: That is an operational question, in terms of how we're using capabilities.

SCHUMER: So you won't answer whether it is allowed and you won't answer whether it's been done. I mean, isn't part of your—in all due respect, as somebody who genuinely likes you, but isn't this part of your job, to answer a question like this?

GONZALES: Of course it is, Senator.

SCHUMER: But you're not answering it.

GONZALES: Well, I'm not saying that I will not answer the question. . . .

SCHUMER: OK. All right. Next, different issue.

Now FISA makes public every year the number of applications. In 2004, there were 1,758 applications. Why can't we know how many under this program? Why should one be any more classified than the other?

GONZALES: I don't know whether or not I have a good answer for you, Senator.

SCHUMER: I don't think you do.

GONZALES: The information is classified, and I certainly would not be at liberty to talk about it here in this public forum.

SCHUMER: And I understand this isn't exactly your domain, but I can't even think of a rationale why one should be classified and one should be made routinely public. Both involve wiretaps, both involve terrorism, both involve protecting American security, and we've been doing the FISA one all along. I'm sure if the—well, let me ask you this. If the administration thought that revealing the FISA number would damage security, wouldn't they move to classify it?

GONZALES: I think maybe—of course, now I'm going to give you an answer. Perhaps it has to do with the fact that FISA, of course, is much, much broader. We're talking about enemies beyond Al Qaida. We're talking about domestic surveillance. We're talking about surveillance that may exist in peacetime, not just in wartime. And so perhaps the equities are different in making that information available to Congress. . . .

SCHUMER: When Frank Church was speaking at the hearing that Senator Kennedy, I think, talked about much earlier this morning, he said the NSA's, quote, "capability at any time could be turned around on the American people and no American would have any privacy left—such is the capability to monitor everything: telephone conversations, telegrams, it doesn't matter, there would be no place to hide." Now it's 31 years later and we have even more technology. So the potential that Senator Church mentioned for abuse is greater. So let me ask you these questions. I'm going to ask a few of them so you can answer them together.

Have there been any abuses of the NSA surveillance program? Have there been any investigations arising from concerns about abuse of NSA program? Has there been any disciplinary action taken against any official for abuses of the program?

GONZALES: Senator, I think that . . .

SCHUMER: Because this gets to another thing. This is what we're worried about.

Most of us—I think all of us—want to give the president the power he needs to protect us. I certainly do. But we also want to make sure there are no abuses. And so if there have been some abuses, we ought to know about it. And it might make your case to say, "Yes, we found an abuse or a potential abuse and we snuffed it out." Tell me what the story is.

GONZALES: Well, I do not have answers to all those questions. I'd like to remind people that, of course, even in the area of criminal law enforcement, when you talk about probable cause, sometimes there are mistakes made, as you know.

SCHUMER: No question—no one's perfect.

**GONZALES:** A mistake has to be one that would be made by a reasonable man. And so when you ask, "Have there been abuses?," these are all investigations, disciplinary action . . .

**SCHUMER:** So has there been—yes, this is something you ought to know, if there's been any disciplinary action, because I take it that would be taken . . .

**GONZALES:** Not necessarily. I think the NSA, I think, has a regimen in place where they ensure that people are abiding by agency policies and regulations.

**SCHUMER:** If I asked those two questions about the Justice Department, any investigations arising out of concerns about abuse of NSA surveillance or any disciplinary action taken against official, in either case by the Justice Department, you would know the answer to that.

**GONZALES:** I'd probably know the answer to that. To my knowledge, no. . . .

**GRAHAM:** I want to talk to you exclusively about inherent power and your view of it and the administration's view of it and share some thoughts about my view of it. The signing statement issued by the administration on the McCain language prohibiting cruel, inhumane, and degrading treatment—are you familiar with the administration's signing statement?

**GONZALES:** I am familiar with it, Senator.

**GRAHAM:** What does that mean?

**GONZALES:** The entirety of the statement, Senator?

**GRAHAM:** It was sort of an assertion that the president's inherent authority may allow him to ignore the dictates of the statute. Does it mean that, or did I misunderstand it?

**GONZALES:** Well, of course, it may mean that this president—first of all, no president can waive constitutional authority of the executive branch.

**GRAHAM:** And my question is very simple but very important: Is it the position of the administration that an enactment by Congress prohibiting the cruel, inhumane, and degrading treatment of a detainee intrudes on the inherent power of the president to conduct the war?

**GONZALES:** Senator, I don't know whether or not we have done that specific analysis.

# DOCUMENT 10.14

The intelligence analyst Wayne E. White's testimony was the only official record of a document entitled "Iraq, the Middle East and Change: No Dominoes" issued on February 26, 2003, for internal Bush administration consumption. White had been the deputy director of the State Department's Office of Analysis for the Near East and South Asia in the Bureau of Intelligence and Research. His report warned specifically that it would be nearly impossible to develop liberal democracy in Iraq and the region and that any new democracies would likely be anti-American. After details of the report were leaked to the press in 2003, President Bush publicly rejected its findings, and Newt Gingrich, the Republican former House speaker, called the leaks treasonous. In his 2006 testimony, White pointed to the administration's ideological agenda for reshaping the Middle East and the ways in which it insisted on complete secrecy and dismissed prewar intelligence reporting that did not conform to that agenda.

---

WAYNE E. WHITE, TESTIMONY TO SENATE DEMOCRATIC POLICY COMMITTEE DURING "OVERSIGHT HEARING ON PRE-WAR INTELLIGENCE RELATING TO IRAQ," JUNE 26, 2006

Good Afternoon, Mr. Chairman, Senator Bingaman, Senator Feinstein, and others.

Unlike some others testifying today, I come before this group having had far less involvement in some of the more notorious pre–Iraq War intelligence issues.

Nonetheless, I believe I have some insights worth sharing in the context of this hearing relating to several important areas.

One key point that must be noted concerning pre-war decision-making is not only that it was made by a group of policymakers who often turned a blind eye to intelligence inconsistent with their Middle East agenda. Equally disturbing is that the most senior officials involved—the President, the Vice-President, Defense Secretary Rumsfeld, and then-NSC Director Rice—had relatively little past experience with the complex politics of the Middle East region, let alone Iraq—a MAJOR impediment to sound policymaking if one already does not have an open mind and one is agenda-driven.

Clearly, as is strongly implied above, it is my belief that some officials did intervene in the process of intelligence analysis in order to shape it to serve a regional agenda. The harassment of a friend, Bureau of Intelligence & Research (INR) analyst Christian Westermann, by State Department Undersecretary Bolton was just one example of this broader problem. Mr. Westermann told me back in 2003 that it was his belief that some other intelligence community analysts who denied, at least early on, as having been pressured to produce analysis more supportive of the Administration's agenda were, in fact, almost certainly pressured.

How much difference that made in what was actually produced by these intelligence professionals is another issue. But even at this late date, public admissions that pressure was involved are probably running far behind the full measure of pressure actually applied.

Another example of undue (and damaging) interference was, of course, the creation of Doug Feith's intelligence shop in the Pentagon, almost certainly in an effort to end-run established—and far more professional—intelligence channels. The extent of this operation's overall influence within senior echelons of the Administration also probably is not fully appreciated, even today.

Warning signs also were ignored or belittled. The INR/Energy Department footnote in the Fall 2002 National Intelligence Estimate on Iraq WMD stating that there was little or no evidence that Iraq had an active nuclear weapons program was either ignored or allegedly, repeat allegedly, not read by at least one key decision-maker. To have shoved aside the Energy Department's views, in the face of its well-known technical capabilities with which to assess intercepted Iraqi-bound aluminum tubes, for example, is deeply disturbing and indicative of the atmosphere prevailing in 2002 and early 2003.

My own formal February 2003 INR Analysis "Iraq, the Middle East and Change: No Dominoes" warned that even a successful effort in Iraq, both militarily and politically, would not only fail to trigger a tsunami of democracy in the region, but potentially could endanger longstanding U.S. allies in the Middle East, like Jordan, not the region's anti-U.S. autocrats.

I must add that the conclusions of this study were not all that extraordinary, for decision-makers with open minds, that is. Polling for a number of years and by a variety of polling sources had revealed clearly that the region's populations were (and are) predominantly more anti-American, anti-Israeli, and militantly Islamic than their existing governments.

So, even if democracy had taken hold in various Middle East states, the result would have been governments more anti-American, anti-Israeli and militantly Islamic than those previously in power, as with Hamas in the Palestinian context.

In other states viewed as candidates for democratization, ethno-sectarian strife is either well under way (Iraq) or looming (Lebanon). And, finally, with respect to Egypt, a state initially—and naively—showcased by the Administration as a promising case related to emerging democracy, heavy-handed Egyptian government obstructionism has become a serious impediment.

I should make clear that I have nothing against increased Islamic activism per se, but, to cite just one aspect of the American political agenda around the world, women's rights, Islamist regimes have demonstrated far less interest in this issue than their secular counterparts. To cite another downside, Islamists also often tend to be somewhat more anti-Israeli and anti-American than their secular counterparts.

Something else should be added about my February 2003 assessment. Its existence was almost certainly known to Administration policymakers because, although not the result of any action on my part, its contents were leaked to the *Los Angeles Times* in early March 2003, causing a bit of an embarrassing public stir.

Another issue I should touch upon is that of pre-war preparedness. The Administration consistently denies charges that forces allotted to the Iraqi campaign were insufficient. This is false. I would like to provide just one example I believe not previously aired that strongly suggested to me that resources were stretched terribly thin.

I should digress a bit and explain that until December 2002, my Office Director and our veteran Iraq Analyst in INR's Office of Analysis for the Near East & South Asia dealt with virtually all Iraq-related matters. As Deputy Director, I was asked to concentrate on most other office issues, especially the region more broadly. I was generally aware of what was going on with respect to Iraq, but not, as they say, "in the flow."

Only when the Iraq workload began to overwhelm these two officials was I asked to attend some significant meetings related to Iraq. One was a forum for largely operational political-military issues, with CENTCOM playing the lead role—a perfect fit for a military buff like myself with considerable prior experience in Iraqi affairs.

To my shock, I discovered that CENTCOM was hoping to rely on NGO's (Non-Government Organizations, like the Red Cross) for the treatment of Iraqi military and civilian wounded. In two separate meetings, I reminded CENTCOM officers in no uncertain terms of their responsibilities under the 2nd and 4th Geneva Conventions of 1949 regarding these duties and that NGO's almost never operate on active battlefields in any case.

In retrospect, I cannot bring myself to believe that CENTCOM was thoroughly unaware of its responsibilities under international law, but instead probably was stretched so thin because of the limited U.S. military resources assigned to the Iraq campaign that officers were desperately casting about for ways in which to pass along to others certain basic duties.

As requested, I also will touch upon both intelligence and policy perceptions of the Iraq insurgency in 2003. It was my overall impression that most of those within the Administration and the Intelligence Community initially dismissed the emerging insurgency as being comprised of only so-called "Former Regime Elements," plus some so-called "Foreign Fighters." The thinking was to hunt down and destroy "Former Regime Elements" and close the Syrian border to "Foreign Fighters," destroying those who had already entered the country, after which the insurgency should diminish in strength.

This analysis was one-dimensional and badly flawed. I encountered this line of thinking among virtually all around the table in the first meeting to coordinate what would become three months of deliberations over a National Intelligence Estimate on this issue requested by CENTCOM in July 2003. I argued that the insurgency had deep roots in generic opposition to foreign occupation among a very proud people, broad-based Sunni Arab anger over being disenfranchised, joblessness, lack of public services, and, what I termed "Pissed Off Iraqis," or POI's, for lack of a better term. POI's are people who lost relatives in the war, whose relatives were arrested and taken away to Abu Grhaib and other military holding areas, those imprisoned and released (many of whom were innocent), those whose property had been destroyed or damaged by Coalition action during the war or in

| 563

the course of anti-insurgency operations, etc., etc. In other words, the insurgent recruiting pool was (and is) not only potentially vast, but renewable.

I was pessimistic as early as late April 2003 about our chances for success in Iraq. As a matter of fact, I personally came to believe at that time that our chances for success in Iraq already might have been reduced to little more than 50/50.

That conclusion was grounded on the tremendous impact of the devastation wrought by widespread looting that Coalition forces did virtually nothing to stop—something fairly consistently belittled. The looting utterly devastated Iraq's power grid, government ministries, the educational system, state industries, etc. Simply getting the country back to where it was just before the war would prove, even now in certain sectors, a mission impossible. As a result the supply of so-called "Pissed-Off" Iraqis would be that much more plentiful and continuous.

The Administration continues to claim that the appalling state of Iraq's basic infrastructure is largely the result of 12 years of UN sanctions. In reality, much of what severely damaged Iraq's infrastructure was looting and subsequent, ongoing sabotage on the part of insurgents or criminal elements, direct consequences of the 2003 war, not sanctions.

In addition, few people are aware that when Ambassador Bremer made one of his early 2003 mistakes, the wholesale dismissal of the Iraqi Army, he also effectively demobilized Iraq's border brigades. They were an element of the Iraqi Army. Their absence helped open the door to hordes of "Foreign Fighters."

In closing, let me mention a factor—a major blind-spot of sorts—that bears on so much of what has happened and is happening today. As I have noted, Iraqis are an extraordinarily proud people. They also are very disciplined and tough, sometimes dubbed the "Prussians" of the Arab world by other Arabs.

In the 1991 Gulf War, Iraq was largely a pushover militarily, something played out weekly on the Military and History Channels. But that was only true because the average Iraqi soldier recognized that fighting the U.S., U.K., many European powers, and a vast and truly united global coalition under the aegis of the United Nations was clearly hopeless.

Too many of our military people (and others) took the poor showing of Iraqi soldiers in that war—and the relatively ineffective conventional Iraqi resistance in the 2003 campaign (for similar reasons)—as the true measure of the average Iraqi war-fighter.

What Iraqis are really capable of militarily man per man was demonstrated in the 8-year Iran-Iraq War in which Iraqis largely stood their ground despite horrific losses. They did so because they knew they had a very real chance of winning, and did.

At the very beginning of the 2003 War, British forces were compelled to repeatedly re-take the fairly small, largely Sunni Arab port city of Umm Qasr just over the Kuwaiti border from Iraqis fighting as guerrillas. I knew then and there that we could have a serious problem on our hands.

These first insurgents, fighting out of uniform from windows, behind corners, and on their home turf had discovered that they had a chance to inflict significant damage on a technologically far superior foe. I quickly warned around the first week or 10 days of the war, in a formal INR Assessment, that this spelled danger as we moved farther north, especially into Iraq's Sunni Arab heartland.

Nonetheless, probably because of all that "shock and awe," Umm Qasr (and one or two other problem towns along the way) became the exception. Only in the first months after the end of the conventional campaign did the broader Sunni Arab insurgency begin to take shape and gain momentum.

My warning was accurate, but just a tad premature. . . .

# ★ CHAPTER 11 ★

# THE LIMITS OF PREEMPTION

## THE UNITED STATES IN THE WORLD

THIS BOOK HAS TREATED the invasion of Iraq as a case study of a preemptive war. Any case study is both a particular moment in history and the consequence of a prior set of actions and forces. The Bush administration decided to launch the war, and historians will rightly assess the country's forty-third president in light of his responsibility for that decision. If we are to understand why he chose that particular course of action, we must consider such matters as the influence of neoconservatism, the impact of the terrorist attacks of September 11, 2001, the drive to construct a "unitary executive," the pursuit of oil and international hegemony, and more. At the same time, the policy of any president is powerfully shaped by historical precedents, the structure of the international system, the actions of other states, and a host of other factors that affect the possibilities—and the limits—of action.

Consideration of long-standing patterns in U.S. foreign policy is as important as consideration of those matters that were particular to the Bush administration. While the invasion of Iraq marked a new stage in world politics, it also echoed older forms of imperialism and militarism. Great powers have pursued hegemony throughout history, and the United States was no exception. Indeed, President Bush's invasion of Iraq was not the first "regime change," or even the first preemptive war, launched by the United States. But his administration was unique in proclaiming an official doctrine of preemption that directly challenged the traditions of international politics that had structured the state system since the 1648 Treaty of Westphalia. A crucial element of an explicit drive for global dominance, preemption was also an assault on the core principles of the UN Charter.

With no other superpower to check its ambitions, the Bush administration launched two wars within a year and a half, occupied Iraq, and pursued "full spectrum dominance" both in international affairs and in space.[1] Direct use and routinization of "enhanced interrogation techniques"—torture by another name—was also new, although Washington had trained, encouraged, and financed the use of torture by partner forces in earlier anticommunist wars. And, as is often the case in U.S. history, criticism, protest, and resistance to the war and its methods arose before and during the conflict. Important sectors of U.S. society argued that the policies of the administration betrayed domestic and international values expressed by religious traditions, the Constitution, the Bill of Rights, and international law and institutions. These voices represented the "other tradition" of the United States, one that espoused diplomacy in foreign relations and a "good neighbor policy" toward other countries rather than belligerence and militarism. Nevertheless, the Bush administration remained committed to unilateralism and preemption—particularly with regard to the "war on terror," the war in Iraq, and the methods used to wage them—despite Supreme Court rulings, congressional opposition, public disapproval, and international isolation.

The "other" tradition's powerful commitment to human rights, peaceful | 567
resolution of conflict, justice, and international cooperation has long been central to U.S. history. Critical voices and political dissent have repeatedly arisen to challenge prevailing domestic or foreign policies. With the scourge of slavery came the abolitionists; with foreign wars and interventions came political protest and vibrant antiwar movements. Such debates reflected the complexity and diversity of U.S. society, the conflicting interests of different economic and political sectors, and the complicated history of U.S. democracy. Arguments about the proper role for the United States in the world have raged since the country was born, and they will continue to do so long after the Iraq War has come to an end.

As we have shown, the Bush administration took office with a deep distrust of a law-governed world order. It quickly withdrew from several important treaties and claimed the exclusive right to launch attacks or wage wars as it saw fit, without UN authorization. After September 11, it moved secretly to lift many lawful restraints governing the CIA and the military. Administration lawyers, political appointees who shared Bush and Cheney's ideas of expansive executive power, bypassed normal governmental procedures and rejected two centuries of constitutional and international law by seeking to legalize torture and brutality. Nevertheless, despite—or because

---

1. The Defense Department includes the military control of space as part of full spectrum dominance in "Joint Vision 2020."

of—such methods, terrorism seemed to be growing. In 2006 a National Intelligence Estimate leaked to the press suggested that the war in Iraq was fueling, not weakening, Islamic radicalism.[2] The U.S. public was subject to sharp reversals of civil liberties as well, as the administration secretly authorized new surveillance programs and data-mining operations, ignored laws passed by Congress by using presidential "signing statements" and secret legal opinions, and claimed executive power beyond all previous limits.

Any country's history is marked by a struggle between different impulses. From time to time the outcomes of such struggles shape the future in powerful ways. The Iraq War represented such a historical moment. The administration spoke as if U.S. history had led inevitably to its positions and policies, but the problematic character of its claims was not lost on serious observers. Alongside its record of military intervention over the years, the United States had also played a key role in forming the United Nations and establishing many of the international system's most important institutions and covenants. The intensifying debate about the Bush administration's preemptive invasion and occupation of Iraq exposed the fault lines of U.S. history and its dual traditions with striking clarity.

## SEEING HISTORICAL PATTERNS

The founders of the United States wanted the young country to represent a set of revolutionary new ideals: the right of a people to rebel against tyranny, a concept of rights as universal and self-evident, a break with the class conflicts and oppression of Europe, and a social contract offering opportunity, equality, and freedom. Fresh from resisting King George's authoritarian rule, they feared the formation of new concentrations of political, economic, or military power domestically, and structured the new government to prevent them. Soon after the Constitution was prepared, Benjamin Franklin famously cautioned his fellow citizens that the United States would be "a republic, if you can keep it." Most rights and freedoms were limited to white male property owners at first, but excluded groups would later use those concepts and ideals to claim their own democratic rights in a process that deepened U.S. democracy.

In one of the ironic twists of U.S. history, important periods of democratic progress at home occurred while the government was moving to extend U.S. influence, power, and commercial interests abroad, often through intervention. This was especially the case in U.S. relations with Latin America, where Washington first exercised an expansionist role in pursuit of its economic, military, and political interests. Important U.S. leaders argued

---

2. "Intelligence Report Finds War Increasing Terrorist Threat," *PBS Online NewsHour,* September 25, 2006.

that domestic security and prosperity required the spread of private enterprise and unobstructed access to raw materials and markets around the world. These long-term policy goals predated the Cold War and persisted in the twenty-first century.

The dual traditions in U.S. foreign and domestic policy were apparent almost from the birth of the new nation. With the Monroe Doctrine of 1823, Washington asserted the right of the United States to its own sphere of influence in Latin America and warned away possible European competitors. In the mid-nineteenth century, the Polk administration, under the banner of Manifest Destiny, seized half of Mexico's territory. Yet Abraham Lincoln and Henry David Thoreau were leading voices opposing the war with Mexico, and in 1848 Congress went so far as to censure Polk for starting an unconstitutional war. After the nation had settled the matter of slavery with the Civil War, the tensions between democracy and empire resurfaced. By the end of the century, industrialization was intensifying tendencies that had been present for decades. Political and cultural assumptions of U.S. superiority, as expressed in Manifest Destiny, also played a role. The 1898 Spanish-American War marked the first time that the United States acquired colonial possessions:, Puerto Rico, the Philippines, and Guam; Cuba became a quasi-colony. But prominent critics, including Mark Twain and Jane Addams—both of whom later served as vice presidents of the national Anti-Imperialist League—deplored the emergence of the United States as a colonial power. Even William Graham Sumner, a leading Social Darwinist of the period, warned that democracy and empire were incompatible.[3]

These arguments, which echoed disputes as old as the Roman Republic and Empire, were never resolved. Under the so-called 1904 Roosevelt corollary, the Monroe Doctrine was reconfigured to justify an expanding array of U.S. interests and to claim permanent "international police power" in Latin America. Theodore Roosevelt proclaimed that, in order to safeguard Latin America's welfare, the United States had the right to intervene in the region in cases of "chronic wrongdoing" or "impotence." In a formulation that may sound familiar to contemporary readers, the president argued that U.S. police power and virtual trusteeship of the hemisphere served the interests of humanity at large. With the democratic upsurge that accompanied the New Deal, a significant change came with Franklin Delano Roosevelt's Good Neighbor Policy of hemispheric nonintervention in 1933. The push and pull of the two traditions continued.

| 569

---

3. For important studies of the tension between democracy and empire see, among others, the three books by Chalmers Johnson: *Blowback: The Causes and Consequences of American Empire* (New York: Henry Holt, 2000); *The Sorrows of Empire: Militarism, Secrecy, and the End of the Republic* (New York: Holt, 2004); and *Nemesis: The Last Days of the American Republic* (New York: Holt, 2008); in addition to Brian Loveman, ed., *Strategy for Empire: U.S. Regional Security Policy in the Post–Cold War Era* (Lanham, MD: Rowman & Littlefield, 2004).

After World War II, with Europe in ruins and a Cold War taking shape, officials in Washington began to redefine U.S. interests as global, and not simply regional, in scope. An intensifying conflict with the Soviet Union led to calls for new forms of warfare, including covert operations and counterinsurgency. The clash between opposing visions of the U.S. role in the world became even more pronounced and, with the advent of nuclear weapons, even more consequential.

## CONTAINMENT VERSUS ROLLBACK: CONFLICTING VISIONS OF AMERICA'S GLOBAL ROLE

As the Cold War grew more volatile during the 1950s, a debate pitted officials espousing George Kennan's policy of "containment" against Secretary of State John Foster Dulles's more aggressive desire to "roll back" socialist or nationalist governments. Containment implied constraining the USSR from its perceived expansionism, with the hope of inducing fundamental changes in its behavior, weakening it internally, and denying it strategic possibilities. Containment included a variety of policies, such as arms-control agreements, nuclear-deterrence strategies, anti-Soviet alliances like NATO, and a number of other treaties. Containment implied recognition of existing states and was part of a general attempt to avoid direct confrontation with Moscow. But "rollback" was a much more offensive and belligerent strategy, with proactive measures to undermine nationalist, neutralist, and revolutionary forces and overthrow regimes that seemed to challenge U.S. interests even outside the Soviet sphere of influence, whether or not they posed a military threat. As Washington debated in 2001 and 2002 whether to contain or overthrow Saddam Hussein's regime, George W. Bush's doctrine of preemption implicitly drew upon earlier theories of rollback.

570 |

Both rollback and preemption employed alarmist language warning of imminent threats and implacable enemies. International treaties and organizations were judged ineffectual and untrustworthy, and reliance was placed on U.S. military power and the willingness to use it. This approach was summed up in a particularly stark fashion in Paul Nitze's famous National Security Council Paper No. 68, a 1950 document that warned of permanent hostility and the possibility of direct confrontation with the USSR in a battle for world hegemony. NSC-68 played a key role in creating the Cold War climate. It also anticipated many of the arguments that the Project for the New American Century, and later the Bush administration, would deploy to raise public support for a preemptive invasion of Iraq. Picturing a world of permanent danger and mortal threat, NSC-68 described the Cold War as a global clash of unlimited scope and magnitude between the virtuous United States and a menacing enemy "animated by a new fanatic faith, antithetical to our own, and seek[ing] to impose its absolute authority on the rest of the world."

Cold War strategy documents also made clear that Washington sought to preserve access to the world's raw materials and other resources and secure capitalist investment worldwide, as well as to promote U.S.-style liberal democracies where possible. But anticommunism often overrode a verbal commitment to democracy. If Washington saw a threat from nationalist or revolutionary governments, it often sided with brutal and repressive anticommunist allies.

The Cold War era was more than the confrontation between the United States and the Soviet Union, however. It was also a time of rising nationalism and anti-colonialism in the developing world. Nationalists sought to end their countries' dependent status, control their own national resources, limit the influence of major powers and foreign corporations, and determine their own political futures. For policymakers in Washington, such aspirations often seemed to challenge U.S. interests. Even regimes that could best be described as nationalist in orientation were viewed through a Cold War prism and portrayed as threats to economic liberty or as Soviet surrogates. As we have seen, such arguments helped create the conditions for the 1953 CIA-led overthrow of Prime Minister Mohammed Mossadegh in Iran, who had nationalized his country's oil. That coup had dramatic effects on decades of Persian Gulf history, directly contributing to the 1979 Iranian revolution against Shah Reza Pahlavi. The "modernizing" and brutal shah, installed by the West in 1953, had not objected when U.S. companies gained control of some 60 percent of Iran's oil after Mossadegh's ouster. Washington did something similar in Guatemala in 1954. President Jacobo Arbenz, a nationalist former military officer elected in 1950, acted to extend civil and political rights and modernize the semi-feudal social structure of his country through a series of economic measures designed to improve conditions for the large mass of impoverished peasants. An agrarian reform program that aimed to break the dominance of the country's landed oligarchy—2.2 percent of the population owned 70 percent of the arable land—attracted the hostility of the powerful United Fruit Company of Boston, which also controlled vast holdings in Guatemala. Arbenz was also regarded as insufficiently anticommunist after four communists were elected to a Congress of fifty-eight members. In 1954, the CIA carried out its first covert operation in the Americas when it organized his overthrow. Forty years of brutal military regimes followed.

These two "regime changes" were early examples of covert U.S. operations in the developing world aimed at "rolling back" governments not to Washington's liking. Indeed, the United States continued to pursue rollback in subsequent decades, usually through covert operations, in an ongoing attempt to shape political outcomes. To this end, Washington launched successful campaigns to undermine such nationalist leaders as Patrice Lumumba in Congo (1960), Sukarno in Indonesia (1967), and Salvador Allende in Chile (1973); there were also continuous efforts to roll back revolutionary governments, as in Cuba (through the Bay of Pigs Invasion and

| 571

Operation Mongoose in the 1960s) and Nicaragua (via the Contra war in the 1980s).

But there were always protests and countervailing tendencies at work. As soon as the United States emerged as a world power, its citizens began energetic debates about foreign policy, and many warned that the pursuit of empire abroad would undermine democracy at home. Sectors of the U.S. public argued, in the "alternative" U.S. tradition, that democratic values should be reflected in both foreign and domestic policy. Such debates became more momentous after the United States emerged as a superpower. As the Vietnam War began to threaten domestic progress, Martin Luther King Jr., in one of the most important speeches in the country's history, declared his "independence from the war in Vietnam" three years after he was awarded the Nobel Peace Prize. Later, responding to widespread public protest against the Vietnam War, the Watergate scandal, and revelations about CIA assassination plots, President Jimmy Carter called for a new foreign policy based on respect for other nations and support for democracy and human rights. His preference for "soft power," cooperation, alliances, and nonmilitary solutions to global conflicts earned him the contempt of hard-line conservatives.

In the 1980s another group of aggressive military and policy figures, several associated with right-wing think tanks such as the American Enterprise Institute, sought to reshape U.S. policy once again. The Committee of Santa Fe issued a clarion call for remilitarizing the United States and reasserting U.S. power worldwide to reverse what its members saw as the Carter administration's weaknesses. They argued that the United States needed to regain control of Latin America, its traditional "backyard," and use it to project U.S. power worldwide. The Committee's "New Inter-American Policy for the Eighties" had a pronounced impact on the Reagan administration, much as the Project for the New American Century would have on the Bush administration twenty years later.[4] These debates mirrored the complexities and contradictions of American democratic thought and action and the conflicting impulses of democracy and empire. But Franklin, Jefferson, Lincoln, Addams, Paine, FDR, King, and Carter represented an American tradition that was just as vibrant and authentic as that claimed by the Cold Warriors, the neoconservatives, and the Bush administration.

## THE UNIPOLAR MOMENT

By 2008, there were signs that the international system that had taken shape after the collapse of the Soviet Union in 1991 was changing, as the outlines of a new balance of forces began to appear: China was developing

---

4. Committee of Santa Fe, "A New Inter-American Policy for the Eighties" (Washington, DC: Council for Inter-American Security, 1980).

rapidly, Russia was showing signs of resurgence, European nations were taking increasingly different policy positions from Washington, and Latin American governments were asserting their own independent policies. A more multinational world seemed to be coming into view as President Bush, belatedly more receptive to negotiation and compromise, saw his term in office draw to a close. The administration's international isolation, its military and political failures, and its domestic unpopularity were reflected in its eleventh-hour attempts to negotiate terms it had been unable to impose unilaterally. But its allies in Baghdad, looking forward to a new U.S. president and sensing the end of Bush's doctrine of unilateralism and preemption, insisted that Washington agree to an explicit timeline to exit the country. After hard negotiations, a Status of Forces Agreement between the two countries was signed in November 2008. Its compromises and uncertainties notwithstanding, the agreement markedly limited the previously unchallenged and open-ended U.S. role in Iraq and granted Baghdad significant authority over U.S. military operations. It had specific requirements for removing U.S. troops from Iraqi cities, required U.S. withdrawal by 2011, mandated respect for Iraqi laws and sovereignty, and obligated Washington to turn over to Iraqi authorities, in some circumstances, soldiers or private contractors who had committed crimes. The Bush administration had resisted all these demands for years, but the world had changed since the president first envisioned a "New American Century."

The Bush presidency was a notable departure from previous administrations, characterized as it was by repeated efforts to broaden presidential powers and weaken those of Congress and the courts as it pursued a unilateral and preemptive foreign policy. Convinced that history had offered a unique opportunity to restructure international and domestic politics, the administration had pursued an ambitious agenda whose radicalism became increasingly clear. Exploiting and amplifying the fears of a traumatized country, it had launched a preemptive war with the promise that removing Saddam Hussein and bringing "democracy" to Iraq would promote international stability, deal a blow to international terrorism, safeguard the Persian Gulf, promote the welfare of the Iraqi people, protect the U.S. economy, enhance domestic freedom, and guarantee a peaceful world under U.S. hegemony. Few, if any, of its sweeping claims came to pass. On the contrary, the invasion of Iraq destabilized international politics, brought chaos to the Persian Gulf, strengthened international terrorism, devastated Iraqi society, damaged the U.S. economy, threatened its democracy, and made the United States an international pariah. Preemption and "regime change" had weakened, not strengthened, U.S. security.

## FINAL THOUGHTS

The war in Iraq was always about much more than U.S. history, international relations, the Bush administration, or the particular issues raised in this book. It was about the sort of nation and the sort of world the American people wanted to live in. The war raised profound questions that urgently demanded answers. Did the United States really want to dominate the world? Did other peoples have the right to determine their own national directions? Were domestic democracy and prosperity compatible with militarism and expansionism? Were Americans willing to live with a government that insisted on unchallenged military dominance, invasions, and interventions; that rejected diplomacy; and that routinely degraded democratic rights in the face of challenges? Were they prepared to pay the human, physical, and moral costs of empire?

After eight years of President Bush and almost six years of a preemptive war that had left hundreds of thousands dead or wounded, two million refugees scattered throughout the Middle East, a shattered Iraq whose recovery would take decades, a destabilized arc of countries stretching from Lebanon to Pakistan, and a divided, isolated, demoralized, and weakened United States, the electorate seemed ready to answer these questions. It did so in 2008 in an election that represented a decisive repudiation of Bush's policies. As his administration came to a close, its neoconservative dream that a single superpower would reorder the world in the image of U.S.-style capitalism and liberalism was in ruins. With Barack Obama's resounding electoral victory, it appeared that, for the moment at least, the American people wanted their "other" historical tradition to prevail: the one that respected civil liberties, democracy, and economic development at home; supported strong international institutions; valued international law; used the enormous power of the country peacefully; and acted as a good neighbor in a law-governed world.

Whether the new administration would reorient U.S. foreign policy and reconstruct the institutions dedicated to peace and justice at home and abroad remained to be seen. But the new president's early measures were promising. In his first days, Obama issued executive orders to close Guantánamo within a year, to halt military tribunals, to outlaw overseas CIA prisons, and to nullify every legal opinion on interrogations issued by the executive branch after 2001. He also reiterated one of his central campaign pledges: that U.S. combat forces would leave Iraq within sixteen months (although he also said he would augment U.S. military efforts in Afghanistan). President Obama seemed to be committed to ending the Bush administration's misbegotten adventure in Iraq. But the war's costs and consequences were certain to reverberate in Iraq, the United States, and the entire world for many years to come. As always, an informed and engaged citizenry would be required to hold leaders accountable, sort out what had happened, decide whether preemption was a viable strategy, and repair the damage done by the Bush administration's invasion and occupation of Iraq.

National Defense University Press for excerpt from *Shock and Awe: Achieving Rapid Dominance,* by Harlan K. Ullman and James P. Wade, October 1996. Copyright © 1996 by National Defense University.

National Lawyer's Guild for excerpt from "White Paper on the Law of Torture and Holding Accountable Those Who Are Complicit in Approving Torture of Persons in U.S. Custody," by Jeanne Mirer and the National Lawyer's Guild, May 2008.

NBC News for excerpted interview with Secretary of State Madeleine Albright, *Meet the Press,* January 2, 2000. Copyright © 2005 by NBC Universal, Inc. All rights reserved.

The *New York Times* for "The Words That Were Used," by Matthew Ericson/New York Times, January 29, 2008; "Text of U.S. Security Adviser's Iraq Memo," November 29, 2006; "The Times and Iraq," May 26, 2004; "The Right Way to Change a Regime," by James A. Baker III, August 25, 2002; "Bombing Iraq Isn't Enough," by William Kristol and Robert Kagan, January 30, 1998; and "U.S. Strategy Plan Calls for Insuring No Rivals Develop," by Patrick E. Tyler, March 8, 1992. Copyright © 2008, 2006, 2004, 2002, 1998, 1992 by the New York Times.

PLATFORM for table of "Foreign Investment in the World's Major Oil Reserves," from *Crude Designs: The Rip-off of Iraq's Oil Wealth,* by Greg Muttitt, November 2005. Published by PLATFORM with Global Policy Forum, Institute for Policy Studies, www.carbonweb.org.

Paul Wolfowitz for "Rebuilding the Anti-Saddam Coalition," originally published in the *Wall Street Journal,* November 18, 1997. Copyright © 1997 by Paul Wolfowitz.

Raed Jarrar for the English translation of "Letter from 108 Iraqi Technical, Academic, and Economic Experts Opposed to Oil Privatization," published July 16, 2007, by Hands Off Iraqi Oil. English translation copyright © 2007 by Raed Jarrar. www.handsoffiraqioil.org.

RAND Corporation for excerpt from "How Terrorist Groups End: Lessons for Countering al Qa'eda," by Seth G. Jones and Martin C. Libicki, 2008. Copyright © 2008 by RAND Corporation.

Random House, Inc. for excerpt from *A World Transformed,* by George H. W. Bush and Brent Scowcroft. Copyright © 1998 by George H. W. Bush and Brent Scowcroft. Used by permission of Alfred A. Knopf, a division of Random House, Inc.

Robert Parry for "Gore's Other Global Warning: Iraq War," published February 25, 2007, by Consortium News. http://www.consortiumnews.com.

*Small Wars Journal* for "Waterboarding is Torture . . . Period," by Malcolm Nance, October 31, 2007. Copyright © 2007 by Small Wars Foundation. www.smallwarsjournal.com.

United Nations for "Security Council Resolution 1566," October 8, 2004; "Press Encounter with the Secretary-General at the Security Council Stakeout," March 17, 2003; "Spain, United Kingdom of Great Britain and Northern Ireland and United States of America: Draft Resolution to Security Council," March 7, 2003; and excerpt from "Security Council Hears over 60 Speakers in Two-Day Debate on Iraq's Disarmament: Many Say Use of Force Should Be Last Resort, Others Urge Swift Action," February 19, 2003.

Permissions Acknowledgments

United States Agency for International Development for excerpt from "Options for Developing a Long Term Sustainable Iraqi Oil Industry," sector study prepared by BearingPoint, December 19, 2003.

United Steelworkers for "United Steelworkers Letter to Congress Opposing Privatization of Iraqi Oil Industry," July 31, 2007.

*Wall Street Journal* for "Don't Attack Saddam," by Brent Scowcroft, August 15, 2002. Copyright © 2002 by Dow Jones & Company, Inc.

*Washington Post* for "The Axis of Petulance," by Charles Krauthammer, March 1, 2002. Copyright © 2002 by the Washington Post.

William Kristol for "Letter to President Clinton from the Project for the New American Century," January 26, 1998; and "Statement of Principles," June 3, 1997. Copyright © 1998, 1997 by the Project for a New American Century.

World Council of Churches for "Statement against Military Action in Iraq," February 21, 2003. Copyright © 2003 by World Council of Churches.

# ★ INDEX ★

| 589